NEW DIRECTIONS

IN JEWISH PHILOSOPHY

New Directions in Jewish Philosophy

Edited by
Aaron W. Hughes
and Elliot R. Wolfson

INDIANA UNIVERSITY PRESS
Bloomington and Indianapolis

This book is a publication of

Indiana University Press
601 North Morton Street
Bloomington, IN 47404-3797 USA

www.iupress.indiana.edu

Telephone orders   800-842-6796
Fax orders   812-855-7931
Orders by e-mail   iuporder@indiana.edu

© 2010 by Indiana University Press
All rights reserved

♾The paper used in this publication meets the minimum
requirements of the American National Standard for Information
Sciences—Permanence of Paper for Printed Library Materials,
ANSI Z39.48-1992.

Manufactured in the United States of America

Library of Congress Cataloging-in-Publication Data

New directions in Jewish philosophy / edited by Aaron W. Hughes
and Elliot R. Wolfson.
p. cm.
Includes bibliographical references and index.
ISBN 978-0-253-30031-7 (cloth : alk. paper) —
ISBN 978-0-253-22164-3 (pbk. : alk. paper)
1. Philosophy, Jewish. I. Hughes, Aaron W., date
II. Wolfson, Elliot R.
B154.N49 2009
181'.06—dc22

2009025666

1 2 3 4 5   15 14 13 12 11 10

To Friendship

To think is not to possess the objects of thought; it is to use them to mark out a realm to think about which we therefore are not yet thinking about.

—MERLEAU-PONTY,
"THE PHILOSOPHER AND HIS SHADOW"

CONTENTS

NEW DIRECTIONS
IN JEWISH PHILOSOPHY

INTRODUCTION

CHARTING AN ALTERNATIVE COURSE FOR THE STUDY OF JEWISH PHILOSOPHY

Aaron W. Hughes and Elliot R. Wolfson

THE STATUS OF JEWISH PHILOSOPHY IN THE UNIVERSITY CURRICULUM IS ambiguous. It is often regarded as too technical or philosophical for Jewish Studies and, at the same time, as too Jewish for philosophy departments. The traditional tendency has been to account for this ambiguity by turning to history, showing the intellectual contexts that inspired Jews to philosophize, the various controversies this gave rise to, and their ultimate resolutions. This historical turn, however, risks mistaking Jewish philosophy as part of history (be it intellectual history or the history of ideas), and not as part of philosophy. There are many reasons for the confusions that both led to and emerge from this mistake, most of which date to the foundation of the modern discipline of Jewish Studies (*Wissenschaft des Judentums*) in the nineteenth century.[1]

Because of its problematic relationship to philosophy, if and when Jewish philosophy is taught at all, it is usually in departments of Religious Studies, History, and Hebrew and Judaic Studies. Whereas the first is often most concerned with religious identity, the second with the historical record, and the third with matters of Jewish cultural formation, the assumptions mentioned above are often reinscribed or reinstated, further attesting to the problematic status of Jewish philosophy within the university curriculum. Such curricular moves often succeed in defanging the intellectual rigor of Jewish philosophy, making it part of the historical project of how Jews understood themselves, their traditions, and their texts in the face of non-Jewish ideas encountered through diasporic existence.[2] In departments of Religious Studies, Jewish philosophy risks being subsumed under the insipid slogan of "World Philosophy," "Comparative Philosophy of Religion," or "World Philosophies."[3] In such courses identity often trumps ideas—or, alternatively, the permutations that philosophical ideas undergo by different religious or ethnic groups are regarded as "quirky" or "eccentric" departures from their lofty heights (i.e., as un-contaminated by religion) within ancient Greek thought. Moreover, when medieval philosophy courses are actually taught, Jewish philosophy is either ignored completely or a Jewish representative, usually Maimonides, is often invoked in order to show either the perceived diversity of medieval philosophy beyond the Christian traditions (e.g., Scholasticism) or to re-flect the multiculturalism of the contemporary university.

Missing in all of these formulations, however, is Jewish philosophy as a living and engaged practice.[4] Even if we are not willing to accept Pierre Hadot's celebrated depiction of philosophy—understood primarily as the contemplative study of nature—in the Greco-Roman context as consisting of "spiritual exercises" aimed at transforming the inner life of the practi-tioner, it nevertheless seems legitimate to embrace his conception of phi-losophy as a "way of life."[5] A crucial implication of Hadot's approach, as he himself makes clear, is that the study of philosophy is not merely "his-torical," but it is a venue to offer contemporary readers a "model of life."[6] Applying this standard, we must ask, What does it mean to philosophize from a hermeneutical standpoint demarcated as distinctively Jewish? Can one study something called "the history of Jewish philosophy" philosophi-cally? How does Jewish philosophy intersect with, subvert, or offer alter-natives to something called general or non-Jewish philosophy? How might Jewish philosophy converse with other disciplines in the humanities? Even more fundamentally, we must ponder, what is Jewish philosophy? Can a philosophy be particularized in this way? Is there a Muslim phi-losophy? A Christian philosophy? Is it not the case that a Jew, a Muslim, or Christian philosopher would first have to inquire into the human con-dition more generally, and only then inquire on that basis into the condi-tion of the Jew, Muslim, or Christian? How are we to conceive primarily of a thought that is delimited by a specific cultural formation or religious tradition? Is it not the case that the various subjects included in the rubric of philosophy—logic, epistemology, ontology, aesthetics, or ethics—are for good reason considered universal and therefore resist culturally specific delimitation?

We ask the question again: Can there be a Jewish philosophy?[7] Surely, we would not want to say that every Jew who is a philosopher is neces-sarily a Jewish philosopher in the sense that he or she articulates a Jewish philosophy—Spinoza or Derrida, in contrast to Maimonides or Levinas—any more than we want to say a Jew who is a mathematician professes a Jewish mathematics, that a Jew who is a physicist does Jewish physics, or that a Jew who writes poetry necessarily produces Jewish poetry. If we would not want to say that any philosophy produced by a Jew is ipso facto Jewish philosophy, are we prepared to say that a non-Jew cannot produce Jewish philosophy?[8] Perhaps it would be better to speak of the philosophy (or philosophies) of Judaism rather than Jewish philosophy. And indeed, in 1933 Julius Guttmann published a book called *Die Philosophie des Judentums*. The "philosophy of Judaism," as opposed to "Jewish philosophy," implies two things: (a) the philosophical interpretation of Judaism, or better, the attempt to articulate the basic tenets of Judaism in a philosophical idiom; and (b) the attempt to consider the fundamental philosophical questions from a Jewish standpoint.[9] However, a consequence of the shift in terminology is the assumption that the genuinely philosophical side of so-called Jewish philosophers is derived from the outside, that Judaism is the subject of philosophical inquiry, and that any philosophy of Judaism is a religious philosophy, in the same way that Corbin argued that Islamic philosophy is a "philosophy whose development, and whose modalities, are essentially linked to the religious and spiritual fact of Islam."[10] Consider Guttmann's own words:

> Since the days of antiquity, Jewish philosophy was essentially a philosophy of Judaism. Even during the Middle Ages—which knew something like a total, all-embracing culture based on religion—philosophy rarely transcended its religious center. This religious orientation constitutes the distinctive character of Jewish philosophy. . . . In this respect the philosophy of Judaism, whatever the differences in content deriving from the specific doctrines and the concepts of authority of the religions concerned, is formally similar to that of Christianity or Islam. . . . The great majority of Jewish thinkers made the philosophical justification of Judaism their main subject.[11]

In a similar vein, Alexander Altmann observed, "It would be futile to attempt a presentation of Judaism as a philosophic system, or to speak of Jewish philosophy in the same sense as one speaks of American, English, French, or German philosophy. Judaism is a religion, and the truth it teaches are religious truths. They spring from the source of religious experience, not from pure reason."[12] According to Altmann, just as a philosopher of religion philosophizes about religion, but the truths of the religion are separate from philosophy, so a philosophy of Judaism is a philosophizing about Judaism, but the truths of Judaism are derived independently. On this score, a philosophy of Judaism, and even more so a Jewish philosophy, cannot be philosophy in its authentic sense, a universal curiosity and a universal questioning about the nature of reality.[13] At best, the philosophy of Judaism would amount to the philosophical explication of Judaism, a rethinking of the fundamental tenets of the faith, and therefore it will be limited by specific historical and cultural circumstances. This is precisely the conclusion articulated by Leon Roth:

We have seen enough to suggest that, however much we use the term "Jewish philosophy," the most we should intend by it is a philosophy of Judaism, that is, a discussion of the answers offered by Judaism to some of the general problems of life and thought; and we must recognize that this is not philosophy in the authentic historical sense of a universal curiosity and a universal questioning into the widest aspects of human experience. It is on the contrary a restricted study of certain historical ideas severely limited in relevance and space and time. Now it may possibly be that these historical ideas are of a universal interest, even of a universal importance. But this is a matter of enquiry and discussion. It is not self-evident truth.[14]

While we embrace the mandate to put into question the nature of Jewish philosophizing—and indeed, it is this openness that we seek to preserve both with respect to the past and with respect to the future—the essays gathered together in this volume seek a taxonomy that shifts the emphasis from seeing philosophy itself as a derivative to a native dimension of the Jewish religious sensibility. Rather than locating the philosophic element in some foreign domain, we look to situate it within the culture itself, though we do not want to leave the impression that we think a hard-and-fast line dividing inside and outside can be drawn. At best, the spatial demarcation applied to the life of the human spirit is a relative judgment: what is "outside" at one historical stage becomes appropriated and assimilated into the "inside" at another. The process of internalization of an external influence occurs by means of a creative leap through which the boundaries are traversed, resulting in the destabilization of the inside/outside dichotomy. To the extent that this destabilization is mollified and the outside becomes inside, the cultural balance is regained temporarily, so that for the moment one knows one's bearings.[15] Instead of thinking of Jewish philosophy as providing a Jewish context for philosophy, we are operating with a notion of philosophical reasoning that is shaped by the singularity of a specific cultural matrix, and it is from the standpoint of this particularity that the universal is to be thought.

The study of Jewish philosophy, as mentioned, has traditionally attracted scholars working in departments of Religion, History, Judaic Studies, and, to a lesser extent, Philosophy. Increasingly, however, scholars in English, French, and German departments are interested in Jewish philosophy, especially modern Jewish philosophy, as a resource for a variety of critical discourses. Whereas the more traditional model of Jewish philosophy focuses on concerns particular to Judaism and Jewish Studies (i.e., ethnicity and the politics of identity), the essays collected here seek a broader scope, one that enables us to begin re-framing the field in light of language, poetics, aesthetics, and visual culture.

Such nontraditional phenomena, however, are usually associated, whether correctly or incorrectly, with Continental philosophy or with Postmodernism. Without denying the singular and significant contribution of the attempt on the part of some scholars to shape the contours of a Jewish postmodernist discourse, the driving force behind this volume is the desire to rethink the discipline more broadly. Rather than imposing the hermeneutical presuppositions of this particular enterprise on the contributors, we have opted instead for a methodological openness that would facilitate a reexamination of the philosophical import of Jewish philosophy. This is certainly not to claim that there are not other equally appropriate or valid ways to approach this material. It is a testament to the dynamism of Jewish philosophy that it can be explored scientifically,[16] ethically,[17] theologically,[18] or from the perspective of gender studies.[19] However, rarely is Jewish philosophy, especially in the premodern period, examined from the perspectives of literary theory or Continental philosophy. Rather than claim to be critical of these other approaches, our hope is that this volume will add a new voice to the existing polyphony.

IMPETUS FOR THE VOLUME

New Directions in Jewish Philosophy provides a first attempt, a set of initial soundings, to redress some of the oversights, lacunae, and assumptions that we contend characterize the study of Jewish philosophy. Framed most broadly now, but to be discussed in greater detail below, we seek to temper what we consider to be an overwhelming reliance on historical context, construed in a predominantly temporal-spatial proximity and, especially in the case of medieval philosophy, on philology.

The historical record has done much for Jewish philosophy. It has articulated a set of books deemed canonical; it has produced a series of thinkers, in chronological succession, who bring philosophical method to Jewish questions;[20] it has fitted these individuals into larger, non-Jewish philosophical "schools"; it has bequeathed to us a series of methodologies that proclaim the best way to explore the data that has been constructed as Jewish and philosophical; and it has, in the process, imagined that very something that we today call "Jewish philosophy."

Yet this imagining or set of imaginings has created, from the present gazing backwards, a rather rigid line stretching from Levinas back to Philo. This line is too straight; its borders are vigilantly policed to ensure that only the "philosophical" be allowed in, and all else—the "mystical," the "midrashic," the "religious"—be checked at the door. The regnant discourses have, moreover, established a hierarchical series of questions that determine what should be or will be of significance. For example, in the medieval period, the grand themes of metaphysics and ontology are paramount, whereas in the modern period, pride of place is customarily given to ethics.

How does memory fare at this border? If to study Jewish philosophy is to study history, where is the desire of memory? How do we fit language, especially language's relationship to a particular people or set of truth claims, into this equation? Where are we to put all of those nontraditional aspects of Jewish philosophy that have been left out of the so-called canon? If history and philosophy can, at times, illumine one another, their lights ultimately emerge and shine from different angles.

This raises the question of the nature of the relationship between philosophy and context. Much writing on Jewish philosophy, whether in the medieval or in the modern period, stresses the contextual configuration of individual thinkers vis-à-vis the outside. Thus, Ibn Ezra is understood as the Jewish Avicenna, Maimonides as the Jewish instantiation of Alfarabi or Averroes, Hermann Cohen as Kant's Jewish representative, or Franz Rosenzweig as preferring Jewish thoughts or ideas that bear an affinity to the non-Jewish Heidegger. But all of these "equivalences" come with a cost: the cost of oversimplification when adjectives (e.g., "Neoplatonic," "Aristotelian," "Kantian," "Idealist") suffice to cover up or blur the complexities within each thinker's corpus; the cost of reductionism when the role of Jewish philosophy is regarded as little more than a tool of acculturation; the cost of misunderstanding Jewish philosophy and Jewish philosophers as simply providing non-Jewish ideas in Jewish guises.

The choice of contextualization is always a matter of degrees, of the choices that we make, of what we deem significant or not. Paul Franks frames contextualization in the following terms:

> It also makes a difference who is trying to achieve understanding, and in what capacity. If, say, you are the official historian of the city of Württemberg, then you should not be criticized for the choice—which might rightly be called parochial—to place Hegel in just that context. This would be an odd choice, however, if you were, say, a philosopher considering the import of Hegel's teleology for contemporary philosophy of mind.[21]

Such parochialism, however, has played a large role in the study of Jewish philosophy. It risks misunderstanding thinkers, Jewish or otherwise, in the larger and more general flow of ideas. Often implicit in this flow is, if not evolution, then at least a certain progressivism. The closer thinkers are to our times, the better their philosophy is, the more realistic their concerns, and so on.

This is certainly not a call to jettison history or context. Both have been tremendously useful in elucidating *certain* problems, bringing various filiations to light, and supplying much-needed intellectual, sociological, cultural, and religious interconnections to an otherwise diffuse set of texts. Having said this, however, this volume is a reminder that such historical and contextual interconnections must not come at the expense of the concomitant philosophical reflections that emerge from this activity.

Yet, if history and the historical record represent one set of obstacles to a full or holistic appreciation of Jewish philosophy, analytical philosophy's complete disregard for things religious or ethnic cannot be our default position. While analytical philosophy tends to take for granted that philosophical problems can be answered as timeless questions without reference to context or presuppositions that were historically formed, this is but an unintentional corrective to the often narrow contextualization and parochial understanding of what is going on in the field of Jewish philosophy, such that the originality of the thought being studied, its potential for intervening in perennial philosophical questions, might well be obscured.

Charting a course between intellectual history's attention to context and analytical philosophy's leveling of the particular, we seek here a middle path, one that acknowledges historicity in human intellectual activity but does not reduce such activity to it. Not so much interested in the truth claims of Jewish philosophers, many in the present volume wish to explore some of the closet assumptions, unchecked inconsistencies, and potential paradoxes that arise in this literature, both medieval and modern.

Beginning A/New

There currently exist many overviews of Jewish philosophy, which represent a great deal of stocktaking, of consolidations of the field, and all of which tend to over-rely on historicism. Our volume, by contrast, is suspicious of such claims. We are interested in what is new, and as such our claims are future-orientated. We seek here to question the traditional order of things, not to buy into it and accept it as part of the natural order. Our goal is to begin to interrogate Jewish philosophy by calling into question its organizing principles, its taxonomies, its assumptions, and, ultimately, the way it problematically falls between various disciplinary boundaries.

Accordingly, we seek to establish new conceptual models, modes of analysis, and theoretical paradigms to apply to the study of Jewish philosophy. Moving away from the customary historical scope and chrono-logical presentation of data, this volume seeks new and dynamic ways to engage the material both to specialists in the field and to those in cognate disciplines with an interest in Jewish philosophy and critical theory. The overarching goal of the project is to sustain the study of Jewish philosophy in the present and set an agenda for future research.

Previous large-scale treatments of Jewish philosophy, including sur-veys, tend to focus on a particular era, introducing a series of individuals or "schools" (e.g., Jewish Neoplatonists) that are presented chronologically.[22] Our volume, as may be seen from the table of contents, avoids such a historical treatment and instead examines Jewish philosophy from a va-riety of interdisciplinary perspectives. In so doing, the chapters seek to move beyond traditional assumptions (e.g., the privileging of metaphysics over aesthetics, intellect over imagination) and categories (e.g., rational-ism, theology), including the customary taxonomical arrangement or pre-sentation of Jewish philosophy (e.g., ancient, medieval, renaissance, early modern, modern; or, alternatively, *kalām,* Neoplatonism, Aristotelian, a hybrid of philosophy and kabbalah, Kantianism, neo-Kantianism, Exis-tentialism, Postmodernism).

New Directions in Jewish Philosophy provides an alternate approach to Jewish philosophy, one that emphasizes precisely the type of philosophical thinking that is otherwise examined from historical and textual perspec-tives. Since the philosophical component of Jewish philosophy tends to be underemphasized, the validity and dynamism of its arguments are often ignored in favor of a focus on individuals and their historical idiosyncra-sies. A philologically or historically oriented approach to Jewish philoso-phy, as opposed to a problem-oriented one, risks calcifying the dynamics of (Jewish) philosophical practice, mistaking the historical and the tem-poral for the philosophical. Within this context, the study of Jewish phi-losophy customarily proceeds by examining, in their historical contexts, individuals who have responded to various sets of non-Jewish ideas. Al-though not all of the contributors to this volume are willing to jettison the historical and contextual record, many question it and prefer to move it from center stage.

"OLD" AND "NEW"

Any volume devoted to "new" themes must necessarily turn to the past, the habitual, the "old." How have things proceeded? How have we arrived here from there? Although on one level a volume such as this, devoted to a realignment of trajectories and a refocus of questions, might well indicate the general health of a subdiscipline known as Jewish philosophy; framed differently, it might also point to its general lethargy and decay. In his posthumously published *Das Büchlein vom gesunden und kranken Menschenverstand,* Franz Rosenzweig uses an apt (and perhaps prescient) metaphor to describe the numbness associated with the traditional way of doing things. Rather than connect us to life, the habitual all too often isolates us, removes us from life's dynamic rhythms. He writes:

> The philosopher cannot wait. His kind of wonder does not differ from the wonder of others. However, he is unwilling to accept the process of life and the passing of the numbness wonder has brought. Such relief comes too slowly. He insists on a solution immediately—at the very instant of his being overcome—and at the very place wonder struck him. He stands quiet, motionless. He separates his experience of wonder from the continuous stream of life, isolating it.[23]

Perhaps, following Rosenzweig, we could intimate that the largest plight currently facing the study of Jewish philosophy is how to reconnect it to life. How can we make the dynamism of Jewish philosophy, taken from different times and places, relevant to us? How can we do this so that we do not smother philosophy with philology or historical contexts, yet at the same time take account of each? It is precisely this goal that we have set for ourselves in the present volume. While we certainly do not think that we can cure the study of Jewish philosophy with one volume, we do offer this collection as a way, to again use the metaphor of Rosenzweig, of convalescence, of adding an important corrective to the traditional way of doing or engaging Jewish philosophy.

Any volume devoted to the "new" must accordingly distance itself from the "old," its past. Unfortunately, this often means proceeding by means of negation: whereas the customary way to look at Jewish philosophy was or has been "x," we, on the contrary, have "not-x" as our point of departure. For instance, the old way of doing Jewish philosophy is characterized by that which is historical, philological, overly descriptive, contextual, and so on. The approaches taken by the contributors to this volume, however, are imaginative, poetic, and, in some instances, contextless. This approach would mean that we have proceeded with a negative objective in the distance. To proceed on a negative footing, however, leads surely to stumbling, to infirmity, and, to use the metaphor of Rosenzweig, to further paralysis.

Rather than frame our collection this way, perhaps it is better to offer it as a corrective, a collection of essays that seeks to redress certain oversights, thereby contributing to our total understanding of the practice, composition, and ultimate vitality of Jewish philosophy.

TRADITIONAL TAXONOMIES OF JEWISH PHILOSOPHY

The overriding historiographical assumption that has shaped the study of
Jewish philosophy has been that philosophy as such is not indigenous to
Judaism as a religious and sociopolitical culture. A consequence of this assumption is that every philosophical expression in Jewish history has been
treated as a derivative attempt (at times overtly apologetic) to reinterpret
the main tenets of Judaism in light of a prevailing conceptual scheme that
is extrinsic. Historically, the main taxonomical schemes employed to account for Jewish philosophy in Late Antiquity, the Middle Ages, and the
Renaissance have been Aristotelianism, Neoplatonism, and Stoicism, and,
in the Modern period, Idealism, Phenomenology, Existentialism, and Hermeneutics. In addition, the development of Jewish philosophy, particularly but not exclusively in the medieval period, has often been examined
from the vantage point of responding to theological concerns expressed
in other religions, especially the other two Abrahamic faiths, Islam and
Christianity.

There is surely truth to both of these assumptions, but it leaves open
the question of the very enterprise of Jewish philosophy. Is there nothing
native that might be claimed as philosophical within Judaism without being either secondary or responsive? In *Open Wounds*, David Patterson addresses the issue in the following way:

> If we cannot determine what makes Jewish thought Jewish, then the testi-
> mony that makes the Jewish people a people apart will be lost. . . . If we are
> to deal with it in any responsible fashion, then Jewish thought cannot be de-
> fined by the accidents of nature attached to the thinker: the fact that a Jew
> has a thought, in other words, does not make it a Jewish thought. . . . And
> the key to the truth of the Jew—the key to the identity of the Jew—is the
> Torah that the Nazis sought to erase from the face of the earth. Fackenheim
> rightly declared that "nothing so powerfully makes a philosopher *Jewish* as
> Torah." Because the Divine prohibition against murder is revealed in the To-
> rah that defines Judaism, I take that absolute prohibition to be a cornerstone
> of Jewish thinking. Because the Torah is written in the holy tongue, I take
> the Hebrew language to be a key to the categories that shape Jewish think-
> ing. And because this thinking has developed over the centuries in the works
> of the Jewish sages, I take those texts to be among the defining elements of
> Jewish thought. This does not mean that Jewish thought, over the centuries,
> has not been influenced by other ways of thinking; but Jewish thinkers have
> always grounded their thinking in Torah. . . . Jewish thought, then, is a
> thinking that on some level takes the teachings and commandments of To-
> rah to be absolute, that incorporates Hebraic categories into its thinking, and
> that is informed by the *sifrei kodesh*, the texts of the sacred tradition.[24]

In the rest of the book, Patterson works out in more detail what he considers to be the standpoint of Jewish thought: the unconditional regard for the other, both the Absolute Other, or God, and the irreducible alterity of one's fellow human being, deeply influenced, as he is, by Levinas. Leaving aside the credibility of this stance, we want to focus on what he takes to be the constitutional aspects of Jewish thought: (1) adherence to Torah (both in terms of belief and action); (2) reliance on Hebrew as the sacred language; (3) indebtedness to a canon of sacred texts. The first criterion is elementary but also not so simple, for what is the nature of Torah? How do we draw the lines of interpretation that determine the textual contours? The second criterion is reasonable enough, but it raises the larger question of the relationship of thought and language, and a particular language that is unique to a specific ethnos. The third matter is instructive, since it would comport Jewish thought as a form of textual reasoning, but it is still imperative to inquire what is the ultimate basis for a thought to be considered Jewish—the text or an idea independent of the text? At stake here is the matter of "Jewish particularity," which has been a major concern in modern and postmodern Jewish philosophy. Does Judaism resist assimilation into a universal, or is the mandate for Jews to become like the other?

WRITING ABOUT THE HISTORY OF JEWISH PHILOSOPHY PHILOSOPHICALLY

So where does this leave us? Is Jewish philosophy an academic practice? A literary one? A religious one? For many of us in religious studies departments, the study and/or practice of Jewish philosophy straddles the age-old tension of "religious studies" or "theology," "insider" vis-à-vis "outsider." But this tension is surely a faulty one, one that—to return to Rosenzweig again—perhaps need not occupy us at all:

> The real question arises because the human always senses his own lack of power whenever he stands before God, and thus necessarily must await and request the first step from God. And yet at the same time he hears that which he cannot help but hear: that God demands the first step from him, from the human. No theory can get away from this, neither one that seeks to discredit the demanding voice of God that is heard nor one that seeks to discredit the perceived lack of power as a deception of Satan. And of course absolutely not one that might steer between such a crude alternative through clever distribution or a meticulous apportionment of roles. Instead the matter remains an unending conversation.[25]

Jewish philosophy is about uncovering God's traces in the world and in the word. It is about thinking through the ramifications of a particular set of claims, using the universal as a map. It represents a thinking about alterity, both of the non-self and of the quintessential other. The "Jewishness" of Jewish philosophy, accordingly, must always be negotiated from the standpoint of preserving the identity of difference in the difference of identity. The task of a genuine philosophical engagement is to fashion the state of interiority from the perspective of the exterior without reducing the former to the latter. Not everything of philosophical import in Judaism is reducible to something else, but nothing of note is hermetically sealed from that mutual reciprocity.

Perhaps it is best to frame some of the issues that concern us here as a series of questions: How do we write about Jewish philosophy and Jewish philosophers as if they were not simply a set of data? Can one use the canon of Jewish philosophy, the very canon that has been constructed chronologically, to think about philosophical questions that are not confined solely to the historical epoch in which they were created and developed? Can Jewish philosophers be put in conversation with one another, and with non-Jewish philosophers, in ways that cross temporal and geographical boundaries?[26] Moreover, can this canon, conceived of broadly and openly as opposed to narrowly, do so in ways that the questions to be asked (and answered) are not just of the past or gazing toward it, but questions that concern us now and ones that are also future-directed?

Furthermore, can this broadly understood canon of Jewish philosophy reorient (non-Jewish) philosophy? The struggle with God's radical transcendence, the need to mediate the ontological gap between this world and the divine world, concern for the other, and the attunement to the fragility and aporia of language—all serve to show how, at least potentially, the contours of philosophy morph and change shape in its confrontation with one of its perennial others.[27] In a similar vein, Judaism does not create and sustain a particular and particularistic space that somehow remains outside of or immune from philosophy's more universal concerns. The philosophy/Judaism binary, perhaps best articulated for Jewish philosophy, at least, in Strauss's formulation of the Athens/Jerusalem divide,[28] is in many ways a false one. Yet it is nonetheless a formulation that has functioned as a pole around which much speculation has revolved. To use Martin Kavka's words:

> Without Athens, Jerusalem (Judaism) risks being unable to articulate the meaning of its own religious practices, becoming no more than a set of customs divorced from their ultimate source, a sedimented series of rote actions that can create an identity for its practitioners only through the profane category of "culture."[29]

The complex interactions between Judaism and philosophy demand further exploration rather than another repetition of a slogan that neatly reinforces their mutual incompatibilities. Since neither philosophy nor Judaism simply assimilates the other, it becomes necessary to explore how each changes in relationship to the other. Perhaps it is these explorations that most enable us to mine the veins that connect Judaism and philosophy while at the same time maintaining the porous boundaries that separate them.

Such questions and issues—sometimes directly, sometimes indirectly— illumine the chapters of the present volume. Framed generally, thinking about how we might write non-historically, or at least anachronistically, about the history of Jewish philosophy allows for further philosophical reflection on Judaism. This, in turn, permits us to conceptualize more clearly something of the nature of the relationship, as complex and fractured as it often is, between Judaism and Western culture.

WHAT FOLLOWS

All of the authors assembled here were asked to address the following set of questions: What is the major lacuna that you witness in your respective subfield of Jewish philosophy? What traditional assumptions have created such a lacuna? How can these assumptions be redressed? And, most importantly: If redressed, what would the future study of Jewish philosophy look like? When read together, then, these essays boldly chart a new and creative course for the study of Jewish philosophy.

Contributors have composed their chapters based on what they perceive to be pressing issues in the study of their respective subfields. In addition, each contributor has begun the process of rethinking the assumptions and discourses that have traditionally driven research in those subfields. Many of the authors have chosen to frame these issues, and subsequently undertake responses to them, in different ways. As such, there is no uniform structure that each chapter reproduces. Rather, each author examines his or her particular subfield using the disciplinary tools and vocabularies unique to it.

The overarching goal of the volume, therefore, is an important, timely, and creative one. We seek to reinvigorate the study of Jewish philosophy by moving beyond the traditional *Wissenschaft* model, a model that has driven virtually every treatment of Jewish philosophy writ large. This volume, in short, does not obsess about understanding the past on its own terms or employ strict chronological assumptions used to quantify this past. Rather, the essays collected here expand the contours of Jewish philosophy—redefining its canon, articulating a new set of questions, showing its counterpoints with other disciplines—as a way to demonstrate the vitality and originality of the topic.

Toward the Future Past

The commonsense conception of time, which is generally accepted by scholars as well, rests on a triadic division aligned in a linear fashion. On this score, the present is determined by the past, and the future by the present. The hermeneutic underlying the reconsideration of Jewish philosophy proffered in this volume rests on an alternative temporality. Past and future should not be considered respectively as the beginning and end of a closed circuit, but rather as termini of a path that remains open in both directions. Not only does this justify the methodological juxtaposition of medieval and modern thinkers, but it disrupts the causal assumption that the thinking of the former is to be elucidated by the latter. The swerve of time is such that extending back through memory is itself stretching forward through expectation. The future we set out to discover is a protention recollected in the past, just as the past we set out to recover is a retention anticipated in the future. The hope of this collection, therefore, is to inaugurate the future by initiating the past. Through the portal of this double opening, we may lay claim to a present that holds the promise of what has always been what is yet to come.

Notes

1. This is not the place to trace this history. Relevant literature may be found, for example, in Shmuel Feiner, *Haskalah and History: The Emergence of a Modern Jewish Historical Consciousness*, translated by Chaya Naor and Sondra Silverston (Oxford: Littman Library of Jewish Civilization, 2002), 1–8; David N. Myers, *Resisting History: Historicism and Its Discontents in German-Jewish Thought* (Princeton, N.J. : Princeton University Press, 2003), 1–34; and the recently published anthology, *Modern Judaism and Historical Consciousness: Identities, Encounters, Perspectives*, edited by Andreas Gotzmann and Christian Wiese (Leiden: Brill, 2007).

2. Reminiscent of this is Julius Guttmann's formulation: "The Jewish people did not begin to philosophize because of an irresistible urge to do so. They received philosophy from outside sources, and the history of Jewish philosophy is a history of the successive absorptions of foreign ideas which were transformed and adapted according to specific Jewish points of view." See his *Philosophies of Judaism: A History of Jewish Philosophy from Biblical Times to Franz Rosenzweig*, translated by David W. Silverman (New York: Schocken Books, 1964), 3.

3. E.g., Ninian Smart, *World Philosophies*, 2nd ed., edited by Oliver Leaman (New York and London: Routledge, 2008).

4. Even the title of Hilary Putnam's book, although promising much, is less interested in exploring Jewish philosophy as a "guide" than in proffering an introduction to Jewish philosophy, albeit in an ahistorical manner. Moreover, by Jewish philosophy, he means modern Jewish philosophy. See his *Jewish Philosophy as a Guide to Life: Rosenzweig, Buber, Levinas, Wittgenstein* (Bloomington: Indiana University Press, 2008).

5. Pierre Hadot, *Philosophy as a Way of Life,* edited by Arnold Davidson and translated by Michael Chase (Oxford: Blackwell, 1995); idem, *The Inner Citadel: The Meditations of Marcus Aurelius,* translated by Michael Chase (Cambridge, Mass.: Harvard University Press, 1998), 35–53; idem, *What Is Ancient Philosophy?* translated by Michael Chase (Cambridge, Mass.: Harvard University Press, 2002), 207–11; idem, *The Veil of Isis: An Essay on the History of the Idea of Nature,* translated by Michael Chase (Cambridge, Mass.: Harvard University Press, 2006), 182–89.

6. Hadot, *Philosophy as a Way of Life,* 208.

7. For a sustained reflection on this question, which presents a historical review of many of the major scholars who have weighed in on the topic, see Raphael Jospe, *Jewish Philosophy: Foundations and Extensions,* vol. 1, *General Questions and Considerations* (Lanham, Md.: University Press of America, 2008), 5–53,

8. See Jospe, *Jewish Philosophy,* xv.

9. This is also the perspective introduced by Steven Schwarzschild's concept of the "Jewish twist" that Jewish philosophers introduce into the non-Jewish philosophical systems in which they work. See, e.g., *The Pursuit of the Ideal: Jewish Writings of Steven Schwarzschild,* edited by Menachem Kellner (Albany: SUNY Press, 1990), 139.

10. Henry Corbin, *History of Islamic Philosophy,* translated by Liadain Sherrard with the assistance of Philip Sherrard (London: Kegan Paul International, 1993), xiv.

11. Guttmann, *Philosophies of Judaism,* 4, 55.

12. Alexander Altmann, "Judaism and World Philosophy," in *The Jews: Their History, Culture, and Religion,* edited by Louis Finkelstein (Philadelphia: Jewish Publication Society of America, 1950), 2:954.

13. To this chorus of voices we could also add the following from Colette Sirat: "Thus one can say that the history of Jewish philosophy in the Middle Ages is the history of the effort of Jews to reconcile philosophy (or a system of rationalist thought) and Scripture . . . the harmonizing of these two systems of thought in one unique verity was the theme of almost all Jewish medieval philosophy." See her *A History of Jewish Philosophy in the Middle Ages* (Cambridge: Cambridge University Press and Editions de la Maison des Sciences de l'Homme, 1985), 5.

14. Leon Roth, *Is There a Jewish Philosophy? Rethinking Fundamentals* (London: Littman Library of Jewish Civilization, 1999), 7–8.

15. Elliot R. Wolfson, "Hebraic and Hellenic Conceptions of Wisdom in *Sefer ha-Bahir,*" *Poetics Today* 19 (1998): 172.

16. E.g., Norbert M. Samuelson, *Jewish Faith and Modern Science: On the Death and Rebirth of Jewish Philosophy* (New York: Rowman and Littlefield, 2008).

17. E.g., David Novak, *Natural Law in Judaism* (Cambridge: Cambridge University Press, 1998); Elliot Dorff, *Love Your Neighbor and Yourself: A Jewish Approach to Modern Personal Ethics* (New York: Jewish Publication Society of America, 2006).

18. E.g., *Textual Reasonings: Jewish Philosophy and Text Study at the End of the Twentieth Century,* edited by Nancy Levene and Peter Ochs (Grand Rapids, Mich.: Eerdmans, 2002).

19. E.g., *Women and Gender in Jewish Philosophy,* edited by Hava Tirosh-Samuelson (Bloomington: Indiana University Press, 2004).

20. When their interest in Jewish questions seems to be minor—as in the case of

Shlomo ibn Gabirol's *Fons Vitae* or Judah Abravanel's *Dialoghi d'Amore*—these thinkers' inclusion in the "canon" has been questioned. See Aaron W. Hughes, *The Art of Dialogue in Jewish Philosophy* (Bloomington: Indiana University Press, 2008), 120–25.

21. Paul Franks, "What Is Context?" *Jewish Quarterly Review* 96, no. 3 (2006): 387. This essay is part of a review symposium devoted to Peter Eli Gordon, *Rosenzweig and Heidegger: Between Judaism and German Philosophy* (Berkeley: University of California Press, 2003).

22. The main surveys devoted to Jewish philosophy are primarily focused on individual philosophers, presented in chronological order. For medieval Jewish philosophy, see Isaac Husik, *A History of Medieval Jewish Philosophy* (Philadelphia: Jewish Publication Society of America, 1948); Colette Sirat, *A History of Jewish Philosophy in the Middle Ages; The Cambridge Companion to Medieval Jewish Philosophy,* edited by Daniel H. Frank and Oliver Leaman (Cambridge: Cambridge University Press, 2003); and *The Cambridge History of Medieval Jewish Philosophy,* edited by Steven Nadler and Tamar Rudavsky (Cambridge: Cambridge University Press, 2009).

For survey treatments of modern Jewish philosophy that work on the same historicist assumptions, see Nathan Rotenstreich, *Jewish Philosophy in Modern Times: From Mendelssohn to Rosenzweig* (New York: Holt, Rinehart, and Winston, 1968); Norbert Samuelson, *An Introduction to Modern Jewish Philosophy* (Albany: State University of New York Press, 1989); *The Cambridge Companion to Modern Jewish Philosophy,* edited by Michael L. Morgan and Peter Eli Gordon (Cambridge: Cambridge University Press, 2007).

Surveys of the entire gamut of Jewish philosophy from antiquity to the present include Julius Guttmann, *Philosophies of Judaism* (1944); *Routledge History of Jewish Philosophy,* edited by Daniel H. Frank and Oliver Leaman (London: Routledge, 1997); Norbert Samuelson, *Jewish Philosophy: An Historical Introduction* (New York: Continuum, 2004).

23. Franz Rosenzweig, *Understanding the Sick and the Healthy: A View of World, Man, and God,* translated and with an introduction by Nahum Glazer (Cambridge, Mass.: Harvard University Press, 1999), 40.

24. David Patterson, *Open Wounds: The Crisis of Jewish Thought in the Aftermath of Auschwitz* (Seattle: University of Washington Press, 2006), 20–21.

25. Franz Rosenzweig, *Jehuda Halevi: Zweiundneunzig Hymnen und Gedichte,* in *Der Mensch und sein Werk: Gesammelte Schriften,* 4.1, edited by Rafael Rosenzweig (The Hague: Martinus Nijhoff, 1983). English translation in Barbara Ellen Galli, *Franz Rosenzweig and Jehuda Halevi: Translating, Translations, and Translators* (Montreal and Kingston: McGill-Queen's University Press, 1995), 194–95.

26. For a philosophical justification of this, consult Elliot R. Wolfson, *Language, Eros, Being: Kabbalistic Hermeneutics and Poetic Imagination* (New York: Fordham University Press, 2005), xv–xxxi.

27. This is explored nicely in Robert Gibbs, *Correlations in Rosenzweig and Levinas* (Princeton, N.J.: Princeton University Press, 1992). See especially his comments and agenda for the future on 255–59.

28. E.g., Leo Strauss, *Jerusalem and Athens: Some Preliminary Reflections* (Frank Cohen Public Lectures in Judaic Affairs; New York: City College, 1967).

29. Martin Kavka, *Jewish Messianism and the History of Jewish Philosophy* (Cambridge: Cambridge University Press, 2004), 2. In this regard, also see the comments in Daniel Rynhold, *Two Models of Jewish Philosophy: Justifying One's Practices* (Oxford: Oxford University Press, 2005), 6–21.

PART 1

THE PAST CONFRONTS THE PRESENT, THE PRESENT CONFRONTS ITS PAST: CHALLENGING CANONICITY

1

SCREENING THE CANON: LEVINAS AND MEDIEVAL JEWISH PHILOSOPHY

Martin Kavka

ALTHOUGH THE WORK OF EMMANUEL LEVINAS IS NOW WELL ENSCONCED in the canon of Jewish philosophy, the task of relating him to other thinkers in this canon remains difficult. Part of this is because, given the fact that the vast majority of his writings are constructive, we simply do not have very much Levinasian commentary on other thinkers in the canon. His most detailed remarks are about Buber,[1] but given the paucity of references to Judaism among those remarks, scholars still have to exert energy to pursue the issue of how Levinas's predominantly critical view of Buber relates to issues that the canon of Jewish philosophy has long held dear, and even the issue of whether Levinas's argument against Buber is a fair one. (For example, what does Levinas's comment that "Buber has never brought out in a positive way the spiritual element in which the I-Thou relationship is produced"[2] mean for discussions of law and commandedness in Jewish philosophy?) And while Levinas wrote an equal amount of material about Rosenzweig,[3] the introductory function of those essays means that they skim the surface of Rosenzweig's texts more than they delve into them. This makes analysis difficult, although at least in this case scholars have begun to assess the validity of Levinas's impression of Rosenzweig.[4] Otherwise, Levinas made a smattering of remarks about Moses Mendelssohn,[5] Emil Fackenheim,[6] and Hermann Cohen,[7] as well as various comments on Spinoza.[8] In terms of premodern thinkers, Levinas was most substantive in a tantalizingly brief discussion of Halevi and Maimonides;[9] the other references that Levinas made to them simply careen past their thought.[10]

This situation is dispiriting, because it suggests that the most prominent new feature in the discipline of Jewish philosophy in the last twenty years—the addition of Levinas to its canon—may be difficult to sustain, because scholars have only a few traces to follow for mapping Levinas vis-à-vis other thinkers in the canon. This is not to say that Levinas does not belong in the canon; it is to say that the phenomenon of Levinas's entry into the canon may show that the logic of the canon of Jewish philosophy is based in the material conditions of the academy (the need to produce more figures in the canon, the need to transcend the assimilationist overtones of liberal philosophical theology), rather than in a tradition of ideas that are passed on from generation to generation of thinkers within the canon. Even on those rare occasions when Levinas did explicitly take up the theme of the meaning of "Jewish philosophy," there is a suspicion of the phrase as implying assimilation to the West, as expressing an assumption that Judaism and philosophy are as easily translatable into each other as two Romance languages. For Levinas, Judaism was not inherently philosophical, nor is reason something that, in the style of Hermann Cohen, scholars can portray as proceeding "out of the sources of Judaism." Rather, Levinas understood both Judaism and Western philosophy as engaging in structurally similar forms of thinking. They both consist of texts that point to that which cannot be brought to presence, and thus they oscillate—albeit in different styles—between the explicitative dimension of the deictic act of pointing and the essentially hidden nature of that toward which the philosopher, or the Jewish thinker, points. This seems to me to be the upshot of the following passages from the 1985 interview with Françoise Armengaud published as "On Jewish Philosophy":

> Does this distinction between Judaism and philosophical reflection immediately emerge as a major conflict? We may start out (and this was the case with me, since you wish to speak of me) in a world in which Judaism was lived, and in a very natural way: not all, or not only, in what is called piety or rigorous ritualism, but above all with the sense that belonging to humanity means to be answerable to an order of supreme responsibility. . . . Philosophy speaks of it [the drama of human existence] also, but in another language that always makes itself explicit, bringing its terms into harmony and formulating problems where there are breaks in the coherence. But has the handing down of Scriptures ever taken place without transmission through that language of interpretation? . . . No doubt you know Rashi's expression "These verses cry out, 'Interpret us!'" This is not yet a philosophical reading, but it is probably the acquisition of one of its virtues. . . . But one day it is discovered that philosophy too is a plural, that its truth hides itself and involves strata, [that] it unceasingly examines itself thoroughly, that its texts are inconsistent and that internal difficulties torment [*travaillent*] systems.[11]

On this reading, Jewish philosophy would be a discipline in which Judaism gnaws at philosophy, showing the essential hiddenness of its truth, and philosophy gnaws at Judaism, showing the essential hiddenness of *its* truth. "Jewish philosophy" would not be an oxymoron, but only because the identical structure of truth in both Judaism and philosophy would entail that the ethē of various cultures have their origin in a truth that is hidden. For truth to be so radically transcendent means that we have no right to posit it as being anything other than single. (If there were multiple hidden originary truths, how could we tell them apart in the absence of any light?) Different cultures would thus be expressions of the same, while being free to maintain the diverse and idiosyncratic nature of those expressions. Yet nowhere did Levinas show, through careful and extensive textual analysis of any thinkers in the canon of Jewish philosophy, that his vision of Jewish philosophy has anything in common with that of a strand of thinkers in the canon.

The stakes here are not insignificant. Without a way to situate Levinas in the history of Jewish philosophy—to give him a genealogy—the temptation is to see him as constituting a new direction in Jewish philosophy only by virtue of leaving the tradition of "Jewish philosophy" behind. This glass is half empty: such a degree of novelty is enough to seriously and permanently maim a field of inquiry by raising the specter that Levinas's arguments are best understood, not as truth claims, but as contingent historical expressions. Nonetheless, while this glass is also half full—the opportunity for scholars to try to give him such a genealogy is a bounteous one—in this essay, I would like to make another type of argument. I will argue that if Levinas does offer a new direction for practitioners in the discipline of Jewish philosophy, then that new direction arises from an inherently muddy relation to the canon that allows scholars-practitioners of Jewish philosophy to seize, with confidence, any one of a wide variety of orientations to that canon, *even if no canonical text is the sole and immediate cause of taking up that orientation.* In other words, what Levinas's relation to the canon authorizes is the autonomy and agency of practitioners in the field. (This is true even if a practitioner exercises that agency to argue for its having been limited by another, or by God.)

It is not clear to me that such a "new direction" in Jewish philosophy is really new. It might be an expression of what Jewish philosophy has always said. Levinas's muddy or tenuous relationship to other figures in the canon—let me be blunt and speak of his misreadings of them—may disclose a structure that has always been the case in Jewish philosophy. To make such an argument is to go against Levinas, for it involves denying the validity of some of his remarks about figures in that canon. But it also continues Levinas's tendency—and certainly that of many contemporary scholars, perhaps of other philosophers in the canon, and of non-philosophical accounts of Judaism—to think out of a belief in the spontaneity of the Jewish tradition. Receiving the content of the Jewish philosophical tradition in the form of a uniform canon is to foist "deadly decay" onto it, to use a phrase of Gershom Scholem.[12] For a believing Jewish philosopher to take that canon in new directions is to act on an assumption that religious truth must be mediated and othered in its reception in order to maintain its transcendent source. If the transcendence of its source is to be maintained over the course of history, it must be continually mediated and othered in new fashions. Believers (whether or not they are philosophers) may engage in this act of shifting tradition as they receive it by attesting to the infinity of the divine word; scholars of Jewish philosophy may do the same as they argue for better ways to portray this infinity in philosophical language and give their arguments noble ancestors from the canon of Jewish philosophy. Yet to do these things is to misread the past, and willfully so. It is to assume, whether consciously or unconsciously, that misreading is necessary for a "tradition" to remain fresh, even if that misreading is occluded by an author's claim to be expressing something essential to the Jewish, or the Jewish philosophical, tradition. In "The Builders," Franz Rosenzweig wrote that "the teaching itself is unknowable; it is only my and your and our knowledge."[13] This is as true of the Jewish philosophical canon as it is, on Rosenzweig's view, of Torah. However, recognizing the unknowability of a philosophical or theological teaching is only possible when "my" knowledge is particularized by its departure from "yours," when one community's claim of "our" knowledge differs from another's. Showing Jewish philosophers' misreadings of other Jewish philosophers can therefore be seen as a "theological" activity of attesting to the transcendence of that which Jewish philosophy seeks to express, although non-theologians who study Jewish philosophy might very well engage in the same activity in a "secular" manner so as to display the constructed nature of the canon of Jewish philosophy.

To read Levinas's place in the Jewish philosophical canon in this manner is to begin to carve out a view of the canon as something other than that screen of reason or Enlightenment that has unfortunately all too often been seen as hiding Jews from the Jewish tradition. Instead, the canon becomes a screen onto which practitioners *project* the Jewish tradition, othering it in the course of vivifying it: creating and defending a rich variety of ways to identify themselves as inflected by that tradition, arguing about the salutary or unsalutary effects of those identifications, and using the canon and its arguments to justify their loves (including, but not limited to, their love of that canon itself as the environment in which they make their dwelling).[14]

*   *   *

The most apt place to begin reading Levinas in this manner is that place in his corpus where he claimed his filiations in the canon of Jewish philosophy most clearly. This is in the Armengaud interview, in response to a question of whether he prefers Halevi or Maimonides. There he appeared to claim a closer proximity of his own thinking to Halevi than to the cognitivism or intellectualism of Maimonides. It is a strange passage, as is the interview as a whole, despite its being the most sustained treatment of Jewish philosophy in Levinas's writings. It seems to mark a reversal of sentiments that Levinas held earlier in his career, when he was critical of Halevi and lionized Maimonides. In "God and Philosophy," published in 1975, Levinas described his entire project in anti-Halevian terms:

> To ask oneself, as we are attempting to do here, whether God cannot be uttered in a reasonable discourse that would be neither ontology nor faith, is implicitly to doubt the formal opposition, established by Yehuda Halevi and taken up by Pascal, between, on the one hand, the God of Abraham, Isaac, and Jacob, invoked without philosophy in faith, and on the other the god of the philosophers. It is to doubt that this opposition constitutes an alternative.[15]

And in the 1957 essay "A Religion for Adults," Levinas wrote of Maimonides as the figure par excellence of the resemblance between the Jew and the "Greek," or Western: "It is not by virtue of simple chance that the way towards the synthesis of Jewish revelation and Greek thought was masterfully traced by Maimonides."[16] Maimonides would not have been able to engage in this synthetic act had there not already been some substantial inner affinity between Judaism and philosophy. Nevertheless, Levinas's mind had changed by 1985. The passage deserves to be quoted at length:

> I do not know whether that division into two [Halevi and Maimonides] is definitive. . . . [I]t is an extremely important division, however. On one side there is the great philosophical tradition that finds intelligibility, rationality and sense [sens] in knowledge [savoir]. In Maimonides, spirituality is understanding [le connaître] par excellence. It is knowledge in which being is present to the intellect [esprit], in which that presence of being to the intellect is the truth of being, i.e., truth's placing itself in the open. It is as if, since then, "being" meant presence, even though called "eternity": its exposure to thought and its exposition on the scale of thought, its assimilation by thought and immanence, in which the transcendence of God can signify only negatively. This still leaves open the question of how that transcendence per se was ever able to let thought know of its very separation. . . . Yehuda Halevi passes for a mystic, but he acknowledged the science [savoir] of the philosophers to a great extent, and he never developed the theme of pure and simple union with God, the disappearance of the thinker in the thought. What we can retain in his Kuzari is his description of the relationship with what he calls "the divine order [l'ordre de Dieu]": inyan elohi. This relationship is not spoken of in terms of an indeterminate coinciding with transcendence and the infinite, but in terms such as "association" (hithabrut) and "proximity" (hitqarvut). It is as if these social meanings of the relationship did not express privations of

understanding, the least desirable forms of knowledge, but were rather possessed of their own sovereign positivity. What matters to me in that work,
in which many significant features are only suggested (as well as many others which are unacceptable to me), is this possibility of an original thinking
and intelligibility other than the immanence of knowledge. (And there is
no question here of dispensing with knowledge just for the sake of opposing
Maimonides.) The proximity and sociality that the philosophers will seek
in *knowledge* will appear in Yehuda Halevi as irreducible possibilities of the
meaningful [*sensé*]. Sociality *with* transcendence![17]

It appears that the reversal could not be greater.

By this time, Maimonides had become for Levinas a representative
of all the pitfalls of intellectualism. The problem of such a mode of doing philosophy is that it adheres to an Aristotelian model of knowledge,
most clearly delineated in *De Anima* III:5 (430a), in which there is no difference between the cognizing subject, the act of cognition, and the cognized object. This means that the self, when it is understood according to
a hierarchy that privileges the intellectual, sees the course of its life as oriented around intellectual activity as a vehicle of self-transcendence. While
this view of knowledge does not claim that an object is equivalent to the
mental concept of that object, it does claim that knowledge is the path to
actuality (for both the potentially cognizing subject and the potentially
cognized object), and that knowledge allows one to conquer spatiotem-
poral limitation, since mind is immortal and eternal. As Levinas stated in
"Philosophy and the Idea of Infinity," originally published in 1957:

> The freedom of the investigator, the thinker on whom no constraint weighs,
> is expressed in truth. What else is this freedom but the thinking being's re-
> fusal to be alienated in the adherence, the preserving of his nature, his iden-
> tity, the feat of remaining the same despite the unknown lands into which
> thought seems to lead? Perceived in this way, philosophy would be engaged
> in reducing to the same all that is opposed to it as *other*. It would be moving
> toward *autonomy*, a stage in which nothing irreducible would limit thought
> any longer.[18]

A description of philosophy as primarily oriented toward attaining autonomy in this sense is not foreign to Maimonides, who indeed described
the human intellect in *The Guide of the Perplexed* (I:68) according to this
model. In the case of the knowledge of the whatness of a piece of wood,
Maimonides wrote: "[F]or the intellect *in actu* is nothing but that which
has been intellectually cognized, and the thing by means of which the
form of wood was intellectually cognized and made abstract, that thing
being the intellectually cognizing subject, is also indubitably identical with
the intellect realized *in actu*."[19] Knowledge is how the self transcends its
own situation of being constrained by the world. For Maimonides in this

part of the *Guide,* knowing in this manner was understood as *imitatio Dei,* since the divine intellect and the human intellect were described in structurally similar terms.[20] In addition, there are Neoplatonic elements in the *Guide* that heighten the stakes of intellectual activity as self-transcendence: an object is cognized only when it is stripped of its matter and represented as pure form in the mind. Because matter has the status of evil and non-being in Plotinus (e.g., "When something is absolutely deficient—and this is matter—this is essential evil without any share in good, for matter has not even being . . . the true way of speaking is to say it 'is not'"),[21] the conversion of an object into pure form through the act of cognition is given an ethical urgency.

Levinas's praise for Halevi requires a bit more extensive unpacking than his criticism of Maimonides. The Jewish sage who instructs the Khazar king in Halevi's *Kuzari* asserts that "logical demonstration [*al-istidlāl*] leads astray," especially when practiced to the extent that philosophers do.[22] And in spite of Levinas's frequent refusal of a contradictory relation between philosophy and the Bible, there are overlaps between the vociferous criticism of philosophy in the *Kuzari* and Levinas's thought. At the opening of the *Kuzari,* the philosopher who describes the telos of the philosophical life to the Khazar king claims that "there conjoins with the perfect one a light from the divine nature which is called the Active Intellect. His passive intellect conjoins with it in a conjunction of union [*ittiṣāl; ittiḥād*], to the point at which the individual regards himself as that Active Intellect, with no distinction between them."[23] Thus, while the philosopher refuses to posit any identity between the person perfected through philosophical training and God, the philosopher does use unitive rhetoric to describe an individual's relation with the lowest of the separate intellects emanated from God, namely, the Active Intellect that governs this sublunar world. The Jewish sage in the *Kuzari,* on the other hand, refuses to deploy unitive rhetoric, referring simply to the possibility of conjunction (*ittiṣāl*)—what Levinas termed "association"—with the ʾamr ilāhī, literally, "divine thing" or "divine command." This term remains vague. Harry Wolfson translated it as "divine will," Howard Kreisel refers to it as "divine matter," while Diana Lobel translates it simply as "the divine."[24] On most occasions in the *Kuzari,* Halevi used the term to refer to something that is divine yet distinct from God, although there are also passages in which it seems to be a name for God.[25] Herbert Davidson helpfully defined the ʾamr ilāhī as a "direct divine causality" that either allows individuals to achieve a divine degree of existence or exercises providence over the people of Israel.[26]

Levinas also posited a similarity between his own thinking and that of Halevi on the issue of "proximity" as an apt description for the relationship with the *ʾamr ilāhī*. This similarity does indeed exist, although the best evidence for it is one important passage in the *Kuzari* in which conjunction with the *ʾamr ilāhī* is described in the language of nearness:

> Now all that our promises imply is that we shall become connected with the *ʾamr ilāhī* by means of prophecy, or something nearly approaching it, and also through our relation to the *ʾamr ilāhī*, as displayed to us in grand and awe-inspiring miracles. . . . The promises of this Law are all included under one principle: the anticipation of drawing near to the Lord and his angels. One who has arrived at this degree need not fear death; our Law has demonstrated this plainly.[27]

In addition, the link between conjunction and the commanded life that Halevi made in this passage implies that there is a communal context for an individual's conjunction with the *ʾamr ilāhī*. Although Halevi often wrote of *ittiṣāl* as occurring on an individual basis, he also posited that "we still hold a connection with that *ʾamr ilāhī* through the laws which He has placed as a link between us and Him."[28] This would justify, to some extent, Levinas's description of *ittiṣāl* in the Armengaud interview as "social."

The final element of Levinas's later revised opinion of Halevi that requires glossing is his description of *ittiṣāl* as being superior to the order of knowledge. It is indeed the case that at one brief point in the *Kuzari*, Halevi wrote that the "ʾamr *ilāhī* can only enter a soul that [already] contains intellect."[29] Yet, given the fact that Halevi described the mitzvoth as sufficient for attaining conjunction with the *ʾamr ilāhī*, it seems odd to make a certain level of intellectual perfection a prerequisite for conjunction with the divine. Rather, it must be the case that, given Halevi's belief that this kind of conjunction is greater in degree and in kind than any conjunction with the Active Intellect, and in order to defend the rightness of the mitzvoth, conjunction with the divine must somehow subsume intellect. The Active Intellect and the *ʾamr ilāhī* operate similarly, as the Jewish sage makes clear at *Kuzari* II:14: "For the *ʾamr ilāhī* is, so to speak, waiting for whomever, such as the prophets and pious friends of God, is worthy to attach to him, and become a God to him, just as the intellect, so to speak, waits for those such as philosophers, whose natural qualities have become perfected and whose souls and moral qualities have become temperate, that it may dwell in him perfectly."[30] Just as a philosopher's intellectual perfection requires the perfection of moral habits to become worthy of intellectual perfection, so does a prophet's conjunction with the *ʾamr ilāhī* require the perfection of habits through the life of mitzvoth to become worthy of that conjunction. Neither did Halevi make it possible to understand him as saying that the life of mitzvoth has intellectual side effects: "One can only come near to God"—and such language of nearness calls to mind

Halevi's description of conjunction with the *ʾamr ilāhī*—"by the commandments of God, and there is no way to knowledge of the commandments of God except by way of prophecy, not by speculation or cleverness."[31] The religious life is thus wholly outside the life of speculation and philosophy.

Nevertheless, even given the ability to defend Levinas's descriptions of Maimonides and Halevi in this passage, it is unclear to me that Levinas was actually correct in aligning himself with Halevi and not Maimonides. For Halevi, *ittiṣāl* was often connected with attaining prophecy; as stated above, "prophecy, or something nearly approaching it" is the result of the commanded life, whether for elites or for the masses. For this reason and others, Shlomo Pines wrote that the *ʾamr ilāhī* "may in many cases be translated as a divine influx conferring prophethood."[32] Given that "prophecy" is also an important term in the Levinasian corpus, especially in his post-1970 writings,[33] it would follow that the Levinas-Halevi connection could be defended far more strongly if their views of prophecy overlapped in significant ways. Yet outside of a rhetorical link between prophecy and witness, there is no substantive overlap between the two.

*   *   *

The lengthiest articulation of Levinas' view of prophecy appears near the end of his second magnum opus, *Otherwise Than Being*. Yet just because it is lengthy does not mean that it is all that clear. The ostensible definition reads as follows: "One could call 'prophecy' [*prophétisme*] this reversal [*retournement*] in which the perception of an order coincides with the signification, made by the one who obeys it, of this order. And thus prophecy would be the very animation [*psychisme*] of the soul [*l'âme*]—the other in the same—and all the spirituality of humankind would be prophetic."[34] A hint on how to gloss these two sentences comes several paragraphs onward in this section of *Otherwise Than Being*, where Levinas was clearer, in writing of "the anachronism of inspiration or of prophecy" or of "the inspiration or prophecy of all language," that "prophecy" and "inspiration" are to be understood as synonyms.[35] Now earlier in *Otherwise Than Being*, Levinas had used "inspiration" to describe the basis of selfhood in terms of sensibility, that is, the fact that the self is opened out into the world and to others before it understands itself in terms of self-consciousness, implying that a self only comes to think of itself as a subject through its acts of response. As a result, the realm of property and mineness that Levinas identified as "the Same"—because the world becomes comprehended, and mine, through acts of cognition—can only be identified as such on the basis of the self's being "exposed" to the world. The "other" is in the "same," as the condition of its (the same's) possibility. This structure of selfhood implies that the self is unable to become a subject that develops projects for self-making without having already adventured into otherness. It cannot be for itself without existing at least implicitly for the other, and it is in this existing-for-others that it is truly itself. Therefore, Levinas could write (albeit in a poetic style marked by its hyperbole), "through [*par*] the other and for the other, but without alienation: inspired."[36] For Levinas to have troped "the other in the same" as "inspiration" is to hark back to Genesis 2:7 ("He [God] blew into his [Adam's] nostrils the breath of life, and he became a living being"). The "other in the same" is a structure in which "inspiration vivifies [*suscite*] respiration";[37] my breath is not truly my own, but is given to me from that which is other than myself.

Levinas's other-centered ethics—his argument that we should, as a matter of praxis, substitute ourselves for others—is a way of bringing this implicit structure of selfhood into explicit relief. But this argument, expressed as it is in hyperbolic language, is also a call and an act of prophetic signification. We can thus define prophecy for Levinas as an act of bringing the fact of inspiration (the fact that the other precedes the same, that inspiration precedes and thus gives life to respiration as God gives life to Adam) to the fore of sentences that signify. To return to the long and complex definition of prophecy in *Otherwise Than Being* quoted earlier, prophecy would be a "reversal" away from an account of a subject that understands itself as autonomous and that understands its self-expressions as dependent upon its knowledge of the meaning of objects. In addition, it would be a "reversal" away from an account of the self that, in the act of perceiving objects, would determine their essence by examining their properties and would thus see itself as prior to, and more fundamental than, the world. The "reversal" would be a return to the self as it fundamentally exists; it would attest to the fact that expressivity[38] is given to the self from outside, and it would do so explicitly. Prophecy would be any speech-act that is uttered in the awareness that there is an order (here understood in the sense of "stratum") outside and before that in which the self determines itself and its world in its freedom; it would verbalize this awareness in terms opposed to that of freedom, namely, the heteronomous language of order (here understood in the sense of "command"); it would signify this awareness in speaking to others of its obeying this commandedness. If the arena of human spirituality can be described as attesting to this order and the ways in which it determines and guides possibilities for human self-understanding, then there is no reason not to identify prophecy with this entire realm of human culture.

Levinas's discussion of prophecy in *Otherwise Than Being* is situated within a longer discussion of witness, which is defined as a "way for a command to reverberate in the mouth of the very one who obeys."[39] Because the prophet speaks a command of which it is not the author, the prophet serves as witness to this author. However, it is not a witness in the sense that it *sees* the author; rather, it is a witness insofar as its speech is a mark that a command has been given. The witness to a contract is not a witness because she or he has laid eyes on that document. The witness gives testimony (as a *témoin,* "witness" in French) that she or he is certain (*gewiß,* the German word etymologically related to the English "witness") that the parties to the contract have made promises to each other, and thus verifies the contract. In parallel fashion, the Levinasian prophet is not the witness to a promise; the act of witnessing or attesting consists of nothing more (and nothing less) than the act of verification, in and through the nature of prophetic speech, that a command has taken place.[40]

> In my "Here I am" [Is. 6:8], at first present in the accusative, I give evidence of [*témoigne de*] the Infinite. . . . "Here I am, in the name of God," without referring myself directly to Its presence. "Here I am"; nothing more! The word "God" is still absent from the phrase in which God comes for the first time to be mingled with words. It does not at all state "I believe in God." To bear witness to [*témoigner de*] God is not precisely to state this extraordinary word. . . . As a sign given to the other of this very signification, the "here I am" signifies me in the name of God, at the service of those who look at me, without having anything with which to identify myself except the sound of my voice or the figure of my gesture.[41]

Note that the identity of the commander remains unspoken in Levinas's account of prophetic speech, or at the very least, the identity of the commander is immaterial to the fact that the prophet has been commanded. The prophet knows only that she or he has been sent, that she or he speaks in someone else's name and not for the prophet's own self. A commander would only act in human history insofar as it would ground prophets', and their audiences', acts of other-centered ethics.

As stated earlier, Levinas at one point in *Otherwise Than Being* wrote of "the inspiration or prophecy of all language." All language can be analyzed as prophetic speech insofar as linguistic expression is not primarily an innocent invocation of concepts that the speaker and hearer share. If this were the case, there would be no need for language (and no problem of other minds). Language cannot be conceptualized without a structure in which the self speaks *to* another, existing *for* another and only able to identify itself as speaker in this act of extending itself out of itself, in an act of "overflowing [*épanchement*]"[42] to another. Nevertheless, it behooves readers of Levinas to distinguish between "the prophetic" as a structure that the analyst of language and language-users can unveil and make explicit, and "prophetic" as an adjective that we can use to distinguish explicitly prophetic speech from nonprophetic speech. We know that Levinas assumes such a distinction from his last invocation of prophecy in *Otherwise Than Being*:

> Language would exceed the limits of what is thought by suggesting . . . an implication of a meaning distinct from that which comes to signs from . . . the logical definition of a concept. This quality [of language] is laid bare in the poetic said, and the interpretation it calls for ad infinitum. It is shown in the prophetic said, scorning [*méprisant*] its circumstances [*conditions*] in a sort of levitation.[43]

If the prophetic could be immediately identified as such by all hearers of language, then there would be no reason to distinguish between prophetic and poetic statements as Levinas does here; all statements would be prophetic.[44] The "prophetic said"—an utterance that enacts prophecy through a call to a community or a culture to follow certain thematized sets of rules in a determinate way of life, not unlike those philosophical systems that believe thought to mirror nature[45]—belies the origin of its call (that which exceeds that which can be thought). It therefore exists in two orders simultaneously: that of natural causation (the sociopolitical order in which a prophetic call is either heard or ignored) and that of non-natural causation (that which inspires the prophet). For this reason, the prophetic said is described as existing in a kind of levitation. It is neither stuck to the ground by ordinary gravity, nor does it float up, up, and away into the heavens; it remains on earth, possibly audible in language in a mode that also testifies to its height over its audience.

The prophetic said attests to its height in two ways: through its form and through its content. In its form, as stated earlier, it speaks, not for itself, but in the name of that by whom the prophet has been "deranged, awoken, transcended";[46] it testifies to an experience in which the prophet has been taken out of himself. This is a standard piece of non-philosophical scholarship on Israelite prophetic literature: "The tremendous power of the divine claim over Israelite prophets results in a striking state of self-surrender. The singular self shudderingly succumbs to the force of a divine presence that finds thereby both a 'mouth' and a means of earthly expression."[47] In its content, it is countercultural. Indeed, Levinas believes that whenever prophetic speech takes the side of earthly power, it exposes itself as false prophecy.[48] True prophecy, in acknowledging that its source cannot be digested in a system of rules, pushes for new rules that go beyond the limits of the law. Thus, while it is always a danger that the radicality of other-centered ethics might evaporate in any order of justice (even one that is more just than that at present, or even one that is perfectly just), there is also

the eventual possibility for "goodness" to be understood in the guise of prophetic voices reverberating imperiously beneath the profundities of established laws. Voices that do not come, like a legislation beneath legislation, to
be formulated once again in the guise of logical rules, whatever be their invitations to loving-kindness and mercy—to *ḥesed* and *raḥamim,* according to
the expressions of the Hebrew Bible—which are heard within the rigorous
mediation of the just law. But mercy-for-the-other-person, going beyond the
rigorous limit that designates justice, responds to these invitations, whether
by the resources or by the poverty of my uniqueness as an I, in which God
can come to mind.[49]

All morality systems were for Levinas by their very nature nonprophetic, whether they represent the ideologies of those in power or of
those who are powerless. If even a radical ethics of loving-kindness or
mercy is the result of calculation—say, a decision that members of one's
religious community should not merely tithe but donate a majority of their
salaries to charitable organizations—then the origin of inspiration that
cannot be grasped or calculated by the understanding is not the origin of
the believer's acts. For God to come to mind in the life of a community, the
only answer to "What is to be done?" can be "More."

It is not clear to me that this account of prophecy is a purely descriptive
one. Prophecy is the expression of inspiration, yet insofar as "inspiration"
refers to the priority of alterity, prophecy is not something that can signify
in an obvious way to an audience that has not been trained to think of alterity as that which is prior. It does not depend on charisma (although that
might help). It does not depend on how the prophet makes his or her audience feel (although that might help). It does not depend on the images
that the prophet invokes (although that might help). It does not depend on
the good-naturedness or the good-heartedness of the prophet (although
that might help). The one who utters the prophetic said, as well as the
ones who acknowledge the prophetic said as prophetic, require training.
Perhaps this training might be poetic or even Talmudic; such regimens of
learning that the meaning of a text cannot be fully exhausted in a single
interpretation are paths toward an awareness of the primacy of alterity. Yet
for Levinas, especially in *Otherwise Than Being,* it is clear that this training
is philosophical, and specifically, phenomenological. The statement that
language is inherently prophetic can only be recognized as a true statement by the reader who has worked through the previous pages of *Otherwise Than Being* and who has thereby learned, for example, that (a) if the
self were an independent subject, the phenomenologist Edmund Husserl
would not have had to explain our consciousness of time by recourse to a
"primal impression" that comes from I-know-not-where;[50] (b) if the other
were not prior, we would not be able to explain the immediate nature of

sensations of taste or smell, which imply that the self does not have concepts of yeastiness or oakiness before those acts of sensation, and is thus fundamentally constituted by sensibility;[51] (c) if the self were essentially intellectual, if its concrete embodiment were irrelevant, the experience of the pregnant woman would not be one in which she endures disturbances from another in her womb.[52]

These phenomenological analyses have ethical implications once we make explicit in our lives the structures of selfhood that must be the case once we acknowledge such facts about time, taste, or maternity. Indeed, we could not be ethical without such philosophical training in attending to and understanding the implications of our embodiment.[53] Phenomenology, for Levinas, is a precondition of something like the return of prophetic speech to our social and political lives. To do phenomenology

> is above all to search for and recall . . . the human or interhuman intrigue which is the concreteness of its unthought; this concreteness is the necessary mise-en-scène from which abstractions are detached in the "said" of words and propositions. It is to search for the human or interhuman intrigue as the fabric of ultimate intelligibility. And perhaps it is also the way for the wisdom of heaven to return to earth.[54]

This last sentence has two echoes in ancient Judaic literature. The first is to Job 28, a poem that assumes the departure of wisdom from the earth (unlike Proverbs 8 or the opening of Genesis Rabbah, which see wisdom as present in creation): "Where can wisdom be found, where is the place of understanding?" (Job 28:12). After claiming that humans cannot find wisdom through any natural means, that only God knows its place (28:23), the poem concludes in its closing verse (most likely added to the poem by a later redactor) that "fear of the Lord is wisdom, to shun evil is understanding." Thus, the return of wisdom is linked both to ethics and to the awareness of the impossibility of containing transcendence in humanly constructed categories. The second echo is to Ben Sira 24, in which wisdom is identified with the Torah (24:23–34); here the Torah-observant sage taps into wisdom that "runs over, like the Euphrates, with understanding" (24:26) and is thereby able to claim that "I will again pour out teaching like prophecy, and leave it to all future generations" (24:34). Yet the link in Levinas's account of phenomenology between the hoped-for return of heavenly wisdom to earth with an examination of what earthly existence already signifies, through analyses of embodiment and types of sensation, hints that he provides a way to reconcile these ancient texts, which see the acquisition of wisdom by humans as a future occurrence, with other texts, which see wisdom as available now, "playing in His in-

habited world, finding delight with humankind" (Prov 8:31). For Levinas, the account of prophecy is a normative one, offered in the hope that
wisdom will return and prophetic speech will be uttered when, through
philosophical training, we learn that wisdom has been in some sense coyly
with us in its very absence or that wisdom was "playing in front of Him all
the time" (Prov 8:30).[55]

To sum up, there are three primary elements to the Levinasian discourse of prophecy: (1) a description of prophetic witness, not as an act of
seeing or *vision*, but as an act of *saying* or *attesting* to the fundamentally heteronomous nature of human existence, because all language is "in the
name of God"; (2) a description of the prophet's community-creating and
community-oriented acts as fundamentally countercultural, organized
against the amassing of power and authority; and (3) an argument that
both the prophet and the audience need philosophical training—in particular, in a certain kind of way of doing phenomenology—in order to be
sure that the content of prophetic statements is coherent with a right way
of life.

In all three of these respects, Levinas's discourse of prophecy contains
elements that are pointedly opposed to that found in Halevi. First, while
it is true that Halevi conjoined prophetic testimony (*shahāda*) and prophetic witness (*mushāhada*) in the *Kuzari*'s primary discussion of prophecy
at IV:3[56]—"for they [prophets] witness things about which they testify to
one another"—it remains the case that prophetic witness for Halevi is a vision of something that has sensuous content. The Halevian prophet sees
something in the moment of prophecy, while the Levinasian prophet can
only attest to that which transcends through phenomenological analysis.
At least that much seems to be apparent in the following extended passage
from the *Kuzari:*

> Upon the noblest of his creatures God bestowed an "inner eye" that sees all
> things in their unchanging reality; the intellect learns by means of it the es-
> sence of these things. One for whom this [inner] eye has been created is a
> clear-sighted person in truth, and he sees all [other] people as blind, and he
> guides them and shows them the right way. This "eye" is almost [*yushiku
> ʿinna*] the imaginative faculty insofar as it serves the intellect. And he sees a
> great fearsome form that points to indisputable truths. The greatest proof of
> their truth is that this entire species agrees upon these forms—that is, all of
> the prophets witness things about which they testify to one another, just as
> we do with our sensory objects. We testify about the sweetness of honey and
> the bitterness of colocynth; if someone contradicts us we say that he deviates
> from what is natural. They [the prophets] without doubt saw the divine world
> with an "inner eye." They saw forms that were appropriate to their nature
> and to which they were accustomed. They described in corporeal terms what

they saw. These descriptions are true in regard to what estimation, imagination and the senses grasp, but they are not true in regard to the essence that the intellect grasps.[57]

There are some good reasons to read this passage as not about vision. After all, if prophecy is only true in accordance with the imagination, and if the imaginative faculty is secondary to the intellect—as is implicit in Halevi's assertion that the corporeal images that the prophet sees are figural—then it might not be the case that the prophet in Halevi actually has a vision of anything objective. This would open up the possibility of describing what God does in bestowing the "inner eye" in other terms, perhaps focusing on what a prophetic community hears (e.g., at Mount Sinai, per Halevi at *Kuzari* I:87), in a manner that would increase the proximity between Levinas and Halevi. Nevertheless, taking this path would require us to assume that Halevi was being disingenuous when he wrote, in accordance with various Sufi texts, that the prophets "without doubt saw the divine world with an inner eye." There is a way of reading these two passages as coherent, on the assumption that the "inner eye" cannot be *identical* to the imaginative faculty; if that were the case, there would be no need for Halevi to describe the "inner eye" as a special faculty. Rather, it seems to be the case that the "inner eye" is *similar to,* "almost," the imaginative faculty insofar as it provides the intellect with images from which the intellect can grasp essences.[58] It is not a perfected imaginative faculty, but a different kind of faculty that has the same function as the imaginative faculty without being a distinctly human sense, as the imagination is. For this reason, Halevi could assert that the prophet sees the divine world, which is incorporeal, at the same time that he could assert that the prophet expresses what he sees in corporeal terms. The inner eye allows both for a certain kind of seeing and for the generation of corporeal images that lead to a certain kind of saying. The fact that the *descriptions* of what the inner eye sees are not true descriptions of the essence of what the prophet has seen, because they are descriptions of corporeal objects, does not entail that the *visions* of the inner eye are visions of corporeal objects.[59] Thus one should say, along with Elliot Wolfson, that in the *Kuzari* "spiritual vision has an object that is outside the mind, an object that is incorporeal."[60] No such visionary power is ascribed by Levinas to the prophet.

With regard to effects of prophecy in Levinas and Halevi, there are again surface similarities that cover more significant differences. Prophecy in Levinas orients the religious life away from theologoumena, since "to bear witness to God is precisely not to state this extraordinary word."[61] It maintains the transcendence of God in a way that philosophy (on Levinas's view) does not, given its tendency to reduce God to a concept, when

"God" is "a proper and unique noun not entering into any grammatical category." Insofar as the discussion of prophecy in the fourth part of the *Kuzari* has its root in a discussion of divine names that claims that YHVH is a proper noun—"prophecy" is the answer to the Khazar king's asking, "How can I personalize one whom one cannot indicate?"[62]—the contours of the context for the discussions of prophecy in Levinas and Halevi are somewhat similar. Prophecy in both figures is a way of attesting to the uniqueness of that which transcends for the benefit of the community to which the prophet speaks. Nevertheless, in Halevi, as stated above, YHVH is only personalizable because the prophet has had a personal encounter with the divine presence in which he has witnessed the divine world. More importantly, the verification of prophecy in Halevi solidifies the power of religious leaders insofar as the prophet's message is only believed to the degree that the prophet says things that are in agreement with earlier prophets. Those who have seen the divine world see the same thing with their inner eye and must therefore develop images of that world that cohere with each other. Prophecy in Halevi underscores the power of tradition insofar as that tradition attests to the possibility of immediate encounters with the divine and the providential benefits of acknowledging the power of tradition.

Near the end of the *Kuzari*, before the Jewish sage leaves for the Holy Land (because it is only there that human faculties can be perfect), he states that even though the visible Shekhinah is absent from the people of Israel, it is still "best to refer everything to God."[63] Yet one of the benefits of referring everything to God and acknowledging the providential framework of existence is that it brings about the presence of the Shekhinah:

> Imagine God's providence and guidance removed for an instant; the whole world would be destroyed. If the pious person meditates on this in all his movements, he acknowledges the Creator's participation in them, for He first created them, and now provides them with his unceasing support necessary for their perfection. Then it is as if the divine Presence [*sakīna*] is with him continually, and the angels virtually accompany him. If he strengthens his piety, and he abides in places worthy of the Shekhinah, they accompany him in reality, and he sees them with his own eyes, just below the degree of prophecy.[64]

In addition, even though Halevi here described the vision of the Shekhinah as just below prophetic witness, elsewhere in the *Kuzari* he claimed that the presence of the Shekhinah is the cause of prophetic witness.[65] This acknowledgment of providence and its historical benefits for the people of Israel is not present in Levinas in the same manner. For Levinas, prophecy was fundamentally about interruption—about the interruption of the subject by the other person, thereby ethically orienting the self (a dimension

of the "social" being wholly absent in the *Kuzari,* despite Levinas's claim
to the contrary)—and for Levinas, the interruption is also an interruption
of prophecy. In other words, while for Levinas, prophecy is a challenge to
earthly powers, it is also a challenge to its own power when it seeks to in-
stantiate itself in earthly institutions. The prophetic statement that attests
to the fact of transcendence must aim to incarnate itself in a system of justice at the same time that it cannot do so if it is to remain transcendent.
"The forgetting of the self moves justice," wrote Levinas.[66] Yet insofar as
justice requires a system of laws that is ordinary and logical, it cannot incarnate a discourse that testifies to the extraordinary.[67] At best, all that one
can hope for is a cycle of a "periodic return" in which prophetic speech
contests the very institutions that it has helped to create. To the extent
that Levinasian prophecy allows for a traditional sort of religious thought,
centered around a God who can be described in some sense as "personal,"
it does not embolden that tradition as much as does Halevi's discourse of
prophecy. Certainly, it does not aim at a state of affairs in which the divine presence is with a people, whether or not that people is the people of
Israel, so as to maximize their historical power.

When it comes to the issue of the preparation for prophecy, the difference between Levinas and Halevi is stark. As I argued earlier, knowledge
of phenomenological philosophy is a prerequisite for knowing what is at
stake in prophecy—namely, the priority of alterity—and indeed is a prerequisite for uttering prophetic statements. To phrase the issue most baldly,
in *Otherwise Than Being* one can learn to prophesy. No such philosophical
prerequisite for prophecy exists in Halevi; neither is prophecy the result of
a cultivation of human faculties:

> The gift of prophecy was retained among Abraham's descendants in Pales-
> tine, the property of many as long as they remained in the land and fulfilled
> the required conditions: purity, worship, and sacrifices, and above all the rev-
> erence of the Shekhinah. For the *ʾamr ilāhī* singles out one who is worthy of
> its conjoining with him and becoming his lord, as in the case of the prophets
> and the pious, just as the [Active] Intellect singles out one of perfect natural
> qualities, a well-balanced soul and moral traits, to inhabit it in a perfect man-
> ner, as in the case of the philosophers.[68]

Intellectual perfection is completely divorced from prophecy in this passage of the *Kuzari.* The perfection that is associated with prophecy is, by
virtue of its being only structurally analogous to (and lesser than) the intellectual perfection that philosophy can achieve, by definition *other than*
intellectual perfection.

To a great extent, to point out the significant divergences between
Levinas and Halevi is nothing other than to point out that Levinas was a
modern thinker and thus ensconced in very different concerns than Halevi

was. Nevertheless, it is also to point out that the proximity between Levinas and Maimonides is greater than it would appear from Levinas's assertion in the section of "On Jewish Philosophy" quoted near the beginning of this essay. This is most obviously the case as regards the issue of whether prophecy is a natural or supernatural perfection. For Maimonides in *The Guide of the Perplexed*, the traditional Jewish view of prophecy is largely in agreement with the dominant view in the Neoplatonized Aristotelian philosophy of his time. In opposition to Halevi's account of prophecy, in which the divine wills who is or is not to be a prophet, Maimonides argued that "prophecy is a certain perfection in the nature of man. This perfection is not achieved in any individual from among men except after a [philosophical] training that makes that which exists in the potentiality of the species pass into actuality, provided an obstacle due to temperament or to some external cause does not hinder this." The only difference between Judaism and philosophy on the nature of prophecy is that "we [Jews] believe that it may happen that one who is fit for prophecy and prepared for it should not become a prophet, namely, on account of the divine will."[69] The divine will only chooses who *is not* to become a prophet, not who *is* to become a prophet, and there is no prophecy without philosophical training.

Yet the extent of this increase in proximity between Levinas and Maimonides is minimal. It remains the case that for Maimonides too, prophecy was largely about vision; the highest nine of the eleven degrees of prophecy that Maimonides detailed in II:45 of the *Guide* involve veridical dreams or prophetic visions.[70] Still, it might be possible, given the overlap between Levinas and Maimonides on the issue of the philosophical training of the prophet, to translate Levinasian prophecy into Maimonidean language as an overflow from God that perfects a person's rational and imaginative faculties, thereby enabling the prophet to influence others.[71] This would involve describing Levinas's hyperbolic prose, and its effect on readers, as a set of images rooted in Levinas's own phenomenological acumen. (It would also necessitate labeling Levinas a prophet.) Nevertheless, it would remain the case that acquiring intellectual perfection means different things for Maimonides and Levinas, simply because Levinas's account of prophecy as bolstering other-centered ethics involves, as all of Levinas's writings do, the rejection of the primacy of abstract form in philosophy.[72] Despite Levinas's greater proximity to Maimonidean intellectualism than he claimed in "On Jewish Philosophy," the increase is minimal.

One might want to counter this claim and argue for a thicker intimacy between Levinas and Maimonides on the basis of those remarks that Levinas made, both at a later point in "On Jewish Philosophy" and in the discussion following the delivery of the paper "Transcendence and Intelligibility" in 1983, in which he raised the possibility of reading Maimonides as a thinker of other-centered ethics. First, the passage from "On Jewish Philosophy":

> And in Maimonides himself . . . everything culminates in the formulation of the negative attributes. But the possibility of this knowledge is maintained as the ethical stance [*comportement*] of benevolence (*hesed*), justice (*mishpat*) and equity (*tsedaqah*), as "for the other." The imitation of God! The love of one's neighbor is at the summit of a life devoted to supreme knowledge. This is a remarkable reversal, unless we are to question the sincerity of this teacher, suggesting that he may have spoken otherwise than he thought, to avoid unsettling pious minds.[73]

Next, the relevant exchange from the discussion following "Transcendence and Intelligibility," which harks back to an earlier point in that discussion at which Levinas distinguished between his notion of prophecy and oracular concepts of prophecy, saying "I am always troubled when one speaks of 'the presence of God'":[74]

> *Esther Starobinski:* I would like to come back to what you said about prophecy. You describe it in its ethical sense. But there is also in Jewish thought an intellectualist interpretation: prophecy as a perfectly purified intelligence.
> *Emmanuel Levinas:* That is Maimonides!
> *E.S.:* Do you see in such an interpretation something foreign to Judaism or something that is integrated there?
> *E.L.:* I do not have the impertinence to contest Maimonides. Prophecy may precisely signify this perfectly purified intelligence. I think that in its ethical signification this notion of purity and this superlative are less metaphorical.[75]

In both of these passages, Levinas dealt with the vexed issue of the nature of human perfection in the *Guide*. In the midst of the closing section of the *Guide*, Maimonides claimed that "the true human perfection consists in the acquisition of the rational virtues,"[76] and that this perfection is higher than perfection in the moral virtues. Such an assertion is consistent with the overall intellectualist tenor of the text. Nevertheless, in the final sentences, Maimonides also cited Jeremiah 9:22–23 in support of the contention that God "means that it is My purpose that there should come from you 'lovingkindness [*hesed*], righteousness [*tsedaqah*] and judgment [*mishpat*] in the earth' (Jer. 9:23) in the way we have explained with regard to the thirteen attributes [*middot*]: namely, that the purpose should be assimilation to them and that this should be our way of life."[77] The moral virtues seem, in the final accounting, to come out on top, in contradiction to Maimonides' earlier intellectualist claim.

Levinas himself would be a Maimonidean, *if* Maimonides were anti-intellectualist. The two brief remarks, in "On Jewish Philosophy" and the exchange with Starobinski, seem to suggest that Levinas himself cannot decide on this issue. In the former interview, Levinas's own position is best described as that of the pious minds who would be upset by Maimonides' intellectualist denigration of ethics. Levinas identified with Halevi, despite elements in Maimonides' thinking that are proximate to Levinas's own, because Maimonides was not seriously and systematically supporting other-centered ethics. In the exchange with Starobinski, Levinas seemed to be open to the possibility that intellectualism and ethics are linked. If this were to be the case, other-centered ethics would be a less abstract, less "metaphorical," account of what is at stake in prophecy, for the intellectual perfection that leads to prophecy cannot but perform itself in other-centered ethical acts. But scholars of Jewish philosophy should not, through esoteric readings or other acts of acrobatic litheness, run with possibilities here. For Maimonides was neither exoterically nor esoterically arguing for an other-centered ethics at the center of the religious life. As Herbert Davidson has argued in his classic article on ethics in Maimonides,[78] for humans to assimilate their acts to God's acts is also to act from the same grounds that God does. And as Maimonides argued in *Guide* I:54, because God is one, God does not have multiple passions or aptitudes of the soul. As a result, God's actions do not have their ground in "any passion whatever, may He be exalted above every deficiency."[79] This means that the prophet who imitates God should act similarly:

> It behooves the governor of a city, if he is a prophet, to acquire similarity to these attributes, so that these actions may proceed from him according to a determined measure and according to the deserts of the people who are affected by them and not merely because of his following a passion. He should not let loose the reins of anger nor let passion gain mastery over him, for all passions are evil; but, on the contrary, he should guard against them as far as this lies within the capacity of man.[80]

For Maimonides, the ethical element in prophecy involved *not* being for the other. It is already to know what the proper measure of action is, and to know what is a deserved response to another's act. Indeed, to be a prophet is neither to be for the other nor for oneself; it is to be for God. This being-for-God may indeed benefit others, but this benefit would not be due to acknowledging the primacy of alterity.

Still, one might seek to argue for proximity between Maimonides and Levinas by bolstering the importance of phenomenological aptitude as a preparation for Levinasian prophecy. For in *Otherwise Than Being*, other-centered ethics was not the result of an encounter with another person that inflamed the passions and gave rise to a conversion away from self-centeredness. It is the result of philosophical reflection that leads one to acknowledge that the self is always subject to that which is, and those who are, exterior to it. If this were not to be the case, there would have been no reason for Levinas to spend over a dozen pages analyzing the nature of time near the beginning of that book; nor would he have begun the analysis of sensibility by pointing out facts about what it means to sense heat, taste, or smell.[81] (Such senses are not ethical. We say that a rose smells good; we do not say that we do good to roses when we stop and smell them.) Would it not be possible, then, to say that Levinas's other-centered ethics too would have its basis in a self's knowledge of what is to be done and how to respond to a situation? To say that ethics consists in being for the other as much as one is humanly capable, and perhaps in striving to expand that capability, is not to root ethics in a passion.

Such an argument may, indeed, work—I must confess that it is an argument that I hold dear—but it would come up short against a more formidable difference between Levinas and Maimonides, namely, that of elitism. (I thank Oona Eisenstadt for raising this issue in conversation; it is of such importance that I cannot relegate my gratitude to a footnote.) For Maimonides, the ability to imitate God's dispassionate nature was limited to cultural leaders, whether politicians or philosophers; he could not imagine the masses extirpating their passions. Yet for Levinas, there was no such limit. Maimonides believed that the true human perfection is also the most rare; Levinas believed, because his phenomenological philosophy aims at unpacking the concrete and not the abstract, that there is no one who cannot come to know that existence is for the other. This difference is clearest in their different interpretations of Amos 3:8. There are several occasions in Levinas's discussions of prophecy in which he cited this verse ("The Lord God has spoken; who would not prophesy?"). On one occasion, it is to support the claim that "in principle the human spirit as such is open to inspiration, that man as such is potentially a prophet";[82] more often, it is to support the somewhat stronger claim that "all men are prophets."[83] Individuals, through philosophical preparation, can come to acknowledge that their language is spoken in the name of a God who has already spoken; such an acknowledgment cannot occur without the corollary that language has been prophetic all along, that we have been prophets but have not made use of that gift to direct the future of history. Prophecy becomes the domain of all language-users; the ability to utter prophetic statements is not excluded from any on the basis of their intellectual capacity or their ethnic identity. For Levinas, Amos posited prophecy "as the fundamental fact of man's humanity"[84] or "simply the fact of having an ear."[85]

When Maimonides cited this verse at the end of II:37 of *The Guide of the Perplexed*, it was to explain why prophets might be unsuccessful in persuading their audiences to agree with them. When a prophet receives an overflow from the divine of a sufficiently great quantity, he cannot but "address a call to the people, teach them, and let his own perfection overflow toward them."[86] Nevertheless, the people may not listen to the prophet. Even though they may reject him, and even though it may be prudent for the prophet to cease his prophecy, such a prudential decision is impossible in light of the urge to speak that has been implanted in the prophet without his consent. Maimonides cites Jeremiah's lament (20:8–9) that "the word of the Lord causes me constant disgrace and contempt. I thought, 'I will not mention Him, no more will I speak in His name.'" The citation to Amos 3:8 is yet another proof text for this claim. As a result, his citation is to be understood as saying, "The Lord God has spoken *to me*, and not to you. There are others to whom God has spoken (but not you); and they are compelled to speak prophetically." Because Maimonides saw prophecy as contingent upon an individual's perfection of both his rational and imaginative faculties,[87] prophecy, even in the loosest of senses, could never become equivalent with language use. Maimonides' investment in citing Amos was an investment in salvaging the elite status of the prophet when he suffers historical misfortune, for example, rejection from his audience. One might think that a prophet's failure to redirect a community's ethos would signify that he does not possess the degree of intellectual or imaginative perfection that Maimonides alleges; thus, to speak of prophetic speech as coerced explains away the apparent imprudence of the prophet. But such failure seems not to have been a real possibility for Levinas. When all language-users are seen as prophets, either actually or potentially, the possibility of an audience's rejection of the prophet is minimized, and hope in the possibility of a better future for a community is strengthened.[88] For Levinas to be interpreted as a Maimonidean in this regard would be to sacrifice hope in the future, hope that war is not permanently possible,[89] hope that divine providence can be social and not simply individual.[90]

* * *

In conclusion, we cannot show a seamless connection between Levinas and the two foremost thinkers in the canon of medieval Jewish philosophy. We cannot say that Levinas was genuinely aligned with Halevi. And while there are some minimal overlaps between Levinas and Maimonides resulting from their open appreciation for certain philosophers and philosophical practice, neither is it possible to say that Levinas was exoterically attached to Halevi while esoterically Maimonidean. Finally, we cannot say that Levinas succeeded in showing that the dichotomy between Halevi and Maimonides is minimal, as he hints in the opening of his response to Armengaud, or even if such a goal was his intent. What we can say is that the case of Levinas is yet another piece of evidence in support of the contention that traditions are constructed. We do not assimilate to them; we assimilate them to ourselves. Levinas was a modern,[91] detached from the past (as we all are) simply because he was not contemporary with that past. He attempted to hide this detachment behind the screen of the canon of Jewish philosophy and expressed that detachment by screening his own concerns onto that canon through the medium of philosophy. Yet, given the vibrancy of scholarly debates on the relationship between "Judaism" and "philosophy" in the major figures in this canon from Philo to Derrida, there is no reason to quarantine Levinas with the charge that he is atypical in this regard. Such is the bugbear of all who make claims about Judaism after emancipation, or even after the Babylonian exile. Because those about whom scholars of Jewish philosophy write are not *us* (in spite of scholars' reflexive tendency to use the present tense when writing about them), we can never receive their wisdom directly. The canon of Jewish philosophy can never be anything more than a screen that gives itself to us when we read, discuss, write about, or publish essays on the texts that compose it. But for those who cannot tolerate living in the disorder of detachment from past and future, who need to reach out to the absolute, the canon of Jewish philosophy is a necessary tool for self-making, and can never be anything less than that screen.

May we scholars of Jewish philosophy have the courage to honor our forebears by screening our canon, reading from out of our own non-neutral positions—even if this means being untrue to the texts that we read, or even if this means being untrue to ourselves (out of shame at such naked subjectivism)—and pushing Jewish philosophy into new directions as a result. Some would describe such a labor in secular terms, speaking of scholars' own constructive position within the history of ideas. Others, on the other hand, might well describe this act of freeing ourselves from being determined solely by the past, insofar as this makes possible a future that is discontinuous with the present, as an act that can build communities' confidence in the possibility of a future manifestation of a redeeming presence.[92]

NOTES

1. For the primary essays on Buber, see "Martin Buber et la théorie de la connaissance" and "Dialogue avec Martin Buber," in *Noms propres* (Montpellier: Fata Morgana, 1976), 23–48; "Martin Buber and the Theory of Knowledge" and "Dialogue with Martin Buber" in *Proper Names,* translated by Michael Smith (Stanford, Calif.: Stanford University Press, 1996), 17–39. See also "La pensée de Martin Buber et la judaïsme contemporaine," "Martin Buber, Gabriel Marcel et la philosophie," and "A pro-

pos de Buber: quelques notes," all in *Hors sujet* (Montpellier: Fata Morgana, 1987), 15–69; "Martin Buber's Thought and Contemporary Judaism," "Martin Buber, Gabriel Marcel, and Philosophy," and "Apropos of Buber: Some Notes," all in *Outside the Subject,* translated by Michael B. Smith (Stanford, Calif.: Stanford University Press, 1995), 4–48.

See also the following other books and essays of Levinas. In French, *Totalité et l'infini* (The Hague: Martinus Nijhoff, 1961), 40–41 and 129; *Autrement qu'être, ou au-delà de l'essence* (The Hague: Martinus Nijhoff, 1974), 15; *Le temps et l'autre* (Paris: PUF, 1983), 89; "La dialogue: conscience de soi et proximité du prochain," in *De Dieu qui vient à l'idée* (Paris: Vrin, 1986), 211–30; "Le mot je, le mot tu, le mot Dieu," in *Altérité et transcendance* (Montpellier: Fata Morgana, 1995), 104–6; "Transcendance et hau-teur," in *Levinas,* edited by Catherine Chalier and Miguel Abensour (Paris: L'Herne, 1991), 103. In English, see *Totality and Infinity,* translated by Alphonso Lingis (Pitts-burgh: Duquesne University Press, 1969), 68–69 and 155; *Otherwise Than Being,* trans-lated by Lingis (Pittsburgh: Duquesne University Press, 1981), 13; *Time and the Other,* translated by Richard A. Cohen (Pittsburgh: Duquesne University Press, 1987), 93–94; "Dialogue: Self-Consciousness and Proximity of the Neighbor," in *Of God Who Comes to Mind,* translated by Bettina Bergo (Stanford, Calif.: Stanford University Press, 1998), 137–51; "The Word I, the Word You, the Word God," in *Alterity and Transcendence,* translated by Michael B. Smith (New York: Columbia University Press, 1999), 93–95; "Transcendence and Height," in *Basic Philosophical Writings,* eds. Adriaan T. Peperzak, Simon Critchley, and Robert Bernasconi (Bloomington: Indiana University Press, 1996), 20.

See also the remarks in the following interviews. In languages other than En-glish: François Poirié, *Emmanuel Levinas, qui êtes-vous?* (Lyon: La Manufacture, 1987), 123–25; "Intention, Ereignis und die Andere," in *Humanismus des anderen Menschen,* edited by Ludwig Wenzler (Hamburg: Felix Meiner, 1989), 136–37; "La proximité de l'autre," in *Altérité et transcendance,* 110–12; "Philosophie, justice et amour," in *Entre nous* (Paris: Grasset, 1991), 137–38. In English, "Interview with François Poirié," and "Intention, Event and the Other," in *Is It Righteous to Be? Interviews with Emmanuel Levi-nas,* edited by Jill Robbins (Stanford, Calif.: Stanford University Press, 2001), 72ff. and 145ff.; "The Proximity of the Other," in *Alterity and Transcendence,* 99–102; and "Phi-losophy, Justice and Love," in *Entre Nous,* translated by Michael B. Smith and Barbara Harshav (New York: Columbia University Press, 1998), 119.

2. Levinas, *Autrement qu'être,* 15; *Otherwise Than Being,* 13.

3. For the primary essays on Rosenzweig, see Levinas, "Entre deux mondes: la voie de Franz Rosenzweig," in *Difficile liberté* (Paris: Albin Michel, 1976), 235–60; "Franz Rosenzweig: une pensée juive moderne," in *Hors sujet,* 73–96; "La philosophie de Franz Rosenzweig," in *A l'heure des nations* (Paris: Minuit, 1988), 175–85. In En-glish, see Levinas, "Between Two Worlds: The Way of Franz Rosenzweig," in *Diffi-cult Freedom,* translated by Seán Hand (Baltimore: Johns Hopkins University Press, 1990), 181–201; "Franz Rosenzweig: A Modern Jewish Thinker," in *Outside the Subject,* 49–66; "The Philosophy of Franz Rosenzweig," in *In the Time of the Nations,* translated by Michael B. Smith (Bloomington: Indiana University Press, 1994), 150–60.

For references in other books and essays see, in French, *Totalité et l'infini,* xvi; *Difficile liberté,* 207; "Diachronie et representation," in *Entre nous,* 196; "La dialogue," 221–22; "Façon de parler," in *De Dieu qui vient à l'idée,* 268–69. In English, see *Totality and Infinity,* 28; *Difficult Freedom,* 157; "Diachrony and Representation" in *Entre Nous,* 176; "Dialogue: Self-Consciousness and the Proximity of the Neighbor" and "Manner of Speaking," in *Of God Who Comes to Mind,* 144–45 and 210–11.

For references in interviews, see "Judaïsme 'et' christianisme," in *A l'heure des nations,* 189–95, and its expanded German form in *Zeitgewinn: Messianisches Denken nach Franz Rosenzweig,* edited by Gotthard Fuchs and Hans Hermann Henrix (Frankfurt: Josef Knecht, 1987), 163–84; Poirié, 121–22; "Intention, Ereignis, und der Andere," 138 and 141; "Philosophie, justice et amour," 137; Solomon Malka, *Lire Levinas* (Paris: Cerf, 1989), 105–106; "L'Autre, utopie et justice," in *Entre nous,* 263–64; *Éthique et infini: dialogues avec Philippe Nemo* (Paris: Fayard, 1982), 80. In English, see "Judaism and Christianity," in *In the Time of the Nations,* 161–66, and its expanded form as "Judaism and Christianity after Franz Rosenzweig," in *Is It Righteous to Be?* 255–67; "Interview with François Poirié," 71; "Intention, Event and the Other," 147 and 150; "Philosophy, Justice, and Love," 118; "Interview with Salomon Malka," in *Is It Righteous to Be?* 94–95; "The Other, Utopia, and Justice," in *Entre Nous,* 233; "Diachrony and Representation" in *Entre Nous,* 176; "Dialogue: Self-Consciousness and the Proximity of the Neighbor" and "Manner of Speaking," in *Of God Who Comes to Mind,* 144–45 and 210–11; *Ethics and Infinity,* translated by Richard A. Cohen (Pittsburgh: Duquesne University Press, 1985), 75–76.

4. For intellectual-historical criticisms of Levinas's encomium to Rosenzweig, see Peter E. Gordon, *Rosenzweig and Heidegger: Between Judaism and German Philosophy* (Berkeley: University of California Press, 2003), 9–11, and Samuel Moyn, *Origins of the Other: Emmanuel Levinas Between Revelation and Ethics* (Ithaca, N.Y.: Cornell University Press, 2005), 113–63. For philosophically based criticisms of the encomium, see Martin Kavka, *Jewish Messianism and the History of Jewish Philosophy* (Cambridge: Cambridge University Press, 2004), 129–92, and David Novak, *Natural Law in Judaism* (Cambridge: Cambridge University Press, 1998), 66ff., especially when read in the context of 142ff. Whether these criticisms are, at the end of the day, criticisms of Levinas, as opposed to criticisms of self-styled "Levinasians," remains unclear. Moyn points out Levinas's detachment from certain aspects of Rosenzweig at 162; one could also point to the following sentence in the interview with Poirié: "I don't follow Rosenzweig all the time, by the way, although I have adopted certain of the fundamental positions of his purely theoretical thinking" (Poirié, 121–22; "Interview with François Poirié," 71).

5. See "La pensée de Moses Mendelssohn," in *A l'heure des nations,* 159–68; "Pour un humanisme hebraique," in *Difficile liberté,* 351; "Moses Mendelssohn's Thought," in *In the Time of the Nations,* 136–45; "For A Jewish Humanism," in *Difficult Freedom,* 274.

6. See "La souffrance inutile," in *Entre nous,* 115–18; "Useless Suffering," in *Entre Nous,* 97–100.

7. See *La théorie de l'intuition dans la phenomenology de Husserl* (Paris: Alcan, 1930), 17; *Totalité et l'infini,* 43; *Dieu, la mort, et le temps* (Paris: Grasset, 1993), 229–30; *The Theory of Intuition in Husserl's Phenomenology,* translated by André Orianne (Evanston, Ill.: Northwestern University Press, 1973), xxv; *Totality and Infinity,* 71; *God, Death and Time,* translated by Bettina Bergo (Stanford, Calif.: Stanford University Press, 2000), 200. See also Edith Wyschogrod's 1980 article "The Moral Self: Levinas and Hermann Cohen," reprinted in *Crossover Queries: Dwelling With Negatives, Embodying Philosophy's Others* (New York: Fordham University Press, 2006), 405–22, an article that only touches on Judaism obliquely, through a brief analysis of messianic society in Cohen and Levinas (412).

8. Most of these comments claim a close filiation between Spinoza and Heidegger or Hegel. See *Totalité et l'infini,* 59, 75, 78, 92, 193; *Autrement qu'être,* 222; "Judaïsme et revolution" and "Désacralisation et désensorcellement," in *Du sacré au saint* (Paris: Minuit, 1977), 31 and 99; "La pensée de Martin Buber et la judaïsme contemporain," 27; "Réflexions sur la 'technique' phénoménologique," in *En découvrant l'existence avec*

Husserl et Heidegger (Paris: Vrin, 1967); 120; Poirié, 107; "La vocation de l'autre," in *Racismes: l'autre et son visage,* edited by Emmanuel Hirsch (Paris: Cerf, 1988), 101; "Infini," "La proximité de l'autre" and "Le philosophe et la mort," in *Altérité et transcendance,* 71, 82–84, 108, 161, and 169; "Sein-zum-Tod und 'Du sollst nicht töten,'" in *Französischen Philosophen im Gespräch,* edited by Florian Rötzer (Munich: Klaus Boer, 1987), 96–97; *Dieu, la mort et le temps,* 21. In English, see *Totality and Infinity,* 87, 102, 105, 119, 217; *Otherwise Than Being,* 176; "Judaism and Revolution" and "Desacralization and Disenchantment," in *Nine Talmudic Readings,* translated by Annette Aronowicz (Bloomington: Indiana University Press, 1990), 105–6, 147; "Martin Buber's Thought and Contemporary Judaism," 14; "Reflections on Phenomenological 'Technique,'" in *Discovering Existence with Husserl* (Evanston, Ill.: Northwestern University Press, 1998), 100; "Interview with François Poirié," "The Vocation of the Other," and "Being-Toward-Death and 'Thou Shalt Not Kill,'" in *Is It Righteous to Be?* 59, 113, and 136; "Infinity," "The Proximity of the Other" and "The Philosopher and Death," in *Alterity and Transcendence,* 55, 68–71, 97, 155 and 166; *God, Death, and Time,* 12.

For more interesting comments, see "Idéologie et idéalisme," in *De Dieu qui vient à l'idée,* 22; "L'arrière-plan de Spinoza," in *Au-delà du verset* (Paris: Minuit, 1982), 201–6; "Jean Lacroix: Philosophie et religion," in *Noms propres,* 119–30; "Existentialisme et antisémitisme," in *Les imprévus de l'histoire* (Montpellier: Fata Morgana, 1994), 121–22, and the important remarks, made early in Levinas's career, found in "Le cas Spinoza" and "Avez-vous relu Baruch?" in *Difficile liberté,* 142–59. See also Levinas's review of Harry A. Wolfson's *Spinoza* in *Revue des études juives* 1 (1937): 114–19. In English, see "Ideology and Idealism," in *Of God Who Comes to Mind,* 6; "Spinoza's Background," in *Beyond the Verse: Talmudic Readings and Lectures,* translated by Gary D. Mole (Bloomington: Indiana University Press, 1994), 168–73; "Jean Lacroix: Philosophy and Religion," in *Proper Names,* 80–89; "Existentialism and Antisemitism," in *Unforeseen History,* translated by Nidra Poller (Urbana: University of Illinois Press, 2004), 74–75; "The Spinoza Case" and "Have You Reread Baruch?" in *Difficult Freedom,* 106–18.

See also Michel Juffé, "Levinas as (mis)Reader of Spinoza," in *Levinas Studies* 2 (2007): 153–73.

9. See "Sur la philosophie juive," in *A l'heure des nations,* 199–203; "On Jewish Philosophy," in *In the Time of the Nations,* 169–72.

10. For additional references to Halevi, see "Dieu et la philosphie," in *De Dieu qui vient à l'idée,* 96–97 and *Autrement,* 232; "God and Philosophy," in *Of God Who Comes to Mind,* 57 and *Otherwise Than Being,* 184.

For additional references to Maimonides, see "L'actualité de Maïmonide," *Paix et Droit* 15, no. 4 (April 1935): 6–7, reprinted in *Emmanuel Levinas,* edited by Catherine Chalier and Miguel Abensour (Paris: Cahiers de L'Herne, 1991), 142–44; "Une religion d'adultes," "Textes messianiques," and "Pour un humanisme hébraïque," in *Difficile liberté,* 30, 83, and 351; "Envers autrui," in *Quatre lectures talmudiques* (Paris: Minuit, 1968), 33; "Le nom de Dieu d'après quelques texts talmudiques," "La revelation dans la tradition juive," and "L'état de César et l'état de David," in *Au-delà du verset,* 147, 175, and 213–15; "Mépris de la Thora comme idolâtrie" and "Une figure et une époque" in *A l'heure des nations,* 71 and 172; "Questions et réponses," in *De Dieu qui vient à l'idée,* 149–50; *Transcendance et intelligibilité* (Geneva: Labor et Fides, 1996), 63; Malka, *Lire Levinas,* 114; "La laïcité et la pensée d'Israël," in *Les imprévus de l'histoire,* 191. In English, see "A Religion for Adults," "For a Jewish Humanism," and "Messianic Texts," in *Difficult Freedom,* 15, 274, and 296–97 n.1; "Toward the Other," in *Nine Talmudic Readings,* 14; "The Name of God According to a Few Talmudic Texts," "Revelation in the Jewish Tradition," and "The State of Caesar and the State of David," in *Beyond The Verse,* 119,

145, 181–82; "Contempt for the Torah as Idolatry" and "A Figure and a Period," in *In the Time of the Nations*, 59 and 149; "Questions and Answers," in *Of God Who Comes to Mind*, 94; "Discussion following 'Transcendence and Intelligibility'," in *Is It Righteous to Be?* 283; "Interview with Salomon Malka," 102; "Secularism and the Thought of Israel," in *Unforeseen History*, 122. See also Edith Wyschogrod's 1982 "Interview with Emmanuel Levinas," reprinted in *Crossover Queries*, 288.

For suggestive links between Maimonides and Levinas, see the following essays in Wyschogrod's *Crossover Queries:* "Intending Transcendence, Desiring God," 25–26; "Corporeality and the Glory of the Infinite in the Philosophy of Levinas," passim; "Postmodernism and the Desire for God," 311–12. For a suggestive treatment of Levinas's 1935 article on Maimonides, see Moyn, 189–90.

11. Levinas, "Sur la philosphie juive," 198–99; "On Jewish Philosophy," 167–69. On many occasions in this essay I have emended published translations from the French. I do not read either Arabic or Judeo-Arabic, so citations from Halevi and Maimonides are indebted to existing translations as well as to the essays and books of scholars who have emended existing translations.

12. The quotation is from Gershom Scholem, "Revelation and Tradition as Religious Categories in Judaism," translated by Henry Schwarzschild and Michael A. Meyer, in *The Messianic Idea in Judaism and Other Essays on Jewish Spirituality* (New York: Schocken, 1971), 292. For a treatment of this essay, see Michael Morgan, *Interim Judaism: Jewish Thought in a Century of Crisis* (Bloomington: Indiana University Press, 2001), 57–59. For a treatment of this essay with specific reference to Levinas, see Richard A. Cohen, *Ethics, Exegesis and Philosophy: Interpretation after Levinas* (Cambridge: Cambridge University Press, 2001), 216ff. In this essay, I agree with Cohen's statement (226) that "exegesis is the effort not to reduce transcendence," but voice my doubt as to whether this effort can avoid misreading and express a hope that exposing misreading might be of both scholarly and theological value.

13. Franz Rosenzweig, "Die Bauleute," in *Zweistromland: Kleinere Schriften zu Glauben und Denken*, ed. Reinhold and Annemarie Mayer (Dordrecht: Martinus Nijhoff, 1984), 702. Either purposefully or accidentally, Nahum Glatzer omitted this sentence from his translation of "The Builders" in the volume published as *On Jewish Learning*.

14. In other words, I see no reason why Jewish philosophy cannot fulfill the same function that Daniel Boyarin sees Jewish cultural studies as fulfilling, in "Justify My Love," in *Unheroic Conduct: The Rise of Heterosexuality and the Invention of the Jewish Man* (Berkeley: University of California Press, 1997), xiii–xxiv. In future work, I hope to describe Jewish philosophy as a discipline that works according to the logic of disidentification articulated most clearly in José Esteban Muñoz's *Disidentifications: Queers of Color and the Performance of Politics* (Minneapolis: University of Minnesota Press, 1999), and defend a claim that "disidentification" is a more apt term than philosophical "counternarrative," used by Michael Mack in *German Idealism and the Jew* (Chicago: University of Chicago Press, 2003) or some other variant on Amos Funkenstein's notion of "counterhistory," because it expresses the (very Levinasian) idea that the independent subject arises out of, without ever completely abandoning, a relation of dependence. Jewish philosophy has never been a masculine science, no matter how much it may have strained to appear as one. (Even its frequent "butch" appearance is dependent on others' charges of effeminacy.)

15. Levinas, "Dieu et la philosophie," 96–97; "God and Philosophy," 57.

16. Levinas, "Une religion d'adultes," 30; "A Religion for Adults," 15.

17. Levinas, "Sur la philosophie juive," 200–201; "On Jewish Philosophy," 169–70.

18. Levinas, "Philosophie et l'idée de l'infini," in *En découvrant l'existence avec Husserl et Heidegger*, 165–66; "Philosophy and the Idea of Infinity," in *Collected Philosophical Papers*, translated by Alphonso Lingis (Dordrecht: Martinus Nijhoff, 1987), 48.

19. Moses Maimonides, *The Guide of the Perplexed*, translated by Shlomo Pines (Chicago: University of Chicago Press, 1963), 164.

20. Ibid., 165. This passage creates problems for the customary understanding of Maimonides' so-called "negative theology." For one attempt to solve this problem, see Diana Lobel, "'Silence Is Praise to You': Maimonides on Negative Theology, Looseness of Expression, and Religious Experience," *American Catholic Philosophical Quarterly* 76, no. 1 (2002): 25–51.

21. Plotinus, *Enneads* I.8.5.8–10.

22. Yehuda Halevi, *Kuzari*, IV:3. See the Hirschfeld translation (New York: Schocken, 1964), 199, which I have altered to match that of Diana Lobel in *Between Mysticism and Philosophy: Sufi Language of Religious Experience in Judah Ha-Levi's* Kuzari (Albany: SUNY Press, 2000), 73.

23. Halevi, *Kuzari*, I:1. See Hirschfeld, 37; Lobel, 22.

24. Harry A. Wolfson, "Hallevi and Maimonides on Prophecy," in *Studies in Religious Philosophy*, edited by Isadore Twersky and George H. Williams (Cambridge, Mass.: Harvard University Press, 1973), 1:60–119, esp. 96; Howard Kreisel, *Prophecy: The History of an Idea in Medieval Jewish Philosophy* (Dordrecht: Kluwer Academic Publishers, 2001), 137; Lobel, *Between Mysticism and Philosophy*, 30.

25. Kreisel, 137; Herbert Davidson, "The Active Intellect in the *Cuzari* and Hallevi's Theory of Causality," *Revue des études juives* 131 (1973): 391ff.

26. Davidson, "Active Intellect," 395.

27. Halevi, *Kuzari*, I:109. See Hirschfeld, 75–76; Lobel, *Between Mysticism and Philosophy*, 51.

28. Halevi, *Kuzari*, II:34. See Hirschfeld, 108.

29. Halevi, *Kuzari*, II:26. See Hirschfeld, 103; here I have followed the translation of Davidson, "Active Intellect," 383.

30. Halevi, *Kuzari*, II:14. See Hirschfeld, 92; Lobel, *Between Mysticism and Philosophy*, 33.

31. Halevi, *Kuzari* III:53. See Hirschfeld, 183; Lobel, *Between Mysticism and Philosophy*, 85.

32. Shlomo Pines, "Shīʿite Terms and Conceptions in the Kuzari," *Jerusalem Studies in Arabic and Islam* 2 (1980): 165–251, qtd. at 177.

33. See *Autrement qu'être*, 190–94 and 216; "Avant-propos," "De la lecture juive des Écritures," "La revelation dans la tradition juive," and "Politique après!" in *Au'delà du verset*, 7–11, 136–38, 173–75, and 223; "Avant-propos" and "Dieu et la philosophie," in *De Dieu qui vient à l'idée*, 13 and 123–26; *Transcendance et intelligibilité*, 37 and 63ff.; "Philosophie, justice, et amour" and "De l'un à l'autre," in *Entre nous*, 124 and 175; *Ethique et infini*, 121–22; "Pour une place dans la Bible," "Mépris de la Thora comme idolâtrie," "Au-dela du souvenir," and "De l'éthique a l'exégèse," in *A l'heure des nations*, 28–32, 77, 100, and 129–30; "Violence du visage," in *Altérité et transcendance*, 182; "L'ancien et le nouveau," in *L'ancien et le nouveau*, edited by Joseph Doré (Paris: Cerf, 1982), 37; "Entretien," in *Répondre d'autrui*, edited by Jean-Christophe Aeschlimann (Neuchâtel: Baconnière, 1989), 11; *Dieu, la mort et le temps*, 163.

In English, see *Otherwise Than Being*, 149–52 and 170; "Foreword," "On the Jewish Reading of Scriptures," "Revelation in the Jewish Tradition," and "Politics After!" in *Beyond the Verse*, x–xiv, 110ff., 143–45, 189–90, 210–11; "Foreword" and "God and

Philosophy," in *Of God Who Comes to Mind*, xv and 75–77; "Being-for-the-Other" and "Discussion following 'Transcendence and Intelligibility,'" in *Is It Righteous to Be?* 116, 269–70 and 283ff.; "Philosophy, Justice, and Love" and "From the One to the Other," in *Entre Nous*, 106 and 152ff., 11; *Ethics and Infinity*, 113–14; "For a Place in the Bible," "Contempt for the Torah as Idolatry," "Beyond Memory," and "From Ethics to Exegesis," in *In the Time of the Nations*, 19–23, 64–65, 86 and 111–12; "Violence of the Face," in *Alterity and Transcendence*, 181; "The Old and the New," in *Time and the Other*, 137–38; *God, Death and Time*, 142.

34. Levinas, *Autrement qu'être*, 190; Levinas, *Otherwise Than Being*, 149. In translating *psychisme* as "animation," I am following John Llewelyn, *The Hypocritical Imagination: Between Kant and Levinas* (London: Routledge, 2000), 28.

35. Levinas, *Autrement*, 192 and 194; Levinas, *Otherwise*, 150 and 152.

36. Levinas, *Autrement*, 146; Levinas, *Otherwise*, 114.

37. Levinas, *Autrement*, 147; Levinas, *Otherwise*, 116.

38. Note that Levinas also uses "signification" and "expressivity" as synonyms. See Levinas, *Autrement*, 17; Levinas, *Otherwise*, 14.

39. Levinas, *Autrement*, 187; Levinas, *Otherwise*, 147.

40. As such, the Levinasian rhetoric of the "witness" should be seen as parallel to the rhetoric of verification (*Bewährung*) that we find in the closing pages of both Martin Buber's *I and Thou* and Franz Rosenzweig's *Star of Redemption*.

41. Levinas, *Autrement*, 190; Levinas, *Otherwise*, 149.

42. Ibid.

43. Levinas, *Autrement*, 215–16; Levinas, *Otherwise*, 169–70.

44. I must admit here that my interpretation is on somewhat shaky ground. In other places in the Levinasian corpus, he describes prophetic inspiration as that which allows its statements to be "ever renewable through exegesis." In this case, the prophetic said and the poetic said would be marked by the same characteristic, making the task of identifying the difference between them difficult. Nevertheless, I think that it is important to be able to distinguish between sentences that express the inspiration of language in their content (those spoken by prophets) and those that do not (those spoken by, say, Donald Trump). See "De l'éthique à l'exégèse," 129; "From Ethics to Exegesis," 112.

45. This definition of the "said" is a gloss on "Dieu et la philosphie"; "God and Philosophy," 74.

46. Levinas, "De la lecture juive des Écritures," 138 n.10; Levinas, "On The Jewish Reading of the Scriptures," 210 n. 11. In this footnote, Levinas also claims that ethics appears as the prophetic.

47. Michael Fishbane, "Biblical Prophecy as a Religious Phenomenon," in *Jewish Spirituality: From the Bible through the Middle Ages*, edited by Arthur Green (New York: Crossroad, 1986), 66.

48. "Let us not forget the constant existence of false prophets who flatter kings. Only the true prophet addresses the king and the people without wanting to please them, and reminds them of ethics." Levinas, "Philosophie, Justice et Amour," 124; Levinas, "Philosophy, Justice and Love," 106.

49. Levinas, "Entretien," 11; "Being-for-the-Other," 116.

50. Levinas, *Autrement qu'être*, 40ff. and *Otherwise Than Being*, 32ff., as well as "Intentionalité et sensation," in *En découvrant l'existence avec Husserl et Heidegger*, 145–62 and "Intentionality and Sensation," in *Discovering Existence with Husserl*, 135–50. See also Martin Kavka, *Jewish Messianism and the History of Philosophy*, 166–72.

51. Levinas, *Autrement qu'être,* 79ff. and 91ff.; *Otherwise Than Being,* 62ff. and 72ff. See also Martin Kavka, "Levinas Between Monotheism and Cosmotheism," *Levinas Studies* 2 (2007): 79–103, esp. 94–99.

52. Levinas, *Autrement qu'être,* 94ff.; *Otherwise Than Being,* 75ff. See also Lisa Guenther, *The Gift of the Other: Levinas and the Politics of Reproduction* (Albany: SUNY Press, 2006), 105ff., and Claire Elise Katz, *Levinas, Judaism and the Feminine: The Silent Footsteps of Rebecca* (Bloomington: Indiana University Press, 2003), 129–55.

53. One might argue that Levinas also believes that talmudic training, in which one acquires one of the virtues that is also available through philosophical training, might have the same function of inculcating ethics. For reasons that I articulate in "Is There a Warrant for Levinas' Talmudic Readings?" in *Journal of Jewish Thought And Philosophy* 14:1–2 (2006): 153–73, I believe that Levinas's talmudic readings, in their lack of fealty to the text, are contingent upon a prior philosophical orientation.

54. Levinas, *Transcendance et intelligibilité, suivi d'un entretien* (Geneva: Labor et Fides, 1984), 28; Levinas, "Transcendence and Intelligibility," translated by Simon Critchley and Tamra Wright in *Basic Philosophical Writings,* 158.

55. For a brief survey of wisdom in biblical and intertestamental literature, see Peter Schäfer, *Mirror of His Beauty: Feminine Images of God from the Bible to the Early Kabbalah* (Princeton, N.J.: Princeton University Press, 2002), 19–38. (I have used Schäfer's translations from the Hebrew Bible here.) On the vexed status of Ben Sira in rabbinic literature, see Benjamin G. Wright, "B. Sanhedrin 100b and Rabbinic Knowledge of Ben Sira," in *Treasures of Wisdom: Studies in Ben Sira and the Book of Wisdom,* edited by N. Calduch-Benages and J. Vermeylen (Leuven: Peeters, 1999), 41–50.

56. See Lobel, *Between Mysticism and Philosophy,* 104.

57. Halevi, *Kuzari* IV:3. The translation takes elements from Kreisel, *Prophecy,* 127, and Lobel, *Between Mysticism and Philosophy,* 104, 108, and 109; see also Hirschfeld, 207.

58. For a more detailed account of the relationship between the imagination and the intellect in Avicenna, see, e.g., Herbert Davidson, *Alfarabi, Avicenna, and Averroes on Intellect* (New York: Oxford University Press, 1992), 95ff. For another example of Halevi's borrowing from Avicenna, see Lobel, *Between Mysticism and Philosophy,* 137ff.

59. For a different view, see Kreisel, *Prophecy,* 129.

60. Elliot Wolfson, *Through a Speculum That Shines: Vision and Imagination in Medieval Jewish Mysticism* (Princeton, N.J.: Princeton University Press, 1994), 167, and "Merkavah Traditions in Philosophical Garb: Judah Halevi Reconsidered," *Proceedings of the American Academy of Jewish Research* 57 (1991): 213.

61. Levinas, *Autrement qu'être,* 190; Levinas, *Otherwise Than Being,* 149.

62. Halevi, *Kuzari,* IV:2. Translation taken from Lobel, *Between Mysticism and Philosophy,* 98; see also Hirschfeld, 199.

63. Halevi, *Kuzari,* V:20; Hirschfeld, 290. See also V:23.

64. Halevi, *Kuzari,* III:11. Translation taken from Lobel, *Between Mysticism and Philosophy,* 134; see also Hirschfeld, 146.

65. Halevi, *Kuzari,* II:14; see Hirschfeld, 89. See also Davidson, "The Active Intellect in the *Cuzari* and Hallevi's Theory of Causality," 390.

66. Levinas, *Autrement qu'être,* 203; Levinas, *Otherwise Than Being,* 159.

67. For this reason, Levinas's remark in "Politics After!" that the state of Israel "will have to incarnate the prophetic moral code and the idea of its peace" must refer to an imperative that is impossible to realize. See "Politique après!" 228; "Politics After!" 194.

68. Halevi, *Kuzari* II.14. The translation takes elements from Hirschfeld, 91–92, and Kreisel, *Prophecy,* 123.

69. Maimonides, *The Guide of the Perplexed,* translated by Shlomo Pines (Chicago: University of Chicago Press, 1960), 361.

70. Ibid., 396–402.

71. Ibid., 373ff. See Charles Raffel, "Providence as Consequent upon the Intellect: Maimonides' Theory of Providence," *Association for Jewish Studies Review* 12:1 (1987): 25–71, esp. 57ff.

72. See the Levinas and Maimonides texts cited in notes 18 and 19 above.

73. Levinas, "Sur la philosophie juive," 203; "On Jewish Philosophy," 172.

74. Levinas, *Transcendance et intelligibilité,* 37; "Discussion following 'Transcendence and Intelligibility.'" 270.

75. Levinas, *Transcendance et intelligibilité,* 63; "Discussion following 'Transcendence and Intelligibility.'" 283.

76. Maimonides, *Guide,* 635.

77. Ibid., 638.

78. Herbert Davidson, "The Middle Way in Maimonides' Ethics," *Proceedings of the American Academy of Jewish Research* 52 (1987): 31–72.

79. Maimonides, *Guide,* 126.

80. Ibid.

81. Levinas, *Autrement qu'être,* 33–49 and 81–82; *Otherwise Than Being,* 26–38, 65.

82. Levinas, "Révelation dans la tradition juive," 174; "Revelation in the Jewish Tradition," 144.

83. Levinas, "Violence du visage," 182; "Violence of the Face," 181. See also "Dieu et la philosophie," 124, and *Ethique et infini,* 122; "God and Philosophy," 76, and *Ethics and Infinity,* 114.

84. Levinas, *Ethique et infini,* 122; *Ethics and Infinity,* 114.

85. Levinas, *Dieu, la mort et le temps,* 163; *God, Death and Time,* 142.

86. Maimonides, *Guide,* 375.

87. Ibid., 374.

88. For another treatment of Levinas on Amos, see Bettina Bergo, *Levinas Between Ethics and Politics* (Dordrecht: Kluwer, 1999), 222–39. There is one passage in Levinas that implies that he realizes that prophetic speech, or philosophy about prophetic speech, might not hit its mark: "The contribution of each person and period [to a divine message "whose wealth is thereby revealed only in the pluralism of persons and generations"] is confronted with the lessons from everyone else, and from the whole of the past. . . . Hence the commentaries of commentaries, the very structure of the Torah of Israel . . . [which signifies] the participation of the one who receives revelation in the work of Him who is revealed in prophecy. This, no doubt, is also what is meant in the verse from Amos 3:8: 'The Lord God has spoken; who can but prophesy?' The reading of the prophetic text is still to a certain extent prophetic, even if all human beings are not open with the same attentiveness and the same sincerity to the Word that speaks in them. And who, in our days, embraces tradition?" (Levinas, "Avant-propos," in *Au-delà du verset,* 10; Levinas, "Foreword," in *Beyond the Verse,* xiii–xiv).

89. See Levinas, *Totalité et l'infini,* ix; *Totality and Infinity,* 21.

90. See Raffel, "Providence as Consequent upon the Intellect."

91. See Leora Batnitzky, *Leo Strauss and Emmanuel Levinas: Philosophy and the Politics of Revelation* (Cambridge: Cambridge University Press, 2006), 28–53.

92. For more on the redemptive capacity of misreading, see Kavka, "Is There a Warrant for Levinas' Talmudic Readings?" My thanks to Aaron Hughes and Elliot Wolfson for inviting me to contribute to this volume, to Hughes for clarifying a point on Arabic translation along the way, to Matthew Goff for discussing Wisdom litera-

ture with me, and to Nancy Levene and Benjamin Wurgaft for extremely helpful suggestions on a prior draft of this essay (suggestions that I regret not being able to implement more extensively). All responsibility for the remaining weaknesses of this essay remains mine. I dedicate this essay to the wonderful group of women in the field of Jewish philosophy, all of whom have taught me a great deal over the last decade about how to read the canon of Jewish philosophy productively and how to steer it in new directions. Without them—and in specific regard to this essay, without Diana Lobel, Oona Eisenstadt, Bettina Bergo, Claire Katz, Nancy Levene, Laura Levitt, Susan Shapiro, and Randi Rashkover—I am nothing.

2

PRECURSORSHIP AND THE FORGETTING OF HISTORY: FRANZ ROSENZWEIG AND SAADYA GAON ON THE MEMORY OF TRANSLATION

Aaron W. Hughes

In the critic's vocabulary, the word "precursor" is indispensable, but it should be cleansed of all connotations of polemic or rivalry. The fact is that every writer *creates* his own precursors. His work modifies our conception of the past, as it will modify the future.

—JORGE LUIS BORGES

It is that no generation is interested in Art in quite the same way as any other; each generation, like each individual, brings to the contemplation of art its own categories of appreciation, makes its own demands upon art, and has its own uses for art. "Pure" artistic appreciation is to my thinking only an ideal, when not merely a figment, and must be, so long as the appreciation of art is an affair of limited and transient human beings existing in space and time. Both artist and audience are limited. There is for each time, for each artist, a kind of alloy required to make the metal workable into art; and each generation prefers its own alloy to any other. Hence each new master of criticism performs a useful service merely by the fact that his errors are of a different kind from the last; and the longer the sequence of critics we have, the greater amount of correction is possible.

—T. S. ELIOT

CRITICISM—WHETHER LITERARY OR HISTORICAL, PHILOSOPHICAL OR scientific—is obsessed with precursors. The reduction of the present to the reception and adaptation of ideas from the past, a future ultimately contingent upon and determinable by the present and its past, structures our engagement with and in the world. Unraveling a great chain of ideas to isolate who said what before whom comforts us by making us feel that we somehow better understand its formulation and development. Within this context, the genesis of a philosophical principle is often regarded as more important than the principle itself, with later thinkers in danger of becoming little more than the sum of their earlier redactional sources. Genesis and anticipation become essential to our assumptions about the flow of ideas, create an anxiety over influences, and govern the presumed structure of the historical record. Precursors subsequently play a formative role in the construction of the history of philosophy and in the establishment of canonicity, be it corpora or thinkers. Yet, as the above quotation by Borges suggests, precursors need not simply set in motion a set of principles whose concatenations move effortlessly from thinker to thinker in a grand history of ideas. Each writer, consciously or unconsciously, constructs a web whose threads link up those who come before him. As such, the line of precursor-ity is not straight, but disjointed; not forward-moving, but backward-moving.

Does an author need to construct his or her own precursors solely from the past? Can present thinkers anticipate earlier ones? Can those in the future influence us? This essay works on the assumption that they can. Here we must not lose sight of the mediated nature of past and future through the present. Just as the past is constructed through the present, so too will the present be by the past. More specifically, although a tenth-century thinker would, chronologically, be unable to read the work of a twentieth-century one, we today have the luxury of reading both thinkers in such a manner that we can often only get at the earlier thinker through the later one. The latter thus anticipates, influences our reading of the former. Rather than understand the historical record as something moving forward, *Geist*-like, from beginning to end, perhaps it is more appropriate, as the epigraph from T. S. Eliot suggests, to rethink the historicity of the given order, the so-called axioms of the historico-critical record.

What follows is meant to suggest an alternative to the history of Jewish philosophy, one that seeks to liberate a future held hostage to the present, and a present hamstrung by its past. One of the best theoretical formulations of this in recent years is in the work of Elliot R. Wolfson, my co-editor in this project, and someone whose voice belongs beside those of Borges and T.S. Eliot. In what follows, I use as my point of departure his tantalizing formulation:

> The presence of the present yields the present of presence remembering the past that is future and anticipating the future that is past, a presence, that is, enfolded in a double absence that renders the timeline irreversibly reversible. From that standpoint we set out on the path to uncover what may be recovered.[1]

Introduction: Take One

The very construction of a historical canon of Jewish philosophy is contingent upon the establishment of a line of thinkers that, irrespective of time, language, or geography, devotes itself to a series of "philosophical" problems that are customarily taken to justify Jewish particularism in the light of universal categories. Many of these problems, however, are our problems, ones that we have read into the past, and not necessarily the problems of the individuals to whom we have attributed them. The thinkers who make up this line, especially as presented in surveys or in reference works, are often presented chronologically and contextually,[2] put on display, museum-like, in order to show a developmentalism that customarily moves from Kalām to Neoplatonism to Aristotelianism to Renaissance Humanism to Idealism to Existentialism to Modernism to Postmodernism and beyond. Particular Jewish issues usually remain the same (e.g., creation, revelation, redemption), while the non-Jewish philosophical systems that Jews inherit to interpret such issues differ, depending on the century in which a particular thinker happens to find himself.[3]

Immediately, then, we are presented with a set of binaries: Jewish/non-Jewish, religion/philosophy. The "Jewish," like the "religious," is deemed authentic, eternal, and stable, while the "non-Jewish" and the "philosophical" are unstable and fleeting because their paradigms are always shifting, depending on the century and the particular -ism or set of -isms associated with it. What connects the pieces in the museum wing called Jewish philosophy is, quite simply and often unabashedly, ethnicity.[4] An ethnically or historically oriented approach to Jewish philosophy, as opposed to a problem-oriented one, risks calcifying the dynamics of (Jewish) philosophical practice, mistaking the ideal for the real, the historical and the temporal for the philosophical.

All of these binaries make it all too easy for the reader to misunderstand Jewish philosophy as belonging to the discipline of Jewish Studies, Religious Studies, or intellectual history rather than to the discipline of philosophy. The study of Jewish philosophy customarily proceeds by examining various individuals in history who have asked certain types of questions or responded to sets of non-Jewish ideas. But the focus is rarely on the questions asked or why those questions remain worthy ones for us. In many respects, the study of Jewish philosophy is thus reminiscent of what Rorty has called "doxography," the tendency to go through the historical record, "ticking off what various figures traditionally called 'philosophers' had to say about problems traditionally labeled as 'philosophical.'"[5]

A doxographical approach to the study of Jewish philosophy focuses unapologetically on the contexts in which Jewish philosophers lived and wrote, what they had to say about "big ideas," and how dominant non-Jewish philosophical systems provided the tenor of such responses. To stay with Rorty just a little longer:

> Doxography is the attempt to impose a problematic on a canon drawn up without reference to that problematic, or, conversely, to impose a canon on a problematic constructed without reference to that canon.[6]

As in all of the chapters collected here, it is necessary to ask ourselves: How can we think about a so-called canon of Jewish philosophy writ large in ways that are not simply historical in scope and chronological in presentation? Moreover, is it possible to do this in ways that avoid analytical philosophy's tendency to take for granted that philosophical problems can be answered as timeless questions completely devoid of context? Thankfully, there are certainly many ways to respond to this question. The approach that I take here is one that strives for historical and philological accuracy regarding individual thinkers; however, I do not want such accuracy to function as a straightjacket, methodological or otherwise, that would keep us from getting at philosophical ideas that remain unfettered by either history or philology.

INTRODUCTION: TAKE TWO

Because we have largely bought into the great historical project inaugurated by *Wissenschaft des Judentums,* we are all too often suspended within its web of historicism, clinging to its notion that to understand Jewish philosophy properly is to understand it contextually. And once understood contextually, ideas—even if they do not make complete sense to us today or if they appear to us as unsophisticated—must have made sense to those of an earlier era. Thinkers of the past, in other words, are judged by criteria that are different from those used to judge thinkers of the present. At best, we might invoke a Cohenian or Straussian dictum and argue that a particular thinker's ideas are hidden because he departed from mainstream Aristotelianism,[7] or because they somehow threatened the belief of the masses and their orthodoxy.[8] Rarely are we willing to engage earlier thinkers philosophically as philosophers even though we are often quite happy to call them "Jewish philosophers."

In many ways I am invoking the spirit of Cohen and Rosenzweig, two thinkers who, in their break with historicism,[9] looked non-historically to the earlier Jewish philosophical record. Rather than justify Judaism according to its history, they were part of a growing trend to stress the supra-historical character of the tradition. The goal now was less to contextualize premodern Jewish philosophers so as to show the heights Jews could reach if granted freedom, but to use the premoderns as antidotes to contemporary philosophical critiques of Judaism. This could take the form of Cohen's recasting of Maimonides into a Platonist in order to counter Kant's critique of Judaism as nothing more than a series of "statutory laws," or it could be Rosenzweig's construction of Halevi as an anti-philosophical philosopher.[10]

Although one might object *on historical grounds* to Cohen's or Rosenzweig's respective uses of Maimonides or Halevi, in each case the later thinker regarded his "precursor" as providing keys to unlock certain philosophical problems. The history of philosophy, for these individuals, was neither the history of ideas nor intellectual history, but the creation of a living dialogue (*Gespräch*) with sympathetic earlier thinkers regarded as responsible for first articulating a set of problems, which, whether real or imagined, were relevant to modern concerns. In what follows, I join Cohen and Rosenzweig in their mutual suspicion of historicist claims and take their lead in looking for alternative ways to approach the Jewish philosophical record.

INTRODUCTION: TAKE THREE

Conventional wisdom tells us a number of things when it comes to putting Saadya and Rosenzweig in counterpoint. First is the assumption that to do this topic justice I would first have to embed Saadya Gaon (882–942) and Franz Rosenzweig (1886–1929) in their immediate cultural, linguistic, and intellectual milieus—tenth-century Egypt and Babylonia and early twentieth-century Germany respectively. What Arabo-Islamic thinkers did Saadya read? What was Rosenzweig rebelling against? How might the problematics Saadya was working with illumine those of Rosenzweig? In this regard, I might consider "anticipations" or "influences," but only from Saadya to Rosenzweig, and never vice versa.

Secondly, and relatedly, how or why can one compare two thinkers separated by roughly one thousand years? How could understanding Saadya Gaon's questions of biblical translation possibly shed light on those of Franz Rosenzweig? The natural way to proceed would be by showing how and why Rosenzweig read the work of Saadya. However, there is no evidence whatsoever that he did.[11] In fact, there is little evidence that the main theoretical work of Saadya Gaon on translation—the beginning parts of his *Egron*—were even known at the time of Rosenzweig, since they did not exist in the form of a critical edition.

Thirdly, how can we compare a tenth- and a twentieth-century translation of the Bible? Surely Saadya and Rosenzweig read the biblical narrative through different sets of lenses that filtered the expectations they brought to the text and determined what of significance would be taken back from it? They worked, for example, with radically different aesthetics that governed artistic and literary production in their respective cultures. Certainly, both individuals were gifted litterateurs, but their literary assumptions were by no means similar.

Finally, how can one proceed on this line of comparison and contrast without making one of these thinkers the foil for the other? That is— and I think this is certainly the most difficult problem facing a study such as this—is it possible to read them together in a way that does not make Rosenzweig into a crypto-Saadyan or Saadya into a crypto-Rosenzweigian? How, in other words, can one do each of these thinkers justice, yet in ways that do not simply re-inscribe the historical record—the very record beyond which I am attempting to move—for support?

ROSENZWEIG AND SAADYA ON TRANSLATION

Like all Jews who sought to translate the Bible into the vernacular,[12] both Rosenzweig[13] and Saadya were motivated by what they considered to be a general state of neglect of the Hebrew language among their contemporaries. This neglect was not simply a historical process concerning the rise and fall of languages, but it was intimately connected to the unfolding of the universe from an originary point, and the word and world's redemptive return to this point. Although the relationship of language to ontology is perhaps most poetically and articulately described by Rosenzweig, we must not lose sight of the fact that its clearest archival record remains Saadya's *Commentary to the Sefer Yetzirah,* a text that is foundational to all of Saadya's translative and commentarial activity.

Both framed this neglect in terms of forgetting—a forgetting of language, a forgetting of being, and a forgetting of all the religious obligations that flowed from such activity. Forgetting, in turn, was linked to the erasure of both cultural and scriptural memory. Language was not just connected to communication and social entertainment, but it was interwoven with a perceived authenticity, the Jewish ability to be both home and not-home, to be in-time and beyond-time. The ontological filiations between word and world witnessed in Rosenzweig's and Saadya's theories of translation were ultimately grounded in precisely these twin notions of authenticity and memory of a past that would be future. Authenticity and memory, however, were increasingly encroached upon by the claims of German Idealism and Karaism on the level of philosophy, by *Bildung* and *Arabiyya* on the level of cultural aesthetics, and by German and Arabic on the level of language.

The flip side of this forgetting was seen to be a youthful romance with another language, and all of the poetic and rhapsodic infatuations that such a romance entailed. The perceived musicality in the adopted language became associated, falsely, with tone-deafness in the originary one. In order to counteract this, each sought to fabricate harmonic and linguistic flows between Hebrew and their adopted languages by creating a series of channels that would fuse, on the level of semantics, the two languages. Contextually, their translations were certainly related to contemporaneous theories that connected language, linguistic expression, and aesthetics to peoplehood. Whether framed as the inimitability of the Arabic Qurʾān or as the racial and linguistic purity of the German *Volk*, language defined the essential characteristics of Arab-ness or of German-ness. It should come as no surprise, then, that when Saadya and Rosenzweig reflected on Hebrew and its correlations and disparities with Arabic or German, they employed categories derived from their larger surroundings. My interest, however, is less with these larger surroundings than with their individual thinking about language and with how each sought to construct an aesthetics of memory based on a complex dialectic of forgetting and un-forgetting.

For Rosenzweig and Saadya, the task of translating the Bible was both an act of scholarship and one of salvation. To forget the Hebrew of the Bible was tantamount to a loss of memory and all of the national fragmentation that this implied. Translating the Bible into contemporaneous idioms, *if done properly*, could both save the antiquity of Hebrew and yet also forever change the contours of a host language. The originary moment of Hebrew revelation could only be mediated, paradoxically, through German or Arabic. It was the semantics and grammar of the latter languages that pointed to the traces of the former. The antiquity of Hebrew memory, in other words, had to be inscribed within modern forms of German or Arabic. The end result is that the originary moment of revelation came to be imagined as an ongoing modern revelation in which the memory of the past was foregrounded against present concerns that would anticipate a future perfect.

This linguistic foregrounding of past and future in the present formed a clearing in which to isolate a series of reverberations between Jewishness and non-Jewishness. The mediative role offered by translation enabled Hebrew to slip into both the linguistic and ontologic structures of another language, thereby framing Hebrew, and ultimately Judaism, in the light of the other language and illuminating the living quality of this other language through the specter of Hebrew's non-living qualities. This, of course, also functioned as an apologetic claim. The palimpsest of Hebrew emerges as the guarantor and touchstone of vibrancy for other languages, which can only emerge as living and dynamic when the specter of Hebrew breathes life into them from outside the text, from behind the word.

Yet, if Hebrew breathes life into these other languages, it symbiotically requires their word-blood and grammar-cells for nourishment. Hebrew is thus kept alive by means of its relations to other languages. As a result, both Rosenzweig and Saadya pay significant attention to the "space-in-between" the two languages—the silences, the breathings, the formal constraints. It is these phenomena, and not just the transcription of words and the transference of meanings, that provide the various linguistic and semiotic strategies that allow Hebrew to both open up and be opened up by another language.

If one impetus behind Rosenzweig's and Saadya's respective translative activities was to stem the tide of forgetting, another was the desire to (re-)create a series of memories that, while hoary and labyrinthine with distance, were very much grounded in present concerns. The lyricality of a Hebrew transcribed into a staccato Arabic or German enabled the former to embed itself within the contemporary aesthetic ideals of the latter languages. Hebrew's traces now inform other semiotics, other writing; its silent echoes resonating through foreign linguistic articulations. The foreign thus creates the authentic, and the authentic the foreign. The modern establishes the ancient, and the ancient the modern. The past remembered becomes a future anticipated.

For both Rosenzweig and Saadya, Hebrew becomes a constituent part of the *Ursprache*, the potential for language as such, a silence that represents not the absence of language but its fullness.[14] This silent speech functions as the originary poetic language, the language of creation, the language of a Book from which all other books must ultimately derive their potency and their meaning. The Hebrew of the Bible, the Hebrew that defined Judaism and the Jewish people, represents but one idiom of this divine speech that does not speak, thereby making Hebrew (like all languages) translatable, allowing Hebrew to absorb another language and forever change it. According to Rosenzweig,

> [T]he voice of this book [the Bible] [*die Stimme dieses Buches*] is not to be enclosed in any space—not in the inner sanctum of a church, not in the linguistic sanctum of a people, not in the circle of the heavenly images moving above a nation's sky. Rather this voice seeks again and again to resound from outside [*will immer wieder von draußen schallen*]—from outside this church, this people, this heaven. It does not keep its sound from echoing in this or that restricted space, but it wants itself to remain free [*aber sie selber will frei bleiben*]. If somewhere it has become a familiar customary possession, it must again and

anew, as a foreign and unfamiliar sound [*als fremder, unvertrauter Laut*] from outside stir up the complacent satedness of its alleged possessor.[15]

In his *Sefer ha-Egron*, a work meant to create a Hebrew-language lexicon for poets in order to facilitate acrostics and rhyme, Saadya also connects language, translation, and memory/forgetting. He writes that

he who wants to acquire knowledge [*ʿilm*] must study in the companionship of friends, to persevere and not stop lest one forgets the different subjects that make up the science. The prophets exhorted this and it should be clear to the wise: "Blessed is the man who listens to me, watching daily at my gates, waiting at my door" [Prov 8:34]. The prophets also announce that the main sources of remembrance are perseverance [*al-mulāzama*] and exhausting one's energies [*al-mudhābita*]. They also remark that the loss of perseverance is the greatest cause of forgetting [*indirāsa*]: "Where there is no vision, the people cast off restraint, but the one that keeps the law is happy" [Prov 29:18].[16]

In their different ways, Rosenzweig and Saadya signal the radical otherness of biblical language. For Rosenzweig, this language has become too familiar, coming from inside as opposed to from without, fettered by Luther's German translation;[17] for Saadya, it has become too unfamiliar, in danger of fragmentation, of being forgotten through lack of perseverance. The over-vigilance of the former gives way to a dearth of vigilance for the latter. The uncanniness of the biblical narrative risks either being-at-home-in-the-world or falling-through-the-fissures-of-peoplehood. To correct this general state of decay, both Saadya and Rosenzweig sought to translate and maintain the autonomy of Hebrew by hebraizing Arabic and German respectively.

In order to do this, both had to take what they considered to be the essential core of Hebrew revelation and harness it to a new language. That is, they both conceived of translation, not literally, but in ways that reflected—and challenged—contemporary aesthetics. For Rosenzweig, this was done through recreating the rhythm and breath of human speech;[18] for Saadya it was done through rhyme, tonality, and rhythm that could compete with Arabic poetic meter. For Rosenzweig it was taking the biblical narrative back to its ancient origins; for Saadya, it was bringing it up to date using the mesmerizing verse of Arab poets.

Both, then, were presented with the same problem. How, using another language, could one, quite literally, reveal an original? How can one visible, tangible language point to another that is invisible and intangible? How does an unspoken and original language speak in a spoken, living language? What is lost and what gained? Framed somewhat differently, could the latter reveal the palimpsest of the former? How can the act of translation render the specter of the *Ur*-language? If so, what might this say about language? Silence? The space-in-between?

Nineteenth-century German and tenth-century Arabic spun in their languages and syntax all that was artistic and cultural, both marking for its speakers—whether Jew or Gentile—the respective high points of Western civilization. Not to frame Judaism in their grammars was to risk ossification. Moreover, both used the literary features of their profane vernaculars to wax poetic about the contours of Hebrew's sacrality. For Rosenzweig, this meant casting his work in the literary aspects of Schelling's "narrative philosophy" [erzählende Philosophie],[19] an attempt to show how language, including its silences, mediates the various relationships between God, the world, and humans in time, in temporality.

Saadya, in a similar vein, had no choice but to compose his work, both translative and poetic, in a way that revolved around the Arabic term faṣīḥ, a term that subsumed within itself all that was considered good, beautiful, and pure about language. Whereas the Arab grammarians considered the language par excellence to be Arabic, Saadya argued that Hebrew possessed the same properties, and his Egron is, inter alia, an attempt to make the same case for Hebrew. It is, then, like the work of Rosenzweig, a "narrative philosophy" in which is subsumed a theory of God's relationship to humanity through the ontology of language.

CHRONOLOGICAL INVERSIONS: ROSENZWEIG'S PRECURSORSHIP OF SAADYA

The historical study of philosophy in general and of Jewish philosophy in particular prides itself on terms such as "influences" and "anticipations." Earlier thinkers are framed as having envisaged a problem (one that we often articulate from the vantage point of the present) and set out to solve it, and their solutions are viewed either directly as "influences" or indirectly as "anticipations" of what later thinkers will do.[20] Using such a model, we certainly could, without little ado or difficulty, make the claim that the lexicographical and grammatical writings of Saadya Gaon, not to mention his translation of the Bible into Arabic, somehow "anticipate" those of Franz Rosenzweig.[21] "Anticipation" is the word usually invoked to argue that, even though a later author may not have read a particular earlier one, he nonetheless framed his problems in ways that are perhaps not unlike that particular earlier thinker.[22]

Yet what if we follow the path of Rosenzweig and start, not at the beginning, but at the end? Texts demand readers. Each reader reads texts in ways heretofore unread. In this Gadamerian "fusion of horizons" (Horizont-verschmelzung)[23] the past is read using the contours of the present, anticipating a future that must ultimately be past again.[24] Each reading is an invention—an invention of text, of author, and of reader. Each reading, to

invoke Borges, makes its own precursors. We can accordingly read Saadya
Gaon before Franz Rosenzweig, but once we read the latter, we can never
read the former in the same way. If, historically, we must read Rosenzweig
in Saadya's shadow, we can, ahistorically, read Saadya using the light supplied by Rosenzweig.

There is ample reward for such a reading in the works of both Saadya
and Rosenzweig. Both conceptualize language as moving back to an originary point and therefore as not progressing linearly. Language moves
backward, from present usage to past imagining, from the obsoleteness
of the present to the perceived authenticity of the past that is also future.
In so doing, both sought to rethink, and in many instances rewrite, the
languages of their day—whether Arabic or German—as a way, to use the
words of Klaus Reichert, of opening "up new possibilities by recalling old
or lost ones, unused potentialities."[25] In this way, both thinkers project
their own fantasies of authenticity onto an invented past in which a beautiful and authentic Hebrew defined Jewish *Dasein*. As such, both make attempts to invent a Hebrew using another language—indeed, using its very
vocabulary, syntax, and grammar. Hebraized Arabic and Hebraized German point beyond themselves to reveal a glory that was past and that will,
ideally, be future again. To use the words of Rosenzweig:

> And if Judaism is a force of the past, a peculiarity of the present—to us it is the
> goal of every future. And since future, therefore a world of its own, in spite of
> the world that surrounds us. And since a world of its own, therefore rooted in
> the soul of each and everyone in his or her own language.[26]

For Rosenzweig, Judaism's ahistorical language, moving multi-directionally,
vectors the quiddity of Judaism, thereby making it distinct from the manifold cultures that surround it and that seek to appropriate it. Rather than
succumb to these surrounding cultures, Rosenzweig, like Saadya, seeks to
renew Hebrew and all that this language carries with it into the present,
into the future. The great paradox, of course, is that this renewal could
only happen using the existing semiotic structures of living languages already in place—in Rosenzweig's case, German; in Saadya's, Arabic. That
is, one could return to the past's authenticity only through the linguistic
mechanisms of a present host language. Only by getting at Hebrew by linguistically reshaping German and Arabic, would it be possible to prevent
linguistic and cultural acculturation—the retrieval of a past from a present looking toward an uncertain future.

ROSENZWEIG ON TRANSLATION

In "Die Schrift und Luther," Rosenzweig contends that ideas cannot be
rendered free of words: "It is impossible to transmit the content without

at the same time transmitting the form. How something is said is not peripheral to what is said [*Für das, was gesagt wird, ist es nicht nebensächlich, wie es gesagt wird*]."[27] Translation often fails precisely because it is most interested in transmitting content, ideas behind language, as opposed to the very linguistic texture and grammatical forms in which such content is embedded.[28] It is the forms of language that the translator, Hermes-like, must meander between, creating his own channels that permit the transportation of meaning across the chasms of space and time, lest the very words the translator seeks to convey crystallize and shatter. The creation of "a wavelike flow of words through the sentence-bed" [*das wellenhaften Fließen der Worte durch das Satzbett*][29] ensures a dynamic process in which the translator does not passively absorb words [*Wörter*] from the dictionary, but becomes the active creator of ideas [*Worte*].[30] Language thus becomes the quiddity of narration, in which reality is experienced as clothed in the temporality of speech. The art of translation, thus, is indistinct from the act of *Sprachdenken*.

Translation, perhaps owing to its practical necessity, becomes theoretically impossible. Rosenzweig describes it as "serving two masters" (*zwei Herren*),[31] inhabiting two modes-of-being, bespeaking two distinct cultural vocabularies. The translator is thus a facilitator of languages, the creator of new words, new worlds. Because of the intimate connection that Rosenzweig draws between language and ontology, speaking and the unfolding of the world, translation is not simply the act of mediation between people, between languages, or between cultures;[32] rather, translation enables one—as listener, as translator, or as both—to open oneself up to another; and it is in this act of opening up that one encounters the presence of another, and, through this encounter, that one ultimately gazes into the divine countenance.[33]

This encounter can occur because translation takes place around what he conceives to be a single linguisticity that envelops all language, which gives way to an essential unity underpinning all language. In his Afterword to his translation of the Halevi poems, Rosenzweig writes:

> One can translate because in every language is contained the possibility of every other language; one may translate if one can realize this possibility through cultivation of such linguistic fallow land [*durch Urbarmachung solchen sprachlichen Brachlands*]; and one should translate so that the day of the harmony [*Eintracht*] of languages, which can grow only in each individual language, not in the empty space "between" them, may come.[34]

Rosenzweig here uses a series of agricultural metaphors to argue, not for the establishment of a common language that all peoples ideally speak, some form of messianic Esperanto, but to show that what happens in one language will ultimately influence what happens in another. Just as the

Bible forever redirected the linguistic trajectory of the ancient Israelites, it must ultimately do the same for every language into which it is translated. The translator plants one language in the soil of another, where he watches its autochthonous forms grow and flourish.[35] In "Die Schrift und Luther," he switches from agricultural to geological metaphors to describe the translator and his act. The translator must now connect words (*Wörter*) and ideas (*Worte*) between the source and the target languages on the level of roots, which "the surface of words only let us dimly intuit" (*die an der Wortoberfläche nur erahnbare*).[36] These roots, paradoxically, are ultimately responsible for maintaining the boundaries between languages. The unity of languages is supported by *différence,* which facilitates the dynamic motion between them.

Staying with the geological motif a little longer, Rosenzweig argues that it is incumbent upon the translator to pay attention to "the glimmer emanating from the veins of the text itself" (*aber auch von dem Aufschimmern der Adern des Texts selbst darf er das Auge nicht hochmütig abwenden*).[37] This glimmer is presumably that which attracts the translator to the source language in the first place. Yet one must be drawn to this glimmer, not blinded by it. Applying this metaphor to the act of translation, one must not be so bedazzled by the formal and categorical embellishments of the target language, the language into which one translates, that one loses sight of that which one translates. This, according to Rosenzweig, is one of the main problems besetting translation fixated solely on the *Wissenschaft*-based model of philology that sought to harness rather than celebrate this difference.[38] On the contrary, Rosenzweig, both in his Halevi poems and, along with Buber, in his Bible translation, sought to tease out the otherness of Hebrew, making its uncanniness wrench the German out of its familiarity.[39]

It is the shattering of the dialectic between the transgression and nontransgression of linguistic possibility that drives translation forward, forging new inroads into the target language, forever changing its texture. The translator becomes a poet, embracing both the traces of the language to be translated and the new forms into which it must be translated. This becomes an act of perceived authenticity, taking the Jewish past and putting it into a German present with an eye to future renewal. Alternatively, and perhaps equally, it represents the construction of a German future present and its embeddedness in a Hebraic past.[40] In many ways this was the antithesis of what Luther had done when he wrenched the German present from contemporaneous forms and threw it upon a biblical, but not necessarily Hebraic, past.

Near the end of "Die Schrift und Luther," Rosenzweig discusses how in certain roots "the translator reaches the boundary of linguistic possibility [*die Grenze des Sprachmöglichen*], which the root meaning permits him to see beyond but not to walk across." Moses-like, the translator glimpses the text's sacred landscape without ever being able to enter its original form.[41] The translator must orient himself both toward an original that can never be completely rendered anew and also into a new work that must become its own original. There thus emerges a tremendous paradox in Rosenzweig's discussion of translation. On the one hand, translation must not simply be a form of mimesis or "free-rendering" (*nachdichten*) of an original. Yet on the other hand, it must also not be so literal as to deprive the original of its life force. Although he claims in his Afterword to the Halevi poems that his translations "want to be nothing other than translation[s],"[42] Rosenzweig subsequently writes that

> how important the imitation of the rhyme form [*Reimform*] can be is seen even from the fact that in the poems under discussion the rhyme is not merely the mortar that glues one stone to another, as in modern poetic forms, but almost throughout, at least in addition, it is its very building material [*Baumaterial*], the unified tone of which determines the total impression given by the façade.[43]

The translator,[44] thus, must do the impossible, create and destroy language at one and the same time. The creation of one language corresponds to the dismantling of another. At the same time, however, the translator resurrects both languages by establishing a series of trajectories between the language elements of the originary and those of the target. As these elements approach one another, the possibility of their interaction becomes possible, thereby establishing paths between them. These paths (*Bahnen*) subsequently make possible communication between present and past, past and future, future and present. Since the translator is able to let languages speak to one another, using the contours of one to illumine those of the other, and presumably vice versa, his act is a creative and divinely inspired one.

It is also a destructive act, however. In bringing one language to another, both to each other, the translator potentially destroys both in taking them back to their original, to the one language that admits of no peculiarity, no dialects, no idioms.[45] This translative activity, paradoxically, turns on silence. The silences between words, including breath—become, on the level of the text, the silence out of which emerges God's call—the call to which humans move and respond.[46] Just as creation (and revelation) only makes sense in terms of redemption, when speech reverts to silence, so too does translation only make sense when it ceases to be.[47]

In playing with language, translation becomes the putting-into-practice of a method of narration, what Rosenzweig calls "narrative philosophy" (*erzählende Philosophie*): the thinking of time and/or temporally thinking.[48] Since everything that is articulates itself in language, ideas cannot be borne by anything other than words. To use his formulation, "The world is never without the word. Indeed it only exists in the word, and without the word there would be no world" (*die Welt ist nie ohne das Wort, ja sie ist nur im Wort, und ohne das Wort wäre sie selber auch nicht*).[49] Words themselves both create and express this ontological temporality in the three modalities that we experience: that which is always already here (creation), that which is (revelation), and that which is always yet to come (redemption).[50] The translator, as a new thinker, must think in time, must think dialogically: the spontaneity of translating, as opposed to reading, enables the modern, assimilated reader to learn to speak anew with an other, with the past, and ultimately with God.[51] In *Der Stern der Erlösung*, Rosenzweig makes language central to such encounter, for

> to trust [language] is easy, for it is within us and around us [*sie ist in uns und um uns*]; and when it comes to us from the "outside," nothing other than it echoes our "inside" toward the "outside." The word is the same, whether heard or spoken [*Das Wort ist das gleiche wie es gehört und wie es gesprochen wird*]. The ways of God and the ways of man are different, but the word of God and the word of man are the same [*sind das gleiche*]. What man feels in his heart as his own human language is the word that has come from the mouth of God.[52]

Language must be living, not confined to the dictionary. Translation, accordingly, must not simply be about words—replacing a word in one language with its lexicographical synonym in another—but about getting into the linguistic structures, what Rosenzweig calls "contours" (*die Konturen*),[53] and configurations that connect the two languages. Despite the fact that Rosenzweig, as I noted above, spends much time on proclaiming the unity of all languages, he is acutely aware of the differences, of the dissonances, and of the ruptures between them: "Only respect for the distance involved makes it possible to leap over a ditch; he who starts by filling in the ditch cripples the powers of others to leap over it."[54]

This brings us to the monumental task of translating the Bible. Why would one undertake such a task? For whom? For the translator him- or herself? For others? If the former, why go to all the trouble and publish such a multivolume work? Why not just reflect on language, mining root-veins that connect various linguistic structures and permutations without taking this extra step? If the latter, how can such a personal act of living with (at least) two languages, reflecting upon and illuminating their contours, and interacting with them intimately on the level of dialogic, possibly be an inclusive activity? After all, Rosenzweig and Buber intended their Bible translation for those in possession of only one of the languages, the target one (i.e., German).

One can only do this if one has a larger set of theological claims to make. A set of claims that are worth publicizing and disseminating and that would, moreover, reach out, at least in theory, to every (German-speaking) Jew. For Rosenzweig, as I have already argued, this set of claims revolved around notions of Jewish authenticity, an authenticity that could presumably be uncovered from its embeddedness in ancient linguistic root-structures. Uncovering these Hebraic structures once-removed in German translation would, again presumably, facilitate their embrace, while simultaneously renewing German. This twofold goal would ideally get a Jewish readership, paradoxically, to move beyond the German of German, beyond their German translation, to a Hebrew palimpsest.

Translation, from this perspective, is mimetic. A linguistic-turning, a semantic-tuning, creating an estrangement from the familiar, a familiarity with the strange. To do this, one had to write in one language using the structures of another, producing a set of meanings, not of the translation, but of the translated. This has the effect of liberating language in language, of producing meaning in the spaces in-between. To use the words of Rosenzweig, the voice of this book (*die Stimme dieses Buches*), that is, the Bible:

> wants itself to remain free [*sie selber will frei beliben*]. If somewhere it has become a familiar, customary possession, it must again and anew, as a foreign and unfamiliar sound [*als fremder, unvertrauter Laut*] from outside [*von draußen*] stir up the complacent satedness of its alleged possessor.[55]

From the outside, translation must destroy the bonds of quaint possession; from the outside, language must shatter familiarity; from the outside, translation must make the Bible newly approachable, without making it one more book in the cultural "treasure house" (*Schatzhaus*) of the world's literature. And, finally, from the outside, translation must make the reader respond to its language, not simply read its words. This would have the effect of pulling the reader back "outside," to a language that opens up to the horizon of anticipation, to that language that will ultimately bespeak silently.

To even contemplate such a translative project, however, it was first necessary to distance it from its competitors, in particular that of Luther.[56] Although Jews had previously translated the Bible into German,[57] it was the Luther translation that had truly captured a German readership, since it became the "founding book" (*Grundbuch*), as Rosenzweig points out, "not only of a church . . . but of the national language itself" (*nicht nur einer*

Kirche . . . sondern der nationalen Sprache selber).[58] However, to use Rosenzweig's terms, this twofold establishment was ultimately responsible for its becoming a "possession, a national possession" (*Besitz, nationaler Besitz*).[59] In contradistinction, Rosenzweig and Buber sought to reclaim both the German and the Hebrew of the biblical narrative. Gunther Plaut appropriately characterizes the translation as a "work of defiance."[60] Breaking with the more traditional models of German-Jewish acculturation and assimilation, this new translation would maintain Judaism's otherness, its lack of attachment to land, language, and conventional temporality.[61] Buber and Rosenzweig sought to make their translation different from German while at the same time using German, to use language to un-speak language in order to get at the silent speech that offers the potential for constant renewal. This apophatic act uses the one (or both) language(s) to create the possibility of the other (or neither).[62] However, it is paradoxical precisely because it uses the grammar and syntax of the one to reveal the un-grammar and un-syntax of the other. In his Afterword to his Halevi translations, Rosenzweig writes that it is his goal not "to Germanize what is foreign [*das Fremde einzudeutschen*], but rather to make foreign what is German [*das Deutsche umzufremden*]."[63] For German to communicate the orality and antiquity of the Bible, it must be an un-German German, a German that reflected and mirrored the idiosyncrasies of a Jewish minority within its midst. This is why the translation had to be finished by Buber—in Israel, not in Germany—for an audience that, again paradoxically, but this time also tragically, could no longer hear.

In many ways this was tantamount to the further exiling of Hebrew in order to reflect the hebraizing of exile. Exile, for Rosenzweig, is defined by its relationship to *Schrift*, a relationship to both Scripture and writing simultaneously.[64] *Schrift* has priority, an ontological pre-temporality over non-*Schrift*:

> The exiling of the environment is accomplished by means of the constant presence of *Schrift*. With it, a different present slides itself in front of this environment and demotes it to the status of an illusion, or more precisely, a simile. So it is not that *Schrift* is adduced as an illustration (by way of simile) of life in the present; on the contrary, these events serve to elucidate *Schrift* and become a simile for it.[65]

Language takes priority to the all-else. This, of course, takes us back to the original task of the translator: Since ideas cannot be rendered free of words, they must be born in their very fabric.[66] The translative act, like the poetic one, is artistic. Yet at the same time, the genius of the Hebrew language is that those who recite it (but never speak it) must remain fixed either on the page or in the formulaic language of the liturgy. This is not a language of everyday usage or a set of clichés appropriated by the aesthete for social entertainment; on the contrary, Hebrew takes one back to an originary moment in which the present is an illusion, a simile.

In part three, book one of *Stern der Erlösung*, Rosenzweig discusses the three concepts that distinguish the Jewish people from all other nations: land, language, and law. Language, he claims, is—like land and law—something that, for most, is not eternal, but something that lives insofar as a people speaks it. Language thus has a unifying factor, connecting a living people to an often-specific land.[67] Not so with Hebrew, however: "The eternal people lost its own language and everywhere speaks the language of its external destinies, the language of the people with whom it perchance dwells as a guest."[68] Whereas language traditionally locates a people in time, the language of Israel removes itself, and by extension Israel, from time and relocates it in eternity. Because Hebrew is disconnected from time, it lacks the spontaneity of lived encounter. It becomes the language of liturgy, of ritual celebration, but never of daily life. However, by reciting the liturgical character of Hebrew and speaking the host language, "the Jew senses that his everyday language is also still at home in the holy language of his festive hours" (*auch sein Sprachalltag noch heimisch in der heiligen Sprache seiner Feierstunden*).[69] Hebrew thus relies on the vernacular to ground it in the lived experiences of those who can mouth its eternal sounds but never speak them to another, save God.

Accordingly, the Bible demands translation. To reverberate in the ears of contemporaneous Jews, biblical language must intersect with Hebrew and German, un-speaking and speaking simultaneously. The freedom and spontaneity that German affords Buber and Rosenzweig in their translation permits an allusion to, a pointing-toward, the fixed eternality of the Hebrew. This is why Rosenzweig assigns the term "being-in-exile" (*Im-Exil-Sein*) to Jewish poetry and literature. The presence of the scriptural present is foregrounded in the recesses that are embedded within the presented-ness of exilic speech. This has a dream-like effect of making the past present, the future past. This saturation of biblical language has been forgotten in Rosenzweig's time and must be remembered, thereby overcoming the dialectic of home/not-home, speech/silence, Jew/Christian.

So how does one translate the Bible?

If Luther had made the Bible a national possession for the German people, Rosenzweig and Buber sought to reclaim it—not on the level of language, but on that of alterity, one that mirrored Judaism, its language, its situation and, most importantly, its *Im-Exil-Sein*. The Bible translation project, thus, had to reaffirm the Jewish-ness of the work, pointing to the authentic Hebrew residing interstitially between/behind the familiar, although now un-familiar, German. The language of the Bible is, according to Rosenzweig, the lifeblood that nourishes the creative imagination of both Jew and non-Jew. Its language frees language from itself, facilitating non-language, silence. By returning the un-lyricality of modern speech to the *Ursprache* of poetry, what he calls the "mother tongue of the human race" (*die Muttersprache des menschlichen Geschlechts*),[70] the translator mines the origins of language, of communication, of dialogism. In the following quotation, the chthonic depths of language and its ultimate origins in an *Ursprache* are connected by way of the Bible:

> All poetry that has been written in the Bible's light [*Lichtkreis*]—and indeed poetry more than prose, Judah Halevi more than Maimonides, Dante more than Aquinas, Goethe more than Kant—has been animated by the Bible's spirit of prose [*ist von ihrem Geist der Prosa begeistert*]. Henceforth the gate into the nocturnal silence that enveloped the human race in its origins, dividing each from each other, and all from what was outside and what was beyond— henceforth the gate is broken and cannot be altogether closed again: the gate of the word.[71]

The Bible, for Rosenzweig, is the *Hort* ("fortress") of human language. Shattering the dichotomous relations of poetry/un-poetry, prose/un-prose, biblical language is related to prophetic language, *Ursprache*. That which declares the law is ensconced in its rapture. Breaking through into history, biblical language defines both word and world "at the moment of becoming human" (*am Augenblick seiner Menschwerdung*).[72] Becoming fully human requires a movement from death to life, from the ephemeral to the eternal, from German to Hebrew. The way Buber and Rosenzweig went about this was to (re-)create a German that was built on the cadences and rhyme of Hebrew. To use the words of Mara Benjamin, "a German in which the classical Hebrew of Jewish scripture and liturgy formed the horizons of the German language field."[73]

Translation, thus, could not (and cannot) just be literal or prosaic. It must unlock or smash the semantic fetters that embed words. It must transgress punctuation; it must not be enslaved to the philological approach of *Wissenschaft* or source criticism.[74] The "breath of the word" (*Atem des Worts*) must resuscitate language,[75] revivifying a public that "has in reading been read off, read wrong, and read under."[76] The translative act is an act that must walk the razor's edge of harnessing this language at the same moment that it acknowledges its liberation.

SAADYA GAON ON TRANSLATION

Not only did Saadya write the first Hebrew grammar, the first Hebrew lexicon, and one of the earliest commentaries to the *Sefer Yetzirah*, but he also translated the Bible into Arabic. This translation, like that of Rosenzweig and Buber, was not in a vernacular transcribed into Hebrew characters but was written in the characters of the host language.[77] All of these activities, I contend, were intimately connected to one another, and all reflect a common interest in language—its role in creation and its redemptive properties. Indeed, Saadya's Bible translation only makes sense when informed by and understood against a broader context of the ontology and philosophy of language. His translative activity was not simply about finding Arabic equivalents for Hebrew terms; rather, like Rosenzweig, he sought out the linguistic structures and the grammatical configurations that connect two languages. Since language, for Saadya, was responsible for the formation of the universe and everything within it, he was aware that translation was also a creative activity, one that was tied to peoplehood and that was ultimately contingent on a set of aesthetic and literary codes.

In the opening section of the *Egron*, the first Hebrew lexicography as well as the first work of Hebrew poetics, Saadya Gaon emphasizes that the intention behind his composition is to stem forgetting. To do this, he proposes to look into the very fabric of the biblical narrative so as to retrieve both the memory of Hebrew and, in the process, the memory of peoplehood.[78] In the Arabic introduction to the work, he writes that

> one can lose the knowledge of things on account of the reduction of diligence. Public knowledge may be lost on account of leaving this diligence behind. In my time I well understand that The Creator wants me to begin the process [of remembering]. Since many students have lost the knowledge of tradition. The Book of Rhymes (*Kitāb al-atqāl*), the foundational sciences and other matters have disappeared.[79]

Here Saadya implies that Jews of his day lack requisite knowledge of Hebrew. The inability to write poetry using its language, the inability to communicate eloquently in its ancient literary forms, is, as it was for Rosenzweig, not simply a linguistic or philological lacuna. It is symptomatic of a larger issue that connects language to aesthetics, to ontology, to *Dasein*. The neglect of knowledge (*tark al-ʿilm*) is tantamount to the oblivion of knowledge (*nisyān al-ʿilm*).[80] Like Rosenzweig, Saadya uses an agricultural metaphor to convey this when he invokes Proverb 24:30–31: "I passed the field of a lazy man, passed the vineyard of a man lacking sense, and behold it was overgrown with thorns." Here Saadya compares the "lazy man" to his generation of poets and intellectuals who are unwilling or unable to understand Hebrew, compared to a field that, when cultivated, yields the fruits of creativity. It is precisely this activity that Saadya seeks to accomplish in his Bible translation, to sow the un-canny seeds of Hebrew into the fallow, autochthonous lands of Arabic.

Since Hebrew is no longer a spoken language—for this, there exists Arabic—Hebrew runs the risk of ossification, of fragmentation, of dispersion. This also has a cosmic significance, for Hebrew, as Saadya shows in his later *Tafsīr kitāb al-mabādī* ("Commentary to the *Sefer Yetzirah*"),[81] is not simply a conventional language, but that which undergirds the universe, establishing its first principles and maintaining its forms.[82] I submit that, like Rosenzweig, Saadya holds on to the view of Hebrew that falls outside of the scope of rational justification.[83] The restorative and redemptive qualities of translation are archived in the dual roles that Saadya casts for himself in the two introductions to the *Egron*. In the Arabic introduction he compares himself to the Arab Abū Aswad al-Duwālī, the person responsible for composing a treatise so that Arabs would not forget the classical Arabic of the Qurʾān. Yet in the Hebrew introduction he sees himself, prophet-like, as restoring Hebrew, paving the "pathway to redemption."[84]

Language, examining Saadya from the perspective of Rosenzweig, is not innocent. It is not simply about the ability to compose Hebrew verse that can compete with and get the better of the Arab poets.[85] Presumably, Hebrew poets wrote as beautifully in Arabic meter and prosody as the Arabs. Moreover, Saadya's theory of translation was not about the simple transliteration or transmigration of Hebrew words into Arabic. It seems that, on a fundamental level, Saadya was aware of the creative, sustaining, and destructive powers of language in general, but especially of Hebrew, what he calls the "sacred language, which our God selected."[86] Like Rosenzweig, Saadya envisaged himself as re-inventing the language, re-breathing life into its ancient forms, thereby re-establishing the first principles responsible for generating of the universe.

In his introduction to the *Tafsīr kitāb al-mabādī* Saadya discusses various theories of the world's genesis (everything from its eternality to its origination in preexistent matter).[87] After rejecting seven such theories, he turns his attention to one that combines the Pythagorean notion of prime numbers with a Hebraic one that emphasizes the twenty-two letters of the Hebrew alphabet. These principles, according to Saadya, are responsible for the formation of the universe, and their various permutations ultimately establish the physical bodies to be found within it. Later on in the commentary, he argues that there is an analogy between human speech and divine speech. When humans speak the letters of a word, the word—including the letters that form it—takes on a tangible quality that is responsible for vibrating the air surrounding the words/letters and subsequently carrying them into the ear of the person who is listening. In like manner, when God speaks (e.g., Genesis 1:3), the words and the letters do not just resonate ethereally, but form reality.[88]

Indeed, the first four parts of Saadya's *Kitāb fasīḥ lūghat al-ʿibrāniyyin* deal with the twenty-two letters of the Hebrew alphabet, examining the various consonantal makeup of words, showing how letters join and permutate with one another.[89] This corresponds to part two of his commentary to the *Sefer Yetzirah*, in which Saadya argues that the physical properties witnessed in the world correspond to the different combinations of the primary elements that make up physical bodies, which he identifies with the letters of the Hebrew alphabet.[90] He subsequently identifies both of these combinations to the ways that meanings occur from the permutation of letters in words and the transposition of words in sentences.[91]

Letters thus have an existence independent of communication and writing. They are, to paraphrase the *Sefer Yetzirah*, the very building blocks of creation. In the *K. fasīḥ lūghat al-ʿibrāniyyin*, Saadya frequently refers to God as the "Institutor of Speech" (*moletz al-kalām*), the person from whom the twenty-two letters are derived.[92] Despite this, however, in the same work Saadya also contends that language is a conventional phenomenon: since objects have different names in different languages, these names are not based on intrinsic value, but on consensus.[93] All languages, framed in Rosenzweigian parlance, are ultimately one; and it is this aspect of language that enables Saadya, as it did Rosenzweig, to translate between them.

This emphasis on language, on grammar, on the permutations of the various Hebrew letters runs like a vein throughout Saadya's diverse writings.[94] As with Rosenzweig, the translator's skill turns on his ability to manipulate and play with language, in many ways imitating divine activity, by bringing languages together. By putting languages in counterpoint with one another, the translator forges new linguistic possibilities against the larger backdrop of literary worlds. In his treatise devoted to Hebrew grammar, Saadya included, according to Dunash ibn Labrat, a no-longer-extant chapter devoted to linguistic permutations and the interchanging of consonants.[95] The formation of the universe was for Saadya, then, very much a grammatical act on the part of the *moletz al-kalām*. Understanding grammar, language, and the art of translation, therefore, was not just a linguistic act but a cosmological one.

As the *Egron* also shows, however, there are also deep ontological filiations between lexicography and poetics. Language is bound up with aesthetics. Arab grammarians of the period stressed the inimitability of qurʾanic Arabic and its formative role in the establishment of an Arabo(-Islamic) aesthetics. Saadya, of course, argued that Hebrew not only functioned this way in Hebraic culture but actually easily surpassed the linguistic dexterity of Arabic.[96] He does, however, take his cues from the Arab grammarians:

> The children of Ishmael relate how
> One from their midst[97] realized that his generation
> No longer spoke the Arabic language purely [*faṣḥuna*].
> This grieved him and he wrote a small treatise

As a model to get them to speak purely [al-faṣīḥ].
I likewise saw many among the children of Israel
Who are unable to master even the simple rules
Let alone the more difficult ones of our language.
They mispronounce when they speak;
They are mistaken in their word choice;
And when they compose poetry they neglect the foundations of our
    ancestors.[98]

Here, in the Arabic introduction, Saadya provides the reason for under-taking his translative activities. It is both pedagogical and aesthetic, and he takes as his role model an Arab grammarian who undertook the same task. Thus, Saadya envisages himself as the Jewish and Hebrew equivalent of, as I mentioned earlier, Abū Aswad al-Duwālī.[99] Since his contempo-raries no longer understand their originary language and thus lack the aes-thetic sensibilities to communicate, to compose, to create, Saadya sought to remedy this. Whereas Rosenzweig and Buber complained of earlier trans-lations that made Hebrew too *familiar*, Saadya was concerned about Jews who were too *unfamiliar* with the language. Whereas Rosenzweig and Bu-ber sought to make a germanized Hebrew and a hebraized German less fa-miliar, Saadya, as a more conventional linguistic thinker, wanted to famil-iarize a reading public with Hebrew by showing its points of contact with contemporary Arabic poetics and belles-lettres.

Yet in Saadya's Arabic introduction there is no mention of Hebrew's distinctiveness. Hebrew is not framed in the same context as it was in the *Tafsīr kitāb al-mabādī*, for example, as the building block of creation and of all subsequent ontology and epistemology.[100] On the contrary, Saadya writes as a scholar who is trying to prevent the poetic oblivion of Hebrew, framed in exactly the same terms that would be recognizable to Arab grammarians and linguists. In the Hebrew introduction, however, Saadya connects language, peoplehood, and the exiling of both. But whereas Rosenzweig seemed to pride himself on the *Im-Exil-Sein* of Hebrew poetry and literature, Saadya laments the perniciousness of exile's grasp. In this introduction, Saadya is not at all concerned with the larger Arabic context of forgetting, but instead he frames forgetting and memory solely within the context of Israel's *Heilsgeschichte*.

In the Hebrew introduction to the *Egron*, Saadya presents the model for his attempt to revive an ancient and authentic language:

The *Sefer ha-Egron* is in the sacred language
Which God chose from time immemorial, and
In which the angels sing *selah*
All superior men [*bnei eliyon*] worshipped in it.
Our language and a unified vocabulary existed in the land

From the time God created *adam* upon the *adamah*.
He bestowed upon him this wisdom for one thousand
       nine hundred and ninety-six years . . .[101]

All languages, to use the words of Rosenzweig, possess an "essential unity." This unity, for Saadya, is that which defined the world prior to the scattering of the nations after the destruction of Babel and the Jewish people prior to their dwelling among other cultures and languages. The Hebrew language, especially that associated with the biblical narrative, is associated with "home." The myth of a linguistic unity—for Saadya, as for Rosenzweig—couples with a genetic unity that, in turn, functions as a catalyst for contemporaneous Jewish renewal. According to Saadya, linguistic unity was one of the hallmarks of living in the land of Israel from the time of Abraham until just prior to the exile (*galut*):

We did not speak the languages [of our neighbors],
or worship their gods.
From Egypt, our God spoke to us the words of purity [*divrei tzahot*]
in the mouth of his servant, Moses, a man of God.
He spoke laws and judgments [*huqim u-mishpatim*]
From atop Mt. Horeb.
For generations we had deputies who lived
In the land of our heritage.
[Our language] was heard among our kings,
in the songs of the Levites, and in the hymns of our priests.
It was spoken by our prophets, defining their visions[102]

In this passage language is tied to worship. The purity of Hebrew prevents it, and those who speak it, from being co-opted by idolatry, linguistic or religious. In the past, at least according to Saadya's reconstruction, Hebrew—the language of prophecy and of revelation—successfully prevented the ancient Israelites from worshipping other deities, from transgressing the commandments, and, more generally, from coming under the cultural influences of neighboring peoples. His goal in recreating this language through a Bible translation is to show how the highly ornate and literary Arabic language points to, reveals, the distant Hebrew at the same time that it conceals its specter behind its own literary graces.

Saadya connects Hebrew to the trajectories of creation, revelation, and redemption; past, present, and future. Hebrew was the originary language, the language that all humans originally spoke. Hebrew was the language in which God called out to humanity, and the language in which humanity responded to God's call. He juxtaposes this with Hebrew's current state of neglect, which is described as a form of punishment for adopting the languages of other peoples.[103] Saadya sees it as his obligation

To interpret, understand and study [Hebrew]—
Us, our children, our women, our slaves—
So that it will not completely [depart] from our lips.
[Hebrew] is wisdom; the laws of the Torah are our life, our essence
[ḥayyatenu], our light, and our sanctification for eternity [miqdoshenu
      lemeʿolam ve-ʿad ʿolam].[104]

Here Saadya connects the forgetting of language to the forgetting of being. Moreover, he envisages his goal as renewing and reviving Hebrew for the sake of Israel's redemption (yeshuʿata).[105] It seems that the key to renewing Hebrew and ushering in redemption was for Saadya, as indeed it was for Rosenzweig, through language and translation. The creation of a new language, a new Hebrew, that models itself on the literary and aesthetic qualities of another language is an innovative act. The new is cast as ancient only because its ancientness is conceived of in new terms. To conceptualize such a Jewish ontology in the diaspora is contingent upon the memory of a past that is defined by the present, both of which are ultimately shaped by the future.

To do this, Saadya quite literally created a Hebrew grammar developed out of the Arabic. The result is the creation of one of the earliest examples of adab (or belles-lettres) literature written by a Jew.[106] As with Rosenzweig, the translation from Hebrew into another language ultimately turns on aesthetics. The Bible, as the originary language—functioning similarly to the Ursprache in Rosenzweig's parlance—comes to Jews in the present through the veil of another language. This language is not other than the Hebrew of the original, because all languages are ultimately one to the linguistic and literary caresses of a gifted translator. Both Saadya and Rosenzweig have to demonstrate to a readership that is not familiar with the Hebrew original how Hebrew transforms and ultimately breaks out of the semantic and grammatical casing of another language. The written Arabic or German ultimately reveals the Hebrew behind it, which in turn reveals the silent fullness beyond.

Translation is thus about creating a new literary language out of the ashes of old ones. This includes both the original Hebrew and their modern linguistic incarnations. For the new Hebrew, whether in Saadya's florid Hebrew introduction to his Egron or that discovered in his Arabic translation to the Bible, is not the Hebrew of the original. It is a Hebrew twice- or thrice-removed from its source. It is a Hebrew that Saadya himself has developed in light of contemporaneous advances in Arabic grammar and lexicography. If his Arabic contemporaries searched the poetic language of pre-Islamic Arabian poetry as a means to keep the pure Arabic of the Qurʾān alive, Saadya sought to understand the beauty of biblical Hebrew through both Arabic and his own reconstituted Hebrew. And that is certainly what Saadya did:

> When I decided to write this book to facilitate knowledge
> Among all who have chosen the language of the holy angels
> I thought a lot about the speech, pronunciation and utterances
> Found among all the nations.
> All words exist in one of two types: foundational [*yesod*] and
> Additional [*tosefet*] . . . Whereas the former are stable, the latter
> are not.[107]

Here Saadya differentiates between the tri-consonantal root structure on the one hand, and those letters that are added to it in order to designate phenomena such as gender, plurality, and tense. He is thus quite literally constructing or, perhaps better, restoring a primary text using the categories of Arabic lexicography. A literary Hebrew slowly emerges through the linguistic forms and categories of Arabic, the language of Saadya's translation. The Hebrew Bible, then, was a text that could be translated into Arabic. However, in translation, it could also be as forceful as the original.

Translation—for Saadya, as for Rosenzweig—is a nostalgic act. It remembers the way the past was or might have been had things been different. Translation uses one language to invoke the meaning, the nuances, and ultimately the texture of another language. But if Hebrew is changed by being encased in Arabic, the latter—as the work from Rosenzweig makes abundantly clear—must also be forever changed in the process. Arabic is expanded when touched by Hebrew. The latter language can actually become the catalyst for the renewal of the former because, according to Saadya, it now absorbs the purity of Hebrew. In Arabic, Saadya's translation amounts to a copy of a copy—an Arabic memory of what an otherwise unspoken Hebrew should sound like. Saadya's return to the past, his translation of an ancient text into the literary lingua franca of his day was very much a project of modernity, a form of "ancient modernism," to borrow the phrase used of Rosenzweig's translation project.

CONCLUSIONS

Whereas Rosenzweig faced a semantic otherness posed by the radical differences between Indo-European German and Semitic Hebrew, empirically, Saadya's predicament is not nearly as severe. Hebrew and Arabic were cognates, and the former could easily be absorbed into the word structures and semiotics of the latter. However, he still encounters the same problem that, it seems to me, every Jewish translator of the Bible must face: How does one keep open the spaces in-between the languages, the words? How does one create an aesthetically pleasing translation that vectors all of the memories associated with another language and way-of-being in the world? Can an originary language bespeak in another language?

The retrieval of memory, as we have seen here, is tantamount to an aesthetics of forgetting. One must remember a past that will be future, using the colorful sounds and harmonics of a new language that is present. As such, this new language must be wrenched out of its familiarity and differently conceived. The Hebrew must inform this new language, caress it, transform it in the same way that it must ultimately open itself up to the other language. This fusion of languages, paradoxically, creates a past, the concept of a pristine language that is accessible only through a different and a modern language. It is this paradox that both Rosenzweig and Saadya faced, and it seems to me that they could never quite ameliorate the tensions brought on by this paradox. According to their respective models, the Hebrew is, as I have mentioned time and again, a palimpsest, something that, like the *Ursprache,* can be glimpsed at only through the veil of another language. In its sacrality, Hebrew ceases to be a real language; it becomes little more than a specter that translation keeps forever out of reach.[108]

The target language thus conjures up an originary language that does not exist except as an alluring absence. Hebrew's presence resides solely in the verbal, grammatical, and semiotic structures of another text, another language, another mode of expression. It is the exiling of language, using the language of exile. Hebrew remains as a distant memory, one not to be forgotten but also one that is always just out of reach.

In reflecting on the art of memory and translation here, I have also sought to overturn, or at the very least question, the axiom of precursorship, one of the guiding principles that governs the historical study of Jewish philosophy. Rather than have Saadya Gaon, as the earlier thinker, set the frames of reference for this study, I decided to use Rosenzweig as my point of departure, to use his understanding of language, being, and translation as a way of shedding new light on the translative project of Saadya. The results, I trust, will be not so much anachronous as natural. One simply cannot read, from the vantage point of today, Saadya's work on translation—his ontology of language, his linking creation to grammar, his notion of the redemptive value in translation—except through the lens provided by Rosenzweig, much as one cannot translate the Bible, according to Rosenzweig, by circumventing Luther. Saadya's questions, accordingly, are our questions, not a set of curiosities that inhabit one of the dusty backrooms of the museum of Jewish philosophy. By starting with Rosenzweig and moving back to Saadya, we see translation as a philosophical problem and not just a historical one.[109]

NOTES

The first epigraph is from Jorge Luis Borges, "Kafka and His Precursors," in *Everything and Nothing,* translated by Donald A. Yates et al. (New York: New Directions, 1999), 73. The second epigraph is from T. S. Eliot, *Points of View* (New York: Faber and Faber, 1941), 13.

1. Elliot R. Wolfson, *Language, Eros, Being: Kabbalistic Hermeneutics and Poetic Imagination* (New York: Fordham University Press, 2005), xxxi.

2. Chronological and contextual presentations are customary in surveys precisely because these treat a wide range of figures. Yet even works devoted to specific individuals within the Jewish philosophical tradition tend to adopt the contextual approach, and especially to appeal to the system of influences of earlier thinkers.

3. Individually authored surveys include Colette Sirat's *A History of Jewish Philosophy in the Middle Ages* (Cambridge: Cambridge University Press, 1990); Norbert Samuelson's *Jewish Philosophy: An Historical Introduction* (New York: Continuum, 2004); Nathan Rotenstreich's *Jewish Philosophy in Modern Times: From Mendelssohn to Rosenzweig* (New York: Holt, Rinehart, and Winston, 1968); and Norbert Samuelson, *An Introduction to Modern Jewish Philosophy* (Albany: SUNY Press, 1989). Edited volumes include *The Cambridge Companion to Medieval Jewish Philosophy,* edited by Daniel H. Frank and Oliver Leaman (Cambridge: Cambridge University Press, 2003); *The Cambridge Companion to Modern Jewish Philosophy,* edited by Michael L. Morgan and Peter Eli Gordon (Cambridge: Cambridge University Press, 2007); and *The Cambridge History of Jewish Philosophy: The Modern Era,* edited by David Novak and Martin Kavka (forthcoming, 2009).

4. This, despite the fact, that no philosopher in the premodern period would have referred to himself as a "Jewish philosopher" engaged in an activity somehow referred to as "Jewish philosophy."

5. Richard Rorty, "The Historiography of Philosophy: Four Genres," in *Philosophy in History: Essays on the Historiography of Philosophy,* edited by Richard Rorty, J. B. Schneewind, and Quentin Skinner (Cambridge: Cambridge University Press, 1984), 62. Rorty adds that "either we anachronistically impose enough of our problems and vocabulary on the dead to make them conversational partners, or we confine our interpretive activity to making their falsehoods look less silly by placing them in the context of the benighted times in which they were written" (49).

6. Ibid., 62.

7. E.g., Hermann Cohen, *Charakteristik der Ethik Maimunis,* in *Jüdische Schriften* (Berlin: Schwetschke, 1924), 3:264–65. An English translation may be found in *Ethics of Maimonides,* translated by Almut Sh. Bruckstein (Madison: University of Wisconsin Press, 2004), 124–25

8. E.g., Leo Strauss, "The Literary Character of the *Guide of the Perplexed,*" in *Persecution and the Art of Writing* (Chicago: University of Chicago Press, 1988 [1952]).

9. See the formulation in David N. Myers, *Resisting History: Historicism and Its Discontents in German-Jewish Thought* (Princeton, N.J.: Princeton University Press, 2003), 18–34.

10. See my forthcoming "Medieval Philosophers in Modern Jewish Philosophy: A Case Study of Dialogism," in *The Cambridge History of Jewish Philosophy: The Modern Period*, edited by Martin Kavka and David Novak (Cambridge: Cambridge University Press, forthcoming).

11. There are a few hints when, for example, Rosenzweig mentions lexicography (albeit without mentioning Saadya) in the medieval period. See, for example, his comments to Halevi's poem "Ein Sprachkunststück," in *Jehuda Halevi: Zweiundneunzig Hymnen und Gedichte*, in *Der Mensch und sein Werk: Gesammelte Schriften*, 4.1, edited by Rafael Rosenzweig (The Hague: Martinus Nijhoff, 1983), 165–67. English translation in *Ninety-Two Poems and Hymns by Yehuda Halevi*, edited by Richard A. Cohen (Albany: SUNY Press, 2000), 175–77. This poem is not included in Barbara Ellen Galli, *Franz Rosenzweig and Jehuda Halevi: Translating, Translations, and Translators* (Montreal and Kingston: McGill-Queen's University Press, 1995).

12. In this regard, see Edward Breuer, *The Limits of Enlightenment: Jews, Germans, and the Eighteenth-Century Study of Scripture* (Cambridge, Mass.: Harvard University Press, 1996).

13. Here it is important to be clear that Rosenzweig, as should be well known, did not undertake to translate the Bible into German by himself. The main impetus behind the project was Martin Buber, and he was the one that did much of the translative work and who undertook to finish the project after Rosenzweig's death in 1929. Although both Buber and Rosenzweig wrote about their undertaking (collected as *Die Schrift und ihre Verdeustschung*), I choose to focus on Rosenzweig's writings, especially his "Die Schrift und das Wort," "Die Schrift und Luther," and his Afterword to the Halevi translation. When I mention Rosenzweig's "translation," then, it is simply a matter of convenience, and I am not trying to diminish Buber's contribution to the project in any way.

14. I would like to thank Elliot R. Wolfson for this formulation.

15. Franz Rosenzweig, "Die Schrift und Luther," in Martin Buber and Franz Rosenzweig, *Die Schrift und ihre Verdeutschung* (Berlin: Schocken Verlag, 1936), 104–5. An English translation may be found in *Scripture and Translation*, translated by Lawrence Rosenwald and Everett Fox (Bloomington: Indiana University Press, 1994), 56. All future citations from the work of Rosenzweig will give the German title followed by the page number in the German and then the page number from the English (e.g., 104–5/56).

16. Saadya Gaon, *Ha-Egron: Kitāb ʾusūl al-shiʿr al-ʿibrānī*, critical edition with introduction and commentary by Nehemya Allony (Jerusalem: Academy of the Hebrew Language, 1969), Arabic introduction, 148.

17. Although Luther's translation remains incontrovertible and omnipresent, one cannot now translate the Bible into German as if there were no Luther translation. See the comments in Dana Hollander, *Exemplarity and Chosenness: Rosenzweig and Derrida on the Nation of Philosophy* (Stanford, Calif.: Stanford University Press, 2008), 143–46.

18. See the comments in Peter Eli Gordon, *Rosenzweig and Heidegger: Between Judaism and German Philosophy* (Berkeley: University of California Press, 2003), 238–39.

19. Franz Rosenzweig, "Das neue Denken," in *Der Mensch und sein Werk. Gesammelte Schriften*, vol. 3, *Zweistromland. Kleinere Schriften zu Glauben und Denken*, edited by Reinhold and Annemarie Mayer (Dordrecht: Martinus Nijhoff, 1984), 148. "The New Thinking," in *Franz Rosenzweig's "The New Thinking*," edited and translated by Alan Udoff and Barbara E. Galli (Syracuse, N.Y.: Syracuse University Press, 1999), 81.

20. On the history and problems associated with the employment of "influences" in intellectual history, see the classic formulations in Quentin Skinner, "Limits of

Historical Explanation," *Philosophy* 41 (1966): 199–215; idem, "Meaning and Understanding in the History of Ideas," *History and Theory* 8, no. 1 (1969): 3–53. In the latter work, for example, he writes that "A given writer may be 'discovered' to have held
a view, on the strength of some chance similarity of terminology, on some subject to
which he cannot in principle have meant to contribute" (7–8).

21. There is no evidence, however, as far as I am aware, that Rosenzweig read anything by Saadya.

22. Skinner, "Meaning and Understanding in the History of Ideas," 5–12; see
further the comments in *Meaning and Context: Quentin Skinner and His Critics,* edited by
James Tully (Cambridge: Polity Press, 1988); Dominick LaCapra, *Rethinking Intellectual
History: Texts, Contexts, Language* (Ithaca, N.Y.: Cornell University Press, 1983), 56–69

23. Hans-Georg Gadamer, *Wahrheit und Methode* (Tübingen: Mohr, 1990). An English translation may be found in *Truth and Method* (New York: Crossroad, 1982),

24. Here I take my insights from E. R. Wolfson, *Language, Eros, Being,* xv–xxxi.

25. Klaus Reichert, "'It Is Time': The Buber-Rosenzweig Bible Translation in Context," in *The Translatability of Cultures: Figurations of the Space Between,* edited by Sanford
Budick and Wolfgang Iser (Stanford, Calif.: Stanford University Press, 1996), 180.

26. Rosenzweig, "Zeit ists . . . : Gedanken über das jüdische Bildungsproblem des
Augenblicks," in *Zur jüdischen Erziehung* (Berlin: Schocken, 1937), 8. Also in *Gesammelte
Schriften* III: *Zweistromland,* 461–81. Qtd. in Reichert, "'It Is Time,'" 173.

27. Franz Rosenzweig, "Die Schrift und Luther," 113/61. See further, Franz
Rosenzweig, *Der Stern der Erlösung,* in *Der Mensch und sein Werk: Gesammelte Schriften,* edited by Reinhold Meyer (The Hague: Martinus Nijhoff, 1976), 2:275. I have consulted
the English translation found in Franz Rosenzweig, *The Star of Redemption,* translated
by Barbara Galli (Madison: University of Wisconsin Press, 2005), 265.

28. See the comments in Leora Batnitzky, *Idolatry and Representation: The Philosophy
of Franz Rosenzweig Reconsidered* (Princeton, N.J.: Princeton University Press, 2000),
110–11.

29. Rosenzweig, Afterword 4/172. The English page number refers to the Galli
translation. In the original 1927 version, this appeared as an "Afterword," yet in the
version found in his *Gesammelte Schriften,* it appears as "Foreword." I will follow Galli
and refer to it as his "Afterword."

30. See the comments in Rosenzweig, "Afterword," 4/172.

31. Rosenzweig, "Die Schrift und Luther," 88/47.

32. See the comments in Hollander, *Exemplarity and Chosenness,* 141–47

33. Elliot R. Wolfson, "Facing the Effaced: Mystical Eschatology and the Idealistic
Orientation in the Thought of Franz Rosenzweig," *Journal for the History of Modern Theology* 4 (1997), esp. 74–80.

34. Rosenzweig, "Afterword," 3–4/ 171; c.f., "Die Schrift und Luther," 124/67.

35. Reichert, "'It Is Time,'"174.

36. Rosenzweig, "Die Schrift und Luther," 125/67.

37. Ibid., 125/67.

38. Ibid., 110–11/59–60.

39. E.g., Batnitzky, *Idolatry and Representation,* 106–12; Gordon, *Rosenzweig and Heidegger,* 248–57.

40. In this regard, the comments are a propos in Mara Benjamin, "Building a
Zion in German(y): Franz Rosenzweig on Yehudah Halevi," *Jewish Social Studies* 13,
no. 2 (2007): 128–30.

41. Rosenzweig, "Die Schrift und Luther," 126/68.

42. Rosenzweig, "Afterword," 1/169.

43. Ibid., 6–7/174.

44. Here I refer to Rosenzweig's "ideal" translator, and not the many translators of whom he is critical in the Afterword. These translators (e.g., Schulze, Cohn, and Wilamowitz), according to him, have "nothing to say" so they "need not ask anything of the language, and a language whose speaker asks nothing of it becomes frozen into a tool for basic communication" (ibid., 3/171).

45. Ibid., 3/171.

46. E.g., Rosenzweig, *Der Stern der Erlösung*, 198–99/192–93.

47. See the comments in Elliot R. Wolfson, "Light Does Not Talk But Shines: Apophasis and Vision in Rosenzweig's Theopoetic Temporality," chapter 3 of this volume.

48. E.g., Rosenzweig, "Das neue Denken," 148–49/80–83.

49. Rosenzweig, *Der Stern der Erlösung*, 327/312.

50. See the comments in Stéphane Mosès, *System and Revelation: The Philosophy of Franz Rosenzweig*, translated by Catherine Tihanyi (Detroit, Mich.: Wayne State University Press, 1992), 150–52.

51. See the comments in Galli, "The Halevi Book, Rosenzweig, and the *Star,*" in her *Franz Rosenzweig and Jehuda Halevi*, 291.

52. Rosenzweig, *Der Stern der Erlösung*, 167–68/163.

53. Rosenzweig, "Afterword," 4/172.

54. Ibid., 5/173.

55. Rosenzweig, "Die Schrift und Luther," 104–5/56.

56. Gordon, *Rosenzweig and Heidegger*, 249.

57. See W. Gunther Plaut, *German-Jewish Bible Translations: Linguistic Theology as a Political Phenomenon* (New York: Leo Baeck Institute, 1992).

58. Rosenzweig, "Die Schrift und Luther," 95/51.

59. Ibid., 107/57.

60. Plaut, *German-Jewish Bible Translations*, 18.

61. More generally, see *Der Stern der Erlösung*, 331–39/317–24.

62. See the comments in Wolfson, "Light Does Not Talk But Shines."

63. Rosenzweig, "Afterword," 2/170.

64. Ibid., 10/177.

65. Ibid.

66. In *Das neue Denken*, 148/81, Rosenzweig attributes this ability to the "new thinking" that is defined by "narrative philosophy" (*erzählende Philosophie*) or "experiencing philosophy" (*erfahrende Philosophie*).

67. See the comments in Nobert M. Samuelson, *A User's Guide to Franz Rosenzweig's Star of Redemption* (Surrey: Curzon, 1999), 251–52.

68. Rosenzweig, *Der Stern der Erlösung*, 334/320.

69. Ibid., 336/321.

70. Rosenzweig, "Die Schrift und das Wort," 86/45.

71. Ibid., 87/46.

72. Ibid., 86/45.

73. Benjamin, "Building a Zion in German(y)," 136.

74. See Rosenzweig's comments in "Die Einheit der Bibel: Eine Auseinandersetzung mit Orthodoxie und Liberalismus," in *Die Schrift und ihre Verdeutschung*, 46–54/22–26.

75. Rosenzweig, "Die Schrift und das Wort," 84/44.

76. Ibid., 80/42.

77. See the comments in Abraham ibn Ezra, *Commentary to Genesis*, 2:11.

78. Saadya wrote two introductions to the work, one in an ornate vocalized and

accented Hebrew that imitated the biblical narrative, and one in a more prosaic Arabic. The former was written in Egypt when Saadya was around twenty. The latter was written "years later" when he wrote an expanded Hebrew-language lexicon for poets that included, in Arabic, a discussion of rhetoric and poetics. For an illuminating comparison of the two introductions, see Rina Drory, *Models and Contexts: Arabic Literature and its Impact on Medieval Jewish Culture* (Leiden: Brill, 2000), 178–90.

79. Saadya, *Egron,* Arabic introduction, 151.

80. See Drory, *Models and Contacts,* 185–86.

81. On Saadya's attempt to ground the *Sefer Yetzirah* in his philosophical system, see Georges Vajda, "Le Commentaire de Saadia sure le Sefer Yeçirah," *Revue des études juives* 106 (1941): 64–86; Haggai Ben-Shammai, "Saadya's Goal in this *Commentary to the Sefer Yezirah,"* in *A Straight Path: Studies in Medieval Philosophy and Culture in Honor of Arthur Hyman,* edited by Ruth Link-Salinger et al. (Washington, D.C.: Catholic University Press of America, 1988), 1–9.

82. Saadya Gaon, *Sefer Yezirah ʿim perush Rabbenu Saadya ben Yosef Fayyumi,* Arabic text and Hebrew translation by Yosef Kafiḥ (Jerusalem, 1972), introduction, 33–34.

83. An analogy may be found in Abraham Abulafia, who, on the one hand, follows Maimonides and claims that Hebrew is conventional but, on the other, argues that Hebrew is the essential language, the language of creation, revelation, and ultimately of redemption. I thank Elliot R. Wolfson for suggesting this comparison.

84. See the comments in Drory, *Models and Contacts,* 188.

85. This is the opinion of Allony in the introduction to his critical edition of the *Egron.*

86. Saadya, *Egron,* Hebrew introduction, 156.

87. C.f., *Kitāb amānāt wa-al-iʿtiqādāt.* An English translation may be found in *The Book of Beliefs and Opinions,* translated by Samuel Rosenblatt (New Haven, Conn.: Yale University Press, 1976). Requisite secondary literature may be found in Harry A. Wolfson, *Repercussions of the Kalam in Jewish Philosophy* (Cambridge, Mass.: Harvard University Press, 1979); Alexander Altmann, "Saadya's Theory of Revelation: Its Origin and Background," in his *Studies in Religious Philosophy and Mysticism* (Ithaca, N.Y.: Cornell University Press, 1969); Israel Efros, "Saadya's Second Theory of Creation in its Relation to Pythagoreanism and Platonism," in *Louis Ginzburg Jubilee Volume* (New York: American Academy of Jewish Research, 1945), 133–42 (English Section).

88. This is also related to Saadya's concept of the "second air." For requisite secondary literature on this topic, see Harry Austryn Wolfson, "The Kalam Arguments for Creation in Saadia, Averroes, Maimonides, and St. Thomas," reprinted in *Saadia Anniversary Volume* (New York, 1943), 198–245.

89. Saadya Gaon, *Or rishon bi-ḥokhmah ha-lashon: Sefer siḥot lashon ha-ivrim le-rav saadya gaon,* ed. A. Dotan (Jerusalem: World Union of Jewish Studies, 1997). Requisite secondary literature may be found in Henry Malther, *Saadia Gaon: His Life and Works* (Philadelphia: Jewish Publication Society of America, 1921), 139–40; Solomon L. Skoss, "Saadia Gaon, The Earliest Hebrew Grammarian," *PAAJR* 21 (1952): 75–100; 22 (1953): 65–90, and 23 (1954): 59–73; idem, "A Study of Hebrew Vowels from Saadia Gaon's Grammatical Work *Kitab al-Lughah,"* *JQR* 42 (1951–52): 283–317.

90. Saadya, *Tafsīr kitāb al-mabādī,* 121–22.

91. Ibid., 117–19.

92. See the comments in Aron Dotan, "Particularism and Universalism in the Linguistic Theory of Saadia Gaon," *Sefarad* LV.1 (1995): 71–72.

93. Dotan, "Particularism and Universalism," 68–69. Although see my comments in n. 83 above.

94. In the Middle Ages, at least based on the manuscript tradition, Saadya's com-

mentary to the *Sefer Yetzirah* was more popular than his *The Book of Beliefs and Opinions.* See Ronald C. Kiener, "Saadia Gaon and the *Sefer Yezirah:* Translation Theory in Classical Jewish Thought," in *Interpretation in Religion,* edited by Shlomo Biderman and Ben-Ami Scharfstein (Leiden: Brill, 1992), 171.

95. Skoss, "Saadia Gaon, the Earliest Hebrew Grammar," 59.

96. See the comments in Allony, "Translator's Introduction," 28–30.

97. I.e., the aforementioned Abū Aswad al-Duwālī.

98. Saadya, *Egron,* Arabic introduction, 151–53.

99. Drory, *Models and Contacts,* 186.

100. Drory argues that the notion of Arabic as being primarily a communicative language, and therefore clear and understandable, was quite a common one among medieval Hebrew scholars. She contrasts this with the use of Hebrew, which was regarded as more "festive and grandiloquent." See her *Models and Contacts,* 165–77.

101. Saadya, *Egron,* Hebrew introduction, 156.

102. Ibid., 157.

103. Ibid., 158.

104. Ibid., 159.

105. Ibid., 160.

106. Eliezer Schlossberg, "Ten Observations on Rhetoric and Expression by Saadia Gaon," *Journal of Semitic Studies* 38, no. 2 (1993): 269–70.

107. Saadya, *Egron,* Hebrew introduction, 160–61.

108. See the comments in Benjamin, "Building a Zion in German(y)," 131–32.

109. I would like to thank Jennifer M. Hall, Dana Hollandar, and Elliot R. Wolfson for reading and commenting on earlier drafts of this paper. All mistakes are solely my own.

PART 2

TEXT BEYOND TEXT: EMPHASIZING VISION AND THE VISUAL

3

LIGHT DOES NOT TALK
BUT SHINES: APOPHASIS AND
VISION IN ROSENZWEIG'S
THEOPOETIC TEMPORALITY

Elliot R. Wolfson

> There can be *nothing* sacred.
> The sacred cannot be a *thing*.
> The instant alone is sacred,
> which is *nothing* (is not a *thing*).
>
> —GEORGES BATAILLE

IT IS COMMONLY MAINTAINED, AND NOT WITHOUT GOOD REASON, THAT Rosenzweig's *sprachdenken* rests upon the supposition that there are three unsublatable elements—God, human, and world—that emerge from the shattering of the all-encompassing totality presumed by German idealists to be the ultimate reality. In an essay published in 1997, I argued that in the third part of *The Star of Redemption,* especially in the sustained discussion of eternal truth in book three, Rosenzweig embraced a more mystically oriented conception that, in some measure, led to a reappropriation of the very idealism that he set out to repudiate.[1] The characterization of Rosenzweig's understanding of redemption as a kind of *theistic mysticism* was proffered by Gershom Scholem[2] and reiterated by Nahum Glatzer.[3] Support for my contention that the emphasis on the visual at the end of the *Star* betrays an affinity to, if not direct influence of, kabbalah[4] is found in a passing remark that Rosenzweig makes in his commentary to Judah Halevi's poem *liqra't meqor ḥayyei emet aruẓah,* which he translates as *Sehnsucht:*[5] "For this poet, the forerunner of the great Kabbalistic movements for whom the vision of God served as Israel's topical heritage and always to be newly actualized on the holy ground, sleep and dream are the legitimate ways to the goal."[6]

This is a remarkable passage for at least two reasons. First, it demonstrates a subtle grasp of Halevi's protokabbalistic sensibilities, and second, it offers an astoundingly incisive and concise understanding of the centrality of the visionary dimension in the kabbalistic worldview.[7] What is important for our immediate concern, however, is the fact that the vision Rosenzweig articulates in the concluding part of the *Star* is on a par with the vision he ascribes to Halevi and to the kabbalists. That vision, moreover, renders problematic the dialogical thinking that is dependent on the "essential separateness" (*wesenhafte Getrenntheit*) or "transcendence" (*Transcendent*)[8] of each of the elements vis-à-vis the other,[9] a theme that has even been used to justify labeling Rosenzweig as a precursor of postmodern discourse.[10] Rosenzweig thus made good on his promise in the conclusion of the introduction to the *Star* "to find again in this nothing, in this threefold nothing of knowledge [*diesem dreifachen Nichts des Wissens*], the All that we had to cut into pieces."[11] The All is retrieved, but not as the one all-encompassing nothing posited by idealist philosophers, but as a threefold nothing, a nothing aligned individually with each of the basic terms of Rosenzweig's correlative thinking—the nothing of the knowledge of the human or the metaethical, the nothing of the knowledge of the world or the metalogical, and the nothing of the knowledge of God or the metaphysical.[12]

The mystical nature of this reclamation finds support in a letter that Rosenzweig wrote to Margrit Rosenstock-Huessy on February 1, 1919, in which he described the third book of part three of the *Star* as "a 'mysticism,' but one which rests on the ground of all the unmystical which stands 500 pages before it, and then which is also neutralized again through the anti-mystical 'Gate' which yet follows after it."[13] Rosenzweig qualifies the mystical character of his account of redemption by insisting that the way he had to embark upon to get to it and the opening of the gate that follows from it are "unmystical," which is to say, they affirm the factuality (rendering the German *Tatsächlichkeit*, a critical term in Rosenzweig's thinking, as we shall see) of each of the three elements, that is, allowing God to be God, the human to be human, and the world to be world.[14] But the fact is, as his own admission makes clear, the vision of the All that he offers the reader is not unrelated to the ideal of the "ecstatic mystic," who affirms that "everything is God"[15] and, as a consequence, divests the divine of its "one significant function: to be wholly other than the world."[16]

Here it is worth recalling that in the letter to Rudolf Ehrenberg written on November 18, 1917, the "Urzelle" (the germ-cell) of the *Star*, Rosenzweig positioned mysticism between "actual theology" and "actual philosophy."[17] Is this not an appropriate way to characterize his own effort in the *Star*? Consider the description of the "new philosopher" found therein: "Philosophy today requires . . . that 'theologians' do philosophy. But theologians in a different sense, of course. For . . . the theologian whom philosophy requires for the sake of its scientific character is himself a theologian who desires philosophy—out of concern for integrity. What was a demand in the interests of objectivity for philosophy will turn out to be demand in the interests of subjectivity for theology. They complete each other, and together they bring about a new type of philosopher or theologian, situated between theology and philosophy."[18] A similar point is made in the 1925 essay "Das neue Denken," which attempts to offer the reader a guide to reading the *Star:* "Theology may not debase philosophy to play the part of the handmaid, yet just as degrading is the role of charwoman which . . . philosophy has become accustomed to give theology. The true relationship between these two renewed sciences . . . is one of siblings, which must in fact lead to union [of the sciences] within the persons who maintain them. Theological problems want to be translated into human [problems], while human [problems] want to be driven into the theological."[19]

The import of this comment sheds light on another well-known passage in the same essay: Rosenzweig remarks that the *Star* is primarily not a "Jewish book" or a "philosophy of religion," but it is a "system of philosophy," which sought "to bring about the total renewal of thinking."[20] The system propounded by Rosenzweig is situated in the interstice between philosophy and theology,[21] but it emerges from the "intuitive knowledge of experience" (*anschaulichen Wissen der Erfahrung*) of God, human, and world,[22] which serves as the epistemic basis for the vision to come of the All, a seeing of the eternal star in the countenance of the configuration that is (in) truth.[23] That the vision described in the last part of the *Star* is Rosenzweig's attempt to incorporate into his system his own unique mystical experience can be confirmed by another letter to Margrit Rosenstock-Huessy from October 4, 1918, in which he described in extraordinary language having seen the star rotating around itself "with eyes and everything individual in it." By Rosenzweig's own admission, the attempt to write down the nocturnal vision the morning after proved to be a "wholly poor" and fragmentary recounting of the "immediate sight of the whole" (*Anblick des Ganzen*).[24] An allusion to this vision, whence the path goes forth and to which it returns, can be found in another passage in "Das neue Denken." Reflecting on the nature of the philosophic book, of which the *Star* is exemplary, Rosenzweig notes that "the whole [*Ganze*] becomes surveyable at a glance [*Blick*]." This momentary glimpse of the whole in the new thinking is to be contrasted with the conception of totality in the old thinking, insofar as the time of its occurrence "cannot be predicted" and is not "at exactly the same point for two readers."[25] It is nevertheless an integral part of the system that Rosenzweig constructed from his own vision, a "beholding the 'world-likeness in the countenance of God' [*Welt-gleichnisses im Gottesantlitz*]," a "seizing of all being in the immediacy of a moment [*eines Augenblicks*] and blink of an eye [*Augen-blicks*]" in which "the limit of humanity is entered."[26] The broken All is reconfigured in this immediate sight of the whole, the whole that, like the moment in which it is seen, the blink of the eye, is the not yet that has already been and therefore is always still to come.

In this study, I return to that argument but from a different angle, focusing on the implications of Rosenzweig's depiction of the redemptive moment as the "silent illumination [*schweigenden Erleuchtung*] of the wholly fulfilling end."[27] The apophatic vision is an other-worldly state, the "eternal bliss" of the life-beyond-death, not a triumph of death by a return to the vicissitudes of temporal existence, but rather an overcoming of time in the fullness of time that Rosenzweig describes in the ocular terms (derived from the rabbinic depiction of the world-to-come) of the "pious ones" seated "with crowns upon their heads, and their eyes . . . turned toward the brilliance of the divinity become manifest" (*den Lichtglanz der offenbarwordenen Gottheit*).[28] The end, to which is conferred the spectrality by means of which one crosses the "threshold of the supra-world [*Überwelt*], from the miracle [*Wunder*] to the illumination [*Erleuchtung*]," signifies that all three elements are transmogrified and liberated from their own ontic contingency: the human is redeemed "from all singularity and self-seeking," the world "from all thingliness," and God "from all the work of the six days of Creation and from all loving anxiety about our poor soul"; that is, God is unfettered from the imagistic garb of being portrayed "as the Lord" (*als den Herrn*),[29] the personal deity of the Jewish faith, the dialogical presence of the divine other that Rosenzweig placed at the center of his "absolute empiricism."[30]

In Heideggerian terms, Rosenzweig's project could be called an "onto-theology," which has been succinctly characterized as "a philosophical theology in search of a philosophical foundation for the living God, a theological philosophy trying in its reflection on Being to reach a new understanding of the concrete God."[31] I am aware of the fact that Rosenzweig was critical of the metaphysical tradition and its quest for an ontological essence, a point to which I shall return below, but the validity of this claim should not obscure the fact that his own speech-thinking was not only meant to serve as a bridge connecting philosophy and theology, as I have already noted, but it is an experiential mode that presumes that we can attribute a "naturalistic, existential essence" (*naturhaftes, daseiendes Wesen*) to God,[32] and consequently, he is still thinking of being in relation to entity, albeit the supreme entity that cannot be thought.[33] On both of these counts the term "onto-theology" is justified.[34]

The question I wish to put before the reader is whether Rosenzweig succeeds in promoting a way for human beings to access this essence. Does he philosophically articulate (and this is indeed the measure by which his thought needs to be judged) a foundation for belief in a living, concrete God? Expressed in his own theological register, does he account adequately for the real possibility of revelation as an experience of the immediate presence of the transcendent (or perhaps better, transcendence) breaking into history? Is Rosenzweig's radical empiricism sufficient to ground faith in a personal deity with a distinct existentiality, or is his own thinking susceptible to promoting an "atheistic theology" according to which the divine is reduced to a "self-projection of the human into the heaven of myth?"[35] Does he break forth from, or is he inevitably trapped in, the "anthropological modernity," the term he uses to name the third epoch of European philosophy—which complements "cosmological antiquity" and the "theological Middle Ages"—an epoch dominated by the "darling idea" of the "reduction" of experiences of the world and of God to the ego.[36] One might counter that Rosenzweig's embrace of apophaticism is actually an anticipation of more recent attempts to affirm "theology after ontotheology."[37] While I am sympathetic to this point of view, in my mind it still begs the critical question, since even this form of "theological" reflection may not be exempt from the verdict that it is deeply atheological. Clarification of this matter has major implications not only for properly assessing the thought of one of the more profound thinkers of the twentieth century, but for taking stock of the persistent theocentric bias of much of modern, and to some extent postmodern, Jewish religious philosophy, which owes its inspiration to the compelling narrative of Rosenzweig's biography and his effort to revitalize the sacramental life of Judaism in his major work.[38] Tackling this issue head-on may provide an opportunity to set this course on a more even keel.

A responsible and responsive discussion of what is arguably one of the more challenging aspects of Rosenzweig's thought requires a reinvestigation of two major dimensions of his speech-thinking: the relation of hermeneutics and time, and the poetic nature of language. Without a proper grasp of these topics, the reader cannot be expected to understand the turn on Rosenzweig's path that culminates in the overcoming of language as one is rendered speechless in the face of truth, a metaphorical idiom that is hyperliteralized (perhaps due in part to the influence of kabbalistic terminology) in his attempt to render the literal metaphorically. In Rosenzweig's own poetic diction, "The star that travels the path does not stand still for a moment," and thus it cannot be seen by the eye. When, however, the "moment has shut down through its becoming eternal," time permits the eye to see the configuration of truth in that very moment, in the blink-of-the-eye. "The configuration, therefore, more than that which is elemental, more than what is real, is the directly perceptual [*unmittelbar Anchauliche*]." In this direct perception or intuition (*Anschauung*), the very factuality (*Tatsächlichkeit*) that Rosenzweig struggled to affirm,[39] that is, the ontic autonomy of the basic elementals, is "brought to its end," and "then nothing more is heard of thing [*Sache*] or of act [*Tat*]."[40] Redemption at the end restores one to creation at the beginning, and the hidden that became manifest becomes hidden again. The effort of the *Star*, in great measure, is to allow that hiddenness to be revealed as the hiddenness that cannot be revealed but as the hiddenness that is so revealed.

It has been noted that the structure of the book is not linear but circular: the author leads the reader on a journey, the end of which is a return to the beginning.[41] The hermeneutic at work in the *Star* reverses the temporal order, allowing for "a backward movement from the future to the past as opposed to a dialectically forward-moving argument from past to future,"[42] an idea substantiated dramatically by the opening "from death" (*Vom Tode*) and the conclusion "into life" (*Ins Leben*). In a strictly linear pattern, one would expect the progression to be from life to death, but the circular course laid out by Rosenzweig starts with death and ends with life. One might say, therefore, that the *Star* puts into practice Rosenzweig's observation in "Das neue Denken" that in a philosophical book "a sentence does not follow from its predecessor, but, much more likely, from its successor."[43] Even more to the point, in a second passage from that essay, Rosenzweig accepts the recommendation of one of the critics of the *Star* that the potential reader would profit by reading the book "backward and forward."[44] The author has no objection as long as one keeps in mind that it can be read from front to back as well as from back to front, thereby forming a circuitous itinerary rather than a linear trajectory. I would argue, however, that this circularity is not simply going back to where one has been, a mere repetition and recycling of patterns,[45] but it is rather a reverting to where one has never been, and indeed where one can never be, which is precisely the mode of eternality that interrupts and intersects with time, thereby transforming temporality itself into a diremptive mode of luminosity, what I will call a theopoetic[46] temporality, the shining-forth of the nonrepresentable presentness that anticipates the past and recollects the future. The origin, on this account, is determined by the telos, the past shaped by the future.[47] It is worthwhile recalling Rosenzweig's comments in *Das Büchlein vom gesunden und kranken Menscenverstand*, composed in 1921 as a précis of the *Star* to make it more accessible to a wider audience, that an introduction to a book can never be conclusive, since its task is simply to introduce, and hence "the end to which it points serves as final verification. The end validates the beginning."[48] With these words Rosenzweig was certainly offering the potential reader a key to unlocking the intended meaning of his own work.

From that vantage point, I would propose that the terms "linear circularity" or "circular linearity," expressions that I have used to convey the dual deportment of time in kabbalistic lore as an extending line that rotates like a sphere or as a rotating sphere that extends like a line, can be applied to Rosenzweig as well. I note, in passing, that in the entry written by Rosenzweig in his diary on June 22, 1922, he remarked that his attempt to harmonize kabbalah and the "healthy human understanding" related to two key points: first, the "reality of space, that means the inadmissibility of *coincidentia oppositorum*," and second, the "reality of time, that means the inadmissibility of the category of eternity to enter somehow into the occurrence."[49] It is surely not insignificant that with respect to the central categories of space and time, Rosenzweig noted a basic affinity between kabbalah and his new thinking. For the purposes of this essay, the latter is worthy of comment: the quest for truth is Rosenzweig's ultimate concern, and in the final analysis, he gives way to speaking of an eternal truth that comprehends the scope of truth as a whole, even if he continues to insist on an "epistemological incompleteness,"[50] since the whole of truth is not available to us as finite beings subject to generation and decay.[51] But, never losing sight of what he thought was his distinctive contribution, Rosenzweig resolutely maintained that eternity should not be affirmed at the expense of stripping time of its inherent temporal significance. He understood this to be an essential component of the kabbalistic orientation as well, "the inadmissibility of the category of eternity to enter somehow into the occurrence." As the ensuing analysis will suggest, Rosenzweig's indebtedness to kabbalah, or at the very least the affinity of his path to the Jewish esoteric tradition, can be seen in his embrace of an apophatic discourse at the end, and this in spite of his explicit rejection of negative theology at the beginning.

HERMENEUTICS AND TIME

I will commence my analysis with revisiting the question of hermeneutics and time in Rosenzweig's new thinking or, as he alternatively referred to it, his "experiential philosophy" (*erfahrende Philosophie*).[52] The nuances of his approach can be appreciated if one compares it to the still valuable discussion in Gershom Scholem's study, "Revelation and Tradition as Religious Categories in Judaism."[53] Tradition, Scholem argued, is the "special aspect of the process that formed rabbinic Judaism," the hermeneutical method that "embodies the realization of the effectiveness of the Word in every concrete state and relationship entered into by a society."[54] The midrashic mode, which eventually assumed the taxonomic classification "Oral Torah" in the rabbinic lexicon, expands the contents of the Written Torah—and thus, in some measure, reinscribes the text—by applying it to new historical circumstances. Revelation, consequently, is no longer portrayed as "a unique, positively established, and clearly delineated realm of propositions";[55] rather, it is polysemic and multivalent, demanding "commentary in order to be rightly understood and applied—this is the far from self-evident religious doctrine out of which grew both the phenomenon of biblical exegesis and the Jewish tradition which it created. . . . A creative process begins to operate which will permeate and alter tradition— the Midrash: the more regulated *halakhic* and the somewhat freer aggadic exegesis of Scriptures, and the views of the biblical scholars in their various schools, are regarded as implicitly contained in the Written Torah."[56] The midrashic perspective makes

> absolute the concept of tradition in which the meaning of revelation unfolds in the course of historical time—but only because everything that can come to be known has already been deposited in a timeless substratum. In other words, we have arrived at an assumption concerning the nature of truth which is characteristic of rabbinic Judaism (and probably of traditional religious establishment): Truth is given once and for all, and it is laid down with precision. Fundamentally, truth merely needs to be transmitted. . . . The effort of the seeker after truth consists not in having new ideas but rather in subordinating himself to the continuity of the tradition of the divine word and in laying open what he receives from it in the context of his own time. In other words: Not system but *commentary* is the legitimate form through which truth is approached.[57]

Scholem goes so far as to say that this insight is the "most important principle for the kind of productivity we encounter in Jewish literature. Truth must be laid bare in a text in which it already pre-exists."[58]

The locating of rabbinic genius in the domain of commentary as opposed to system accentuates the way in which the midrashic method embraces essentially—an essentiality, I hasten to add, that is essentially inessential, since its essence is always to have been determined by what is yet to be determined—the paradox of discovering anew what was previously given. I concur that recovering truth partakes of the epistemological paradox that what presents itself as new does so precisely because it is old, but I would modify Scholem's assessment by proffering a complementary hermeneutical conception based on a conception of temporality that would not necessitate a bifurcation between a "timeless substratum" of meaning and its unfolding in "historical time." Viewed from the observational post staked by Scholem, it makes perfect sense to raise a question about the possibility of immediacy in one's relationship to the divine, for the "absoluteness of the divine word" that is revealed must always be mediated—that is, translated—so that it might be received. Since every religious experience after revelation is thought to be mediated, what is experienced is the "voice of God rather than the experience of God."[59] The insight regarding the lack of immediacy in religious experience leads Scholem to conclude that tradition "creates productivity through receptivity."[60] The kabbalistic materials only bolster the idea that tradition "is founded upon the dialectic tension" of the "absoluteness" effecting the "unending reflections in the contingencies of fulfillment. Only in the mirroring in which it reflects itself does revelation become practicable and accessible to human action as something concrete." Again, the logical conclusion is drawn categorically: *"There is no immediate, undialectic application of the divine word."*[61]

In response, I would contend that it is not necessary to bifurcate tradition and revelation in the history of Judaism in the way that Scholem suggests, nor is it obvious that the mediated and conditional status of the former inevitably entails the inability to experience the immediacy and unconditionality of the latter. I see little justification, moreover, for distinguishing the experience of the "voice of God" and the "experience of God," since the latter entails, originarily, both epistemic modalities, seeing and hearing, sometimes understood by subsequent commentators (on the basis of Exod 20:15, "And they saw the voices") as an example of synesthesia.

The dialectical resolution tendered by Scholem may be circumvented if one posits a mode of textual reasoning based on a logic that affirms the identity of opposites in the opposition of their identity—the logic of the middle path, or the "logic of not," expressed in the Mahāyāna Buddhist tradition, "A is not A, therefore it is A"[62]—rather than proposing overcoming the divergence of identity and its opposition. If we follow that route, productivity and receptivity need not be understood as antinomical; the rabbinic sensibility is another cultural formation that fosters the collusion of opposites in the sameness of their difference—*ellu we-ellu divrei elohim ḥayyim*, "these and those are the words of a living God."[63] If "this" and "that" are opposing positions, and both the one and the other are true, we must assume that truth contains within itself the prospect of being untrue. Such a hermeneutic, moreover, is based on a varied conception of time that likewise upholds the convergence of the ancient and novel in the variance of their semblance. As I have argued elsewhere, the rabbinic understanding of an ongoing revelation that unfolds through an unbroken chain of interpretation is not based on a static conception of the eternity of Torah set in opposition to time and therefore resistant to the fluctuation of historical contingency. Rather, it is predicated on a conception

of temporality that calls into question the linear model of aligning events
chronoscopically in a sequence stretched invariably between before and
after. The rabbinic hermeneutic champions a notion of time that is circular in its linearity and linear in its circularity.[64] The study of Torah, accordingly, demands that one be able to imagine each day—indeed, each
moment of each day—as a potential recurrence of the Sinaitic theophany.
Each interpretative venture, therefore, is a reenactment of the revelatory
experience, albeit from its unique vantage point.[65] Rendering in a different register the words of Goethe with which Scholem concluded his essay,
"The truth that long ago was found, / Has all noble spirits bound, / The ancient truth, take hold of it" (*Das Wahre war schon längst gefunden, / Hat edle
Geisterschaft verbunden, / Das alte Wahre, fass es an*),[66] I would say that noble
spirits are indeed bound by an ancient truth that was long ago found, but
one can take hold of that truth only as the truth that is yet to be disclosed,
a truth renewed in the gesticulation of its genuine iteration.

On this score, it is well to recall another motto of Goethe, "understanding at the right time" (*Verstehen zur rechten Zeit*), which is invoked by
Rosenzweig in "Das neue Denken,"[67] to corroborate his claim that understanding occurs always in the present, "time in the most temporal sense"
(*Zeit im zeitlichsten Sinn*).[68] This insight runs parallel to Rosenzweig's account of revelation in the *Star*, based on the premise that "God's love is always wholly in the moment and at the point where it loves; and it is only
in the infinity of time, step by step, that it reaches one point after the next
and permeates the totality with soul."[69] The knot of divine love takes an
infinity of time to unravel, but at the core of that love is the utterance of
the divine commandment that "knows only the moment: it waits for the
outcome right within the moment of its growing audible. . . . The commandment is thus—pure present. . . . Revelation is in the present, and indeed it is the present par excellence . . . the presently lived experience."[70] In
this respect, revelation may be compared profitably to music, the art form
wherein "time is the dominant feature," as opposed to the plastic arts that
are aligned with the spatial,[71] for just as the movement of a musical composition "is the only possibility for making objective the temporal succession that otherwise sinks down helplessly into the temporal point of the
present,"[72] so the eruption of the revelatory event must "begin already at
the same moment, in the sinking away it must already begin again; its
perishing must be at the same time a beginning again. . . . So this moment must have more as its content than the mere moment. The moment
shows something always new to the eye every time it opens."[73] This moment, which has the potentiality to be perpetually renewed, and thus carries within itself the "diversity of the old and new," is identified by Rosenzweig as an "hour" or the "fixed moment" in which "its end can flow again

into its beginning because it has a middle, or rather many moments of the middle between its beginning and its end. With beginning, middle and end, it can become what the mere sequence of single ever new moments can never become: a circle that flows back in itself. . . . In the hour, the moment is therefore turned into that which, when it should have perished, always newly begins again and thus into the imperishable, the *nunc stans*, eternity."[74] Compressed in the "single moment" is "pure temporality" (*reinen Zeitlichkeit*)—significantly, this is demarcated as the "purely temporally lived life of Goethe"—whereby "life has become entirely temporal [*das Leben ganz zeitlich oder*], or, put differently, time has an entirely living, an entirely real river flowing through the vast space above the crags of the moment [*die Klippe des Augenblicks*]; no sooner can eternity fall upon time. Life, and all life, must be entirely living [*ganz lebendig*] before it can become eternal life [*ewiges Leben*]."[75] In the moment, the blink-of-the-eye (*Augenblick*), time is fully temporal, and hence eternal, a time beyond the calibration of ordinary time, but a time nonetheless, indeed the fullness of time.

Stéphane Mosès has characterized this "modality of time" in Rosenzweig as *ritual time*, which he further described as "a repetitive time, that is, a *motionless time*, a principle not of change but of permanence." The *"cycle of the liturgical year*," he goes on to say, unveils the "transtemporal dimension" of sacred time, which is eternity, "not a time indefinitely stretched out forward but rather a total immobilization of the present instant, a state of perfect equilibrium absolutely outside the flow of time."[76] I concur that we cannot comprehend Rosenzweig's taking of time seriously unless we factor in the possibility of experiencing what Mosès has called transtemporality, but I question the accuracy of describing the latter as immobile, repetitive, and permanent. These classifications impose on Rosenzweig a binary way of thinking that he sought to transcend. For him there is no permanence but in change, no stasis but in process, no repetition but in innovation, no time but in eternity. In describing the "eternal moment" (*ewige Augenblick*) that bears the "destiny of an infinite now" (*unendliches Nun*),[77] Rosenzweig deals head-on with the paradox of positing a present that is imperishable but passing, overflowing but withholding: "There is only one way out: the moment we are seeking must, since it has flown away, begin again already at the same moment, in the sinking away it must already begin again; its perishing must be at the same time a beginning again."[78] Let us recall Rosenzweig's comments inspired by Halevi's poem *yeqarah shakhnah gewyah*, which he translates as *Der Lohn:*

> Eternity can of course break into every moment, but what it then seizes is only just this moment. Life on the whole is contained in a few moments in such a way that it can grasp them in these moments. At the moment of birth as a life ahead; in one or two moments during life as a decisive one; and in

death as a perfected one. Thus, only in death as a real, "present" whole. This
worldly reality has life only here, and to want here to withdraw it from the
clasp of eternity would mean that life never would be allowed to be an experienced whole.[79]

To unpack the depth of this passage does not fall within the purview of my
immediate concern. But I would underline that this text attests to the inadequacy of separating time and eternity in Rosenzweig's thinking. Eternity erupts into the moment, and by this gesture temporal life becomes
real, a realization that comes to pass fully in clutching the perfect moment
of death in which life may be experienced as whole. Levinas, therefore,
is closer to the mark in describing Rosenzweig's "extasis" of temporality
as the "[u]nexpected meaning of eternity within the very dimensions of
time! We are very far from the atemporal signification of relations inside
a system."[80]

For Rosenzweig, as Levinas well understood, time, and particularly
the sacred time of ritual, is dialogical, or, in his own terms, diachronic,
since the present, time in its most temporal, is a way to, a facing of, the
other. Rosenzweig thus contrasts the "grammatical thinking" (*gramma-
tischem Denken*) of the "speech-thinker" (*Sprachdenker*) and the "logical
thinking" (*logischem Denken*) of the "thinking thinker" (*denkenden Denker*)
on the grounds that the former is in "need of time," which means "being
able to anticipate nothing, having to wait for everything, being dependent on the other for one's own. . . . the difference between old and new,
logical and grammatical thinking does not rest on loud versus quiet, but
rather on needing the other and, what amounts to the same, on taking
time seriously."[81] This sentiment was expressed in slightly different terminology in the following remarkable passage:

> Let us be ourselves and nothing more. Such a moment of existence may be
> nothing but delusion; we shall, however, choose to remain within the mo-
> ment, deceived by it and deceiving it, rather than live in deception above or
> below the moment. Let our personal experience, even though it change from
> instant to instant, be reality. Let man become the bearer of these shifting im-
> ages. . . . Whenever I encounter man, I shall steep my countenance in his
> until it reflects his every feature. . . . Thus, traveling about the earth, I shall
> come face to face with my own Self. The innumerable masks of the innumer-
> able instants, yours and mine, they are my countenance.[82]

Displaying his ability to collapse binaries in a manner that seems to me
more effective than much of the contemporary postmodern discourse,
Rosenzweig affirms that there is a self, but not without the other; there is
identity, but not without difference; there is endurance, but not without
change; there is a countenance, but not without masks; there is an un-
relenting reality, but not without shifting images. All there is to grip is the

moment of existence, a moment that may be nothing but delusion, but still authenticity demands that we choose to live in that moment, to deceive and to be deceived by it. In this momentary deception, the deception of the moment, which persists as what passes, lies the possibility of fidelity to one's self and hence to the other.[83]

The indissoluble link between temporality, alterity, and transcendence in Rosenzweig was correctly discerned by Levinas: "The relation and movement where thought becomes life is not primitively intentionality but Revelation, the crossing of an absolute interval. The ultimate bound [*sic*] of psychism is not the one insuring the unity of the subject, but, so to speak, the tying separation of society, the *dia* of the dialogue, of dia-chrony, of time that Rosenzweig aims to 'take seriously,' the tying separa-tion we call by a well-worn name—love."[84] A discussion of Levinas's re-flections on time obviously is beyond the scope of this essay, but let me cite one articulation that betrays his indebtedness to Rosenzweig. The passage is from the preface that Levinas wrote for the 1979 collection[85] of lectures entitled *Le temps et l'autre:*

> The main thesis caught sight of in *Time and the Other* . . . consists in thinking time not as a degradation of eternity, but as the relationship to *that* which—of itself unassimilable, absolutely other—would not allow itself to be assimilated by experience; or to that which—of itself infinite—would not allow itself to be com-prehended. . . . This impossibility of coinciding and this inadequa-tion are not simply negative notions, but have a meaning in the *phenomenon* of noncoincidence *given* in the dia-chrony of time. Time signifies this always of noncoincidence, but also the always of relationship, an aspiration and an awaiting, a thread finer than an ideal line that diachrony does not cut.[86]

In writing of the phenomenon of noncoincidence, the given that cannot be assimilated by experience or comprehended in accord with the noetic-noematic structure of intentionality, Levinas is undeniably responding to the Husserlian internal time-consciousness.[87] Additionally, however, re-verberations of Rosenzweig, albeit couched in different terminological reg-isters, can be heard in Levinas's opposing the positing of time in opposi-tion to eternity, as well as in his emphasizing the diachronic dimension of time as an opening to the other, the transcendent that resists representa-tion or reification.[88]

Consider one more passage from Levinas in which the attuned ear will detect the trace of this influence: "My profoundest thought, which bears all thought, my thought of the infinite older than the thought of the finite, is the very diachrony of time, non-coincidence, dispossession itself: a way of 'being avowed' prior to every act of consciousness and more pro-foundly than consciousness, through the gratuitousness of time. . . . Inspi-ration is thus the prophetic event of the relation to the new."[89] In the tem-

poral pleroma of the present envisioned by Rosenzweig, the line becomes
a circle, beginning and end meet in, and as a result eliminate, the middle
by inverting the projectile of time and turning one thing into its opposite.[90]
The eternalization of time brought to fruition in the moment of revelation
proleptically anticipates the temporalization of eternity to be realized in
the hour of redemption.[91] In the interim, however, the ecstatic temporality
is lived in and through the diachronic performance of ceremonial acts, and
especially the sacrament of prayer, by which the arrival of the end is accel-
erated and tomorrow is transmuted into today.[92]

Rosenzweig's thinking about time and eternity was informed, at least
in part, by the rabbinic insistence that one can hear again the timbre of
the archaic saying in the "great historical testimony of Revelation, the necessity of which we recognized precisely from the presentness [*Gegenwär-
tigkeit*] of our living experience [*unseres Erlebnisses*]."[93] The presentness of
which Rosenzweig speaks is a *tempus discretum*, or, in Levinasian terms, a
diachrony exemplifying dispossession, noncoincidence, deformalization,
and disfiguration. As Rosenzweig already put it in the "Urzelle":

> So the organizing concept (*Ordnungsbegriff*) of this world is not the univer-
> sal, neither the Arche nor the Telos, neither the natural nor the historical
> unity, but rather the particular, the event, *not beginning or end, but rather middle*
> of the world. The world is "infinite," both from beginning and from end, from
> the beginning infinite in space, toward the end infinite in time. Only from
> the middle arises a limited home in the unlimited world. . . . Viewed from this
> perspective, beginning and end are also transformed for the first time, from
> limit-concepts of infinity to cornerposts of our worldly estate [*Grenzbegriffen
> der Unendlichkeit zu Eckpfeilern unsres Weltbesitzes*], the "beginning" as creation
> [*Schöpfung*], the "end" as salvation [*Erlösung*]. Thus revelation is capable of be-
> ing a *middle* point, a fixed, middle point that cannot be displaced. . . . Reve-
> lation pushes itself into the world as a wedge; the This struggling against the
> This.[94]

Rejecting the old philosophical ideal, Rosenzweig replaces the universal
(*Allgemeine*) with the particular (*Einzelne*), the classifiable general with the
irreducibly singular, the essence (*Wesen*) with the event (*Ereignis*).[95] Reiter-
ating the theme in *Das Büchlein vom gesunden und kranken Menscenverstand*,
Rosenzweig wrote: "The true concern of the philosopher is with the 'essence,' the 'essential' being of his subjects. . . . The singleness and particularity [*Eigenheit*] of the subject detached from time is transformed into a
statement of its particular essence [*Eigentlichkeit des Wesens*]. . . . The terms
of life are not 'essential' but 'real'; they concern not 'essence' but 'fact.' In
spite of this, the philosopher's word remains, 'essential.'"[96]

The actuality (*Wirklichkeit*) of each of the elemental forms is experienced in their relations to one another—only as creation, revelation, and

redemption; to try to grasp any of them in its own essence would result in lack of discernment, God concealing himself, the human self closing up, and the world becoming a visible riddle.[97] The temporal location of the event is always in the middle; indeed, it is only from the delimited possibility of the midpoint (*Mittelpunkt*) of revelation that the limit-concepts of infinity at the beginning and at the end—the former correlated with space and the latter with time—are converted respectively into creation (*Schöpfung*) and redemption (*Erlösung*), the theological concepts that provide the corner posts that uphold the edifice of a world of finitude.

The time of the present, therefore, is a desire for the new that is a desire for the other,[98] a time whose continuity is marked by discontinuity with past and/or future, a time about which one can only be certain of its uncertainty,[99] since it ruptures and cuts the timeline, the moment that, in each moment, returns as something that has never been exactly, on account of its always having been. "The language of love is only present; dream and reality, sleep of the limbs and wakefulness of the heart are inextricably woven one into the other, everything is equally present, equally fleeting and equally alive . . . A shower of imperatives descends and endows with life this eternally green meadow of the present, imperatives from different horizons, but always alluding to the same thing . . . it is always the same one imperative of love."[100] Revelation, therefore, imbibes the paradox of being "always new only because it is immemorially old."[101]

It is germane to recall here Rosenzweig's comments on the poem *ye'iruni be-shimkha ra'ayonai*, "My thoughts have awakened me in your name,"[102] which he translated as *Nachts*, since the "longed for event" (*Ersehnte*) occurred as a "night-vision" that "brought the poet the experience of the sight of God" (*Erlebnis der Gottesschau*). The visionary phenomenon, accordingly, happens in "the state between dream and waking, a state which derives its autonomy from dream and its validity from waking." The experience, moreover, collapses the gap between past and present, as the poet sees God in his heart in such a way that it is as if he were standing again at Sinai. "The experience of today confirms and repeats the historical revelation."[103] To locate the vision of God between dream and wakefulness is analogous to the aforementioned statement in the *Star* according to which dream and reality are interwoven. These are two poetic ways to communicate the convergence of the ideal and the real, an idea that Rosenzweig likely borrowed from Schelling[104] but that also resonates with kabbalistic symbolism. It is precisely in this convergence that one can appreciate the reversibility of time, the construction of the future as the possibility of the past recurring in the present. For Rosenzweig, this paradox can be formulated as well in terms of language. Addressing the thorny question of the relationship of word and thing, he remarked that a thing "possesses equally the right to keep the name it has, and to receive new names. . . . And furthermore each new name must come to terms with the old ones. . . . It is man's privilege to give new names. It is his duty to use the old ones, a duty which he must perform, though unwillingly." The very continuity of humankind—instantiated in the singular person and not in the abstract ideal or essence—depends on the practice of appropriating and translating old names into new terminological designations. "Mankind is always absent. Present is a man, this fellow or that one. The thing, however, is tied to all of mankind by language and by its inherent law of transmission and translation. These linguistic laws require that each new word confront the old. And where does the presence of mankind manifest itself? Not in the word of man, of course, but in that of God."[105]

From this hermeneutic standpoint, the sense of the present, enduring in its evanescence—the return of the same that is always different, different because the same, the same difference—is realized in the act of interpreting the divine commands entrusted in the scriptural text, an exploit of mind that must be positioned at the interface of the verbal and graphic, as the interpreter restores the written trace to the spoken word. Hence, for Rosenzweig, as Fishbane expressed it, "the hermeneutics of reading must therefore serve to recall man to the word of God that summons him into existence. One may therefore say that the horizon of textuality is just this divine-human speech resounding within the text."[106] The interpretive act affords one an opportunity to experience time, and, more specifically, the moment, which encapsulates time in its most elemental cadence, the coming again as novel repetition. The divine word reiterated with each reading of Scripture, therefore, is the word yet to be spoken. The phenomenological cornerstone of Rosenzweig's new thinking rests on the belief in the possibility of experiencing revelation as a genuine contingency at every moment. And just as, temporally, the present is the aperture through which one accesses past and future, so, hermeneutically, revelation is the eventuality that makes creation and redemption possible.[107]

Linguistic Revelation and Metaphoric Poiesis

From the perspective of the history of religions, Rosenzweig grasped the dialogical potential of revelation as a linguistic occurrence—he even coined the phrase "linguistic revelation" (*sprachliche Offenbarung*)[108] as a way of marking that language is not only the primary means of the revelatory experience but its major content. To take in the full import of this claim, one must recall that Rosenzweig, following a much older opinion, views revelation as the historical instantiation of the institution of prophecy, but the latter can be understood only when viewed in conjunction with the notion of miracle, which is essentially a "sign" (*Zeichen*).[109] Rosenzweig concludes, accordingly, that revelation "is entirely a sign, entirely a making visible and a becoming audible of the Providence originally hidden in the mute night of Creation."[110] The innately semiotic nature of revelation is expressed in the translating of the divine intent in both visual and auditory terms. The larger hermeneutical principle at work here is made explicit in the remark of Rosenzweig in his *Die Schrift und Luther* that all speech, which is delimited as dialogic as opposed to monologic speaking, is an act of translation.[111] We may assume, moreover, that for Rosenzweig, in a manner strongly reminiscent of similar claims enunciated by Heidegger[112] and elaborated by Gadamer,[113] every act of translation is an interpretation. The emphasis on the linguistic character of revelation epitomizes the point, for the saying of what was spoken is already translated; that is, the divine word is interpreted speech. Revelation, therefore, is an inherently metaphorical process that yields, in the double sense of engendering and surrendering, an insight into the interweaving pattern of experience and interpretation.[114] It is from this spot that we can discern the mythopoetic tenor of revelation wherein the rift between the ideal and the actual, thought and being, reality and appearance, is bridged, a bridging that undergirds Rosenzweig's celebrated use of the Song of Songs to articulate the analogical deportment of the dialogical encounter between God and human. In the section dedicated to the elucidation of this biblical book, he wrote:

> The allegory of love, as allegory, goes through the whole Revelation [*Das Gleichnis der Liebe geht als Gleichnis durch die ganze Offenbarung hindurch*]. . . . But it is supposed to be more than an allegory. . . . So it is not enough that the relationship of God to man is presented in the allegory of the lover and the beloved; God's word must immediately hold the relationship of the lover to the beloved, without the signifier making any allusion at all to the signified [*das Bedeutende also ohne alle Hindeutung auf das Bedeutete*]. And so we find it in the Song of Songs. It is no longer possible to see in that allegory "only an allegory."[115]

In characterizing the Song of Songs as an "allegory of love," and by considering it an exemplum for revelation as a whole, Rosenzweig is drawing on the traditional interpretation of this text as a transfigurative representation of God's love for Israel in heteroerotic terms.[116] Additionally, he seems to be echoing older rabbinic dicta that extol this book as the holy of holies or as being equivalent to all of Torah.[117] The Song is the "core book of Revelation" (*Kernbuch der Offenbarung*);[118] that is, it is the book that illustrates the metaphorical nature of metaphor most pristinely, since its literal sense is figurative. The distinction between dream and reality, what appears and what is, collapses when the divine word is thought to allude to the relationship of God and human in the erotically charged images of male lover and female beloved.[119] This, I submit, is what Rosenzweig means when he says that the allegory of love is more than an allegory: the assortment of erotic tropes discloses the face of truth in the masking of image. In Rosenzweig's own astonishingly complex and densely poetic language: "The sensuous character of the word [*Sinnlichkeit des Worts*] is full to the brim with its divine supra-sensuous meaning [*göttlichen Übersinn*], like language itself love is at once sensible and supra-sensuous [*die Liebe ist, wie die Sprache selbst, sinnlich-übersinnlich*]. To express it another way: the allegory is not a decorative accessory for love, but essence."[120]

In picturing the divine-human correlation heteroerotically, the diction of the Song concurrently embraces the sensuous and supra-sensuous, a double embrace that is the character of love itself—the language of eros enfolded in and unfolding from the eros of language—and thus Rosenzweig insists that love is "absolutely and essentially allegory [*ganz und gar und wesentlich Gleichnis*]. It is ephemeral only in appearance, but in truth it is eternal [*den sie ist nur scheinbar vergänglich, in Wahrheit aber ewig*]."[121] The allegorical nature of love yields the incongruity of appearing to be transient when it is actually interminable. But this opposition is only apparent, for in truth the distinction between semblance and reality disappears in the simulacrum of allegorical figuration: "That appearance is as necessary as this truth; as love, love could not be eternal if it did not seem to be transitory; but in the mirror of this appearance, truth reflects itself directly [*aber im Spiegel dieses Scheins spiegelt sich unmittelbar die Wahrheit*]."[122] The overlapping of the external and internal meaning conveys to the reader a rudimentary insight regarding the poiesis of Torah more generally: to speak of an unspeakable God—the signifier that makes no allusion to a signified—is to render the imageless in poetic images that juxtapose the ostensibly divergent through the prism of symbolic likeness. The word of revelation perforce must be figurative, but in the speculum of the text, the metaphorical figuration is real, the allegory that cannot be only an allegory.[123]

This is not the appropriate place to elaborate on Rosenzweig's sense of the mythic or poetic—the two terms may be used interchangeably—but it is important to note his indebtedness to Schelling in privileging poetry as the fount of philosophy[124] as well as his insistence that the Jews alone possess the unity of myth that facilitates the coalescence of the universal and particular, a hallmark of the messianic ideal.[125] As Rosenzweig writes, "The concepts of Revelation spring up for the aesthetic theory under the influence of the 'mythical' upon the 'tragic,' hence of the whole upon the spiritual content that is to be poet-ized."[126] Poetry is said to be "at home neither in time nor in space, but where time and space have their inner origin [*inneren Ursprung*], in imagistic thinking [*vorstellenden Denken*]. Poetry is not a kind of art of thought [*Gedankenkunst*], but thinking is its element as space is that of the plastic arts and time is that of music."[127] One may conclude, therefore, that the poetic is essentially at odds with the world, inherently in a state of "uncanniness" or estrangement (*Unheimlichkeit*),[128] a diasporic condition that is natural for the Jews, the "eternal people" (*ewigen Volk*), whose promise of the holy land "never lets it feel entirely at home [*mehr ganz heimisch*] in any other land."[129] The metahistorical reference point in history accorded the Jewish nation renders it as fundamentally alien to the vagaries of the sociopolitical world.[130] Here it is apposite to recall Rosenzweig's remark in the afterword to his translation of ninety-two poems by Halevi:

> All Jewish poetry in exile scorns to ignore this being-in-exile [*Im-Exil-Sein*]. It would have ignored its exile if it ever, like other poetry, took in the world directly. For the world which surrounds it is exile, and is supposed to remain to it. And the moment that it would surrender this attitude, when it would open itself to the inflow of this world, this world would be as a home for it, and it would cease to be exile. This exile of the surrounding world is achieved through the constant presence of the scriptural word [*die ständige Gegenwärtigkeit des Schriftworts*]. With the scriptural word another present thrusts itself in front of the surrounding present and downgrades the latter to an appearance, or more precisely, as parable. Thus it is not that the scriptural word is drawn out as parables for illustrations of present life, but exactly reversed, that events serve as illucidation of the scriptural word and become the parable for this scriptural word.[131]

In the above citation, Rosenzweig contrasts Jewish poetry and other forms of poetry on the grounds that the former is inherently exilic and therefore in a perpetual state of homelessness, whereas the latter takes on the world directly and therefore exhibits a sense of being at home. Bracketing this difference, the implications of the poetic disorientation are drawn clearly by Rosenzweig: the Jewish poet is confronted by the constant presence of the scriptural word, a past that has the potential always to plunge itself into the present and thereby to downgrade the latter into an "appearance" (*Schein*) or a "parable" (*Gleichnis*). What we consider to be reality morphs into a parabolic prism through which the word of Scripture is elucidated. The respective valence accorded reality and appearance in Western philosophical thought is inverted in Rosenzweig's thinking as what appears to be real is rendered really apparent in the speculum of the text. In this mirroring, moreover, the timeline is reversed, and the past is illumined from the present: "When a Jewish poet describes Christianity and Islam through Edom and Ishmael, he is not commenting on the present from

Scripture, but rather on Scripture from the present."[132] The hermeneutical reversibility is a direct consequence of being outside of or at variance with time and space that is integral to the poetic sensibility.

The pairing of poetry (*Dichtung*) and thinking (*Denken*) in Rosenzweig's notion of imagistic thinking—a thinking-in-images—anticipates Heidegger's characterization of the thinking about being as an "original way of poeticizing," the "primordial poetry," which is "prior to the poetics of art."[133] We note the obvious difference between Rosenzweig and Heidegger: one looked to the Bible as the wellspring of mythopoiesis and the other to the parabolic dicta of the ancient Greeks.[134] In spite of this divergence, the affinity is striking.[135] The resemblance is enhanced by the fact that Rosenzweig's insistence on the inseparability of the spatial and temporal coordinates in the poetic—the epic aligned with the former and the lyric with the latter—parallels Heidegger's thinking of timespace (*Zeitraum*) as the lighting/clearing (*Lichtung*) that yields the language to house, and thereby to shelter and to expose, being.[136] It lies beyond the scope of this essay to engage this matter adequately, but suffice it to say that a key facet of the turn on Heidegger's path relates to the affirmation of poetry as the primary linguistic way of appropriating the opening of the ontological horizon, the abyss (*Abgrund*), the originary ground, which is, paradoxically, the absence of ground.[137] Another congruence that is worthy of emphasis is Rosenzweig's expressing the confluence of the spatial and temporal as the convergence of the visual and verbal, a slant that resonates with Heidegger's conception of the essence of language as a saying (*Sage*) that is a showing (*Zeige*).[138] To cite the pertinent formulation of Rosenzweig: "For poetry gives figure [*Gestalt*] and discourse [*Rede*] because it gives more than either: imagistic thinking [*vorstellende Denken*], in which both are alive together."[139]

The commingling of visible form and audible word highlights another essential similarity between revelation and poetry: the allusive idiom of the former, as the elusive intonation of the latter, is concomitantly seen and heard. The intrinsic symmetry between the two, which must be thought from this point of intersection, portends that the two modalities embrace a shared sense of temporality—just as the proper attunement to the revelatory is occasioned by an openness to the moment, so the understanding of the poetic is "strongly conditioned by a certain richness of lived experience [*das Veständnis von Dichtung stark bedingt ist durch einen gewissen Reichtum an Erlebnis*]."[140] The rapture of poetic composition, as the rupture of revelation, issues from and helps give shape to the now of God's address, where the triadic nature of time is eternalized and the unified nature of eternity temporalized.[141] We may assume that the creative spirit is incarnated fully in the poet, since poetry, according to Rosenzweig, is the "living art [*lebendige Kunst*] in the proper sense,"[142] and thus, like the revelation of the divine word, it takes place always in the moment where the verbal image resounds as the visual word, and the visual word is revisioned as the verbal image.

APOPHASIS AND THE ESCHATOLOGICAL OVERCOMING OF WORD BY IMAGE

In the last part of the *Star*, Rosenzweig articulates the eschatological overcoming of word by image, the triumphant manifestation of the light that is beyond language, a visual perception or intuition at the end, the consummation of which is marked by the completion of factuality (*Tatsächlichkeit*) to the point that "nothing more is heard of thing [*Sache*] or of act [*Tat*]."[143] Rosenzweig's elocution is evidently playful, as the perfection of *Tatsächlichkeit* results in the overcoming of both thing (*Sache*) and act (*Tat*), quite literally, a decomposition of the word's hybridity. Perhaps there is here as well an allusion to the scriptural slogan linked to the response of the ancient Israelites to the divine revelation, or more precisely, to hearing the reading of the "book of the covenant" (*sefer ha-berit*) on the part of Moses, "Let us do and let us hear," *na'aseh we-nishma* (Exod 24:7). In Rosenzweig's own provocative and poetic verbalization:

> That which can be looked at is relieved of language, put into relief above it. Light does not talk; but shines. It is not at all turned in on itself; it radiates not inward but outward. Yet its radiating is also not a surrendering of itself, as language is; light does not give itself away, dispose of itself as does language when expressing itself, but it is visible while abiding entirely by itself, it does not exactly radiate outward, it only goes on radiating; it does not radiate like a fountain, but like a face, like an eye radiates, an eye that becomes eloquent without needing to open its lips. There is a silence here that is unlike the speechlessness of the primordial world that has no words yet, but a silence that no longer needs words. It is the silence of perfect understanding. Here, a glance means everything. Nothing teaches more clearly that the world is not yet redeemed than the multiplicity of languages.[144]

Retaining something of the aniconic rendering of revelatory experience proffered by the Deuteronomist and elaborated by a host of later Jewish exegetes, Rosenzweig depicts revelation as the emergence of language from the speechlessness of the primordial world. What is most important about the Sinaitic theophany, accordingly, is not the appearance of the glory, but the communication of the divine word, although, strictly speaking, the latter is itself a form of idolatrous representation.[145] The moment of redemption, however, is marked by a transition from the verbal to the visual, for the light no longer talks but shines. Silence, in other words, is the appropriate way to describe the luminosity of the face, since it is apprehended by the aperture of the eye that gazes rather than by the opening of the lip that speaks. Although the muteness of the protocosmos and the stillness of the hypercosmos are carefully distinguished, there is a sense in which redemption is a return to creation, for the former, like the latter, entails the overcoming of word by light, the triumph of speech by vision.[146] As Rosenzweig puts it:

> We have already seen eternal truth sinking back into the Revelation of divine love: in all things Redemption was nothing but the eternal result of the beginning that is always set anew in the revealing love. In the love, that which was hidden had become manifest. Now this ever renewed beginning sinks back into the secret everlasting beginning of Creation. That which is manifest becomes that which is hidden. And along with Revelation, Redemption therefore also flows back into Creation.[147]

The light of the eternal truth is a reclamation of the divine fiat at creation, encapsulated in the words "Let there be light." From that perspective, one could view creation as pointing to redemption, even as redemption is anticipated in revelation. To express the convergence of the three tenses of time in the eternity that is the truth of the divine, Rosenzweig must turn to the poetic: "The midnight that glitters in eternal starry clarity before our dazzled eyes is the same one that became night in God's bosom before all existence. He is truly the First and the Last One. Before the mountains were born and the earth writhed in labor-pains—from eternity to eternity you were God. And were from all eternity what you be in eternity: truth."[148] The end, as the beginning, is associated with midnight, an image that conveys the paradox of luminal darkness, the moment when the dark is at its brightest.

A common denominator of the three central theological categories in Rosenzweig's thought, and their corresponding temporal modes, is the interplay of concealment and disclosure. Creation is demarcated as the beginning (*Anfang*) in which God speaks and the "shell of the mystery [*die Schale des Geheimnisses*] breaks." In language that reflects the influence of Schelling but is also strikingly close to Lurianic kabbalah, Rosenzweig speaks of creation as "God's birth from out of the foundation [*die Geburt Gottes aus dem Grunde*], his creation before the Creation [*seine Schöpfung vor der Schöpfung*]. . . . The figure [*Gestalt*] of God, until now hidden in the metaphysical beyond of myth, steps into the visible and begins to light up [*aufzuleuchten*]."[149] Creation can be regarded, therefore, as a prediction of revelation, or, alternatively, revelation is the fulfillment of creation, since it is the present in which God is manifest in the "immediacy and pure presentness of the lived experience [*die Unmittelbarkeit und reine Gegenwär-*

tigkeit des Erlebens]. For the being that he now makes known is no longer a being beyond lived experience, this is no longer a being in secret, rather a being which has fully blossomed in this lived experience."[150] Creation and revelation are two stages in the exposure of the concealed, but redemption is characterized as the return to the origin (*Ursprung*) before the beginning (*Anfang*) of creation in which what has come to light again is concealed. The arc of time is balanced on opposite ends by two symmetrically inverse processes: the hidden becoming manifest on one side, and the manifest becoming hidden on the other.

Whether intentional or not, it is with respect to this construct that Rosenzweig's theopoesis divulges its deepest affinity with kabbalistic sensibility. Further support for this contention lies in the fact that the light at the end, the luminosity wherein the manifest is again hidden, is portrayed as the configuration (*Gestalt*) of the divine face, a notion that corresponds to the image of the *parṣuf* that figures prominently in the theosophic symbolism of the kabbalists, especially in certain sections of zoharic literature and in the treatises that expound the kabbalah attributed to the sixteenth-century master Isaac Luria. The proximity of Rosenzweig's characterization of truth in the image of the divine face and the kabbalistic tradition has been noted by a number of scholars.[151] Nevertheless, it is useful to cite Rosenzweig's words verbatim, the very words that serve as the inscription on the "gate" (*Tor*) to which one returns at the terminus of the journey, the passageway to the "No-longer-book" (*Nichtmehrbuch*), the "everyday of life" that is beyond the text:[152]

> That which is eternal had become the configuration in the truth. And truth is nothing other than the countenance of this configuration [*das Antlitz dieser Gestalt*]. Truth alone is its countenance. . . . In the Star of Redemption in which we saw the divine truth become configuration [*die göttliche Wahrheit Gestalt werden*], nothing else lights up than the countenance that God turned shining toward us. We shall now recognize in the divine face [*göttlichen Angesicht*] the Star of Redemption itself as it now finally became clear for us as configuration.[153]

For Rosenzweig, the world of revelation is marked by the privileging of the auditory over the visual, exemplified by Deuteronomy 4:12, which he paraphrases as "No figure have you seen, speech only have you heard," but the "word grows silent in the afterworld and supra-world," such that in the redeemed world language is overcome by light, a theme that is linked exegetically to the entreaty in the priestly blessing in Numbers 6:25, which is rendered as "May he let his countenance shine upon you."[154] In the lighting-up of the divine face is true knowledge of truth, that is, knowing the apparent truth as it truly appears in the constellation of truth that is God. In consonance with the prophetic, apocalyptic, and mystical visionary traditions that stretch from antiquity through the Middle Ages, and in some respects consistent with the ocularcentric bias of Western philosophical culture, Rosenzweig depicts this highest knowledge as a form of seeing wherein one apprehends the "final clarity of transexperienced truth [*übererfahrenen Wahrheit*],"[155] that is, a truth experienced beyond the contours of experience.

But what does one see in this seeing? From one perspective, the response is obvious, the luminosity of the face; but from another perspective, the matter is more complex, for this very illumination is also troped visually as the manifest becoming hidden, and verbally as the word growing into silence. How is the manifest becoming hidden to be envisioned? Is this not a seeing of the unseen, a vision that could be accorded only to one whose vision is blind-sighted? Is this not an affirmation that is negation? Is Rosenzweig not guilty of embracing at the end the apophasis he seemed to reject in the opening paragraph of the first book of part one of the *Star*? "About God we know nothing," he begins, quickly adding, "But this not-knowing is a not-knowing about God [*Aber dieses Nichtwissen ist Nichtwissen von Gott*]. As such it is the beginning of our knowledge about him. The beginning, not the end." From Rosenzweig's vantage point, it is appropriate to place this not-knowing at the beginning of knowledge, but to do so at the end, to make ignorance the end of human striving, is the "fundamental idea" (*Grundgedanke*) of negative theology, a "way that leads from a found something [*vorgefundenen Etwas*] to the nothing [*Nichts*] and at the end of which atheism and mysticism can shake hands."[156] The concluding remark is particularly noteworthy, for in Rosenzweig's mind, the apophasis to which the philosophical path (exemplified by Maimonides in the Jewish tradition) leads, the proposition that God can be defined only in his indefinable nature, is notionally on a par with both the mystical sense of the ineffable and the atheistic lack of belief, the conviction of faith and the skepticism of doubt.[157]

It is instructive to recall a second passage in the *Star*, in which Rosenzweig proclaims that the basic confession of Islam, "God is God," is not a "confession of faith, but rather a confession of unbelief; in its tautology, it confesses not the revealed God, but the hidden God; Nicholas of Cusa rightly declares that both the pagan and the atheist confess this." An "authentic confession of faith" would require the "unification of two things," and hence "it always testifies that the personal experience of love must be more than a personal experience."[158] Leaving aside the patently prejudicial interpretation of Islam,[159] what is important for our purposes is to note the juxtaposition of the pagan and the atheist, which parallels the alternative pairing of the atheist and the mystic. In this connection, it is of interest to recall a strikingly similar comment made by Derrida: "Like a certain mysticism, apophatic discourse has always been suspected of atheism."[160] Derrida supports his contention by mentioning Heidegger's citation of a remark of Leibniz concerning Angelus Silesius (Johannes Scheffler), the seventeenth-century German mystic-poet: "With every mystic there are some places that are extraordinarily bold, full of difficult metaphors and inclining to Godlessness, just as I have seen in the German poems of a certain Angelus Silesius, poems beautiful besides."[161]

Beyond mystical agnosticism, or learned ignorance, the unsaying of apophatic discourse bespeaks a lack of belief fitting the atheist. In a move that is typical of Derrida's penchant for paradox, he inverts the analogy: "If on the one hand apophasis inclines almost toward atheism, can't one say that, on the other hand or thereby, the extreme and most consequent forms of declared atheism will have always testified to the most intense desire of God?"[162] Derrida captures well the paradoxical implications of apophatic discourse and the implicit reversal of absence and presence: God is most present in the place from which God is most absent. When looked at from that vantage point, the denial of belief is the strongest avowal thereof. One might wonder if Rosenzweig did not himself have such a reversal in mind when he stated in the last paragraph of the introduction to part three of the *Star* that divine truth (*göttliche Wahrheit*) "hides from the one who reaches for it with one hand only. . . . It wants to be implored with both hands. To the one who calls to it with the double prayer of the believer and of the unbeliever, it will not be denied. God gives of his wisdom to the one as to the other, to belief as to unbelief, but to both only when their prayer comes jointly before him."[163]

To return to the matter of nothing. Philosophy is a dead end, for it terminates in negative theology, claiming that all we can know about God is that we do not know. Rosenzweig assures the reader that the way he is taking, by contrast, will lead "from the nothing to the something [*vom Nichts zum Etwas*]." The aim of his thinking "is not a negative concept, but a most positive one. We are seeking God, as we shall later see the world and man, precisely not within a one and universal All, as one concept among others; if we wanted this, then of course the negative theology of Nicholas of Cusa or of the man from Königsberg would be the only scientific goal; for then the negative would already be fixed as the goal at thinking's point of departure; one concept among others is always negative, at least in its opposition to the others; and if it claims to be unconditional, then science can only deal with an unconditional—nothingness."[164] Rosenzweig insightfully links the scientific goal with negative theology, whether the standard expression thereof in Nicholas of Cusa or in the less expected version of Immanuel Kant, referred to allusively as the "man from Königsberg." This identification rests on the assumption that negation is fixed as the goal in one's departure on the path. The unconditional, scientifically, could be nothing but nothingness, which, rendered theologically, amounts to the idealistic subsumption of God, world, and human within "the one and universal All" (*des einen und allgemeinen Alls*). From Rosenzweig's stand-point, however, this presupposition must be renounced, because the three elements are correlative but ontically distinct. The God sought by the new thinking is "dependent on itself alone in its absolute factuality [*absoluten Tatsächlichkeit*]—if the expression is not misleading—precisely, that is, in its 'positivity' [*Positivität*]. That is why we must put the nothing of the sought-after concept at the beginning: we must get it behind us; for ahead of us lies a something as a goal: the reality of God [*die Wirklichkeit Gottes*]."[165]

Ostensibly, there does not seem to be any ambivalence or ambiguity on Rosenzweig's part. Apophasis must be cast away in favor of a kata-phatic quest for the reality of God, which is described as well as factuality and positivity. Rosenzweig's point is consistent with the view expressed by Cohen in his essay "Charakteristik der Ethik Maimunis" (1908): "We can-not deny, however, that from the perspective of a person's absolute faith in God, the zeal for the doctrine of negative attributes spells something rather suspicious and oppressive. We are bidden to put our trust in the content of revelation, relying but upon its rational moorings, and yet we deprive ra-tional cognition of its positive conceptuality: what foundation remains at our disposal for knowing God if we are left to operate merely with nega-tive attributes? Would it not appear that a latent trait of aversion and of dis-trust against the very foundation of the God-concept, against its cognitive validity, prevailed throughout this entire Maimonidean argument?"[166] Rosenzweig does not explicitly evoke the name of Maimonides, but it is plausible to assume that he would have agreed with Cohen regarding the probable influence of the *via negativa* of the great medieval Jewish sage on the formation of the *docta ignorantia* by Cusanus,[167] though the diver-gence between the two is also noted.[168] Be that as it may, the crucial point that Rosenzweig shares with Cohen is the sense that if negative theology is the logical conclusion of philosophical theology, then rationalism is it-self an affront to the cognitive validity of the God-concept and a challenge to a Judaism that is grounded in an absolute faith in the factuality of God based on a revelatory encounter, the conviction regarding the divine be-ing whence all theological conceptions are to be adduced.

But Rosenzweig is more subtle than first impressions might suggest, and as the continuation of his own text makes clear, he was indebted to Cohen's interpretation of the Maimonidean negative theology in light of the Platonic conception of the Good as the non-foundation or, con-strued more literally, the non-hypothesis (*to anhypotheton*).[169] This concep-tion resonates with Cohen's understanding of the Jewish idea of origin, which accords priority to what is unknown over what is known, as well as with his own notion of a "new thinking" predicated on seeing the aught (*Ichts*) as originating in the naught (*Nichts*), which is further delineated as the "naught of knowledge," that is, a negation that yields an affirmation in virtue of negating itself as negation and hence merely appears to be a negation.[170] As Rosenzweig expressed the point: "In the first place then, God is a nothing for us, his nothing [*sein Nichts*]. From the nothing to the 'something,' or, more strictly: from the nothing to what is not nothing— for we are not seeking a 'something'—there are two ways, the way of affirmation and the way of negation. The affirmation, that is to say of what is sought after, of the not-nothing; the negation, that is to say of what is presupposed, the nothing."[171] Two ways are distinguished, the way of affirmation (*der Weg der Bejahung*), and the way of negation (*der Weg der Verneinung*); the former leads to the not-nothing (*Nichnichts*), and the latter to the nothing (*Nichts*).

What kind of affirmation is contained in this neologism, the not-nothing? The German *Nichnichts* is even more evocative than its English rendering, since it is a compound word without any hyphenation. Rosenzweig is adamant that the two ways "are as different from each other and even as opposite to each other as—well, as precisely Yes and No."[172] This comment notwithstanding, Rosenzweig's insistence that the path progressing from nothing to something must be understood as one that traverses from nothing to not-nothing raises questions about the validity of setting the two ways in diametric opposition. If the Yes applies to not-nothing and the No to nothing, then the way of affirmation is itself a form of negation, albeit a negation of negation, a delimitation of something that exceeds language and can thus be best demarcated in the double negative, a modality of thinking that belongs to the apophatic discourse of negative theology.[173] Rosenzweig articulates the point in the continuation of the passage:

> To affirm the not-nothing [*Bejahung des Nichnichts*] is to posit an infinite [*ein Unendliches*]—like affirmation that takes place through negation [*wie jede Bejahung, die durch Verneinung geschieht*]: to negate the nothing [*Verneinung des Nichts*] is to posit—like all negation—something limited, finite, determinate. So we see the something in a twofold figure and in a twofold relationship to the nothing: on the one hand, it is its inhabitant, and on the other hand, it escapes from it. As inhabitant of the nothing, the something is the entire plentitude of all that is—not nothing . . . but as an escaped prisoner who has just broken out of the prison of the nothing, the something is nothing other than the event of this liberation from the nothing. . . . Endlessly, then, the essence springs up from the nothing; in a sharp delimitation the action separates from it. For the essence one asks about the origin, and for action about the beginning.[174]

Affirmation takes place through negation. The "something" that is affirmed is viewed through a twofold prism in relation to the "nothing," either as inhabitant or as escapee. With respect to the former, the some-thing is the "not nothing" (*nicht Nichts*), that is, the infinite or the "entire plentitude of all that is" (*die ganze Fülle alles dessen*); and with respect to the latter, the something is naught but the deliverance from this nothing, which yields the finite being. The something that inhabits the fullness that is within God is identified further as the "origin" (*Ursprung*) whence issues forth the "essence" (*Wesen*), whereas the something that escapes therefrom is the action (*Tat*) to which is assigned a "beginning" (*Anfang*).

Rosenzweig's indebtedness to Cohen's principle of origin (*Ursprung-sprinzip*) in his attempt to deduce a positive God-concept from an aborigi-nal void has been duly noted.[175] Rosenzweig was assuredly persuaded by Cohen's discussion of the concept of the originative principle, the nature of the divine being, and the problem of the nothing. For Cohen, noth-ing, which he relates philologically to the Hebrew *ayin*, "in no way means merely nothing; it means, rather, unquestionably relative infinity of priva-tion. The latter, however, is not found within becoming, with matter, with the nonexistent primeval substance, but rather within the unique being of God. . . . The finite is to attain its originative principle in the infinite, in the negation of privation."[176] Without denying this influence, I would sug-gest, in addition, that there is a conspicuous affinity between Rosenzweig and kabbalistic theosophy. After all, Cohen's principle is related to the ap-propriation of an infinitesimal calculus, which implies, mathematically, that the origin of the objective realm is in that which is not.[177] For Rosen-zweig, the matter is not simply the derivation of something from nothing, but rather the positing of an origin that is not-nothing, an essence whose essence is not to be an essence. This notion of an inessential essence, I sur-mise, corresponds to *Ein Sof*, the origin that has no limit, and the action to the sefirotic gradations, whose emanation from the infinite marks the be-ginning of the process of delimitation.

Support for this contention is found in the passage from Rosenzweig's diary that I mentioned briefly in the first section of this essay: "The true predecessors of my problem are nevertheless in the Kabbala. However I show that the problem of Kabbala is not specifically theological (but En Sof appears in the same way with regards to M[an] and W[orld] and in the pri-ority of the theological which the Kabbala presents, the real time can only be based on (that which really happens not that which unfolds itself, etc.) which contradicts the pure theory of Potency."[178] The passage, which was written in 1922, parallels the discussion in the *Star* of the not-nothing, the infinite that precedes the binary division into Yes and No. Rivka Horwitz suggested that since Rosenzweig did not avail himself of the kabbalistic ter-minology in the *Star* but only in the diary entry, it is likely that he learnt of the Jewish mystical teaching after composing his magnum opus.[179] While this conjecture is possible, it seems to me unnecessary. As Idel already pointed out,[180] there is a passage in the "Urzelle" that demonstrates that Rosenzweig was already familiar to some extent with the teaching of Lurianic kabbalah, specifically the "interiorization of God [*Verinnerung Gottes*], which *precedes* not merely His self-externalization [*Selbstentäusserung*], but rather even His self," an idea that he explicitly links, moreover, to the "dark ground" (*dunkeln Grund*) of Schelling's thought.[181] I would suggest, therefore, that he was probably aware of the kabbalistic resonance of his thought from an earlier period of his life, but for some reason, he chose to conceal that in the *Star*. In a manner similar to many kabbalists, though likely indicating the influence of Cohen as well, Rosenzweig clearly differentiates between the beginning and the origin: the former denotes a temporal moment, the point of creation of something from nothing, in contrast to the latter, which is before any temporal demarcation, the creation before creation, the essence that springs forth endlessly from the not-nothing that is the source of the nothing that is everything. With regard to this basic distinction in kabbalistic writings, moreover, there is a close affinity between Rosenzweig and Heidegger as well.[182] Perhaps, in a distinctly Heideggerian turn of phrase, we should speak of Rosenzweig's *Nichnichts* as the nothing that nothings, the nothing that reveals itself as nothing in the guise of nothing.[183] The nothing that comes from the not-nothing, consequently, should not be understood in the Hegelian sense as "an unveiling of the essence of pure being,"[184] but rather in the Schellingian (or kabbalistic) sense of the "self-externalization" (*Sich-äusserns*) of God from the "primordial No" (*Urnein*),[185] the "self-configuring" (*Selbtsgestaltung*) or the "self-revelation of God's freedom before Creation" (*vorschöpferische Sichselbst-offenbaren der göttlichen Freiheit*).[186] The power of God that is revealed from its hiddenness at the beginning of creation can be considered an "essential attribute" (*wesenhafte Eigenschaft*), but it originates in an event (*Ereignis*) that internally is an act of "pure arbitrariness" (*reine Wilkür*) or "absolute freedom" (*bedingungslose Freiheit*) and externally an act of "pure necessity" (*reiner Notwendigkeit*).[187] The essential attribute is essentially inessential, for its essence consists of its being an inherently necessary randomness that cannot be predicted or calculated, the ground of being that is not-nothing.

The two ways specified by Rosenzweig should not be set in binary opposition. As he himself writes: "That which came out as Yes appears as No, and vice versa, just as we unpack things we put into a suitcase in the order that is opposite to how we packed them. . . . the No is not the 'antithesis' of the Yes; on the contrary, facing the nothing, the No has the same immediacy as the Yes; and for its confrontation with the Yes, it does not presuppose the Yes itself, but only the emergence of the Yes from out

of the nothing."[188] Rosenzweig offers a trivial example to illustrate a profound philosophical point: the respective processes of packing and unpacking leave the impression that one order is opposite to the other, but in
fact, these orders are not oppositional at all. The sense of apparent opposition arises from the temporal sequencing, a matter that is a pure contingency and not reflective of an inherent dichotomy. Analogously, as Rosenzweig emphasizes, it is possible to read a text from beginning to end or
from end to beginning. As I have argued elsewhere, "the ability to read
bi-directionally presumes an open circle, which of necessity entails the
impossibility of determining the end from the beginning or the beginning from the end; the reversibility of the timeline does not imply clo-
sure at either terminus, but rather an ever-changing flux that destabilizes
the model of an irreversible succession proceeding unilaterally from start
to finish."[189] The same logic of reversibility is at play in Rosenzweig's description of the relationship of the Yes and the No: the latter presupposes
the materialization of the former from the nothing that is something, just
as the former presupposes the materialization of the latter from the something that is nothing. Yes and No appear to be the antithesis of one another, but they are not antithetical. Rosenzweig adamantly avers that the
Yes does not come from the No as if it were "torn from God in a spasm
of self-negation" (*Krampf der Selbstverneinung*),[190] but, given his own delineation of the Yes as the not-nothing, the quintessential double negative, one cannot help but comprehend this advent as an act of negation.
To be sure, what is negated is not a self but an essence that can only be demarcated as the not-nothing, that is, a nothing negated of and by its own
nothingness.

Bearing this is mind, we can understand how the conclusion of the
Star is anticipated in its inception. In this connection, it is worth recalling
the instructive remark made by Rosenzweig in "Das neue Denken" that
any philosophical book requires that the reader "does not understand the
beginning, or, at the very least, [that one] understands it wrongly." Rosenzweig illustrates the point from the discussion regarding the concept of
nothingness (*der Begriff des Nichts*) in the *Star*, "the 'nothingnesses,' which
here seems to be only a methodological auxiliary concept, first reveals its
contentful significance only in the short concluding paragraph of the volume, and its ultimate meaning only in the concluding book of the whole.
What is said here is nothing other than a *reductio ad absurdum* and, at the
same time, a rescue of the old philosophy."[191] The import of Rosenzweig's
analysis of the nothing at the beginning—the rescue of the old philosophy
that his new thinking will execute—can only be elicited from the discussion at the end. The disclosure of the face of God that will shine in the es-
chaton is itself a form of concealment, the manifestation becoming hid-

den and the speech leading to silence. To be granted a vision of the face inscribed within the contours of the star is to behold the inexpressible truth.

It is understandable why Rosenzweig begins with a rejection of negative theology—affirming our inability to know God is the limit to where philosophy goes—but it is not clear that he has presented the apophatic dimension of the philosophical tradition accurately. More importantly, his own sense of affirmation as the negation of negation, which is reflected in his characterization of the end as a silence that no longer needs words, is itself a form of apophasis that embraces the mystical. As I have noted already, this end is depicted by Rosenzweig as the discernment that God is truth. It might appear that this apprehension is kataphatic in nature: "That by which we had to designate God's essence, the last thing that we know of him as the Lord of what is last, of the one life perfected in supra-worldly fashion in the All: that he is truth—this last conception of the essence slips through our fingers. For if God is truth—what is said with this about his 'essence'? Nothing more than this, that he is the original ground of truth, and all truth is truth only through this, it comes from him."[192] The essentiality of God is linked to his being the ground of truth, and this would ostensibly provide the ideational basis for a theocentric orientation, which is seemingly articulated by Rosenzweig in his claim that the "divine essentiality [*göttliche Wesenheit*] is really nothing more than the divine self-revealing [*göttliche Sich-Offenbaren*]."

The kataphatic theology, which is close in tone to Schelling and Lurianic kabbalah, can be cast propositionally in the declaration that "God is truth." If we probe more carefully, however, we discover that Rosenzweig approaches an articulation that is reminiscent of the *via negativa* of Maimonides: "God is truth—this sentence with which we thought we had risen to the utmost of knowledge—if we see more closely what truth really is, then we find that that sentence brings back to us in different words only what is most intimately familiar of our experience; the apparent knowledge about the essence turns into the near, immediate experience of his action; that he is truth tells us finally nothing however other than that he—loves."[193] The "apparent knowledge" of God's essence amounts to the "near, immediate experience" of divine action, expressed especially in the form of love, rather than any positive delineation of that essence. It should come as no surprise, then, that Rosenzweig informs us that by gathering this "last knowledge about God's essence" (*letzte Wissen um Gottes Wesenheit*), "we could venture back . . . into that first non-knowledge [*erste Nichterkenntnis*], into the knowledge of his nothing [*die Erkenntnis seines Nichts*], which was our starting point."[194] In going forward, one goes back, retracing steps to where one could have never been, and thus one discerns that the knowledge of the divine essence ascertained at the end is identical to the non-knowledge available at the beginning, the knowledge of his nothing, a nothing that can only be in virtue of not being, the not-nothing. Still struggling to demarcate his path as distinct from idealistic philosophy, Rosenzweig remarks that paganism finds the "All" in that nothing, whereas revelation, the basic postulate that accords theism meaning, taught us to recognize the "hidden God" (*verborgenen Gott*), that is, the "hidden one who is nothing other than the not yet manifest one [*der noch nicht offenbare*]. . . . The nothing of our knowledge about him thus became for us a meaningful nothing [*inhaltsreichen Nichts*], the mysterious prediction of what we have been experiencing in the revealing."[195]

The notion of the not-yet translates the apophatic into a kataphatic register. As Martin Kavka astutely discerned, the meontological sign of the not-yet in Rosenzweig, as in Levinas, albeit differently, entails a "temporalization of the concept of nonbeing" that "justifies a structure of messianic or eschatological anticipation."[196] By turning nothing to not-yet, the negative holds within its nonbeing the potential for all that comes to be; to translate the metaphysical idea theologically, that which is hidden reveals itself through continuous manifestations. The disclosures, however, are themselves a form of concealment, indeed, the concealment of concealment, for what is revealed is always the not-nothing that is not yet. In spite of his initial rejection of negative theology, the swerve of Rosenzweig's path winds its way to an apophasis of apophasis: "That God is nothing becomes just as much a figurative sentence as the other one, that he is truth."[197] Both propositions, that "God is nothing," which is assigned to the beginning, and that "God is the truth," which is affixed to the end, must be taken figuratively. To render either literally would be to veil the truth unveiled in the mirror of truth and thereby lapse into the mistaken dichotomization of appearance and reality.

So what, then, asks Rosenzweig, is nothing? His response quintessentially performs the dialectic of concealment doubling itself to reveal what it conceals in the concealing of what it reveals: "Already in this very question the single answer that would let the nothing remain nothing is forbidden, the answer: nothing. For nothing can never designate the essence, never be predicate."[198] To inquire about the nature of nothing is to presume that nothing is something, but for nothing to be nothing, it must be no thing. Any attempt to articulate this truism, to put the comportment of nothing into propositional logic with a subject and predicate connected by a copula will fail. Language has reached its limit, though the very failure of language holds the promise of language, the "true mystery" by which the "word speaks," an articulation that determines the very boundary beyond which lies that which speech "can neither reach nor perceive," that which is "cast away from its luminous and audible sphere, into the cold dread of the nothing," the "decisive anticipation . . . where the Kingdom to come is actually coming and where eternity is actual reality."[199] Nothing is not some thing; it is the eventuality of something, indeed, of everything that originates in the origin that is not-nothing, the not-yet that is the "ever-repeated present, the eternal, wherein beginning and end meet, the imperishable in the today."[200] We can pronounce that "nothing is God," but this sentence, Rosenzweig insists, "is as little an absurdity as the sentence of idealism that truth is God; it is simply, like the former one—false. Exactly like truth, the nothing is of course not at all finally a self-supporting subject; it is merely a fact, the awaiting of a something, it is not anything yet. . . . Of God alone can it be said that he is the nothing; it would be the first knowledge of his essence."[201] By now, however, we know that this claim to knowledge of the divine essence intends its very opposite, for the essence of God is such that there is no essence to be known. As I noted above, for Rosenzweig, attested already in the "Urzelle," the organizing concept is event (*Ereignis*) as opposed to essence (*Wesen*).[202] Nevertheless, he wrote repeatedly of God's essence, though this is an essence that is not knowable, for the essence of this essence is what-shall-become-in-having-already-been. Alternatively expressed, the truth of God is contained in the compresence of the three temporal modes, an idea traditionally offered by rabbinic interpreters as the meaning of the Tetragrammaton.[203] To say of God that "He is" implies that the "actual has-been," the "actual is," and the "actual becoming" are all together as one.[204]

Rosenzweig cannot elude the double bind of apophasis, even as he tried to disentangle it. The signpost of redemption, "God is truth," is the only admissible answer to the theological question, "What is God?" And this answer, Rosenzweig maintains, "leads the mystical question about his supra-worldly essence, this last question, back into the living experience of his actions, so the answer 'he is nothing' leads to the abstract question about his primordial worldly essence, this first question—towards—the same experience."[205] The experience to which Rosenzweig refers is the experience of revelation, the dialogical expression of divine love, which is not a thing but an event, not spatial facticity but temporal factuality. Revelation is the immediacy that provides the cement to mend the "primeval break" of the All, for by affirming the real possibility of revelation as transcendence entering into dialogical relation with the human being in the world, the three modes of time, beginning, middle, and end, all "become equally immediate, that is to say equally incapable of being mediated, no longer to be mediated because they are themselves already centers—and now the All, the once shattered, has grown together again."[206] This passage must be read intertextually with the statement at the end of the in-

troduction to the book to which I have already referred: "The nothing of
our knowledge is not a singular nothing, but a threefold one. Hence, it contains in itself the promise of definability. And that is why we may hope, as
did Faust, to find again in this nothing, in this threefold nothing of knowledge, the All that we had to cut into pieces."[207]

The multiplication of nothing, however, leaves one with nothing, indeed more nothing, three times more than nothing. What would be unveiled in this veiling of nothing but nothing veiled in the unveiling of
nothing? In the middle that is revelation, writes Rosenzweig, beginning
(creation) and end (redemption) rise "out of their hiddenness into the
manifest," but in so doing, that "which is manifest becomes that which
is hidden."[208] If the hidden that is manifest becomes hidden again, if the
"light breaking / darkness unutterable" at the beginning recycles to the
"unutterable darkness / breaking light" at the end,[209] then Rosenzweig's
new thinking is inescapably enmeshed in the duplicity of secrecy that is endemic to apophatic theology. The meontological temporalization of nonbeing may facilitate the possibility of encounter with transcendence, embodied linguistically in the erotic metaphors of the Song of Songs, but the
price to be paid for grounding the openness to the other in a negative theology[210] is the potential undoing of the dialogical in the discernment that
what is disclosed is the face of truth that can only be rendered metaphorically.[211] The eternal forms (*ewigen Gestalten*), which will be manifest in
the futurity of redemption, are the figures (*Bildern*) in which the "three
invisible-secret sources" (*drei unsichtbar-geheimen Quellen*) that feed the
stream of actuality (*der Strom der Wirklichkeit*) become themselves figural
(*selbst bildhaft*), and "the constant course of life rounds itself off into recurrent form [*der stete Ablauf des Lebens rundet sich zur wiederkehrenden Form*]."[212]
The metaphysical concept of actual presence is transposed into a semiotic
trope of mythopoetic metaphoricization. But all three invisible secrets (*un-
sichtbaren Geheimnisse*) lie beyond—and indeed may be extracted ontically
from—the factuality of their imaginative realization. Through the world-
time of Judaism and Christianity, what is real "takes figural shape as a
formed copy [*geformten Abbild*]. In their God, their world, and their man,
there becomes expressible the secret of God, of man, of world, which is
only experienceable, but not expressible, in the course of life. What God,
what the world, what man 'is,' we do not know, only what they do, or
what is done to them. . . . In place of the existing substances [*seienden Sub-
stanzen*], which are everlasting only as secret preconditions of the very renewed actuality [*geheime Voraussetzungen der allzeiterneuerten Wirklichkeit*],
enter forms [*Gestalten*] that eternally mirror this ever renewed actuality
[*die diese allzeiterneuerte Wirklichkeit ewig spiegeln*]."[213] A substantialist ontology is replaced by a notion of actuality that is based on the temporality

lived and narrated in the "eternal clock-faces" (*ewigen Zifferblätter*) of the two liturgical communities, the eternal life of Judaism and the eternal way of Christianity. The pulse of time is measured from the perspective of this (dia)chronic mirroring, the unremitting dissimulation of forms that appear to be true in the truth of their appearance.

Derrida's observations regarding Angelus Silesius may well apply to Rosenzweig: "Not only God but the deity surpasses knowledge, the singularity of the unknown God overflows the essence and the divinity, thwarting in this manner the oppositions of the negative and the positive, of being and nothingness, of thing and nothing—thus transcending all the theological attributes."[214] As it happens, Derrida reached a similar conclusion in a passing reference to Rosenzweig's call to the originary *yes*, which ostensibly rejects the apophatic. According to Derrida, this inceptual invocation is "an event or advent of the *yes* which might be *neither* Judaic *nor* Christian, not yet or no longer simply one or the other," and hence it brings us "not to some ontological or transcendental condition of possibility, but to the 'quasi' which I've been insinuating for some time now ('quasi transcendental' or 'quasi ontological'), which could harmonize the originary eventness of the event with the fabulous narrative or with the fable inscribed in the *yes* at the origin of every word (*fari*)." The "originary word" (*Urwort*) both "belongs to" and is "foreign to" language. What is declaimed in the beginning, therefore, is an "inaudible term," a "language without language," a word that "belongs without belonging to that totality which it simultaneously institutes and opens. It exceeds and incises language, to which it remains nonetheless immanent; like language's first dweller, the first to step out of its home. . . . But its intrinsic double nature is already discernable, or more precisely, it is already confirmed. It is and is not of language, it both merges and does not merge with its utterance in a natural language."[215] The figurative status of the configuration of the divine face beheld in the star puts into play the possibility that the ultimate truth is that there is no truth, just as knowledge of the essence consists of becoming cognizant of the fact that there is no essence to be known. "That God is nothing becomes just as much a figurative sentence as the other one, that he is truth."[216] This dissimilitude may be the inexorable consequence of negative theology.[217] In spite of Rosenzweig's painstaking effort to advocate that the personal God of Judaism (and Christianity as well) cannot be "only an allegory," that revelation must consist of the unmediated bond between God and human that rests on the self-disclosure of the former to the latter and the consequent courage of the latter to bow down in worship before the former,[218] it is not clear that theistic language for him is anything but metaphorical, for there is no reality but the naught that is not-nothing, the nothing that is not, not even nothing. As Rosenzweig speculated in *Büchlein vom gesunden und kranken Menschenverstand,* if *nothing* is truly the order that is the essence behind appearance, then it is possible that "appearance is everything and everything is only appearance," that "there is nothing beyond appearance, not even something 'wholly other,'" that the human being, itself reduced to mere appearance, "reflects a segment of the mirage, or, indeed (why not?) the complete mirage," that "God is merely the shadow cast by the frame of the mirror, or possibly the reflection of the mirror's glass."[219]

In the last analysis, it is legitimate to wonder if the theism championed by Rosenzweig is not prone to being itself an *as if* construct, the "panacea for doubt" of the philosophical temperament that obscures the empirical tangibility of an event and thereby inverts "healthy common sense" into "sick reason."[220] To avoid potential misunderstanding, which has already been reflected back to me by some who have heard my argument, I am well aware that the whole point of Rosenzweig's new thinking is to turn our attention away from "essence" to "event," to ascribe to theological language the role of marking "experiences of meetings" rather than "experiences of an objective kind," as he accounts for biblical anthropomorphisms.[221] I well appreciate that from his standpoint the human being is "the single protection against the backsliding into polytheism, which indeed is nothing but consolidation of a genuine present revelation of the real God to a lasting image of God."[222] Rosenzweig's labors, therefore, must be judged in terms of leading the way to an experience of encountering this "real God" (*wirklichen Gottes*) rather than an experience of an essence that is naught but an "image of God" (*Gottesbild*).[223] Yet to think in his footsteps—the thinking that is the highest mode of thanking—imposes on us the demand to inquire if it is feasible to speak of such a meeting when our ability to assert anything positive about the "reality" of God is compromised. Is Rosenzweig not subject to the same quandary as Maimonides, that is, does the insistence on the radical incomparability of God not render all predication inappropriate? And if this is so, God-talk, theistically conceived, would be meaningful in some social, psychological, or political sense or perhaps as a form of apophatic discourse, the saying of the unsaid in the unsaying of the said.[224] Would apophasis not be the inevitable conclusion of such an uncompromising disbanding of the anthropomorphically inflected tropes of the tradition? But are these not the very rhetorical patterns that provide the eidetic underpinning for the ontic possibility of meeting a *real God,* a God to whom "phenomenological concreteness" (in the Levinasian sense) may be attributed?[225] In spite of his unfaltering effort to make a credible philosophical case for the theological belief in a revelatory experience that preserves the otherness of the divine vis-à-vis the human—thereby anticipating the contemporary "rediscovery of negative theology" that has resulted in the narrowing of the gulf between theology and philosophy[226]—does Rosenzweig, ultimately, succumb to the conversion of theology into anthropology along the lines of Feuerbach, for whom the consciousness of the Infinite (which is offered as a definition of religion) amounts to the consciousness of the infinity of consciousness, and hence the God of traditional monotheism is no more than an outward projection of human nature?[227] Or, to appropriate the terminology of Habermas, is Rosenzweig not guilty of a postmetaphysical "linguistification of the sacred" that would render the ontotheological experience of the divine presence that he so passionately desired untenable?[228]

Eschewing the possibility of an a-theological ontology, which has been associated with Heidegger,[229] Rosenzweig seems nevertheless to be ensnared in the clench of an atheistic theology. Is there anything to affirm as real but the "name-less, transcendent nothing," a belief that Rosenzweig characterized as the "diseased thought" of the philistine?[230] Perhaps this is the drift of the gloss made by Rosenzweig regarding the *absolute factuality* of God, "if the expression is not misleading."[231] To the best of my knowledge, Rosenzweigian scholars have not heeded this stipulation. The expression may indeed be misleading, since it is not feasible to speak of God's factuality—the "dark chaos of the particular" (*dunkles Chaos des Besonderen*)[232]—prior to or dissociated from the theopoetic confabulation of the divine in the guise of creation, redemption, and revelation.[233] Let us recall Rosenzweig's remark that the enemy "is not idealism as such," but the "assumption that it is possible for something to exist beyond reality." Realism and idealism—indeed, any *ism*—are equally unacceptable, for they both promote an "essence" that abstracts from life, and hence they "fail to conciliate thought and action."[234]

Is Rosenzweig subject to the very malady of spirit that he earnestly sought to alleviate? There is an aside made toward the end of "Atheistic Theology," the essay that set Rosenzweig on the course to articulate a new thinking that would uphold the possibility of revelation, which indicates that he was acutely aware of the risk of lapsing into the posture that he criticized: "That the light of God is the human soul and that only the rays of that light, which the soul needs for the illumination of its earthly way, are visible—this fundamental idea of our philosophy—was and is just as susceptible as its mystical parallels to an atheistic stamp."[235] In this utterly honest and prescient moment, Rosenzweig foresaw that the commitment to the belief that the light of God is the human soul[236] propels his own path perilously close to the "secret abysses of the nothing,"[237] the unfathomable ground where mysticism and atheism insidiously shake hands.

NOTES

1. Elliot R. Wolfson, "Facing the Effaced: Mystical Eschatology and the Idealistic Orientation in the Thought of Franz Rosenzweig," *Zeitschrift für Neure Theologiegeschichte* 4 (1997): 39–81. For a more typical presentation of Rosenzweig, and one that unfortunately did not take my study into account, see Michael Mack, "Franz Rosenzweig's and Emmanuel Levinas's Critique of German Idealism's Pseudotheology," *Journal of Religion* 83 (2003): 56–78. See also Peter E. Gordon, "Rosenzweig Redux: The Reception of German-Jewish Thought," *Jewish Social Studies* 8 (2001): 8–9, 32–33.

2. Gershom Scholem, *The Messianic Idea in Judaism and Other Essays in Jewish Spirituality* (New York: Schocken Books, 1971), 322.

3. Nahum N. Glatzer, "Was Franz Rosenzweig a Mystic?" in *Studies in Jewish Religious and Intellectual History Presented to Alexander Altmann on the Occasion of His Seventieth Birthday*, edited by Siegfried Stein and Raphael Loewe (Tuscaloosa: University of Alabama Press, 1979), 131. On the depiction of the *Star* as promoting a philosophically mystical doctrine, see also Kenneth Hart Green, "The Notion of Truth in Franz Rosenzweig's *The Star of Redemption*: A Philosophical Enquiry," *Modern Judaism* 7 (1987): 317–18. Although Glatzer applies the Scholemian characterization "theistic mysticism" to Rosenzweig, he categorically denies that he was a mystic. See, additionally, the comments of Nahum N. Glatzer in the introduction to his *Franz Rosenzweig: His Life and Thought* (Philadelphia: Jewish Publication Society of America, 1953), xxvii. In contrast to Leo Baeck, Hermann Cohen, and Martin Buber, "Rosenzweig is distinguished . . . by his more radical break with the past and his renascence of theological concepts that were last alive in the long-forgotten sphere of independent, dialectical Kabbalah. (This parallel, first recognized by Gershom G. Scholem, is doubly significant, since Rosenzweig never was a mystic.)"

4. Wolfson, "Facing the Effaced," 74–81. The question of the influence of kabbalah on Rosenzweig has been discussed by several other scholars. See Gershom Scholem, "Franz Rosenzweig and His Book *The Star of Redemption*," in The *Philosophy of Franz Rosenzweig*, edited by Paul Mendes-Flohr (Hanover, NH: University Press of New England, 1988), 20–41, esp. 35–39; Warren Zen Harvey, "How Much Kabbalah in *The Star of Redemption*?" *Immanuel* 1 (1987): 128–34; Moshe Idel, "Rosenzweig and the Kabbalah," in *The Philosophy of Franz Rosenzweig*, edited by Paul Mendes-Flohr (Hanover, N.H.: University Press of New England, 1988), 162–71; Rivka Horwitz, "From Hegelianism to a Revolutionary Understanding of Judaism: Franz Rosenzweig's Attitude toward Kabbala and Myth," *Modern Judaism* 26 (2006): 31–54, and the Hebrew version in *Judaism, Topics, Fragments, Faces, Identities: Jubilee Volume in Honor of Rivka*, edited by Haviva Pedaya and Ephraim Meir (Beer-Sheva: Ben-Gurion University of the Negev Press, 2007), 43–71. See also Barbara E. Galli, "Franz Rosenzweig's Theory of Translation Through Kabbalistic Motifs," in *The Legacy of Franz Rosenzweig: Collected Essays*, edited by Luc Anckaert, Martin Brasser, and Norbert Samuelson (Leuven: Leuven University Press, 2004), 189–97; Renate Schindler, *Zeit, Geschichte, Ewigkeit in Franz Rosenzweig's Stern der Erlösung* (Berlin: Parerga Verlag GmbH, 2007), 232–35; and the additional references cited below, n. 151.

Rosenzweig's understanding of kabbalah is attested as well in his passing remark in the brief note on anthropomorphism published initially in *Der Morgen* 4, Heft 5 (1928) and a second time in Franz Rosenzweig, *Kleinere Schriften* (Berlin: Schocken Verlag, 1937), 525–33, esp. 531–32. See the English version "A Note on Anthropomorphisms in Response to the *Encyclopedia Judaica*'s Article," in Franz Rosenzweig,

God, Man, and the World: Lectures and Essays, edited and translated by Barbara E. Galli, with a foreword by Michael Oppenheim (Syracuse, N.Y.: Syracuse University Press, 1998), 143:

> The philosophy peaks in the—so far as possible in Judaism—successful attempt of Maimonides to codify dogmatically the "incorporeality" of God. The answer is given this time by the high- and late-Kabbala. Simply because it took over from philosophy of religion the concept of "absolutely without attributes," a Godhead to be determined only negatively, kabbalistically expressed, the Ain Sof [the Infinite], the Absolute, it discovered under this highest rung an ever more variegated throng of heavenly rungs beneath and between.

Rosenzweig goes on to say that the "last degenerations" (*letzten Ausartungen*) of the Kabbalah belong to the "third epoch" of the battle against anthropomorphism within Judaism. As he further surmises on the basis of personal experience, the answer to this perplexing problem will likely "be given by the great ones who get baptized [i.e., Jewish converts to Christianity] of the nineteenth and unfortunately also the twentieth century" (144).

Here is not the place to enter into a lengthy discourse about the affinity that Rosenzweig seems to have grasped between the anthropomorphic tendency of the kabbalistic imaginary and the incarnational appeal of Christianity for some Jews. See Idel, "Rosenzweig and the Kabbalah," 169–70; Sandu Frunză, "Aspects of the Connections Between Judaism and Christianity in Franz Rosenzweig's Philosophy," in *Essays in Honor of Moshe Idel,* edited by Sandu Frunză and Mihaela Frunză (Cluj-Napoca: Provo Press, 2008), 200–227, esp. 221–22. For discussion of the beginning of the aforecited passage of Rosenzweig and the *Shiʿur Qomah* tradition, see Paul Franks, "Everyday Speech and Revelatory Speech in Rosenzweig and Wittgenstein," *Philosophy Today* 50 (2006): 35. A more extensive discussion of Rosenzweig's attitude to the *Shiʿur Qomah* speculation, viewed from the perspective of his overall understanding of biblical anthropomorphisms, is offered by Paul Franks, "Talking of Eyebrows: Religion and the Space of Reasons after Wittgenstein, Rosenzweig, and Diamond," in *Religion and Wittgenstein's Legacy,* edited by Dewi Z. Phillips and Mario von der Ruhr (Burlington: Ashgate, 2004), 150–54. Franks notes, inter alia, that even though Rosenzweig's "approach to biblical talk about God" is "quite opposed" to Maimonides and "much closer" to Wittgenstein, he nonetheless "endorses Maimonides' judgement of the *Shiʿur Qomah* traditions" (150). I will briefly note, as will become evident in the course of this study, that in spite of the seemingly vast difference between the Maimonidean and Rosenzweigian interpretations of scriptural discourse about the divine, both thinkers end up affirming a contemplative seeing beyond language as the culminating mode of liturgical worship. I have previously noted the conceptual affinities between Rosenzweig and the kabbalists with respect to the mythopoetic construction of the symbolic form of the divine anthropos ("Facing the Effaced," 79–80, a discussion that, lamentably, is completely ignored by Franks in his analysis of the development of the *Shiʿur Qomah* anthropomorphisms in the Idrot sections of the zoharic compilation), but this should not blind one from the notional proximity of the *via negativa* of Maimonides, which itself exerted a great influence on the kabbalistic sensibility, and the apophaticism affirmed by Rosenzweig. On the repercussions of the Maimonidean apophatic theology on the kabbalists, see Elliot R. Wolfson, "*Via Negativa* in Maimonides and Its Impact on Thirteenth-Century Kabbalah," *Maimonidean Studies* 5 (2008): 393–442.

5. Barbara E. Galli, *Franz Rosenzweig and Jehuda Halevi: Translating, Translations, and Translators*, foreword by Paul Mendes-Flohr (Montreal: McGill-Queen's University Press, 1995), 20–21; German original in Franz Rosenzweig, *Der Mensch und sein Werk: Gesammelte Schriften IV. Sprachdenken im Übersetzen, 1: Band Hymnen und Gedichte des Jehuda Halevi,* edited by Reinhold and Annemarie Mayer (Dordrecht: Martinus Nijhoff, 1984), 27.

6. Galli, *Franz Rosenzweig and Jehuda Halevi,* 187.

7. I have dedicated many of my studies to elucidate the point, but none as extensively as Elliot R. Wolfson, *Through a Speculum That Shines: Vision and Imagination in Medieval Judaism* (Princeton, N.J.: Princeton University Press, 1994). Halevi is discussed on 173–87.

8. Franz Rosenzweig, "The New Thinking," in *Philosophical and Theological Writings,* translated and edited, with notes and commentary, by Paul W. Franks and Michael L. Morgan (Indianapolis: Hackett Publishing Company, 2000), 119. The original German of this essay, which appeared in *Der Morgen* 1, no. 4 (1925): 426–51, has been reprinted in several collections. I have consulted Rosenzweig, *Kleinere Schriften,* 373–98.

9. For a critique of such a reading, see Benjamin Pollock, *Franz Rosenzweig and the Systematic Task of Philosophy* (Cambridge: Cambridge University Press, 2009), 258–311.

10. Galli, *Franz Rosenzweig and Jehuda Halevi,* 317–18. A reading of Rosenzweig as a postmodern philosopher was proffered by Robert Gibbs, *Correlations in Rosenzweig and Levinas* (Princeton, N.J.: Princeton University Press, 1992), 10, 20-22, 55, 120, but see the challenge offered by Gordon, "Rosenzweig Redux," 33. Another attempt to interpret Rosenzweig as a postmodern Jewish thinker is offered by Yudit Kornberg Greenberg, *Better Than Wine: Love, Poetry, and Prayer in the Thought of Franz Rosenzweig* (Atlanta, Ga.: Scholars Press, 1996), 139–150.

11. Franz Rosenzweig, *The Star of Redemption,* translated by Barbara E. Galli (Madison: University of Wisconsin Press, 2005), 29; *Der Stern der Erlösung* (Frankfurt am Main: Suhrkamp Verlag, 1990), 24. References to the former will henceforth be cited as *SR* and to the latter as *SE*. It is of interest to recall the remark of Karl Löwith, "F. Rosenzweig and M. Heidegger on Temporality and Eternity," *Philosophy and Phenomenological Research* 3 (1942): 55–56, that Rosenzweig and Heidegger shared the aim of replacing the "all-too-many things" with "the one that is necessary at a time which is driving toward decisions because the traditional contents of modern civilization no longer prove indisputable." For the revised version, see idem, *Nature, History, and Existentialism,* edited by Arnold Levison (Evanston, Ill.: Northwestern University Press, 1966), 54–55.

12. Norbert Samuelson, "The Concept of 'Nichts' in Rosenzweig's *Star of Redemption,*" in *Der Philosoph Franz Rosenzweig (1886–1929): Internationaler Kongreß-Kassel 1986,* 2 vols., edited by Wolfdietrich Schmied-Kowarzik (Freiburg: Verlag Karl Alber, 1988), 643–56. See also the brief introduction to the selection from Rosenzweig's *Star* included in *On What Cannot Be Said: Apophatic Discourses in Philosophy, Religion, Literature, and the Arts,* vol. 2, edited with theoretical and critical essays by William Franke (Notre Dame, Ind.: University of Notre Dame, 2007), 139–44. For points of difference between my approach and that of Franke, see below nn. 173 and 211. On the influence of Kant with regard to the threefold formulation of the nought in Rosenzweig, see Else-Rahel Freund, *Franz Rosenzweig's Philosophy of Existence: An Analysis of* The Star of Redemption (The Hague: Martinus Nijhoff, 1979), 87–88.

13. *Die "Gritli"-Briefe. Briefe an Margrit Rosenstock-Huessy,* edited by Inken Rühle and Reinhold Mayer, with a preface by Rafael Rosenzweig (Tübingen: Bilam Verlag, 2002), 227, cited in Pollock, *Franz Rosenzweig,* 397 n. 3, and then again, with analysis, on 419.

14. Rosenzweig, "The New Thinking," 115. See ibid., 116–17: "Experience (*Er-*

fahrung), no matter how deeply it may penetrate, discovers only the human in man, only worldliness in the world, only divinity in God. And only God in divinity, only in the world worldliness, and only in man the human." And ibid., 118: "To the question of essence there are only tautological answers. God is only divine, man only human, the world only worldly; one can drill shafts into them as deeply as one wants, one always finds the same again." Rosenzweig's understanding of the mystical as an effacing of the autonomy of one of the three basic elements that are in correlation (God, human, or world) was anticipated by Hermann Cohen. See, e.g., *Reason and Hope: Selections from the Jewish Writings of Hermann Cohen*, translated by Eva Jospe (New York: W.W. Norton, 1971), 84: "But whenever God and man, or God and nature are equated, mysticism inevitably ensues. It turns the moral into the supernatural, and the supernatural into the natural."

15. Rosenzweig, "The New Thinking," 116. In that context, the mystic is described as the "associate" of the pantheist, who affirms the subsumption of everything into divinity, and the atheist is associated with the materialist, who maintains that the human is a product of nature and God "nothing but its reflection." By contrast, in the beginning of the first book of the *Star*, Rosenzweig links the mystic and the atheist (see below at n. 156).

16. Franz Rosenzweig, *Understanding the Sick and the Healthy: A View of World, Man, and God*, translated and with an introduction by Nahum Glatzer, and with an introduction by Hilary Putnam (Cambridge, Mass.: Harvard University Press, 1999), 68.

17. Rosenzweig, "'Urzelle' to the *Star of Redemption*," in *Philosophical and Theological Writings*, 71. See also the curious, and to my knowledge somewhat neglected, comments of Rosenzweig on 69–70. The two base-points of the triangle of the sciences are identified as faith and unfaith, or as theology and philosophy. The *salto mortale*, i.e., the life-risking leap (a phrase made famous by Jacobi, as the editors remark on 69 n. 49), on the triangle's summit is linked to theosophy. Despite Rosenzweig's self-acknowledged bewilderment and resistance to the pinnacle of the sciences, it seems to me that his own thinking in the *Star* occupies the same place as theosophy, that is, the midpoint positioned between the two bases of philosophy and theology. It is not inconsequential that he declares his interest in pursuing Steinerian theosophy in more serious manner (71–72). See below, n. 173.

18. *SR*, 116. It is of interest to recall here the following description of the relationship of scholasticism and mysticism in medieval Christian philosophy offered by Martin Heidegger, "Supplements to *The Doctrine of Categories and Meaning in Duns Scotus*," in *Becoming Heidegger: On the Trail of His Early Occasional Writings, 1910–1927*, edited by Theodore Kisiel and Thomas Sheehan (Evanston, Ill.: Northwestern University Press, 2007), 85: "Philosophy as a rationalistic structure, detached from life, is *powerless;* mysticism as irrational experience is *aimless*" (emphasis in the original).

19. Rosenzweig, "The New Thinking," 129.

20. Ibid., 110. According to his own account (111–12), the system in the *Star* comprises three of the four elements usually found in a philosophical system: logic, ethics, and aesthetics; the only element missing is a philosophy of religion. Toward the end of the essay (131), Rosenzweig does finally accept the designation of the *Star* as a "Jewish book." He explains, however, that this does not imply that it deals with "Jewish things," but that the "old Jewish words" are deployed to express what it has to say. "Like things in general, Jewish things have always passed away; yet Jewish words, even when old, share the eternal youth of the word, and if the world is opened up to them, they will renew the world." See the passage from the *Star* cited below at n. 100, and on the question of the "Jewishness" of the "new philosophy," see the letter of

Rosenzweig to Rudolf Hallo, written on February 4, 1923, in Franz Rosenzweig, *Briefe*, edited by Edith Rosenzweig (Berlin: Schocken Verlag, 1935), 475–77, partially translated in Harold M. Stahmer, "'Speech-Letters' and 'Speech-Thinking': Franz Rosenzweig and Eugen Rosenstock-Huessy," *Modern Judaism* 4 (1984): 64. For discussion of Rosenzweig's objection to branding the Star as a "Jewish book," see Gordon, "Rosenzweig Redux," 15–17.

21. On Rosenzweig's positioning his new thinking in the interstitial space between philosophy and theology, see Eric L. Santner, "Miracles Happen: Benjamin, Rosenzweig, Freud, and the Matter of the Neighbor," in Slavoj Žižek, Eric L. Santner, and Kenneth Reinhard, *The Neighbor: Three Inquiries in Political Theology* (Chicago: University of Chicago Press, 2005), 82.

22. Rosenzweig, "The New Thinking," 118 (*Kleinere Schriften*, 380).

23. *SR*, 441.

24. *Die "Gritli"-Briefe*, 159–60, cited in Pollock, *Franz Rosenzweig*, 258–59.

25. Rosenzweig, "The New Thinking," 114 (*Kleinere Schriften*, 377).

26. Ibid., 136 (*Kleinere Schriften*, 397).

27. *SR*, 312 [*SE*, 327].

28. *SR*, 271 [*SE*, 282]. Rosenzweig paraphrased the well-known depiction of the world-to-come transmitted in the name of Rav in Babylonian Talmud, Berakhot 17a. See Zachary Braiterman, "'Into Life'? Franz Rosenzweig and the Figure of Death," *AJS Review* 23 (1998): 203–21; idem, *The Shape of Revelation: Aesthetics and Modern Jewish Thought* (Stanford, Calif.: Stanford University Press, 2007), 118–19.

29. *SR*, 280 [*SE*, 291].

30. On the notion of "absolute empiricism," see Schindler, *Zeit, Geschichte, Ewigkeit*, 114–23.

31. Laurens ten Kate, "The Gift of Loss: A Study of the Fugitive God in Bataille's Atheology, With References to Jean-Luc Nancy," in *Flight of the Gods: Philosophical Perspectives on Negative Theology*, edited by Ilse N. Bulhof and Laurens ten Kate (New York: Fordham University Press, 2000), 277. On the concept of philosophical theology in Rosenzweig and his sources, see Bernhard Casper, "Die Gründung einer philosophischen Theologie im Ereignis," *Dialegesesthai* 2003, available at http://mondodomani .org/dialegesthai/bc01.htm. In spite of Heidegger's critique of onto-theology, there is a point of resemblance between him and Rosenzweig on the need to translate the philosophical into the theological and the theological into the philosophical. See Löwith, "F. Rosenzweig and M. Heidegger," 56, and idem, *Nature, History, and Existentialism*, 55. Löwith correctly notes, however, that "Heidegger's attitude towards Christianity is an estrangement and Rosenzweig's attitude towards Judaism a return." And see the elaboration on the opposed goals of the two thinkers in Löwith, "F. Rosenzweig and M. Heidegger," 61–75; idem, *Nature, History, and Existentialism*, 60–76.

32. Here I have accepted the rendering in Franz Rosenzweig, *The Star of Redemption*, translated by William Hallo (New York: Holt, Rinehart, and Winston, 1970), 17 [*SE*, 19]. Galli, *SR*, 24, translates: "his essence by nature, his essence that is there."

33. On this dimension of the onto-theological, see Jean-Luc Marion, "Thomas Aquinas and Onto-theo-logy," in *Mystics: Presence and Aporia*, edited by Michael Kessler and Christian Sheppard (Chicago and London: University of Chicago Press, 2003), 38–74, esp. 39–40. Also instructive is the essay by Ben Vedder, "The Disappearance of Philosophical Theology in Hermeneutic Philosophy: Historicizing and Hermeneuticizing the Philosophical Idea of God," in *Religious Experience and the End of Metaphysics*, edited by Jeffrey Bloechl (Bloomington: Indiana University Press, 2003), 14–30. The phe-

nomenon described by Vedder is precisely what Rosenzweig resists in his affirmation of a desired new union between philosophy and theology, a desire that, in my judgment, kept him bound to the onto-theological even as he roundly criticized the metaphysics of presence, especially as it was articulated in nineteenth-century German Idealism, thereby privileging event (*Ereignis*) over essence (*Wesen*).

34. My approach is thus quite different from the Wittgensteinian reading of Rosenzweig's alleged critique of the notion of essence and the implied "absurdity of metaphysics" proffered by Hilary Putnam, "Introduction," in Rosenzweig, *Understanding the Sick and the Healthy*, 3–9. For a more extensive comparison of Rosenzweig and Wittgenstein, see Hilary Putnam, *Jewish Philosophy as a Guide to Life: Rosenzweig, Buber, Levinas, Wittgenstein* (Bloomington: Indiana University Press, 2008), 9–36. For a similar orientation, see Franks, "Everyday Speech." Compare Gordon, "Rosenzweig Redux," 29–30. For a useful discussion that sheds light on the approach of Putnam and Franks, see Henry Ruf, "The Origin of the Debate over Ontotheology and Deconstruction in the Texts of Wittgenstein and Derrida," in *Religion, Ontotheology, and Deconstruction*, edited by Henry Ruf (New York: Paragon House, 1989), 3–42.

35. Rosenzweig, "Atheistic Theology," in *Philosophical and Theological Writings*, 17.

36. Rosenzweig, "The New Thinking," 115. See also idem, *Understanding the Sick*, 66: "The world is appearance, illusion. However, it does appear to me; this is more than mere illusion. This is 'essence,' and it is concluded that the 'ego' is the essence of the world. All the wisdom of philosophy can be summed up in this sentence." Needless to say, it is precisely this reductionism that Rosenzweig opposes as the inevitable outcome of the "fallacious enterprise" of philosophical speculation: "And so the 'ego' is thwarted in its attempt to become the essence of the world; it turns out to be nothing. It is neither 'subject' nor 'object'—nothing. To justify its claims it must be nothing. The result: the essence of the world is 'nothing'; nothing is at the core of the 'world of appearance.' . . . This much philosophy understood correctly—the world must be something other than it appears to be. But this something cannot be identified with the Self" (67).

37. Mary-Jane Rubenstein, "Unknow Thyself: Apophaticism, Deconstruction, and Theology After Ontotheology," *Modern Theology* 19 (2003): 387–417. See also David Tracy, "The Post-Modern Re-Naming of God as Incomprehensible and Hidden," *Cross Currents* 50 (2000): 240–47; Richard Kearney, *The God Who May Be: A Hermeneutics of Religion* (Bloomington: Indiana University Press, 2001); Clayton Crockett, "Post-Modernism and Its Secrets: Religion without Religion," *Cross Currents* 52 (2003): 499–515; John D. Caputo, *The Weakness of God: A Theology of the Event* (Bloomington: Indiana University Press, 2006). Similar attempts have been made to base a feminist theology on the apophatic tradition. See, e.g., Ann-Marie Priest, "Woman as God, God as Woman: Mysticism, Negative Theology, and Luce Irigaray," *Journal of Religion* 83 (2003): 1–23, and Catherine Keller, *Face of the Deep: A Theology of Becoming* (London: Routledge, 2003), 200–212. For critical assessments of the endeavor to construct a negative atheology rooted in the hermeneutical principles of Derridean deconstruction, see Robert S. Gall, "Of/From Theology and Deconstruction," *Journal of the American Academy of Religion* 58 (1990): 413–37; Siebren Miedema and Gert J. J. Biesta, "Jacque Derrida's Religion Without Religion and the Im/Possibility of Religious Education," *Religious Education* 99 (2004): 23–37. The appropriation of apophasis on the part of feminist theologians is a subject that requires a careful analysis that cannot be taken up in earnest in this context. For a complex and theoretically nuanced example of this approach, see Catherine Keller, "The Apophasis of Gender: A Fourfold Unsaying of Feminist Theology," *Journal of the American Academy of Religion* 76 (2008): 905–33.

38. The following assessment of Michael P. Steinberg, *Judaism Musical and Unmusical* (Chicago: University of Chicago Press, 2007), 201, can be considered a succinct formulation of the prevailing approach to Rosenzweig: "*The Star of Redemption* attracts devotion more because of the work's renowned difficulty and esotericism than despite of these qualities. The work can be described, I would hazard, as an existential argument for the resacralization of Jewish life. In this respect, it parallels Rosenzweig's own biographical trajectory from his near conversion to Protestantism in 1913 through a rigorously deliberate agenda of reinvestiture in Jewish practice and ritual. It parallels also the desire for resacralization among present-day readers." I do not know why the author thinks his view is risky, since what he articulates confirms the standard understanding of Rosenzweig that has prevailed in the field. Compare the discussion of the "hagiographic impulse" in scholarship on Rosenzweig and the emphasis placed on his "return" to Judaism as a motivating force in the Weimar-era Jewish renaissance in Gordon, "Rosenzweig Redux," 4–17. I do not fully agree with Gordon's assessment that "the hagiographic 'aura' that once illuminated Rosenzweig's memory has now decayed, yielding scholarship less responsive to social needs but also—for that very reason perhaps—more balanced in appraisal" (24).

39. Rosenzweig introduced the notion of "pure factuality" (*reine Tatsächlichkeit*) in the "Urzelle," 67. See the extensive philological-textual discussion in n. 45 ad locum, and ibid., 69, where the "pure factuality" is described further as "something for itself," a philosophical *salto mortale* (see above, n. 17). See also Rosenzweig's 1925 essay "The New Thinking," 135: "What was put into the *Star of Redemption* was, at the beginning, the experience of factuality prior to all of actual experience's matters of fact. [The experience] of factuality that forces upon thinking, instead of its favorite word 'really,' the little word 'and,' the basic word of all experience, to which its tongue is unaccustomed." See Freund, *Franz Rosenzweig's Philosophy of Existence*, 86–87.

40. *SR*, 313 [*SE*, 328].

41. Peter E. Gordon, *Rosenzweig and Heidegger: Between Judaism and German Philosophy* (Berkeley: University of California Press, 2003), 175–77.

42. Leora Batnitzky, *Idolatry and Representation: The Philosophy of Franz Rosenzweig Reconsidered* (Princeton, N.J.: Princeton University Press, 2000), 66. On the hermeneutic of reading backwards in Rosenzweig, see also Elliot R. Wolfson, *Alef, Mem, Tau: Kabbalistic Musings on Time, Truth, and Death* (Berkeley: University of California Press 2005), 59.

43. Rosenzweig, "The New Thinking," 113. This comment is also referenced by Batnitzky, *Idolatry*, 64.

44. Rosenzweig, "The New Thinking," 134.

45. Zachary Braiterman, "Cyclical Motions and the Force of Repetition in the Thought of Franz Rosenzweig," in *Beginning/Again: Toward a Hermeneutics of Jewish Texts*, edited by Aryeh Cohen and Shaul Magid (New York: Seven Bridges Press, 2002), 215–38; idem, *Shape of Revelation*, 135–65.

46. The source that seems to have given the expression "theopoetic" the most currency in scholarly discourse is Amos N. Wilder, *Theopoetic: Theology and the Religious Imagination* (Philadelphia: Fortress Press, 1976). As Wilder recounts in the foreword (iv), he picked up the expressions "theopoetic" and "theopoesis" from Stanley Hopper and his students in discussions on hermeneutics and language that took place at Drew University and Syracuse University. I initially came across the term in Catherine Keller, *God and Power: Counter-Apocalyptic Journeys* (Minneapolis: Fortress Press, 2005), 140, 145–46, 149–52. On the utilization of this expression, note should also be made

of David L. Miller, *Hells and Holy Ghosts: A Theopoetics of Christian Belief* (Nashville, Tenn.: Abingdon Press, 1989); and idem, *Christs: Meditations on Archetypal Images in Christian Theology* (New Orleans, LA: Spring Journal Books, 2005), xviii. I thank Virginia Burrus for reminding me of these later references. Given Rosenzweig's privileging of poetry as the art form that shows the greatest affinity with the theological category of experience, I would suggest that "theopoetics" is an excellent tag to apply to his thinking.

47. For the background of this way of conceiving temporality, see Almut Sh. Bruckstein, "On Jewish Hermeneutics: Maimonides and Bachya as Vectors in Cohen's Philosophy of Origin," in *Hermann Cohen's Philosophy of Religion: International Conference in Jerusalem 1996*, edited by Stéphane Mosès and Hartwig Wiedebach (Hildensheim: Georg Olms Verlag, 1997), 35–50.

48. Rosenzweig, *Understanding the Sick*, 36.

49. Text cited in Horwitz, "From Hegelianism," 41.

50. Batnitzky, *Idolatry*, 70.

51. Green, "Notion of Truth," 297–323.

52. Rosenzweig, "The New Thinking," 117 (*Kleinere Schriften*, 379). See Reiner Wiehl, "Experience in Rosenzweig's New Thinking," in *The Philosophy of Franz Rosenzweig*, 42–68.

53. Scholem, *Messianic Idea*, 282–303.

54. Ibid., 284.

55. Ibid., 286.

56. Ibid., 287–288 (emphasis in original).

57. Ibid., 289 (emphasis in original).

58. Ibid., 289–290.

59. Ibid., 292 (emphasis added).

60. Ibid., 297.

61. Ibid., 296 (emphasis added).

62. Shigenori Nagatomo, "The Logic of the *Diamond Sutra*: A is not A, therefore it is A," *Asian Philosophy* 10 (2000): 213–44.

63. Palestinian Talmud, Berakhot 1:3, 3b; Babylonian Talmud, Eruvin 13b, Giṭṭin 6b. In the former two contexts, these words, it will be recalled, are attributed to the *bat qol*, the heavenly voice.

64. Wolfson, *Alef, Mem, Tau*, 60.

65. Ibid., 64–65.

66. Scholem, *Messianic Idea*, 303.

67. Rosenzweig, "The New Thinking," 123.

68. Rosenzweig, "The New Thinking," 131 (*Kleinere Schriften*, 391). See Wolfson, *Alef, Mem, Tau*, 50–51, and Schindler, *Zeit, Geschichte, Ewigkeit*, 81–87.

69. Rosenzweig, *SR*, 177.

70. *SR*, 191, 200.

71. On the contrast between the space of the plastic arts and the time of music, see *SR*, 263.

72. *SR*, 212.

73. *SR*, 307.

74. *SR*, 308.

75. *SR*, 306 [*SE*, 320].

76. Stéphane Mosès, *System and Revelation: The Philosophy of Franz Rosenzweig*, foreword by Emmanuel Levinas, translated by Catherine Tihanyi (Detroit, Mich.: Wayne

State University Press, 1992), 170 (emphasis in the original). A similar position was taken by Manfred H. Vogel, *Rosenzweig on Profane/Secular History* (Atlanta, Ga.: Scholars Press, 1996), 12:

> Now, according to Rosenzweig, Judaism proffers this prefiguration, presentiment, of eternity in the liturgical calendar which it instates. Namely, Rosenzweig contends that in the Jewish calendar of holy, sacred, days . . . a prefiguration of the state of eternity reflects itself. For in ever-repeating itself, year in and year out, in a prescribed order . . . the Jewish liturgical calendar transforms the linear progression of temporality into a cyclical progression; and with regard to a cyclical progression of temporality a good case can be made that it (in contra-distinction to a linear progression) can provide us with an intimation, a prefiguration, of eternity. . . . Cyclical progression is the closest that one can come to the abrogation of progression, i.e., to eternity, while still being within the progression and this clearly should allow us to conclude that Judaism in appropriating a cyclical progression in its liturgical calendar is providing us with a prefiguration of the state of Eternity.

See also Glatzer, *Franz Rosenzweig,* xxv; Catherine Chalier, "Franz Rosenzweig: Temps liturgique et temps historique," *Le Nouveaux Cahiers* 72 (1983): 28–31; Bernhard Casper, "Zeit—Erfahrung—Erlösung. Zur Bedeutung Rosenzweigs angesichts des Denkens des 20. Jahrhunderts," in *Der Philosoph Franz Rosenzweig,* 553–66; Hagai Dagan, "Hatramah and Dehikat ha-Kez in F. Rosenzweig's Concept of Redemption," *Daat* 50–52 (2003): 391–407, esp. 405–406 (Hebrew); Dana Hollander, "On the Significance of the Messianic Idea in Rosenzweig," *Cross Currents* 53 (2004): 555–65, esp. 559–61. For an alternative approach, which emphasizes a tension in Rosenzweig's messianic idea between the temporal and the eternal, the this-worldly and the other-worldly, see Gregory Kaplan, "In the End Shall Christians Become Jews and Jews, Christians? On Franz Rosenzweig's Apocalyptic Eschatology," *Cross Currents* 53 (2004): 511–29.

77. With regard to the "eternal moment," there is a conceptual affinity between Rosenzweig and both Kierkegaard and Nietzsche, as was already noted by Löwith, "F. Rosenzweig and M. Heidegger," 76–77; idem, *Nature, History, and Existentialism,* 77–78. Needless to say, the notion of temporality in Kierkegaard and Nietzsche has been examined by many scholars. For representative studies, see Karl Löwith, *Nietzsche's Philosophy of the Eternal Recurrence of the Same,* translated by J. Harvey Lomax, foreword by Bernd Magnus (Berkeley: University of California Press, 1997), and David J. Kangas, *Kierkegaard's Instant: On Beginnings* (Bloomington: Indiana University Press, 2007).

78. *SR,* 307 [*SE,* 322].

79. Galli, *Franz Rosenzweig and Jehuda Halevi,* 222–23. On the relation of eternity and time, see Galli's discussion, 462–63.

80. Levinas, foreword to Mosès, *System and Revelation,* 21.

81. Rosenzweig, "The New Thinking," 126–27 (*Kleinere Schriften,* 387).

82. Rosenzweig, *Understanding the Sick,* 79.

83. Ibid., 80: "Once again it is language which erects the visible bridge from man to that which is no man, to the 'other.' A person's name, his first name, is so external [*aüsserlich*] to him, that it is sufficient witness to the fact that there is something exterior to man, a 'without' [*Aussen*] surrounding him."

84. Levinas, foreword to Mosès, *System and Revelation,* 22 (emphasis in original). It is worthwhile here to recall the nexus between the present, presence, and relation to the other established by Martin Buber, *I and Thou,* translated, with a prologue and

notes, by Walter Kaufmann (New York: Charles Scribner's Sons, 1970), 63–64: "The present—not that which is like a point and merely designates whatever our thoughts may posit as the end of 'elapsed' time, the fiction of the fixed lapse, but the actual and fulfilled present—exists only insofar as presentness, encounter, and relation exist. Only as the You becomes present does presence come into being. . . . Presence is not what is evanescent and passes but what confronts us, waiting and enduring. . . . What is essential is lived in the present, objects in the past." In the third part of *I and Thou*, Buber develops the notion of God as the eternal Thou, an absolute presence that can never by its own nature become an it, an object subject to spatial and temporal conditionality: "Every You in the world is compelled by its nature to become a thing for us or at least to enter again and again into thinghood. . . . Only one You never ceases, in accordance with its nature to be You for us. To be sure, whoever knows God also knows God's remoteness and the agony of drought upon a frightened heart, but not the loss of presence. . . . The eternal You is You by its very nature; only *our* nature forces us to draw it into the It-world and It-speech. The It-world coheres in space and time. The You-world does not cohere in either. It coheres in the center in which the extended lines of relationships intersect: in the eternal You" (147–48, emphasis in the original).

Buber's depiction of God as the absolute presence encountered in the moment was developed, in part due to the influence of Rosenzweig, in the fifth of the eight lectures he delivered at the *Freies Jüdisches Lehrhaus* in Frankfurt between January 15 and March 12, 1922. See Rivka Horwitz, *Buber's Way to "I and Thou": An Historical Analysis and the First Publication of Martin Buber's Lectures "Religion als Gegenwart"* (Heidelberg: Verlag Lambert Schneider, 1978), 36, 107–10. On the presence of God and the relation of time and eternity, see also Buber's remarks in the seventh lecture, ibid., 131, and the relevant comments on Buber's idea of the realization of God in the ever-present moment of revelation, which is compared to Nietzsche's doctrine of "the eternal return of the same," in Paul Mendes-Flohr, *From Mysticism to Dialogue: Martin Buber's Transformation of German Social Thought* (Detroit, Mich.: Wayne State University Press, 1989), 118–19.

85. The essays included in *Le temps et l'autre* were lectures delivered in 1946–47 at the Philosophical College and then published in the 1948 collection *Le Choix-Le Monde-L'Existence.* They were reissued with a preface by Levinas under the new title in 1979. See Emmanuel Levinas, *Time and the Other,* translated by Richard A. Cohen (Pittsburgh: Duquesne University Press, 1987), 29–30.

86. Levinas, *Time and the Other,* 31–32 (emphasis in original).

87. The relation of Levinas to Husserl is a matter that has been engaged by numerous scholars from varied methodological perspectives. Here I mention three especially insightful essays by Edith Wyschogrod, "Husserl and the Problem of Ontology" in *Emmanuel Levinas: The Problem of Ethical Metaphysics,* 2nd ed. (New York: Fordham University Press, 2000), 28–55; "Intending Transcendence: Desiring God"; and "Corporeality and the Glory of the Infinite in the Philosophy of Levinas," both included in *Crossing Queries: Dwelling with Negatives, Embodying Philosophy's Others* (New York: Fordham University Press, 2006), 13–44.

88. On the relation of diachrony, alterity, and transcendence, see Levinas, *Time and the Other,* 105–109, 133–38. The number of scholars who have discussed the theme of time in the thought of Levinas is too vast to delineate in this note. For a brief analysis of the specific nexus between temporality and alterity in Rosenzweig and Levinas, see Wolfson, *Alef, Mem, Tau,* 49–54.

89. Levinas, *Time and the Other,* 137.

90. One of the boldest expositions of eternity in terms of the temporal inversion of beginning and end, emblematized more concretely by the symbol and ritual of Sabbath, is offered by Rosenzweig in a section in the last part of the *Star*, 442–43, titled "God's time" (*Gottes Zeit*). For analysis of this passage, see Wolfson, "Facing the Effaced," 56–57.

91. For a slightly different formulation of this point, see Fishbane, *Garments of Torah*, 145 n. 15.

92. *SR*, 306: "Eternity . . . must be hastened, it must always be capable of coming as early as 'today'; only through it is it eternity." And *SR*, 307: "But more is to be demanded of it . . . to hasten the future, to make eternity into the very nearest thing, into the today." Compare Levinas, *Time and the Other*, 122: "What is new is what is present—or on the point of presenting itself. The elements of experience and those of dispositions are old to the extent that they withdraw from presence, which constitutes the zero point in the scale of time: the point where what is comes to be—or is the point of being produced. The present is the future making itself present."

93. *SR*, 213 [*SE*, 221].

94. Rosenzweig, "Urzelle," 63, 65 (emphasis in original); German in *Kleinere Schriften*, 365–66, 368.

95. See Rosenzweig, "The New Thinking," 115: "All philosophy asked about 'essence.' It is by this question that it distinguishes itself from the unphilosophical thinking of healthy human understanding." The use of the term *Ereignis* in Rosenzweig calls to mind the same term in the thought of Heidegger. For a detailed analysis of this topic, see Bernhard Casper, "'Ereignis': Bemerkungen zu Franz Rosenzweig und Martin Heidegger," in *Jüdisches Denken in einer Welt ohne Gott: Festschrift für Stéphane Mosès*, edited by Jens Mattern, Gabriel Motzkin, and Shimon Sandbank (Berlin: Verlag Vorwerk 8, 2000), 67–77.

96. Rosenzweig, *Understanding the Sick*, 41–42. On Rosenzweig's critique of philosophical essentialism, see Franks, "Everyday Speech," 25–27.

97. Rosenzweig, "The New Thinking," 125.

98. Levinas, *Time and the Other*, 119.

99. On the conceptual identity of time and uncertainty, related to a nonlinear mode of thinking, attested especially in poetic writings, see the thoughtful essay by Maria L. Assad, "Time and Uncertainty: A Metaphorical Equation," in *Time and Uncertainty*, edited by Paul Harris and Michael Crawford (Leiden: Brill, 2004), 19–30.

100. *SR*, 217–18.

101. *SR*, 121. See the passage from "The New Thinking" cited above, n. 20.

102. Galli, *Franz Rosenzweig and Jehuda Halevi*, 20–21. For discussion of Halevi's poem, see Wolfson, *Through a Speculum*, 174–75.

103. Galli, *Franz Rosenzweig and Jehuda Halevi*, 187–88; Rosenzweig, *Gesammelte Schriften IV*, 28–29.

104. Myriam Bienenstock, "Recalling the Past in Rosenzweig's *Star of Redemption*," *Modern Judaism* 23 (2003): 235, noted that Rosenzweig "understood the meaning of Schelling's identity thesis—the thesis of identity between thought and being, between the *ideal* and the *real*," and consequently, "he could develop a conception of myth very close to Schelling's 'tautegory,' a conception according to which mythical representations are ideal, internal to consciousness, as well as real, external to it. A reading of the first part of *Star of Redemption* shows that for Rosenzweig too, as for Schelling, mythical representations are experienced in consciousness but also have at their basis an objectively real theogony, the history of real gods." As I argue below, it is not clear to me

that, in the final analysis, Rosenzweig was able to affirm this sense of reality external to consciousness.

105. Rosenzweig, *Understanding the Sick,* 72.

106. Fishbane, *Garments of Torah,* 106.

107. I have here reworked with slight emendation a section of my "Introduction," in Galli's translation of the *Star,* xix. The subject of time and interpretation has been the focus of many hermeneutical studies. See, for instance, David Wood, *The Deconstruction of Time* (Evanston Ill.: Northwestern University Press, 2001), 319–34.

108. *SR,* 263 [*SE,* 273].

109. *SR,* 104–105 [*SE,* 105]. See Batnitzky, *Idolatry,* 40–54, esp. 42; Santner, "Miracles Happen," 83–88. On Rosenzweig's understanding of "miracle" as a boundary concept in philosophy, see Wiehl, "Experience," 62–68.

110. *SR,* 120–21.

111. This work was published separately in Berlin in 1926. I have utilized the version included in Rosenzweig, *Die Schrift,* 51–77, the slightly edited Hebrew translation in Rosenzweig, *Naharayim,* 41–55, and the English translation included in Martin Buber and Franz Rosenzweig, *Scripture and Translation,* translated by Lawrence Rosenwald and Everett Fox (Bloomington: Indiana University Press, 1994), 47–69. For an extensive analysis of Rosenzweig's philosophy of translation, see Galli, *Franz Rosenzweig and Jehuda Halevi,* 322–59. See also the discussion of Rosenzweig's hermeneutics as a "proliferating translatability" in Wolfgang Iser, *The Range of Interpretation* (New York: Columbia University Press, 2000), 113–44; and further discussions in Dana Hollander, "Franz Rosenzweig on Nation, Translation, and Judaism," *Philosophy Today* 38 (1994): 380–89; Hans-Christoph Askani, *Das Problem der Übersetzung, dargestellt an Franz Rosenzweig* (Tübingen: Mohr Siebeck, 1997); Leora Batnitzky, *Idolatry,* 105–41; idem, "Franz Rosenzweig on Translation and Exile," *Jewish Studies Quarterly* 14 (2007): 131–43; Mara H. Benjamin, *Rosenzweig's Bible: Reinventing Scripture for Jewish Modernity* (Cambridge: Cambridge University Press, 2009), 103–34.

112. See, for instance, Martin Heidegger, *Early Greek Thinking,* translated by David Farrell Krell and Frank A. Capuzzi (New York: Harper & Row, 1975), 13–58, esp. 18–19; idem, *Parmenides,* translated by André Schuwer and Richard Rojcewicz (Bloomington: Indiana University Press, 1992), 12–13; and the extensive discussion on hermeneutics and the philosophy of translation in Miles Groth, *Translating Heidegger* (Amherst, Mass.: Humanity Books, 2204), 115–63. The affinity between Heidegger and Rosenzweig on this point has been noted by Peter E. Gordon, "Rosenzweig and Heidegger: Translation, Ontology, and the Anxiety of Affiliation," *New German Critique* 77 (1999): 113–48, and idem, *Rosenzweig and Heidegger,* 273–74.

113. Hans-Georg Gadamer, *Truth and Method* (New York: Crossroad, 1982), 345–51, and the study of John Sallis, "The Hermeneutics of Translation," in *Language and Linguisticality in Gadamer's Hermeneutics,* edited by Lawrence K. Schmidt (Lanham, Md.: Lexington Books, 2000), 67–76. On interpretation as a mode of translation, see also Iser, *Range of Interpretation,* 5–12. Batnitzky, "Rosenzweig on Translation," 141–42, contrasts the relation between speech and translation in Rosenzweig and Gadamer. According to Batnitzky, Gadamer privileges speech, whereas Rosenzweig makes translation primary. See idem, *Idolatry,* 108–9. In my assessment, Gadamer (and Heidegger as well) would have agreed with Rosenzweig's sense that all speech is "dialogic speaking and thus—translation" (*Scripture and Translation,* 47), the very assumption that makes translation both impossible and necessary. See Rosenzweig's "Afterword" to the translation of Halevi's poems in Galli, *Franz Rosenzweig and Jehuda Halevi,* 170 (original Ger-

man in Rosenzweig, *Kleinere Schriften*, 202): "Will this not be asking something impossible of language with this task to reflect the foreign tone in its foreignness [*den fremden Ton in seiner Fremdheit wiederzugeben*]: not to Germanize what is foreign, but rather to make foreign what is German [*also nicht das Fremde einzudeutschen, sondern das Deutsche umzufremden*]? Not the impossible, but rather the requisite, and the requisite not merely in translating. The creative achievement of translating can lie nowhere else than where the creative achievement of speaking itself lies."

114. Rosenzweig would have agreed with Gadamer's assertion in *Truth and Method*, 442, that the "hermeneutical experience" is "also an event of a genuine experience." The affinities and differences between Gadamer's hermeneutical approach and Rosenzweig are explored further by Batnitzky, *Idolatry*, 44–46, 69, and 71.

115. *SR*, 213 [*SE*, 221–22].

116. The transfiguration of the erotic imagery of the Song in later midrashic and poetic texts is explored by Michael Fishbane, "The Song of Songs and Ancient Jewish Religiosity: Between Eros and History," in *Von Enoch bis Kafka: Festschrift für Karl E. Grözinger zum 60. Geburtstag*, edited by Manfred Voigts (Wiesbaden: Harrassowitz Verlag, 2002), 69–81.

117. Elliot R. Wolfson, *Language, Eros, Being: Kabbalistic Hermeneutics and Poetic Imagination* (New York: Fordham University Press, 2005), 336.

118. *SR*, 217 [*SE*, 225]. To transpose the idiom more literally, I have modified Galli's translation "the essential book of Revelation." The meaning is not substantially altered. For an alternative rendering, see Hallo's translation of *Star*, 202: "the focal book of revelation." And see Inken Rühle, "Das Hohelied—ein weltliches Liebeslied als Kernbuch der Offenbraung? Zur Bedeutung der Auslegungsgeschichte von *Schir haSchirim* im *Stern der Erlosüung*," in *Rosenzweig als Leser: Kontextuelle Kommentare zum "Stern der Erlosüng*," edited by Martin Brasser (Tübingen: Max Niemeyer Verlag, 2004), 453–79.

119. Wolfson, "Facing the Effaced," 77–78. In that study, I focused on the same passage of the *Star* that I interpret again in this context. To me, it is the crucial statement to understand Rosenzweig's theopoetics. The position I have taken is intermediate between the perspective of Mosès, *System and Revelation*, 102–103, and that of Samuel Moyn, *Origins of the Other: Emmanuel Levinas between Revelation and Ethics* (Ithaca, N.Y.: Cornell University Press, 2005), 150. According to the former, Rosenzweig's portrayal of love as a metaphor for revelation implies that the analysis of God's love for the human being is "only anthropomorphic in appearance," whereas according to the latter, the reverse is true and hence "human love is metaphorical of divine love." For an elaboration of his thesis, see Samuel Moyn, "Divine and Human Love: Franz Rosenzweig's History of the Song of Songs," *Jewish Studies Quarterly* 12 (2005): 194–212. On the comparison of Rosenzweig's use of the term *Gleichnis* in his interpretation of the Song of Songs to Scholem's understanding of the kabbalistic symbol as the expression of the inexpressible, see Benjamin, *Rosenzweig's Bible*, 60-61. The author makes no mention of my previous discussion of this matter in "Facing the Effaced" or in the study cited below in n. 123.

120. *SR*, 216 [*SE*, 224].

121. Ibid. [*SE*, 224].

122. Ibid. [*SE*, 224].

123. See Elliot R. Wolfson, "Suffering Eros and Textual Incarnation: A Kristevan Reading of Kabbalistic Poetics," in *Toward a Theology of Eros: Transfiguring Passion at the Limits of Discipline*, edited by Virginia Burrus and Catherine Keller (New York: Fordham University Press, 2006), 342–43, 346–53. See also Rühle, "Das Hohelied," 472–78.

Worthy of recollection here is the discussion of lyric poetry as the most suitable expression of the human love of God, in Hermann Cohen, *Religion of Reason Out of the Sources of Judaism*, translated by Simon Kaplan (Atlanta, Ga.: Scholars Press, 1995), 373–74. It is reasonable to assume that the reading of the erotic metaphors in the Song proffered by Rosenzweig reflects the discussion of Cohen, though the matter requires a more sustained reflection than I can offer here. See the discussion of lyric poetry and prayer in Andrea Poma, *Yearning for Form and Other Essays on Hermann Cohen's Thought* (Dordrecht: Springer, 2006), 227–41. Finally, I would add that Rosenzweig's perspective, if I have understood it properly, seems to me very close to the observation of Gadamer regarding the reformation of intuition through metaphor in his essay "Intuition and Vividness," translated by Dan Tate, in Hans-Georg Gadamer, *The Relevance of the Beautiful and Other Essays*, edited with an introduction by Robert Bernasconi (Cambridge: Cambridge University Press, 1986), 169–70: "For the theory of metaphor, Kant's remark in Section 59 [of the *Critique of Judgment*] seems to me most profound: that metaphor at bottom makes no comparison of content, but rather undertakes the 'transference of reflection upon an object of intuition to a quite different concept to which perhaps an intuition can never directly correspond.' Does not the poet do that with every word? The poet suspends every direct correspondence and thereby awakens intuition." See below, n. 134.

124. Franz Rosenzweig, "Das Älteste Systemprogramm des deutschen Idealismus: Ein handschriftlicher Fund," in *Kleinere Schriften*, 230–77, esp. 252–57; and compare Ernest Rubinstein, *An Episode of Jewish Romanticism: Franz Rosenzweig's* The Star of Redemption (Albany: SUNY Press, 1999), 221–22; Gordon, *Rosenzweig and Heidegger*, 126–29. For discussion of the intellectual background of Schelling on this point, see Theodore D. George, "A Monstrous Absolute: Schelling, Kant, and the Poetic Turn in Philosophy," in *Schelling Now: Contemporary Readings*, edited by Jason M. Wirth (Bloomington: Indiana University Press, 2005), 135–46. Many have discussed Rosenzweig's indebtedness to Schelling, and here I offer a highly select enumeration of some of the relevant sources: Moshe Schwarcz, *From Myth to Revelation* (Tel-Aviv: Ha-Kibbutz ha-Meyuhad, 1978; Hebrew); Freund, *Franz Rosenzweig's Philosophy of Existence*; Wolfdietrich Schmied-Kowarzik, "Vom Totalexperiment des Glaubens. Kritisches zur positive Philosophie Schellings und Rosenzweigs," in *Der Philosoph Franz Rosenzweig*, 771–99; Robert Gibbs, "The Limits of Thought: Rosenzweig, Schelling, and Cohen," *Zeitschrift für Philosophische Forschung* 43 (1989): 618–40; Rubinstein, *An Episode of Jewish Romanticism*; Benny Lévy, "Philosophie de la Révélation? Schelling, Rosenzweig, Levinas," *Cahiers d'Études Lévinassinnes* 2 (2003): 283–383; Bienenstock, "'Recalling the Past," 234–37; idem, "Auf Schellings Spuren im Stern der Erlösung," in *Rosenzweig als Leser*, 273–90; Schindler, *Zeit, Geschichte, Ewigkeit*, 229–46.

125. *SR*, 348–49, and see analysis in William Kluback, "Time and History: The Conflict Between Hermann Cohen and Franz Rosenzweig," in *Der Philosoph Franz Rosenzweig*, 801–13; Von Ulrich Hortian, "Zeit und Geschichte bei Franz Rosenzweig und Walter Benjamin," in *Der Philosoph Franz Rosenzweig*, 815–27, esp. 819–20; Wolfson, "Facing the Effaced," 60–61.

126. *SR*, 206. Here it is also pertinent to recall Rosenzweig's description in the outline for a series of lectures at the Berlin Lehrhaus (delivered from January-March 1921) on the ritual life of Judaism as "wholly artwork" (*ganz Kuntswerk*), cited by Batnitzky, "Rosenzweig on Translation," 137. See also Angel E. Garrido-Maturano, "Die Erfüllung der Kunst im Schweigen: Bemerkungen zu Franz Rosenzweigs Theorie der Kunst," in *Théologie Négative*, edited by Marco M. Olivetti (Milan: CEDAM, 2002), 695–720, esp. 706–9.

127. *SR*, 263 [*SE*, 273]. On the link between the Jewish national spirit, the art of music, and the sense of time, see the comments of Martin Buber in his 1911 essay "Renewal of Judaism," in *On Judaism*, edited by Nahum N. Glatzer (New York: Schocken Books, 1967), 49.

128. On the notion of Jewish *Unheimlichkeit* in Rosenzweig's thinking, see Leora Batnitzky, "Rosenzweig's Aesthetic Theory and Jewish Unheimlichkeit," *New German Critique* 77 (1999): 87–122; idem, "Rosenzweig on Translation," 138–41. For an analysis of the broader cultural context of this image, see Susan Shapiro, "The Uncanny Jew: A Brief History of an Image," *Judaism* 46 (1997): 63–78. Eric L. Santner, *On the Psychotheology of Everyday Life: Reflections on Freud and Rosenzweig* (Chicago: University of Chicago Press, 2001), 5–8, 23–24, notes the matter of the *Unheimlichkeit* in Rosenzweig in more general terms with respect to the sense of the uncanny, the impenetrability of the other, that is internal to any construction of identity.

129. *SR*, 319 [*SE*, 333].

130. Alexander Altmann, "Franz Rosenzweig on History," in *Between East and West: Essays Dedicated to the Memory of Bela Horovitz*, edited by Alexander Altmann (London: East and West Library, 1958), 194–214, reprinted in *The Philosophy of Franz Rosenzweig*, 124–37. See also Glatzer, *Franz Rosenzweig*, xxv; Paul Mendes-Flohr, "Franz Rosenzweig and the Crisis of Historicism," in *Philosophy of Franz Rosenzweig*, 138–61; Steven T. Katz, "On Historicism and Eternity: Reflections on the 100th Birthday of Franz Rosenzweig," in *Der Philosoph Franz Rosenzweig*, 745–69; Amos Funkenstein, "An Escape from History: Rosenzweig on the Destiny of Judaism," *History and Memory* 2 (1990): 117–35; Vogel, *Rosenzweig on Profane/Secular History*; Wolfson, "Facing the Effaced," 55–63; Gordon, "Rosenzweig Redux," 18; David N. Myers, *Resisting History: Historicism and Its Discontents in German-Jewish Thought* (Princeton, N.J.: Princeton University Press, 2003), 68–101.

131. Galli, *Franz Rosenzweig and Jehuda Halevi*, 177 (*Kleinere Schriften*, 210).

132. Ibid.

133. Heidegger, *Early Greek Thinking*, 19. Needless to say, the bibliography on Heidegger's poetics is extensive. Here I mention only a modest number of relevant studies: Walter Biemel, "Poetry and Language in Heidegger," in *On Heidegger and Language*, edited and translated by Joseph J. Kockelmans (Evanston, Ill.: Northwestern University Press, 1972), 65–105; Véronique M. Fóti, *Heidegger and the Poets: Poiēsis/Sophia/Technē* (Atlantic Highlands, N.J.: Humanities Press, 1992); Krzysztof Ziarek, *Inflected Language: Toward a Hermeneutics of Nearness: Heidegger, Levinas, Stevens, Celan* (Albany: SUNY Press, 1994), 21–42; Marc Froment-Meurice, *That Is to Say: Heidegger's Poetics*, translated by Jan Plu (Stanford, Calif.: Stanford University Press, 1998); Jennifer Anna Gosetti-Ferencei, *Heidegger, Hölderin, and the Subject of Poetic Language: Towards a New Poetics of Dasein* (New York: Fordham University Press, 2004); and see my own discussion in *Language, Eros, Being*, 17–25, and the accompanying notes on 412–19.

134. Gordon, *Rosenzweig and Heidegger*, 130–31. Rosenzweig's views on poetry can also be compared effectively to the reflections of Gadamer on this matter. For a useful analysis of the latter, see Gerald L. Bruns, "The Remembrance of Language: An Introduction to Gadamer's Poetics," in Hans-Georg Gadamer, *Gadamer on Celan: "Who Am I and Who Are You?" and Other Essays*, translated and edited by Richard Heinemann and Bruce Krajewski (Albany: SUNY Press, 1997), 1–51.

135. As is well known, in a brief note dictated from his deathbed, which was occasioned by the second edition of Hermann Cohen's *Religion der Vernunft aus den Quellen des Judentums*, but which also included his reflections on the confrontation that took place in Davos, Switzerland, between Ernst Cassirer and Martin Heidegger (based on

the report by Hermann Herrigel in the *Frankfurter Zeitung* of April 22, 1929), Rosenzweig noted some similarities between Heidegger's thought and Cohen's theory of correlation as well as his own new thinking. The text, "Vertauschte Fronten," written in May 1929, was first published in *Der Morgen* 6, no. 6 (April 1930): 85–87, reprinted in *Kleinere Schriften*, 354–56, and again in Franz Rosenzweig, *Der Mensch und sein Werk: Gesammelte Schriften III. Zweistromland: Kleinere Schriften zu Glauben und Denken*, edited by Reinhold and Annemarie Mayer (Dordrecht: Martinus Nijhoff, 1984), 323–26. An English translation, "Transposed Fronts," appears in *Philosophical and Theological Writings*, 146–52. For further discussion, see Freund, *Franz Rosenzweig's Philosophy of Existence*, 78; Steven S. Schwarzschild, "Franz Rosenzweig and Martin Heidegger: The German and the Jewish Turn to Ethnicism," in *Der Philosoph Franz Rosenzweig*, 887–89; Gordon, "Rosenzweig and Heidegger," 113–14; idem, *Rosenzweig and Heidegger*, 275–304; Moyn, *Origins*, 114–15.

As could have been expected, Gordon's book has commanded a fair amount of critical assessment, since it is the first major monograph on the topic, though important observations regarding the intellectual kinship and difference between Heidegger and Rosenzweig have been made by previous scholars, for instance, Löwith, "F. Rosenzweig and M. Heidegger," 53–77, and idem, *Nature, History, and Existentialism*, 51–78; Freund, *Franz Rosenzweig's Philosophy of Existence*, 7–8, 89, 132, 146; Alan Udoff, "Rosenzweig's Heidegger Reception and the re-Origination of Jewish Thinking," in *Der Philosoph Franz Rosenzweig*, 923–50. For some reviews of Gordon, see Charles R. Bambach, "Athens and Jerusalem: Rosenzweig, Heidegger, and the Search for an Origin," *History and Theory* 44 (2005): 271–88; Martin Ritter, "Peter Eli Gordon, *Rosenzweig and Heidegger: Between Judaism and German Philosophy* (2003)," *Hebraic Political Studies* 1 (2006): 238–48; the "Review Forum" (with contributions by Paul Franks, Samuel Moyn, Bettina Bergo, and a response by Gordon), *Jewish Quarterly Review* 96 (2006): 387–422; Nitzan Lebovic, "Review of Peter Eli Gordon, *Rosenzweig and Heidegger: Between Judaism and German Philosophy*," *H-German, H-Net Reviews in the Humanities and Social Sciences* (June 2006), available at www.hnet.msu.edu/reviews; Gregory Kaplan, "Review of Peter Eli Gordon, *Rosenzweig and Heidegger: Between Judaism and German Philosophy*," *Studies in Contemporary Judaism* 22 (2008): 319–23.

136. For discussion of this Heideggerian theme, with citation of relevant sources, see Wolfson, *Alef, Mem, Tau*, 42–46. It is worthwhile considering the following comment of Rosenzweig, in *Understanding the Sick*, 74, in light of the Heideggerian orientation toward language, being, and human existence:

> The world is real only insofar as it enters into this process, a process which brings all of it within the context of the human word and God's sentence. The world as such does not exist. To speak of the world is to speak of a world which is ours and God's. It becomes the world as it becomes man's and God's world. Every word spoken within its confines furthers this end. This is the ultimate secret of the world. Or rather, this would be its ultimate secret, if there were anything secret. But common sense blurts out this secret every day. . . . We face the world each day innocently and fearlessly, considering it as the ultimate that it is; we confront all of its reality, willing to submit to each name. We are certain that our names are the names of things and that the name we bestow will be confirmed by God.

Heidegger would have rejected the onto-theological tenor of Rosenzweig's account, but there is a basic affinity between the two thinkers with regard to the positing of a world that is independent of and yet only realized through the human act of naming.

On the affinities between Rosenzweig and Heidegger related to the poetic nature of thought and its inflection in language, see Glatzer, *Franz Rosenzweig*, xxvi; Yudit Kornberg Greenberg, "Martin Heidegger and Franz Rosenzweig on the Limits of Language and Poetry," *History of European Ideas* 20 (1993): 791–800; idem, *Better Than Wine: Love, Poetry, and Prayer in the Thought of Franz Rosenzweig* (Atlanta, Ga.: Scholars Press, 1996), 52–56. With respect to the nexus between language and being, we can detect a similarity in the *Sprachdenken* affirmed respectively by Heidegger and Rosenzweig, on the one hand, and the kabbalah, on the other hand. See Wolfson, *Language, Eros, Being*, 10–25. It is of interest to recall here the observation of Scholem, "Franz Rosenzweig and His Book," 25, that "in his comments both on language and on time-bound thought, Rosenzweig is in very close agreement with the disdained Kabbalah." My student, Dirk Hartwig, has recently drawn my attention to the monograph of Johanna Junk, *Metapher und Sprachmagie, Heidegger und die Kabbala: Eine philosophische Untersuchung* (Bodenheim: Syndikat Buchgesellschaft, 1998). Even though the author does not engage the kabbalistic texts independently, many of the conclusions she reached, as well her interpretive strategies (including a comparative analysis of Heidegger and Wittgenstein), are corroborated by my own work.

137. See, for instance, Martin Heidegger, *Poetry, Language, Thought*, translated by Albert Hofstadter (New York: Harper & Row, 1971), 92.

138. Martin Heidegger, *On the Way to Language*, translated by Peter D. Hertz (San Francisco: Harper & Row, 1971), 123, and see analysis and citation of other relevant sources in Wolfson, *Language, Eros, Being*, 14–17.

139. *SR*, 263 [*SE*, 273].

140. Ibid.

141. Galli, *Franz Rosenzweig and Jehuda Halevi*, 340: "Only through the creative spirit can and do past, present, and future find for themselves a certain mutuality. Eternity *and* time, that is, the oneness of eternality and the plurality of the tenses, interconnect and are bridged by the creative spirit." See above, n. 78.

142. *SR*, 263 [*SE*, 273].

143. *SR*, 313 [*SE*, 328].

144. Ibid.

145. This obvious point was made explicitly by Cohen, *Religion of Reason*, 73–74. See also the more extensive discussion of religion as idolatry and negative theology in the fourth chapter of Hermann Cohen, *Ethics of Maimonides*, translated with commentary by Almut Sh. Bruckstein (Madison: University of Wisconsin Press, 2004), 77–105.

146. Rosenzweig offers a terse summary of his view of the messianic future in the commentary to Judah Halevi's poem *yashen we-libbo er*, which he renders as *Auf*, "No longer a dialogue . . . but only one is still speaking, the One. Thus no longer present tense, but rather future, no longer drama, but rather vision" (Galli, *Franz Rosenzweig and Jehuda Halevi*, 258).

147. *SR*, 440.

148. Ibid.

149. Ibid., 123–24 [*SE*, 124–25]. See Luca Bertolino, "'Schöpfung aus Nichts' in Franz Rosenzweigs Stern der Erlösung," *Jewish Studies Quarterly* 13 (2006): 247–64, esp. 260–62; Schindler, *Zeit, Geschichte, Ewigkeit*, 154–61, esp. 157–58.

150. *SR*, 196 [*SE*, 203].

151. Richard A. Cohen, *Elevations: The Height of the Good in Rosenzweig and Levinas* (Chicago: University of Chicago Press, 1994), 241–73; Kornberg Greenberg, *Better Than Wine*, 113–18; Wolfson, "Facing the Effaced," 74–76; Horwitz, "From Hegelianism," 45–46.

152. Rosenzweig, "The New Thinking," 136 (*Kleinere Schriften*, 397).

153. *SR*, 441 [*SE*, 465].

154. Ibid.

155. Rosenzweig, "The New Thinking," 136 (*Kleinere Schriften*, 396).

156. *SR*, 31 [*SE*, 25]. See above, n. 15, and the citation below in n. 225.

157. In this regard, it is of interest to note the view of Arthur H. Armstrong, *Plotinian and Christian Studies* (London: Variorum Reprints, 1970), 185–88, that apophatic theology and moderate skepticism were two closely aligned trends of thinking that emerged from Platonism. For citation and analysis of some of the relevant texts, see John P. Kenney, "The Critical Value of Negative Theology," *Harvard Theological Review* 86 (1993): 441–43.

158. *SR*, 196.

159. Regarding this subject, see Shlomo Pines, "Islam According to *The Star of Redemption:* Toward a Study of Franz Rosenzweig's Sources and Biases," *Bar-Ilan Yearbook* 22–23 (1987–88): 303–14 (Hebrew), and the German version, "Der Islam im 'Stern der Erlösung'. Eine Untersuchung zu Tendenzen und Quellen Franz Rosenzweigs," *Hebräische Beiträge zur Wissenschaft des Judentums* 3–5 (1987–89): 138–48; Gil Anidjar, *The Jew, the Arab: A History of the Enemy* (Stanford, Calif.: Stanford University Press, 2003), 87–98; Yossef Schwartz, "Die Entfremdete Nähe: Rosenzweigs Blick auf den Islam," in *Franz Rosenzweig "Innerlich Bleibt die Welt Eine": Ausgewählte zum Islam*, edited by Gesine Palmer and Yossef Schwartz (Berlin: Philo, 2003), 113–47.

160. Jacques Derrida, *On the Name*, edited by Thomas Dutoit, translated by David Wood, John P. Leavey Jr., and Ian McLeod (Stanford, Calif.: Stanford University Press, 1995), 36. See also idem, "How to Avoid Speaking: Denials," in *Derrida and Negative Theology*, edited by Howard Coward and Toby Foshay (Albany: SUNY Press, 1992), 73–142. The bibliography on Derridean deconstruction and the apophatic orientation is quite extensive. I will mention here only a sampling of available scholarly treatments: Kevin Hart, *The Trespass of the Sign: Deconstruction, Theology, and Philosophy* (Cambridge: Cambridge University Press, 1989), 183–94; Toby Foshay, "Introduction: Denegation and Resentment," in *Derrida and Negative Theology*, 1–24; David E. Klemm, "Open Secrets: Derrida and Negative Theology," in *Negation and Theology*, edited by Robert P. Scharlemann (Charlottesville: University Press of Virginia, 1992), 8–24; Mark C. Taylor, *Nots* (Chicago: University of Chicago, 1993), 33–39, 46–50; Martin C. Srajek, *In the Margins of Deconstruction: Jewish Conceptions of Ethics in Emmanuel Levinas and Jacques Derrida* (Dordrecht: Kluwer Academic Publishers, 1997), 214–33, 255–57; Shira Wolosky, "An 'Other' Negative Theology: On Derrida's 'How To Avoid Speaking: Denials'," *Poetics Today* 19 (1998): 261–80; Jean-Luc Marion, "In the Name: How To Avoid Speaking of 'Negative Theology,'" in *God, the Gift, and Postmodernism*, edited by John D. Caputo and Michael J. Scanlon (Bloomington: Indiana University Press, 1999), 20–53; Hent de Vries, *Philosophy and the Turn to Religion* (Baltimore: John Hopkins University Press, 1999), 305–58; idem, "The Theology of the Sign and the Sign of Theology: The Apophatics of Deconstruction," in *Flight of the Gods*, 166–94; Ilse N. Bulhof, "Being Open as a Form of Negative Theology: On Nominalism, Negative Theology, and Derrida's Performative Interpretation of Khôra," op. cit., 195–222; John D. Caputo, *The Prayers and Tears of Jacques Derrida: Religion without Religion* (Bloomington: Indiana University Press, 1997), 1–68; idem, "Shedding Tears Beyond Being: Derrida's Experience of Prayer," in *Théologie Négative*, 861–80; Rubenstein, "Unknow Thyself"; Dirk Westerkamp, *Via Negativa: Sprache und Methode der negativen Theologie* (Munich: Wilhelm Fink Verlag, 2006), 200–209; Anslem K. Min, "Naming the Unnameable God: Levinas, Derrida, and Marion," *International Journal for Philosophy of Religion* 60 (2006): 99–116.

161. Martin Heidegger, *The Principle of Reason*, translated by Reginald Lilly (Bloomington: Indiana University Press, 1992), 35.

162. Derrida, *On the Name,* 36. Here it is of interest to recall the observation of Jean-Luc Nancy, *Dis-Enclosure: The Deconstruction of Christianity,* translated by Bettina Bego, Gabriel Malenfant, and Michael B. Smith (New York: Fordham University Press, 2008), 15, that "the unique *thēos,* deprived of appearance [*figure*] and name, really represents an invention, even the invention of 'god' in general. There is neither 'the god' nor 'the divine,' not even perhaps 'the gods': these do not come first or, again, they do not quite exist so long as there are people or the species of immortal figures. . . . We must therefore suppose that the invention of 'atheism' is contemporaneous and correlative with the invention of 'theism.' Both terms, in effect, have their unity in the principal paradigm or premise [*paradigme principiel*]."

163. *SR,* 314–15. One should also bear in mind here the well-known remark of Rosenzweig in his commentary to Judah Halevi's poem *yonat reḥoqim naggeni heṭivi,* which he renders as *Die Frohe Botschaft:* "For the expectation of the Messiah, by which and for the sake of which Judaism lives, would be an empty theologoumenon, a mere 'idea,' idle babble—if it were not over and over again made real and unreal, illusion and disillusion in the form of 'the false Messiah.' The false Messiah is as old as the hope of the genuine one. He is the changing form of the enduring hope" (Galli, *Franz Rosenzweig and Jehuda Halevi,* 259).

164. *SR,* 31 [*SE,* 25].

165. Ibid. [*SE,* 25–26].

166. Cohen, *Ethics of Maimonides,* 83.

167. Ibid., 85. See also *Reason and Hope,* 178, and discussion in Michael Zank, *The Idea of Atonement in the Philosophy of Hermann Cohen* (Providence, R.I.: Brown Judaic Studies, 2000), 354–55.

168. Cohen, *Ethics of Maimonides,* 85–86: "Nicholas of Cusa could afford to play with the ambiguities of pantheism in a daring and meaningful fashion since he could use them to expound the mystery of the trinity. In contrast, Maimonides guards himself against the serpent of pantheism, although he is not disinclined toward the enchantment of neo-Platonism." And see Cohen's summation on 98–99:

> As a result of all these reflections, we may conclude that the negative attributes, of which Maimonides could avail himself, must inevitably take as their premise and prerequisite the privative attributes, in so far as we relate them to God. . . . Instead of saying that Maimonides advocates the doctrine of negative attributes, we ought to say that he admits only those negative attributes that imply the negation of a privative attribute. Maimonides proposes by no means merely a *docta ignorantia.* . . . He is not even ultimately concerned only with the unknowability of God's essence. Rather, by multiplying negations, Maimonides promotes the true, seminal (ethical) cognition of God. . . . Jewish philosophy prior to Maimonides had followed the path indicated by the neo-Platonists who had advocated the doctrine of negative attributes. . . . Maimonides' criticism, however, expresses itself more pointedly and more radically. He puts forward his critique even at the risk of exposing himself to the suspicion of dispensing with the knowledge of God and of depriving it of all content. Why does he commit himself to this course and why did he feel impelled to do so? We know the focus of his thinking: it lies in ethics. Consequently, he has to negate, concerning the content of Knowing God, anything based upon privation . . . in that it creates a link between God and something else by analogy or through any other relationship. . . . Maimonides relates God exclusively to ethics. Hence the only admissible divine attributes are attributes of action.

While I appreciate the motivation for Cohen to forge an intrinsic connection between the Maimonidean *via negativa* and ethics, such that the grounding of the ethical rests on a lack of knowledge of the divine that facilitates the functioning of goodness as the transcendental limit (ibid., 102), I am not convinced of the soundness or accuracy of this interpretation, either textually or conceptually, but this is a matter that cannot be pursued here. On the approach of Maimonides to the problem of the negative attribution, see the discussion in Cohen, *Religion of Reason,* 61–66.

169. Cohen, *Ethics of Maimonides,* 86–87: "Let us recall, however, how even Plato formulates his idea of the Good in seemingly negative terms as non-foundation. . . . I would venture to propose that in similar fashion, Maimonides by no means conceives of the negative attributes in a purely negative vein, but rather relates them to infinite judgment, which only apparently takes on the form of negation in that its formulation employs a negating principle."

170. Ibid., 88: "Hence, Maimonides was able to find in Plato as well as in neo-Platonism the point of departure and support for developing his own fundamental doctrine of Knowing God: it is not through negation, but rather through a negation that is only apparent, that we attain a true and fast affirmation of God." See Bruckstein, "On Jewish Hermeneutics," 42–46. On Rosenzweig's indebtedness to Cohen in this matter of the nothing and the principle of the origin (*Ursprung*), see the comments of Bruckstein, op. cit., 88–89, 102. See, however, Ernest Rubinstein, *An Episode of Jewish Romanticism,* 186. The author notes the influence of Cohen on Rosenzweig's attempt to philosophize anew from the standpoint of the particular Naught, but he also emphasizes that the deduction of reality from nothing is not the latter's own project. See also Westerkamp, *Via Negativa,* 188–91.

171. *SR*, 31–32.

172. Ibid., 32.

173. Consider the observation of Armstrong, *Plotinian and Christian Studies,* 185, that negative theology consists "in a critical negation of all affirmations which one can make about God, followed by an equally critical negation of our negations." The comment is cited by Kenney, "Critical Value," 440. After finishing this study, I happened upon the essay by William Franke, "Franz Rosenzweig and the Emergence of a Post-secular Philosophy of the Unsayable," *International Journal for Philosophy of Religion* 58 (2005): 161–80. While we approach the subject from different angles, there is a fundamental agreement with regard to Rosenzweig's embrace of an apophatic logic or grammar (169), according to which any form of discourse is a linguistic delimitation of an infinitely unsayable ground. My own thesis accords with the following observations of Franke:

> Because language remains conversant with the nothing of its elements, a linguistic thinking is able to keep in view, peripherally at least, the Nothing underlying every revelation, every articulation of being and essence. From beyond all manner of verbal determinations, in which our experience consists, language can recall and call forth the unrepresentable, unsayable sea of Nothing on which it surfs and skims. Only this skipping and skidding of language demarcates temporally the eternal abyss of nothing—that is, nothing sayable—which is otherwise imperceptible, giving it positive inflections by delimitation and qualification. . . . To know nothing of God is a way of being in relation to the whole of life and existence as infinite and unknowable. . . . This unknowing is far more vital and potent than any positive knowing—in fact, all positive knowing is contained proleptically therein and can only be a working out and an articulating of a relation to some virtual wholeness

that is as such unsayable. . . . For Rosenzweig, knowledge and its articulation in language, the whole intricate network of mutual relations and disclosure of things, is a veiling of the separate, unspeakable reality of each of his
elements—God, World, Man—which are *not* as such, all one, *not* any All. In
the relations of Creation, Revelation, and Redemption, these elements are
disclosed and articulated in relation to one another, but in themselves they
remain pure enigma, each an ineffable mystery that no concept can grasp
(170–172, emphasis in the original).

I concur as well with Franke's conclusion that Rosenzweig "effectively gives a philosophical rationale for the sorts of theosophies that have traditionally been overtly
apophatic in purport and intent," though I would, however, respectfully disagree with
the statement that "Rosenzweig does not present his philosophy expressly as apophatic" (177). My own analysis herein argues, to the contrary, that apophasis is the
key to understanding how Rosenzweig presented his thought. To be sure, in consonance with this philosophical orientation, the explicit articulation is concomitantly a
saying and an unsaying.

    174. *SR*, 32 [*SE*, 26].

    175. Peter E. Gordon, "Science, Finitude, and Infinity: Neo-Kantianism and the
Birth of Existentialism," *Jewish Social Studies* 6 (1999): 3053; Moyn, *Origins*, 145; Schindler, *Zeit, Geschichte, Ewigkeit*, 132–35.

    176. Cohen, *Religion of Reason*, 66.

    177. Martin Kavka, *Jewish Messianism and the History of Philosophy* (Cambridge:
Cambridge University Press, 2004), 135–36.

    178. As cited in Horwitz, "From Hegelianism," 40.

    179. Ibid.

    180. Moshe Idel, "Rosenzweig and the Kabbalah," 166–67. Horwitz, "From Hege-
lianism," 37–38, notes this passage and refers to Idel's work, but she still suggests that
Rosenzweig was not familiar with the Lurianic teaching at the time that he composed
the *Star*.

    181. Rosenzweig, *Philosophical and Theological Writings*, 56–57. I have made use of
the version of the original German in *Kleinere Schriften*, 360. For discussion of this passage, see also Schindler, *Zeit, Geschichte, Ewigkeit*, 232–33.

    182. Wolfson, *Alef, Mem, Tau*, 119–22. On Heidegger, Rosenzweig, and the kab-
balah, see above, n. 136.

    183. Freund, *Franz Rosenzweig's Philosophy of Existence*, 89, asserts that the Nought
affirmed by Rosenzweig is "completely different" from "the Nought of which Martin
Heidegger speaks. . . . Heidegger's Nought also is not a formal one; it signifies an absolute, real Nought, a *nihil absolutum*, that one can also perceive as death. The state of
being contained within this Nought is called existence. . . . In the case of Rosenzweig,
however, the Nought with which the construction begins comes into action only when
the consciousness of being is already well established. It is placed before this being that
precedes thought merely hypothetically in order to make possible the conceptual, constructive re-creation of the experienced threefold being. . . . If the Nought of Heidegger
is an extra-conceptual, non-rational Nought, then the Nought of Rosenzweig is a conceived Nought that is not purely formal only because of the devaluation of thinking itself." In the case of Rosenzweig, insofar as "thinking is subordinate to the factuality
that is prior to thinking," the Nought is conceived as Nought on the basis of something
experienced, and it is therefore "differential." Freund does admit, however, that only
"when faith negates thinking as a whole, does the Nought of Rosenzweig also assume

LIGHT DOES NOT TALK BUT SHINES 145

the features of a real Nought, a 'dark depth,' by which it them moves nearer to the Nought of Heidegger." In my judgment, the concluding sentence is crucial, and I concur that Rosenzweig ends up in a position that is very close to Heidegger, and both of them can be viewed as creative interpreters of Schelling.

184. *SR*, 27.
185. Ibid., 124 [*SE*, 125].
186. Ibid., 126 [*SE*, 128].
187. Ibid., 126–127 [*SE*, 128].
188. Ibid., 124.
189. Wolfson, *Alef, Mem, Tau*, 59.
190. *SR*, 124 [*SE*, 125].
191. Rosenzweig, "The New Thinking," 114–15.
192. *SR*, 411.
193. Ibid., 411 [*SE*, 432].
194. Ibid.
195. Ibid, 411–12 [*SE*, 433].
196. Kavka, *Jewish Messianism*, 14, and the elaboration of the argument on 135–57.
197. *SR*, 412.
198. Ibid.
199. Ibid., 255. Aaron W. Hughes, *The Art of Dialogue in Jewish Philosophy* (Bloomington: Indiana University Press, 2008), 173–74, correctly notes that, for Rosenzweig, the dialogic gives way to silence, but that silence, paradoxically, can only be glimpsed from the vantage point of anticipation, which requires speech for its articulation. Instead of thinking of silence and language as binary oppositions, we should think of language that "both speaks and unspeaks, says and unsays." At the "heart of Rosenzweig's thought," therefore, is the "anticipation of language for speaking" that is, at the same time, "a silence that articulates." A similar sentiment was expressed by Kornberg Greenberg, *Better Than Wine*, 63, when she noted that, in contrast to Heidegger and Levinas, "for Rosenzweig, silence is a great moment of bliss. This moment is in the realm of linguistic *manifestation* rather than in the sphere of concealment" (emphasis in the original). See also Franke, "Franz Rosenzweig," 175: "The only articulable, systematizable knowledge is knowledge of what is *not* man, *not* world, *not* God, for these elements are all in their own nature unknowable. To this extent, everything within the purview of language and revelation is but a reference to what is not . . . every determination in language is but a delimitation of something that exceeds language" (emphasis in the original).
200. *SR*, 309.
201. Ibid., 412.
202. See above, n. 94.
203. Wolfson, *Alef, Mem, Tau*, 74, 76, 92, 93, 108, 109, and the corresponding notes for references to primary sources.
204. Rosenzweig, "The New Thinking," 136.
205. *SR*, 412–13.
206. Ibid.
207. Ibid., 29.
208. Ibid., 413.
209. From my poem that Galli included in the "Translator's Acknowledgments" in *SR*, x.
210. For a more hopeful assessment of this possibility, see Ilse N. Bulhof, "Negative Theology as Spirituality: Deep Openness," in *Théologie Négative*, 423–41.

211. See, however, Franke, "Franz Rosenzweig," 174–75:

> Negative Theology claims no positive knowledge of God, but it does so in
> order to free the relation to God from all the pretences of finite concepts so as
> to all the inconceivable *reality or irreality* of divinity to be fully experienced, or
> at least sensed, in unknowing. This is essentially what Rosenzweig's whole
> philosophy does. In positioning himself against a certain narrow formula-
> tion of negative theology, Rosenzweig is actually renovating the deeper in-
> sight of apophatic thinking in all ages. His thinking opens upon what can-
> not be said and makes that the basis for all that is in any way affirmed. . . .
> It is a knowing of the nothingness of our knowledge, but this itself opens to
> a revelation of the positive relatedness of all things, of their forming an All,
> after all—albeit an All that cannot be said, one that can be grasped by nei-
> ther thought nor word (emphasis added).

There is much in this statement that overlaps with my own analysis, but there is
one critical difference. Franke does not seem to appreciate the extent to which this
apophatic turn challenges the theistic faith that Rosenzweig sought to affirm against
the prevalent atheistic theologies of his day. From that standpoint, it is not sufficient to
speak of the "inconceivable reality or irreality of divinity to be fully experienced," nor
is it satisfactory to depict revelation as an opening to the All that is beyond reason and
language. What is lost is the personal God of the Jewish tradition. I concur that Rosenzweig's thought does renovate the "deeper insight of apophatic thinking," but it is important to understand how this conflicts with his own stated goal vis-à-vis the liturgical and ritual demands of Judaism.

212. Rosenzweig, "The New Thinking," 131 (*Kleinere Schriften,* 391–92).

213. Ibid., 132 (*Kleinere Schriften,* 392).

214. Derrida, *On the Name,* 52.

215. Jacques Derrida, "A Number of Yes (Nombre de Oui)," in *Deconstruction: A
Reader,* edited by Martin McQuillan (New York: Routledge, 2000), 100–101. I thank
Gregory Kaplan for drawing this essay to my attention.

216. See above, n. 197.

217. François Nault, "Le Discours de la doublure: Nietzsche et la théologie négative," *Religiogiques* 12 (1995): 273–94.

218. Based on Rosenzweig's account of revelation in his commentary to Halevi's
poem *ye'iruni be-shimkha ra'ayoni,* rendered as *Nachts,* which I will cite in full: "God reveals in revelation always only just this—revelation. In other words, he reveals always
only Himself to the human, to the human only. The accusative and dative in its union
is the peculiar content of revelation. Whatever does not follow immediately from this
bond established here between God and human, whatever cannot verify its unmedi-
atedness to this bond, does not belong to it. The problem has not been solved for the
seer of the vision, but rather—it moves into the past. The miracle does not astonish
him, but rather the vision has given him the courage to bow down before the source of
the miracle. Out of the problem of thought has arisen a strength of heart" (Galli, *Franz
Rosenzweig and Jehuda Halevi,* 187–88). See analysis of Franks and Morgan, *Philosophical
and Theological Writings,* 87–88, and Franks, "Everyday Speech," 30.

219. Rosenzweig, *Understanding the Sick,* 68.

220. Ibid., 45, 53, 55.

221. Rosenzweig, "A Note on Anthropomorphisms," 138. I am not persuaded by
the reading of this passage offered by Franks, "Everyday Speech," 31–32. That is to say,
I do not impute to the author a misreading, but I do not think he has pushed Rosen-

zweig hard enough, and hence he does not interrogate the philosophical tenability of revelatory speech, an interrogation that is justified by Rosenzweig's sway of thinking. See my comments above, n. 211.

222. Rosenzweig, "A Note on Anthropomorphisms," 144–45.

223. Based on the German original in Rosenzweig, *Kleinere Schriften*, 533.

224. Wolfson, "*Via Negativa*," 407–15. See, by contrast, Hilary Putnam, "On Negative Theology," *Faith and Philosophy* 14 (1997): 419. Putnam concludes his essay on the *via negativa* in Maimonides by referring to Rosenzweig's insistence (read in a distinctly Wittgensteinian way; see above, n. 34) that it is the "primal right" of human beings "to give names, to create and speak languages—but our language is also the language that we use to speak to God, and that God uses to speak to us in scripture. *That* religious language connects us to God is something one can feel with one's whole being, not something that one can *explain. Pace,* Maimonides, it is not the theoretical intellect that connects us to the Divine" (emphasis in the original). I do not disagree with the final statement, which does mark an essential difference between Maimonides and Rosenzweig, but Putnam's presentation relates to only a part of the whole story. One cannot ignore Rosenzweig's complex discussion of negative theology at the beginning of the *Star* and his embrace of silence at the end. The positive affirmation of language has to be examined within the framework of these apophatic bookends. Putnam's position, without explicit reference to Rosenzweig, is reiterated in his "God and the Philosophers," *Midwest Studies in Philosophy* 21 (1997): 175–87.

225. Theo de Boer, "Levinas and Negative Theology," in *Théologie Négative,* 849–59. The interpretation of Levinas offered in the concluding paragraph underscores the similarity of his thought to Rosenzweig: "There is a line from negative theology to atheism. What is the relevance of an abstract Being that we cannot know? Negative theology can however also be a first step to a metaphysics of non-indifference. Scepticism regarding the super-essence turns into testimony of a trace left behind by Transcendence in concrete individuals" (859).

226. Lieven Boeve, "The Rediscovery of Negative Theology Today: The Narrow Gulf Between Theology and Philosophy," in *Théologie Négative,* 443–59. See idem, "Christus Postmodernus: An Attempt at Apophatic Christology," in *The Myriad Christ: Plurality and the Quest for Unity in Contemporary Christology,* edited by Terrence Merrigan and Jacques Haers (Leuven: Peeters Press, 2000), 577–93; and idem, "Negative Theology and Theological Hermeneutics: The Particularity of Naming God," *Journal of Philosophy and Scripture* 3 (2006): 1–13. For an alternative approach, see William Franke, "Apophasis and the Turn of Philosophy to Religion: From Negative Theology to Postmodern Negation of Theology," *International Journal for Philosophy of Religion* 60 (2006): 61–76.

227. In "The New Thinking," Rosenzweig credits Feuerbach for anticipating the distinctiveness of the I and Thou, the critical component of Cohen's theory of correlation that serves as the basis for his own dialogical philosophy. See *Philosophical and Theological Writings,* 127; Freund, *Franz Rosenzweig's Philosophy of Existence,* 142–43; Kornberg Greenberg, *Better Than Wine,* 5, 22–24. On anthropomorphism and the need for religious illusion in Feuerbach's thought, see Van A. Harvey, *Feuerbach and the Interpretation of Religion* (Cambridge: Cambridge University Press, 1995), 281–309; and compare the innovative analysis in Jeffrey J. Kripal, *The Serpent's Gift: Gnostic Reflections on the Study of Religion* (Chicago: University of Chicago Press, 2007), 59–89.

228. See discussion of this theme in Eduardo Mendieta, "Modernity's Religion: Habermas and the Linguistification of the Sacred," in *Perspectives on Habermas,* edited by Lewis Edwin Hahn (Chicago: Open Court, 2000), 123–38. Also relevant is the es-

say by Wendell S. Dietrich, "Is Rosenzweig an Ethical Monotheist? A Debate with the New Francophone Literature," in *Der Philosoph Franz Rosenzweig,* 891–900. The author points out the extent to which Rosenzweig departs from the nineteenth-century portrayal of Judaism as an ethical monotheism, focusing on the eclipse of the ethical. My analysis raises questions about the legitimacy of the term "monotheism," at least if it is interpreted literally.

229. Ben Vedder, "The Possibility of an A-Theological Ontology: Heidegger's Changing Position," in *Théologie Négative,* 757–68.

230. Rosenzweig, *Understanding the Sick,* 57.

231. See reference above at n. 165.

232. *SR,* 153 [*SE,* 157]. Mack, "Franz Rosenzweig's and Emmanuel Levinas's Critique," 60, detects in these words an allusion to Schelling's departure from German transcendental philosophy by his assuming that the divine nature is constituted by chaos and materiality.

233. Cohen, *Religion of Reason,* 65, wrote that mythology is "overcome through the definition of God." For Rosenzweig, not only is it not the case that the definition of God overcomes mythology, but the former is impossible without the latter, and the *Star* can be seen as an effort to reclaim the mythologic in a meaningful way.

234. Rosenzweig, *Understanding the Sick,* 57.

235. Rosenzweig, "Atheistic Theology," 24.

236. *SR,* 121: "The word of God is Revelation only because at the same time it is the word of Creation. God said: Let there be light—and what is the light of God? It is man's soul."

237. Ibid., 119.

4

TEXTUAL BODY LANDSCAPES AND THE ARTIST'S GEOMETRY OF TALMUD: *ATELIER*-WORK WITH THE MATERIALITY OF SCRIPTURE

Almut Sh. Bruckstein

Salvation [in Jewish mysticism] comes about through the containment of the feminine in the masculine, the neutralization of female powers. Suffering the suffering of this axiom is a first step on the path to redeeming an ancient wisdom, tiredly waiting to be liberated from the confinement of its own textual embodiment.

—ELLIOT R. WOLFSON

INTRODUCTION/POST-SCRIPTUM

IN THIS CHAPTER I EXPLORE THE EDGES OF SEVERAL REALMS OF (JEWISH) philosophical discourse simultaneously, seeking to offer a rather personal philosophical and artistic path "in-between" the phenomena of image and Script, letter and body, matter and mind. I am thereby moving in-between the dead ends of an aporia that is painful alike to the integrity of reason and to the integrity of (Jewish) tradition, an aporia tied to the exclusive nature of such central concepts as Oneness and Truth, Justice and Mankind, the Love of Humanity and Holiness, concepts whose majestic ethical sublimity seems to be inextricably linked to a rhetoric of war, a rhetoric prone to violence and a relentless annihilation of difference.[1] The present essay continues a theme developed in my recent work, *Vom Aufstand der Bilder: Materialien zu Rembrandt und Midrasch* (The Uprising of Images: Materials on Rembrandt and Midrash), in which I advance a theory of (Jewish) aesthetics based on a phenomenology of text and body as material surface matter addressing textual and visual sources in equal measure. *Vom Aufstand der Bilder* addresses the deadlocks of universalism in Jewish philosophy, seeking a way out of the violent conceptual presuppositions of Oneness through a hermeneutics of the visual field, which allows for a

Parastou Forouhar. *Schriftraum.* By permission of the artist.

perceptive glance at the simultaneity of differences blurring the boundaries between text and image:

> Roland Barthes characterizes the semantic structure of the visual field, more
> specifically of painting, as a non-predicative language, as a "utopia of the
> text." [*The Uprising of Images*] elaborates the significance and non-significance
> of visual imagery and of textual surface-structures in Jewish tradition touch-
> ing upon a pre-lingual ground of indeterminacy associated with an art of
> reading or interpretation that amounts to an art of tactility, or touch; an in-
> determinacy that leaves the correlation between signifier and signified that
> characterizes any material surface structure principally open. The congeni-
> ality of painting as a "utopia of the text" (Roland Barthes) with a "perfect
> text," as conceived of in Midrash and Kabbalah (*Torah Kelulah*) or in Muslim
> sources (the holy Qurʾān), lies in the non-predictable, non-foundational sur-
> face structure of matter that is text surface and pictorial surface at the same
> time.[2]

"ONENESS" AND "THE WEST": THE CULTURAL-
POLITICAL DIMENSIONS OF AN AESTHETIC CRITIQUE

The concept of the perfect text as material surface structure or body-
landscape as set out in this contribution employs a hermeneutics of the

visual field and of tangency, advancing a free interplay of veiling and unveiling, figure and ground, signifier and signified apart from the patristic
definitions of reason, in which the *logos* assumes its place with Christ, and
apart from the Platonic-Freudian concept of an engendered mankind signified by the logos/phallus as the one and only signifier. I am thus seeking to transgress, or rather question, the boundaries of "Oneness" on a
double ground: that of the alleged rationalism of Europe and the West,
projecting its claims to reason, democracy, and its achievements of a secular Enlightenment onto an appropriation of Hellenistic, biblical, and patristic sources. This process unfolds to the detriment of a once-prominent
Judeo-Arabic alliance, whose sources were increasingly eradicated as Jewish tradition in the twentieth century was subjected to the allegedly Judeo-
Christian agenda of Western modernity, often instrumentalized in a violent political conflict between "Western" and "Islamic" countries. The
claim to one mankind, one vision of democracy, one power, one God,
one world order, turns out to be an engendered one, one that hides/veils/
reveals "femininity" as the foundational question of alterity. In this essay, the trope of the "perfect text" appears as an artistic, material opening, seeking to demonstrate a movement, gesture, or glance in-between
image and text, following the lure of that foundational alterity, materiality, or femininity that is revealed and concealed in the process of writing, painting, drawing, and engraving and that is akin to a caress whose
flip side is the violence of the one imposing himself on the other. This essay thus takes on the character of a collage, presenting pictorial and textual matters as a double grounding, as two constitutive moments of beginning and procedure. Visual matters are set free from their illustrative
status. The phenomenological congeniality of pictorial and textual materiality emerges within the texture of a semantic whole, provoking and demanding a reading that cultivates the visual imagination as its own constitutive element.

    Taking as my point of departure two contemporary artists from the
Middle East who focus on the activity of "writing,"[3] I seek to provide an
alternative to the ways in which art forms like calligraphy and writing
are put up in opposition to painting and other forms of pictorial or sculptured artistic expression. The alleged bifurcation of body and book, text
and image often serves to underscore an opposition of West and East,
Christianity and Islam. Thereby the specific development of Renaissance
painting—suggesting a central perspective to the beholder that results in
a "naturalist" perception of the external world—is widely believed to represent not only the visual imagination in Christian contexts but also the
concept of "image" at large.[4]

THE "PERFECT TEXT": JEWISH-MUSLIM CONGENIALITIES WITH MODERN EUROPEAN ART

In the face of such a reading, my own work carves out a Jewish-Muslim liaison or congeniality, demonstrating the autonomy of a visual imagination and pictorial representation that remains free from the rather exclusive commitment of the central beholder's perspective that went unchallenged in the history of Western art until the nineteenth and twentieth centuries. Only when surrealists and abstract expressionists started to criticize systematically the "illusionary" nature of the allegedly objective correlations between nature and its representation in the pictorial arts of the West,[5] did another correlation come into view: that of modern European art and extra-European sources uncommitted to the fixation of the logos, of reason and central perspective within the politico-theological frameworks of Christian culture.[6] There is an underlying phenomenological congeniality in the bodily gesture—beyond "influence" or "chance"—in Vincent van Gogh's reflections of the Japanese Gutai Group,[7] or in Paul Klee's work mirroring the structures of Arabic calligraphy and Egyptian hieroglyphs. Elliot R. Wolfson's work provides a landmark of orientation as to how medieval kabbalist, Sufi, and Judeo-Arabic sources on the visual imagination touch upon contemporary gender discussions, semiotics, phenomenology, and aesthetics. It seems to me that an investigation into the *phenomenological* relationship between the principles of modern European art and the classical sources of Muslim and Jewish philosophy theology and mysticism still remains a desideratum.[8]

This essay is a transitional one, indicating a future project in between the visual arts and the talmudic tractate *Berakhot* that I am presently working on. At stake is demonstrating a kind of Jewish philosophy that incorporates a "fourth dimension"—the dimension of time—into the heart of its own movement of thought. The framework of the visual and performing arts, beyond the confines of the text, is constitutive for the kind of engagement with talmudic texts that I envision for my own future work. Significantly, this essay ends not only with Rosenzweig's "wall of images" as a metaphor for the relationship between matter and mind, but also with the presentation of a new platform for Jewish-Muslim cooperation in philosophy and art—an *atelier* in which the gesture of artistic and philosophical expression is intimately tied to what mystical sources term the "process of creation."

Joseph Semah's Folios of Talmud

An Introduction to the Principle of Relative Expression is the title of an artwork by the Iraqi-Jewish artist Joseph Semah, exhibiting a series of pages of the Babylonian Talmud covered with black oil. We see pages from the talmudic tractate *Pessaʾim* in which the *Gemara* as well as the traditional commentary of Rashi (1040–1105) and the Tosafists are each covered up with black glue, thereby forming a unique geometrical pattern, different on every single page.

Revelare: *To Reveal, to Disclose, to Cover Up*

By blackening and erasing the multiple textual faces of the *Gemara*, the artist radicalizes a traditional hermeneutical practice in rabbinic and kabbalistic literature. According to midrashic and kabbalistic sources, the process of revealing the significance of the text does not consist of a simple and abstract disclosure of meaning but rather, paradoxically, in an act of overwriting, or cover-up: the activity of writing ab-originally covers empty spaces, cracks, and fissures in-between preceding lines, words, and letters with interpretation and commentary. The text itself, even the so-called original text, emerges thus as a material trace, a signature, an imprint, a visual crystallization upon something that went before, ever re-veiling, that is, revealing meaning hidden within the traces of who or what came before and passed by. A moment of indeterminacy is at work in this process of writing/reading, un/covering the ephemeral traces of a receding matter whose origins cannot be contained. As Wolfson expresses it:

> That the other voices of interpretation cannot be predicted is integral to the indeterminacy/spontaneity that marks the way of the path. Here we touch upon the nexus of time and reading, the sense in which reading embraces the flow of temporality in its bringing to light what has been laid away, the superfluity of meaning, determinate in its unpredictability and predictable in its indeterminacy, an implication of Derrida's manner of reading but an idea implied already in Rosenzweig's *Sprachdenken*.[9]

In the midst of this material gesture, writing points beyond itself, to the spiritual realm, holding in, however, what it conceals in the very materiality of black or colored ink on white or colored parchment or paper.[10]

Gershom Scholem's Turn against Idealism

In "Revelation and Tradition as Religious Categories in Judaism" (1970),[11] Gershom Scholem suggests a material hermeneutics of rabbinic commen-

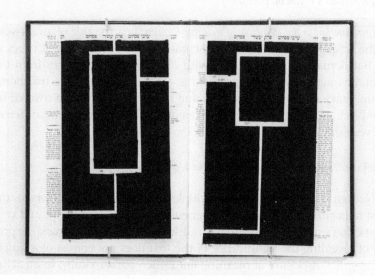

Joseph Semah. *An Introduction to the Principle of Relative Expression* (YaKNeHaZ) 24.2.1979. Black oil sticks on Talmud Bavli. Tractate Pesaḥim, 40 × 54 × 4 cm. By permission of the artist.

tary, prominent among masters of twelfth- and thirteenth-century kabbalistic traditions. There the process of over-writing text with commentary assumes the status of the very act of creation. The written Torah thereby takes on a deep transparency, the abysmal in-between space between letters, white-in-black, in which all creative commentary and interpretation originates and upon which it is inscribed.[12] In a revolutionary gesture, much in line with the mainstream turn to myth and nationalism in Germany and France in the early twentieth century,[13] Scholem contrasts this material process of commentary to both German-Jewish and Judeo-Arabic universalist Enlightenment traditions, whose most outstanding expression Scholem finds in the rationalist reception history of Maimonides in the nineteenth century. Hermann Cohen, in his reading of Maimonides of 1908, sees all interpretation and commentary in Jewish tradition as being rooted in the one and all-encompassing source of human reason;[14] in his introduction to *The Guide of the Perplexed,* Maimonides points to language and even Scripture as to an unavoidable material compromise with the physical conditions of the human body, a nod to the weaknesses of the human condition that to his deep irritation seems to be inherent in the transmission of the prophetic teaching itself.[15] Against this background, harking back to twelfth- and thirteenth-century kabbalistic and Neoplatonic sources, Scholem advances the physical and aesthetic specificities of the Hebrew language and of Hebrew letters in their concrete visual shape as constitutive points of departure for the tradition and transmission of sanctified texts in Jewish tradition.[16] This anti-idealist turn converges with a critique of universalism at large that reverts to the specificities of language, place, and peoplehood away from the cosmopolitan ideals of German-Jewish scholarship of the nineteenth and early twentieth centuries.[17] Oral tradition is now claimed to originate, not in the infinite ideality of human reason to which the specificities of language are but insignificant material remnants of an otherwise autonomous spirit, but rather in the infinite material transparency of the space in-between letters, wherein the very concrete shape and form of the letters serve as delineating marks of interpretative departure. It is a material kind of nothingness upon which interpretation and commentary is inscribed—"black fire upon white fire," according to rabbinic and midrashic sources.[18]

> We might say that Hebrew letters for kabbalists are excitation nodes that generate visual and sonic aftershocks, producing semblance of light and resonance of sound expressive of infinity. . . . Matter, on this account, is a cloak, a veil, through which the luminous form-shadows of the Hebrew letters are concomitantly concealed and revealed.[19]

The "whiteness of Scripture" indicates the perpetual illegibility of the original text—an illegibility that is radically exposed by the artwork of Joseph Semah. Semah's work of oil-covered talmudic pages radicalizes the materialist hermeneutical agenda of Scripture's visual performance while questioning the all-too-particularist turn that Kabbalah scholarship took with Scholem's homecoming to Israel. Joseph Semah's geometric patterns of Talmud put to the extreme the essential indeterminacy of the text in the same way that Daniel Boyarin portrays as a central feature of rabbinic literary tradition as opposed to the Hellenistic concept of reason that is located as the "logos" at the very heart of Christian Trinitarian dogma.[20] The opaqueness of Joseph Semah's artwork suggests an absence of preconceived sense that is radically opposed to any allegorical or idealist readings of text, leaving the relationship between signifier and signified principally open, while presenting a definite although illegible material form. It is this aesthetic suggestion reflected back on the visual shape of letters, the art of writing, and the very phenomenon of the line in the visual arts at large that I take as my point of departure for this first investigation into the correlation of textual and visual arts in Jewish (and Islamic) tradition, taking my cue from the material body-landscape of the text rather than from its philological, historical, or traditional interpretations.[21]

SEMIOTICS OF HOLINESS:
A JEWISH-MUSLIM PERSPECTIVE

The phenomenon of a traditional yet illegible Script, in which criteria of geometry and visual form may override the sensibilities of both orthography and content, corresponds with the aesthetic and theological surplus value of Hebrew and Arabic letters. "There is a critical difference that distinguishes Christianity from the various forms of mystical devotion that evolved historically in Judaism and Islam," writes Wolfson.[22] The letters and their specific bodies, according to Jewish and Islamic medieval kabbalistic and Sufi sources, are not meant to serve as the means for verbal communication only, but rather they testify to the material traces of divine self-disclosure.[23]

> The divine word originally conveys an infinite plenitude, but this message—and this is the main point—is incomprehensible! It's a kind of communication that serves no communicative purpose. Only by ascribing an interpretation to this scriptural form, this form—that is essentially autonomous—turns to be communication too.[24]

Scripture carries an aesthetic surplus of visual form, precisely because the literal configurations revealing themselves in the body-landscapes of Scripture and its semiotic textures are divine. Wolfson states that "Jews and Muslims provided alternative narratives to account for the commingling of the corporeal and transcendent, the visible and invisible, the literal and spiritual."[25]

According to contemporary work in Islamic art history, Jewish mysticism, and Qurʾanic studies, the phenomenon of the written word in Jewish and Islamic tradition, whether it is the Qurʾān or the Torah, reverses the relationship of the "word that became flesh" as it is presented in classical Christian doctrine: here it is not the divine word, the logos, that became flesh in Christ (incarnation), but rather the poetic body of God that reveals itself in the holy book, the written word, whose every little dot and detail therefore assumes significance far beyond the question of its verbal meaning. "Both narratives . . . presume a correlation of body and book but in an inverse manner: for Christians, the literal body is embodied in the book of the body; for Jews, the literal body is embodied in the body of the book."

> From the standpoint of medieval Sufis and kabbalists, the innumerable transmutations of meaning stem from the fact that each sign/letter is a component of the textual corpus that constitutes the name of the nameless, the veil that renders the invisible visible and the visible invisible. . . . Read esoterically, the

Arabic letters—bones, tissue, and sinews of the Qurʾanic body—are signs
that point to the unseen and thereby reveal the light by concealing it. . . . In
a similar vein, the letters of the matrix text, Torah for kabbalist, Qurʾān for
Sufi, reveal and conceal the divine essence, the *face* beyond all veils, the pre/
face, devoid of form, the pre/text, devoid of letter.[26]

Against all fundamentalist directions of reading, it is not a divine "message" that is communicated here, but rather the self-revelatory body of the
divine word harboring all of creation within its semiotic texture, whether
it carries meaning, reason, a legible message, or none of these.

Kabbalists and Sufi would agree that if one remains bound to the letters of
the scriptural text, then one is fettered by an idolatry of the book . . . but
both would also insist that the way beyond letters (scripted and/or voiced) is
by way of letters, visual-auditory signs, semiotic ciphers at once visible and
audible . . . that communicate the incommunicable not through a . . . model
of symbolic logic but through a . . . model of poetic allusion.[27]

Elliot R. Wolfson's work on Jewish mysticism and Richard Ettinghausen's work on Arabic epigraphy and calligraphy[28] share a common
agenda that I take as the point of departure for my argument here: "Readability was only a secondary concern. The *Gestalt* of the inscription as a
whole"[29] presents the essential element. The visual, trans-verbal nature of
calligraphy deserves to be taken into account when the general and specific character of inscriptions within Muslim society is examined.[30]

Pure Painting and the Utopia of the Text

Letters and bodily signs in both Sufi and Jewish mysticism and Islamic
calligraphy in particular point to a utopia of the text whose self-referential
perfection paradoxically testifies to the autonomy of its visual form and
to the integrity of its material letter-landscape. Roland Barthes elaborates this utopia with reference to both ancient and contemporary ideo-
graphic writing systems in which the gesture of the calligrapher/painter
leaves an ephemeral material trace, moving in correlation with his body.
To Roland Barthes, the *Dessins automatiques* of the surrealists, like those of
André Masson, present a prime example for a semiography that exposes
the visual autonomy of the letter:

The semiography of André Masson corrects thousands of years in the history of writing by referring us not to any origin [of text] (the origin does not
interest us) but rather to the *body*. His work tells us that *for Scripture to be revealed in its truth* (and not in its instrumentality) *it must be illegible*. The semio-
graph (Masson) knowingly and through sovereign work produces illegible
stuff: he disconnects the urge of writing from any imagined communication (from readability). Thus the semiography of Masson—directly emerg-

ing from an in-significant practice (painting)—instantly performs the utopia of the text.[31]

Precisely *because* Jewish and Islamic mysticism disentangle themselves from the patristic and rationalist search for the logos, they can claim the autonomy of a visual and audio semiotics of Scripture beyond the limitations of rational or verbal meaning.[32] This semiotics in its visual dimension becomes a principle of surrealist painting in twentieth-century Europe, where the constitutive meaning of the non-mimetic line for painting was exemplarily expressed by Kandinsky's "Point and Line to Surface" in 1926.[33] The correlation between Sufi theology and surrealist painting was explored by the Syrian poet Adonis in his book *Sufism and Surrealism*, published in Beirut (1995),[34] which Abdul-Rahim Al-Shaikh elaborates upon in a recent piece devoted to "The Sufi's Dance."[35]

Scripture as Artistic Procedure

Phenomenologically speaking, there emerges a form of writing in which the boundaries between writing and pure art, even pure painting, seem to be blurred. Roland Barthes establishes this phenomenological argument fervently in his essay on the semiography of André Masson:

> Something is about to emerge that leaves the boundaries between literature and painting obsolete; in the place of these ancient divinities it advances a kind of "Ergography," the text as artistic procedure, the work as textual artefact.[36]

Visual poetry and holy texts are about to merge. Pure painting, in its refusal of any mimicry, advances to become itself a "poetic language."[37]

SPLINTERING THE LOGOS AND KEEPING SECRETS CONCEALED

It is important to note, as many scholars of Jewish and Islamic mysticism have done, that this kind of materiality, this kind of material trace that constitutes the text, whether it be a letter or line or dot or any other semiotic sign, points to a transcendence that cannot but be expressed by way of a garment, a veil, or some other form of physical trace, gesture, signature, or bodily movement.

> Just as the Qurʾān is the book that manifests the invisible deity through verbal images, so the cosmos is a book that unveils the divine presence through veils of phenomenal existence. . . . Two Qurʾanic motifs are combined here: the identification of cosmic phenomena as signs pointing to the unicity of all

André Masson, *Dessin automatique,* 1924–1925, Stiftung Sammlung Dieter
Scharf, Kupferstichkabinett, Berlin. By permission of bpk / Kupferstichkabinett,
SMB, Stiftung Sammlung Dieter Scharf zur Erinnerung an Otto Gerstenberg /
Jörg P. Anders.

being, and the idea of the heavenly book, primordial scripture, inscribed by
the divine pen, *qalam* (Q 68:1).[38]

From this perspective, Scripture transcends its functionality as semiotic
system: it emerges a transcendental universe made of letter-signs which
derive their significance from a supra-natural beauty.[39]

In his work on Sufi theology, calligraphy, and body movement,
Abdul-Rahim al-Shaikh demonstrates an equation between Qurʾanic writing as signature of creation—material traces testifying to the absence of
divine penmanship—and the Sufi's dance embodying a choreographic
signature of cosmic perfection, manifesting and transforming traces of
nothingness into the very ephemerality of the Sema movement.[40] The
dancer thereby assumes the function of the *calamus* [writing instrument]
about which the tenth-century calligrapher and writer from Baghdad,

Al-Tawhidi says in the name of Ibrahim b. al Abbas: "The calamus speaks and is silent. It stays in one place and travels. It is present and absent. It is far away and near at hand. . . . It keeps secrets concealed."[41]

The European Enlightenment—A Fateful Aporia

This kind of transcendentalism that remains conscious of the constitutive meaning of the *material gesture* of writing as the very core of revelation is not identical—in fact, is diametrically opposed—to the Hellenistic transcendentalism adopted by Maimonides and Averroes in equal measure, searching for the logos "behind," "above," or "beneath" the material traces of bodily language.[42] The refusal to seek out the logos and thereby to reject any one unifying central message underlying the holy text or cosmic creation characterizes rabbinic hermeneutics and Ashʾarite atomism alike.[43] Daniel Boyarin ascribes this process of "splintering the logos" to an intense and critical response of rabbinic tradition to fourth-century patristic theology and its delineation of the logos within the confines of patristic Trinitarian dogma.[44] Retrieving this critique of logocentrism from fourth-century rabbinic history, Boyarin exposes an aporia of rationalism that is working its way through all of European philosophical history, culminating in what is known as Western Enlightenment and the very concept of (Western) modernity. Trying to get hold of reason without getting contaminated by any trace of materialism, Enlightenment traditions, whether (Judeo-)Arab or German(-Jewish), get entangled in a fateful deadlock, an unbending negation of materiality; of body, letter, image, matter; of (sexual) difference, the visual imagination, and femininity, since femininity represents matter from the very inception of philosophical history. What ensues from the denial of matter and from the pursuit of an unveiled spiritual truth is a theological and political bifurcation, a dialectic deadlock of oppositions, a spiritual and political quest dividing the world into body and spirit, matter and form, activity and passivity, above and below, male and female, good and evil. The European Enlightenment radicalizes this agenda by claiming that there is only one spirit, one gender, that is, one mankind, one God (namely, the logos defined as Christ), one world, one truth.

ONE GENDER: LEAVING OTHERNESS TO NAUGHT

The idea of one mankind and of humanity derives its power from the concept of universality and oneness. The idea of oneness, of one mankind (one gender), writes Luce Irigaray, *"holds nothing outside itself.* It neither in-

dicates nor indexes anything *other* than itself, however akin. And it needs
no heterogeneous *vehicle,* no foreign *receptacle,* in order to signify and represent itself. . . . [It is] an ideal that will not submit to being determined
by the diversity of any matter."[45] The idea of one mankind, of one reason,
the logos itself, leaves otherness to naught, nothing, absence, or death. Irigaray, a critic of Jacques Lacan, connects this discourse about the unbending nature of the logos, of the one that knows no other than itself, in an in-
genious way with the Freudian dogma of the male phallus being the one
and only signifier of gender, of that male gender compared to which any
other is defined merely by lack, absence, castration:

> The desire for the same, for the self-identical, the self (as) same, and again of
> the similar, the *alter ego* and, to put it in a nutshell, the desire for the auto . . . ,
> the homo . . . the male, dominates the representational economy (of the phal-
> lus). . . . In this proliferating desire of the same, death will be the only repre-
> sentative of an outside, of a heterogeneity, of an Other: woman will assume
> the function of representing death (death of the male organ, which is) cas-
> tration.[46]

The woman, representing matter, being defined philosophically as lack of
form and ontologically as lack of the male organ, provides the passive receptacle of the intellect and the phallus alike, whether this be in Aristotelian, Neoplatonic, or Freudian terms.

> Hence, woman does not take an active part in the development of history,
> for she is never anything but the still undifferentiated opaqueness of sen-
> sible matter . . . She is . . . that resisting remainder of a corporeality to which
> his passion for sameness is still sensitive, or again his double, the lining of his
> coat.[47]

One Logos and One Gender—An Aristotelian Freudian Alliance

In modern Europe, Aristotle and Freud are made to testify together to this
theologico-political alliance, dividing the world into intellectual power
and sexual drives, male and female, phallus and the lack of it, west and
east, north and south, civilized and barbarian, Christian and not Christian, human and not human. The pursuit of pure spirit, of bare truth, and
of unveiled transcendence results in the violence of one mankind that
knows no other. However, it is not a feminist critique that I wish to emphasize at this point. Rather, it seems to me that when Irigaray lays open this
modern liaison between Aristotle and Freud, this liaison between one logos, one mankind, and one gender, when she therefore speaks about her,
the woman, as *"that resisting remainder of a corporeality,"*[48] she brings to the

fore those Jewish and Islamic philosophers and mystics who, in opposition to the patristic search for the one and unifying fundamental verbal message of the holy text, invoked a multifaceted semiotic significance of the text, its letters and visual forms, claiming them as remnants of materiality in the hermeneutical process of revelation, signalizing a material trace or signature, pointing to a transcendence whose absence or loss becomes visible on paper or parchment, engraved upon wood, metal, skin, or other matter.

Graphein: *"To touch the Surface"*

Femininity—"that resisting remainder of corporeality." Femininity seems to be reminiscent of those material traces that Sufi and kabbalah masters in Jewish and Islamic mysticism encountered in the lines and dots of the letters outlining the holy text, taking them seriously as visual, figurative, and often untranslatable and even illegible signs of the prophetic teaching, residues of materiality in the very process of revelation. Within the veil that reveals, matter and spirit touch in a subversive manner, upsetting the division of pure and impure, male and female, body and spirit, maintaining a texture, *métissage,* mélange of immanent transcendence, of transcendental immanence. The surface structure of an object, whether text, image, or skin, resists and does not give in to the grip of preconceived concepts, but demands an art of sensuous touch, knowing how to oscillate between matter and spirit, surface and depth.[49]

Veiling Femininity

Keeping and defending the veil as a surface structure of matter in the very process of revelation thus becomes an act of subversion, since the materiality of the veil, whether it consists of dots, lines and letters of ink, images of color, textiles of wool, or facial features of skin, questions the unrestricted rule of the abstract, male order of the one God. The acknowledgement of the slightest material resistance to the purity of monotheistic abstraction, according to Neoplatonic doctrine, means to touch upon the eruptive and dangerous nature of a different order, an order in which matter, that is, femininity, takes on a constitutive role.

Consequently, medieval Jewish mystics set strict limits to feminine autonomy when dealing with the "feminine" configurations of Jewish traditional life such as Torah, Sabbath, and the Shekhinah, the Beloved of God. Elliot R. Wolfson's work on twelfth- and thirteenth-century Jewish mysticism points to the phallocentric symbolic structure of kabbalistic language, putting an end to the naive association of Jewish mysticism with a

celebration of femininity in Jewish mysticism.[50] His work has given way
to a rigorous philosophical engagement with modern and contemporary
phenomenological traditions and its critical reflections on the constructions of gender, body, and language.

Playful Twists

Ironically, however, following the logic of suppression, the patriarchic
guardians of God use none other than the veil, the garment, this subversive mélange of body and spirit with its inherent resistance to the denial of
matter, as a means of silencing the heterogeneity of the feminine.

If we were now to take up this veil as a female asset, a playful accessory of self-assertion, of public affirmation of visible alterity, as a socio-
political performative spot of heterogeneity and difference, portraying it as
a second skin, controlled by an activity from *within* the feminine, outside
the grip of patriarchic discipline, we would be playing with the structures
of subversion inherent in the hermeneutical processes of veiling and unveiling at the very heart of knowing (God) in classical Jewish and Islamic
texts. Nilüfer Göle's sociological work on the "modern *mahrem*"[51] and a recent exhibition of the same name in Istanbul that exhibited works by the
Iranian artist Parastou Forouhar and other playful installations of female
veilings[52] are exemplary gestures of (feminine) self-assertion. They demonstrate an undefeatable alterity actively entering the space in-between
philosophy and art, deconstructing the violent grip of homogeneity and
sameness so characteristic of collective identities and their violent constructions of narrative histories.

Atelier-*Work with Rabbinic Literature*

In my own work, I find myself increasingly surrounded by a space defined
not only by texts and text scholars but also by artists and institutional set-
tings of the visual and performing arts.[53] In the 1920s, Aby Warburg's pictorial map advanced an associative logic for the display of disparate objects and art-crafts from various disciplines and periods of time, guided by
iconographic formulas of human gestures. Analogously in method, one
could imagine an approach to studying talmudic texts that leads one from
one topical site to another, connecting seemingly unrelated talmudic matters by an associative detour through related poetic, philosophical, and
artistic sources disparate in scope and context.[54] The artwork of Joseph
Semah on Tractate Pessaḥim suggests a movement or path for studying
rabbinic texts that is determined by tactile rather than philological structures of text. Orientation within the textual landscape of Talmud—this

Parastou Forouhar. *Bismarck*. Serie Okzidentalismus, Rom 2006. By permission of the artist.

is what Semah seems to suggest—amounts to a *spatial* orientation in between disparate knots, fields, and clusters of thematic density connected
through "white" threads, strings, and lines: paths of relativity or nothingness not unlike the "naught of knowledge" that Jewish neo-Kantians such
as Hermann Cohen and Walter Benjamin associated with the *temporal* in-
vestigative energy of *questioning* the order of any preconceived symbolic
conventions.[55]

The in-between space of the artist's white-in-black advances the indeterminacy of new knowledge hinging on those constitutive moments
of nothingness embodied in the learner's questions and external associations when touching the surface of the text. The variety of thematic issues
within the narration of talmudic discourse, which often poses a kaleido-
scope of disparate topical order, presents itself from the artist's perspective
like a visual body-landscape in which heterogeneous objects in all their
topical heterogeneity *leave space for one another*. The artist advances a spatial
order in which artistic performance affirms the simultaneous presence of
heterogeneous objects in a homogeneous place, taking his cue from the
specific measurements of the talmudic text itself.

Such a performative affirmation of a heterogeneously structured space
suggests a *change of place* with respect to future negotiations of classical Jewish texts and traditions with far-reaching cultural-political consequences.
Moving away from the textual realm in which questions of truth are inextricably bound to bifurcating notions of one God, one mankind, one
people, the artist calls for a novel negotiation of rabbinic literature within
the context of the visual and performing arts, suggesting a transition away
from the classical *bet ha-midrash* into a space defined by the heterogeneous
presence of multiple material objects that leave room for one another, even
when clashing in color, texture, and form—just like in the working space
of the artist itself (the *atelier*) where artwork is being produced.

A *"Wall of Images"*: An Epistemological Suggestion based on
The Star of Redemption

Surprisingly, it was Franz Rosenzweig who, in his search for a post-idealist
"new thinking," suggested an "empty wall full of paintings" as an epistemological model for his own deconstruction of the all-embracing "All," the
totalitarian idea of Oneness.[56] In his *Star of Redemption*, Rosenzweig advises
his readers not to imagine the truth as a kind of fresco in which "wall and
image merge into a unity," but rather to visualize it as an empty wall full of
paintings. To be sure, the "empty wall full of paintings" is meant by Rosenzweig as a metaphor when he says, "One could not hang up the painting
if the wall was not there, but the painting has nothing to do with the wall.

The wall had no objections if next to this one, or instead of this one, there were other paintings hung on the wall. . . . In this way, oneness escapes from the all. . . . [The painting] *leaves space* besides itself."[57]

The manifold and multifaceted material presence of objects taking definite spatial positions while allowing for topical contradictions puts up a resistance to the violent appropriation that the idea of "oneness" exerts on its subjects. Such material presence makes room for an ontological difference appearing from within the transcendental materiality of the body—whether it is text or image, letter or skin. In Rosenzweig's words, the painting "leaves space besides itself." I am suggesting an institutional move: Creating a new space for the negotiation of Jewish literary traditions within the contexts of the visual arts amounts to an affirmation of the particular in which "universality" is safeguarded not by concepts but rather by the human gestures that make up the grammar of artistic expression, unbound by the limitations of truth, collective identity, language, or ethnic belonging. Rosenzweig—just like the artist Joseph Semah—proposes a visual/material particularity within the artist's *atelier*, the gallery, the museum, affirming the simultaneous presence of various objects in the eyes of the beholder. In this new space, it is the artist who, together with the scholar, becomes the new guardian of a particularism that knows how to safeguard the dignity, the integrity, and the inviolability of any body-surface (whether text, artwork, or skin) without giving up the universal gestures of humanity that Maimonides subsumes under the expression *ha'inyan ha'enoschi*—the "matter of humanity."[58]

NOTES

The epigraph is from Elliot R. Wolfson, *Language, Eros, Being: Kabbalistic Hermeneutics and Poetic Imagination* (New York: Fordham University Press, 2005), 390.

1. The sublimity of the ethical has been the subject of much of my earlier work on Hermann Cohen and his neo-Kantian universalistic reading of Maimonides and medieval Jewish philosophy: Almut Sh. Bruckstein, *Hermann Cohen: Ethics of Maimonides*, translated with commentary by Almut Sh. Bruckstein, foreword by Robert Gibbs (Madison: University of Wisconsin Press, 2004). For a critical discussion of the interrelation between monotheism and violence, see Jan Assmann, *Of God and Gods: Egypt, Israel, and the Rise of Monotheism* (Madison: University of Wisconsin Press, 2008). For a radical critique of the Freudian-Platonic (engendered) concept of mankind, see Luce Irigaray, *Speculum of the Other Woman*, translated by Gillian C. Gill (Ithaca, N.Y.: Cornell University Press, 1985).

2. Almut Sh. Bruckstein, *Vom Aufstand der Bilder: Materialien zu Rembrandt und Midrasch, mit einer Skizze zur Gründung einer jüdisch-islamischen Werkstatt für Philosophie und Kunst* (Munich: Wilhelm Fink, 2007).

3. I invoke images of the Iraqi-born Jewish artist Joseph Semah (Amsterdam) and the Iranian, Frankfurt-based artist Parastou Forouhar, who is presented here twice, with a calligraphic work in the beginning and a rather ironic installation toward the end. I thank both artists for their generous permissions to reprint their work in this piece.

4. Hans Belting, in his recent book *Florenz and Bagdad: Eine westöstliche Geschichte des Blicks* (München: C.H. Beck, 2008), presents a fascinating link between Renaissance painting's discovery of the central perspective and the tenth-century Persian scientist Alhazen and his theory of optics and light. He demonstrates how the adoption of the beholder's central perspective in Italian Renaissance painting coincides with the logocentric perspectives of Christian scholasticism. Within this insightful analysis I remain unconvinced by Belting's main contention that the very concept of the image and its significance for the representation of the visual imagination remains a characteristic feature of "Western art" committed to a "naturalist" perfection of the image as opposed to "Islamic art," which "knows no images." When we keep the relationship between "Florence and Baghdad" in mind, however, it might indeed prove productive to investigate the constitutive meaning of the mental image, of averting the glance, and of "not-seeing" for Islamic theology and art, and to relate this classical critique of the visual representation to the artistic deconstruction of "illusionist" naturalist painting in twentieth-century Western art itself.

5. See Joseph Leo Körner, "Paul Klee and the Image of the Book," in *Paul Klee: Legends of the Sign,* edited by Rainer Crone and Joseph Leo Koerner (New York: Columbia University Press, 1991).

6. An interesting detail in Belting's *Florenz und Bagdad* is that Jesuit missionaries in China included the commitment to central perspective in the visual arts into their missionary program.

7. See Ming Tiampo, "Gutai and Informal Post-War Art in Japan and France 1945–1965" (Ph.D. diss., Northwestern University, 2003).

8. An important contribution in this respect is Adonis's book *Sufism and Surrealism* (1995), see discussion below; see also Gülru Necipoglu, "L'idée de décor dans les régimes de visualité islamiques," in *Purs Décors? Arts de l'Islam, regards du XIX,* edited by Rémi Labrusse (Paris: Musée du Louvre Éditions—Les Arts Decoratifs, 2007), 10–23, esp. 11–12: "L'apperception mystico-intellectuelle de la beauté visuelle, partant de l'autonomie esthétique de la forme, la situé au sein d'un système cosmologique unitaire qui s'ouvre sur le transcendant."

9. Wolfson, *Language, Eros, Being,* 113. Among the numerous contributions to Kabbalah scholarship, Wolfson's work assumes a rigorous philosophical engagement with the post-structuralist presuppositions of Scripture as presented by Jacques Derrida. In his encyclopedic engagement of contemporary positions in various fields of discourse, such as phenomenology, psychoanalysis, medieval rabbinic and Islamic studies, gender studies, or poetry, Wolfson establishes the field of kabbalistic studies as part of an encyclopedic and cosmopolitan cultural agenda, undoing the turn to myth and national homecoming advanced by Scholem when he turned from Berlin to Jerusalem, an alliance of kabbalah and nationalism that still marks most of Kabbalah scholarship today. The gist of this essay as well as of my own forthcoming work on the visual landscapes of Talmud owes so much to the philosophical work of both Derrida and Wolfson that a documentation of every single trace of reference becomes impossible.

10. See Wolfson, "Re/Covering the Un/Covered: Taking Hold of Letting-Go" in *Language, Eros, Being,* 111–17.

11. Originally published in German in *Über einige Grundbegriffe des Judentums*

168 ALMUT SH. BRUCKSTEIN

(Frankfurt a. M: Suhrkamp, 1970), 90–120. English edition, "Revelation and Tradition as Religious Categories in Judaism," in Gershom Scholem, *The Messianic Idea in Judaism and Other Essays on Jewish Spirituality*, with a foreword by Arthur Hertzberg (New York: Schocken, 1995), 282–303.

12. For the aesthetic implications of Scholem's work on Jewish mysticism, see the chapter "Moses at Sinai—A Theory of Painting?" in Bruckstein, *Vom Aufstand der Bilder*, esp. 62–68.

13. Scholem introduces his entry "Jewish Mysticism and Kabbalah" in the encyclopedic handbook *The Jewish People, Past and Present* (New York, 1946) with the following general assertion: "In its development, the movement of Jewish mysticism was characterized by an ever-growing tendency to become a social and national factor." Steven M. Wasserstrom comments: "These spiritual nationalisms emerged not only internally from their respective spiritual traditions but were perhaps primarily borrowed from contemporary French and German traditions. See Wasserstrom, *Religion after Religion: Gershom Scholem, Mircea Eliade, and Henry Corbin at Eranos* (Princeton, N.J.: Princeton University Press, 1999), 129.

14. Hermann Cohen's reading of Maimonides became essential for Jewish philosophy in the twentieth century at large, determining the position of such different thinkers such as Walter Benjamin, Theodor W. Adorno, Franz Rosenzweig, Leo Strauss, and Emmanuel Levinas.

15. Moses Maimonides, *The Guide of the Perplexed*, translated with an introduction and notes by Shlomo Pines (Chicago: University of Chicago Press, 1963), 8–9. See also the argument presented in my *Hermann Cohen: Ethics of Maimonides*, 115–16.

16. Gershom Scholem, *On the Kabbalah and Its Symbolism*, with a foreword by Bernard McGinn (New York: Schocken, 1996), 49–50. For a sharpened perspective in the light of modern and contemporary philosophical sources, see E. R. Wolfson, "Hebrew and the Semiotics of Creation," in *Language, Eros, Being*, 197–202 and passim. The fact that even the most sublime (God) remains associated with the materiality of the four letters of his name is the subject of far-reaching discussions of the relationship between body and spirit, male and female in Neoplatonic and kabbalistic sources.

17. E.g., Almut Sh. Bruckstein, "Versuch einer Topographie zur jüdischen Hermeneutik," *Judaica* 56 (2000): 154–77.

18. Gershom Scholem, "The Significance of Torah in Jewish Mysticism," *On the Kabbalah and its Symbolism*, 37–44; see also Betty Rojtman, *Black Fire on White Fire: An Essay on Jewish Hermeneutics, from Midrash to Kabbalah* (Berkeley: University of California Press, 1998); Moshe Idel, *Absorbing Perfections: Kabbalah and Interpretation*, foreword by Harold Bloom (New Haven, Conn.: Yale University Press, 2002), 48–59; 447–52 and passim.

19. Elliot R. Wolfson, *Language, Eros, Being*, 201.

20. Daniel Boyarin, *Border Lines: The Partition of Judaeo-Christianity* (Philadelphia: University of Pennsylvania Press, 2004), 165–201, esp. 182–92; first in idem, *Den Logos zersplittern. Zur Genealogie der Nichtbestimmbarkeit des Textsinns im Midrasch*, translated by Dirk Westerkamp, ha-atelier essays no. 3 (Berlin: Philo, 2002).

21. This essay presents preparatory material for my forthcoming talmudic readings of TB *Berakhot* 54a, based on materials from poetry, philosophy, and the visual arts.

22. Elliot R. Wolfson, *Language, Eros, Being*, 190.

23. See Aaron W. Hughes, *The Texture of the Divine: Imagination in Medieval Islamic and Jewish Thought* (Bloomington: Indiana University Press, 2004), esp. 48–80.

24. Gershom Scholem, "Offenbarung und Tradition als religiöse Kategorien im Judentum," in Gershom Scholem, *Judaica 4,* edited by Rolf Tiedemann (Frankfurt a. M.: Suhrkamp, 1984), 212, my translation; English edition: Gershom Scholem, "Revelation and Tradition as Religious Categories in Judaism," 294.

25. Elliot R. Wolfson, *Language, Eros, Being,* 190.

26. Ibid., 205–6. Wolfson engages Ibn Arabi and other classical Arabic sources to advance a parallel universe of Jewish and Sufi mysticism; for a critique of the semiotic manifestations of the divine within the Qurʾanic tradition and their contemporary ahistorical traditionalist reception history, see Angelika Neuwirth, "Scripture and Body: Some Thoughts about Qurʾanic Monotheism" (unpublished lecture delivered at the international conference on "Edward Said: Critical Accounts on (Post) Modernity," December 15–17, 2007, at Birzeit University). I thank Angelika Neuwirth for letting me see the unpublished German version of this paper. By claiming that "oral tradition" represents a unique feature of Islamic tradition, contrasting it to the "written tablets" of "Judaism," Neuwirth, however, leaves aside the rabbinic tradition that asserts the central significance of *tora she be'al pe,* "oral tradition," for the entire postbiblical Jewish tradition; even the idea of reenacting revelation continuously anew by reciting the Holy Writ in liturgical contexts is a feature of both Jewish and Islamic traditional practice and cannot be ascribed one-sidedly to Islamic tradition. Several generations of Jewish scholarship have emphasized the predominance of the oral/ liturgical/musical over the visual/written aspects of Jewish tradition. "Never read, always sing!" With these words Rosenzweig—who ironically thought that Islamic tradition knows nothing of an "oral tradition"—advances the hermeneutical predominance of the oral over the written tradition in Judaism, taking this to be the essence of any Jewish learning. On Rosenzweig's critique of Islamic tradition "lacking an oral tradition," see Rosenzweig *Der Stern der Erlösung,* with an introduction by Reinhold Mayer (Frankfurt a. M.: Suhrkamp, 1990), 185–86; about the paramount importance of the recitation of the Qurʾān and the theological and aesthetic specifics of its oral transmission, cf. Navid Kermani, *Gott ist schön. Das Ästhetische Erleben des Koran* (München: C. H. Beck, 1999). For a brilliant analysis of Rosenzweig's ideological reading of Islam within nineteenth-century orientalism and the colonial and nationalist constructions of European modernity, see Yossef Schwarz, "Alienated Closeness: A Glance upon Islam," in Franz Rosenzweig, *"Innerlich bleibt die Welt eine." Ausgewählte Schriften zum Islam,* edited, introduced, and with an afterword by Gesine Palmer and Yossef Schwarz (Berlin: Philo, 2003), 111–47. For more references on the primal significance of the oral tradition as a hermeneutical principle in Jewish tradition, see Almut Sh. Bruckstein, *Die Maske des Moses. Studien in jüdischer Hermeneutik* (Berlin: Philo, 2001/2007), 89–103, and passim. The working out of parallel hermeneutical structures of Jewish and Islamic oral traditions would be of utmost importance for a future agenda of shared Jewish-Muslim scholarship.

27. Elliot R. Wolfson, "Flesh Become Word: Textual Embodiment and Poetic Incarnation," in *Eros, Language, Being,* 190–260, esp. 206. Angelika Neuwirth cites Harry A. Wolfson's coining the term "inlibration" for Jewish and Muslim tradition; see Neuwirth, "Scripture and Body," n. 7 of the unpublished manuscript.

28. Richard Ettinghausen, "Arabic Epigraphy: Communication or Symbolic Affirmation," in *Near Eastern Numismatics, Iconography, Epigraphy and History: Studies in Honor of George C. Miles,* edited by Dickram K. Kouymjian (Beirut: American University of Beirut, 1974), 297–317.

29. Ibid., 306.

30. Ibid., 317.

31. Roland Barthes, *Der entgegenkommende und der stumpfe Sinn. Kritische Essays III,* translated from the French by Dieter Hornig (Frankfurt a. M.: Suhrkamp, 1990), 161–62; for the original French, see Roland Barthes, *L'obvie et l'obtus: Essais critiques* 3 (Paris: Ed. du Seuil, 1982).

32. For an extended hermeneutical argument proposing the juxtaposition of Jewish and Muslim mystics with universal rationalism, see Bruckstein, *Vom Aufstand der Bilder,* 13–33.

33. Kandinsky, *Punkt und Linie zu Fläche. Beitrag zur Analyse der malerischen Elemente,* "Bauhaus Bücher," vol. 9, edited by Walter Gropius and L. Moholy-Nagy (München: Albert Langen, 1926).

34. The French-Syrian poet and writer Adonis sees in the autonomous visual semiotics of both Islamic calligraphy and surrealist painting a hermeneutical openness related to the hermeneutics of the visual field at large, especially with relation to the unconscious; see Adonis, *Sufism and Surrealism,* translated from the Arabic by Judith Cumberbatch (London: SAQI, 2005).

35. Abdul-Rahim Al-Shaikh, "The Sufi's Dance," lecture delivered at ha'atelier— platform for philosophy and art in Berlin, September 2007, forthcoming in *ha'atelier essay series* 2009. I am grateful to the author for his generosity in sharing his thoughts with me on this topic.

36. Roland Barthes, *Der entgegenkommende und der stumpfe Sinn,* 159.

37. Barnett Newman, *Selected Writings and Interviews,* edited by John P. O'Neill (New York: Knopf, 1990).

38. Elliot R. Wolfson, *Language, Eros, Being,* 206–7.

39. Angelika Neuwirth, "Scripture and Body: Some Thoughts about Qurʾanic Monotheism."

40. The Sema movement of the Sufis' dance signifies devotion to God and a celebration of his oneness in whirling motion.

41. Franz Rosenthal, "Abu Hayan al Tawhidi on Penmanship," *Ars Islamica,* 13–14 (1948): 18.

42. The search for the logos behind or beneath the text is not to be confused with the invigorating Jewish and Muslim practice of inhaling breath—*pneuma*—vocal tunes into the Hebrew or Arabic text which consists of consonant letters only. Both the Torah and the Qurʾān are brought alive in liturgical contexts by oral recitation in which the text is enlivened by the breath of the reader audibly carrying the vocals into its texture in oral tradition. According to the medieval Bible commentator Ibn Ezra, the consonants represent the body of the text, whereas the vocals, the *pneumata,* which are inextricable bound to the voice of the reader, represent its life and soul. Thus the text is brought to life when it is audibly recited in the community by its readers or studied in oral tradition. See Bruckstein, *Die Maske des Moses,* 100–101, for further references.

43. See, for example, the discussion of creator, soul, matter, time, and space as mutually independent principles in al-Razi's cosmogony according to Shlomo Pines, *Studies in Islamic Atomism,* translated from German by Michael Schwarz, edited by Tzvi Langermann (Jerusalem: Magnes Press, 1997), 67–69 and passim.

44. Daniel Boyarin, *Border Lines,* 151–225.

45. Luce Irigaray, *Speculum of the Other Woman,* 298.

46. Ibid., 26–27.

47. Ibid., 224.

48. Ibid.

49. Goerges Didi-Huberman, *Die leibhaftige Malerei,* translated from the French by Michael Wetzel (München: Wilhelm Fink Verlag, 2002), 28. See also Bruckstein, *Vom Aufstand der Bilder,* 66 and 122–23; Jacques Derrida, *Grammatologie* (Frankfurt a. M.: Suhrkamp, 1974), 278; English *Of Grammatology,* translated by Gayatri Chakravorty Spivak (Baltimore: Johns Hopkins University Press, 1974).

50. Elliot R. Wolfson, *Circle in the Square: Studies in the Use of Gender in Kabbalistic Symbolism* (Albany: SUNY Press, 1995), 79–121, and passim.

51. Nilüfer Göle, *Schleier und Republik. Die muslimische Frau in der modernen Türkei* (München: Babel, 1995).

52. "Modern Mahrem: Islamic Veilings and Secular Imaginaries," exhibition curated by Emre Baykal and Nilüfer Göle, santralistanbul, Istanbul, 2007.

53. For the activities of *ha'atelier,* an international platform for Jewish-Muslim cooperations in the humanities and the visual arts, see www.ha-atelier.de. Ha'atelier—platform for philosophy and art was founded by the author in 2001; see also Bruckstein, *Vom Aufstand der Bilder,* 127–33.

54. The rabbinic scholar Max Kadushin describes this process or movement of thought as analogous to the functioning of an organic system, see Max Kadushin, *Organic Thinking* (New York: Jewish Theological Seminary, 1938).

55. It is obvious that spatial and temporal structures are not opposed to one another in this context since the temporal element is essential to the moment of indeterminacy here invoked.

56. Leora Batnizky draws attention to the fact that "Rosenzweig's description of the artwork parallels his description of the Jewish people." See Batnizky, *Idolatry and Representation: The Philosophy of Franz Rosenzweig Reconsidered* (Princeton, N.J.: Princeton University Press, 2000), 98. For a discussion of Batnizky's thesis within my own talmudic reading of TB *Berakhoth* 54a, see Bruckstein, *Vom Aufstand der Bilder,* 107–9.

57. Franz Rosenzweig, *Der Stern der Erlösung,* 14, 16 (his emphasis).

58. For my friend and colleague Elliot R. Wolfson and the artist Parastou Forouhar.

PART 3

OTHERS CONFRONT JEWISH PHILOSOPHY, JEWISH PHILOSOPHY ABSORBS ITS OTHERS

5

CONSTRUCTION OF ANIMALS IN MEDIEVAL JEWISH PHILOSOPHY

Kalman P. Bland

There are times in life when the question of knowing if one can think differently than one thinks, and perceive differently than one sees, is absolutely necessary if one is to go on looking and reflecting at all. . . . In what does [philosophy] consist, if not in the endeavor to know how and to what extent it might be possible to think differently, instead of legitimating what is already known? . . . [Philosophy] is entitled to explore what might be changed, in its own thought, through the practice of a knowledge that is foreign to it.

"Now," said [Socrates], "if you wish to find this out easily, do not consider the question with regard to men only, but with regard to all animals and plants, to all things which may be said to have birth."

HISTORIOGRAPHY AND REJUVENATION OF RESEARCH PARADIGMS

THE IMPULSE TO PURSUE NEW DIRECTIONS IN THE STUDY OF MEDIEVAL Jewish philosophy neither originates in a vacuum nor requires starting from scratch. The impulse is more reformative than revolutionary, partly because many of the old compass-points and traditional coordinates for historiography still hold true: medieval Jewish philosophy was indeed launched in, and flourished in, Arabophone, Islamicate environments; medieval Jewish philosophy was indeed the cultural enterprise of discovering and adjudicating conceptual differences distinguishing "revelation" in the form of biblical-talmudic traditions from "reason" in the form of Greek procedures and doctrines as formulated by Plato, Aristotle, Plotinus, and their various commentators, both polytheist and monotheist. Isaac Husik was not entirely off the mark when he declared, in 1916, that "revelation and reason, religion and philosophy, faith and knowledge, authority and independent reflection are the various expressions for the dualism in mediaeval thought, which the philosophers and theologians of the time endeavored to reduce to a monism or a unity. . . . Philo in Alexandria and

Maimonides in Fostat were the products not of the Bible and the Talmud alone, but of a combination of Hebraism and Hellenism, pure in the case of Philo, mixed with spirit of Islam in Maimonides."[1]

Neither was Julius Guttmann entirely off the mark, first in German in 1933 and again in Hebrew in 1963, when he insisted that "the Jewish people did not begin to philosophize because of an irresistible urge to do so. They received philosophy from outside sources, and the history of Jewish philosophy is a history of successive absorptions of foreign ideas which were then transformed and adapted according to specific Jewish points of view. Such a process first took place during the Hellenistic period. . . . [Greek] philosophy penetrated Jewish intellectual life a second time in the Middle Ages. It was Greek philosophy at second hand, for the philosophic revival took place within the orbit of Islamic culture and was heavily indebted to Islamic philosophy, which, in its turn, derived from Greek systems of thought. . . . Even during the Middle Ages—which knew something like a total, all-embracing culture based on religion—philosophy rarely transcended its religious center. This religious orientation constitutes the distinctive character of Jewish philosophy, whether it was concerned with using philosophic ideas to establish or justify Jewish doctrines, or with reconciling the contradictions between religious truth and scientific truth."[2]

Neither was Harry A. Wolfson entirely off the mark, in 1948, when he invented the "synthetic medieval philosopher" who subscribed to a number of characteristic "doctrines," "teachings," or "common principles," which are anchored in sacred Scripture and in the light of which "every branch of pagan Greek philosophy—its epistemology, its metaphysics, its physics, and its ethics" was revised. These scripturally based doctrines, articulating the intellectual contents of revelation, "furnish . . . enough materials for an orderly description of the world . . . an explanation of those things [the synthetic philosopher] wants to know about the world, how it came into being and how it is governed, [and] . . . rules for the guidance of man in his various relations to his fellow men." The work of "reason" in the form of pagan Greek philosophy is therefore identical with the work of "revelation" in the form of Scripture: "to discover . . . truths . . . to discover the nature of the world, to describe it, to explain it, and to lay down rules for the conduct of mankind." "Scripture, to our synthetic philosopher, however, is always true, if only its language could be properly understood; reason would always be true, if only it were not misguided by the body in which it is encased. In the proper study of the relation of Scripture to reason, therefore, Scripture has to be interpreted in the light of what is most evidently true in reason, and reason has to be corrected in the light of what is most evidently the true teaching of Scripture."[3]

Neither was Leo Strauss entirely off the mark in 1967 when, articulating the differences between Hellenism and Hebraism, he argued that "the least one would have to say is that according to Plato the cosmic gods are of much higher rank than the traditional gods, the Greek gods. Inasmuch as the cosmic gods are accessible to man as man—to his observations and calculations—, whereas the Greek gods are accessible only to the Greeks through Greek traditions, one may ascribe in comic exaggeration the worship of cosmic gods to the barbarians. . . . It goes without saying that according to the Bible the God Who manifests Himself as far as He wills, Who is not universally worshipped as such, is the only true god. The Platonic statement taken in conjunction with the biblical statement brings out the fundamental opposition of Athens at its peak to Jerusalem: the opposition of the God or gods of the philosophers to the God of Abraham, Isaac, and Jacob, the opposition of Reason and Revelation."[4]

Neither was Colette Sirat entirely off the mark in 1985, when she summarized her predecessors, reasserting a cluster of well-established truisms: (1) "During the Middle Ages, 'philosophy' . . . referred to the 'explanations of the world,' the 'systems of thought' elaborated by the Greeks, which reached their culmination in the fifth and fourth centuries BC with Plato and Aristotle." (2) "This God of the philosophers is essentially different from the God of the Bible." (3) "Maimonides . . . did not innovate very much in philosophical thought; he took over the 'philosophy,' the 'science,' as it was expounded by the Arab philosophers; but he wished to show not only that this philosophy did not contradict the revealed text but that the revealed text alludes and leads to it. . . . This means that a given philosophy, appearing at a certain moment of human history, was brought into connection with the Jewish tradition, and the traits common to certain texts of the Hebrew heritage and to this system of thought were emphasized." (4) "Thus one can say that the history of Jewish philosophy in the Middle Ages is the history of the effort of the Jews to reconcile philosophy (or a system of rationalist thought) and Scripture. According to the various philosophers, the effort was more or less successful; the different elements, philosophical or religious, assumed greater or lesser importance, but the harmonizing of these two systems of thought in one unique verity was the theme of almost all Jewish medieval philosophy. And when the accepted philosophy was called into doubt, this was in the name of reason."[5]

These five opinions, or master narratives plotting the tale of medieval Jewish philosophy, are not perfectly congruent. Husik and Sirat prefer to see the medieval Jewish philosophic enterprise as the effort to harmonize, reconcile, or reduce to a monism the differences between Jewish and Greek traditions; Guttmann acknowledges that some of those cultural differences amount to doctrinal contradictions; Strauss stresses the radical incommensurability that perennially segregates the traditions; and Wolfson prefers to see medieval Jewish philosophy as yet another episode in which Greek principles concerning epistemology, metaphysics, physics, and ethics are chastened into becoming the subordinated handmaiden of Hebrew Scripture.[6] These significant differences nevertheless pale in comparison to their similarity. Common to all five of the paradigmatic, consensual renditions of medieval Jewish philosophy are an emphasis on the doctrine of God and the assumption that ancient Greek philosophy may be reduced to a collection of epistemological "principles," "teachings," "doctrines," "systems of thought," "ideas," "scientific truths," or rational "explanations of the world." With the notable exception of Wolfson, who at least acknowledged ancient Greek philosophic preoccupation with ethics, in theory if not applied practice, historians of medieval Jewish philosophy have tended to restrict Greek philosophy to exclusive concern with cognition, scientific knowledge, or cosmological explanation, and unquestioned reliance on the supremacy of pure reason.

As Pierre Hadot has meticulously shown, this reductive assumption is typical of the "scholastic *teaching* of philosophy . . . which has always had a tendency to emphasize the theoretical, abstract, and conceptual side of philosophy."[7] Favoring theoretical abstraction, the "scholastic teaching of philosophy has obscured" what Hadot identifies as "a way of life" or "praxis" that features "spiritual exercises" enabling people to "develop a *habitus,* or new capacity to judge and criticize; and to *transform,*—that is, to change people's way of living and of seeing the world."[8] In Hadot's view, ancient Greek philosophy is misconstrued when scholars fail to discern its sociological, soteriological, and existential implications or fail to recognize philosophy's resemblance to what today we might fairly classify as religion, a practical "way of life." Adjusting our view of Greek philosophy to accord with Hadot's analysis necessarily entails a paradigm shift, or modification, in our approach to the study of medieval Jewish philosophic texts. If the modern study of medieval Jewish philosophy is beginning to show its age, the case for making that shift is compelling.

The shift would be neither idiosyncratic nor unattractive to comparativists. Heinrich Zimmer, the distinguished historian of Indian thought, anticipated Hadot's perception of ancient Greek philosophy. In a monograph published in 1951, Zimmer noticed that

> Indian philosophy . . . has had, and still does, its own disciplines of psychology, ethics, physics, and metaphysical theory. But the primary concern—in striking contrast to the modern philosophers of the West—has always been, not information, but transformation: a radical changing of man's nature and, therewith, a renovation of his understanding both of the outer

world and of his own existence; a transformation as complete as possible, such as will amount when successful to a total conversion or rebirth. In this respect Indian philosophy sides with religion to a far greater extent than does the critical, secularized thinking of the modern West. It is on the side of such ancient philosophers as Pythagoras, Empedocles, Plato, the Stoics, Epicurus, and his followers, Plotinus and the Neoplatonic thinkers. We recognize the point of view again in St. Augustine, the medieval mystics such as Meister Eckhart, and such later mystics as Jacob Böhme of Silesia. Among the Romantic philosophers it reappears in Schopenhauer.[9]

To Zimmer's list, Hadot added the names of "Montaigne, Descartes, Kant, . . . [and] many other thinkers, as different as Rousseau, Shaftesbury, . . . Emerson, Thoreau, Kierkegaard, Marx, Nietzsche, William James, Bergson, Wittgenstein, Merleau-Ponty, and still others. All, in one way or another, were influenced by the model of ancient [Graeco-Roman] philosophy, and conceived of philosophy not only as a concrete, practical activity but also of a transformation of our way of inhabiting and perceiving the world."[10]

Neither would the proposed shift in research paradigms be anachronistic or ahistorical. Medieval Jewish echoes of Hadot's and Zimmer's notion of philosophy as a transformative way of life and their partiality for lists reverberate in Judah Halevi's *Kuzari*. Halevi's trans-confessional philosopher concisely alludes to "the cheerful soul" of the perfected man whose intellect has conjoined with the Active Intellect and who therefore "pays no attention to the passing away of his body and his organs since he and [the Active Intellect] are one and the same thing. His soul enjoys an excellent state during his lifetime, as he comes to belong to the company of Hermes, Asclepius, Socrates, Plato, and Aristotle; indeed, he, they, and all those who have achieved their rank as well as the Active Intellect are one and the same thing."[11] Halevi's philosopher also stipulates that the preconditions and consequences of this way of life are "contentment, humility, meekness, and every other praiseworthy inclination." It is a way of life devoted exclusively to the acquisition of metaphysical and cosmological truths, together with "purity of soul," an exemplary ethical way of life conducted without concern for particularisms of any sort, whether religious or ethnic.[12]

The literary echoes of Halevi's universalizing philosopher assure us that a redescription of medieval Jewish philosophy along the lines suggest by Hadot is appropriate and capable of yielding rich dividends. The redescription is likely to correct the tendency of modern scholars, from Husik to Sirat, to discount or overlook medieval Jewish responses to artifacts and art forms, just as it is likely to correct the tendency of modern scholars to deprive medieval Jewish philosophies of ethics and politics of the "attention" they "deserve."[13] The redescription promises to rejuvenate the modern study of medieval Jewish thought by offering new points of departure and shedding fresh light on old topics.

ANIMALS IN PLACES OF PAIN AND PLEASURE

For the point of departure in this essay, I have chosen Socrates, Aesop, and animal fables. Eventually, they will lead to an encounter with the enchanting beguilements of medieval Hebrew literature, especially its braided conceptions of spatiality, violence, pleasure, and death as they converge in the social construction of non-human animals as humanity's Same and Other.[14] In the *Phaedo*, Plato reports that Socrates spent his final days in a heterotopic space that makes a difference: Death Row in Athens. Socrates was pondering, among other questions, the coincidence of pain and pleasure. "And I think," Socrates said, "if Aesop had thought of them, he would have made a fable [*muthon*] telling how they were at war and god wished to reconcile them, and when he could not do that, he fastened their heads together and for that reason, when one of them comes to anyone, the other follows after. Just so it seems in my case, after pain was in my leg on account of the fetter, pleasure appears to have come after." Cebes, one of Socrates' visitors, exploited the opportunity. "By Zeus, Socrates, I am glad you reminded me. Several others have asked about the poems you have composed, the metrical versions of Aesop and the hymn to Apollo . . . why you, who never wrote any poetry before, composed these verses after you came to prison?" Socrates replied that a life-long, recurrent dream compelled him. "Socrates," the dream demanded, "make music and work at it." Prior to the trial and festival that delayed his execution, Socrates explained, he thought that by "music" philosophizing was meant. After the trial and awaiting execution, Socrates continued, he reconsidered his life's vocation and thought it prudent to take the dream literally by composing poetical verses. "So first I composed a hymn to the god whose festival it was; and after the god, considering that a poet, if he really is to be a poet, must compose myths and not speeches, since I was not a maker of myths, I took the myths of Aesop, which I had in hand and knew, and turned into verse the first I came upon."[15]

Which of Aesop's myths did Socrates versify? Plato does not say, but we might as well ask which kind of apple alerted Newton to gravity's attraction or which verse of Scripture prompted late ancient rabbis to compose midrash.

Giving license to imagination, it may be remembered that Aesop told the tale of two species, mice and men, and two spaces, town and country:

the tale of a field mouse who invited his friend, the town mouse, to join him for dinner in the country. The town mouse was unsatisfied by the meager fare of raw barley and corn. Because he considered the rustic diet fit only for ants, he persuaded the field mouse to join him in town for proper dining. The urbane menu included "some beans and bread flour, together with some dates, a cheese, honey and fruit. The field mouse was filled with wonder and blessed him with all his heart, cursing his own lot. Just as they were preparing to start their meal, a man suddenly opened the door. Alarmed by the noise, the mice rushed fearfully into the crevices. Then, as they crept out again to taste some dried figs, someone else came into the room and started to look for something. So they again rushed down the holes to hide. Then the field mouse, forgetting his hunger, sighed, and said to his erstwhile companion. 'Farewell my friend. You can eat your fill and be glad of heart, but at the price of a thousand fears and dangers. I, poor little thing, will go on nibbling barley and corn without fear or suspicion of anyone.'"[16]

The fable broadcasts philosophy. As Socrates once taught and philosophic field mice always rediscover, it is divinely ordained and therefore timelessly true for all animals, humans included, that we ought to live fearlessly and that pleasure and pain are determined by place and human activity.

Socrates may have added that fables, like all myths, constitute a deceptively profound genre.[17] At one level, fables edify and entertain; they convey prudential wisdom rather than traffic in information; they challenge us to suspend disbelief; they are charming projections of human foible and virtue. Barely disguised morality plays, fables pretend that animals are humans. At another level, fables stubbornly resist allegorization. They prefer being taken literally. The fantastic component of animals conversing in human language signals a refusal to dilute the doctrine that space, drama, and emotion shape the life of all creatures.[18] Fables therefore mock human pretensions of uniqueness and grandeur. By insisting that animals are moral agents who speak, fables destabilize conventional rationality;[19] they disrupt so-called common sense.[20] A form of "spiritual exercise" described by Hadot, fables assert themselves as transformative "efforts to practice objectivity in judgment," as liberating "efforts to become aware of our situation in the universe. Such an exercise of wisdom [is] thus an attempt to render oneself open to the universal."[21]

When Berakhiah ha-Naqdan, in the twelfth century, retold Aesop's mouse fable in Hebrew, things had changed, but not altogether. Space still made a difference. Creatures from the habitat of town still found life in the habitat of wilderness uncomfortable; creatures from the habitat of wilderness still found life in the habitat of town intolerable. Space was still simultaneously "a social product (or outcome) and a shaping force (or medium) in social life."[22] Creatures still traveled from place to place to satisfy multiple needs; space was still the dramatic site of adventure, pleasure, and pain; and, as usual, natural creatures still had far more to fear from mankind than from the rest of nature.

In Berakhiah's version, the town mouse "journeyed from his native place to visit his kin in another city." Stopping for the night in the forest, where he saw "country mice disporting themselves in their soul's paradise," the town mouse "lodged with a country mouse with whom he took pleasure." Their food was spare, "herbs and the like, and the root of the broom." Said the town mouse to the forest mouse, in Moses Hadas's charming translation, "Thy foot shall follow in my steps; tomorrow shalt thou journey with me and I will make thee drink of my beverages and thou shalt eat of my viands. Better for thee will be a day in my courts than a thousand in the forest midst straitness and oppression, in the blast of the storm wind, and in the lack of food. . . . Come with me and lift thy head high; I will bestow dainty sweetmeats upon thy soul." When the two mice arrived at *Bet Lehem*, Bethlehem, literally the House of Bread, the city mouse said, "I have compassion upon thee; lo, all my house is before thee—eat as is thy pleasure." So the mice proceeded to eat, drink, and make merry, "with flour and bread and flesh and fish," until a man entered the room to fetch his food and supply his board. Immediately, the town mouse fled, hiding in his shelter; the country mouse followed suit. As soon as the man departed, the mice left the safety of their hiding place. The town mouse pounced on the food, but the forest mouse stayed put, watching from a safe distance to see what might befall his companion. The forest mouse "quivered with dread of the man he had seen; his flesh trembled and his spirit was crushed for the path he had taken, and he regretted his rational choice (*maḥavshavo*)."

When the town mouse finished stuffing himself and returned to their hiding place, the forest mouse waxed eloquent, declaiming, "Happy is he who departs hence in peace and is no longer in fear and dread. From the moment I forsook my lodging the iniquity of my steps has encompassed me. . . . I will no longer tarry with thee. Terror has breached our covenant. Come to the rock, hide thee in the dust from before the man, lest he gather thee in his trap, lest the lurker stir from his ambush. All thy life is vexation and wrath; but bread in secret is sweet. Why hast thou slandered the forest? Better a dry crust and tranquility therewith than a house filled with the sacrifices of contention. From every man that approaches thou fleest in panic and in breathlessness takest refuge in one tent then another. In my place I shall find song and joyful shouting, the beauty of Carmel and Sharon."[23]

In the version of this amusing tale told by Horace in *Satires,* the details differ but the upshot remains unchanged. The sybaritic city-slicker mouse puts a rhetorical question to the abstemious country mouse—"Wouldn't you put people and the city above these wild woods?"[24]—to which the country mouse replies with a resounding and sagacious, No, for I repudiate the city. The country mouse refuses "to slander the forest," where wealth happily means nothing and men to be feared do not live.

The country mouse ought to have known better. Men do not live in the forest, but they visit it, doing what cannot be done in cities. Judah al-Harizi (1170–1235) explored this territory in the twenty-fifth chapter, or Gate, of his collection of *maqamat,* the justly famous Hebrew *Book of Takhemoni.* He reversed the polarity from pleasure to pain, showing that wild spaces, precisely because they are innocent and idyllic, invite dreadful human activity. As if the landscape itself were alive, even inanimate stones have reason to fear the ubiquitous terror of human violence. Setting the scene, Heman the Ezrahite, one of al-Harizi's poetic alter egos, speaks: "Journeying from Ashkelon to the Valley of Ayalon we camped upon a pleasant green, and spoke, each man, of places he had seen or things he had heard; whereupon an old man chanced by, whose flashing eye hinted a vision none else could descry. Let me tell you, he ventured, what my eyes have seen here, for I have not been here in many a year. Long since, I passed this place and, lifting my eyes, saw a champion of the hunt who could the desert lion outface; who, with a roar, could mountain peaks displace. . . . Behold, the hero a-horse on his raging course, falcon to hand; and to shoulder, the source of quick death—his quiver. Shiver, now, rocks at his stallion's attack: fall back, lest flint hooves grind you to powder. Hunter and horn roar louder and louder: leaping on mountains, he halloos, he yells, flushing conies and hares, and wide-eyed gazelles, and the trembling hart."

"Now a trail wound deep to the mountain's heart, to a large, rocky glen and, therein, a covert den where none intruded. Here safe and secluded, lay a camp of deer, tranquil all, large and small, old and young, the fawn nudged gently by the mother's joying tongue, the grazing roe, the watchful buck, the suckling fawn, and mother giving suck. Blest be the babes, now seeking rest upon their mother's breasts, now sweetly sleeping; then waking, leaping, mother dancing at their sides, now faster, now slower, neck craning higher, now lower, not knowing that her sun will soon set in their tears, that their doomsday nears. Even as she runs from them, faces them, even as she kisses, embraces them, Death's arrow thrums: he comes. The hero comes!"

So well-prepared by the poet, need we guess what ensues? Let Heman's old man, the trickster, the other of al-Harizi's poetic alter egos, complete the tale. "Now weary unto death, their sun set, flanks throbbing, wet with blood and sweat, the deer are hard beset on every side by the flash of the warrior's steel, by wheeling falcon and the hounds hot zeal. Hound at neck and hound at heel, barking, nipping. Lunging, gripping, rending, ripping thighs, throats, paps, their legs collapse, as many are taken in Death's traps. Growls and barking drown their silent moans as their flesh is ripped from their twitching bones. Yes, the maddened pack pulls their bowels apart, drinks down the blood of fawn and hart, and all for no sin on their part."[25]

Were the function of these mouse tales and hunting scenes to verify that premodern fabulists and poets perceived mankind as the wanton scourge of space, as the dreadful destroyer of natural life in both urban and undomesticated locations, similar examples could easily be multiplied. Numerous examples nevertheless fail to tell the whole story. To the question posed by Horace's town mouse, who was habituated to life in fear while consuming urban dainties—"Wouldn't you put people and the city above these wild woods?"—not every medieval Jewish poet or philosopher replied with a No. Many of them, indeed, "slandered the forest" precisely because they were infatuated by the city, finding pleasure rather than pain in the presence of urbanized mankind.

Dan Pagis (1930–1986), no mean poet himself and scholarly historian of medieval Hebrew poetry, noted that secular poetry composed by Moses ibn Ezra (1055–1135), like all medieval Hebrew poetry devoted to life's physical pleasures, knew nothing of the nineteenth-century's Romantic, humanly untouched, idyllic landscape. According to Pagis, the medieval poets, steeped in Spanish courtier culture, delighted in nature only insofar as they perceived it to be a carefully groomed backdrop to highly refined human pursuits. Rather than naturalizing human culture, the medieval poets socialized, politicized, or aestheticized natural landscapes. Forging their metaphors, they praised nature by likening it to skilled artisans or political leaders with whom nature itself competes.[26] "The Garden Dressed in a Coat of Many Colors," by Moses ibn Ezra, in T. Carmi's translation, for example: *"Katnot passim lavash ha-gan. . . .* The garden put on a coat of many colors, and its grass garments were like robes of brocade. All the trees dressed in chequered tunics and showed their wonders to every eye. The new blossoms all came forth in honour of Time renewed, coming gaily to welcome him. But at their head advanced the rose, king of them all, for his throne was set on high. He came out from the guard of leaves and cast aside his prison-clothes. Whoever does not drink his wine upon the rose-bed—that man will surely bear his guilt."[27]

Another example: the culturally saturated, unapologetically anthropomorphic poem *"Katav Stav,"* "Winter Wrote," by Solomon ibn Gabirol

(1021–1055), again in T. Carmi's translation: "With the *ink* of its showers and rains, with the *quill* of its lightning, with the *hand* of its clouds, winter *wrote a letter* upon the garden, in purple and blue. No artist could ever conceive the like of that. And this is why the earth, grown *jealous* of the sky, *embroidered* stars in the folds of the flower-beds."[28]

Raymond Scheindlin, another keen observer of medieval Arabic and Hebrew poetry, reminds us that goats, fawns, and gazelles served as conventional medieval metaphors signifying the luscious body of the beloved. He also calls our attention to the erotic implications of the medieval preference for human culture over untamed, uncourtly naturalism. In "Fawns of the Palace and Fawns of the Field," Scheindlin analyzed *"Neum asher ben yehudah"* or "Asher in the Harem," the twelfth-century Hebrew *maqama* composed by Shlomo ibn Tzaqbel (d. 1123).[29] The dramatic plot pivots on the difference between beauties of the indoor harem and beauties of the out-of-doors. The crucial lines, spoken by a stunningly beautiful woman, are these: "My master! I am but a mountain-goat of the chamber, a gazelle of the court. I have never dwelt in the forest, nor have I known the cloven mountains. I am a girl of the palace, in opulence bred."[30]

In the course of his discussion, Scheindlin cites a parallel poem composed by Todros Abulafia (1247–1295), "that unabashedly salacious rake of a poet": "When I was yet without wisdom and sense, my heart would run after every beautiful girl. When it was young, it loved the ladies, and clung to mountain goats not a few. To satisfy its lust was its only desire, with everyone of lovely face and form. It made no distinction between lowborn and noble, a patrician's daughter of imposing state. When the season of youth passed, when it was like a passenger with his carriage hitched, my heart thought over my wicked deeds. And shame nearly covered my face. I stopped loving any girl except a noble girl, a princess kept indoors."[31] Like Todros Abulafia after him, the fictitious Asher ben Yehudah finally learned to replace his addiction to beauties in the outdoors with exclusive devotion to sophisticated and noble "fawns of the palace." "Oh you who run to hunt fair gazelles on fragrant hills or on the forest floor, Have done, for they are kept in harem rooms, they pass their lives behind the palace door."[32]

This complementary ensemble of mouse fables, poetry of the hunt, and poetry of erotic preference suggests an analytic field where three sets of independent variables converge in defining geography: universal pain and pleasure, human presence and human absence, town and country.[33] At one extreme, the mouse fables and hunting scene suggest that for all natural creatures the maximal pleasure is to be found in the wild, far away from interaction with mankind, while maximal pain is to be found in proximity to mankind. At the other extreme, the erotic poetry suggests that, for actual humans or metaphorical animals, maximal pleasure is to be found in elaborate sites of human settlement far away from untamed nature. Occupying a midpoint, the opening lines of the hunting scene suggest that pleasure is also to be found while "camping on a pleasant green" in the untamed countryside. Like Boccacio's *Decameron* or Chaucer's *Canterbury Tales* or the genre of Arabic and Hebrew *maqama*, the opening lines of al-Harizi's hunting scene situate pleasure in the countryside less because of the idyllic and refreshing landscape and more because of the sociable company of congenial fellow travelers who pause to swap tales of impressive sites seen and dramatic sounds heard for mutual entertainment or edification.

Regardless of their position on the analytic spectrum generated by the three sets of independent variables, all of the medieval Hebrew texts exhibit a geography of pathos. They all presuppose a deeply ingrained conceptual distinction between town and country.[34] They affirm that space is the site of social, political, or aesthetic drama and therefore that all space is inescapably produced by mankind.[35] The texts agree that all animals, including the human, are subject to pleasure and pain. The texts also anthropomorphically personify nature, implying that space not only sets the scene for pleasure and pain but that space itself may be subject to a similar range of feelings.

This geography of pathos is a far cry from competing notions of space in technical, or scholastic, medieval Jewish thought. According to the Aristotelian philosophers, space is the imaginary geometric boundary, vessel, envelope, or "surrounding limit" (*takhlit maqif*) between any physical entity and its immediately contiguous environment.[36] Unlike the medieval geography of pathos, the competing medieval philosophic concept of space is impersonal, abstract, and dispassionate. The Aristotelians, tending toward cosmic perspective and universality, nevertheless seem oblivious to earth's geography as the zone of pain and pleasure for all creatures.

ANIMALS IN DEATH

In the twelfth century, Abraham ibn Ezra gave voice to a commonplace of dualistic metaphysics when he identified the "glory and majesty" mentioned in Psalms 8 with "the power of the living soul (*neshamah*) that [God] breathed into [man], for it is supernal and not bodily, and therefore not subject to death."[37] Moses Maimonides (1138–1204) was verbalizing a closely related medieval commonplace when he argued that "man possesses as his proprium something in him that is very strange as it is not found in anything else that exists under the sphere of the moon, namely, intellectual apprehension. In the exercise of this, no sense, no part of the body, none of the extremities are used; and therefore this apprehension was likened unto the apprehension of the deity. . . . It was because . . . of the divine intellect conjoined with man, that it is said of the latter that he 'is in the image of God and in His likeness,' not that God, may He be exalted, is a body and possesses a shape."[38]

Another ambassador for prevailing dualism was Jacob Anatoli, the thirteenth-century Jewish translator, physician, and philosopher active in southern France and Italy. Presupposing the hierarchic scale of nature or the great chain of being, Anatoli measured mankind against the lower realm of inanimate "mountains and valleys," the higher animate realm of plants, and the even higher realm of "sensate animals" (hay margish). Although he conceded that human beings were animals of some sort, he concluded that a human being, the "rational/speaking animal" (hay medabber), cannot be compared with any of these other earthly composites. Anatoli insisted that "man is the most glorious [nikhbad] of all, since it falls within his power to choose the correct path and to know truths. Choice entails providential reward and punishment [gemul]."[39]

These and similar passages were well known by Jewish intellectuals. Their thoughts were both inspired and reinforced by Islamic renditions of Greek philosophy. Ibn Rushd, Averroes (1126–1198), an Andalusian, the single most authoritative medieval commentator on the Arabic Aristotle, reasoned that non-human animals neither conceive abstract ideas nor understand forms of art. Deploying a dietary metaphor, he articulated the implications of epistemological dualism for the human-animal boundary in these uncompromising terms:

> In man, the [five senses] perceive the differences in objects and the particular ideas represented by them. These [ideas] would be, with respect to the object of sense, as the fruit is to the rind. In other animals, however, the [senses] perceive only external properties, and with reference to the object of their senses their relationship is that of the rind to the fruit. The proof of this can be seen in the fact that animals are not moved by these senses as man is moved by them, for man will be stirred by the sound of melodies, while animals will not be stirred, unless we use the term "stirred" with regard to them in an equivocal sense. Similarly, man is moved by the sight of colors and figures in a manner in which animals are not moved.[40]

Marginalized, obscured, or forgotten by Ibn Rushd and like-minded medieval philosophers were the animals charmed by the music of Orpheus,[41] the speckled goats bred with the help of Jacob's rods,[42] or the birds tricked by Zeuxis the painter.[43] Never before had the gap between humanity and animals been wider or deeper.[44]

By the seventeenth century, Jewish scholars had inherited a rich legacy of arguments and authorities establishing the absolute superiority of human beings over the beasts. As Elliot R. Wolfson has persuasively ar-

gued, many of those arguments were not universalist, but rather chauvin-
istic, exclusively Jewish, or "ethnocentric."[45] Rabbi Manasseh ben Israel,
famous for his campaign with Cromwell to win readmission to England
for the Jews,[46] drew upon that legacy to compose a homiletic essay based
on the opening chapters of Genesis that outlined no fewer than ten essential and traditional differences between (Jewish) human beings and
beasts. Among his narcissistic, Judeocentric, or anthropocentric arguments, Rabbi Manasseh explained that just as God is the final cause and
ultimate aim (*takhlit*) of all creatures, since "all existents ascend toward
God," so too is humanity the final cause and ultimate aim of all the lower
creatures. Moreover, just as God "rules and governs all creatures," so too
does "humanity rule and govern all the lower creatures." Regarding this
sovereignty, Rabbi Manasseh emphasized that human superiority was a
function of the soul directly conferred by God, since in purely physical
terms, no human body is a match for the various animals and predators,
"as everyday occurrences prove." When, however, the human soul is perfected, "no creature has the power to raise a limb to injure a human." It
therefore follows, according to Rabbi Manasseh's reasoning, "that the human soul is divine, for if the human soul were like the soul of any other
animal, why should sovereignty be ascribed to the human soul and why
did God permit human beings to slaughter and eat the animals?" Rabbi
Manasseh also noted that "human beings alone are endowed with free
will and choice, whereas animals have only instinct, or natural inclination (*netiyʿah tivʿit*)," to guide their behavior. Similarly, only human beings
are endowed with speech, as "Aristotle taught in the *Politics*," all assertions
to the contrary ascribing speech to animals being mere rhetorical flourish, hyperbole, or "tall-tales [*guzma*]." Finally, Rabbi Manasseh remarked
that only man and woman were given their generic names directly by
God, in contrast to all the other animals that were named by Adam in the
Garden, thereby signifying human superiority over all other creatures.[47]
Rabbi Manasseh, the sage of Amsterdam, anchored in the conventional
thought of tradition, unequivocally rejected the comparison of humans
with animals.

Rabbi Manasseh's contemporary, the philosopher René Descartes, was
no less grounded in the conventions of tradition that taught the absolute
superiority of human beings over the animals. Like Rabbi Manasseh, Descartes clearly, distinctly, and dogmatically minded the comparison of humans *with* animals. But unlike Rabbi Manasseh, who merely harvested
the traditional arguments, leaving them intact, Descartes pruned and
grafted. He propagated new stock. He excised the organic metaphor of instinct, or natural inclination, and replaced it with the technological metaphor of mechanism to explain animal behavior. With Descartes' help, me-

dieval cosmological and epistemological dualism was guaranteed several centuries of continued vitality.[48] Descartes reduced animals to machines. He restricted cogitation to human minds.[49]

Because the gap between humans and animals had taken the metaphysical turn, medieval and early modern critics of medieval dualism could not rehash traditional appeals to the non-pejorative, homogenizing dust of common mortality forcefully articulated in Ecclesiastes 3:18–21: "So I decided, as regards the children of Adam, to dissociate them [from] divine beings [elohim]. And to face the fact that they are beasts [behemah]. For with respect to the fate of the children of Adam and the fate of beasts, they have one and the same fate: as the one dies so does the other, and both have the same life breath, so that man's superiority or advantage [mutar] amounts to nothing, for everything is vaporously futile. Everything goes to one and the same place, everything comes from the dust of the earth and returns to the dust of the earth." Regardless of their diverse motives, premodern thinkers who recognized continuities between humans and animals and therefore relished the comparison of humans *with* animals were obliged to be inventive. They would have to augment Ecclesiastes by designing innovative rhetorical weapons capable of toppling the metaphysical buttresses that supported previously established cultural intuitions of human superiority. In turn, these established intuitions rested on longstanding socioeconomic realities: urban settlement, omnivorous human diet, fashions in human clothing, memories of the ancient sacrificial cult, domestication of animals for agriculture and transportation, and training of animals for hunting and war.[50] Resisting this formidable cluster of conceptual and socioeconomic realities presented a formidable challenge.

Necessity being the mother of invention, the new weapons were not long in coming. Nudged forward by the emergence of mechanistic worldviews, the gradual shift from traditional belief to modern secularism and the assault against vitalism were well underway. Yirmiyahu Yovel, a modern historian of ideas, accurately identified the protagonists and deftly summarized their revolutionary accomplishment: "Machiavelli and Hobbes, Spinoza, Darwin, Marx, Nietzsche, Freud, perhaps Heidegger, and Sartre were all bound by a philosophy that challenges the 'divine part' in man and its alleged origin in a transcendent realm; each worked to shatter complacent self-images and comforting illusions and claimed to have discovered something dark and unsettling about the structure of man and his world."[51]

Yovel's references to Spinoza, Darwin, and Freud are particularly helpful. Darwin finished Spinoza's monistic work.[52] Darwin also bridged the gap made wider by Descartes, who had perpetuated medieval distinctions between humans and animals by denying rationality to animals and defining them as mere machines. Freud, another of Spinoza's disciples, put Darwin's controversial achievement famously:

> In the course of centuries the *naïve* self-love of man has had to submit to two major blows at the hand of science. The first was when they learnt that our earth is not the centre of the universe but only a tiny fragment of a cosmic system of scarcely imaginable vastness. . . . The second blow fell when biological research destroyed man's supposedly privileged place in creation and proved his descent from the animal kingdom and his ineradicable animal nature. This revaluation has been accomplished in our days by Darwin, Wallace, and their predecessors, though not without the most violent contemporary opposition.[53]

The modern phase of the revolt against medieval dualism, featuring the comparison of humans *with* animals, is well known.[54] The medieval phase of the revolt against dualism remains something of a terra incognita in the history of Jewish ideas. Venturing to map this terrain will not be futile. Two arguments are reassuring: modern historians of medieval ideas can safely assume that medieval Jewish scholars were intimately familiar with the text of Ecclesiastes that lumped humanity with the beasts; they can also safely assume that Spinoza, Darwin, Nietzsche, and Freud might find precursors and kindred spirits in the medieval, so-called credulous Age of Faith.[55] It is to that relatively unknown, heterodox terrain in medieval Jewish thought that I now turn my attention.

To sample *medieval* shattering of "complacent self-images" and *medieval* disclosure of "something dark and unsettling about the structure of man and his world," consider a poem composed by an extraordinary Jew from Andalusia, the warrior, poet, diplomat, and sage, Shmuel ha-Nagid (993–1056).[56] The poetic scene evokes Nietzsche's abrasive claim that righteous morality originated in the muck of commercial transactions.[57] Shmuel described a bazaar, a *souk/shouk*, a "butchers' market" where countless "sheep, cattle . . . and fowl were all awaiting" slaughter. "Blood congealed on blood." Nearby, there were "fishmongers and fishermen," bakeries and incessant "ovens":

> Men were bearing home their kill; Men were hawking beasts they had
>   hunted;
> I stood alone musing, still. Then speaking to the crowd I said,
> "Why should these beasts be snatched away from life to die?
> How do they differ from you? They die and are born.
> They sleep and wake at morn. They sit. They stand.
> Because the Rock made them tasty morsels for you, He did not destroy
>   them.
> Had He but given them the spirit, they would have killed their killers.

They have soul, like you; also heart, like you, to make them wander the
    earth.
Never's a time when mortals do not die, never a time when begetters do not
    beget.
To this clear heads must attend, even princes boasting their glory.
Were they to understand the universal secret (*sod ha-ʿolam*), they would
    know
that all this applies to every man.[58]

Shmuel's poem resembles an anvil. Anvils are not bashful. Struck
by the smith's hammer, they clang. Shmuel's poem, a meditation on the
universal inevitability of death, is not bashful. Comparing humans *with*
beasts, the poem clangs, tolls, and peals. Once, it explicitly challenges its
audience to acknowledge that there is no "difference" (*hevdel*) between humans and animals. Twice, it reminds vendors and shoppers in the market, the scene of bloody carnage, that they and the animals are identical
in birth and death. Twice, it uses the phrase "like you" (*kakhem*), admon-
ishing shoppers, vendors, fishermen, and hunters that humans and animals possess souls and hearts that drive them to the same life of wan-
dering, refugees escaping troubles here, seekers of vital needs there. Four
additional parallels are drawn. Rhetorical merisms, paired opposites representing the whole, they underscore the sameness of bodily behavior and
quotidian routine: sleeping and rising, sitting and standing.

Sixteen times, one for each of its sixteen lines, the final word or rhyming syllable is *dam*, meaning "blood." Were this number of emphatic cadences inadequate, line three deploys the word "blood" three times. By
the time the poem reaches its last word, *ha-adam*, literally meaning "man,"
the word has been transformed phonetically into meaning "the bloody
one" (*ha-dam*). In this clashing finale, the poem utterly shocks by sub-
verting orthodoxy. It lifted its closing phrase from the very end of Ecclesiastes: "Revere God and observe His commandments, for all this applies
to every man." Rather than endorsing this expected biblical "exhortation
to piety,"[59] Shmuel's poem shrinks mankind to the two implications of
bloodiness: naturalistic description of inevitable death, and moral condemnation of wanton slaughter. Marking inevitable death, bloodiness signifies physiological, psychological, and existential identity with the beasts.
Marking ruthless slaughter, bloodiness signifies mankind's arrogant butchery. Compared to the poem's scathing critique of human egotism, Ecclesiastes went easy on human vanity. Puncturing our specious pride, Ecclesiastes bluntly affirmed mankind's common dustiness and mortality with
animals. Stressing mortality, Shmuel's poem is similarly blunt. Unlike Ecclesiastes, however, Shmuel's poem denounces mankind's uncaring markets and unsympathetic shedding of animal blood.

That the poem's main targets are human arrogance and lack of compassion is made clear by the absence of calls to modify or revolutionize
the social order. The poem no more objects to hunting and fishing than
it condemns the relatively innocuous practice of baking bread. It rebukes
arrogance, not the food cycle; it excoriates cruelty, not the institution of
abattoirs. The poem neither advocates vegetarianism nor demands the
elimination of all commerce. Instead, it seeks to provoke a profound change
in human self-awareness and moral sensibility. The poem defies conventional blindness to human community with the animals and demands
that mankind forgo complacent ignorance and understand the "universal secret" of commonality between human and beast. Operating as a rhetorical mechanism for the artful transmission of philosophic universalism and the liberating transformation of human consciousness, Shmuel's
poem exemplifies Hadot's felicitously termed late-ancient practice of "spiritual exercises."[60]

Conspicuously absent from Shmuel's poem is any allusion to the "image of God." Affirmations of a God-given superiority, as they did for Rabbi
Manasseh and the traditionalists, would justify markets and butchery. The
poem, however, makes no appeal to exalted human status. The poem does
not invoke the naturalistic Aristotelian doctrine that ascribed humanity's
uniquely upright posture and uniquely rational capacities to the subtle
mixture of bodily elements and natural heat.[61] Neither does the poem invoke any of the other conventional medieval claims to human superiority,
including moral agency, religiosity, or "saintliness."[62] The socioeconomic
subordination of animals is explained in strictly theocentric terms. To
the question of why these animals are "snatched away from life to die,"
the poem replies by invoking God's will and God's will alone. The poem
thereby raises the terrifying prospect of revenge and reversal of fortune:
Were God to permit them, animals would requite humanity measure for
measure, transforming human killers into the killed. The poem, therefore, neither (anachronistically) advocates animal rights nor indulges in
romantic idealization or "bambification" of the beasts.[63]

Written in full recognition that animals have sufficient reason for re-
prisal and that no "difference" (*hevdel*) obtains between predators, whether
human or animal, the poem discloses Shmuel's conscience-stricken declaration of the "universal secret" (*sod ῾olam*): Animals mirror humanity. In
the social order, tables get turned, hunters inevitably become the hunted,
eaters eventually become the eaten. Our fate, then, like that of animals,
is precariously contingent and inescapably mortal. No wonder that thinking about animals "tends to produce a combination of resistance and
anxiety."[64] At any rate, thinking about or with animals produced Shmuel's

poem, the stunning product of his mindful comparison of humans *with* animals.

Shmuel also expected to die. He believed that his soul would be judged in the afterlife. If found worthy, reward would follow; if found guilty, punishment instead. In 1054, two years before his death, he composed these contemplative lines:

> . . . worst of all, most bitter fate of all: I shall have to rise from my musty grave to stand in judgment, while all my deeds are weighed in a balance, my merits on this scale and my sins on another. But perhaps an angel will speak up in my favor and add weight to my virtues. He will remind my Rock, as I am being judged, that I pored over the Scriptures and expounded the Law. And I shall then hear: 'God has already approved what you have done.' Thus shall the scales be tipped, and my good deeds will outweigh my crimes. I shall rejoice that I am being taken away by the glory of God. I shall rejoice as my moon and sun are taken away.[65]

It is altogether unlikely that Shmuel believed in a similar eschatology for animals.

Like Moses Maimonides, medieval Jewish thinkers denied that animals were subject to individualized reward and punishment in the afterlife.[66] Did Shmuel both believe and disbelieve in the comparison of humans *with* animals? The citations suggest that he entertained both opinions: one poem affirms humanity's difference from animals with respect to moral accountability in the afterlife; the other poem affirms humanity's commonality with animals with respect to blood.

We are aware of the contradiction, but was he? The question is unanswerable. Not every poet is a logician; not every poem is an exercise in systematic theology. We are also well advised never to mistake the character speaking within a poem for the poet's own self.[67] Shmuel may have articulated both opinions without feeling the need for reconciling them.[68] Seeking to fathom Shmuel's mind, we cannot achieve mathematical certainty, but we can read his poems, the products of his supple imagination. One of those poems was occasioned by the pious expectation of impending death and final judgment. Another was occasioned by the utter shock of pondering a bloody marketplace. That poem places Shmuel squarely in the camp of thinkers who confront the universality of death, defy conventional theological assurances of human superiority, and neither avoid the necessity nor mind the disruptive consequences of comparing humans *with* animals.

Shmuel's unsettling discovery of the "universal secret" was partially enabled by a combination of familiarity with quotidian marketplaces and knowledge of Ecclesiastes. The discovery was therefore not unique. It was readily available to other medieval Jewish intellectuals as well. In twelfth-century Spain, Judah al-Harizi uncovered the "secret" while meditating on the noble pastime of chase or hunt. He gave voice to those irrepressible and horrifying meditations in the *Book of Tahkemoni*. After graphically describing the wanton slaughter of innocent deer by the "heroic" hunter and his trained birds and dogs, al-Harizi put these stunning words in the mouth of Hever the Kenite, his spokesman:

> Praise God . . . whose justice rules the earth—though it be veiled from man. Who can grasp our Maker's plan, that makes one creature another's prey, for the killer's life sweeps blameless lives away? He fashions fangs to dismay the weak, yes slay the weak; casts kid and dam to riving claw and beak, gives the young and feeble unto the command of the murderer's hand. Who shall illumine God's laws, that fling the suckling to the lion's jaws? Yes, one creature feeds another, but in the end, each is the other's brother: all wend earthward, all descend, all feed slug and maggot in the end. . . . All creatures are food; Death's hungry eye, Death's falcon eye, has scanned them. The weakest feed the strong. Such are God's laws. None can withstand them. The killers wreak their worst designs. . . . Yet though they snare and feed, the hunter Death shall snare and brand them. Eater and eaten shall perish both, the selfsame Death command them. All praise to God, whose ways are hid; no one can understand them.[69]

Hever's speech and Shmuel's poem use similar means to reach similar ends. They both begin with graphic descriptions of mankind's treatment of animals, here in the hunting scene, there in the marketplace; they both allude to Ecclesiastes, refusing to invoke the "image of God" or affirm humanity's superiority over the animals; and they both conclude that death is the common destiny of human and beast alike. What Hever calls "God's laws," Shmuel terms the "universal secret." Shmuel declares that "never's a time when mortals do not die"; Hever proclaims that "all wend earthward, all descend, all feed slug and maggot in the end."

Hever's speech and Shmuel's poem also differ. Despite the bloodiness of the scene, Shmuel's marketplace remains morally neutral, a necessary evil, or simply God's sanctioned way of guaranteeing human sustenance. Shmuel does not call for the elimination of slaughter houses or marketplaces. In Shmuel's poem, two other things never happen: questions of guilt or innocence relating to the human actors and animal victims are never raised, and God's justice is never challenged. The contrast is stark: Hever despises the savagery of hunting for mere sport. Equally significant, Hever's thoughts, unlike Shmuel's poem, are preoccupied with guilt and innocence. Hever struggles with the perennial challenge of theodicy, stumbling over language that reconciles God's justice with "the suffering of innocents,"[70] whether human or animal.

To assume that Shmuel intended his marketplace poetically to represent life itself would be gratuitous. His marketplace stubbornly remains an actual marketplace and nothing more. Again, the contrast is stark. Al-Harizi's poetic vision was apparently more ambitious than Shmuel's, on par with al-Harizi's more complex preoccupation with human guilt, innocence, and suffering; the universality of death; and God's justice. Al-Harizi's hunting scene, like Shmuel's marketplace, was also intended to be taken literally. It was meant to describe the actual slaughter of innocent deer by an actual hunter accompanied by actual hounds and birds. Hever's closing remarks, however, indicate that the hunt also served as apt metaphor, symbol, allegory, or parable for life itself. Some modern critics propose that the victimized deer were possibly meant to be an allegory for the innocent suffering of the Jewish people throughout their history.[71] It is more likely, however, that al-Harizi's imagination was less parochial. His moral vision was universal. His concerns were both trans-ethnic and trans-species. Hever's attention is focused exclusively on death, the same death that awaits all Jews, whether innocent or guilty; the same death that awaits all human beings, whether Jewish or Gentile, innocent or guilty, hunter or hunted; and the same death that awaits all animals, whether predator or prey, large or small, strong or weak, mild or ferocious. Focused on the universality of death, Hever's thoughts also belong to Hadot's genre of "spiritual exercises."

Shmuel's poem slightly softens the blow by remarking the hypothetical: "Had [God] but given [animals] the spirit, they would have killed their killers." Hever's remarks proclaim the factual. Hunting and predation are merely two of Death's ways. Eventually, the killers do indeed become the killed, in one fashion or another, for Death commands all creatures, fulfilling "God's law." The law ordains that innocent victims, whether human or animal, will suffer and die, just as the law ordains that the unconscionable hunter who wantonly killed the deer or the unjust persecutor who oppressed human victims will inevitably be hunted and brought to death by Death. Like Ecclesiastes, Hever refused counterfeit consolations based on the illusion of just compensation in the afterlife.[72] Like Ecclesiastes and Shmuel ha-Nagid, Hever the Kenite, al-Harizi's eloquent speaker, unflinchingly championed the comparison of humanity *with* the beasts.

Regarding the common destiny of human beings and beasts, Ecclesiastes remarked that they share "one and the same fate." Medieval Hebrew poetry corroborated this truth poetically; medieval Hebrew fables confirmed it fabulously, seeing life empathetically from the perspective of the animals and therefore without the false consolations of conventional theology. In fables, animals know that even the most fit do not survive the inexorable and universal cycle of eaters becoming the eaten. Let one example suffice. In the twelfth century, Berakhiah ha-Naqdan related the tale of the wily fox who tried persuading the fish to stop consuming one another, come ashore, and live under his peaceful reign. One fish spoke sagaciously for them all:

> If thou wilt verily rule over us, wilt thou indeed ordain peace for us? Even when we abide in quiet waters, surrounded by our kin and in peace, the robber assails us, the destroyer arises against us, and we live in terror of men's snares. Many fisherman fish for us, many hunters hunt us; we all roar like bears. If you had experience of our plight, your anguish would equal ours. If now by thy cunning thou devourest spoil, when thou hast done spoiling thou shalt thyself be spoiled, for suddenly thy creditors shall rise up against thee and thy ways will not prosper. How dost thou spread a web of deceit against us and count thyself secure in a land of peace? Surely the fowl of the heavens and the fish of the sea and the beast of the field are all ambushed and hunted, and even humans quarrel for the envy that is between them. But there be higher than they, and he that is higher than the highest regardeth.[73]

More prosaically but not less powerfully, similar conclusions regarding the universal food chain were reached in tenth-century Iraq, in the city of Basra, home to a fraternity of Muslims known as the "Pure Brethren," the *Ikhwan al-Safā*, authors of the extended fable known as "The Case of the Animals versus Man before the King of the Jinn." One of the fable's heroic characters, a sagacious and eloquent frog, is credited with these observations: "All animals of the sea flee in terror before the sea serpent, but he fears nothing, save only a tiny beast somewhat resembling a gnat or mosquito. . . . Once it stings him, its poison creeps through his body and he dies. The same is true with birds as predators . . . when [they] die, they are at last eaten by the smallest, the ants, flies, and worms." As the frog continues, the empirical evidence mounts, and the argument escalates: "So too is the life's course of human beings. For they eat the flesh of kids and lambs, sheep and cattle, birds and the rest. Then when they die, they are consumed in their graves and coffins by worms, ants, and flies." Having come this far, the frog draws the unsettling, inexorable conclusion:

> We have heard, your Majesty, that these humans claim to be our masters and that we and all the other animals are slaves to them. Do they not consider the give and take of animals' lives, which I have described? Is there any difference between them and the rest in this regard? Sometimes they are the eaters, but sometimes they are the eaten. So on what account do the sons of Adam claim superiority over us and all the other animals? Their end is the same as ours. And it is said, "Their works will bear their signet marks. All of them were formed from earth, and the earth is their destiny."[74]

Four hundred years later, in fourteenth-century southern France, the Arabophone frog from Basra learned to speak Hebrew with the help of his translator, Qalonymus ben Qalonymus.[75] The frog's arguments were given a fresh hearing and a wider audience. Featuring the comparison of humans *with* animals and exploiting the inevitability of death in order to civilize humanity, the arguments would not have struck late-medieval Jewish audiences as being unfamiliar or unwelcome. Earlier medieval Hebrew poetry and fables engaged in similar "spiritual exercises." Perhaps identifying with the frog's plight, late-medieval Jewish audiences might have suspended disbelief and forgotten that animals cannot speak reasonably. Perhaps other audiences, as well, might admire the frog's heterodoxy and courageous eloquence. He spoke irksome truth to pretentious power. Let medieval, fabulous frogs have their timeless, fabular say. To conclude this exploratory attempt to redescribe medieval Jewish philosophy along the lines suggested by Pierre Hadot, let the frog from Basra have the final word.

NOTES

The first epigraph is from Michel Foucault, *The Use of Pleasure: The History of Sexuality*, vol. 2, translated by Robert Hurley (New York: Vintage Books, 1990), 8–9. The second epigraph is from Plato, *Phaedo* 70D. See *Plato I*, translated by H. N. Fowler (Cambridge, Mass.: Harvard University Press, 1914), 244–45.

1. Isaac Husik, *A History of Mediaeval Jewish Philosophy* (New York: Atheneum, 1969 [Macmillan, 1916]), xiii, xvi.

2. Julius Guttmann, *Philosophies of Judaism: A History of Jewish Philosophy from Biblical Times to Franz Rosenzweig*, translated by David W. Silverman (New York: Schocken Books, 1973), 3–4.

3. Harry A. Wolfson, *Philo: Foundations of Religious Philosophy in Judaism, Christianity, and Islam* (Cambridge, Mass.: Harvard University Press, 1948), 2:445–47.

4. Leo Strauss, "Jerusalem and Athens: Some Preliminary Reflections" in *Studies in Platonic Political Philosophy* (Chicago: University of Chicago Press, 1983), 166.

5. Colette Sirat, *A History of Jewish Philosophy in the Middle Ages* (New York: Cambridge University Press, 1985), 1–5.

6. For a divergent historiographical account, altogether thoughtful and thought provoking, see Jonathan Cohen, *Philosophers and Scholars: Wolfson, Guttmann, and Strauss on the History of Jewish Philosophy*, translated by Rachel Yarden (New York: Lexington Books, 2007).

7. Pierre Hadot, *What Is Ancient Philosophy?* translated by Michael Chase (Cambridge, Mass.: Belknap Press of Harvard University Press, 2002), 273. See also idem, *Philosophy as a Way of Life: Spiritual Exercises from Socrates to Foucault*, edited and introduced by Arnold I. Davidson (Cambridge: Blackwell, 1995).

8. Hadot, *What is Ancient Philosophy?* 274

9. Heinrich Zimmer, *Philosophies of India*, edited by Joseph Campbell (New York: Meridian Books, 1956 [1951]), 4.

10. Hadot, *What Is Ancient Philosophy?* 270.

11. For the classical genealogy of this emphasis on unity, see Philip Merlan, *Mono-*

psychism Mysticism Metaconsciousness: Problems of the Soul in the Neoaristotelian and Neoplatonic Tradition (The Hague: Martinus Nijhoff, 1963).

12. Judah Halevi, *The Book of Refutation and Proof of the Despised Faith (The Book of the Khazars)*, edited by David H. Baneth (Jerusalem: Magnes Press, 1977), 1:1. The bulk of this English translation is excerpted from Sirat, *History of Jewish Philosophy in the Middle Ages*, 2–3.

13. See the editor's introductory comments in *Averroes' Middle Commentary on Aristotle's Nicomachean Ethics in the Hebrew Version of Samuel Ben Yehudah*, edited and introduced by Lawrence V. Berman (Jerusalem: Israel Academy of Sciences and Humanities, 1999), 49. For an attempt to correct the historical record on matters aesthetic, see Kalman P. Bland, *The Artless Jew: Medieval and Modern Affirmations and Denials of the Visual* (Princeton, N.J.: Princeton University Press, 2000).

14. For the conception of non-human animals as Same and Other, I have profited from Wendy Doniger O'Flaherty, *Other People's Myths: The Cave of Echoes* (Chicago: University of Chicago Press, 1988), 75–96, especially 80–81, where she argues that "animals and gods are two closely related communities poised like guardians on the threshold of either side of our human community, two Others by which we define ourselves. Aristotle remarked that a man who could not live in society was either a beast or a god." Her bibliographic reference inexplicably refers to "Aristotle, *Nicomachean Ethics* 10.28." Perhaps she was alluding to *Politics* I:1 [1253a25–29]: "while a man who is incapable of entering into partnership, or who is so self-sufficing that he has no need to do so, is no part of a state, so that he must either be a lower animal or a god." See Aristotle, *Politics*, translated by H. Rackham (Cambridge, Mass.: Harvard University Press, 1944), 12–13. Alternatively, she may have been alluding to *Nicomachean Ethics* 10:8, 7–8 [1178b7–32], which was well known to medieval Jewish philosophers in Hebrew translation. See *Averroes' Middle Commentary on Aristotle's Nicomachean Ethics in the Hebrew Version of Samuel Ben Judah*, edited by Lawrence V. Berman, 342–44. For a guide in tracking Aristotle's influential discussion of human perfection, happiness, or ultimate felicity, see Hava Tirosh-Samuelson, *Happiness in Premodern Judaism: Virtue, Knowledge, and Well-Being* (Cincinnati, Ohio: Hebrew Union College Press, 2003).

15. *Phaedo* 59b–60b in Plato, *Euthyphro, Apology, Crito, Phaedo, Phaedrus*, translated by H. N. Fowler (Cambridge, Mass.: Harvard University Press, 1982), 209–13.

16. Aesop, *The Complete Fables*, translated by Olivia and Robert Temple (New York: Penguin Books, 1998), 178–79. For the versified form of the Greek original, see Ésope, *Fables*, edited and translated by Émile Chambre (Paris: Société D'édition "Les Belles Lettres": 1957), 107–8.

17. For an appreciation of storytelling, the genus of fiction to which animal fables belong as species par excellence, I am currently indebted to several profound discussions: Walter Benjamin, "The Storyteller: Reflections on the Works of Nikolai Leskov," *Illuminations*, translated by Harry Zohn, edited and introduced by Hannah Arendt (New York: Schocken Books, 1968), 83–109: Elaine Scarry, "A Defense of Poesy (The Treatise of Julia)," *On Nineteen Eighty-Four: Orwell and Our Future*, edited by Abbot Gleason, Jack Goldsmith, and Martha Nussbaum (Princeton, N.J.: Princeton University Press, 2005), 13–28; and Robert Cover, *Narrative, Violence, and the Law*, edited by Martha Minow et al. (Ann Arbor: University of Michigan Press, 1992), 95–172.

18. For primary texts in Latin, English translations, and learned analysis of medieval animals who converse in human language, see Jan M. Ziolkowski, *Talking Animals: Medieval Latin Beast Poetry, 750–1150* (Philadelphia: University of Pennsylvania Press, 1993). I am grateful to Professor Edwin D. Craun, my colleague at the National Humanities Center in 2002–2003, for calling this text to my attention.

19. For my appreciation of philosophy's insistence on exploring the limitations of abstract rationality and philosophy's strategic alliance with drama, theatre, and film-making to realize its anti-intellectualist aims, I am indebted to the lively discussion in "Let's Make More Movies" by Paul Feyerabend in *The Owl of Minerva: Philosophers on Philosophy,* edited by Charles J. Bontempo and S. Jack Odell (New York: McGraw-Hill, 1975), 201–21.

20. Ibn Sina, the great Islamic philosopher, composed a fable, "The Recital of the Bird," that features talking birds. Imagining the skeptical response of his convention-ally rational audience, Ibn Sina invented their response to the fable: "I see that thou art somewhat out of thy wits, unless sheer madness hath befallen thee. Come now! It is not thou who didst take flight; it is thy reason that has taken flight . . . How should a man fly? And how should a bird fall to speaking?" To which Ibn Sina sagaciously re-sponded, "Oh, what a waste of words! And with what a miserable result! The worst kind of discourse is this chatter with which people are so liberal without any occasion." For an English translation of the text, bibliographic references, and critical discussion, see Henry Corbin, *Avicenna and the Visionary Recital,* translated by Willard R. Trask (New York: Pantheon Books, 1960), 165–203.

21. Pierre Hadot, *Philosophy as a Way of Life,* 212. For more analysis of "spiritual ex-ercises," see Hadot's *What Is Ancient Philosophy?*

22. Edward D. Soja, *Postmodern Geographies: The Reassertion of Space in Critical Social Theory* (New York: Verso, 1989), 7.

23. *Fables of a Jewish Aesop Translated from the Fox Fables of Berechiah ha-Nakdan,* translated by Moses Hadas (New York: Columbia University Press, 1967), 25–26. For the Hebrew original, see *Mishle Shuʿalim le-Rabbi Berakhiah ha-Naqdan,* edited by A. M. Haberman (Jerusalem: Schocken Press, 1946), 18–19. For exhaustive critical discussion, see Haim Schwarzbaum, *The Mishle Shuʿalim (Fox Fables) of Rabbi Berachiah Ha-Nakdan: A Study in Comparative Folklore and Fable Lore* (Kiron: Institute for Jewish and Arab Folklore, 1979), 61–64.

24. *Satires* II: 6 in Horace, *Satires, Epistles and Ars Poetica,* translated by H. Rushton Fairclough (Cambridge, Mass.: Harvard University Press, 1978), 218.

25. Judah al-Harizi, *The Book of Tahkemoni: Jewish Tales from Medieval Spain,* trans-lated by David S. Segal (Portland: Littman Library of Jewish Civilization, 2001), 224–27. For the original Hebrew and a more literal English rendition, see *The Tahkemoni of Judah Al-Harizi,* translated by Victor E. Reichert (Jerusalem: Raphael Haim Cohen's Ltd., 1973), 2:122–28, [Hebrew: 43b–44a].

26. Dan Pagis, *Secular Poetry and Poetic Theory in Moses Ibn Ezra and His Contempo-raries* [Hebrew] (Jerusalem: Bialik Institute, 1970), 256–57.

27. T. Carmi, *The Penguin Book of Hebrew Verse* (New York: Penguin Books, 1981), 323.

28. Ibid., 310.

29. For the Hebrew original, see Hayyim Schirman, *Ha-Shirah Ha-ʿIvrit Be-Sefarad Uve-Provens* (Jerusalem: Mosad Bialik, 1959), 1:554–65. For a witty English poetic ren-dition, see Raymond Scheindlin, "Asher in the Harem by Solomon Ibn Saqbel" in *Rab-binic Fantasies,* edited by David Stern and Mark J. Mirsky (New Haven, Conn.: Yale Uni-versity Press, 1990), 253–67. For a prose rendition, see David S. Segal, "*Mahberet neum ʿasher ben yehuda* of Solomon Ibn Saqbel: A Study of Scriptural Citation Clusters," in *Journal of the American Oriental Society* 102 (1982): 17–26.

30. Raymond P. Scheindlin, "Fawns of the Palace and Fawns of the Field," *Proof-texts* 6 (1986): 195.

31. Ibid., 199.

32. Ibid., 195.

33. In selecting and analyzing this ensemble of texts, I was unable to incorporate the arguments and conclusions reached in two recent publications by Jonathan P. Decter, *Iberian Jewish Literature: Between al-Andalus and Christian Europe* (Bloomington: Indiana University Press, 2007) and "Landscape and Culture in the Medieval Hebrew Rhymed Narrative," *Jewish Studies Quarterly* 14 (2007): 257–85. Our points of departure and critical frameworks differ, but our conclusions appear to be complementary.

34. That the town-country distinction pervaded medieval consciousness is easy to show. See, for example, the illuminating study of this *topos* in Islamic thought by Gordon D. Newby, "Ibn Khaldun and Frederick Jackson Turner: Islam and the Frontier Experience," in *Ibn Khaldun and Islamic Ideology*, edited by Bruce B. Lawrence (Leiden: Brill, 1984), 122–32. For detailed discussions of Ibn Khaldun's terminology and its counterparts in medieval Latin literature, see Muhsin Mahdi, *Ibn Khaldun's Philosophy of History* (Chicago: University of Chicago Press, 1964), 184–87, 190–204.

35. For theoretical elaborations of the sociopolitical foundations for the conceptualization of space, see Henri Lefebvre, *The Production of Space*, translated by Donald Nicholson-Smith (Cambridge: Blackwell, 1991); Michel Serres, *The Parasite*, translated by Lawrence R. Schehr (Baltimore: Johns Hopkins Press, 1982); idem, "The Algebra of Literature: The Wolf's Game" in *Textual Strategies: Perspectives in Post-Structuralist Criticism*, edited by Josué V. Harari (Ithaca, N.Y.: Cornell University Press, 1979), 260–76.

36. The *locus classicus* in Aristotle is *Physics* IV:1–4. For texts and critical discussion, see Harry A. Wolfson, *Crescas' Critique of Aristotle* (Cambridge, Mass.: Harvard University Press, 1929), 44–45, 153–57, 354–65, and passim, as well as the still-useful Israel Efros, *The Problem of Space in Jewish Medieval Philosophy* (New York: Columbia University Press, 1917).

37. See Ibn Ezra's commentary to Psalms 8:6 in any edition of a rabbinic Bible.

38. Moses Maimonides, The *Guide of the Perplexed*, translated by Shlomo Pines (Chicago: University of Chicago Press, 1963), 23 [Book I:2].

39. Jacob Anatoli, *Sefer Malmad Hatalmidim*, (M'kize Nirdamim: Lyck, 1866; Reprint Jerusalem, 1968), 13a.

40. Averroes, *Epitome of Parva Naturalia*, translated by Harry Blumberg (Cambridge, Mass.: Medieval Academy of America, 1961), 20–21.

41. For summaries and references, see Robert Graves, *The Greek Myths* (Harmondsworth, Middlesex: Penguin Books, 1960), 1:111–15.

42. See Genesis 30: 31–43. For discussion, see Bland, *Artless Jew*, 149–51.

43. See Pliny, *Natural History*, translated by H. Rackham (Cambridge, Mass.: Harvard University Press, 1968), 9:309–10 [Book XXXV:36]. Pliny's passage enjoys frequent citation and discussion. For references to the critical discussion and a particularly insightful analysis of the original source, see W. J. T. Mitchell, *Picture Theory* (Chicago: University of Chicago Press, 1994), 334–44.

44. For indications of the biblical and rabbinic assessments of animals, see Elijah J. Schochet, *Animal Life in Jewish Tradition* (New York: Ktav Publishing House, 1984). For the Greek traditions, see Richard Sorabji, *Animal Minds and Human Morals: The Origins of the Western Debate*. For an overview of the medieval Latin traditions, see Joyce E. Salisbury, *The Beast Within: Animals in the Middle Ages* (New York: Routledge, 1994).

45. See Elliot R. Wolfson, *Venturing Beyond: Law and Mortality in Kabbalistic Mysticism* (New York: Oxford University Press, 2006), 42–58, 73–80, 90–124, esp. 107, n. 374. As Wolfson notes, Menasseh ben Israel is "an interesting example" of the phenomenon by which "the anthropological position of the *Zohar*, which predominantly restricts the application of the term *adam* to the Jewish soul, is regurgitated frequently

in kabbalistic works as well as other homiletical or expository works." To be added to the non-kabbalistic authorities discussed by Wolfson, one might add Rabbi David Kimhi's ad locum commentary to Ezekiel 34:31 ["You are called men, but the idolaters are not called men"]. In the case of Rabbi Manasseh, Wolfson correctly observes an ambiguity, since that seventeenth-century sage "is not always consistent as there are passages wherein he articulates a more universalistic approach to the nature of humanity."

46. For biographical data and description of the English campaign that ended in failure, see the still-standard monograph by Cecil Roth, *A Life of Menasseh Ben Israel: Rabbi, Printer, and Diplomat* (Philadelphia: Jewish Publication Society, 1934). For a sampling of current trends in scholarship, see the superb collection of essays in *Menasseh ben Israel and His World*, edited by Yosef Kaplan, Henry Méchoulan, and Richard H. Popkin (Leiden: Brill, 1989).

47. Menasseh ben Israel, *Sefer Nishmat Hayyim* (Amsterdam, 1652 [reprint New York, 1982]), 1–4 [Book I:1]. Menasseh's reference to Aristotle's *Politics* appears to be Book I: 1.10: "For nature, as we declare, does nothing without purpose; and man alone of the animals possesses speech [*logon*] . . . but speech is designed to indicate the advantageous and the harmful, and therefore also the right and the wrong; for it is the special property of man in distinction from the other animals that he alone has perception of good and bad and right and wrong and the other moral qualities." See Aristotle, *Politics*, translated by H. Rackham (Cambridge, Mass.: Harvard University Press, 1932), 11 [=1253a7–18].

48. For a philosophically adept and close reading of the Cartesian texts themselves, see Gordon Baker and Katherine J. Morris, *Descartes' Dualism* (New York: Routledge, 1996). For philosophically acute and historically sophisticated discussions of the medieval background and early modern reactions to Descartes' epistemological and psychophysical dualism, see Marlene Rozemond, *Descartes's Dualism* (Cambridge, Mass.: Harvard University Press, 1998); Norman Diamond, "Thoughtless Brutes," in *Proceedings and Addresses of the American Philosophical Association*, 46 (1972–73): 5–20; and Stephen Toulmin and June Goodfield, *The Architecture of Matter* (Chicago: University of Chicago Press, 1962), 165–69, 307–31.

49. For a compendium of the Renaissance Humanist traditions related to animals explicitly overturned by Descartes, see "Apology for Raymond Sebond" in *The Complete Essays of Montaigne*, translated by Donald M. Frame (Stanford, Calif.: Stanford University Press, 1965), 319–457. For an unforgettable sketch of the striking differences separating Humanists from Rationalists, Montaigne from Descartes, see Stephen Toulmin, *Cosmopolis: The Hidden Agenda of Modernity* (New York: Free Press, 1990), 22–42. For an earlier, explicit, witty, and learned refutation of Cartesian biology, see the fable of "The Two Rats, the Fox, and the Egg" embedded in La Fontaine's "Discourse to Madame de la Sabière," in *The Complete Fables of Jean de la Fontaine*, edited and translated by Norman B. Spector (Evanston, Ill.: Northwestern University Press, 1988), 487–99. For the broader historical and cultural context responsible for the formation and reception of Descartes' controversial ideas, see Leonora Cohen Rosenfield, *From Beast-Machine to Man-Machine: Animal Soul in French Letters from Descartes to La Mettrie* (New York: Oxford, 1941), and George Boas, *The Happy Beast in French Thought of the Seventeenth Century* (Baltimore: Johns Hopkins University Press, 1933).

50. For indications of the ubiquity and importance of animals in medieval daily life, see Salisbury, *The Beast Within*, 1–76.

51. Yirmiahu Yovel, *Spinoza and Other Heretics: The Adventures of Immanence* (Princeton, N.J.: Princeton University Press, 1989), 109.

52. See Wolfson, *Philo: Foundations of Religious Philosophy*, 2:458–60. Wolfson argued that Spinoza overturned the dualistic religious philosophy created by Philo that dominated Western thought for seventeen centuries.

53. Sigmund Freud, *Introductory Lectures on Psychoanalysis*, translated by James Strachey (New York: W.W. Norton, 1966), 285 [Lecture XVIII, end].

54. For a sampling of the vast literature, see Arthur A. Lovejoy, *The Revolt Against Dualism* (Lasalle, Ill.: Open Court, 1960); Antonio Damasio, *Descartes' Error: Emotion, Reason, and the Human Brain* (New York: G.P. Putnam, 1994), and Daniel Dennett, *Darwin's Dangerous Idea: Evolution and the Meanings of Life* (New York: Simon and Schuster, 1995).

55. To cite only one of countless demonstrations, see Jeffrey J. Cohen, *Medieval Identity Machines* (Minneapolis: University of Minnesota Press, 2003).

56. For biographical data, aesthetic evaluation, and abundant sampling of the poetry in English translation, see Peter Cole, *Selected Poems of Shmuel HaNagid* (Princeton, N.J.: Princeton University Press, 1996), and Leon J. Weinberger, *Jewish Prince in Moslem Spain: Selected Poems of Samuel ibn Nagrela* (Tuscaloosa: University of Alabama Press, 1973). For a bracing revisionist view of the traditional historiography that tendentiously idealized Shmuel without considering all of the relevant evidence, see David J. Wasserstein, "Samuel ibn Naghrila Ha-Nagid and Islamic Historiography in Al-Andalus," *Al-Qantara* 14 (1993): 109–25. Also indispensable is Ross Brann, *Power in Portrayal: Representations of Jews and Muslims in Eleventh- and Twelfth-Century Islamic Spain* (Princeton, N.J.: Princeton University Press, 2002), 1–53, passim.

57. Friedrich Nietzsche, *On the Genealogy of Morals*, translated by Walter Kaufmann (New York: Vantage Books, 1989), 70–71 [Second Essay, 8]: "Setting prices, determining values, contriving equivalences, exchanging—these preoccupied the earliest thinking of man to so great an extent that in a certain sense they constitute thinking *as such* . . . here likewise, we may suppose, did human pride, the feeling of superiority in relation to other animals, have its first beginnings."

58. For the original Hebrew text, critical discussion, and elegant English translation that I have substantially modified in places, tending toward prosaic literalism, see Raymond P. Scheindlin, *Wine, Women, and Death: Medieval Hebrew Poems on the Good Life* (New York: Oxford University Press, 1999), 159–61.

59. Ibid., 161. I owe this phrase, the word count of *dam*, and the notion of subversion to Scheindlin's acute formal analysis. He is surely correct in stressing the poem's insistence on the mortality common to humankind and animals. I diverge from his perceptive reading of the poem when he concludes that "all this has been said before" in the biblical book of Ecclesiastes. Shmuel's poem is equally insistent on the moral condemnation of human savagery and the denial of man's superiority over animals, regardless of what that superiority might be. Ecclesiastes never went so far. It has not "been said before."

60. See Pierre Hadot, *What is Ancient Philosophy?* passim; see also his *Philosophy as a Way of Life*, passim.

61. See Gad Freudenthal, *Aristotle's Theory of Divine Substance: Heat and Pneuma, Form and Soul* (Oxford: Clarendon Press, 1995), 56–70.

62. For an English translation of the Arabic text roughly contemporaneous with Shmuel's poem that offers the most thorough medieval inventory of human claims and animal counter-claims to human superiority over the animals, see *The Case of the Animals vs Man Before the King of the Jinn: A 10th Century Ecological Fable of the Pure Brethren of Basra*, translated by Lenn E. Goodman (Boston: Twayne Publishers, 1978). The capstone argument, featuring saintliness, runs as follows: "[Among mankind], the saints

of God [are] the choice flower of his creation, the best, the purest, . . . God's elect. These folks have noble attributes, fair characters, pious acts, diverse sciences, sovereign insights, royal traits, just and holy lives" (202). For the Arabic original, see *Rasa'il Ikhwan al-Safa'* (Beirut: Dar Sadir, 1957), 2:376–77. For the fourteenth-century translation from Arabic into Hebrew by Qalonymos ben Qalonymos (b. 1287) by which it came to be known in late medieval Jewish circles, see, *Sefer Iggereth Ba'ale Hayyim*, Bibliothèque Nationale (Paris), Hebrew MS 899, f. 66v. The Hebrew text is also available in several published editions. See, e.g., *Sefer Iggereth Ba'ale Hayyim* (Warsaw: n.p., 1877), 80. In the monograph on which I am now working, I hope to deal with this spectacular text, this fable to end all fables, at greater length.

63. For "bambification," see Frans De Waal, *The Ape and the Sushi Master* (New York: Basic Books, 2001), 71–74.

64. See the foreword by W. J. T. Mitchell in Cary Wolfe, *Animal Rites: American Culture, the Discourse of Species, and Posthumanist Theory* (Chicago: University of Chicago Press, 2003), ix. Wolfe's book is an eye-opener with respect to contemporary society. Mitchell's remarks (adventitiously and happily) are as pertinent to medieval culture as they are to the modern and postmodern societies he explicitly addresses. This sort of wide-ranging historical applicability is the sign of sound theory.

65. For the Hebrew text and English translation, which I have slightly modified, see Carmi, *Penguin Book of Hebrew Verse*, 298–301.

66. See Moses Maimonides, *The Guide for the Perplexed* III:17. Maimonides associated the belief in divine providence or eschatological reward and punishment for individualized animal souls with the Islamic sect of Mutazilite theologians. Maimonides vehemently denied that Jewish belief agreed with the anti-Aristotelian, Mutazilite view. He maintained that individualized providence is restricted to mankind, which is thereby "permitted and even enjoined to kill animals and employ them usefully" while avoiding all unnecessary cruelty. Contrary to Maimonides' explicit claims, a modern scholar ascribes the belief in reward and punishment for animals in the afterlife to four medieval, Gaonic, Jewish thinkers. So far, I have checked his references to Saadya and found no evidence of such claims. The remaining three sources have yet to be tracked down for verification. See E. J. Schochet, *Animal Life in Jewish Tradition*, 208. For further and illuminating discussion of this vexatious issue, see Daniel Lasker, "The Theory of Compensation ('Iwad) in Rabbanite and Karaite Thought: Animal Sacrifices, Ritual Slaughter, and Circumcision," *Jewish Studies Quarterly* 11 (2004): 59–72.

67. Formulating methodological caution, I am guided by this forceful reminder: "That characters in a literary work should voice opinions appropriate to them rather than to their creator is an elementary matter of literary decorum, the neglect of which may lead to mistaken history as well as questionable criticism." See *The Romance of the Rose by Guillaume De Lorris and Jean De Meun*, translated by Charles Dahlberg (Princeton, N.J.: Princeton University Press, 1995), 10.

68. Instead of emphasizing poetic license that is capable of imagining unresolved contradictions, some scholars think of this quality of mind as characteristically medieval, as Abelardian "sic et non." See María Rosa Menocal, *The Ornament of the World: How Muslims, Jews and Christians Created a Culture of Tolerance in Medieval Spain* (Boston: Little, Brown and Company, 2002), 182.

69. Judah al-Harizi, *The Book of Tahkemoni*, 226–27 [Gate Twenty-Five]. The Hebrew original and a far more literal English translation may be found in Reichert, *The Tahkemoni of Judah Al-Harizi: An English Translation* II, 43b–44a.

70. See the translator's perceptive remarks in David S. Segal, *Book of Tahkemoni*, 541–44.

71. Ibid., 543, n. 7.

72. As David S. Segal forcefully argues, Al-Harizi "undercut his justification of God; chose not to content the reader with the well-known dictum, far less offensive than his flawed whitewash, of 'It is not given us to explain the tranquility of the wicked nor the torments of the righteous' (Mishnah *Avot* 4:15); and, finally, chose not to include any of the myriad rabbinic sources that speak of the rewarding of the just and the punishment of the wicked in the world to come, in the varied understandings of that state." See Segal, *Book of Tahkemoni*, 543.

73. Berakhiah Ha-Naqdan, *Fables of a Jewish Aesop*, 16–17. For the original Hebrew, see *Mishle Shuʿalim*, 13–14.

74. *The Case of the Animals vs. Man*, 133 [English]; *Rasaʾil*, 296–97 [Arabic]; Paris MS 899, ff.41v–42r [Hebrew]; *Sefer Iggereth Baʿale Hayyim*, 46–47 [Hebrew].

75. For a biographical and bibliographic sketch, see Sirat, *History of Jewish Philosophy in the Middle Ages*, 329–30, 443.

6

SHARING SECRETS:
INTER-CONFESSIONAL PHILOSOPHY
AS DIALOGICAL PRACTICE

Steven M. Wasserstrom

SECRECY PERMEATED THE INTELLECTUAL CULTURE OF MEDIEVAL ISLAMICATE civilization, an inter-religious civilization subsuming Jews as well as Muslims.[1] The secret truth with which I am concerned here is not the hidden content of secret monotheistic messages but rather the public act of sharing them.[2] The cult of secrecy, the cultural agreement that secrets should be shared, crossed intra-Islamicate religious boundaries.[3] I sketch here an episode in the historical sociology of inter-religious contact between Muslim and Jew.

Such shared secrecy is a paradoxical communication: On the face of it, secrets do not mean what they say. Everyone, Muslim or Jew, could enjoy the cover thus provided by secrets. In short, concealing, or "secrecy," facilitated revealing, or "sharing."[4] If such mutually intentional indeterminacy comprised a nearly universal phenomenon among Jewish and Muslim elites in this period, then what meaning shall we seek in this universality?

In the following essay, I limit myself primarily to the late twelfth and early thirteenth centuries, an era conventionally said to mark not only the end of the so-called Golden Age of the Jews of Spain but also more generally that of Islamic-Judaic philosophy and mysticism. High point or not, my concern lies with this moment, a brief cultural opening when mysticism, philosophy, and the occult sciences made both rival and overlapping claims on the center of authority. To achieve and sustain their authority, mystics, philosophers, and hermetics often were constrained to learn "secrets" from adherents of foreign religions.

My interest lies in the cross-fertilization between claims to a single truth and inter-confessional sharing of general truths, between social submission to one's scriptural community and intellectual recognition of a trans-scriptural authority.[5] Specifically, then, I will concentrate on the interplay between philosophical esotericism and mystical esotericism, on the rise of the individual and its literary expressions, and, finally, I shall locate them in a transition from twelfth-century philosophical esotericism to thirteenth-century mystical esotericism.

DREAMT RECEPTIONS

Aristotle's ghostly afterlife in the medieval Muslim world was dramatized in a few posthumous appearances. In the first of these, a reliable reporter concerning the arrival of Greek learning in Muslim lands tells us that the Caliph al-Maʾmun

> saw in a dream the likeness of a man white in color, with a ruddy complexion, broad forehead, joined eyebrows, bald head, bloodshot eyes and good qualities, sitting on his bed. Al-Maʾmun related, "It was as though I was in front of him, filled with fear of him. Then I said, 'Who are you?' He replied, 'I am Aristotle.' Then I was delighted with him and said, 'Oh Sage, may I ask you a question?' He said, 'Ask it.' Then I asked, 'What is good?' He replied, 'What is good in the mind.' I said again, 'Then what is next?' He answered, 'What is good in the law.' I said, 'Then what next?' He replied, 'What is good with the public.' I said, 'Then what more?' He answered, 'More? There is no more.'"[6]

This ninth-century Caliph, purportedly inspired by his encounter with a foreign freethinker who lived 1,300 years before him, immediately wrote a letter to the neighboring Byzantine emperor requesting that he provide him with manuscripts of Greek philosophy. Upon their arrival, he instituted a school, the "House of Wisdom" (*Bait al-Ḥikma*), dedicated to their translation and study.

Muslim mystics also claimed that they, like the philosophers, were the elite who could seize directly the inner meaning of the divine text. Some mystics also seized upon Aristotle as a perfect expositor of this perfect vision. I will restrict myself to one example. After a night of spiritualistic practices designed to induce a kind of trance, the twelfth-century hermetic Shihāb al-Din Yaḥya ibn Ḥabash al-Suhrawardī, "in a state of veiling pleasure, shining thunderbolt and flashing light," dreamt of Aristotle. Suhrawardī asked Aristotle "the question of knowledge" (*masʾalat al-ʿilm*), to which the ancient Greek sage replied "Go back to your own soul."[7] For this philosophically inclined mystic, the ancient sage possessed the insight to penetrate to the heart of things, located now in his own soul.[8]

The secret that Aristotle imparted to Suhrawardī in his dream does not refer to law, or to ethics, or to any aspect of Muslim community life as did the secret in the dream of the Caliph al-Maʾmun. Aristotle was now appearing in mystical dreams teaching a kind of inwardness, a going back "to your own soul."⁹ The first dream marks the beginning of the Islamic absorption of Aristotle; the second marks its effective end. In the first instance, Aristotle was dreamt to legitimate a policy of state. But in Suhrawardī's dream, two centuries later, Aristotle's ghost was called to authorize a personal, if not private, quest. And indeed, the after-image of Aristotle, now privatized, never again came to challenge seriously the public standing of Islamic fundamentals.[10]

It is both instructive and amusing, by the way, to note that the most popular Islamicate apparitions of Aristotle had nothing to do with him. The most influential neo-Platonic work of the Muslim and Jewish middle ages, *The Theology of Aristotle*, was actually versions of Plotinus' *Enneads* misattributed to Aristotle.[11] In a related text, written in Arabic probably in the ninth century, a swooning Aristotle delivers his dying wisdom while periodically reviving himself by sniffing an apple.[12] The afterlife of Aristotle was not without its ironies.

One of the ironies of the foregoing narrative is that "the greatest figure of the 13th century was not a man, but a ghost: the ghost of Aristotle whom both the Christian St. Thomas Aquinas, the Jew Moses Maimonides and the Muslim Averroës were to call, simply, 'The Philosopher.'"[13] In the fourth century, Augustine claimed disingenuously that he learned nothing from Aristotle.[14] By the early fourteenth century, Dante tells a different story—tellingly, once again, in the form of a visionary dream. In the *Inferno* (IV:131), Dante has arrived at a noble castle, a symbol of human wisdom, a very different kind of *Bait Ḥikma*. Here he envisions none other than Aristotle: "When I raised my brows a bit more, I saw the master of those who know, seated amid the philosophic family; all regard him, all do him honor."[15] Dante's characterization of the Aristotle he encounters as "the master of those who know" is a far cry from Augustine's scorn.

Aristotle's *Nachleben* unfolded in the philosophical anthropomorphisms of dream. Through their respective dream-meetings with Aristotle, al-Maʾmun, Suhrawardī, and Dante encountered *philosophia* in the guise of its ancient master. These representatives of their day confronted The Philosopher face to face—*as individuals*.

MAN TAMANTAQA TAZANDAQA:
THE CHALLENGE OF THE SCIENCES

I move now to the "translation movement," that is, the movement to translate the Greek sciences into Arabic between the eighth and tenth centuries. From an Islamic and Jewish perspective, the foreign sciences, inasmuch as they were Greek, were pagan. Even so, Jews Judaized and Muslims Islamicized the encyclopedic array of physical sciences inherited from Greece.[16] But both monotheisms also remained normatively wary of the so-called "foreign sciences" (Heb: ḥokhmot ḥitzoniot).[17] As one well-known Arabic maxim expressed this wariness, *Man tamantaqa tazandaqa, "He who practices logic becomes a heretic."*[18] The landmark Islamic rejection of philosophy was al-Ghazali's monumental eleventh-century *The Incoherence of the Philosophers.*[19] The mythological analogue of this cognitive rebuttal, perhaps, was the tradition that Muḥammad the Prophet said that *had Aristotle lived to hear the Qur'ān, he would have converted to Islam.*[20]

That being noted, a countercurrent was also underway. The motif of the wise pagan simultaneously became popular among Jewish and Muslim writers of the tenth to twelfth centuries. And the wisest pagan was, of course, Aristotle. In certain respects, then, Aristotle lingered as "the hidden king of thought"—to borrow the phrase Hannah Arendt applied to Martin Heidegger.[21]

ESOTERIZATION

This ambivalence, this attraction to and countervailing reaction against pagan philosophy, stimulated a certain sequestration of discourse. Aristotle could still be invoked, but usually only non-theologically, only "scientifically," due to official constraints. The challenge was clear. If Aristotelian science succeeded in establishing "generic religion," natural religion, or philosophical religion as such—not to speak of a "pure philosophy"— the autonomy of each monotheistic revelation would have been subverted: monotheistic leaders therefore officially rebuffed these pagan challenges whenever they could.

On the other hand, philosophy—if it may be attributed agency—did colonize some intellectual elites, both Jewish and Muslim. According to the (in)famous "Persecution and the Art of Writing" of Leo Strauss, fear of the persecution resulting from a perception that they trafficked in free thought compelled these intellectuals to obfuscate their ultimate philosophical intentions.[22] Since philosophers usually claimed also to speak on behalf of their respective religions, they all the more cunningly tended to obscure the "pagan" dimension of their authority. At the same time, they strengthened their respective claims to be definitively authoritative expositors of their own monotheisms.

Meanwhile, mystics, on their own distinctive grounds, analogously asserted totalizing claims to authority. And so, by the twelfth century, contending elites exploited secrecy respectively to monopolize, rather than popularize, the perennial teachings of monotheism. These latter-day revolutionaries—philosophers and mystics—arrogated the secrets of tradition respectively to themselves. This process might be termed *esoterization*.

Such esoterization is sometimes explained as indexing the very multiplicity, as such, of scripture-based reading communities. D. P. Walker observes that

> in the history of any revealed religion the question of esoteric, disguised language is likely to be of cardinal importance, for this reason: if the revelation were utterly clear and convincing, then there would be only one religion and everybody would be bound to believe in it; since there have always been several competing religions and at least some unbelievers, the revelation must in every case be supposed to be to some degree obscure, in order to account for this fact.[23]

Walker's principle of esotericism, that *there have always been several competing religions and so the revelation must be obscure to account for the very multiplicity of religions*, takes as its *primordium* the human fact of confessional diversity. For the moment, I mark this context: Esoterization, the systematizing of this discovered obscurity, has its inter-religious history.[24]

BETWEEN INDIVIDUALS:
THE AUTOBIOGRAPHICAL SELF IN DIALOGUE

Understanding this trans-confessional context is essential if we are to integrate esoterization within a historical sociology of monotheism. Toward this end, I want next to consider the role played by emergent forms of the self. Peter Brown noted these forms emerging in twelfth-century Europe, where parallel shifts were underway: "The supernatural becomes an awareness of the individual's own potentiality, salvaged by being raised above the ambiguities and illusions of the natural world. Angels wither away in the mind and art of the 12th century—ancient symbols of the non-human, they are rapidly replaced by symbols of the idealized human."[25]

A second kind of transition, experienced by Jewish intellectuals of this period, was observed by Moshe Perlmann:

> We may note, in this connection, that the [Jewish] individual reappears, what with the greater mobility, physical and intellectual, and with the breaking down of old rigors. Thus individual authorship reappears, after centuries which knew only anonymous bodies of traditional lore (Talmudic, Midrashic; cf. ḥadīth in Islam). Now poets, thinkers, commentators, legists, and grammarians emerge, each insisting on making his distinct individual mark known and felt.[26]

Leo Strauss hinted at a third reason for the emergence of a deepened (and more public) inner life cultivated by certain twelfth-century philosophers: "The precarious status of philosophy in Judaism as well as in Islam was not in every respect a misfortune for philosophy. The official recognition of philosophy in the Christian world made philosophy subject to ecclesiastical supervision. The precarious character of philosophy in the Islamic-Jewish world guaranteed its private character and therewith its inner freedom from supervision."[27]

Related to these three factors was the practice of private study itself. As Arthur Hyman put it, "The study of philosophy was private because philosophic training was generally limited to a gifted few, because students required teachers whom only well-to-do families could afford, and perhaps most importantly, because philosophic studies were often suspect by lay and rabbinic authorities."[28] Similarly, in the Muslim world, as recent studies of the educational systems show, philosophy played little to no part in most curricula.[29]

Maimonides' philosophy, in all these respects, typifies such individualizing tendencies.[30] His is, from one perspective, a philosophy of solitude, drawing in places from the Andalusian philosopher Ibn Bājja, whose masterpiece was titled *The Governance of the Solitary*.[31] *The Guide for the Perplexed* addresses a single correspondent.[32] Presumably, the good Platonic philosopher is to ripen, so to speak, in solitude, but then share the fruits of contemplation with the polis. The published work of philosophy, however, is purported to be a publication for one. This epistolary conceit seems to mark the shift toward the new individual. In short, Maimonides and Ibn Ṭufayl, Jewish and Muslim Andalusian contemporaries, authored their philosophical classics in the form of epistolary treatises purporting to answer questions put to them by correspondents.[33] These Jewish and Muslim contemporaries, who may have known each other, wrote their respective masterpieces, that is, framed as letters to a student or intimate friend. As with the Ismāʿīlī Naṣīr al-Dīn al-Ṭūsī, they could clarify "the aim of the sciences and their secrets" as "spiritual doctors" who alone could rectify the inner ailments of new individual intellectuals.[34]

For all these (and other) reasons, it is reasonable to speak of the inkling of an emergence of an "individual" in this period.[35] The "private character" and consequent "inner freedom" of Islamicate thinkers can furthermore be supported by certain of its literary expressions.[36] Moreover, an explicitly literary expression, the genre of spiritual autobiography, emerges in this period.[37] For present purposes, I note that the individual's "revealing" his life story typically coincided with a plea to protect spiritual secrets.[38] Already in the eleventh century, the mystical intellectual al-Ghazālī, in the introduction to his celebrated autobiography, announced his intention to clarify "the aim of the sciences *and their secrets*."[39] One of the earlier forms of the spiritual autobiography seems to have been the "initiatic romance" of the early Ismāʿīlī missionaries.[40] The influential thinkers al-Ghazālī and Avicenna, acutely sensitive to the Ismāʿīlī mission, wrote autobiographies, as did several philosophers who followed them.[41] Characteristic of this genre are assertions made by Naṣīr al-Dīn al-Tūsī in his autobiography: "For intelligent people there is no secret which has to be kept more hidden than the secret of belief and religious doctrine. Indeed, what harmful consequences would follow if the ordinary, ignorant folk were to become aware of these things requires no explanation."[42] Al-Tūsī goes on to justify the very composition of his autobiography as a confession before his "spiritual doctor."[43] That is, one to one—from individual to individual.

DIALOGUE AS GENRE AND AS METAPHOR IN SHAHRASTĀNĪ AND HALEVI

In literary terms, perhaps the most effective device was the dialogue. Two Jewish-Muslim pairs exemplify the ways in which twelfth-century "individuals" used such devices as means to express themselves to each other, one to one. I refer to the Muslim Shahrastānī (1086–1153) and the Jew Yehuda Halevi (1075–1141). In both cases, one-to-one interactions, either in the metaphors of fictional dialogues or in the genre of letters, provided the literary framework for expressing philosophical secrets.[44]

The dialogue is a striking case of the deployment of fictions for esoteric purposes.[45] Shahrastānī's fictional debate between the Sabeans and the Brahmans and Halevi's fictional dialogue with the Khazar king self-reflexively utilized a "conversation with the pagan" motif in order to expose critically the beliefs and practices of foreign sciences and religions.[46] In the two centuries preceding them, such paradigmatic pagans as Brahmans (Ibn al-Rawāndī), Babylonians (Ibn Waḥshiyya), Persians (Nizāmī, Bahram Gur, Kai Khusraw), had been treated extensively in various genres. But now, in the twelfth century, this convention was taken to a new level of subtlety.

Shahrastānī and Halevi shared at least four important features in their respectively innovative dialogues with the pagan: a rejection of philosophy as the ultimate intellectual path, an influence by Ismāʿīlism, a *détente* between philosophy and mysticism, and an interest in a comprehensive theory of religion. Both worked out these common interests under the cover of theological leadership within their respective religions. Conversations with the pagan written by Shahrastānī and Halevi were philosophical dialogues problematizing the plurality of revelations even as they espoused a trans-confessional prophetology. To be sure, Shahrastānī was an Ashʿari (orthodox) theologian, while the unmistakable surface intention of Halevi's *Kuzari* was the defense of rabbinic Judaism. Nevertheless—

and perhaps precisely for this reason—to the extent that they asserted an anthropology of the prophet in general, and not only a chauvinism of one's own local prophet, they transgressed confessional boundaries in a way that perhaps needed to be concealed.

Like the autobiography, the dialogue was favored by Ismāʿīlī missionaries, who used it to convey, among other things, a veiled message about their mission.[47] The shared "secrets" of Shahrastānī and Halevi were indeed inspired by, even as they transcended, the doctrine of righteous dissimulation (taqiyya) enjoined by such Shiʿites as the Ismāʿīlīs.[48]

THE HERMETIC QUESTION

In addition to the dream, the autobiography, the dialogue, and the letter as expressions of a new kind of monotheistic individual, hermeticists specialized in a practice that, I think, reveals rather explicitly their interest in the emerging individual. I refer to the conjuration of a second self, or astral self. The mid-twelfth-century philosopher Abūl Barakāt al-Baghdādī (d. 1164/65), "an example par excellence of the type of personal philosopher" and who was a Jew who converted to Islam, also employed the notion of "perfect nature."[49] He asserted that the "spiritual teacher [muʿallim] is a "[being] who guides [souls] and consoles them. This friend and guide was known as 'perfect Nature' (al-tibāʿ al-tāmm)."[50] Zakariyā ibn Muḥammad ibn Maḥmud al-Qazwīnī (c. 1203–1283), writing on the "wonders of creation" (ʿAjaʾib al-makhlūqāt), cites this "perfect nature" as that of contemporary philosophers of nature.[51] Contemporaries of Qazwīnī, the poet Nizāmī (1141–1209) and the polymath Fahkr al-dīn al-Rāzī (1149–1210), also explored the personalization practices of astral magic.[52] Fakhr al-Dīn was a student of Abūl-Barakāt al-Baghdādī and probably knew Suhrawardī in Marāgha. Qazwīnī similarly cites both of these philosophers.[53] The point here is that an individualized philosophical practice of the astral self emerged quite certainly in the mid-twelfth century as part of a curriculum incorporating Avicenna, astral magic, and Ismāʿīlī angelology. This curriculum, first, was shared by Jews and Muslims; second, was transmitted from individual to individual; and third, was considered to be a matter of secrets.

HERMETICISM AS ALTERNATIVE

To this point I have suggested that social, literary, philosophical, and psychological evidence reveals nuances of emergent individuality in the twelfth century. Space is limited here, but one could also, for example, examine contemporaneous cultures of friendship and the practices of initiation.[54] A comparison of flourishing traveler's literature and of long-distance correspondence in the twelfth century would provide related contexts.[55] And in particular, the very concept of the "stranger," so important as a self-designation in this period, suggests a distinct alienation on the part of certain social groups, whose individual members felt that they did not "fit in."[56]

Given these constraints, the inner life of the emergent individual was perhaps inevitably ambivalent.[57] Philosophy *did* present what seemed, in theory, a pagan challenge to monotheistic revelation. But critical inquiry nevertheless seduced serious monotheistic thinkers even when they explicitly rejected *philosophia* as an autonomous life practice. This, at least, was the way that such Jews as Yehuda Halevi and such Muslims as Shah-rastānī reacted to its challenge.[58] Inter-confessional conversation partners, in short, equally needed working intellectual tools. And they did share them with each other.

But such individual solutions also brought new collective challenges. Philosophical affronts to religious absolutism could not be proclaimed naively or explicitly. The result can be stated almost as a law of the time: The more open their thought, the less open their expression of that thought. This inverse correlation between content and form intensified the torsion of their esoterization.

However, there was—to switch metaphors—a middle ground. Some, neither philosophers nor mystics, but still philosophical and esoteric, were "in conversation with" ancient idioms of hermeticism.[59] Shahrastānī, Suhrawardī, Halevi, Ibn Ṭufayl, and Ibn Sabʿīn fit in this category. For present purposes, the occult sciences of "hermeticism" tended to coincide with "philosophical mysticism" or "rational mysticism."[60] The pragmatic realities of inter-religious symbiosis produced glimmers of this philosophical religion—a kind of "cognitive theism."[61] I prefer to term this middle position between philosophy and mysticism occupied by occult science as *hermetic*.

Hermetic expressions included the submerging of the self in fictional form—a vision like Suhrawardī's, a novel like Ibn Ṭufayl's, or a dialogue like Halevi's; the perfection of such self-consciously self-styled esoteric complexity; the fictional identification with a fictional history, usually pagan; and, finally, the emergence of a visionary "self," typify this twelfth-century Jewish-Muslim hermeticism.[62] The hermetics, neither philosophers nor kabbalists nor Sufis, identified themselves with an ancient elite, but now operating invisibly within their own religious communities. Because they were also in some fundamental sense extra-territorial, hermetics resorted to camouflage, especially to the concealing coverage extended over them by philosophical fictions. These hermetics identified with an idealized prophetology beyond parochial manifestations. More to the present point, in order to dramatize this meta-narrative, they purveyed secrets inter-confessionally.

All the more interesting, then, is their *failure*. The hermetics failed, insofar as their philosophic mysticism was not pursued in scale. Nonetheless, however still poorly understood as historical forces, it is clear that they played a key role in forcing the problem of the science of religion. Recent scholarship on early modern European alchemy provides paradigms for a properly historical study of the medieval Islamicate occult sciences.[63] The present state of research, immature as it is, suggests that hermetic occult sciences presumed a scientifically generalizable account of religion that, however briefly, transposed inter-religious encounters from the realm of the polemic and apologetic into the inter-religious discourses of the fictive and the visionary. Muslim sciences of foreign religions were taken to a dazzling new height, in particular by Shahrastānī, a gifted and dispassionate historian of world religions possessing discernible hermetic sympathies.[64] But his achievement marked an end, not a beginning. It remains for scholarship to understand how and in what sense the thirteenth-century efflorescence of theosophy succeeded this fleeting stage of inter-confessional hermeticism.

REFLECTIONS ON JEWISH PHILOSOPHY AS INTER-RELIGION

Inter-confessional sharing raised self-consciously the problem of multiple revelations. Not enmity but sharing is the point. There is a social reality of religion as inter-religion, that there is virtually no religious situation that is not a situation of contact.[65] Or, as Elliot Wolfson puts it, "The truthfulness of religious experience is not to be discovered in the indivisibility of one tradition but in the crevices between traditions. Without acknowledging these cracks there can be no hope for repair."[66] Quite distinct from a putatively sacral isolation, the social actor, in fact, locates his or her fate by orienteering the dense social atmosphere of complicated relations. This point is now nicely elucidated by Kocku von Stuckrad in his "integrative model" of "discursive transfers."[67] Our research and reflection cannot conclude whether witches fly, but it can explicate friendships between spell-casters and hex-makers—it can locate witches as neighbors.[68]

IMPLICATIONS FOR RETHINKING JEWISH PHILOSOPHY

I have argued in this chapter that a social practice of "doing" medieval Jewish philosophy, "thinking with" medieval Jewish philosophers, might benefit from modest revision. The notion of a purely intra-Judaic history of Jewish philosophy may make faith-sense in theological terms, perhaps, but not empirical sense in sociological terms. Nor is a larger framework construed as "history of thought" adequate. This latter construction adds "mystics" and "hermetics" to the mix of elite intellectuals without addressing the larger historiographical problem. I have suggested that an amplified re-reading of the shared past should incorporate the history of media, of occult sciences, and of interpersonal relations, all of which were social processes transcending any one exclusive confessional possession or elite cohort.

Shared learning between Jews and Muslims arose on several cusps at once: between East and West, between ancient and modern, between philosophy and mysticism, and between Muslim and Jew. Cusp, crossroad, whatever metaphor we employ will be inadequate but will at least point toward the fructifying location that characterizes shared secrets between Muslim and Jew. Jews and Muslims met in that space, taught each other, and agreed to keep that sharing to themselves as an elite. The ancient esoteric "art of writing," described by the Jewish philosopher Leo Strauss, was designed for a closed society, for such a social elite governing, or hoping to govern, from the top of a social hierarchy. But Strauss's programmatic and reductive description misses the complexity of private social interactions between Muslim and Jew. To posit a singular essence to the esoteric secret is historically unusable for doing Jewish philosophy. Such a claim is neither susceptible to research nor amenable to analysis. Nonetheless, it may be responsible to speak of a certain "content" to the secret. And that may be individual practice itself.

I submit that the rise of the individual, of privacy, of reading, themselves as social phenomena, explain both mystical and philosophical esoterization. The most full-blown of esoteric claims, Carl Schmitt's political theology, casts secrecy "as a figure of religious antagonism."[69] He notoriously asserted that the "the enemy is our own question as figure."[70] Schmitt explains the "theologico-political predicament" in terms of enmity; Strauss, in terms of persecution. Both no doubt were determinants. But along with these constrictive impulses came expansive social realities, necessary realities, of sharing across religious boundaries. For present purposes, it suffices in this context to note that the singular form "art" distorts the plural social reality; there were various arts of writing, not just one.[71]

More generally, a historical sociology of religious philosophy and of philosophical practice predicated on this account of social reality accounts for shared secrets by correlating them within the full range of sociologically indexed needs. Among others, the needs of emigration, friendship, schooling, access to books, leisure for research and contemplation, freedom from persecution, curiosity, and sheer intellectual hunger—discovering, encountering, incorporating the foreign—in other words, some sort of dialogue or the other—drove this Jewish-Muslim symbiosis. One significance of this well-known descriptive fact is, I believe, that the trans-confessional approach implies a need "for the species," that is, to be empowered by the general case.

How groups—elites, sects, or "religions"—ground themselves on some godly foundation; how a society ultimately wields revealed values; how we invoke transcendental validation for action—these perennial challenges are complicated by two sorts of concrete obstacles. One obstacle derives from the apparent dead end of an incommensurable absolutism, ostensibly equally valid, asserted by one's opposite number in another religion. The other is the even more vexing problem of direct experience of the divine, especially the resulting, often disillusioning conclusion that the godhead is both above morals and beyond cognition.[72] These two sorts of discouragement, the one inter-religious and the other visionary, comprise the "theologico-political predicament" of the twelfth century as it gave way to thirteenth-century theosophy in crescendo. The era from the end of antiquity and the rise of Islam up to the thirteenth century was characterized both by inter-religious cross-fertilization—what Goitein termed "creative symbiosis"—and by the progressive dominion of mysticism—what Scholem called "the mystical theology of Judaism." But this sharp tapering off of the inter-confessional, with its even sharper ascent of mystical supremacisms, peaked in the brief apotheosis of thirteenth-century theosophy.

Among the challenges twelfth-century intellectuals struggled to confront were the *geographical problem* of emigration (demographic transfers were underway); the *metaphysical problem* of intermediation (the precise mechanism of the relation between human and divine); the *scientific problem* of comprehensivism (a comprehensive account of all forms of knowledge); the *social problem* of ecumenicism (in a pluralistic environment); and, finally, the *political problem* of esoterism itself (secrets are powerful, so how much such power do you share?). With such challenges, it is no small wonder that their ambitions toward comprehensive integration exceeded their grasp.

Perhaps the most fortunate paradox of the succeeding theosophical hubris is that they published the secrets. With the daring thirteenth-century publications of ibn al-ʿArabī and Moshe de León, "ancient" secrets were now "revealed." The esoteric cat was out of the inter-confessional bag.[73] In the transition from the twelfth to the thirteenth centuries, a dangerous secret nonetheless continued to be the very act of sharing itself. Perhaps the conceit of secrecy, esoterism, had been a function of inter-religious sharing all along. What secrecy hid was its own act of communication. Ironically, then, when the tipping point came, when twelfth-century eso-terization outran the transitionally hermetic inter-confessional sciences and gave way to full-blown ultra-confessional theosophies of the thir-teenth century, the result was a return to an even better defended (if itself still transient) absolutism.

A DIGRESSION ON "ESOTERICISM" IN THE WORK OF SHLOMO PINES AND HENRY CORBIN

Understanding of this social change was authoritatively provided by great scholars who elided the social basis for the change. To clarify this point, I contrast the respective scholarly practices of Shlomo Pines and Henry Corbin.

Shlomo Pines (1908–1990) was born in Paris, raised in Russia, and trained in Germany. He began his work life in Paris, after which he spent his career in Israel, writing primarily in English, Hebrew, and French con-cerning issues of Greek, Latin, Persian, Hebrew, and Arabic philosophy, science, and religion. Pines was simultaneously historian of science, histo-rian of philosophy, and historian of religions.

He was also both "Judaist" and "Islamicist." On principle (if always only implicitly), he negated the differences between religious traditions as being merely conventional.[74] His history of religious ideas concentrated ex-clusively on inter-religious transmission. This macroscopic pattern char-acterizing his corpus implies that he not only understood the scientific status of the imaginative faculty but also practiced it. He never explic-itly announced his formative presupposition, that this faculty is uniquely equipped to trace the flow-points of religious traditions upstream to their cognitive sources. If his work concerns anything, it is these conjunctural moments of communication when one tradition suddenly lights up with the illumination streaming out of its preceding vessel.

Through the act of scholarship—what, with deceptive blandness, he called "the scientific experience"—Pines implemented a catalytic proce-dure to locate ideas not only in their definitive moments of emergence but throughout their life histories as well. The last phase of his career was de-voted to undertaking colossal surveys—on freedom, the limitations of hu-man knowledge, good and evil vs. true and false—in which the history of an idea is encompassed, thus to become available for contemplation as a singularly perceptible form.

Pines was, I suggest, among the greatest unknown "pure" philoso-phers of the twentieth century. While he was at once historian of science, historian of philosophy, and historian of religions, his philosophical "way of life" was a *via contemplativa* in which living connections of ideas are observed impassively, without editorial comment on "the whole," but by which means the whole can be approached nonetheless.

This binocular vision—a micrological gaze that simultaneously apprehends a totality—could not proceed syllogistically. His "scientific experience" was not instrumentally cognitive but rather imaginative. He wrote not a page of philosophy as such, but rather he microscopically traced a trans-religious history of ideas. These were, however, *his* ideas, living ideas that existed together in the pleroma that is the history of thought. I suggest that Pines was almost uniquely equipped to understand the uses of the Islamicate imagination—because he practiced it. Elemental intellection, for Pines, proceeded in a movingly static atomism, where ideas, even the noblest figments of the imagination, like absolute time and absolute space, progressed unimpeded by communal or doctrinal constraints, emanating freely from mind to mind. There is, in a sense, no motion, no impetus, in the forward thrust of ideas: each in itself is still and whole; but the observer, the contemplative scientist, *sees* the movement progressively streaming there. Or at least so (in my reading) said Shlomo Pines.

Pines, from start to finish, shared with Leo Strauss an instructive aversion—apparently born from their shared coming-of-age in Weimar Germany—a repulsion in the face of "a world on the edge of an abyss, the world of the nihilists, of frenzied technology, of unrestrained will to power and of destructive philosophy."[75] Pines answered this inferno with, of all things, a serene scholarship. By contrast to Strauss, however, he concluded that the deepest problem was not the "theologico-political predicament" of paganism vs. monotheism but rather that of philosophy vs. technology.[76] That is, Pines identified the "Sabean" science of theurgy as one claiming efficaciously to draw down astral powers. In other words, if for Strauss the master key to the history of philosophy was politics, for Pines it was natural science. The claim of theurgy, then, was not metaphysical for Pines, not theoretical but rather practical: theurgy is a technique that *works*.

This *telos* (*tachlis*) is central to understanding Pines' practice of philosophy. For this group, what Pines blandly called "the scientific experience" amounted to a virtually theurgical condition. His concept of imagination was neither aesthetic nor ethic. It was ontic. And this pure being could be recapitulated in the act of understanding, in the science of connecting ideas to their sources, in the contemplative following of intellective forms across the winding paths of their transmission.

A last word. It should not be shocking to lift Pines' philological labors into this diaphanous light. The two leitmotifs that I have identified, those of *freedom* and *imagination,* are required for the philologist to succeed, if not thrive: *freedom* here is understood as non-dogmatically derived principles of selection, and *imagination* means the capacity to perceive otherwise imperceptible connections.

For Pines' correspondingly free and imaginative reading of the anti-Aristotelian trajectory in Islamicate thought—his particular province of scientific attention—physics can not "explain" the physical universe, neither time nor space—nor, for that matter, psychology. Since the Aristotelian Maimonides defined prophethood as a psycho-political phenomenon, the question then became one of representation: how does the prophet authoritatively persuade a community that he reveals to them the veritable secrets of creation? Pines pointedly rejected the option, vital in his day, to solve this problem by resurrecting prophethood in himself, that is, by himself prophesying.

Such prophesying was the option embraced by his brilliant contemporary, Henry Corbin. I have dealt with Corbin more fully elsewhere, so I will simply sketch the apposite contrast here. Corbin's mysto-centric prophetism presumes his own inspiration as an indispensable point of orientation into the work he publishes. If one does not accept a priori his mastery of the un-researchable depths beyond "mere" analytic access, the historical connections he makes come unglued; they are held together by poetic visionary connections, as he himself powerfully insisted. The critiques of Muhsin Mahdi and Dmitri Gutas have, to my mind, demonstrated the empirical sins of Corbin's version of the history of philosophy.[77]

One might legitimately respond that Corbin was not "doing history" but rather "doing philosophy." But Corbin undid history in order to redo philosophy: the result was his own post-historical "prophetic philosophy." By contrast, Pines integrated "doing history" and "doing philosophy" in such a way that both were clarified as a consequence; he was both more historical and more philosophical than Corbin. Corbin's esotericism, to be sure, works effectively, but only for those who presuppose its veracity. For the purposes of understanding the Muhammad revered by millions of Muslims, or the functional dominance of sharia, or the everyday piety of such Muslims, Corbin's visionary utterances—which are denuded of Muhammad and sharia and everyday life—are virtually useless.

None of this is to deny that for understanding medieval Islamicate philosophy we need Corbins as well as Pineses (so to speak). As long as students are taught to distinguish between "prophetic philosophy," which is a function of genuine afflatus, and inter-religious critique, which is a practice of inquiry and reflection, a healthy dialectical progress of knowledge will proceed. The preference stated here for a practice aligned with what Pines called "the scientific experience" should not be taken to suggest that an authentic visionary practice must be expunged from our seminars.

CONCLUSIONS

I venture some conclusions of a more general order.

Paolo Rossi argues that the spread of such a cultural consensus on secrecy was indeed pervasive, but it was also, eventually, disastrous:

> The idea that there was a secret knowledge of essential things—the spread of which would be disastrous—for centuries formed a dominant paradigm in European culture. Only the spread of this paradigm of secrecy, and its persistence and historical continuity, could explain the controversial force found in so many of the theories advanced by the so-called founders of the modern world: they unanimously rejected the idea upon which this secrecy was founded; namely, the difference between the learned few, or "true men," and the *promiscuum hominum genus,* or ignorant masses.[78]

Inter-confessional relations—that is, the cultural universal of inter-religious contact—bore putatively secret truths. A shared presumption of the secret truth of public revelations emerged from inter-religious meetings.[79] Construed this way, it follows that a dialogical practice of philosophy should reject the epistemic primacy of esoteric secrets, that is, should reject the secret as being the essence of religious change. Such occultation of agency I consider closer to conspiracy theory than to a serious historical sociology of religious philosophies.[80] Whether understood in historical or mystical terms, sharing *was* the secret.

Jewish law recognizes two fundamental sorts of relations, those between human and human, and those between human and divine. The esoteric and the inter-confessional may be said to operate as complementary poles, with the esoteric functioning as a vertical axis between human and divine, while the inter-confessional marks an horizontal axis between human and human.[81] So too, in religious history, divine secrets seemed to descend from a source out of sight, even while inter-religious relations continued on the ground.

In conclusion, it must be remembered that there was, as Harry A. Wolfson influentially contended, no "pure" philosophy in the monotheistic world until the appearance of Baruch Spinoza in the seventeenth century. An "impure" or mixed philosophical practice was the norm. The foregoing social description, then, is not historicism, not contextualism, not constructivism, and not reductionism. What I propose is a practice of Jewish philosophy that respects its own dialectic between "deep" content and "superficial" forms of transmission. Polarizing this complex social reality in terms of the antagonism between religion and philosophy, or reason and revelation, or Muslim and Jew distorts our understanding of the past and therefore our practice in the present.[82]

NOTES

1. For esotericism in late antiquity, see the important work of Guy G. Stroumsa, *Hidden Wisdom: Esoteric Traditions and the Roots of Christian Mysticism* (Leiden: Brill, 1996). For the medieval European "cult of secrecy," see Richard Kieckhefer, *Magic in the Middle Ages* (Cambridge: Cambridge University Press, 1990), esp. 140–44. For general orientation, see the collection edited by Guy G. Stroumsa and Hans G. Kippenberg, *Secrecy and Concealment: Studies in the History of Mediterranean and Near Eastern Religions* (Studies in the History of Religions 65; Leiden: Brill, 1995), and *Rending the Veil: Concealment and Secrecy in the History of Religions,* edited by Elliot R. Wolfson (New York: Seven Bridges Press, 1999).

2. Rather than identifying the content of secrets, it is more useful to speak of the "esoteric knowledge," which Moshe Halbertal schematizes specifically for the period under consideration here: "The remarkably varied structure of esoteric knowledge includes multiple complex techniques for approaching the hidden: the adoption of a precise and strict method of thought in order to penetrate the deep metaphysical structure of being, entering alternative states of consciousness to facilitate insights from other planes, the use of various magical techniques, the interpretation of dreams and their analysis for the purpose of revealing the repressed level of the self in order to overcome internal censorship, and many, many others." Moshe Halbertal, *Concealment and Revelation: Esotericism in Jewish Thought and Its Philosophical Implications,* translated by Jackie Feldman (Princeton, N.J.: Princeton University Press, 2007), 2.

3. Paul Christopher Johnson dubs this syndrome "secretism." See his *Secrets, Gossip, and Gods: The Transformation of Brazilian Candomblé* (New York: Oxford University Press, 2002), 23. For a current review from a broader perspective, see Ann Williams Duncan, "Religion and Secrecy: A Bibliographic Essay," *Journal of the American Academy of Religion* 74 (2006): 469–82.

4. Elliot R. Wolfson has made major contributions to understanding the dialectic of revealed and concealed, one extensive enough that, to be adequate, must restrict itself to nothing less than his ample bibliography. On the principles of his work, I have made a tentative assessment in my "Melancholy Jouissance and the Study of Kabbalah: A Review Essay of Elliot R. Wolfson, *Alef, Mem, Tau,*" *Association for Jewish Studies Review* 32.2 (2008): 389–96.

5. For the Jewish-Islamic problem of "free thought," "heresy," and "relativism," see Dominique Urvoy, *Les penseurs libres dans l'Islam classique* (Paris: Albin Michel, 1997), and Sarah Stroumsa, "On Jewish Intellectuals Who Converted in the Early Middle Ages," in *The Jews of Medieval Islam: Community, Society, and Identity,* edited by Daniel Frank (Leiden: Brill, 1995), 179–97. I thank Professor Stroumsa for sending me an offprint of her important study. See more fully Sarah Stroumsa, *Freethinkers of Islam* (Leiden: Brill, 1999).

6. For a detailed analysis of this "fictitious history," see Dimitri Gutas, *Greek Thought, Arab Culture: The Graeco-Arabic Translation Movement in Baghdad and Early 'Abbāsid Society (2nd–4th/8th–10th C.)* (New York: Routledge, 1998), 100.

7. *Opera* I, 70; Hossein Ziai, " Beyond Philosophy," in *Myth and Philosophy,* edited by Frank Reynolds and David Tracy (Albany: SUNY Press, 1990), 225.

8. See below for an elaboration of this hermetic projection of the self.

222   STEVEN M. WASSERSTROM

9. See John Walbridge, *Leaven of the Ancients: Suhrawardi and the Heritage of the Greeks* (Albany: SUNY, 1999), 270 n. 3, on this sense of *"nafs."* See also the significant parallels in Juda ben Nissim ibn Malka and Isaac of Acre, cited by Moshe Idel in "The Kabbalah in Morocco, A Survey," in *Morocco. Jews and Art in a Muslim Land,* edited by Vivian Mann (New York: Merrell/The Jewish Museum, 2000), 106–24.

10. The Khazar king of the anti-Aristotelian *Kuzari* also enjoyed a revelatory dream, but, like that of Suhrawardī, it amounts to a rejection of Aristotle.

11. See the overview by Remi Brague, "La philosophie dans la *théologie d'Aristote.* Pour un inventaire," *Documenti e studi sulla tradizione filosofica medievale* 8 (1997): 365–87.

12. Sources are provided in Walbridge, *Leaven of Ancients,* 256–57.

13. Conveniently reproduced in Anne Freemantle, *The Age of Belief* (New York: New American Library, 1954), 109.

14. "When I was about twenty years of age Aristotle's book on the '10 Categories' came into my hands. Whenever my teacher at Carthage and others who were reputed to be scholars mentioned this book, their cheeks would swell with self-importance, so that the title alone was enough to make me stand agape, as though I were poised over some wonderful divine mystery. I managed to read it and understand it without help, though I now ask myself what advantage I gained from doing so. . . . What profit did this study bring me? None." Augustine, *Confessions,* translated by Henry Chadwick (Oxford: Oxford University Press, 1991), IV:16. On the Arabic reception of the *Categories,* see the discoveries reported in Syed Nomanul Haq, *Names, Natures and Things: The Alchemist Jābir ibn Ḥayyān and his* Kitāb al-Aḥjār *(Book of Stones)* (Dordrecht: Kluwer, 1994), 230–42.

15. "The historian is in danger of forgetting that his subjects spent much of their time asleep, and that, when asleep, they had dreams." Peter Brown, *The World of Late Antiquity* (London: Thames and Hudson, 1971), 49. The three appearances I use as examples were, of course, not the physiological epiphenomena of sleep, but rather, literary set-pieces.

16. See, for example, Mauro Zonta, "Mineralogy, Botany and Zoology in Medieval Hebrew Encyclopedias: 'Descriptive' and 'theoretical' approaches to Arabic Sources," *Arabic Sciences and Philosophy* 6 (1996): 263–315.

17. For a significant revision to the standard treatment, that of Ignaz Goldziher, see "The Attitude of Orthodox Islam toward the 'Ancient Sciences,'" in *Studies on Islam,* edited by Merlin L. Swartz (Oxford: Oxford, 1981 [1916]), 185–215. See also Gutas, *Greek Thought, Arabic Culture,* 165–75.

18. Goldziher, "The Attitude of Orthodox Islam toward the 'Ancient Sciences,'" 198.

19. See the superb edition and translation by my teacher, Michael E. Marmura: *The Incoherence of the Philosophers* (Provo, UT: Brigham Young University Press, 1997).

20. *Rasaʾil Ikhwān al-Safāʾ,* cited in Ian R. Netton, *Muslim Neoplatonists: An Introduction to the Thought of the Brethren of Purity (Ikhwān al-Safaʾ),* (Edinburgh: Edinburgh University Press, 1991), 19.

21. Hannah Arendt, "Martin Heidegger at Eighty," *New York Review of Books,* 21 October 1971, 49–54.

22. "Persecution and the Art of Writing," in Leo Strauss, *Persecution and the Art of Writing* (Westport, Conn.: Greenwood, 1973).

23. "Esoteric Symbolism," chapter 15 in D. P. Walker, *Music, Spirit, and Language in the Renaissance,* edited by Penelope Gouk (London: Variorum Reprints, 1985).

24. See my discussion of the de-reification of secrets in the conclusion of *Religion after Religion: Gershom Scholem, Mircea Eliade and Henry Corbin at Eranos* (Princeton, N.J.: Princeton University Press, 1999).

25. Peter Brown, "Society and the Supernatural: A Medieval Change," *Daedalus* 104 (1975): 133–51.

26. Moshe Perlmann, "Medieval Polemics Between Islam and Judaism," in *Religion in a Religious Age*, edited by S. D. Goitein (Cambridge, Mass.: Association for Jewish Studies, 1974), 105.

27. Strauss, *Persecution and the Art of Writing*, 21. Behind these shrewd but ultimately superficial remarks, compare the sociological density of S. D. Goitein, *Mediterranean Society*, vol. 5, *The Individual* (Berkeley: University of California Press, 1988). For a substantial contribution to this question, see Thomas F. Glick,"'My Master, the Jew,' Observations on Interfaith Scholarly Interaction in the Middle Ages," in *Jews, Muslims and Christians in and around the Crown of Aragon, Essays in Honour of Professor Elena Lourie*, edited by Harvey J. Hames (Leiden: Brill, 2004), 157–82.

28. Arthur Hyman, "Jewish Aristotelianism: Trends from the 12th through the 14th Centuries," in *Judaeo-Arabic Studies. Proceedings of the Founding Conference of the Society for Judaeo-Arabic Studies*, edited by Norman Golb (Amsterdam: Harwood, 1997), 200–201.

29. See, for example, Jonathan Berkey, *The Transmission of Knowledge in Medieval Cairo: A Social History of Islamic Education* (Princeton, N.J.: Princeton University Press, 1992), 13.

30. The literature on Maimonides' "secrets" is vast and continues to grow. See Avraham Nuriel, *Concealed and Revealed in Medieval Jewish Philosophy* (Jerusalem: Magnes Press, 2000) [Hebrew].

31. Ralph Lerner, "Maimonides' Governance of the Solitary," in *Perspectives on Maimonides: Philosophical and Historical Studies*, edited by Joel L. Kraemer (Oxford: Littmann Library, 1991).

32. My own encounter with philosophy came first in the person of Marvin Fox, a neighbor during my formative years and a beloved first teacher at university. On the medieval epistolary conceit of philosophy as one-to-one communication, see the studies by Steven Harvey, "The Author's Introduction as a Key to Understanding Trends in Islamic Philosophy," in *Words, Texts and Concepts Cruising the Mediterranean Sea: Studies on the Sources, Contents and Influences of Islamic Civilization and Arabic Philosophy and Science, Dedicated to Gerhard Endress on his Sixty-Fifth Birthday*, edited by R. Arnzen and J. Thielmann (Orientalia Lovaniensia Analecta 139) (Leuven: Peeters, 2004), 15–33, and idem, "Die Einleitung des Autors als Schlüssel zum Verstehen von Strömungen mittelalterlicher jüdischer Philosophie: Von Saadia Gaon bis Ibn Daʾud," *Im Gespräch* 6 (2003): 54–68.

33. The initiatic epistle is a genre received from antiquity. See especially, M. Grignaschi, "Le roman épistolaire classique conservé dans la version arabe de Sālim Abū-L-ʿAlāʾ," *Le Muséon* 80 (1967): 211–69. For letter writing in the period under discussion here, see especially Goitein. One of the few studies of the relationship between Maimonides and Ibn Ṭufayl has been undertaken by Lenn Goodman, whose latest work on this question can be found in *Jewish and Islamic Philosophy: Crosspollinations in the Classic Age* (New Brunswick, N.J.: Rutgers University Press, 1999).

34. There are arguable Ismāʿīlī elements in the works of Halevi and Maimonides. For some of the shared background, see Hans Daiber, "The Ismāʿīlī Background of Fārābī's Political Philosophy: Abū Hātim ar-Rāzī as a forerunner of Fārābī," *Gottes ist der Orient. Gottes est der Okzident. Festschrift für Abdoldjavad Falaturi zum 65. Geburtstag*, edited by Udo Tworsuchka (Köln, Wien: Böhlau Verlag, 1991), 143–51, at 147.

35. Another indicator of individuality in this period is the ownership and reproduction of books, which, as Beit-Arié observes, were "produced as a private enterprise."

See Malachi Beit-Arié, "The Individualistic Nature of Hebrew Medieval Book Production and Consumption," *Tzion* 65 (2000): 441–51 [Hebrew].

36. Ruqayya Yasmine Khan, "The Significance of Secrets in the Medieval Arabic Romances," *Journal of Arabic Literature* 31 (2000): 238–54.

37. See the important remarks of Dmitri Gutas on Ibn Ṭufayl, suggesting that the real innovation in the trajectory from Avicenna to Rāzī was that of autobiography. Dimitri Gutas, "Ibn Ṭufayl on Ibn Sina's Eastern Philosophy," *ORIENS* 34 (1994): 222–41. See also the provocative suggestions in this regard by Paul Kraus, "The 'Controversies' of Fakhr al-Dīn Rāzī," *Islamic Culture* 12 (1938): 131–53, at 141; Franz Rosenthal, "Die arabische Autobiographie," *Analecta Orientalia* 14 (1937): 1–40. *Edebiyât*, vol. 7 (1997), edited by Dwight Reynolds and Devin Stewart, is devoted to Arabic autobiography; *Middle Eastern Lives*, edited by Martin Kramer (Syracuse: Syracuse University Press, 1991); S. Ghamdi, "Autobiography in Classical Arabic Literature: An Ignored Literary Genre" (Ph.D. diss., Indiana University 1989); Louis Pouzet, "Remarques sur l'autobiographie dans le monde arabo-musulman au Moyen-Âge," in *Philosophy and Arts in the Islamic World,* edited by U. Vermeulen and D. de Smet (Leuven: Peeters, 1998), 97–107. I thank Michael Feener for help in locating these latter sources.

38. Another contemporaneous "spiritual autobiography" of relevance is the *Ifḥām al-Yahūd* of Samauʾal al-Maghribī, which in fact may have (in part) been composed as a response to the *Kuzari.* Even more apposite to the present discussion is the Barzawayh story in Ibn al-Muqaffaʿ's *Kalila wa-Dimna,* which Samauʾal al-Maghribī claimed persuaded him to convert to Islam. See the instructive comments by Sarah Stroumsa, "On Jewish Intellectuals Who Converted in the Early Middle Ages," in *Jews of Medieval Islam,* 193–96. Note that Stroumsa refers to the Barzawayh story as a "spiritual autobiography" (193).

39. See the useful discussion by Gutas, "Ibn Ṭufayl on Ibn Sina's Eastern Philosophy," 238 n. 31.

40. See the synopsis of this genre in Heinz Halm, *The Fatimids and Their Traditions of Learning* (New York: I. B. Tauris, 1997).

41. Including the Jewish apostate Samauʿal al-Maghribī and the Muslim scientist ʿAbd al-Laṭīf al-Baghdādī. See also the 1295 "philosophical conversion" of Saʿīd ibn Ḥasan of Alexandria, in his *Masālik al-Naẓar (Ways of Understanding).* See I. Goldziher, "Saʿīd b. Ḥasan d'Alexandrie," *REJ* 30 (1895): 1–23.

42. Naṣīr al-Dīn al-Ṭūsī, *Contemplation and Action: The Spiritual Autobiography of a Muslim Scholar,* edited and translated by S. J. Badakhchani (London and New York: I. B. Tauris, 1998), 24.

43. Ibid., 25.

44. For the Jewish dialogues, see Aaron W. Hughes, *The Art of Dialogue in Jewish Philosophy* (Bloomington: Indiana University Press, 2008). My primary concern in the present paper lies with the inter-religious dialogue per se, but Hughes's work is especially important for studying the relation between the philosophical dialogue and the inter-religious dialogue. I have not undertaken that study here, other than to observe that the latter was a stimulus to the former.

45. A broadly comparative study of the medieval inter-confessional dialogue is long overdue. From the Christian side, one would include Petrus Alfonsi, Abelard, Nicolas of Cusa, and Reuchlin's *De Arte Cabbalistica,* among others. See Ulrich Berner, "Zur Geschichte und Problematik des interreligiösen Dialoges," in *Tradition und Translation. Festschrift für Carsten Colpe zum 65. Geburtstag,* edited by C. Elsas et al. (Berlin/New York: De Gruyter, 1994), 391–405. Raymond Lull wrote at least five inter-confessional dialogues. See Roberto J. González-Casanova's "Raymond Lull's Rhetorical Ambiva-

lence toward the Jews: Utopia and Polemic in Medieval Iberian Missionary Discourse," in *Encuentros and Desencuentros: Spanish Jewish Cultural Interaction Throughout History*, edited by C. C. Parrondo et al. (Tel Aviv: University Publishing Projects, 2000), 381–413, at 385–86.

46. Shlomo Pines undertook a rich comparison of the two at various points in his lengthy article, "Shiʿite Terms and Conceptions in Judah Halevi's *Kuzari*," *JSAI* 2 (1980): 165–251, reprinted in Shlomo Pines, *Studies in the History of Jewish Thought*, edited by W. Z. Harvey and M. Idel (Jerusalem: Magnes Press, 1997), 219–306.

47. Diane Steigerwald notes that *Umm al-Kitāb* resembles *Kitāb al-ʿālīm waʾl-Ghulām*. See her *Majlis: Discours sur l'ordre et a création* (Saint-Nicolas, QC: Les Presses de l'Université, 1998), 57 n. 42. See more fully, idem, "The Divine Word (*Kalima*) in Shahrastānī's *Majlis*," *Studies in Religion/Sciences Religieuses* 25 (1996): 335–52.

48. See Diane Steigerwald, "La dissimulation (*taqiyya*) de la foi dans le shiʿisme ismaélien," *Studies in Religion/Sciences Religieuses* 27 (1988): 39–59.

49. Corbin, *History of Islamic Philosophy*, translated by Liadain Sherrard with the assistance of Philip Sherrard (London: Kegan Paul International in association with Islamic Publications for the Institute of Ismaili Studies, 1993), 177.

50. Ibid., 178. This association with "taʿlīm" is particularly important, since it may signal an association with Nizārī doctrine, especially that of Ḥasan al-Ṣabbāḥ. As this imam put it, "There is no way to knowledge (*taʿlīm*) even with reason and speculation except with the teaching of a trustworthy teacher (*muʿallimin sādiq*)." Cited in M. G. S. Hodgson, *The Order of Assassins: The Struggle of the Early* Nizārī Ismāʿīlīs *against the Islamic World* (Gravenhage: Mouton, 1955), 325.

51. Toufy Fahd, *La divination arabe* (Leiden: Brill, 1966), 51, citing on *al-tibāʿ al-tāmm* in Qazwīnī, I:317–22: "Certaines philosophes, ajout-t-il, vont jusquʿà dire que les âmes rationelles constituent un genre, comprenant des espèces subdivisées en individus qui ne diffèrent les uns des autres que par le nombre. Chacque espèce se présente comme l'enfant (*walad*) de l'un des esprits célestes. C'est ce que les praticiens des talismans appellent 'la nature parfaite' (*al-tibāʿ al-tāmm*). Cet esprit réalise le perfectionnement des âmes don't il a la charge." The implications of Qazwīnī's astral studies are elaborated more recently in Anna Caiozzo "Quatre signes d'un zodiaque caché. Les porteurs du Trône divin dans les cosmographies en arabe et en persan d'époque médiévale," *Les annales islamologiques* 33 (1999): 1–29; idem, "Les talismans des planètes dans les cosmographies en persan d'époque médievale," *Der Islam* 77, no. 2 (2000): 221–63; and idem, "Rituels théophaniques imagés et pratiques magiques: les anges planétaires dans le manuscrit Persan 174 de Paris," *Studia Iranica* 29, no. 1 (2000): 109–40.

52. Ziva Vesel, "Réminiscences de la magie asrale dans les *Haft Peykar* de Nezami," *Studia Iranica* 24 (1995): 7–17, esp. n. 14, and "The Persian translation of Fakhr al-Dīn Rāzī's *al-Sirr al-Maktūm* ('The occult secret') for Iltutmish," in *Confluence of Cultures: French Contributions to Indo-Persian Studies*, edited by Francoise Delvoye (Tehran: Institute Français de Recherche en Iran, 1994), 14–22. For Nizami's hermeticism, see his tale "Seventy Sages Deny the Doctrines of Hermes and Perish," discussed in J. Christoph Bürgel, "Occult Sciences in the *Iskandarnameh* of Nizami," in *The Poetry of Nizami Ganjavi: Knowledge, Love, and Rhetoric*, edited by K. Talattof and J. W. Clinton (New York: Palgrave, 2000), 132–33.

53. For example, a biographical report on Suhrawardī cited in Henry Corbin, *En Islam Iranien* (Paris: Gallimard, 1972), 2:13 n. 5.

54. For friendship, see the moving materials gathered in Goitein, *Mediterranean Society: The Individual*, 272–307. I hope to treat initiation on another occasion. Let me

simply say here that social history does not corroborate the assertions of René Guénon: "In the end, the real secret, the only secret that can never be betrayed in any way, resides uniquely in the inexpressible, which is by the same token incommunicable: and every truth of a transcendent order necessarily partakes of the inexpressible; it is essentially in this fact that the profound significance of the initiatic secret really lies; no kind of exterior secret can ever have any value except as an image or symbol of the initiatic secret." *The Reign of Quantity and the Signs of the Times,* translated from the French by Lord Northbourne (Baltimore: Penguin Books, 1972), 106.

55. *Jewish Travellers in the Middle Ages: 19 Firsthand Accounts,* edited by Elkan Nathan Adler (New York: Dover, 1987 [1930]), to be compared with *Golden Roads: Migration, Pilgrimage and Travel in Medieval and Modern Islam,* edited by Ian Netton (London: Curzon, 1993), and *Muslim Travellers: Pilgrimage, Migration and the Religious Imagination,* edited by Dale Eickelman and James Piscatori (Berkeley: University of California Press, 1990).

56. See Franz Rosenthal, "The Stranger in Medieval Islam," *Arabica* 44 (1997): 35–75, and, more specifically for the present discussion, Maribel Fierro, "Spiritual Alienation and Political Activism: The *Guraba*ʾin al-Andalus During the Sixth/Twelfth Century," *Arabica* 46 (2000): 230–60.

57. The complexity of the emergent twelfth-century individual has been amply revealed in the new study by Hamid Dabashi, *Truth and Narrative: The Untimely Thoughts of ʿAyn al-Qudat al-Hamadhani* (Richmond Surrey: Curzon, 1999); thus, chapter 1 of this volume is titled "The Birth of an Individual" (64–109), and chapter 10, "The Death of an Individual" (475–537). Dabashi emphasizes ʿAyn al-Quḍāt's (1098–1131) "self-confidence, a brilliant, breath-taking birth of a confident individuality" (331). Elsewhere he speaks of his "reconstitution of an individualistic epistemic legitimacy" (409).

58. See my "The Compunctious Philosopher? Recent Studies on Judah Halevi's *Kuzari*" [A Review Essay], *Medieval Encounters,* 4 (1998): 284–96.

59. I hope to elaborate the history of Jewish Islamicate hermeticism elsewhere. For now, see Paola Carusi, "Harmis al-Harāmisa dans l'alchimie islamique. Une recherche par auteur et par sujet," *Early Science and Medicine* [Fascicle 2: Special issue on Alchemy and Hermeticism, edited by Michela Pereira] (May, 2000): 121–30. See also Vincent J. Cornell, "The Way of the Axial Intellect: The Islamic Hermetism of Ibn Sabʿīn," *Journal of the Muhyiddin Ibn Arabic Society* 22 (1997): 42–79. I thank Professor Cornell for sending me an offprint of this groundbreaking article.

60. On this latter term, see Moshe Idel, "Abulafia's Secrets of the Guide: A Linguistic Turn," *Revue de métaphysique et de morale* 4 (1998): 495–528, at 496. "The Third Force" is a term employed for the seventeenth century by Richard Popkin.

61. As Kenneth Hart Green has dubbed Leo Strauss's worldview in his *Jew and Philosopher: The Return to Maimonides in the Jewish Thought of Leo Strauss* (Albany: SUNY Press, 1993), 27. Thus, on Remi Brague's reading of Strauss, "Maimonides wanted to maintain religion's political role, to favor in religion that which aims more or less toward philosophy, and to neutralize what could harm the civil or religious community whose health is the first condition of the philosopher's life and of the philosophical life. It is a question of making a *fiction* of religion, in the juridical sense of the term: to change the subjacent principle while dissimulating this change by conserving the formula whose original sense is henceforth out-of-date." See Brague, "Leo Strauss and Maimonides," in *Leo Strauss's Thought: Toward a Critical Engagement,* edited by Alan Udoff (Boulder, Colo.: Lynne Rienner Publishers, 1991) 93–114, at 103 (emphasis in original).

62. For one of the best studies on this question, without reference to the "hermetic" per se, see Aviezer Ravitzky, "The Secrets of the *Guide to the Perplexed:* Between the Thirteenth and the Twentieth Centuries," in *Studies in Maimonides,* edited by Isadore Twersky (Cambridge, Mass.: Harvard University Press, 1990), 159–207. See, more generally, Dov Schwartz, *Contradiction and Concealment in Medieval Jewish Thought* [Hebrew] (Ramat-Gan, 2002). Schwartz has made major contributions to the study of medieval Jewish Islamicate hermeticism.

63. See, for example, Bruce T. Moran, *Distilling Knowledge: Alchemy, Chemistry, and the Scientific Revolution* (Cambridge, Mass.: Harvard University Press, 2005); William R. Newman and Lawrence M. Principe, *Alchemy Tried in the Fire: Starkey, Boyle and the Fate of Helmontian Chymistry* (Chicago: University of Chicago Press, 2002); Tara Nummedal, *Alchemy and Authority in the Holy Roman Empire* (Chicago: University of Chicago Press, 2007), and Pamela H. Smith, *The Business of Alchemy: Science and Culture in the Holy Roman Empire* (Princeton, N.J.: Princeton University Press, 1997).

64. See my translation in *Judaism in Practice,* edited by Lawrence Fine (Princeton, N.J.: Princeton University Press), 229–37.

65. As I argue in "Nine Theses on the Study of Religion," in *Rethinking Religion 101: Critical Issues in Religious Studies,* edited by Bradford Verter and Johannes Wolfart (Cambridge: Cambridge University Press), forthcoming.

66. Elliot R. Wolfson, "Lying on the Path," *AJS Newsletter* (2002).

67. Kocku von Stuckrad, "Western Esotericism: Towards an Integrative Model of Interpretation," *Religion* 35, no. 2 (2005): 78–97, at 84–87.

68. Robin Briggs, *Witches and Neighbors* (New York: Viking, 1996), and idem, *Thinking with Demons* (New York: Oxford University Press, 1999).

69. As per the discussion on Jan Assman, *Moses the Egyptian: The Memory of Egypt in Western Monotheism* (Cambridge, Mass.: Harvard University Press, 1997), 212.

70. Heinrich Meier, *The Lesson of Carl Schmitt: Four Chapters on the Distinction Between Political Theology and Political Philosophy,* translated by Marcus Brainard (Chicago: University of Chicago Press, 1998), 44.

71. In addition to their distorting effects, I note other reasons why the esoteric art of writing may properly be considered as a "weak" discourse. The arts of esoteric writing are weak as writing inasmuch as they are stylistically reactionary, dismissive of the reader, and thus intentionally diminish their own readership. Socially, they are peripheral, all the more so as social organization trends toward an open society. And they are "weak thought" intellectually, as it were, because they constrict the deployment of their own strengths.

72. Some subsequent repercussions can be gleaned from William Eamon, *Science and the Secrets of Nature: Books of Secrets in Early Modern Culture* (Princeton, N.J.: Princeton University Press, 1994); Perez Zagorin, *Ways of Lying: Dissimulation, Persecution, and Conformity in Early Modern Europe* (Cambridge, Mass.: Harvard University Press, 1990); Antoine Faivre, "The Notions of Concealment and Secrecy in Modern Esoteric Currents since the Renaissance (A Methodological Approach)," in *Rending the Veil,* edited by Elliot R. Wolfson, 155–77.

73. For the subsequent period, see Miriam Eliav-Feldon, "Invented Identities: Credulity in the Age of Prophecy and Exploration," *Journal of Early Modern History* 3 (1999): 203–32, and Sylvia Berti, "Unmasking the Truth: the Theme of Imposture in Early Modern European Culture, 1660–1730," in *Everything Connects: In Conference with Richard H. Popkin: Essays in His Honor,* edited by James Force and David S. Katz (Leiden: Brill, 1999), 19–37. See also Elisheva Carlebach, "Attribution of Secrecy and Perceptions of Jewry," *Jewish Social Studies* 2 (1996): 115–36.

74. Pines cited Strauss to the effect that Hellenistic philosophers thought that choices between religious systems were ridiculous. See Shlomo Pines, "Notes sur la doctrine de la prophétie et la réhabilitation de la matière dans le Kuzari," *Mélanges de philosophie et de littérature juives* 1 (1957): 254.

75. Pines' eulogy for Strauss. For some perspective on the rhetorical constraints of a *hesped,* see Marvin Fox, "The Rav as Maspid," *Tradition* 30, no. 4 (1996): 164–81.

76. I attempt to substantiate this claim in "The Function of the Imagination in Islamicate Philosophy According to Shlomo Pines," forthcoming.

77. Muhsin Mahdi, "Orientalism and the Study of Islamic Philosophy," *Journal of Islamic Studies* 1, no. 1 (1990): 73–98, and Dmitri Gutas, "The Study of Arabic Philosophy in the Twentieth Century: An Essay on the Historiography of Arabic Philosophy," *British Journal of Middle Eastern Studies* 29 (2002): 5–25.

78. Paolo Rossi, *The Birth of Modern Science* (Oxford: Blackwell, 2000), 18.

79. The perspective espoused here is that of the history of religions after Mircea Eliade. It is at bottom a comparative perspective, though not archetypalist. I reverse the "psychoanalysis in reverse" of Eliade. See the conclusions to my *Religion after Religion,* 237–51.

80. For an interesting reflection of the tension between "sharing" (interconfessionalism) and "secrets" (esoterism) see al-Harizi's *Takhemoni,* especially in the discussion of Ross Brann, *Power in the Portrayal: Representations of Jews and Muslims in 11th and 12th Century Islamic Spain* (Princeton, N.J.: Princeton University Press, 2002).

81. These may be seen to correspond to the two types of esotericism, according to Scholem: "Intentional esotericism, based on the writer's decision (to engage in concealment for socio-political purposes) and esotericism that is essential to the subject under discussion (which cannot be expressed directly and adequately, but only indirectly, through symbols)." *The Kabbalah in Gerona* [Hebrew], edited by Yosef Ben-Shlomo (Jerusalem: Akademon, 1963–64), 16–24, cited by Yair Lorberbaum, "On Contradictions, Rationality, Dialectics, and Esotericism in Maimonides's *Guide of the Perplexed,*" *Review of Metaphysics* 55, no. 4 (2002): 711–51, at 747 n. 83.

82. This chapter originated as a public lecture and retains the tone of oral delivery. Versions of this lecture were delivered at the University of British Columbia; the University of Chicago; St. Michael's College, Vermont; and the University of Pisa, Italy. I thank my hosts on those occasions: John P. Kenney, Willis Johnson, Richard Menkis, and Cristiano Grottanelli. The Stillman Drake Fund at Reed College provided time for its completion, and Kathy Kennedy, Vahid Brown, and Michael Salk provided indispensable support.

7

ETHICAL-POLITICAL UNIVERSALITY OUT OF THE SOURCES OF JUDAISM: READING HERMANN COHEN'S 1888 AFFIDAVIT IN AND OUT OF CONTEXT

Dana Hollander

COMMENTING IN 1927 ON THE SUPPOSEDLY WANING NEO-KANTIAN MOVE-ment in philosophy and on the movement that was supposedly seeking to take the place of that "renewal of Kant," namely, a "renewal" or revival (*Erneuerung*) of Hegel, Martin Heidegger writes:

> These renewals even for the most part flatter themselves on wanting to keep alive and cultivate the reverence and appreciation of the past. But at bottom such renewals are the greatest disrespect the past can suffer, insofar as it is degraded into a tool and servant of a fashion. The basic presupposition for being able to take the past seriously lies in willing not to make one's job easier than did those who are supposed to be renewed. This means that we must first press forward to the real content of the problems they laid hold of, not in order to stay with that content and bedeck it with modern ornaments, but in order to dislodge/move forward [*von der Stelle bringen*] the problems thus grasped.[1]

The positive counterpart of this negative recommendation follows a few pages later:

> It is always a sign of the greatness of a productive achievement when it can let issue from itself the demand to be understood better than it understood itself. Irrelevancies have no need of a higher understanding.[2]

I should like to think of the guideline articulated here by Heidegger for working with philosophical texts as the standard by which we ought to measure our work on Jewish philosophers. To extend Heidegger's complaint about philosophical revivals somewhat: mere retrievals of thinkers of the past, whether in the service of illuminating some historical "context," or in order to assess to what degree "traditional" views of Judaism or "traditionally" Jewish views on some matter or other have been either preserved or abandoned, will always remain philosophically unsatisfying. As

Heidegger articulates so well, such efforts fail not because philosophy "as such" is supposed to make progress with its questions and is supposed to eschew a merely antiquarian cultivation of artifacts of the past. (It would obviously run counter to Heidegger's purpose to seek to establish philosophy instead as simply a positivist science among others, whose task would be to make continual progress toward certain knowledge about the matters under its jurisdiction.) Rather, part of the risk in seeing the past thinker in light of either a "context" or a "tradition" is that doing so fixes that context or tradition as something whose contours are already known. By contrast, when we seek to reactivate or make effective, in a transformative way, past philosophical insights for present and future thought, we thereby also give those past phenomena their due, not least by opening ourselves up to new understandings of what they actually were.

This is also the gist of a methodological remark that Emmanuel Levinas makes in his first public "talmudic reading," in which he comments on what it means to read a talmudic text for the *"philosophical* problems" it articulates. Anticipating objections from those "fanatics of historical method" who might find that his philosophically oriented reading is guilty of "perpetrating anachronisms," Levinas explains that while historical method presupposes "that it is forbidden for inspired thought [*la pensée géniale*] to anticipate the meaning of all experience and that . . . there . . . exist thoughts unthinkable before their time has been attained,"

> we begin from the idea that inspired thought is a thought in which everything has been thought, even industrial society and modern technocracy.[3]

To approach a corpus as if it has potentially already thought everything—to ask, How can we understand what is being said here in light of what is a question for us today?—is to activate and pay tribute to the significance of that corpus for philosophy.

At the same time, the past thinker and his or her world is a "source" for us as philosophers. In his posthumous work, *Religion of Reason Out of the Sources of Judaism,* Hermann Cohen formulates the problem of how philosophers approach sources when he considers how "literary sources" inform the project of understanding "the concept of Judaism": "History as such is not decisive about the essence and distinctiveness of the concept," in part because the concept "has perhaps not yet been brought about and accomplished in the course of history thus far." Thus, while the "literary sources" or "literary history" of Judaism may be seen as "the factor by virtue of which the *Faktum* is accomplished," those historical sources "never [have] the value of criterion—which can reside only in the concept, as problem and method, as task and presupposition."[4] For this reason, to approach a source with a view to understanding its significance for a concept is to "pro-ject" (*vor-werfen*) that concept ahead, or to anticipate it in the sense of "foreclosure" (*vorwegnehmen*), in one's treatment of the source.[5]

In what follows, I attempt to study a work by Hermann Cohen—the affidavit he wrote for the so-called Marburg Antisemitism Trial of 1888[6]—as a source in Cohen's sense. This was the first among several works by Cohen—spanning his entire career—that investigate the idea of love-of-neighbor in the Jewish tradition and the significance of the "neighbor" and related categories for ethics. Reading this text, like reading any text, necessitates what is generally termed "understanding it in its context." On one level, this will mean attempting to understand the more or less immediate discursive framework in which this affidavit was an intervention: a particular trial that was itself a function of two determinate historical phenomena: (1) the legal institution of the secularized criminal offense of blasphemy or insult against a religion; and (2) the use of this institution by Jews in nineteenth- and early twentieth-century Germany as a way of combating antisemitism. Relying on the results of historical research, I shall point out the legal and political conditions of this trial. This allows me to interpret Cohen's intervention otherwise than as simply exemplifying the purported "context" that he has often been taken to represent: an apologetic stance that seeks above all to harmonize a universal morality with the Jewish religion—in the service of furthering the cause of Jewish integration into the non-Jewish world. Instead, I will show Cohen to be breaking with the paradigm of what has recently been termed "tolerance discourse," in order to assert an ideal of ethical-political universality "out of the sources of Judaism."

I.

Whoever publicly, by insulting expressions, blasphemes God, causes scandal [*Ärgernis*], or whoever publicly insults one of the Christian churches or another existing religious association enjoying incorporation rights within the territory of the Reich, or its institutions and customs, and likewise, whoever, in a church or in another place designated for religious gatherings acts in a profane manner, shall be punished by imprisonment not to exceed three years.[7]

Thus reads the text of a German law prohibiting blasphemy, the public profanation or offense against God, or against the Christian church, or against other religions to which church-like rights are extended. It is not quite a contemporary law—although a significantly altered successor-law is still on the books in today's Federal Republic—but it is almost contemporary, and certainly modern: In the wording I have cited,[8] the law, known as the "Gotteslästerungsparagraph" (Law Against Blasphemy), or alternatively as the law against insults of a religion (against *Religionsbeschimpfungen*), appears as Section 166 of the Criminal Code (*Strafgesetzbuch*) enacted in the German Reich in 1871, and it remained in effect until the 1960s.[9]

It is perhaps a curious thing that a modern secular state—secular, at least, in the sense of having no official state church—should have need of a law against blasphemy, a need to treat offenses against religion as a punishable crime. In the context of a religiously pluralist society—which is also clearly envisioned by the text of Section 166 in that it names other incorporated religions alongside the Christian churches as possible victims of blasphemous offenses—we might expect the state to limit the protection of religious institutions and practice to the kinds of legislation that are well known to us as the traditional guarantors of religious freedom. These would be typified (certainly from an American perspective) by the First Amendment to the U.S. Constitution, which is limited to the negative determinations that there shall be "no law respecting an establishment of religion" and no law "prohibiting the free exercise [of religion]," and the positive guarantees of "freedom of speech," including religious self-expression and "the right of the people peaceably to assemble" for religious or other purposes. This schema, consisting of a series of public, or state, guarantees of freedoms or protections for institutions and practices deemed religious, seems to make unnecessary the criminalization of expressions directed against such institutions and practices.

Blasphemy, after all, is an offense of biblical origin, an offense against God, and in particular, a profanation of God's name upon which God decrees a punishment of death. In the originary instance in Leviticus 24:10–23, we are told of "a man whose mother was an Israelite and whose father was an Egyptian" who "[comes] out among the people of Israel" and in a fight with "a certain Israelite" "blasphemed the Name in a curse" (or: "in blasphemy pronounced the Name"). This man is brought to Moses and is held "until the decision should be made clear." God's punishment, communicated to Moses, is death by stoning, to be carried out by the entire congregation, from which issues a general decree about what is to be done in cases of blasphemy:

> One who blasphemes the name of the LORD shall be put to death; the whole congregation shall stone the blasphemer. Aliens as well as citizens, when they blaspheme the Name, shall be put to death. (Lev 24:16)

In a modern secular framework, however, one that claims independence from divine authority, it is hard to see why God or the church should demand worldly protection from human insult. As Leonard Levy asks in his major study of the history of blasphemy, "If vengeance belongs to the supernatural governor of life, why invoke the criminal law?"[10]

Of course, we know that the history, not to mention the contemporary reality, of the modern state's assertion of its independence from religious authority is not at all a story of uniformly clean divisions of a religious from a purely secular realm, and that each modern system of church-state separation evidences its own ambivalences at different stages of its history and to the present day. Already the Bible includes passages in which offenses against worldly authority are linked to blasphemy[11]—early evidence, perhaps, in favor of the view, reminiscent of Carl Schmitt's fundamental thesis about political theology, that secularization of authority is at the very least not completely achievable (though, of course, Schmitt himself would go further to argue that the very project of secularization is both questionable and undesirable). A case in point for the ambivalence of such church-state separation is the fact that Section 166 was routinely employed in Wilhelmine and Weimar Germany in ongoing defense initiatives against antisemitism. For whereas the biblical crime of blasphemy presupposes a single divine authority, and a worldly authority that is merely its extension, Section 166, as we have seen, reflects an evolution according to which it is not only "the Christian churches" but also "other religious associations" that merit protection against attack or profanation on the part of private individuals or entities. That is, an offense whose original purpose was to help secure allegiance to a single authority, to the one God, became employable as an instrument in the service of religious pluralism, the protection of multiple religious entities—at least insofar as such entities had otherwise already been granted institutional recognition on the part of state authorities, such as was the case for Judaism in the Wilhelmine Reich.[12]

By the time Hermann Cohen was called to be an expert witness at the Marburg Antisemitism Trial—a Section 166 trial—a pattern was beginning to establish itself among Jews seeking legal remedies against the growing wave of antisemitic attacks that grew out of the growing traction of antisemitism as a political movement. The accused was a schoolteacher who was reported to have claimed publicly (specifically at an antisemitic rally) that the Talmud specified that Mosaic law was binding only for interactions among Jews and thus condoned crimes against non-Jews.[13] Such claims were quite typical of antisemitic polemics of the period: this was the age in which Rohling's anti-Talmud tract, *Der Talmudjude* (published in 1871 and reprinted many times), popularized older Talmud denunciations whose purpose was to portray Jews as evildoers. A representative of the local Jewish community documented what was said at the antisemitic

rally and brought it to the attention of authorities, who subsequently ini-
tiated proceedings. Numerous similar cases were tried in the following
years, and the sequence of events at Marburg became formalized by the
Centralverein deutscher Staatsbürger jüdischen Glaubens (CV), founded
in 1893 as a Jewish organization one of whose central tasks was anti-
defamation: the CV established a legal defense department whose job was
to solicit and receive reports about antisemitic incidents in order to examine them for the purpose of seeking legal remedies where appropriate.[14]

II.

Thus, if the original offense of blasphemy had, in its formulation as a
worldly criminal offense, been extended to encompass not only offenses
against the Christian God and the Christian church but also offenses
against recognized non-Christian religions, it is striking that in 1888 the
process of bringing an accusation against a supposed slanderer of Judaism
led to a situation in which Cohen was in effect a Jewish expert witness
called to account for whether Judaism, and in particular Jewish law, was
in its turn sufficiently hospitable to the non-Jew. Thus, the trial was the
site of a turning of the tables. While its official legal purpose was to protect Judaism from attack, its effect was to put Judaism on trial, as it were,
for its purported hostility to Christians.

As it happens, Hermann Cohen was able to take this turning of the
tables against the scope and meaning of Jewish law very seriously and to
respond to it in a very systematic way. His affidavit, which he also published in pamphlet form under the title "Love-of-Neighbor in the Talmud,"
was the first in a series of considerations of neighbor-love that Cohen
undertook during his lifetime, culminating in the chapter on "The Discovery of the Human Being as Fellow-Human-Being" in *Religion of Reason Out
of the Sources of Judaism*. In the 1888 affidavit, as in subsequent discussions,
it is evident that developing a correct understanding of the concepts of
neighbor and neighbor-love became for Cohen an interpretative task that
goes to the heart of both the issue of philosophical methodology in general
and the problem of how to philosophically ground ethics.

In what follows, I sketch out the substance of Cohen's understanding
of neighbor-love from the point of view of the method and the ethical philosophy he developed in his systematic works (well after the time of the
Marburg trial) and then link this understanding back to how his remarks
on neighbor-love function in the discursive framework of the 1888 trial.

While Kant, in his metaphysics and epistemology, located human cognition neither solely in sense-based intuition nor in thought-based con-

ceptualization, but in a complex combination of the two, Cohen's brand of
Neo-Kantianism was rooted in a clear privileging of concept, of thought,
over sensory intuition, a privileging that was meant to avoid what Cohen
saw as an unsatisfactory tension between the two aspects in Kant's thinking. Moreover, Cohen typifies a shift in philosophy in an age in which the
empirical sciences were flourishing and in which philosophy was called
in a new way to account for the continuities and discontinuities between
its method and that of the sciences.[15] In Cohen's philosophy, this impact of
the sciences makes itself felt in his elaboration of a philosophical method
that begins not from sensory perception but from a *Faktum,* "fact," that issues from science—and in particular, in the case of theoretical philosophy,
from mathematics, which he terms "the organon of thinking."

In analogous fashion, Cohen develops an ethics that builds upon
Kantian notions of freedom and autonomy but that is also undergirded by
science, in this case the science of law, which he terms the "mathematics
of the human sciences."[16] That is, rather than examining laws or political
institutions against the background of ethical principles arrived at based
on a model of individual moral agency, Cohen proposes law as the arena in
which ethical principles are generated.[17] This is a departure from the philosophy of Kant, for whom existing law has no significance for the ethi-
cality of the actions of an autonomous (i.e., self-legislating) subject. Thus,
for Cohen, it is by reflecting on legal or juridical institutions and relationships that I can come to an understanding of what the good is. This methodological move on Cohen's part represents an understanding of ethical
action as from the outset operating in a social-juridical sphere. For example, in his major book on ethics, *Ethik des reinen Willens* (1904/1907;
Ethics of the Pure Will), Cohen calls attention to the word *action* as having both the sense of "acting" and the sense of a legal action (*ERW* 64).
This latter meaning allows him to differentiate actions from merely empirical, observable behaviors, and to highlight the fact that action can be
taken only by virtue of actionability, only because I have a prior right to
a trial (*Gerichtsanspruch*), that is, only by virtue of a juridical institution or
relationship in which I find myself. Other examples that are especially
highlighted by Cohen as models of legal action are the contract—which
he understands as a legal claim that binds an "I" to a "you" as its counterpart (*ERW* 248)—and the cooperative (*Genossenschaft*), which yields a productive concept of ethical subjectivity in that it is a "juridical person," an
abstraction, as opposed to a physical individual or a human being (*ERW*
229–30). For Cohen, what these concepts share, their advantage as coming
from the juridical realm, is that they point to a universality (*Allheit*) that
the concept of the individual—even when it is generalized into the cosmopolitan idea of humanity—cannot grasp (*ERW* 14, 231).

Given that ethics is directed toward universality and that it is rooted in relation, it is also significant for our discussion of Cohen's writings on the neighbor that for him the "I," insofar as it is a category of ethics, originates in the other person, or alter ego. This other is not an empirical thing that is encountered a posteriori, but is the counterpart of the "I," separate from it but linked to it by what Cohen calls a "correlation." This correlation makes possible ethical action, which, as we saw, is rooted in legal action or actionability (*ERW* 210–13).

At the point in *Ethics of the Pure Will* at which he introduces the idea of the self-other correlation, Cohen announces: "We are standing at a crossroads of systematic ethics," namely, the very point "at which it diverges from religion." To be sure, Cohen writes, the one God of monotheism corresponds from the start to a unity of humankind across the multiplicity of individuals and peoples. But this has meant that the problem of the other has been understood in a way that is misleading from the point of view of the ethics that Cohen is seeking to develop. For the other in the religious context is the stranger or foreigner, initially encountered as a challenge to the unity of humanity, in that the stranger "initially appears foreign as such; he appears different from one's own people and from one's own faith." This is why the Bible seeks to dispel this appearance, this prejudice by decreeing that "the stranger shall be to you as the native among you" (Lev. 19:34; cited in *ERW* 214). Cohen concedes that such pronouncements evoke sympathy—the same sympathy, he adds, that the biblical prophets call for when they evoke, together with the foreigner, the figures of the widow and the orphan—and that, based on such sympathy, they are supposed to engender a hospitality that allows the native to extend the scope of the law to encompass the foreign. These are "sublime ideas," capable of captivating us and reverberating in our hearts, but, Cohen writes, a sober look at the contemporary political hostility to foreigners makes evident that they have had no impact at all. Similarly, the idea of love that is employed by religion is admirable as far as it goes, but insofar as it is an affect, it cannot serve as the basis for ethics.[18] If the other or the stranger are to be ethically significant, this is because they are concepts of law (or of legal science) and thus belong to the political realm from the outset, and not because they are objects of love (*ERW* 216).

Furthermore, Cohen adds that the danger of appealing to love is nowhere as evident as in the command to love thy neighbor—or at least in the discourse surrounding this command—since "neighbor"—in German "der Nächste"—has traditionally been misconstrued as the one who is "nearest" to me, that is, in terms of proximity or nearness. But surely, Cohen protests, ethical obligation cannot be a matter of degrees of nearness, or of "more or less." This, he adds, is evident in the history of mistranslations of the command to "love your neighbor [in Hebrew: your *re'a*] as yourself." While *re'a*, according to Cohen, means simply "other" or "another," the Septuagint renders it as *plesios* (neighbor), the Latin Vulgate as *amicus* (friend), and Luther's translation goes so far as to use the superlative *Nächster*, "the nearest." In all of these translations, what is suggested is that the other whom I shall love is someone who is close to me, related to me in some way; and for Cohen, this misinterpretation simply mirrors the failure of ethics throughout the history of politics (*ERW* 218–19). Wherever differences of degree are invoked, wherever nearness is a criterion, ethical rigor is endangered (*ERW* 217).

But while in the *Ethics* Cohen rejects the ethical relevance of the category of the neighbor, in his 1888 affidavit, as well as in those essays on "the neighbor" that follow the two editions of the *Ethics*,[19] the concept of neighbor-love represents a constitutive principle of ethics. While in the *Ethics*, the work in which he elaborates his ethical philosophy, Cohen contents himself with briefly linking Kant's lack of attention to law as a possible ground of ethics to a prejudice (traceable to a Pauline prejudice) against Judaism as a "statutory," law-based religion (*ERW* 267–69), it is in the "neighbor" writings that we can see Cohen cashing out his insights about legal categories yielding ethical principles specifically with respect to Jewish law. This allows him to move past the naïve and ethically ineffectual religious view of the neighbor that he laid out in the *Ethics*. Thus, while in the passage I just discussed from that work, the very fact that the term *re'a* has been mired in a history of misunderstandings according to which neighbor-love is a matter of degrees of nearness makes the notion in itself corruptible and serves to disqualify it as an ethical category, the texts on neighbor-love provide detailed accounts of why "neighbor" is a mistranslation, and of the negative consequences and implications of that mistranslation. Moreover, in that Cohen in those texts seeks to retrieve an authentic understanding of the neighbor from Jewish sources and against Christian-theological misreadings, he is in effect extending his insights on how law yields the *Fakta* for ethics.

At the 1888 trial, Cohen is led to reflect on love-of-neighbor as he contends with the substance of what the accused is supposed to have said about Mosaic law: that it applies only to interactions among Jews. The historical translation of *re'a* as "neighbor" is problematic, he states, and has led in particular to a widespread misreading of the command as applying only to the fellow Israelite/Jew, and not to the non-Jew. But Cohen makes clear at the outset of his testimony that he is answering the court's questions not as an expert in "Semitic philology" nor as an expert in "Jewish dogmatics" or in Talmud, but as a philosopher. Accordingly, he classifies the historic distortion of biblical neighbor-love as commanded only toward fellow

Jews as mistaken, not because it is a false comparison of the ethical precepts of the Jewish versus the Christian religion—a comparison pertaining to the "content" of the respective ethical obligations. Rather, the mistake for Cohen lies in comparing moral systems by virtue of their content,
rather than in how they are grounded (their *Begründung*), their underlying
moral principles:

> The historical human being is under the sway of a prejudice that moral sys
> tems, whether philosophical or religious, differ principally in regard to the
> *content* of their moral precepts; and the opinion that the difference lies, and
> can lie, and must lie in the content has damaged the well-known philo
> sophical discussion that, by way of the question regarding the *human propen
> sity to morality*, runs through the history of modern ethics.
>   But the difference among moral systems by no means resides primarily
> in the content of precepts, but principally in their *foundation* [*Begründung*]
> and derivation from a general basic idea, the so-called moral principle. . . . It
> is thus the task of moral philosophy everywhere to discover the governing
> principle—and with it to thereby illuminate historical research.[20]

We may see what Cohen does here as being in line with his methodological considerations at the opening of the *Religion:* the biblical and talmudic material, as what he would later call "sources of Judaism," is subject to
philosophical considerations about Judaism and ethics, such that neighbor-
love may be recognized as the "fundamental form of monotheistic morality" (NT 148). That is, for Cohen, neighbor-love is not just one teaching
among others that happens to be, historically or philologically, present in
the literary corpus. For Cohen, it is constitutive of ethics as such.

We may further observe that by opting out of the business of comparing the ethical "content" of Judaism with that of Christianity, Cohen
is avoiding making an argument based on an empirically based apologetic
line of reasoning. He bypasses the court's question, an empirical question
about talmudic morality, and redirects the inquiry from one that would
be designed to show how the Jewish religion could be harmonized with a
universal morality, to an inquiry into the grounding of morality as such.
In this sense, we may say that Cohen is opting out of what the political
theorist Wendy Brown, treating modern and contemporary Western attitudes toward religious and cultural difference, has recently called "tolerance discourse." Building on the observation that tolerance as a public or
political discourse always marks its object as "deviant, marginal, or undesirable by virtue of being tolerated," Brown argues that tolerance discourse should be seen "as a strand of depoliticization in liberal democracies." One of the mechanisms of tolerance discourse that Brown identifies
is its tendency to "naturalize or culturalize" the sources of group conflict.
Thus, essentialized group identities are envisioned as being, by virtue of
essential differences from each other, inherently in conflict. Such con-

flicts then call for the practice of tolerance in order to harmonize the differ-ences.[21] The notion of tolerance is therefore predicated upon, and must in that sense presuppose and produce as naturally preexisting, the conflicts that it is supposedly designed to address—above all, that between cultural particularity and universality. That is, the notion of tolerance posits a uni-versality with respect to which the object of tolerance functions as a par-ticular. To tolerate the particular thus amounts to a claim about the extent to which that particular conforms to the universal.

Drawing on Brown's observation allows us to see that when the Mar-burg court called for a statement as to whether the defendant's alleged claim—that the Talmud sanctions wrongdoing toward non-Jews—was true, a juridical-discursive framework was produced in which, depending on the answer to that question, the particular ethical code could either be reconciled with, or "tolerated" by the universal order, or be found lacking. In answering as a philosopher, Cohen refuses to engage in a comparison of ethical "contents" and thus refuses "tolerance discourse" in order to be able to bring out the moral principles that he views as undergirding Judaism. As we will see, this results in a view of Judaism not as a particularity that makes a bid for tolerance within the Christian order but as a moral system that is constitutive of ethical universality as such. This line of argument is consistent with the way in which Cohen motivates his innovative inter-pretation of the neighbor in the *Ethics,* where he opposes what he sees as the standard religious framing of the neighbor as worthy of ethical treat-ment in light of his degree of similarity to myself, and of the stranger as an object of sympathy, to which the native law may opt to extend its hos-pitality.

Importantly for what we have learned about the methodological role of law in his much-later *Ethics,* Cohen goes on to link the essential equiva-lence between love-of-neighbor and love-of-the-stranger (NT 148–50) with two important juridical categories: (1) the biblical term *ger,* which is the term usually translated as 'alien' or 'stranger' in Leviticus 19:33–34[22] and which Cohen translates into German as "Beisaß-Fremdling," mean-ing "resident-alien"; and (2) its talmudic transformation (Cohen calls it a *Präzisierung,* a specification or more precise formulation) into the cate-gory of the Noahide, an "institution of state law" (*staatsrechtliche Institu-tion*). The Noahide, or "son of Noah," is of course traditionally defined as a non-Jew whose status is equivalent to that of a Jew and who is bound by seven laws that are regarded as binding on all humankind (and that have frequently been equated with the modern-day notion of natural law[23]). Cohen underscores the fact that this is a legal category—the Noahide is defined as a citizen of the state (*Staatsbürger*), and thus his status is irre-spective of his faith or belief (*Glaube*) (NT 158)—and he cites a number of quite diverse legal sources to support this interpretation (NT 159ff.). Thus,

Cohen shifts the questions of the court, which challenge Judaism to defend its moral stance toward non-Jews under the guise of defending Judaism from public attack by non-Jews and which thus purport to be about moral differences between Jews and non-Jews, to one concerning law and politics. As I will seek to clarify in the next section, his affidavit challenges the "tolerance" paradigm according to which the "particular" ethics of Judaism would have to be reconciled to a universal norm, by asserting Judaism as a "source" for a politics of universality.

III.

According to one standard interpretation, Hermann Cohen's contribution to Jewish philosophy consists of having theorized Judaism as an "ethical monotheism," enabling an appreciation for the legacy of Western philosophy and that of Jewish religion as harmonious in their common orientation toward the good and toward messianic peace. When seen under this optic, Cohen's participation in the 1888 trial may appear as a more or less conventional apologetics for Jewish religion in the face of attack. Such a characterization would certainly be in line with the discursive framework of the trial I described earlier, in which what was formally a case against a "blasphemer" of Judaism becomes—by means of what I termed a "turning of the tables"—an occasion for putting Judaism itself on trial. Given the massive corpus of anti-Jewish commonplaces, drawn from the popular antisemitic and anti-talmudic literature, that was mobilized at the trial, Cohen could have focused his testimony and affidavit exclusively on point-by-point refutations; and indeed, his testimony and especially his affidavit—which was composed also in reaction to Lagarde's affidavit/testimony—contains many detailed defenses of what Jewish law says about treatment of the non-Jew. Instead, I am arguing that the core of what Cohen accomplishes in his affidavit is not a defense of Jewish ethics but a political-juridical critique of the institution of the secularized blasphemy trial and of the concept of religion that undergirds it—one that remains relevant for contemporary debates about how we conceive of religious and other differences within political life.

Section 166, the law against blasphemy, places in parallel three offenses: (1) "causing scandal/nuisance" (*Ärgernis*) by "blaspheming God in public insulting expressions"; (2) publicly insulting either (a) a church or (b) any other "religious association" (*Religionsgesellschaft*) or its institutions and customs; and (3) acting in a profane manner in a church or another place designated for religious gatherings. In designating the second of these offenses, the law was presumably meant to protect the religions from public insult. But the law does not quite say that the object of insult is the religion per se. Rather, for the purposes of the second offense, the entity capable of sustaining insult is the "religious association."[24]

At the Marburg Antisemitism Trial, part of the task of the expert witnesses was to consider whether, in denouncing the Talmud as being hostile to non-Jews, the accused was in fact insulting Judaism. The court's question on this subject was formulated as follows:

> Whether the prescriptions contained in the Talmud, pertaining to religion/ faith [*Glaube*] and to morals, are to be regarded as binding commands for believing/practicing [*gläubige*] Jews and whether an insult of the Talmud is to be regarded as an insult of the Jewish religious community [*Religionsgemein-schaft*], or of an institution of the same. (NT 145)

Taking the law's term *Religionsgesellschaft*, "religious association," as its basis, the court refers to *die jüdische Religionsgemeinschaft*, "the Jewish religious community," as the possible object of insult. There is a slight terminological slide here: While the law refers to "religious associations"— the official entities representing the doctrines and interests of a religion, as a church does—the court's question refers to a "religious community," a grouping of adherents. If the object of insult is now the religious group rather than the religion as such, this shift is reinforced by the fact that the court's question about whether insulting the Talmud amounts to insulting the religious group is combined with a question about the relationship between talmudic prescriptions and the members of that group, the "practicing Jews" or "believers" (*gläubige Juden*).

In his initial, formal answer to the court's question, Cohen in part does what one might expect him to do given the range of different Jewish practices that exist in modern times: he explains why, although the Talmud is binding law only in certain respects and for certain aspects of Jewish practice, and although it is acknowledged as such by different Jews to varying degrees, it is nevertheless identified with Judaism in a way that means that any Jew would, and ought to, perceive an offense against the Talmud as an "offense against the Jewish religious community" (NT 150–51). But the rationale Cohen gives for this answer also consists in problematizing the term used in the question, *gläubiger Jude*, "believing/ practicing Jew," in its alignment with the other key term "religious community." In a formulation that is so sophisticated and academic that it seems designed to put the term "believing Jew" out of commission for legal purposes, Cohen writes:

> The nexus of thought on the basis of which an individual who is born into a religious community reckons himself as a member of that community is the product of an ideal construction that practices historical critique on the tra-

ditional sources, their expressions, and their systematics, as they have come about historically. The concept "believing Jew" may also be taken in this sense. (NT 150)

For Cohen, then, Jewish membership is something that applies to individuals who are born into a faith only by virtue of an "ideal construction" that is based on instituting a relationship of "historical critique" vis-à-vis the tradition. A consequence of this is that it is not up to religious or church authorities to define what constitutes a believer:

For no religion is it customary to leave the definition of believer up to the church [*Landeskirche,* i.e., the church of a given province, region, or state/ country]. (NT 150)

Although for Cohen the concept of the "believing Jew" "ought to be most impartially derivable" from the ways in which the congregation/ community (*Gemeinde*) is instituted by the Talmud and in other ways (NT 150–51), he casts doubt on the viability of this concept as a legal category. How can Cohen nevertheless conclude, in answer to the court's first question, that "every Jew with an interest in the honor of his faith feels himself to be connected to the Talmud to the extent that he feels an 'insult' of the Talmud with respect to its foundational moral concepts to be an 'insult of the Jewish religious community'"?

Looking only at his formal answer to the first of the court's questions will not suffice here. Rather, we must turn to what appears in this document to be Cohen's "defense" of Judaism as not mandating conduct that is hostile to non-Jews. Cohen begins to mount this defense in the introductory section of his affidavit, which precedes both of his formal answers to the court's two questions. There, as discussed above, he lays out some basic principles for what it means for him to address the court specifically as a philosopher. Among the matters Cohen seeks to clarify is that of the relationship between religion and morals. It is in this connection that Cohen first cites love-of-neighbor as "the fundamental form of monotheistic morality" and makes his argument against Christian misreadings of "the neighbor" as the kinsman. This is also where Cohen first articulates his view—which he will flesh out in greater detail in response to the court's second question—that the idea of neighbor-love is developed in conjunction with that of love of the stranger. Indeed, he goes so far as to accord to stranger-love a "creative" role in the emergence of neighbor-love. Who is "the stranger" who is to be loved, such that "the concept of the human being as the neighbor" may emerge? It is someone who may be foreign either by virtue of his nationality or by virtue of his religion or faith (*Glaube*) (NT 149–50). Having thus broached the topic of the neighbor and the stranger—the neighbor (*der Nächste*) who is decidedly not the "near" (*nahe*) or the "nearest" (*nächste*) one—Cohen writes:

> With this now I am approaching/nearing [*nähere ich mich*] the questions posed by the Royal Regional Court, which are linked to the concept of the "believing Jew" [*gläubiger Jude*]. (NT 150)

Why should elaborating the concept of love of the neighbor/stranger be an approach toward the way in which the court's questions invoke the "believing Jew"? The connection is forged by Cohen in his discussion of neighbor-love, which, as we saw, comprises for him the concepts of the *ger* and the Noahide. Though this discussion formally serves as Cohen's answer to the court's second question (whether the Talmud says that Mosaic law applies only to interactions among Jews), Cohen here implicitly revisits the category of *gläubiger Jude* that he had problematized in connection with the first question. From an examination of the sources, he concludes that "the Noahide is thus not a believer [*Gläubiger*], but nevertheless a citizen of the state [*Staatsbürger*]" (NT 159); that is, that the status of Noahide is a legal status irrespective of faith.[25] Cohen views this as a true innovation: he writes that "this institution represents a singular *Faktum* in the history of the politics of religion," whose ethical-political potential derives from "the power of the basic monotheistic idea" (NT 159).

Let us return to our earlier question: why Cohen can affirm that to insult the Talmud is indeed an "insult of the Jewish religious community," given that he has called into question the viability of the category "believing Jew." Given the reach of what Cohen argues about the talmudic institution of the Noahide—that it lies at the core of the monotheistic idea and is generative of what we might call political justice as such—Cohen's affirmation that an "insult" has taken place should not be taken simply as a diagnosis of subjective Jewish sensibilities. Rather, by calling into question the category "believing Jew" while arguing for the monumental talmudic contribution to the history of civil law, Cohen implies that the "insult" does not concern someone's "religious feeling." What is "insulted" here is a sensibility (if one could still call it that) for morality as such, as a pro-ject to which Judaism and humanity are directed. Rather than simply responding to the task explicitly assigned by the law and the court, that of establishing whether a particular group has sustained insult, Cohen directs his answer primarily at demonstrating a universal, philosophical truth—in which Judaism has a share.

If we recall Wendy Brown's characterization of "tolerance discourse" as a means of depoliticization, it is striking that Cohen goes on to elaborate that as a legal institution, the category of the Noahide goes beyond tolerance: the Noahide is not "tolerated" based on his particularity or his divergence; his status is simply (a priori) equivalent to that of the Jew: "The Noahide thus does not enjoy tolerance, neither on the part of the state nor on the part of religion, but is, as a person in the moral sense [*sittliche Person*], equivalent to the Jew" (NT 160).

What Cohen says here amounts to an implicit critique of the institution of the Section 166 trial. Such a trial is supposed to be a legal means of tolerating the non-Christian other, the one with a divergent faith or religious practice. But, as Cohen implies, it falls short of the demand of true civil equality before the law, which is what the categories of the Noahide and the *ger toshav* represent in his view. Thus, if we consider Cohen's critical reading of the court's term "believing Jew" in conjunction with his analysis of the legal institution of the Noahide—a conjunction he himself makes by announcing that in broaching the topic of neighbor- and stranger-love, of nearness and distance, "I am approaching/nearing the questions posed by the [court], which are linked to the concept of the 'believing Jew'"—we can see that Cohen is not merely defending Judaism as upholding a universal morality in that it makes juridical provisions for the non-Jew. Rather, Cohen is here effecting a political critique of the secularized blasphemy trial for its reliance on religious categories, or on the category of religion—categories that are ineffectual for achieving a political-juridical result, or, to use Brown's language, categories that "depoliticize" the true conflict that Jews faced in the German political-legal system.

CONCLUSION

In looking at the Marburg Antisemitism Trial, which was the concrete juridical context in which Cohen first developed his core ideas about "the neighbor," I find it significant that the institution of laws against blasphemy in a purportedly religiously neutral state represented a reversal of sorts, such that the means of defending the one God or religion was transformed into a tool for the maintenance of religious pluralism. I have also identified a second reversal, in that the trial displaced the purported objective of exposing an offense against Judaism by instead turning the tables on Judaism and putting Jewish exclusivity on trial, as it were. Thus, on one level, Cohen offered his analyses of neighbor-love as defenses of Judaism as essentially hospitable to non-Jewish otherness. But I have signaled a third and final turning of the tables, which shows us a side of Cohen's intervention that goes beyond the role of apologist for particular Jewish morals in light of universal values and disrupts the terms of what has been called in our own time "tolerance discourse." Cohen's answers to the court, read in conjunction with each other, turn out to be a critical commentary on the legal conception of the Jew with which the court operates, and on the incoherence of the institution of the secularized blasphemy trial, which—as Cohen's sensitivity to the ethical dimensions of law enabled him to notice—diminishes the effectiveness of political-legal categories by virtue of its appeal to supposedly religious ones.

Cohen's 1888 affidavit, along with associated works on neighbor-love, thus merits retrieval not as one more piece of evidence in the service of a contextualist narrative about the accommodation of Jews in the Christian (increasingly) liberal-democratic polity, but for how it contributes to our reflections on the politics and depoliticizations of Western modern thinking about religious difference. A politics of true universality, for Cohen, does not take account of the particular sensibilities of the Jew who is to be integrated or accommodated, nor does it seek to evaluate the degree to which Judaism is compatible with existing ethical-political norms. Rather, it shows how the Jewish sources function to establish and advance such norms in the first place and thus draws on the Jewish sources in order to further the cause of universal ethical-political justice.[26]

NOTES

1. Heidegger, *Die Grundprobleme der Phänomenologie.* Gesamtausgabe, vol. 24 (Frankfurt am Main: Klostermann, 1975), 141. English: *The Basic Problems of Phenomenology,* translated by Albert Hofstadter, rev. ed. (Bloomington: Indiana University Press, 1988), 100–101. This work is Heidegger's lecture course of Summer Semester 1927. Note that throughout the present essay, I draw on published translations where available and modify them where necessary.

2. Ibid., 157; *Basic Problems,* 111.

3. Emmanuel Levinas, "Textes Messianiques" (1960–61/1963), in *Difficile Liberté. Essais sur le judaïsme,* 3rd rev. ed. (Paris: Albin Michel, 1976), 101–102. English: "Messianic Texts," *Difficult Freedom,* translated by Seán Hand (Baltimore: Johns Hopkins University Press, 1990), 68.

4. As Andrea Poma has helpfully explained, Cohen developed Kant's transcendental method such that the first step toward determining the conditions of possibility for knowledge consists in identifying a *Faktum* or "fact" of science in order to "[justify] its possibility." See Andrea Poma, *The Critical Philosophy of Hermann Cohen,* translated by John Denton (1988; Albany: SUNY Press, 1997), 48–49. As we will see further on, for Cohen the method of ethics takes as its starting point the *Faktum* supplied by the science of law (*Rechtswissenschaft;* see Poma, 111, 121). In this passage from *Religion of Reason,* Cohen seems to treat the literary history of Judaism as similarly yielding the *Faktum* from which we can determine the conditions of possibility of knowing Judaism. Hermann Cohen, *Religion der Vernunft aus den Quellen des Judentums,* 2nd

DANA HOLLANDER

ed. (Frankfurt am Main: J. Kauffmann, 1929; repr. Wiesbaden: Fourier, 1978), 4; *Religion of Reason Out of the Sources of Judaism,* translated by Simon Kaplan (Atlanta: Scholars Press, 1995), 3.

5. Cohen, *Religion der Vernunft,* 3: "Es kann nimmermehr gelingen, aus den literarischen Quellen einen einheitlichen Begriff des Judentums zu entwickeln, wenn dieser nicht selbst . . . als der ideale Vorwurf vorweggenommen wird."

6. In calling the trial by this name, I am following the lead of Ulrich Sieg (see note 13).

7. Section 166 of the German Criminal Code of 1871, cited according to *Strafgesetzbuch mit 777 Nebengesetzen* (Munich and Berlin: Biederstein, 1949), 51. My English translation partly follows the one given in *The Statutory Criminal Law of Germany: A Translation of the German Criminal Code of 1871 with Amendments* (Washington, DC: War Department, 1946), 109–10.

8. There was a slight change of wording in 1953, when the phrase "another existing religious association enjoying incorporation rights within the territory of the Reich" was replaced with "another religious association existing in the state." Sieghart Ott, "Ist die Strafbarkeit der Religionsbeschimpfung mit dem Grundgesetz vereinbar?" in *Neues Juristisches Wochenblatt,* Heft 14/15 (1966): 639.

9. Werner Schilling, *Gotteslästerung strafbar? Religionswissenschaftliche, theologische und juristische Studie zum Begriff der Gotteslästerung und zur Würdigung von Religionsschutznormen im Strafgesetz* (Munich: Claudius, 1966), 93. Cf. *Strafgesetzbuch mit 77 Nebengesetzen,* 17th ed. (Munich and Berlin: Biederstein, 1949).

10. Leonard Levy, *Blasphemy: Verbal Offense Against the Sacred* (Chapel Hill: University of North Carolina Press, 1993), 3.

For an expression of this sentiment that is culturally and historically closer to the era I am focusing on, see the account of "Pflichten und Gesetze der Noachiden" offered by H. S. Hirschfeld, a rabbi in Gleiwitz, who interprets the Noahide laws—one of which is, according to rabbinic tradition, the prohibition against blasphemy—as being an instance of natural law, which means that while God rewards transgressions on the part of Jews against Jewish law, only "nature" can reward or punish non-Jews, who are bound by the Noahide laws, which is to say that the transgression already "carries the punishment in itself." Consequently, if a civil punishment is enacted for such misdeeds, it is to be seen as a redundant "complement" to what has already taken place. "Pflichten und Gesetze der Noachiden," *Jeschurun. Zeitschrift für die Wissenschaft des Judenthums,* edited by Joseph Kobak, vol. 4 (1864), 1–19, at 5.

11. Exodus 22:27 and Isaiah 8:21, as pointed out by Kaufmann Kohler and David Werner Amram in "Blasphemy," *The Jewish Encyclopedia* (New York: Funk & Wagnalls, 1901–1906; cited from http://www.jewishencyclopedia.com).

12. Ismar Schorsch writes that "as early as 1882 the Imperial Court [*the Reichsgericht*—D. H.] had recognized Judaism in Prussia as an incorporated religious community and therefore protected by Section 166." *Jewish Reactions to German Anti-Semitism, 1870–1914* (New York: Columbia University Press, 1972), 129. For the decision in question, see *Entscheidungen des Reichsgerichts in Strafsachen* 6 (1882): 77ff.

13. Details of the case are summarized in the editorial note to the posthumous edition of Cohen's "Die Nächstenliebe im Talmud," *Jüdische Schriften* (Berlin: Schwetschke, 1924), 1:338–39, and are laid out in greater detail by Ulrich Sieg in: "'Der Wissenschaft und dem Leben tut dasselbe not: Ehrfurcht vor der Wahrheit.' Hermann Cohens Gutachten im Marburger Antisemitismusprozeß 1888," in *Philosophisches Denken—Politisches Wirken. Hermann-Cohen-Kolloquium Marburg 1992,* edited by Reinhard Brandt

and Franz Orlik (Hildesheim: Olms, 1993), 221–49; and "Der Talmud vor Gericht. Die ideengeschichtliche Bedeutung des Marburger Antisemitismusprozesses," in *Religiöse Minderheiten. Potentiale für Konflikt und Frieden,* edited by Hans-Martin Barth and Christoph Elsas (Hamburg: EB-Verlag, 2004), 128–43.

14. See Schorsch, *Jewish Reactions to German Anti-Semitism,* 123ff.

15. A point made by Michael Zank in his article "Cohen, Hermann," in *Routledge Encyclopedia of Philosophy,* www.rep.routledge.com. Students of recent Continental thought will recognize "Neo-Kantianism" as the name of those philosophical approaches that phenomenology and hermeneutics classically pitted themselves against. The reference I made at the opening of this paper to Heidegger's 1927 lecture course provides a classic example for how the Neo-Kantians are regularly referred to as evidencing the tendency toward sheer positivism and scientism in philosophy—while the phenomenological-hermeneutic tradition was predicated on the view that philosophy is essentially different from the approaches of the natural sciences (as was systematically argued by Dilthey). By contrast, Cohen explicitly insists on the analogous methodology of the natural and the human sciences as a desideratum for the foundation of ethics. Hermann Cohen, *Ethik des reinen Willens* (1904/1907), 5th ed., *Werke,* vol. 7 (Hildesheim: Olms, 1981), 28. Hereafter abbreviated *ERW.*

16. For a look at how Cohen makes this point as an explicit corrective to Kant, see, for instance, *ERW* 227–28.

17. See Helmut Holzhey, "Die praktische Philosophie des Marburger Neukantianismus," in *Neukantianismus. Perspektiven und Probleme,* edited by E. W. Orth and H. Holzhey (Würzburg: Königshausen & Neumann, 1994), 149ff.; Ulrich Hommes, "Das Problem des Rechts und die Philosophie der Subjektivität," *Philosophisches Jahrbuch* 70 (1962/63): 326ff.; Robert Gibbs, "Jurisprudence Is the Organon of Ethics: Kant and Cohen on Ethics, Law, and Religion," in *Hermann Cohen's Critical Idealism,* edited by R. Munk (Heidelberg: Springer, 2005); Gianna Gigliotti, "Ethik und das Faktum der Rechtswissenschaft bei Hermann Cohen," in *Ethischer Sozialismus. Zur politischen Philosophie des Neukantianismus,* edited by H. Holzhey (Frankfurt am Main: Suhrkamp, 1994); Manfred Pascher, *Einführung in den Neukantianismus. Kontext, Grundpositionen, praktische Philosophie* (Munich: Wilhelm Fink Verlag, 1997), 85–91; Eggert Winter, *Ethik und Rechtswissenschaft: eine historisch-systematische Untersuchung zur Ethik-Konzeption des Marburger Neukantianismus im Werke Hermann Cohens* (Berlin: Duncker & Humblot, 1980), 235–38.

18. This view of Cohen's is in line with that of Kant: Although for Kant, moral actions imply a relationship between the agent and the principles under which they may be judged moral, whether that relationship is one of love or inclination is not relevant to whether they are moral. See Immanuel Kant, *Kritik der praktischen Vernunft,* Akademie-Ausgabe, 5:79.

19. "Zum Prioritätsstreit über das Gebot der Nächstenliebe" (1894) and "Gesinnung" (1910) in *Jüdische Schriften,* vol. 1; "Der Nächste. Bibelexegese und Literaturgeschichte" (1914/1916), in *Werke,* vol. 16: *Kleinere Schriften V, 1913–1915* (Hildesheim: Olms, 1997). See also "Die Entdeckung des Menschen als des Mitmenschen" ("The Discovery of Man as Fellowman"), chap. 8 of *Religion of Reason.*

20. "Die Nächstenliebe im Talmud" (1888), *Jüdische Schriften,* 1:146–47. Hereafter abbreviated NT.

21. Wendy Brown, *Regulating Aversion: Tolerance in the Age of Identity and Empire* (Princeton, N.J.: Princeton University Press, 2006), 14–15.

22. In the Revised JPS translation: "[33] When a stranger resides with you in your

land, you shall not wrong him. [34] The stranger who resides with you shall be to you as one of your citizens; you shall love him as yourself, for you were strangers in the land of Egypt." (The NRSV translation uses "alien.")

23. Christoph Schulte, in an effort to understand Cohen's apparent association of Noahide law with natural law, has explored the history and the limits of such an association in "Noachidische Gebote und Naturrecht," in *"Religion der Vernunft aus den Quellen des Judentums." Tradition und Ursprungsdenken in Hermann Cohens Spätwerk. "Religion of Reason Out of the Sources of Judaism. Tradition and the Concept of Origin in Hermann Cohen's Later Work,*edited by H. Holzhey, G. Motzkin, and H. Wiedebach (Hildesheim: Olms, 2000). In the same volume, David Novak goes so far as to assert that Noahide law provides Cohen with the exemplary "legal source" that allows him to see jurisprudence as a source for ethics in general. "Das noachidische Naturrecht bei Hermann Cohen," ibid., 231.

Steven Schwarzschild, on the other hand, has argued that while Noahide law does engage the problems of natural law, Cohen's ethical theory must be read as opposing natural law—or that it remains at best "ambiguous" in its position on natural law. "Do Noachites Have to Believe in Revelation? (A Passage in Dispute between Maimonides, Spinoza, Mendelssohn, and Hermann Cohen): A Contribution to a Jewish View of Natural Law" (1962), in *The Pursuit of the Ideal: Jewish Writings of Steven Schwarzschild,* edited by Menachem Kellner (Albany: SUNY Press, 1990), 29–59; at 49–51, 54ff.

For an informative discussion of this "ambiguous" status of natural law in *Ethics of the Pure Will,* see Peter A. Schmid, "Das Naturrecht in der Rechtsethik Hermann Cohens," *Zeitschrift für philosophische Forschung* 47, no. 3 (1993): 408–21.

24. Looking at the German legal literature surrounding Section 166 around the turn of the century, when a reform of the criminal code was being debated, it is evident that at the time, legal scholars were preoccupied with the tensions surrounding the formulation of this offense and were asking whether the object of the offense had been, or could be, coherently identified. Based on the history leading up the formulation of Section 166 and on its interpretation by the Reichsgericht, it was regularly noted that the state's motives for protecting religion were to ensure peace among the religions, to protect religious observance from disruption, to acknowledge the ethical and social value of religion, and to protect "religious feeling." One commentator particularly underscores the tenuousness of making "mere feeling" the object of a legal offense. Another plainly states that religion itself is clearly not sufficiently definable to be a viable object of offense and regards the recourse to "religious peace" and "religious feeling" as indicative of the helplessness of those who had drafted and applied the law when faced with the task of justifying it—to the point that he recommends abolishing the second Section 166 offense, "public insult against a religion." Similarly to the slide (described below) at the Marburg Antisemitism Trial from viewing the target of the purported offense as "the religious association" (as per the letter of the law) to viewing the target as "the religious community," this legal and interpretative history of Section 166 reflects a tendency to view religion as a matter of private identity—and the adherent as worthy of protection as an individual—rather than as a sacred entity as a matter of public-political fact. See Adolf Moser, *Religion und Strafrecht insbesondere die Gotteslästerung* (Breslau, 1909); Eduard Kohlrausch, *Die Beschimpfung von Religionsgesellschaften. Ein Beitrag zur Strafrechtsreform* (Tübingen: Mohr Siebeck, 1908).

The legal defense department of the CV evidently also relied on the category of "religious feeling" in determining whether Jews had been victims under Section 166: Eugen Fuchs, the director of that department, writes in his twenty-five-year retrospective on its work: "Es galt, den Organen der Rechtspflege darzutun, daß der Jude von heute . . . wie jeder andere Staatsbürger Anspruch darauf hat, daß sein religiöses Empfinden nicht verletzt . . . wird" (*Ein Vierteljahrundert im Kampf um das Recht und die Zukunft der deutschen Juden* [Berlin, 1918], 29).

25. For a reading that similarly highlights this aspect of Cohen's interpretation of Noahide law in the 1888 affidavit, see David Novak, "Universal Moral Law in the Theology of Hermann Cohen," *Modern Judaism* 1 (1981): 104–5; and idem, chap. 14 of *The Image of the Non-Jew in Judaism* (New York and Toronto: Edwin Mellen, 1983), 387–88.

26. I would like to thank Aaron W. Hughes and Randi Rashkover for helpful discussions that contributed much to the writing of this essay.

PART 4

NEW TAKES ON OLD PROBLEMS

8

WHAT IS THE SOPHIST?
WHO IS THE RABBI?

Sergey Dolgopolski

Who is the rabbi?

— *Babylonian Talmud* (*Pes.* 115a, *Yom* 39a, *Qid*, 15a . . .)

. . . and make plain by argument what he is.

— Plato, *The Sophist* (218c)

The first question in the title is from Plato's dialogue The Sophist;[1] the second cites the Babylonian Talmud, a series of—as I will argue— virtual discourses within rabbinic academies in Late Antiquity. Hitherto taken separately, those two questions have invited quite familiar answers: one asks for the personal name of a rabbi behind a given statement in the Mishnah, a third-century codex for rabbinical courts; the other, for a definition of the sophist. However, if put together, these questions create further questions about themselves: Does not the "sophist" also attach to a personal name, or is it not at least a title given to a man? And does not the Talmud also seek to connect a definition (or rather, a given position) to a name, or rather, to a title? Both call for the elucidation of a particular kind of subject position.[2] Taken together, the two questions can illuminate each other and thus perhaps also invite a very different and less familiar answer. I want to listen carefully to that answer.[3]

VIRTUALITY IN PHILOSOPHY AND IN THE TALMUD: A MUTUAL HERMENEUTICS

Studies in philosophy and studies in the Talmud have long been predominantly mutually detached. If this detachment had not happened, both fields might have looked different. This detachment calls for both analysis and undoing. In what follows, I examine different philosophers and philosophies from the various perspectives that emerge from the Talmud and its learners; and at the same time, I will examine the Talmud from various perspectives located in philosophy. This will not only explore Talmudic perspectives on philosophy and philosophical perspective on the Talmud and its commentary, but also, and more importantly, it will interrogate the boundaries that have traditionally and academically been established between these two fields.

Such an inquiry concerns the virtual—or, as it has hitherto been predominantly interpreted, "anonymous"[4]—character of the faces or voices behind arguments featured in so many pages of the Talmud and its commentary, but it also concerns, as I will argue, the voices within a philosophical dialogue such as *The Sophist*. I should first explain what is gained in substituting "anonymous" with "virtual" when studying the Talmud. Moving from anonymity to virtuality allows us to shift focus from a literary-historical analysis of genesis to a literary-philosophical analysis of form. Literary-historical scholarship of the Talmud has isolated an important symptom. The talmudic arguments have an effect (and hence imply an agent) not ascribable to anyone on the list of talmudic personae, either named personae (earlier masters—*tannaim* and *amoraim*) or unnamed (the later masters—*savoraim*). Scholars interpret this symptom as an effect of "redaction" and think of it in empirical terms of historically existing external agents, "redactors," an anonymous group of people located in one[5] or several[6] chronological loci of the Talmud's history. They subsequently refer to these redactors with a neologism, "*stammʾaim*."

The concept of redaction, as crucial as it was, united two incompatible effects—interpreting and emending[7] done by a subject who paradoxically would neither identify him- or herself with the master (as pure emendation would assume) nor claim his/her own listed identity (as pure interpretation would require). This paradox has many repercussions. Producing multiple competing redactions of the teachings of earlier masters, the *amoraim*—whom the redactors would rather found in an unsolvable disagreement than allow one of them to be wrong—was a part of the redactors' modus operandi. Did the produced versions of the *amoraim*'s polemical exchanges restore (emend) the original or interpret it? Literary-historical scholars explicitly asked, but programmatically did not answer, a similar question about the listed masters "redacting" the "corrupted" memories of *tannaim:* Did the masters restore ("emend") a "corrupted" teaching, or rather interpret it?[8] The same pertains to the work of unlisted redactors. Do they interpret/explicate the arguments of the *amoraim,* or rather emend/restore the original arguments in their full? In this case too, the question remains unanswered. It must remain so, because answering either in favor of emendation or in favor of interpretation undermines the concept of redaction altogether. In the framework of a literary-historical

theory of redaction, the choice of "emendation or interpretation" represents an antinomy.

It is probably better, and indeed intellectually more honest, to keep
this antinomy unresolved than to undermine the theory of redaction that
articulated it. Yet is there not another way? A symptom that was established but not resolved in a particular theoretical framework might call for
an analysis within a more general theoretical framework. A move from
anonymity to virtuality provides one. I propose that the notion of virtuality can help reconsider the antinomy through extending the discussion
of the talmudic arguments from a particular literary-historical framework
to a broader field of literary-philosophical analysis.

Returning the Talmud to the broader framework of literary-philosophical theory will also have implications for another particular theory.
I refer to a scholastic-ontological notion of the virtual agent, who produces effects in a reality of which s/he is not an actual part. Conceived
scholastically as neither real nor potential, the virtual agent is more than
a merely potential force because s/he acts in reality, but is less than a real
agent because s/he is not a part of reality that s/he affects.[9] A virtual agent
acts and, both more specifically and more importantly, speaks in reality
without existing in it. As I will argue, in excess of particular boundaries of
scholastic ontology and literary-historical theory of redaction, the virtual
agent can speak as the sophist does, that is, without being at all. What this
means, however, is that we are moving from two particular theories—one
of anonymous redactors, and the other of scholastic virtual agents—to a
broader literary, philosophical, rhetorical, and ultimately talmudic theory
of virtuality. This signals a movement from the two particular theories of
anonymous redactors and virtual agents to a more general theory of virtuality that deals with both speaking and arguing without being.

I will shortly start outlining the movement from anonymity to virtuality.[10] But before I do, let me explain a more general theoretical reason
for the broadening substitution of "the virtual" for more common and traditional terms. On computer screens, where we today tend to locate virtuality, the virtual limits itself—practically and normatively—to only one
frontal view at a very limited distance and with an exposure for only a
very short time and/or with a very high speed of comprehension. However, this is only one kind of virtuality. There are other, much older kinds
that can perhaps teach us important lessons about new virtual times and
spaces, while the knowledge of the new can help us better to discern the
old. Older forms of virtuality are not necessarily wedded to visual mediation. They work on different speeds and hence both assume and require
different regimes of attention, but they still follow the laws of the virtual,
which perhaps, precisely because of the slower speeds they display in their

older sites, makes them more accessible for analysis and understanding. Therefore, older forms of virtuality give us a chance to understand them along with their contemporary forms before they "understand" us[11]—that is, before a perhaps more obvious but also less reliable view of the nature of virtuality takes control of how we understand the virtual, new in light of the old, or the old in light of the new.

As noted, this process works in the other direction as well. The new virtuality makes us look at the older versions of the virtual in ways we did not know before, in part because we were either unable to recognize the older forms as virtual or because we merely failed to appreciate their role and importance.

What follows is an attempt to discern the older forms of the virtual, using the lens of its newer forms and approaching the distortions and aberrations that the newer can create as a heuristic tool. I propose to call this a mutual hermeneutics of the virtual, a mutually hermeneutical illumination of the relationships between philosophy and the Talmud.[12] Through the lens of this specific problem of virtuality in the contemporary study of the Talmud, I will look at the role virtual arguments play in philosophy as an intellectual genre and see what that can help us to learn about virtual arguments in the Talmud.

Through the issue of virtual arguments I will also make a more general claim. My approach here is to situate talmudic discourse vis-à-vis the oppositions between dialogue/oration, philosophy/sophistry, orthodoxy/heterodoxy, and being/nonbeing. Plato's project of philosophy, unlike sophistry, privileges a form of dialogue, in which a philosopher helps his partner to give birth to the right opinion about the truth of what really is. Plato prefers this form over that of sophistic oration, in which a sage, in his view, only manipulates right and wrong opinions without any extra value given to what truly is, and therefore the sage allegedly sinks into the depth of nonbeing. My principal argument is that any choice between being and nonbeing, dialogue and oration, philosophy and sophistry does not allow disagreement to be what it is in the Talmud—that is, a goal and not only a means. This disengages talmudic discourse from both philosophy and its privileged others—sophistry, to name but one of them.

Seeing that disengagement transforms the question of the relationship between the Talmud and philosophy and its others from the hitherto dominant chronology-based comparative approaches into a different kind of question altogether.

As I will explain, in approaching the relationship between philosophy and the Talmud from the perspective of a mutual hermeneutics of virtuality, we will encounter a number of road signs that point to the paths by which we can arrive at that question. My task is to follow those signs and to go where they lead: to the larger realm of inquiry to which the Talmud belongs, along with both philosophy and its others, which include, to start expanding the list, not only sophistry, but also philodoxy and orthodoxy—the embrace of opinions or arguments as such, regardless of their truth, and the combating of heresies. I will proceed through a series of case studies structured along the lines of an inquiry that is hermeneutical in method in the sense that Heidegger proposes, rather than chronological-historical.[13] That is, while a historical analysis normatively proceeds from that which is earlier to that which is later, a hermeneutical inquiry moves from what is clearer and more readily accessible to what is more obscure and thus more difficult to grasp. This often means going from what is later to what is earlier, or in any other direction, regardless of chronological order.

What follows is a study concerned with virtual characters *in* or *of* both talmudic and philosophical arguments, an étude or essay centered around the specific issue of virtuality in the Talmud, philosophy, and the privileged others thereof, among which sophistry is the first.[14]

TWO TRADITIONS VERSUS A MUTUAL HERMENEUTICS

Whether the relationship between the Talmud and philosophy has been predominantly approached in terms of a direct comparison or as a question of appropriation/rejection of one of the traditions within the framework of the other, an underlying assumption has almost always been that there were two separate traditions to compare or to appropriate. This assumption has taken for granted that the two entities are different from one another not only in terms of their histories but also in terms of intellectual characteristics empirically derived from their historical analysis.

These assumptions have prevented an examination of the two traditions either in terms of their histories or in terms of their conceptual formations. Philosophy has been approached as a living tradition ramified in a complex but still linear history of unique and often intellectually self-sufficient masterpieces, while the Talmud has been predominantly treated as one collective masterpiece, a record of arguments (with neither a pronounced nor a historically attested author, either individual or collective), surrounded, but never surpassed by its commentaries, which always remain attached to it. (Perhaps exactly because of the presumably secondary character of the commentaries, historians of the Talmud have carefully differentiated the commentaries from the masterpiece, while traditional adepts of the Talmud have insisted on an unbreakable continuity between them.)

The path of mutual hermeneutics is different. Instead of a direct comparison between philosophy and Talmud, and instead of looking at the appropriation or denial of one tradition by the other, it approaches the traditions of the Talmud and philosophy from their own perspectives, asking how and to what degree each of the traditions can discern the other. A way to realize such an approach is to ask two mutually related questions, which are indeed only marks of a larger set of questions about the relationship between the Talmud and philosophy: What can the Talmud tell us about the tradition of philosophy? And what can philosophy tell about the tradition of the Talmud?

A more hermeneutically specific way to address this set of questions is to ask: What light, or possibly darkness, can be discovered in a foundational text of philosophy such as, for example, Plato's dialogue *The Sophist*, if that text is looked upon from the perspective of both the academic and the traditional study of the Talmud? A similar, if not necessarily symmetrical question would be: What does a Talmudic discussion entail if looked upon from the perspective of philosophers, sophists and, most importantly, from the perspective of the question of being that *The Sophist* introduces once and forever both in philosophy and in its history?

Asked in this way, these questions are by definition not chronological-historical. I am asking, not what Plato can tell us about the Talmud, but what his treatment of the question of being and of sophistry can teach us about it. Likewise, I am not asking what the Talmud or the tradition of its learning tells us about Plato's philosophy, but what Talmud as an intellectual practice, indeed as a version of hermeneutics, can teach us about Plato.[15]

A purely hermeneutical rather than chronology-oriented approach, however, risks the allegation of anachronism. I here join in an alliance with Elliot R. Wolfson's response to a similar charge. In his "Prologue" to *Language, Eros, Being,* he defends the use of recent intellectual achievements in both philosophy and science to interpret the earlier masters of mysticism.[16] Reduced to empirical philology (glossed as a discipline studying the authorial intent), hermeneutics inevitably subscribes to a linear conception of time having just three dimensions: past, present, and future. Wolfson firmly opposes such reduction. In his re-reading of Merleau-Ponty's philosophy of perception in the context of both philosophical and scientific notions of reversibility of time, he proves linear dimensions of time insufficient to grasp the workings of time in full. Itself never timeless, time always involves a perceptual and therefore only a partial exposition of either what is perceived to be or of the perceiving being. Just as the three dimensions of space—length, width, and height—do not suffice to perceive an object in full but only one aspect of it in time, we still perceive the object, not the aspects of it. Accordingly, the three dimensions of time do not suffice to get a correct grasp of time, forcefully reducing it to a line— direct, inverted, or curved. In contrast, a correct grasp of time must allow for what cannot be fully perceived, even from a hypothetically eternal point of view of an architect. If so, the allegation of anachronism concerns only the first three dimensions of time, while hermeneutics has to do with the fourth.[17] On these grounds, Wolfson effectively re-inscribes empirical philology into the broader field of the hermeneutics of time, thereby re- serving chronology for empirical philology and its continuation in herme- neutics for what he sees as both philosophical and mystical inquiry, and what I propose to investigate vis-à-vis yet another intellectual tradition— that of Talmud. With this, I return to the above hermeneutical questions that the traditions of Talmud and Plato's philosophy help to ask about each other.[18]

The answer to these questions is best approached by examining what I am calling the virtuality of arguments and characters in Plato and the Talmud. The issue of virtuality in the Talmud has to do with the character of both the names standing behind Talmudic arguments and of the argu- ments themselves. Virtual characters in the Talmud have been addressed as arguments made in an anonymity that was not so much declared as carefully masked by the names of earlier talmudic masters. Deciphering this palimpsest has been among the central issues in contemporary aca- demic discussion of the Talmud. The arguments of many talmudic mas- ters are made, not directly by them, but rather on their behalf, so that the reader, or rather the learner of the Talmud, often gets different, indeed, conflicting versions of what an argument of a certain talmudic master was in his polemic with another master. This part of talmudic discussion repre- sents a very substantial part of the Talmud and appears even more in the commentaries on arguments either between talmudic masters or between virtual representations of their arguments in the Talmud.

Similarly, the sophist, who is the main target of *The Sophist,* is pres- ent there only virtually. He never becomes present on the stage of the dialogue, nor is he absent from it in the sense of being somewhere else. That, however, in no way prohibits the sophist, which is a title and not a living man, from speaking in the dialogue and from contesting many of the arguments about him. What is more, the sophist is far from the only virtual character in the dialogue. The virtual or hypothetical student of Parmenides is another. The list can continue with other titles or represen- tations of intellectual trends or positions that the Stranger, the most active character, both critiques and dismisses.

The virtual arguments in this philosophical dialogue shed new light on the virtual arguments in the Talmud. It is illuminating to discover the role of virtual argument made on behalf of someone who is programmatically absent[19] from the scene of a philosophical dialogue and to ask what the significance of such programmatic absence was for the progression— indeed, for the success—of the argument. As Plato insists, the genre of dialogue is in no way a form of either contest or competition, which makes it clearer why the sophist, the dialogue's target, cannot be a direct or "real" person in it. After all, he is a prey in the hunt, not a guest at the table.

What can Plato's dialogue, inhabited by such important virtual characters, teach us about talmudic arguments made in virtuality? To answer this question, we need to pay attention to the role and importance of those virtual characters within Plato's dialogue. The virtuality of some of the principal protagonists in Plato's dialogue can help us understand at least two problems involved in the study of the Talmud. These two problems eventually will reemerge as two sides of one and the same problem. The first is discussed in contemporary literary-historical-comparative scholarship. The second, owing to the literary-historical-comparative premises of that discussion, has unfortunately remained unattended.

The first problem concerns the historical existence of hypothetical unnamed people behind the virtual arguments of the talmudic masters. Again, to name the unnamed, contemporary scholars have had to invent a name, calling these people "those without name," or in Modern Hebrew, "סתמאים, stamm'aim." The second problem is the problem of being, or the problem of the ontological status of talmudic arguments. Without turning to Plato, only the first of these two problems both has and could have been considered, because it has been posed in the literary-historical-comparative perspective, which simply did not leave any room for the second problem, much less allowing us to look at the two problems as one.

In *The Sophist*, the question of the existence of the sophist is related to the question of being, because it is related to the speech of the virtual sophist. The connection between Plato's discussion of being and nonbeing and his attempt to identify the sophist proves to be much stronger than has hitherto been recognized by historians of philosophy.[20]

The choice of being versus nonbeing for which Plato advocates is connected to the choice between dialogue and oration. Plato chooses submission and cooperation in a dialogue instead of contest and competitiveness in orations. His choice belongs to the same set of choices that he makes between philosophy versus sophistry and truth versus falsity. The virtual arguments of the sophists present in the text, as well as of the no-less-virtual students of Parmenides and other virtual arguments and/or characters in the dialogue, tightly connect with the Stranger's elaboration on nonbeing. In fact, working only with virtual arguments, which of course is very different from participating in a dialogue, is what enables the Stranger to elaborate on the question of being versus nonbeing. This is not merely a matter of composition but also, and even more so, a matter of strategy—for the sophist, as the target of the dialogue, cannot be its direct participant, yet he still has to be able to argue, even before his identity or even his existence is established. Without his argument about nonbeing, no targeting of him can succeed. The question of nonbeing thus becomes the theme of the virtual defense of the sophist, just as by the same token it becomes the main stake in the Stranger's strategy of catching the sophist in a definition of who he is.

The question of the being and nonbeing of the subject who is present virtually in the text should also be asked in regard to the Talmud. To discern that choice better, we will need to take an even closer look at what is at stake for Plato in allowing for the virtual speech of the sophist.

Doing so not only directly affects the outcome of the effort to identify the sophist but also concerns both the identity and definition of the philosopher—both what he is and who he is. Curing the fear of nonbeing becomes crucial for Plato if he is to identify the sophist or to answer the seemingly naïve question of who he is. The question implies that the sophist exists, while the virtual sophist in the dialogue does not necessarily accept even his own existence, lurking instead in the realm of nonbeing. This allows Plato to deal with the issue of being and nonbeing as a way of identifying the sophist in the first place. To do so, he first has to trap the sophist in the question of who he is. Then, when this most difficult part of the game is over, all he needs to do is explicate the answer to the question, as he does in the end of the dialogue. Yet in doing so, what Plato identifies is not a man of flesh and blood but a personified concept—indeed, a title—which must be allowed to speak even before it is proven to exist. The sophist must speak without being—speak without any person present in speech, speak without being in speech. Plato thus identifies the sophist as a "what" that must also become a virtual "who" in order to participate in the dialogue, using virtual speeches about nonbeing and truth that the Plato's Stranger must make him generate.

Not only must the sophist produce his virtual speech as an apology for nonbeing in general and for his own nonbeing in particular, he must also argue that no speech can be false, but only true. As long as a speech makes some sense, there must be some truth to it. What this means, however, is that *what is* (being) is no different from *what is not* (nonbeing). By implication, the sophist can easily argue, but he cannot *be*—thus successfully avoiding the Stranger.

The Stranger's response to this analysis of nonbeing becomes crucial not only for catching the sophist in the net of the question of who he is but also for establishing the radical difference between the sophist and the philosopher. The question of nonbeing is the site at which the difference between the sophist and the philosopher is established. Plato cannot possibly establish this difference without his own deliberation on nonbeing, which remains dialogical in form but which in its content is a refutation, indeed a contestation, of the position of the sophist. Within the dialogical form, therefore, it is the Stranger who must perform this task.

Far from being only a literary device to catch the sophist in the question of his own identity without either persuading him or entering into a dialogue, Plato's discussion of being versus nonbeing marks a pivotal argumentative step for Plato himself as he delineates who is the sophist and who is the philosopher. Catching the sophist in the question of his own identity lets the philosopher produce an account of his *own* identity. The crucial difference between the sophist and the philosopher is that the sophist hides in the "darkness of nonbeing," where falsity is impossible and thus also undistinguishable from truth. The philosopher, of course, dwells in the "light of being," and therefore both the sophist and the philosopher are very hard to see, especially for the masses, who easily satisfy themselves with no more than convincing opinions about things, without worrying of their truth or falsity. In a different text, Plato pejoratively designates the ways of the masses as "philodoxy"—that is, the embrace of opinions or arguments, not of the truth or falsity that the arguments might entail. While putting a real philosopher and a virtual sophist at the two extremes of the spectrum, Plato needs a representative of philodoxy in the middle. The virtual character of the sophist thus becomes indispensable for creating that spectrum. In one and the same move, the virtuality of the sophist makes the philosopher real, puts him in the light of being, and leaves the philodox Stranger[21] mediating between the two.

What does that connection between the virtual character of the sophist (or of his speech) and his dwelling in darkness of nonbeing teach about the virtual arguments in the Talmud? Can the Talmud's virtual arguments be ontologically qualified as a case of sophistry, rather than of philosophy? Or rather, as philodoxy? Or, what is not very different from the latter, are they a mere play of imagination as Maimonides, for example, would want us to think?[22] To understand the complexity of these questions, let me proceed step by step on the hitherto unpaved road from the question "What is the sophist?" to the question "Who is the rabbi?" That road leads from Plato, via some important milestones, to the Talmud, to Maimonides, and beyond.

Philo of Alexandria will help us to make our first short but very important step on that journey. Despite his admiration of philosophy, Philo is very different from Plato's philosopher. Plato's philosopher primarily discusses issues, not texts.[23] He or she is interested in what is, in being, not in speeches that can entertain what is not, or nonbeing, as well. In contrast, in his allegorical reading, Philo discusses texts as a gateway to discussing issues that a philosopher might also have discussed. This seemingly insignificant difference has a huge implication: Plato's philosopher, by his contrast with the sophists, both initially and ultimately targets what is, or being, as distinct from what is not, or nonbeing. So even if Philo associates his reading of Scripture with the philosophy of being, Plato would still have to place Philo in the ranks of either the sophists or, at best, of the philodox, for Philo has to assume the truth of the text, something that only a sophist might allow but that a philosopher would hardly accept. While Plato thus would identify Philo as a sophist, Philo could hardly agree with that identification. The blind spot between those two is telling. In particular, it helps us to approximate a larger realm or place in which we also can locate the talmudic tradition.

Not entirely unlike Philo, midrash as an exegetical expounding of Scripture, and the Talmud as an exegetical interrogation of the Mishnah, also discuss issues, albeit necessarily through the gateway of a given text from which they begin, proceed, and via which they come to an end. Again, the most important difference lies in the implication: as forms of exegesis, neither midrash nor Talmud necessarily take the discussion in the direction of what is (being) versus what is not (nonbeing), but rather both remain in what Plato classifies as the darkness of nonbeing and sophistry. To complicate things even more, midrash and Talmud never lose sight of the given text: unlike Philo, they use it not only as a gateway but also as a target, and often as a tool.

Like the discourse of the sophist, talmudic discussion works hard to disallow the falsity of a given speech of the Mishnah. But in talmudic discussion, the given nature of the speech is assumed to make it exist or to be and removes it from the realm of nonbeing. The practice of talmudic exegesis therefore can no longer belong to nonbeing alone. Plato, therefore, would again almost inevitably classify exegesis as the practice of sophistry, for it starts from the shaky ground of a text that is either presumed to be not false or reconfirmed as true, instead of discussing the issue or matter directly. Philo, by contrast, classifies his exegesis as philosophy, that is, as a prioritized discussion of being to which nonbeing must be subordinate. In short, midrashic expounding of Scripture and talmudic interrogation of the Mishnah always start from a text, but unlike both Philo and Plato, they also dwell within it, precisely in the dark realm of nonbeing, as Plato (and perhaps even Philo) would see it.

Given the gap between Philo and Plato, the identity of the rabbi in question is therefore hardly that of a philosopher, but even less so that of a sophist. He both emerges from and disappears into the gap between Philo's subscription to Plato's philosophy of being and Plato's implied dismissal of Philo as a sophist. Much less is that rabbi a philodox, a mere middle between the two extremes. Yet the option of philodoxy requires a closer look, which we would be much better equipped to take, not with Philo, but rather with Irenaeus, a second-century church father who, with others, prepared the ground for Christian orthodoxy to emerge. He can be of great help for discerning any orthodoxy and/or philodoxy in the rabbi, for after all, both orthodoxy and philodoxy concentrate on *doxa* and thus can help to illuminate each other.

Is talmudic exegesis a case of philodoxy? What makes the help of Irenaeus indispensable in answering this question is his performance of orthodoxy in its basic sense, as a true opinion that arises, not from stating that opinion directly, but rather primarily from refuting the opinion "falsely claimed to be true," also known as heresy. Our way from Plato to the Talmud therefore might become easier or at least more predictable if we continue it with Irenaeus through his notion of heresy versus orthodoxy.

Irenaeus is an example of a Gentile, that is, of somebody who wants to belong to the covenant with the God of Israel but who pointedly does not want to become a Jew.[24] What allows him to engage with the covenant without becoming its direct subject? His philosophy-oriented refutation of sophistry and philodoxy as heresy is one part of the answer. In performing such a refutation, his own orthodoxy becomes possible. But it is only one part of the answer. A combination of his theology of God as logos with the ontology of God as being rather than nonbeing in his critique of "false knowledge" is the other. But perhaps even more important is the way he resolves the inevitable tension between two imperatives. One is the philosophical imperative to treat the issues, and thus what is versus what is not. The other imperative is exegetical, which in the eyes of Plato would most likely involve either sophistry or, at best, philodoxy.

Philo resolved a similar tension between exegesis and philosophy by discerning and treating the issues as existing above and behind texts, thus in the way of *allegory*. Yet he neither had to position himself as a non-Jew nor was his allegorical reading outside the conventional lineage of the Jewish tradition. He did not need any new covenant for himself. This, however, is not sufficient for a Gentile engaged with a covenant between God and the Jews. Why? Because a Gentile cannot limit him- or herself to just reading already established texts philosophically. Instead, he or she needs to reestablish the texts anew, as a source of a new authority for his or her position as a Gentile engaged with a covenant already designed for those who either are or are willing to become Jews, not for those who want both to be in and to preserve their non-Jewish identity at the same time. Differentiating between philosophy and philodoxy becomes very useful for handling this task. It is precisely knowledge of what is that makes philosophy different from philodoxy. Therefore, the Gentile has to strive for true knowledge, knowledge of what is. At the same time, he or she cannot be Plato's philosopher, for philosophers do not do exegetical work. Instead, he or she has to find a way between philosophy and philodoxy. The result is orthodoxy, a position that can arise only from refuting heterodoxy as heresy, not from any direct philosophical imperative to seek knowledge, for such an imperative would inevitably remain outside of exegesis and thus outside of the Gentile's task.

This might explain why the concept of knowledge comes to the forefront of Irenaeus' intellectual world[25] and why, indeed, he construes and constructs Gnosticism as the main and inevitably virtual target of his refutation. By claiming that the gnostics have knowledge, which, however, happens to be false philosophically, he can prove their knowledge to be false exegetically. Thus, in a negative way, the only way he can use, he establishes his own position, by implication, as orthodox. As we learn from Michael A. Williams, he quite artificially constructs straw men, exegetes of the texts for whom philosophical knowledge was the ultimate value.[26] He even calls them by the name of this most important and most problematic of philosophical concepts—"gnostics," or "those who know"—those who know what is behind what is already revealed in the text.

In this way, Irenaeus creates orthodoxy by refuting the philosophically false knowledge of gnostics as well as by ridiculing their teachings as mere philodoxy. The resulting orthodoxy, however, is neither philosophy nor philodoxy. In fact, his project undermines the difference between the two. This is accomplished in two moves. The first move is a critique of philosophical knowledge of what is, or being, versus what is not, in terms of its dangerous claim to know being beyond what is already revealed in Holy Scripture. The second is his critique of personal authorship. Arguing from their personal philosophical authority, heretic authors create illegitimate additions to what is already made known in revelation. That second move sounds like philosophical critique of sophistry, while the first sounds like a sophistical critique of philosophy—if there can be such a thing at all, for did sophists ever criticize philosophy or could they ever have been interested in that? All this, however, happens for the sake of approaching holy texts, a task that neither philosophy nor sophistry either actually recognized or was potentially able to recognize. The resulting orthodoxy (e.g., the affirmation that the creator of the universe and Christ as Savior are one and the same person in two versions) inevitably calls to mind a similar kind of critique, for it also represents a certain knowledge of being and also extends revelation beyond what is "already revealed" (i.e., beyond Scripture, of course, unless the Gospels are also considered a revelation, a concession that Irenaeus is ready to make, thus allowing the concept of a New Testament to emerge).

Eradicating the difference between the philosophically poor philodox and the anti-philosophically rich sophist, Irenaeus helps us to visit a radically new place that Philo's encounter with Plato did not reach. Instead of a blind spot between Philo's admiration of philosophy and Plato's implicit disqualification of Philo as either a philodox of the holy texts or even a sophist, Irenaeus reveals another blind spot, that of orthodoxy, which is surely not a philodoxy, for he at least theoretically differentiates false opinions from true ones and, refuting the false, reserves room for the true. That truth, however, is maintained, not by philosophical knowledge of what is, but rather by a sophistically performed refutation of the opinions of the others for their reflection of what is not. Orthodoxy thus opens a new empty space created by the sophistical refutation of philosophically false knowledge. This space exists only insofar as and only because there still is something to refute.

Does the rabbi also reside in this space, a space constructed with the blueprints of orthodoxy? If he does, he either maintains it without content—as it should be, for when encountering a heretic, the rabbi limits himself to refuting him—or he fills the room with the opinions of his peers, who disagree one with another. Whether his orthodoxy is empty or full of disagreeing arguments, the rabbi advances the question of being and nonbeing, and thus of virtual arguments, to the forefront of the discussion again.

LANGUAGE AND VIRTUALITY, BEING AND EXEGESIS

So far, our inquiry has shown how the notion of being, or what is, helped Plato to establish himself as a philosopher of light and of being, versus either the sophist, located in darkness and nonbeing, or the philodox, the lover of mere opinions and plausible arguments, regardless of their ultimate truth or falsity. In the taxonomy of the philosopher, the sophist, the philodox, and the orthodox, being, or what is, is thus proved to be a concept with a power greater than even Plato's own (I almost said "orthodox") notion of forms or ideas. The relationships between philosophy, philodoxy, sophistry, and orthodoxy have thus not only been established through the notion of what is, or being, but also have continued in the same way, even when a new (or, from the sophist's point of view, only partially new) element, that of the exegesis of holy texts, entered the game.

The relationship between philosophy and its default others—sophistry and philodoxy—was thus both challenged and complicated in a variety of ways when a new component, that of holy text, with a being of its own and thus with a question of its ontological status (of either being, or nonbeing, or else of opinion) became part of the equation, as also did the new practice of relating and interpreting texts with such a problematic ontological status, the practice of exegetical reading.

As we have seen, for Philo this new component of the holy text called for an allegorical interpretation, which Philo himself deemed philosophical, while Plato would by necessity deem it sophistical, or at best philodoxical. What is more, the very notion of the holy text as speech that cannot be false is very close to the sophistical notion of the impossibility of the falsity of any speech whatsoever, provided that speech can make sense. A remarkable symptomatic and unbridgeable gap exists between these two thinkers: Philo appeals to Plato, while Plato dismisses Philo.

This gap marks the existence of a blind spot between the exegetical and philosophical traditions. It has played itself out in a variety of ways. We have seen it at work with both Irenaeus and the orthodox rabbi who is in disagreement with his peers. One other way in which it has played itself out involves the notion of language itself. Looking at this makes us return to both Philo and Irenaeus, if only for a short time.

For Plato, language mingles with both being and nonbeing alike, thus allowing the sophists or the philodox to tell lies. For Philo, language (at least a certain language) is holy and thus, just as it was for the sophists, cannot tell a lie (albeit, importantly for what will follow, that language can still be understood incorrectly). However, like Plato and unlike the sophists, Philo believes that the holy text must mingle with being only, not with nonbeing. If Plato sees telling no lie as a requirement to tell what is, as opposed to what is not, and the sophists see language's inability to tell a lie as a testimony for nonbeing's parity with what is, Philo allies with Plato. Hence, for Philo nonbeing means a place in which the holy language is read incorrectly; a place that makes one fail to keep the language of Scripture tell us exclusively the truth of what is. Irenaeus cannot be fully content with that, for if the holy text belongs to being, philosophical knowledge prevails over its holiness, a luxury that he, as orthodox, simply cannot afford.

In the Talmud, the relationship between philosophy, philodoxy, being, and language is complicated due to the Talmud's exegetical task. That task applies not only to holy writing but also to the presumably authoritative and yet oral and thus not only authoritatively divine but also intrinsically human tradition of the Mishnah. Since the Mishnah allows and even requires competing interpretations, the Talmud might seem either to take the side of philodoxic indifference to the truth or falsity of knowledge or to execute a sophistical freedom of nonbeing. Either of these options allows talmudists to authorize and reauthorize the oral tradition of the Mishnah through the process of its ongoing sophistical interrogation without the demand for philosophical validity and thus severing any connection with being. However, the Talmud also has an element moving it in the direction of truth and thus away from philodoxy. Once again, Irenaeus can help us to discern this place better.

In Irenaeus, we saw a radically different configuration of philodoxy, philosophy, and the exegetical task, which cannot be even compared to the configuration of the Talmud. He distances himself from knowledge of what is and thus from philosophy, for philosophy represents a danger to his exegetical strategy of treating holy writing as revelation, which, in his view, is already given and thus cannot be extended further—even through philosophically authenticated knowledge. To disallow any application of philosophy to the task of revealing what is, Irenaeus uses the sophistical strategy of refutation. Yet, due to his obligation to revelation in the holy text, and thus to distinguishing truth from falsity, he cannot position himself as a sophist or as philodox. Therefore, he cannot satisfy himself with the refutation of philosophically false knowledge alone, much less with any disagreement with his own peers or friends to whom he writes.

Just as the Stranger talks to Theaetetus, not to the sophist, Irenaeus writes to his friend, not to the gnostics. The latter are as virtual for him as the sophist is for the Stranger. Irenaeus' solution is to establish a new position, that of orthodoxy—a correct opinion guaranteed not by philosophical knowledge, as in Plato, but by the critique and dismissal of any incorrect knowledge about a holy text or what it reveals. Eventually, his design of orthodoxy as an empty space created by means of refuting his virtual gnostics almost inevitably leads to the establishment of a positive opinion about the revealed truth as well, which immediately puts that opinion or its interpretation under the fire of orthodox critique again, for it is constantly haunted by the virtual heretic who stands behind the whole process. This tension, or rather obsessive repetition, resolves itself in Irenaeus' search for authority as opposed to any kind of authorship.

However different he is from the rabbis, Irenaeus indicates something very important about the talmudic tradition. Like him, the rabbis in the Talmud distance themselves from philosophy or its use for furthering revelation as a way of fulfilling the exegetical task, yet unlike Irenaeus, the Talmud does not univocally deny a continuation of revelation by means of, if not philosophy, then sophistry and philodoxy. Both in approaching Scripture in midrash and in approaching Mishnah in the Talmud, the rabbis do what Irenaeus does not: approve the truth of a text through a refutation followed by a defense. By contrast, Irenaeus satisfies himself with refuting heresy alone, using the positive effect of the refutation to anticipate and welcome orthodoxy, even before establishing its positive content. Eventually, the empty space Irenaeus created fills in with a positive "knowledge," or at least with a text, followed by a sophistical fight against the heresies that arise in reading it. In the case of the Talmud, the same place of orthodoxy fills neither with doctrinal or positive statements of faith about God nor with the truth of his revelation, but rather with disagreements between and about the rabbis themselves, including the disagreements about whom they might, virtually, be.

Not fully unlike the case of the sophist, the virtuality of the rabbis' argument becomes indispensable part of who they are, or rather a function of who they are not; for any given argument in either the Mishnah or the Talmud might eventually hark back to any of several possible rabbis, none of whom has to be real, but all of whom are virtual.

A difference between the Palestinian Talmud and the Babylonian Talmud provides a magnifying glass to show the virtuality of the rabbi's being. The earlier version, the Palestinian Talmud, is easier to compare and to juxtapose to Irenaeus' creation of the empty space of orthodoxy surrounded by the ruins of what is first a virtually constructed and then a realistically refuted heresy. The example will show that like Irenaeus in *Against Heresies*, a rabbi in the talmudic record, Rabbi Simlai, produces the empty space of orthodoxy in regard both to heretics and to his students. A later version of the Talmud, the Babylonian Talmud, will help us to show how virtual argument in the Talmud fills in that empty space with refutations now directed not to heretics but rather to peers. Under such circumstances, the arguments (and the addressees) of the refutations and defenses become no less virtual then they were with the heretics and fellows in both Irenaeus and the Palestinian Talmud.

Translated into English, the text in *The Palestinian Talmud*, PT *Berachot* 9:1,[27] reads as follows (its truly fascinating content should excuse the length of the citation):

—How many divinities created the world?—heretics approached Rabbi Simlai[28] with this question.
—Are you asking me?—He said—Go and ask First Adam! For it reads, "if you will ask about first days" etc. "[from the day on which] Elokim created [*bar²u*, plural form of the verb] Adam on the Earth" Yet, it is written there

nothing else but "[from the day on which] Elokim created [*bara*? singular form of the verb] Adam on the Earth."

—But it is written [and reads], "In the beginning Elokim created [*bara*? singular verb form]"—they responded.

—But is it written "created" [*bar²u*, plural verb form]? Nothing is written but "created" [*bara*? singular verb form], he answered.

Rabbi Simlai said [to his students], "Every time the heretics attacked, the answer was found on their side."

—If so, why it is written "Let us make Adam in our image and in our likeness?"—asked the heretics again.

—It is in no way written here "And they created Adam in their image," but rather "And [he], Elokim, created Adam in his image."

[When the heretics left] his students said to him, "You kicked those out with a stick, but what are you going to answer to us?" He said to them, "Earlier, Adam was created from the Earth and Eve was created from Adam, but afterwards, "in our image and in our likeness"—a husband cannot be without his wife, a wife cannot be without her husband, and they both cannot be without divine dwelling between them."[29]

Using the difference between contextual readings of the verb "created"—singular versus plural—which in all cases is spelled the same way, *bar*? with no grammatical indication of number shown in writing, Rabbi Simlai disallows the heretics' use of vocalization to determine the number and returns them back to the limits of how the verb is actually spelled, not to how it is read, thus refuting their attempt to find a second divinity in creation.

Rabbi Simlai is in refutation mode with the heretics and in defense mode with the students, but the space of orthodoxy remains empty with both. With the heretics, he just finds the answers that refute them. With the students, he is responding to (basically providing a support to) their already existing desire. In both cases, orthodoxy is empty. He is obviously not acting as a dialogical philosopher in his openly rhetorical (in Plato's terms, sophistical) contest with the heretics, but he is not in a philosophical dialogue with his students either, because he is following their desire for reassurance, not leading them to any new knowledge. He thus speaks without being. His two capacities—refutation of heretics and defense for his faithful students—produces opinions that do not intersect. Precisely because of that lack of intersection, R. Simlai identifies with no specific opinion/argument that he makes. What it means, however, is that his speaking produces two heterogeneous effects—refutation and defense—in two heterogeneous environments that intersect in no other place than his name. This is only possible if he belongs to none of these environments while still acting in both. He therefore acts as a virtual agent.

Speaking from a position that is perfectly empty in both types of inter-action, he, not unlike the sophist, speaks and acts (i.e., refutes and/or defends) without being. He therefore remains virtual, as Irenaeus' gnostics do, and indeed as does Irenaeus himself, not to mention Plato's sophist, or indeed his philosopher, who acts as no more than a symmetrical function of the sophist. In creating their respective virtual opponents, the Stranger, Irenaeus, and Rabbi Simlai also recreate themselves as virtual subjects.

Virtual argumentation in the Babylonian Talmud, however, creates a different subject position for its participants. Translated into English, the Babylonian Talmud, TB *Megillah* 19b-20a[30] reads as follows:

Mishnah:[31] All are qualified to chant *The Book of Esther* [both initially and after the fact?—S.D.], except for the deaf, imbeciles, and minors. Rabbi Yehuda makes a minor qualify.

Talmud:

—Who is the Rabbi [in the Mishnah] to say a deaf person does not qualify even after the fact?[32]

—"That would be R. Josi, for it is taught in the Mishnah, 'The one, who is [already] chanting the *Shema* prayer and did not make it heard to his own ear, still fulfilled his obligation, said R. Yehuda.[33] R Josi said he did not'"— Said Rab Mathna.

—Why does it have to be R. Josi's? Why does it have to disqualify [the chanting of the deaf] even[34] after the fact?! It may well be Rabbi Yehuda's; and disqualify the chanting of the deaf only initially, thereby intimating it works after the fact!

—Such intimation should not even occur in your mind, because the deaf are mentioned just like imbeciles and minors are; and just as the latter two do not qualify even after the fact, so also the deaf doesn't.

—Yet it still may be that each [in the group] comes out differently!

—It hardly may. Because, in its last phrase, the Mishnah says, "Rabbi Yehuda makes a minor qualify," which must have come from a premise that the first phrase does not make him qualify [at all, even after the fact].

—Yet only the last phrase is [explicitly] R. Yehuda's, which intimates the first phrase would not be his!

—Well, it still might very well be all by R. Yehuda.

—It might not, for the first phrase in the Mishnah is not like the last one. The first forbids and the last permits. For then it would mean mentioning two different kinds of minors!

—Oh, that only means the Mishnah would be corrupted; and here is what it would say as a matter of fact: "All are qualified to chant *The Book of Esther*, except for the deaf, imbeciles and minors. To which minor does that refer? To one who is not yet ready for education; however, if a minor is already ready for education, he is qualified even initially, because Rabbi Yehuda makes the minor qualify."

—Then, where did you end up placing the Mishnah?! In Rabbi Yehuda and in the [case of issues arising] after the fact! But we have a contrary teaching: 'Yehuda the son of Rabbi Shimon Ben Pasi taught that a deaf person who can speak but not hear may set aside the *teruma*-offering"!

—So, whose is the Mishnah then? Paradoxically, if it is of R. Yehuda, it makes [the deaf] qualify after the fact only, not initially. In turn, if it is of

R. Josi, it disqualifies the deaf even after the fact! Rather, it is of R. Yehuda, and makes the deaf fully qualify even initially.

—That would be quite contrary to the following Mishnah, "One should not say his grace after meals silently, and if one did, he did not fulfill his obligation"!

—[Why is that contrary?]

—For, whose can that be? Neither R. Yehuda, nor R. Josi can have it. For in Rabbi Yehuda, the silent grace should work even initially, and for R. Josi, it should not, even after the fact!

—By all means, it would still be of R. Yehuda; and the silent grace after meals works even initially; and there is no difficulty here! The teaching [about *teruma*] indeed expressed the opinion of R. Yehuda, while the other [about the grace after meals] expressed an opinion of his teacher only, as it says in [an apocrypha of *tannaim*], "R. Yehuda says in the name of R. Eleazar the son of Azariah: One who is chanting a *Shema* prayer wants to make it heard to his ear, as it says, 'Listen, Israel, the Lord is Our G-d, The Lord is One'—[which intimates] you should make what gets out of your mouth heard to your ears. R. Meir says, '. . . on which I command you today on your heart' [which intimates that] according to the concentration of our heart is [the value] of our words."

—If you already go that far, you could equally say R. Yehuda [in the teaching about *teruma*-offering] argues just like his teacher, and what was taught [about the grace after meals] is coming from the name of [a different] R. Yehuda, the son of R. Shimon ben Pazi, and is in fact Rabbi Meir.

This text is both a direct example and an immediate context for the question of what or who is, or was, or could be the rabbi. It goes without saying that the "is," or "was," or "could be" get no distinct linguistic expression but are only intimated. I will be interested not in these intimations, however, but in the more explicit "what" and "who" sides of the question. What kind of answer does this question invite in the talmudic discussion above? In response to it, we find a series of possible names of the rabbis, or rather name tags, attached to the tradition recalled. None of the names becomes final, not even the one introduced last. The discussion leaves off with many virtual names precisely because none of them is definitive. Thus, for an answer, we get a host of virtual names, none of which can be fully dismissed and none of which can become the final or acceptable at the expense of others.

Let us appreciate this. The answer to the question comes in a set of virtual names, the collective plurality of which does the expected work. It reaffirms the Mishnah's authority, albeit not by finding a definitive and thus "real" rabbi behind it, but rather through a host of virtual, that is, strongly plausible yet mutually exclusive name tags that thus satisfy the question "Who is the rabbi?" without claiming any philosophical knowledge of the "is."

With such a host of virtual speakers behind the Mishnah, and without any final and thus, as it were, "real" speaker to name, the Mishnah not only emerges as speech without being but also, together with the talmudic discussion of it, loudly calls for a more careful look at the "who" and the "what" in all the other traditions of virtual speaking we have already observed. The "who" and the "what" in these traditions can now be approached afresh, with no imperative connection with either the "is" of the questions or the being that it alleges.

No longer dealing with the question of being or nonbeing invites a discussion of the personality, personal name, intellectual profile, or, if one prefers, the title of the sophist and/or the rabbi. That shift surely involves a mirror effect, because even more importantly, they invite a discussion of the questioner, the one who asks each of the questions. We should always keep in mind, however, that whoever looks in the mirror is never exactly the same as the virtual image he or she sees in it. The simple answer is that it is a philosopher who asks the question "What is the sophist?" and it is a talmudic master or a talmudist who asks the question "Who is the rabbi?"

The "who" and the "what" parts of these questions can therefore be best approximated if the direction of our travel changes and we no longer go from Plato and philosophy to the Talmud, as we did via Philo and Irenaeus, but rather proceed backward, from the Talmud to philosophy. Despite, or precisely due to, his attitude toward the Talmud, Maimonides can hardly be surpassed as a guide on that path. Even if his philosophy is, in a certain sense that I will soon explain, a dismissal of the Talmud, for he replaces it with what he thinks is a philosophically more viable code, his intellectual trajectory still goes in exactly the direction we need to follow: from the Talmud to philosophy. With Maimonides and his later discontents, both talmudic and philosophical, we can attain a better grasp of the "who" and the "what" found both in and behind our questions.

Maimonides helps us to appreciate the personalities and/or intellectual profiles of both the talmudist asking the question "Who is the rabbi?" and the philosopher asking the question "What is the sophist?" He disqualifies the talmudist as a person driven either by *doxa,* that is, by opinion and/or argument, or, as he has it, by "the power of imagination" alone.[35] That philosophical definition, however unpleasant it sounds, will help us to start approximating the profile of the talmudist better.

A distant intellectual relative of Philo and Plato,[36] Maimonides exemplifies a new return from the Talmud to philosophy, now as a way of dismissing the Talmud's open-ended dialectics of legal discussion (without, of course, losing either its authority or its tradition). In that sense, he dismisses the talmudic legal argumentation as bordering on sophistry and/

or imagination,[37] and thus as philodoxy, almost precisely in the ways that Plato dismisses the sophist. Maimonides of course dismisses, not the Talmud as a source of authority, but only the legal dialectics of the talmudists who have no interest in the philosophical tenets that for him illuminate the Law's foundations. Again like Plato, he allies with being, or with what is, making nonbeing only a part of being, which language allows but which philosophy must eradicate. On the other hand, faithful to his exegetical imperative, Maimonides distances himself from the philosophical tradition of searching for truth, holding instead, as Leo Strauss, a contemporary post-Heideggerian interpreter of Maimonides, has argued,[38] that the truth is always already revealed as Scripture, and people need only to understand it—using, of course, the tools of philosophy, not of the Talmud.[39] Strauss suggested that Maimonides considered revelation a given truth to be understood with the help of philosophy and that he treated philosophers without revelation as people who are desperately searching for truth that has already been revealed.

This suggestion helps to determine an important difference in how Plato would classify Maimonides in connection with how Maimonides classifies Plato. The significance of that difference is in its implications. It has to do with the role that misunderstanding or perplexity plays for Maimonides as opposed to its role for Philo as allied with Plato. While for Philo, Scripture is misunderstood if it is not read philosophically, that is, allegorically, so that allegorical reading replaces misunderstanding by what is philosophically correct. For Maimonides, misunderstanding or perplexity is not an extraneous condition to be replaced but the beginning of a true philosophical understanding of Scripture, or in a broader context, a starting point for understanding the revealed truth without substituting the truth of philosophy, but using philosophy as a helper.

As we recall, Philo allied himself with philosophy, although Plato would call him a sophist, because his notion of holy writing (or writing without falsity in it) is what Plato's sophist held about language in general: What can be said cannot be false. In contrast, Plato would hardly call Maimonides a sophist. Maimonides does allow falsity (or seduction, delusion, and hence "perplexity") in the language of the Torah,[40] at least in the way in which people can intelligently misunderstand it. Such perplexity arises if people who are educated enough still do not grasp the full scope of what he calls "co-participant names" in the Torah,[41] or if they do not discern a name as a "borrowed name," or if they fail to isolate names that are dubious in nature and thus find it difficult to determine if they are of the first or the second kind. Most importantly, and what is most strikingly different from Philo, Maimonides allows and even requires educated misunderstanding or perplexity as a condition of the possibility of understanding in philosophical terms—for after all, those who are not educated in philosophy cannot be perplexed. The whole classification of names listed above designates both the conditions of misunderstanding and a way to overcome it.

In addition, unlike Maimonides, Philo did not exactly position himself as a philosopher. While admiring philosophy, he sought only to read or translate holy writing (admittedly a sophistical notion) into the language of philosophy.

From all these differences, there appears an intellectual profile of the philosopher that dismisses, or rather replaces, what Maimonides sees as the "less successful" image of the talmudist. The profile of the dismissed talmudist is thus closer to the sophist or the philodox, not to the "desirable" profile of the philosopher. This is not, of course, to suggest that Maimonides dismisses the Talmud as sophistry. On the contrary, he reestablishes the Talmud as a source of authority. Yet he seriously considers the talmudist's proximity to sophistry—or, in his terms, to the faculty of imagination alone as opposed to the faculty of reason[42]—a serious deficiency. This made Maimonides rewrite the Talmud through the lens of philosophy. The talmudist, then, is to be reinvented by the philosopher, even if Maimonides wants to adjust the profile of the philosopher through the intervention of revelation (of which the Talmud in its pre-given form was not an obvious part).

Maimonides' negative portrayal of the talmudist comes together with his allowance for, and even requirement of, initial perplexities in grasping revelation. This helps to isolate a different, in fact much more positive perspective on the character of the talmudist. This perspective is based on Maimonides' allowance for temporal perplexity, followed by a more precise understanding, which our next guide, Rabbi Izhak Canpanton,[43] transformed from merely an allowance or requirement to an operative tool, indeed, the main device of a rationality that he conceived as both connected to philosophy and differentiated from it.

Responding to Maimonides and at the same time allying with the Tosafists, the medieval commentators of the Talmud, who, unlike the former, considered the Talmud to be not a collection of virtual arguments on different topics around the Mishnah but rather one big argument, consistent and coherent in all its parts (despite all seeming incoherencies that the Tosafists both bring forward and overcome), Canpanton distanced himself from both Maimonides and philosophy. He claimed Talmud to be a rational intellectual art of its own, which Maimonides, as a philosopher, missed in his philosophical thinking of the Talmud as merely a text to be

understood or misunderstood. Against his own will, through his dismissal
of the talmudist in favor of the philosopher of revelation, Maimonides
helped Canpanton to discover the talmudist anew, now as a type different from other types (philosophers, prophets, and people of imagination[44])
that Maimonides was able to identify and also differentiate from any of
the types (philosophers, sophists, the philodox, and the orthodox) that we
have seen before. Help came from Maimonides' (and Plato's) recognition
that language can mingle with nonbeing and thus with a genuine experience of failure (or perplexity), followed by the recuperation of truth.

Talmud, for Canpanton (Talmud without the *the*, as "philosophy" and
"sophistry" are not preceded by *the*) is therefore a case of neither philosophy nor sophistry. Of course, it is not a case of rhetoric/eloquence (terms
for the philosophical interpretation of sophistic speeches) either. First of
all, it is not a case of rhetoric, because philosophy already had defined and
derogated rhetoric as eloquence. Unlike rhetoric (or sophistical eloquence),
Talmud, for Canpanton, is a rational art of disagreement, not a case of nice
speech. Second, the talmudist is neither philosopher nor sophist, both of
whom subscribe to the goal of attaining agreement, either in present or in
the future, either on the basis of being and truth (as does the philosopher)
or on the basis of nonbeing and the impossibility of falsity (as does the
sophist). Unlike them, the talmudist studies the Talmud by targeting the
disagreements found in it not as obstacles to overcome but rather as goals
to attain. For the student, the disagreements in the Talmud come from the
past and have the value of a fait accompli. That is why, for the student of
the Talmud, disagreements are a goal to achieve, not a condition to overcome. A student of the Talmud is to preserve them at all costs, not to take
them to a place of agreement. He or she must thus invest the talmudic disagreements with the assumption of truth, an investment that he or she
will also have to find using the rationality of his or her argument on behalf
of the disagreement. This investment is occasioned, not from the fact of
there being a disagreement, but rather from the student's appreciation that
they come from the past. They have the value of a fact and therefore cannot and should not be changed but only continued, which means "understood better." It is their facticity, in the sense of their *pasticity* (if I may), that
is, their simultaneous pastness and factness, that makes them into a goal
of study. All the talmudist needs to do to the Talmud is to invest intellectually in the permanent truth of its disagreements. That means, for Canpanton, that the talmudist is neither a philosopher of being nor a sophist
of nonbeing, for neither of them can grant a disagreement any truth whatsoever.

This helps us to understand better who stands behind the question
"Who is the sophist?" and who stands behind the question "Who is the

rabbi?" As we have seen, the philosopher emerges from behind the former, and the talmudist from behind the latter. Both are functions of the
virtual arguments and/or characters they both create and encounter. Different from either presence or absence, this virtuality (or respectively, the
figure of a sophist and a rabbi) becomes indispensable for revealing the
philosopher and the talmudist, who are thus no less virtual than the virtual speeches they entertain.

Most importantly for the question of virtuality, it helps to understand
the role of the virtual personalities about whom both the philosopher and
the talmudist ask. Without asking about any biographically "real" sophist
or rabbi, they ask about the truth of their intellectual positions, so that the
name behind the question becomes a title, just as does the name to which
the question refers. In the case of the philosopher, the real question then
is not "What is the sophist?" but rather *who* he is; and in the case of the
talmudist, the real question is also not "Who is the rabbi?" but rather *what*
he is, to which intellectual profile—or rather, as Menachem Kahana[45] has
it, with which cluster of statements, that is, to which name of a rabbi—
does a specific statement in the Mishnah fit better? If what is virtual is not
the same as either what is present or what is absent, what does this say
about the real? Is the talmudist a real sophist, as opposed to the virtual
sophist that Plato produced? If virtuality is more complex than a simple
opposition between what is present and what is absent can allow, it perhaps can also teach us a lesson about reality.

I thus conclude at a point at which the work undertaken here should
continue. The strategy of mutual hermeneutics that I have applied to the
issue of virtuality in the Talmud and in philosophy helps us to discern virtual arguments and/or characters, whereas the simple opposition between
presence and absence (i.e., presence somewhere else) can no longer satisfy
the demand for speech to make sense in which a virtual character and/or
argument is created. The resulting irreducible virtuality of both the argument and of the personality behind it generates a series of configurations
between philosophy and its default others on the one hand, and exegesis,
heresy, orthodoxy, and the Talmud on the other. Those configurations re-
introduce philosophy into the hermeneutical horizon of the Talmud and
the Talmud into the hermeneutical horizon of philosophy, and they do
so in a radically new way in which the hitherto dominant contemporary
intellectual divide between neo-Kantian anthropology (ramified in empirical philological, chronological, and social-cultural readings of the Talmud in terms of its "anonymous redactors") and Heideggerian ontology
(expressed in particular in Heidegger's reading of *The Sophist* in light of the
question of being) shifts from prohibitive to productive. An investigation
of such virtuality can therefore be done only in the way of a mutual her-

meneutics of philosophy and Talmud, that is, in view of a different level of reality to which this virtuality invites us to refer.

Is this reality transcendental? Is it more complex than what either philosophy (including transcendental philosophy) or its default others allow us to entertain? Neither a presence nor an absence, speech without participating in being, an investment in speech well before being, not an elusive ghost, but rather active speaking and arguing happening well before any more common visual expression of the virtual in visual terms, the virtual in philosophy and in the Talmud calls for further analysis, both talmudic and philosophical. This analysis could hardly be done if these disciplines of thinking remain deaf to the virtual speeches that each of them so powerfully creates.

POSTSCRIPT

What comes next? How might mutual hermeneutics help understand the future of Jewish philosophy? How can such an analysis both engage and change the extensive yet primarily empirically based philological scholarship on the relationships, influences, and connections between the Talmud and philosophy?

The program of mutual hermeneutics naturally continues the tradition of academic scholarship of the relationship between talmudic and philosophical traditions done under the premises of empirical philology and respective historical analysis of the texts. For one important instance, Henry Fischel's analysis of the connection with Epicureanism importantly reconstructs both synchronic influence of Epicureanism on the Talmud, and diachronic elision of that influence in later appropriations of earlier traditions in talmudic discourses.[46] In other instances, a connection between the Talmud and philosophy was established in the works of S. Lieberman, D. Daube, S. Fraade, M. Fishbane, M. Jaffe, A. Yaddin, D. Boyarin, and others. Within a completely different set of premises, most brilliantly present in the works of Emmanuel Levinas and Max Kadushin, there developed a tradition of philosophical appropriation/translation of the Talmud with, or sometimes programmatically without, any grounding in empirical-philological study of it. In sum, done either from an empirical-philological or a purely philosophical point of view, exploring connections between the Talmud and different texts of philosophy has a long and rich tradition of scholarship.

Both continuing and revisiting these traditions of scholarship, mutual hermeneutics also represents an important new turn. Stripping the Talmud from the *the*, it moves far away from any attempt to translate the

Talmud into the language of philosophy and from the confines of the exclusivist linearity of philological-chronological inquiry. It therefore anticipates a series of inquiries in which narrowly chronological (and thus reified) notions of the Talmud, philosophy, and philosophy's others in Late Antiquity or in any other given chronological period are to be reconsidered. This allows new light to shine on the question of what Talmud and philosophy are.

More specifically, this kind of work calls for returning the Talmud of Late Antiquity to the field of hermeneutical inquiry, thereby establishing the relationship between Talmud (without the *the*) and philosophy, especially as discernible in the latest contemporary achievements across intellectual genres and practices, including studies of virtuality. This means both using the virtual to think of Talmud, and using both Talmud and philosophy to think about the virtual. If Heidegger found that the essence of technology is "nothing technological," but rather relates to what he calls *das Gestell,* or being supplied, stored, and consumed without being encountered,[47] the next step is to ask if the essence of the virtual is the same as the essence of technology. Rethinking the relationship between Talmud and philosophy along the lines of mutual hermeneutics is an important component in this question.

NOTES

This project was first conceived during the fall of 2005 at the UC Berkeley Center of New Media's semester-long colloquium, in which new media were approached from different disciplinary standpoints, not only and not primarily in their digital avatars, but also and more importantly in terms of the older forms of the new media, from the wheel to the steam engine, from the alphabet to the telegraph, and from the oral form of the Talmud to its ramification in the printed book. I owe my initial question of the relationship between talmudic and philosophical virtuality to the context of this colloquium. Earlier versions of this text were discussed in the Philosophy and Literature Seminar at the Kansas University Hall Center for the Humanities in October 2007 and, in a shortened version, presented at the November 2007 American Academy of Religion convention in San Diego. I am particularly grateful to Paul Franks of the University of Toronto for carefully reading and responding to the text in the early stages of its development, as well as to Daniel Boyarin, Robert Gibbs, Hindy Najman, Benjamin Pollack, Cheryl Lester, and Ilya Dvorkin for a series of conversations that are ramified in the text's present form, with mine, of course, being the sole responsibility for the outcome. I am immensely grateful to Bud Bynack for his editorial suggestions that have helped transform the text from the second part of a larger, book-length project where an expanded version of it eventually will appear, into a stand-alone essay.

1. Unless specified otherwise, *The Sophist* is cited from *Plato, with an English Translation,* vol. 7, edited and translated by Harold North Fowler (Cambridge, Mass.: Harvard University Press, 1977).

2. The term "subject position" is preferred to the term "subject," which is heavily loaded in philosophy. For the present argument, when I employ the term "subject," I do so in a very broad sense and outside of any theoretically charged philosophical usage.

3. The arguments adduced here are part of a larger work in progress, currently titled *Talmud, And, Philosophy.*

4. See, for example, David Halivni, *Mekorot U-Masorot: Beurim Ba-Talmud: Masekhet Shabbat* (Jerusalem: Bet ha-midrash le-rabbanim ba-Amerikah, 1986).

5. Chanoch Albeck, *Einführung in Die Mischna* (Berlin: De Gruyter, 1971); Halivni, *Mekorot U-Masorot.*

6. See, for instance, Christine Elizabeth Hayes, *Gentile Impurities and Jewish Identities: Intermarriage and Conversion from the Bible to the Talmud* (Oxford: Oxford University Press, 2002).

7. See, for example, J. N. Epstein, *Mavo Le-Nusah Ha-Mishnah: Nusah Ha-Mishnah Ve-Gilgula'v Lemi-Yeme Ha-Amoraim Ha-Rishonim Ve-Ad Defuse R. Yo.-T. Lipman Heler (Ba'al To. Y. T.).* Mahad. 3. ed. (Jerusalem: Magnes, 2000).

8. Ibid.

9. On the notion of virtual agency in the scholastic philosophy of Duns Scotus compared with Deleuze's notion of virtuality, see Stephen Crocker, "Into the Interval: On Deleuze's Reversal of Time and Movement," *Continental Philosophy Review* 34 (2001): 45–67. For an exposition of the broader notion of virtuality that arises from that context in Deleuze, see Manuel DeLanda, *Intensive Science and Virtual Philosophy* (New York: Continuum, 2008), 9–55.

10. If continued from this specific point of view of the theory of anonymous redactors, further explaining that transition from a literary-historical theory of anonymous redaction to a broader literary-philosophical, rhetorical, and talmudic analysis of virtuality would involve the following set of observations:

To begin with, the literary-historical theory of redaction already has a passive but strong philosophical commitment. It deploys a philosophical notion of *existence*, understood along the lines of empirical genesis, called "history." Historical explanation of the literary effect of redaction programmatically (and silently) required the anonymous redactors to *exist* historically as opposed to being listed as literary characters within the Talmud. What this means, however, is that instead of going from non-philosophy to philosophy, we are moving from a narrower literary-historical theory that passively subscribes to a philosophical notion of existence, to a broader literary-philosophical (and rhetorical) theory that will actively negotiate that subscription. How does that move take its shape?

Because of redaction theory, we know that the talmudic argument has a force ascribable to no one on the list of the Talmud's personae, named or unnamed. Due to the broadened antinomy of "interpretation versus emendation," we know that the redactors' function is controversial and therefore does not easily ascribe itself to a fixed agent existing in a definite historical period of external reality. Not quite inside and not quite outside, not quite interpreting and not quite emending, the agent is nevertheless in action and is not a mere potentiality. After all, the agent does act and produces a real effect in the argument. A mere potentiality cannot have any effect in reality, yet the agent is actively having its real effect in the ways in which the talmudic arguments operate. It means the agent is neither fully real nor purely potential, for its effects are real, even if we no longer want to call them "redaction." At the first approximation, we deal here with a force, isolated in a literary-historical approach but not successfully explained in it. However, the philosophical tradition of scholasticism knows that force. We talk here about a force neither resolutely real nor remotely potential. In the language of scholastic philosophy such a force, or rather an agent, who acts in reality without being real is virtual. A virtual agent acts in reality without existing in it. (Thinking of the reality of the effect digital virtual characters have upon us can help make this medieval scholastic notion less remote.) Without going ahead of myself, I can only say that while we can successfully start with this philosophical notion of virtuality, we cannot finish with it. A need to reconsider will arise as soon as a more specific configuration of forces, agents, and subject positions in talmudic arguments and philosophical dialogues will mutually shed light on each other at the following stages of the current analysis.

11. The aphorism "to understand them before they 'understand us'" comes from Andrey Platonov, a Russian writer of the first half of the twentieth century. He wrote a dialogue between construction workers and a commissar of the Russian revolution. The latter insistently asked for higher rate of construction; the former responded by asking him to understand them, or else they would threaten to "understand" him (i.e., in the sense of revealing him as a political enemy of the people rather than a true commissar of the revolution). Another way to render what the workers said to the commissar would be "Please get us (meaning our situation) or we will get you (meaning your political hostility to proletarian workers)." This aphorism of Platonov's helps to convey that if we neither understand nor get the older forms of the virtual, we would not be able to get the newer forms either, and if we fail in getting the old, the newer forms of the virtual will "get us" in our thinking about all forms of virtual, both old and new.

12. The hitherto dominant cultural, historical, and empirical philological approaches primarily have subscribed to the methods of comparison between two traditions or fields—philosophical and talmudic—made from a hypothetically possible third point of view, as if the person who draws the comparison has no philosophical, talmudic, or any other premises on which to stand. Because of the problematic character of such comparisons, I take instead a hermeneutical path. The vista point from which I can best introduce this methodological change of perspective comes most readily from Michel Foucault's later turn to genealogical method as a unique combination of a philosopher's sensitivity to concepts with a historian's sensitivity to events.

As Foucault has it, no pure philosopher and no pure historian (including a historian of philosophy) can achieve such a combination, for historians by definition lack what philosophers have, as do philosophers lack what historians possess. I here build upon Foucault's methodological precedent (see his "About the Beginnings or the Hermeneutics of the Self," in Michel Foucault, *Religion and Culture*, selected and edited by Jeremy R. Carrette [New York: Routledge, 1999], 158–82) in order to raise the question of the relationship between the Talmud and philosophy in a new way. Instead of looking at historical appropriations and/or rejections that both the philosophical and talmudic traditions commit with regard to each other, I propose to ask the question of the relationship between Talmud and philosophy using a method similar to Foucault's genealogical one except that, unlike Foucault, I base the method not only on philosophical sensitivity used for reading historical texts but also on talmudic sensitivity used for reading the works of philosophy.

13. See Martin Heidegger, *Plato's Sophist*, translated by Richard Rojcewicz and André Schuwer (Bloomington: Indiana University Press, 1997), 7–8. For scholarship on this approach and its limitations see, for example, Catalin Partenie and Tom Rockmore, *Heidegger and Plato: Toward Dialogue* (Evanston, Ill.: Northwestern University Press, 2005), 112–13.

14. Another such study could have been that of wisdom. For the purposes of illustration of a more general direction in which I go, let me mention, if only in passing, how wisdom is relevant to the issue. However short the intervention of the case of wis-

dom will be, it will help me to start approximating the new question of relationship between Talmud and philosophy.

Wisdom has long been associated with either philosophy or its default others, such as sophistry or rhetoric, and to introduce the last two in the list, philodoxy (love of *doxa*, of opinions or arguments regardless of their truth), as well as orthodoxy, either religious or political. A task of my project is to undo that association of wisdom with either philosophy or its others, or at least to question their self-evident character and, in a larger perspective, to rehabilitate wisdom, using the Talmud as the third point of access to it. I find a heuristic resource for that move in a tradition that was not the other of philosophy but rather its almost always unnoticed third, often mistaken for either philosophy, as in the case of Moshe Chaim Luzzatto, Hermann Cohen, or those historians who connected the Talmud to stoicism, or for rhetoric/sophistry, as in the case of those philosophers (or even Talmud scholars) who took Talmud for either deconstruction or for the language games. (See David Stern, "Midrash and Indeterminacy," *Critical Inquiry* 15, no. 1 [Autumn 1988]). By the third, I of course mean the tradition of the Talmud and its researching and learning.

15. In a sense, these questions mark a continuation of a silent, perhaps too silent, use of talmudic thinking that Harry Wolfson already has demonstrated in his readings of the key figures in the history of philosophy, except that, as Plato might have had it, my inquiry perhaps partakes in the class of history of philosophy but surely does not belong to it. See Harry Austryn Wolfson, *Philosophy of Spinoza* (New York: Meridian Books, 1960) and *The Philosophy of the Church Fathers*, 2nd ed. (Cambridge, Mass.: Harvard University Press, 1964).

16. Elliot R. Wolfson, *Language, Eros, Being: Kabbalistic Hermeneutics and Poetic Imagination* (New York: Fordham University Press, 2005), xv–xxxi.

17. Ibid., xxix–xxxi.

18. I leave it to a different discussion to see if hermeneutics automatically requires an engagement with time. To approach this complicated question is to ask, together with Wolfson, how Heidegger's conception of hermeneutics as a move from what is clearer to what is more obscure connects to (or disconnects from) Husserl's notion of inner time consciousness—two positions with which Wolfson and Merleau-Ponty seem to disengage.

19. The "programmatic absence" should not be confused with a character's either declared or implied being somewhere else. The sophist is not one of the participants in the symposium, but he is not statically away from it either. An object of hunt and a subject of his own speeches, he interacts with the dialogue's participants without being a part of what they are plotting against him. In this sense his absence is programmatic, not just dietetic. It neither means being away nor implies ability, much less will, to sit around the table.

20. Traditionally, the question of the sophist was seen as extraneous to what was construed as the dialogue's central part, ontological criticism of nonbeing. For an account of a traditional scholarship on the issue, see Noboru Nomoti, *The Unity of Plato's Sophist: Between the Sophist and the Philosopher* (Cambridge: Cambridge University Press, 2007), 5–19. The book restores the connection of nonbeing to the sophist, primarily in terms of symmetrical composition of the dialogue (see esp. 40–42).

21. In fact, the position of the Stranger is more complex. As a mediator, he does need a ground of philodoxy, but as someone hunting the sophist he leans toward the reality of philosophy and thus must have a negative attitude to the ground on which he stands. However, this dynamics of the relationship between philosophy and philodoxy goes beyond the scope of the present analysis.

22. Such a suggestion arises from José Faur's interpretation of Maimonides' theory of imagination. See, in particular, the second chapter of his *Homo Mysticus: A Guide to Maimonides's* Guide for the Perplexed (Syracuse, N.Y.: Syracuse University Press, 1998). It is also supported by Leo Strauss's interpretation of Maimonides' views on philosophy and revelation. For Strauss, Maimonides distances himself from philosophy's commitment to searching for truth. Using philosophy as a tool, he appreciates revelation anew, now as the truth that is already given but yet to be understood in philosophical terms. See Leo Strauss, *Philosophy and Law: Contributions to the Understanding of Maimonides and His Predecessors* (Albany: SUNY Press, 1995). As David Hartman shows in his implicit polemics with Strauss, this rethinking of philosophy as a tool to understand revelation also means using philosophy to appreciate haggadic discourses of the rabbis as much more fundamentally important than their intellectual style of "dialectical" argumentation, which, if taken as is, leads to no final truth at the end. See Hartman, *Maimonides: Torah and Philosophic Quest* (Philadelphia: Jewish Publication Society of America, 1976), 28–45. On Maimonides' treatment of haggada, see *Guide* II, 8, 14; Yonah Frenkel, *Darkhe Ha-Agadah Veha-Midrash* (Masadah: Yad la-Talmud, 1991), 504–9. Of course, any limitations of the dialectical and therefore potentially sophistical argumentation in the Talmud do not apply to the sages as the source of authority in the matters of law. (See Maimonides' critique of Acher's exhaustingly unrestricted dialectics in the *Guide* I, 32.) Yet even in the matters of legal tradition, individual sages represented and/or defended particular standpoints coming from the respective traditions that they received and thus acted not on purely philosophically rational grounds. Therefore, Maimonides needs to reformulate their teaching of the law in a new and much less polemical and/or dialectical form; see Hanina Ben-Menahem, "The Second Canonisation of the Talmud," *Cardozo Law Review* 28, no. 1 (2006–2007): 37–51.

23. This remains the case even when a text becomes an issue, as it might when Aristotle discusses tragedy and comedy or when Plato discusses a text from Parmenides in *The Sophist,* or else when philosophers of the Middle Ages discuss the texts of Aristotle or even when the Stoics do the same with the texts of Homer. However, this also must remain beyond the scope of my present argument.

24. This understanding of a Gentile implies Jews and Gentiles sharing the Mosaic law. It is not necessarily unique to Irenaeus but should be distinguished from other approaches that feature a stronger notion of suppression. This matter is, however, beyond the scope of the present discussion. For requisite bibliography, see Philippe Bacq, *De L'ancienne À La Nouvelle Alliance Selon S. Irénée: Unité Du Livre Iv De L'adversus Haereses* (Paris: Lethielleux, 1978), 411–16.

25. See in particular his preface to Book I of *Against Heresies* in *The Ante-Nicene Fathers: Translations of the Writings of the Fathers down to A.D. 325,* edited by Alexander Roberts and James Donaldson (New York: Charles Scribner's Sons, 1899), 1:315–16.

26. Michael A. Williams, *Rethinking "Gnosticism": An Argument for Dismantling a Dubious Category* (Princeton, N.J.: Princeton University Press, 1996), 263–66.

27. Translated from Yaacov Sussmann, *Talmud Yerushalmi: Yotse Le- or 'Al Pi Ketav Yad Skaliger 3 (Or. 4720) Shebe-Sifriyat Ha-Universitah Shel Laiden 'Im Tashlamot Ve-Tikkunim* (Jerusalem: ha-Akademyah le-Lashon ha-'Ivrit, 2001), 65.

28. This might refer to a Palestinian sage from the end of the second and the beginning of the third century.

29. Is his last answer really strong? It is surely pleasing and nice, but is it really strong? It is nice only for those who already said they want to have an answer. So once again, just like he did with the heretics, so also he does with his students. In both instances, R. Simlai remains empty, or works from the position of those with whom he

talks. Heretics wanted a refutation, and he has found it for them; the students want a confirmation, and so they received it. The rabbi nevertheless remains empty.

30. Translated from the London MS, British Library, Harley 5508.

31. Translated from MS Kaufmann A 50, Budapest, Akademia.

32. The phrase "even after the fact" is inserted in the MS.

33. The phrase "said R. Yehuda" is not in the Vilna edition.

34. The word "even" is not in the Vilna edition.

35. For an analysis of Maimonides' understanding of imagination as opposed to apodictic argumentation, see Faur, *Homo Mysticus,* chap. 2.

36. Hermeneutical rather than chronological in its nature, the current argument brackets the question of historical influence of either of these thinkers on Maimonides.

37. As Moshe Idel succinctly presents it in his introduction to a Russian translation of the *Guide,* Maimonides "aims to create a new canon, in which a whole—an intelligible order and definiteness will replace the open-ended, unfinished and somewhat chaotic character of the Talmud or post-Talmudic literature. . . . He finds the highest form of the Torah study not in the endless development of disputations in Talmudic paradigm, but rather in thinking through the spiritual content of the Law." See Maimonides, *Putevoditel' Rasteriannykh / Moshe Ben Maimon (Maimonid),* (Jerusalem and Moscow: Gesharim and Mosty kul'tury, 2003), xiii.

38. Strauss, *Philosophy and Law,* 101–35.

39. A question of whether the philosophical approach of Maimonides is talmudically inflected in terms of its intellectual style remains beyond the current analysis. At this point I can only preliminary submit that in Maimonides, rabbis exemplify a practice of rigorous rational argumentation for the sake of formulating intelligent disagreements between themselves, yet they show no interest in reaching an agreement on the basis of philosophical reason; neither, at least in their legal discussions as opposed to haggadic discourses, do they show interest in the philosophical question of being. For an important distinction in Maimonides' view on legal and haggadic discourses in the Talmud in this regard, see Hartman, *Maimonides: Torah and Philosophic Quest,* 42–45.

40. *The Guide,* Introduction to Part I.

41. משתרכה, or משתתפים in Ibn Tibbon's Hebrew translation of *The Guide.* Michael Schneider explains the difference between this term and the Aristotelian term "homonym." In his view, the latter refers to things bearing the same name, not to the names sharing several different meanings. See his comments in Maimonides, *Putevoditel' Rasteriannykh / Moshe Ben Maimon (Maimonid),* 12.

42. For an analysis of this opposition in Maimonides, see Faur, *Homo Mysticus,* chap. 2.

43. Isaac ben Jacob Canpanton and Shemuel al Valensi, *Darkhe Ha-Talmud,* edited by Y. Sh. Lange (Jerusalem, 1980), 21–26. For secondary literature elucidating this position of Canpanton, see Hayim Zalman Dimitrovski, "Al Derekh Ha-Pilpul," in *Salo Wittmayer Baron Jubilee Volume on the Occasion of his Eightieth Birthday,* edited by Saul Lieberman (Jerusalem: American Academy for Jewish Research, 1975), 111-83 (Heb. section). Also see Daniel Boyarin, *Sephardi Speculation: A Study in Methods of Talmudic Interpretation* (Jerusalem: Institute Ben-Tsevi and Hebrew University, Jerusalem, 1989); idem, "Moslem, Christian, and Jewish Cultural Interaction in Sephardic Talmudic Interpretation," *Review of Rabbinic Judaism: Ancient, Medieval and Modern* 5, no. 1 (2002): 1–34.

44. I once again draw here on the work of Jose Faur, in particular his *Homo Mysticus,* and also idem, *Golden Doves with Silver Dots: Semiotics and Textuality in Rabbinic Tradition* (Atlanta, GA: Scholars Press, 1999).

45. Menachem Kahana, "Intimation of Intention and Compulsion of Divorce—Towards the Transmission of Contradictory Traditions in Late Talmudic Passages," *Tarbiz* 62 (1993): 225–63.

46. Henry A Fischel, *Rabbinic Literature and Greco-Roman Philosophy: A Study of Epicurea and Rhetorica in Early Midrashic Writings* (Leiden: Brill, 1973), 1–35.

47. For the notion of the essence of technology as "nothing technological," see Martin Heidegger, *The Question Concerning Technology, and Other Essays,* translated with an introduction by William Lovitt (New York: Harper and Row, 1977), 4ff. For Heidegger's introduction of the notion of *Gestell* in its original context and terminology, see ibid., 19–21.

9

FORGING A NEW *RIGHTEOUS NATION:* MAIMONIDES' MIDRASHIC INTERWEAVE OF VERSE AND TEXT

James A. Diamond

INTRODUCTION: MEDIEVAL JEWISH PHILOSOPHY SPEAKS INTERTEXTUALLY

THE FOCUS ON CONTRADICTIONS AS THE KEY STRATEGY OF ESOTERICISM in Maimonides' *Guide of the Perplexed* has obsessed traditional commentators and contemporary scholars in their ongoing search for Maimonides' positions on key issues. These positions run the gamut from providence to miracles to creation to prophecy.[1] The understandably seductive lure of "contradictory esotericism" has left the text's self-declared interconnectedness impoverished and demanding of more attention. What is at stake with this aspect of the text, Maimonides cautions, is no less than a grasp "of the totality of this Treatise so that nothing will escape" the reader. In order to avoid misconstruing the treatise's overarching message, the reader is admonished to "connect its chapters one with another; and when reading a given chapter, your intention must be not only to understand the totality of that chapter, but also to grasp each word that occurs in it in the course of the speech, even if that word does not belong to the intention of that chapter."[2] The text cannot be read properly in a progressively linear way and is bound to be partial and misread unless every segmented reading remains tentative and continuously reread in light of each successive reading.

The critical connective thread that weaves itself throughout the work is the relentless referencing of biblical and rabbinic material whose non-philosophical mode of discourse was the impetus for the correspondence that would constitute the *Guide*. Maimonides, I believe, is mandating an intertextual hermeneutic, one that has heretofore been customarily applied solely to the reading of Bible and rabbinic midrash. The *Guide*'s continuously intermittent and sporadic dialogue with the "fractured and unsystematic surfaces" of Bible and midrash, its textual precursors, attenuates the thread of intertextuality that Daniel Boyarin traced from the Bible to midrash into a medieval philosophical text.[3] The particular feature the *Guide* shares with midrash is the pervasive use of scriptural citation that, as in its rabbinic precursor, does not act merely as proof text but generates new meaning out of the tension orchestrated between its setting within the *Guide* and its original context.[4] A citation that appeals simply by virtue of an authoritativeness accepted by both the reader and the writer indicates, as Stefan Morawski acerbically notes, "intellectual torpor and emotional ritual-assiduity," neither of which can Maimonides be accused.[5] Maimonides' engagement with his textual traditions "plays a double role; it both continues and breaches the tradition, that is, it uncovers angles of inquiry which were unknown or forgotten."[6]

The *Guide* presents a sustained philosophical hermeneutic that innovates while anchored in tradition, and in what follows I demonstrate how this actually operates with one such apparent submissive nod to past authority via citation, while at the same time recontextualizing to break with the past. The complexity of this hermeneutic is compounded by the adoption of a midrash-like structure of which Gerald Bruns's characterization of midrash is equally fitting: "The parts are made to relate to one another reflexively, with later texts, for example, throwing light on the earlier, even as they themselves always stand in the light of what precedes them."[7] In this case it is the superscript that will be shown to bear this out, a particularly vital citation, most apt in that it looms behind Maimonides' entire philosophical project and colors every discourse with past tradition in his text. Outside of some of my previous studies,[8] this hermeneutic has not been applied to the Maimonidean corpus to date, an endeavor I believe essential to any reading of Maimonides' misreadings of the foundational texts that preceded him.

MEDIEVAL JEWISH PHILOSOPHY SPEAKS MIDRASHICALLY

Moses Maimonides clearly states his purposes in writing the *Guide of the Perplexed* at the treatise's very outset. These are primarily "to explain the meanings of certain terms occurring in the books of prophecy" (*GP* Intro. 5), and secondarily to offer "the explanation of very obscure parables occurring in the books of the prophets but not explicitly identified there as such" (*GP* 6). His project, *in its entirety,* relates to biblical exegesis both on a micro-level of individual words and a macro-level of passages or units

called "parables," which by definition demand interpretive keys to render
their discursive meaning transparent. The reader is advised that any chapter that does not patently deal with biblical terms does so implicitly as an-
cillary to others that do, or by obliquely hinting at a term intentionally
suppressed for the time being. Such chapters seemingly devoid of biblical
reference might also either "explain one of the parables" or merely "hint
at the fact that a certain story is a parable" (GP 10). No authorial intention
is expressed whatsoever to compile a traditional philosophical treatise, but
rather the intention to engage in that classical Jewish enterprise of biblical
interpretation, or better, of rereading Judaism's sacred texts.[9]

According to Leo Strauss, the *Guide* "is not a philosophic book—a book
written by a philosopher for philosophers—but a Jewish book: a book
written by a Jew for Jews."[10] Maimonides' core subject matter consists exclusively of philosophical issues filtered through Jewish texts, and the existential angst he aims at relieving, the conflict between the Torah and
philosophy, is a Jewish one. What better genre is there to emulate when
it comes to communicating this exquisitely Jewish undertaking than one
that is itself uniquely Jewish? Though a thoroughgoing rationalist, the
language he adopts to convey the universalistic thought of philosophy is
shared with other Jewish movements, even the mystical[11] which he so
virulently opposed in its nascent stages.[12] They all employ the particularistic dialect of the midrashic. In this sense, despite an aversion to various
mystical conceptions of God that offend his philosophical unity, there may
be more continuity between the medieval and philosophical traditions,
as Elliot Wolfson has argued,[13] than the strict dichotomization originally
proposed by Gershom Scholem. One of the staples of midrashic discourse
is biblical recitation whose function is to preserve tradition while at the
same time transforming it to meet new challenges. What has been posited of midrash, whose "simultaneous rejection and preservation of tradition . . . is shown in the all pervasive quotation which forms its very warp
and woof,"[14] is also true of Maimonides' hermeneutical magnum opus. As
a result, it is even more difficult to "disentangle the threads of philosophy
and mysticism,"[15] since the Maimonidean hermeneutic threads its way
into a tight weave between the two. Once this hermeneutic is discerned
and applied, what initially has the veneer of chaos and disorder ultimately
gives way to what Strauss considered the highest form of edification, "enchanting understanding."[16]

Though Maimonides' hermeneutical stance *toward* midrash has been
a subject of scholarly interest,[17] there has been no serious discussion of how
Maimonides himself may have engaged in his own variation of midrashic
discourse. On the one hand, the Rabbis resorted to midrash as a "poeti-

cal conceit," a playful literary tool that imaginatively contorts a verse out of its plain contextual sense into something else entirely, often a moral teaching, but whose meaning cannot escape "someone endowed with understanding."[18] On the other hand, rabbinic midrash was also adopted as an esoteric mode of communicating metaphysical notions so profound and radical as to require concealment from all but the philosophically seasoned elite. Most importantly, of all the genres of literature noted to illustrate the various contradictions that suffuse written works, only midrash categorically shares the esoteric seventh with the *Guide*.[19] By drawing attention to this common feature, Maimonides is claiming much more than merely a shared esoteric strategy to convey philosophical truths. Rather, he is preparing the reader for a midrashic encounter with his own text—a text that consciously eschews a formal philosophical style in favor of one endemic to Jewish writing and one to whose inflections only the highly trained rabbinic ear would be attuned. After all, when reading the *Guide* one must always be cognizant of its epistolary nature and its addressee— a private correspondence with his most beloved and missed student R. Joseph, a disciple possessed of just such an ear. Already in his epistle dedicatory to Joseph, Maimonides signals to this hermeneutic by his desire to satisfy Joseph's quest to *find out acceptable words* (Eccl 12:10). Those *words* are methodologically defined in the next verse as *the words of the wise are like goads, like nails well planted are the words of masters of assemblies.* Referencing Ecclesiastes 12:10 imports a talmudic homily that traces an interpretive dialectic in Torah that will inhere in the *Guide* as well:

> [You might think that] just as the goad can move [and be removed] so the words of the Torah move [and can be removed]—therefore the text says "nails" [which once nailed down cannot be removed]. But [you might think that] just as the nail only diminishes [as it is pounded into the wood] and does not increase, so too the words of the Torah only diminish and do not increase—therefore the text says "well planted." Just as a plant grows and increases so the words of the Torah increase."[20]

The *Guide* intends to model itself on the Torah, which, during the course of its reading, will evoke dialectical tensions graduating from text and verses as exhaustively determinate to ever-increasing meaning that elevates intertextuality to what David Stern has typified of midrash but is equally apt of the *Guide*, "the level of a virtual exegetical principle."[21]

As previously stated, my focus here will be on a verse whose selection as a superscript is designed to intersect across the entire breadth of the treatise, transforming and enhancing its message during the course of reading. Its literary use is patterned after a verse that may instigate a midrashic proem, weave in and out of an intricate web of intertextual allusions spanning across the breadth of the biblical corpus, and be progressively transformed finally into a new sum of its allusive parts.

OPENING AND ENTERING THROUGH THE GATES

The epigraphic verse from Isaiah, *Open ye the gates, that the righteous nation that keepeth faithfulness may enter in* פתחו שערים ויבא גוי צדיק שמר אמנים (26:2), which marks the transition between the introduction and the first chapter of the *Guide,* immediately sets the tone for its midrashic undertaking. Though innocently picking up on the imagery of the introduction, that is, of the text as a key that will unlock gates to areas that prior to the *Guide* were inaccessible, its own meaning unravels along the trajectory of the treatise. What is initially a traditional prayerful supplication for the realization of the book's intended goal becomes progressively enriched at each critical juncture of the reader's journey. Its first hermeneutical enhancement appears in the lexicography. Once chapter 1:22 is read, one can begin to unlock the full meaning of the verse, which itself anticipates unlocking. *Entry* (בא) can be achieved into a place devoid of geography by an entrant that lacks physicality.

An instrumental verse cited to illustrate this metaphoric sense of בא is one that centers on the image of gates that are open to God yet locked to man—[*This gate is locked and will not open and no one can enter through it*] *for the Lord God of Israel enters through it* (Ezek 44:2) (*GP* I:22, 52). Ezekiel's spatial referent is to the eastern gate of the Temple Mount. For Maimonides the temple is oriented westward, with its holiest inner sanctum located in the western precinct to subvert solar worship, the dominant ancient Near Eastern idolatrous cult whose central deity's path naturally orients toward the east (*GP* III:45, 575). The temple's design follows Abraham's iconoclastic efforts to subvert pagan theology by performing an about face on then-current longstanding modes of worship from east to west.[22] The critical element in Abraham's strategy was not to inculcate a preference for west over east but subsisted rather in the turning of his back on the east— that is, the rejection of one spatial vector only as an initial subversive salvo in the ultimate banishment of all space from religious devotion. This facet of the temple captures the essential rationale for Judaism's entire cultic edifice—a concession to the frailty of the human psyche incapable of instantly rejecting what it has long become accustomed to. God, or the ultimate truth in and of the world, remains blind to spatial coordinates and therefore can *enter* through the east. Man, hampered by the exigencies of human nature, must be barred from everything associated with the east and reoriented toward the west so that he can eventually arrive at a point where all geographical coordinates have no bearing on the attainment of the truth of God.[23] The "entry" promised by the introductory verse is to those precincts that will be unlocked by the *Guide*. This portends the placeless place that is the reader's final destination. At the same time it conjures up the Abrahamic model in its identification of those who are qualified to embark on the journey—the willingness to reject tradition and the staples of religious beliefs one was raised on. The verse excludes while it invites.

The invitation is to a process of "opening" to be induced by the text. In addition to the verse's hint at the diminishment of the spatial, this term, as it is reshaped by the *Guide,* envisions the same for the visual in the attainment of its teachings. "Opening" in its metaphorical sense, Maimonides states in the final chapter of his excursus on Ezekiel's Account of the Chariot, is a common prophetic term. The "opening of the heavens" allowing Ezekiel his majestic vision (Ezek 1:1) is akin to the opening of doors and gates found in other passages, including our own epigraphic verse of Isaiah 26:2. Attention is drawn to this prophetic term "openings" as "the key to the whole" of Ezekiel's account (*GP* III:7, 428). It is only the beginning to understand that Ezekiel's vision is to be considered cognitive rather than visual.[24] Without that basic approach, Ezekiel's account, of course, reduces to primitive anthropomorphic nonsense. However, that is not enough. What is substantively critical about the phrase "the heavens were opened" that provides the "key to the whole"? Strait-jacketed both by halakhic constraints on the teaching of the chariot account and by its inherent ineffability (*GP* 415–16), Maimonides has conveyed one of the "chapter headings" to which he has been restricted in divulging the secrets of the Torah or metaphysics. Not only does the heaven's opening signify a noetic enlightenment, but it also marks the removal of an existential barrier. One of the prime examples of the prophetic figurative genre is the heaven opening of Ezekiel 1:1 (*GP* II:47, 408). Proximity to God is achieved when one's reading skills have been honed to the point where the literal and figurative can be clearly discerned, for "then only intelligible beliefs will remain with you, beliefs that are well ordered, and that are pleasing to God. For only truth pleases Him, may He be exalted, and only that which is false angers Him" (409). Divine emotions may initially motivate human aspirations for the truth, but with the acquisition of the truth comes the cognitive awareness that there are no such emotions. Man gains proximity to God by overcoming all those "necessary" incentives such as divine anger that propel man along the path toward such intimacy to begin with.[25]

By citing Isaiah 26:2 as a sister text to Ezekiel 1:1 in illuminating the meaning of prophetic "openings," Maimonides' use of Isaiah as an enticement to the potential readers of his own treatise also acts as a pledge to guide them into the hidden precincts of Ezekiel's visionary legacy. A reading of the *Guide* promises to be an intellectual reenactment of Ezekiel's prophetic revelation, absent though, of its original self-assured certainty. Maimonides' introduction, describing his methodology in decoding Ezekiel's vision, poses the model for the future of Jewish biblical exegesis: "[I]n that which has occurred to me with regard to these matters, I followed conjecture[26] and supposition; no divine revelation has come to me to teach me that the intention in the matter in question was such and such, nor did I receive what I believe in these matters from a teacher" (*GP* 416).

He begins by ruling out both a reenactment of prophecy or suprarational knowledge as well as the natural means of a scholastic tradition. Antithetical to the mystic's approach to the same body of knowledge, it precisely inverts the demand for restrained silence when there is no received tradition on a matter later espoused most prominently by Nahmanides.[27] Positively, the learning process consisted of a combination of "the texts of the prophetic books, the dicta of the *Sages*, together with the speculative premises that I possess" (*GP* 416), that is, the biblical and rabbinic traditions filtered through the sieve of reason to extract the metaphysics of Ezekiel's account. Isaiah's opening, then, is also an endorsement of a biblical hermeneutic that has replaced prophecy and tradition with a reasoned examination of Judaism's formative texts.

The cost of such an approach is its tentativeness. Though Maimonides has convinced himself of the truth of his findings, he admits that "it is possible that they are different and that something else is intended" (*GP* 416). Those readers envisioned by the opening verse must be willing to surrender the certainty of sacred traditions accepted by virtue of the fact they are "handed down" (*mesorah*) in favor of a personal endeavor of self-discovery, the outcome of which will be forever plagued by doubt.[28] The philosophically minded devout Jew that the *Guide* addresses must be aware at the start that it is ultimately an open-ended opening that he seeks. The oppressive political condition of exile that rules out prophetic enlightenment[29] is somewhat alleviated by another means to enlightenment in the combination of text and reason. However, an existential angst persists in that even once the "heartache and great perplexity" over the conflict between one's devotion to the Law and one's own intellect that the *Guide* promises to remedy[30] has been resolved, there still remains the nagging possibility that "something else is intended."

The "gates" have been shut for a very long time, so long that had the *Guide* not appeared, they may have been irreparably fused by the ravages of neglect. What lies behind these gates has not been accessed because of a craving for the real gates that regulated entry to the temple. Those remaining nostalgic for the priestly gatekeepers who discharged their daily duties of opening so that God could be encountered through routine animal sacrifice are barred from the precinct the *Guide's* gates adorn. Its gates cannot be opened by the loud blasts of the ram's horn[31] but by the silent contemplation of the new *tsaddiq* whose entry is no longer qualified by the pedigree or clothing that distinguished the priests of old. Their delegated shifts[32] are now replaced by the new *tsaddiq* who has made the transition from a longing for space to one for something far more transcendent. Only one possessed of *tsedeq* can enter, the precise nature of which will be explored in the discussion that follows.

THE RIGHTEOUS NATION ENVISIONED BY THE *GUIDE*

Tsedeq: *The Move from Ethical to Intellectual Virtue*

The gates open to a *righteous nation*—not just to a select few individuals, but to that company of few who form a community whose characterization as *righteous* (צדיק) can only be discerned once the term is understood in its Maimonidean sense as determined by the *Guide*. The primary meaning of *tsaddiq* appears within an enumeration of the various impediments to mastering the discipline underlying Ezekiel's account or metaphysics. What blocks those who possess the natural aptitude to comprehend this science from reaching their intended goal is the lack of commitment needed to endure the extraordinarily lengthy prerequisites required to attain it. Basing himself on a Solomonic contrast in Proverbs 21:25–26 between the *tsaddiq* and the *sloth* (עצל), they are not one of the *righteous* "who gives everything its due . . . he gives all his time to seeking knowledge and spares no portion of his time for anything else" (*GP* I:34, 76).[33] Here Maimonides has subtly but radically redefined the Jewish "nation" in accord with his rationalist agenda from ethics to intellect, from deed to mind.[34] A Maimonidean *tsaddiq* is one who exerts every effort demanded to comprehend an idea fully. He affords the particular subject matter at hand its due. At the same time he has indicated that quality, outside of political circumstances beyond one's control, necessary for the resumption of prophecy. Slothfulness (*atslut*), or failing to meet the intellectual rigor warranted by an esoteric subject, is the other character trait mentioned alongside sadness and depression that scuttles prophecy.[35]

Cultivation of intellectual "righteousness" is "the cause for prophecy being restored to us in its habitual form as has been promised to us *in the days of the Messiah, may he be revealed soon*" (*GP* II:36, 373). The political dimension of the messianic future, which includes an end to exile and diaspora, the restoration of Jewish political sovereignty, and reestablishment of the monarchy and temple cult are outside the scope of Maimonides' mission. His concern with the *Guide* is to forge the "righteous nation" who can provide that critical intellectual dimension without which the political would be redundant. Unless God miraculously intervenes to interrupt the process, prophecy naturally occurs to those who have undertaken all the necessary steps morally and scholastically to acquire it, "For it is a natural thing that everyone who according to his natural disposition is fit for prophecy and who has been trained in his education and study should become a prophet" (*GP* II:32, 361). Those who enter through the opening provided by the *Guide* to form the righteous nation are the natural heralds of the era when transformative events transpire naturally or, in the wording of the rabbinic maxim Maimonides so favored, as "the world goes its customary way."[36]

Tsedeq *as Justice for the Rational Soul: The Precision of the Proof Text*

The full significance of what this righteous nation embodies would be lost without taking into consideration the *Guide*'s discussion in its penultimate chapter of the meaning of the term *tsedeq*, the action that entitles one to the label *tsaddiq*. It bears the common semantic sense noted previously within the context of intellectual discovery of conceding to "everything its due." More precisely, it is "the granting to everyone who has a right to something, that which he has a right to and giving to every being that which corresponds to his merits" (*GP* III:53, 631). Though the notion of an obligation imposed on one due to the corresponding right of another, such as the payment of a debt or wages for services rendered, would be subsumed under this definition, Maimonides claims this is not its primary biblical meaning: "But in the books of the prophets, fulfilling the duties imposed upon with regard to others is not called *tsedaqah*." Biblical *tsedaqah* exchanges juridical duties for ones that transcend the strictly legalistic, those "imposed upon you on account of moral virtue, such as remedying the injuries of all those who are injured." However, it is not the other, the less fortunate, who imposes any demands, but rather the moral action in aid of another in need is generated by an internal demand of the self, "for when you walk in the way of the moral virtues, you do justice unto your rational soul, giving her the due that is her right."[37] Biblical justice, for Maimonides, is an act satisfying one's own needs, in particular those of the "rational soul" or that facet of a being that constitutes it as human.[38] In this way moral action and intellectual development proceed in tandem, serving the needs of the intellect, allotting it its due in its quest for perfection.[39] Whenever God is said to possess some moral quality such as kindness or

compassion, what such a statement really amounts to is that a natural phenomenon has been observed that would, in the sphere of human actions,
flow from some such quality. The meaning of such statements about God,
however, "is not that He possesses moral qualities, but that He performs actions resembling the actions that in us proceed from moral qualities" (*GP*
I:54, 124). Men normally exhibit moral behavior emotively, whereas God's
actions strictly accord with what reason dictates is appropriate. Genuine
imitatio dei, then, is, as Herbert Davidson has so ably argued, to act morally
but dispassionately.[40]

The three proof texts cited in support of this sense of *tsedeq* are instructive for determining the parameters of the new righteous nation spawned
by the *Guide*. The first is the daily return of debt security to an impoverished borrower whose poverty demands it in consideration of his most rudimentary needs such as night clothes and basic tools of trade.[41] Deuteronomy mandates and regards such considerate treatment to be *a tsedaqah
for you in front of God* (24:13). Firstly, for this instance to endorse credibly
his sense of the term *tsedeq*, Maimonides reads this literally to say that the
beneficiary of the *tsedeq* is the lender (*for you*) and not the poor borrower.
Since halakhically whatever has been pledged must be returned for the
duration of the period it can be utilized, the security is of no benefit to the
lender for the currency of the loan. Because Jewish law also proscribes
charging interest, all ulterior motivations for extending the loan are precluded, rendering it an altruistic act of kindness for one in financial need.
The loan, then, is elevated from a commercial transaction to one of *imitatio dei*. God is called a *tsaddiq* "because of His mercy toward the weak—I refer to the governance of the living being by means of its forces" (*GP* III:53,
632). All living existents in relation to divine omnipotence are considered "weak." God's creation of all living things includes endowing them
with all those natural biological mechanisms ("forces") necessary to sustain themselves. In other words, God has provided living beings in the
world with the basic necessities of life. In this sense the lender-borrower
relationship, where the borrower is impecunious and security guarantees
the loan, mirrors that of the divine-human. The lender is weak vis-à-vis
the borrower; the mandated daily return of security, coupled with the bar
against interest, grounds the loan in the moral virtue of *tsedeq*, or "remedying the injuries of all those who are injured"; the return of security also
allows the borrower to sustain himself just as God programmed all forces
necessary in living beings to do the same.[42]

To qualify as an act of *tsedeq* for Maimonides is to "do justice unto your
rational soul"—it cannot be an emotional act motivated by something like
pity, but rather must be an act that flows from an understanding of the way
God governs the world. A *tsedeq*-based ethics is moored in a reasoned and

logically calculated apprehension of God's attributes of action that grasps God's "providence extending over His creatures as manifested in the act of bringing them into being and in their governance as it is" (*GP* III:54, 638). Only the rational soul can inform such a course of conduct since, as the *Guide* concludes, it "will always have in view *loving kindness, righteousness* [*tsedeq*] *and judgment*, through assimilation to His actions" (ibid.). Divine governance, which translates into actions normally considered as kind or compassionate, actually "proceeds from Him, may He be exalted, in reference to His holy ones, not because of a passion or a change" (*GP* I:54, 125). God acts *dispassionately*, and therefore for human conduct to be considered *imitatio dei* it must also be motivated accordingly.[43] Maimonides crafted his conclusion to link up with the epigraphic verse that contemplates the admission of a *righteous nation*, transforming what initially would have been taken as a religiously conservative phrase implying a community of the devout[44] into a radically new elite fraternity among whom ethics is subsumed within the cognitive realm. They are those whose ethical conduct has been recently described as "consequent morality," or that moral demeanor which *results* from intellectual perfection as opposed to that which is *necessary* for it and therefore precedes it.[45]

The third verse demonstrating Maimonides' sense of *tsedaqah* is *And it shall be a* tsedaqah *to us if we take care to observe [this law before God as He has commanded us]* (Deut. 6:25). Once again, the verse is formulated to suit Maimonides' purpose, since the object of the *tsedeq* is the one who executes the action—that is, a self-referential benefit to the "rational soul." This verse follows a concise retelling of all God has done for Israel in liberating it from slavery and the host of miracles performed on its behalf in order to establish its own homeland in Israel (vv. 21–23). In its original context, the *tsedaqah* of fulfilling God's commandments amounts to a quid pro quo for God's efforts on Israel's behalf. However, this contextual sense of a repayment of debt by Israel to God as a result of an obligation imposed by him has already been ruled out by Maimonides as the biblical sense of *tsedaqah*. Maimonides achieves two goals with the selection of this proof text. One is the normal sense of *tsedaqah* as a return of a favor, which is precluded by the fact that one of the parties is God, who, as perfection *in actu*, cannot possibly have any need for anything outside of himself, nor could anything benefit him, "for He, may He be exalted, would not acquire greater perfection if He were worshipped by all that He has created and were truly apprehended by them, nor would He be attained by a deficiency if nothing whatever existed except He" (*GP* III:13, 451). Observance of divine commands cannot, as is so prominently found in the kabbalistic tradition,[46] have any impact whatsoever on God. Maimonides transforms the traditional rabbinic classification of those commandments which are "between man and God (or *place, maqom*)"[47] into those "whose purpose it is to bring about the achievement of a certain moral quality or of an opinion or the rightness of actions which only concerns the individual himself and his becoming more perfect" (*GP* III:35, 538).[48] There remains only one direction in which the *tsedaqah* can proceed—toward the self. Considering Maimonides' philological treatment of *place* (*maqom*), the traditional euphemism for "God" in the normative category *between man and God*, as bearing a figurative sense of "an individual's rank and situation . . . perfection in some matter" (*GP* I:8, 33), the phrase, as some medieval commentators already noted, reduces to *between man and himself.*[49]

Second is that observance of the mitzvoth as a class are characterized as a *tsedaqah*—that is, the telos of the entire Torah is ultimately to fortify the rational soul. Although the Law aims at two things "welfare of the soul and welfare of the body" (*GP* III:27, 510), the latter is prior but the former is ultimate, since health and political stability are the means toward the "ultimate perfection [which] is to become rational in actu" (511). The body is the means for the mind or, in the phrasing of the new Maimonidean biblical lexicon, any mitzvah performed for the betterment of one's own body (or *bein adam lemaqom*) or another's (*bein adam lechavero*) is a *tsedaqah* for one's own soul, for "once the first perfection [body] has been achieved it is possible to achieve the ultimate [soul], which is indubitably more noble and is the only cause of permanent preservation" (511).[50] Membership in the exclusive club of the "righteous nation" gains entitlement to immortality, since their cultivation of righteousness or *tsedeq* is the "only cause of permanent preservation."[51]

The exegetical manipulation of Deuteronomy 6:25 just described is substantiated by his incorporation of the preceding verse, *And the Lord commanded us to do all these statutes to fear the Lord our God, for our good always, that He might preserve us alive, as it is at this day* (6:24), in the course of his discussion of the two perfections—body and soul. The order of the verse, he claims, endorses his position as to the ultimate end of all the mitzvoth. The phrase *for our good always* refers to a state of being that is endless, or immortality, whose achievement is consequent on attaining intellectual perfection; thus, "He puts the ultimate perfection first because of its nobility; for as we have explained, it is the ultimate end" (*GP* 511). The second phrase, *that He might preserve us alive, as it is at this day,* on the other hand, "refers to the first and corporeal preservation, which lasts for a certain duration and which can only be well ordered through political association" (*GP* 512). The verse and what it signifies is referred to once again in Maimonides' general preface to the section on the rationale for the mitzvoth as a component of his assault on those who subscribe to the view that reasonless commandments render them more godly. It therefore is an overarching verse

that informs the entire system of mitzvoth with the teleology of two perfections.

The nation that Maimonides' envisions, then, is not one simply bound
together by laws and moral virtues that ensure its success as a politically
and socially viable community, for that is transient and eventually disappears with the deaths of its members. It is one that enduringly coheres
through the joint enterprise of amassing knowledge, thereby guaranteeing
its participants' immortality. Politics submits to intellect and the sublime
usurps the pragmatic in the struggle for perfection and a place in eternity.
The opening verse already portends a political association, the majority of
whose constituents largely concern themselves with moral virtue as an
end while fostering the elite few whose immortality they guarantee but
can never aspire to.[52]

The two verses exegetically combine with the epigraphic verse to produce the following propositions:

> Deut 6:24= The Law in sum is formulated to achieve both socio-ethical
> harmony and intellectual perfection. The latter is the end in itself, with the
> former a pragmatic means of accomplishing that end. Only the end of intel-
> lectual perfection warrants a life that succeeds death.
>
> Deut 6:25= The characterization of obedience to the mitzvoth as a
> *tsedaqah* is attributed to the notion that "when you walk in the way of the
> moral virtues, you do justice to your rational soul, giving her the due that is
> her right" (*GP* III:53, 631). Only an awareness of this proposition when per-
> forming all the mitzvoth, including those geared toward ethics and politics,
> leads one to the eternal life promised by verse 24. Treating any of those com-
> mandments as having an end of social utility, kindness, or compassion rather
> than laying the groundwork for achieving the ultimate end of knowledge
> does not qualify it as an act that "does justice to your rational soul" and there-
> fore fails to contribute to the immortal preservation of the soul.
>
> Isa 26:2= The "righteous nation" (*goy tsaddiq*) that Maimonides wishes to
> shape with his *Guide* transcends the socio-political connotations of "nation"
> in its embodiment of the quality of *tsedaqah*. All the actions of the members
> of this polis inure to the enhancement of their rational souls.[53]

This sense of *tsedeq* is not simply confined to the normative dimensions of the Torah but informs the non-legal as well, including narratives
and parables. In this way it is a comprehensive underpinning for both narrative and nomos.[54] Since the majority of prophetic wisdom is couched in
parabolic language, the reader must be constantly on guard to distinguish
between various literary forms and to determine "what has been said by
way of parable, what has been said figuratively, what has been said by way
of a hyperbole, and what has been said exactly according to the first conventional meaning" (*GP* II:47, 409). Failure to detect these literary and
linguistic nuances will result in a misreading, with dire consequences to

the belief system of the reader. Maimonides then draws an unexpected analogy between reader incomprehension of biblical prose and Law, accentuating the damage to the extent of belief "in incorrect opinions that are very remote from the truth and you regard them as Law [sharī'a]" (ibid.). In other words, since the text generating the confusion is the Jew's most sacred and authoritative, any misreading will be dogmatized. The analogy raises the stakes considerably, since the negative implications of narrative misapprehension belie a true apprehension of the Law's purpose: "For the Laws are absolute truth if they are understood in the way they ought to be" (ibid.). There are thus halakhic implications to muddleheadedness about biblical prose.

Two verses are then cited in support of the Law's "absolute truth," both of which import *tsedeq* and therefore all its significations into the discussion: *Thy testimonies are righteous forever and so on* (Ps 119:144), and *I the Lord speak righteousness* (Isa 45:19). Through these proof texts, the *tsedeq* of the mitzvoth seeps into the narrative as well, in that they "do justice to the rational soul" by way of a consciousness of both the two perfections and their respective roles on the hierarchy of means and ends. Biblical parables must also be viewed through the teleological lens of the two perfections, body and soul, politics and metaphysics, means and ends captured by the "apples of gold in silver filigree" metaphor offered in the *Guide*'s Introduction. Silver corresponds to a level of meaning "useful in many respects among which is the welfare of human societies," while gold signifies the internal "concerned with the truth as it is" (*GP* Intro., 6). The parabolic and the normative parallel each other in a multivalenced paradigm[55] where ideal exegesis and conduct must be inspired by *tsedeq*, or doing "justice to the rational soul." In the exercise of both, immortality hangs in the balance, dependent on their grounding in *tsedeq*. The two proof texts are carefully selected to bear this out. Psalm 119:144 characterizes "decrees" as *tsedeq*, while Isaiah 45:19 does so for divine speech representing each critical facet of the Torah—"decrees" are the Laws, while divine speech connotes one of two alternatives, "either will and volition or a notion that has been grasped by the understanding having come from God" (*GP* I:65, 158–59). In the latter case, it would denote prophetic communication, which includes all the parables recorded in the Bible. The second colon of Psalm 119:144, *enable me to understand so that I may live,* suggests that aspect of the commandments which transcends the ethical, social, and political—*understanding*, or that which inculcates true opinions and nourishes the rational soul. As the medieval grammarians and exegetes Abraham ibn Ezra and David Kimhi note, the *forever* in the first colon of the verse, which depicts *decrees*, carries over to the second colon, rendering it *so that I may live forever.*[56]

Maimonides has thus presented, by way of proof text recitation, his own midrashic preservation of a biblical tradition that at the same time, in the delicate interplay of text, proof text, and intertext, accommodates a radically new philosophical agenda. *Tsedeq* is no longer a legal or ethical mode of conduct, but it is a posture vis-à-vis one's own intellect. For laws and narratives to qualify as *tsedeq,* their ultimate intellectual goals must be perceived and assimilated. Only then is there perpetual life for that which succeeds corporeal existence—the rational soul.[57] The "righteous nation" envisioned at the outset of the treatise is the one who will come to abide by this *Weltanschauung.*

The Tsedeq *of Abraham's Visionary Belief*

The proof text sandwiched between the two mentioned, *And he believed in the Lord and it was accounted to him as a tsedaqah* (Gen 15:6), is critical, for unlike the other two, it embodies the *tsedeq* trait in a particular personality, in this case Abraham, the pioneering founder of Judaism. Maimonides' terse explication of this verse is "I mean the virtue of faith"; that is, Abraham's belief is credited as such by the term *tsedaqah.* It is crucial to note that the Arabic term chosen here for belief or faith is *al-īmān* as opposed to another available option, *al-itiqad.* Avraham Nuriel has convincingly argued that the former is used consistently in the colloquial sense of the emotional, psychological, and existential dimensions of faith and trust, while the latter denotes a cognitive certainty about the truth of a proposition[58] or, in Maimonides' words, "belief is the affirmation that what has been represented is outside the mind just as it has been represented in the mind" (*GP* I:50, 109). However, I will argue, its positioning between the other two verses, which have been shown to imbue *tsedeq* with cognition, impels a reconsideration of the simple faith or trust that the term used here (*īmān*) would normally invoke.

The reader is taken back into the original biblical setting of Genesis 15:6, where the "belief" of Abraham emerges out of a *vision of prophecy* introduced by Genesis 15:1, *The word of the Lord came to Abraham in a vision.* The *Guide* must then be consulted to determine what degree of prophecy, from the typologies listed in II:45, classifies this vision. Abraham's "belief" emerges from a group of the four highest degrees, which are eventually collapsed into one class by Maimonides, of prophetic *visions (mareh; mahazeh)* as distinct from prophetic *dreams.* The four subclasses of this eighth-highest category are distinguished by either the form of the communication (parables=eighth) or its purveyor (God, man, angel). What is pertinent for our purposes is the noetic *visionary* origins they all share in common, where "only parables or intellectual unifications[59] are apprehended that give actual cognition of scientific matters similar to those, knowledge of which is obtained through speculation" (*GP* II:45, 403). Actual speech conveyed through an intermediary signals a decline in the caliber of the prophecy, moving away from the rational to the imaginative. In this particular instance of Abrahamic revelation, Maimonides clearly demarcates the end of the *vision* commencing with Genesis 15:1 and the beginning of the *dream* when a *deep sleep fell upon Abram* (15:12).[60] If the *vision* spans verses 15:1 to 15:12, then the verse that recounts Abraham's *belief in the Lord* (15:6) transpires within the *vision*, or within Abraham's consciousness. What triggers that belief is the purely philosophical, like "cognition of scientific matters." This vision then includes a prophetic parable about the nature of authentic faith, or belief in God. Such belief (*īmān* or "belief in") must itself be a consequence of cognizing the nature of God (*itiqad* or "belief that"). Abraham's belief is credited as a *tsedaqah* because it "does justice to his rational soul," that is, it affords his rational faculty its due because it is subsequent to "knowledge which is obtained through speculation" rather than antecedent to it. The new "righteous nation" (*goy tsaddiq*) assembled out of the targeted addressees of the *Guide* is in effect a revitalization of the pristine group drawn together by the trailblazing embodiment of *tsedaqah*, whose spiritual and intellectual legacy hinges on the perpetuation of that very trait—*For I have known him in order that he may command his sons and his house after him to keep the way of the Lord, to do righteousness [tsedaqah] and judgment* (Gen 18:19).[61]

Once the various distinctions between prophetic *dreams* and *visions* have been pieced together throughout Maimonides' excursus on prophecy over the course of five chapters (*GP* III:41–45), and in particular as exemplified by this Abrahamic prophecy, Abraham's *vision/dream* of Genesis 15 becomes profoundly difficult to follow. For but one quandary, if speech is restricted "to *dreams* only," while *visions* entail "the union and overflow of the intellect" (*GP* III:45, 402), how does one sift out the two in a prophecy that is initially identified as a *vision* (Gen 15:1) and immediately followed by a series of speeches and dialogue? What is the content of the *vision* that is explicitly identified as *the speech of God* in verse 15:1? If Abraham's prophetic revelation begins with a vision and then terminates with the sleep of verse 12, "after which it says *And God said*," charted along the way by a progressive intensification of the imaginative intellect, what is the precise line of demarcation between vision and dream? Where can it be plotted on the graph that measures the rational/imaginative intellect quotient? Maimonides would respond in general "that every *vision* in which you find the prophet hearing speech was in its beginning a *vision*, but ended in a state of submersion and became a *dream*." *Visions* deteriorate into *dreams*. He then applies this gradated model to Abraham's vision, which becomes

a *dream* at the juncture of losing waking consciousness altogether, demarcated by *And a deep sleep fell over Abraham* (15:12). Yet there are speeches
in the previous eleven verses. Does Abraham flit in and out of different
states of consciousness? Though the mechanics of Maimonides' prophetic
process is far beyond the scope of this chapter,[62] suffice it to note for present purposes that the two clearly delineated stages of Abraham's dream
correspond to the two classes of mitzvoth, with the first, those *between
man and God*, as already noted, covering those aimed at self-perfection.
Until he is overcome with sleep, the content relates to Abraham personally
(verses 1–5=reproductive capacity; verses 7–11= territorial rights), while
the dream relates to the larger community (the political future of the Israelite nation). The subject matter deteriorates along the declining path
from *vision* to *dream* from self-perfecting cognition to the social/political
condition. Once again, a model of the two perfections is presented in the
personage of Abraham, where the social is *consequent to,* or naturally flows
from, the cognitive.[63]

Why Is Abraham's Belief a Tsedaqah? *Decoding the Parable of Abraham's Vision*

In order for Abraham's *vision* to qualify as such, its content must "give actual
cognition of scientific matters similar to those, knowledge of which is obtained through speculation" (*GP* II:46, 403), despite the fact that it may be
filtered through imaginative modes of communication such as parables.[64]
Abraham's vision here coincides with his portrait in the Mishneh Torah
and the *Guide* as one who discovered, or more appropriately retrieved, the
nature and existence of one Supreme Being through philosophical means
and not revelation or tradition.[65] Except for couching it in parabolic language, the cognitive achievements of Abraham the prophet and Abraham
the philosopher are identical.[66] His philosophical breakthrough and his
subsequent vision are synchronized in their shared "cognition of scientific
matters."[67] In fact, the description of Abraham's experience as a *vision* is the
very proof text cited early on in the *Guide* to illustrate the figurative sense
of its root *ḥazoh* (to vision) as "the grasp of the intellect." It is quoted as an
instance of a metaphorical application for "the apprehension of the heart"
(*GP* I:4, 28), consciously omitting any prophetic connotations and blurring
the distinction between philosopher and prophet even further.[68]

   Once its subject matter is acknowledged, the biblical account of the vision must be subjected to a Maimonidean midrashic hermeneutic to discern those "scientific matters." Only then will the true nature of Abraham's
"righteous belief" crystallize. Here I offer such a hermeneutic for the visionary segment that prefaces that belief. Underscoring the language of vi-

sions as parables constitutes what Maimonides states in his preface that
he will often do—a pared down identification of a passage as a parable
with no further commentary. Such an observation signals the reader to
investigate and decipher, since "remarking that it is a parable will be like
someone's removing a screen from between the eye and a visible thing"
(*GP* 14)

That segment of the vision that precedes the Abrahamic "belief" in
question reads:

1. And afterward the word of the Lord came to Abraham in a vision, saying, "Fear not Abram, for I am your shield; your reward shall be very
   great."
2. But Abram said, "O Lord what can you give me, seeing that I continue
   childless and the one in charge of my house is Damesek Eliezer."
3. And Abram said, "Since you have not granted me offspring, one of my
   house will be my heir."
4. And the word of the Lord said back to him, "This one will not inherit
   from you, but the one who will emerge from your self will be your
   heir."
5. And He took him outside and said, "Look toward the heaven and count
   the stars if you are able to count them. So shall your descendants be."

In order for this vision to comply with the rule that speech does not
occur in visions, its sense must be other than oral or audible. Maimonides
concludes his excursus on prophecy with the lexical nuances of all the
terms for divine speech that often appear in the Bible, including *dibbur.*
Any such *speech* ascribed to God is merely a figurative means of attributing
whatever such speech instigates to God in his capacity as the "First cause
of all things" and not to his direct involvement. Nature runs its own independent course, while each of these terms merely trace all natural causes
and effects back to their originating cause in God, including human actions and volitions.[69] The *word* [*dbr*] *of the Lord* that prompts Abraham's vision, then, is merely a figure of speech that preserves both human independence and freedom and God's ultimate, though remote, control of all
natural events. In other words, God's *word* here really signals Abraham's
autonomous exercise of philosophical concentration. In the same vein, the
"speeches" that follow are metaphors for conceptualizations that crystallize within Abraham's mind.[70]

The key to identifying the "scientific matter" cognized by Abraham
in this vision lies in the opening comforting assurance extended by God
to Abram divided into three clauses: fear not/ I am your shield/ your reward. Each one can be refracted through the prism of the Maimonidean
hermeneutic. The patriarchs' lives, Maimonides posits categorically, pro-

vide "absolute proof of there being an individual providence" (*GP* III:17, 472) that accords with his theory of specialized providence. Though again, this is a subject too complex to be dealt with here,[71] Maimonides sums up his theory succinctly: "Providence is consequent upon the intellect and attached to it. For providence can only come from an intelligent being, from One who is an intellect perfect with a supreme perfection . . . accordingly everyone with whom something of this overflow is united will be reached by providence to the extent to which he is reached by the intellect (474).

The phrase *I am your shield* is the first in a series of proof texts relating to the patriarchs' lives that Maimonides cites when amassing the biblical evidence in corroboration of his theory. These, he writes, are "explicit affirmations of providence watching over them according to the measure of their perfection" (*GP* III:18, 475). What this premiere verse describes in terms of Abraham's experience is both a state of mind and a state of being. The vision is a glimpse into Abraham's intellectual struggle to comprehend the mechanics of divine providence, the precise working out of which we have no better model than Maimonides' own self-described struggle with this "fundamental principle" (*al-qāʿida*).[72] A reasoned process of elimination whereby a number of alternative theories are ruled out is conducted to arrive at the "opinion which is less disgraceful than the preceding opinions and nearer than they to intellectual reasoning" (471). Abraham's vision of the message *I am your shield* indicates a similar cognitive process that led up to a noetic confidence in some "scientific matter"—in this case providence. Since providence is consequent on intellect, that achievement itself draws Abraham within the umbrella of the intellectual overflow that ensures providential protection. The third clause, *your reward shall be very great,* then follows as an effect of perfection, which attracts providence, which in turn allows for a life replete with reward since "everything that is disclosed to a being endowed with the intellect was disclosed to it, is the one accompanied by divine providence which appraises all its actions from the point of view of reward and punishment" (472). Reward, or Abraham's optimistic future, is guaranteed by the success of his intellectual endeavors.

The first clause, *fear not,* now falls into place as an instrumental prerequisite to both the philosophical grasp of providence and its effectuation. Abraham is being told to rid himself of fear, for that gesture of eliminating fear, in its Maimonidean sense, will invite the providence just outlined. Abraham, who within the Maimonidean schema is the quintessential *lover* of God (as opposed to *fearer* of God), is the perfect exemplar for what this entails. Maimonides' formulation of the normative contours of love and fear of God in the Mishneh Torah positions fear as a reflex of love that entails the sober examination of God's creation and extraction of the wisdom it reflects: "When a man contemplates God's great and spectacular works and creations and derives from them His inestimable and infinite wisdom he immediately loves and praises and glorifies and develops an intense longing to know God . . . and when he considers these very things he immediately [*miyad*] recoils in terror and realizes he is a lowly, dark and ignorant creature who faces the Perfect Intellect" (2:2). Fear is the consequential humility of that love, the standard by which Maimonides' promises the opening of vistas to "love God": "In accordance with these I will explain critical principles from God's works so that it will provide an opening for the intellectual *to love God*."[73] Love and fear lead ultimately to an ideal love that integrates both into a reinforced final goal of love.[74] More importantly, this three-staged process of love normatively expresses the model of the *tsaddiq* I have constructed whose morality and ethics is *consequent to* his intellectual perfection.

In the Mishneh Torah, the moral/existential posture of humility is a consequence of profound philosophical investigation that plumbs the depths of creation.[75] Abraham is then portrayed later in the MT as the quintessential lover of God who is emblematic of worship imbued with love and therefore "performs the truth because it is the truth," whom "God called His lover because he served only out of love."[76] To be motivated by truth is of course to know truth, and to know truth is a noetic, not emotive, process. Love of God is directly proportional to knowledge measured on a one-to-one basis: "If a little then a little and if a lot then a lot."[77] *Fear not*, then, is that on which the remainder of the philosophical equation is contingent. Abraham *fears not*, leaving a mode of service that is defined by its alternative of love measured solely in terms of knowledge, the extent of which determines providential sanctuary. Ideal performance of the commandments naturally follows the emulation of Abraham's intellectually constructed standard of love, for "once man loves God with an appropriate love he will immediately [*miyad*] perform all the commandments out of love."[78]

The remainder of the vision up until Abraham's "act of faith" in verse 6 is taken up with the apparent non-philosophical anxiety regarding his own bleak childless state, leaving him no hope of a lasting legacy. His despair invites a divine promise of a striking reversal in fortune, of a future abundantly rich in descendants. Selfish, narrow, and subjective in its concern, it certainly would not seem to qualify as "scientific matters similar to those, knowledge of which is obtained through speculation," the exclusive purview of prophetic "visions." However, given Maimonides' categorical assertion that such is the case, there is an obligation to somehow reconcile this vision with its governing principle. One method of fulfilling that obligation is to heed his warning to all potential readers that "if you wish to grasp the totality of what this treatise contains, so that nothing of

it will escape you, then you must connect its chapters one with another"
(*GP* 15). One of those chapters to which talk of progeny leads is the one
in the *Guide*'s lexicography that centers on the terms for bearing children
(*yalod*) and uncharacteristically does not respond to the anthropomorphic
problems raised by most of the others in the same section. The figurative
sense that is critical for deciphering Abraham's vision is its pedagogical
nuance in which "whoever instructs an individual in some matter and
teaches him an opinion, has, as far as being provided with this opinion is
concerned, as it were engendered that individual" (*GP* I:7, 32).

The visionary exchange between God and Abraham regarding Abraham's reproductive prospects might be a parable alluding to another
corollary of the providential theory assimilated at the outset of the vision. After having achieved self-perfection, both the philosopher and the
prophet can aspire to a degree of perfection that then reverses direction
outward to the perfection of others. They are compelled to "compose
works and teach . . . and let [their] own perfection overflow toward them"
(*GP* II:37, 375). This altruistic perfection is surplus "to the extent that enables them to govern others" (374). This part of the parable further refines
Abraham's grasp of the minutiae of providence. The providential umbrella
under which he has brought himself can be extended to others either by
teaching or by governing others. Abraham's disciples are his metaphoric
children.[79]

By applying the metaphoric code just outlined, the parable consisting
of verses 2 to 4 can be decoded as follows:

2. But Abram said "O Lord what can you give me, seeing that I continue
   childless and the one in charge of my house is Damesek Eliezer."
3. And Abram said, "Since you have not granted me offspring, one of my
   house will be my heir."

Verse 2, buttressed by verse 3, indicates Abraham's angst after having
only assimilated that phase of the theory of providence that relates to self-
perfection. His state of childlessness, translating the father/child simile
into a teacher/disciple one, expresses his own not yet fully matured view
of perfection and providence ending with the self, with no possibility of
widening its scope via the excess perfection that overflows to others.

Here the designation of Eliezer as the sole disappointing heir plays
a role as a signifier in the logic of the parable. He is not Abraham's child
by virtue of the fact that he is not his disciple, particularly in the niceties
of divine providence. His most noteworthy appearance in Maimonides'
Mishneh Torah is in fact as the paradigmatic diviner, a practitioner of pagan magic,[80] and representative of a providential theology that is the very
antithesis of Abraham's. In his general introduction to its rationale, the

Torah's repugnance to all forms of pagan magic, including divination, is part of sustained assault on a perverse theology whereby "certain kinds of harm may be warded off and certain kinds of benefits obtained" through these cultic rituals (*GP* III:37, 542–43). A linchpin of pagan magic is its star-centeredness, which attributes all natural phenomena to the independent sovereignty of innumerable stars. It is therefore inimical to monotheism and its intellectual underpinnings, which mandate an *understanding* of nature to warrant providence: "For they are branches of magical practices, inasmuch as they are things not required by reasoning concerning nature and lead to magical practices that of necessity seek support in astrological notions.[81] Accordingly the matter is turned into a glorification and a worship of the stars" (543). Abraham declares, therefore, that Eliezer is not his child because he has not absorbed any of his teachings, in particular those on providence, and is decidedly not his child in the sense that his belief system of astral worship is anathema to the monotheism he embodies.[82]

God's response to Abraham's despair is couched in kind in parabolic language that can only be decoded in consultation with the Maimonidean lexicon. He reassures Abraham that Eliezer will not be his heir, *this one will not be your heir,* but rather *only that which issues out of your own bowels (*מֵעֶיךָ; *me῾echah) will be your heir.* Bowels is a term that is dealt with when addressing those problematic physiological anthropomorphisms that Maimonides designates as a synonym for *heart.* In this sense "it is a term denoting the intellect" in support of which a number of proof texts are cited, referring to both divine and human "bowels" as a metaphor for intellect (*GP* I:46, 101). One of those, *Your Law is within my bowels* (Ps. 40: 9), is instructive for its meaning in the context of God's pledge to Abraham. As the Psalter's gastronomic metaphor refers to his understanding and intellectual assimilation of the Law's content, so God promises Abraham that what he has achieved intellectually will be successfully passed on through his teaching. Those like Eliezer, who cling to their non-Abrahamic teachings, will of course never qualify as Abraham's *children* in its pedagogical sense. Abraham's progeny is guaranteed by that which issues from his *bowels* as mind, or from his intellect—in the molding of disciples who will preserve his intellectual legacy.

The next verse ensures the survival of Abraham's literally iconoclastic philosophical theology by encouraging the perpetuation of its programmatically reasoned development, by the move from sage to prophet—*He took him outside and said, "Look at the heaven and count the stars, if you are able to count them" and He said to him "so shall be your offspring."* Maimonides would have been attracted to the following prominent rabbinic metaphorical reorientation of the preface—He *took him outside* from its literal spatial transition to an ideological one—*Abandon your allegiance to astral gazing.*[83] Of course, Abraham's philosophical breakthrough was precisely in the rejection of the stars as independent deities. However, since this vision postdates Abraham's discovery of monotheism, it would be difficult to assign it this precise meaning at this mature stage of his career as discoverer and disseminator of the tenets of monotheism. Therefore, consistent with the logic of the vision's symbolism developed thus far, the referent here would be to Abraham's ongoing legacy. It is a reinforcement of the message of the previous segments, which guarantees Eliezer's replacement with true disciples: the star gazers will be usurped by the monotheists.[84] Taking Abraham *outside* symbolizes his escape from what he considered to be a dismal future for his discoveries.[85] Maimonides' midrashic cue may have been another interpretive inflection on transporting Abraham *outside*, rendering it a designation by God that "you are a prophet and not an astrologer."[86] Overcoming the prospect of having no intellectual heirs will be achieved by the transition from a self-perfecting mode to a prophetic one of perfecting others.

The last phrase of the verse, *so shall be your offspring,* normally drawing an analogy between them and the stars, is apposite to the entire segment of the verse that precedes it. Abraham's followers must learn to reason independently toward God's existence, which, as Maimonides repeatedly emphasizes, is inspired by contemplating the heavens and the stars, "for this reason you will find that all the prophets used the stars and the spheres as proofs for the deity's existing necessarily. Thus in the traditional story of Abraham there occurs the tale which is generally known about his contemplation of the stars" (*GP* II:19, 310). The revolution of the heaven "is the greatest proof through which one can know the existence of the deity" (*GP* I:70, 175), and indicates "to those who have knowledge of them and reflect upon them the greatness of Him who caused them to exist and to move" (*GP* I:9, 34). The directive to *look at the heaven* is specifically cited in the lexicography to corroborate a figurative sense of *look (hibit)* "to designate the mind's turning and directing itself to the contemplation of a thing until it grasps it" (*GP* I:4, 28). *So shall be your offspring* refers to the adoption of Abraham's methodical probing of the heavens in constructing an unassailable proof for the existence of God, of his *looking at the heaven.* In so doing, they become his children in the sense of students and colleagues.[87]

Finally, there is the directive to *count the stars, if you are able to count them.* Within the narrative sequence of the vision, this too is the referent of *so shall be your offspring.* In order to qualify as offspring, they must perform the counting and not, as in its literal context, compare to the stars in prolific number. Here is an allusion to another essential aspect of Abraham's reasoned quest for God's existence without which it could never have reached its goal—intellectual humility. Once the philosophical endeavor begins, there is always the danger of exceeding one's capacity, of attempting to grasp what it is not humanly possible to grasp.[88] The prime example Maimonides cites in illustrating the limits of the human intellect is "the number of the stars in the heaven and whether that number is even or odd," knowledge of which is impossible and "there being no gate through which one might enter in order to attain it" (*GP* I:31, 66). The rationally contemplative process must always be tempered by an awareness of the limits of human apprehension signified by the futility of tallying the stars, to which the vision's balk of *if you are able to count them* is a parabolic allusion.

Once the first five verses comprising this phase of the vision have been deciphered, Abraham's act of *faith* as a result can be fully appreciated for what it constitutes. As stated previously, though the Arabic term suggests a "belief in" rather than a "belief that," it is an elevated belief that is reflexive of the "belief that" acuity attained prior to it. That act of faith is the model for the national faith he pioneered. The nature of the "faith" that is the apex of this first phase of Abraham's vision can only be determined by a parabolic reading of the other critical term in the verse, translated to this point as *and it was accounted to him (vayaḥshivehu)*. I believe that Maimonides reads this as an intellectualizing qualifier of Abraham's belief in accordance with the sense that he assigns elsewhere to its root *ḥashav* (*thought*). Though rife with anthropomorphisms, the Bible, Maimonides claims, only uses those which, while as incorrect as others, serve a pedagogical purpose in that they accord with popular notions of perfection rather than deficiency. This rule extends to the "cerebral" activities of God, thus excluding imagination while legitimizing metaphoric, though still anthropomorphic, terms such as *thought*—"Therefore *fancy*, which word means imagination, is not figuratively ascribed to Him, whereas *thought [maḥshavah]* and *comprehension [tevunah]* which words mean reflection and understanding, are figuratively ascribed to Him" (*GP* I:47, 105).

What appears as a divine commendation is really descriptive of the "moral virtue" of Abraham's "faith" as a "reflective" one. It is a faith that "does justice to the rational soul" because it emanates from the rational soul's primary activity of reflection. God's assessment[89] of Abraham's faith is informed by *thought (maḥshavah)*, a knowledge of God's existence and unity so thoroughly convincing as to warrant absolute trust.[90] In this way, Abraham's act of faith in this vision is analogous to his compliance, itself within a vision,[91] with the divine command to slaughter Isaac his son (*aqedah*). The fact that it entailed a number of days travel time signifies that the act "sprang from thought, correct understanding, consideration of the truth of His command," rather than "stupefaction and disturbance in the

absence of exhaustive reflection" (*GP* III:24, 501). As Alexander Altmann
has argued, the prophet is merely a "special class of philosopher" who has
a particular talent for translating what he has cognized into imaginatively
digestible teachings for the philosophically unsophisticated public.[92] The
"simple" act of "faith" (*al-īmān*) in Abraham's vision is then an imaginative
construct of the purely cognitive "faith" (*al-itiqad*) that Abraham personally achieved for the benefit of the public. The *righteous nation (goy tsaddiq)*
envisioned at the outset of the *Guide* is the one that enjoys the *tsedaqah* of
Abraham's pre-imaginative cognitive belief that always trusts in God because of its elite philosophical appreciation of God's nature rather than the
simple post-imaginative trust exhibited by the public that is divorced from
its philosophical roots.

THE FAITHFULNESS OF THE NEW RIGHTEOUS
NATION: SUBVERTING RABBINIC MIDRASH

We now arrive at the final qualifier of the *righteous nation* contemplated
by Maimonides, which is a *keeper of faithfulness* (שמר אמנים), a *faithfulness*
that must be understood as manifesting the Abrahamic faith just examined. Those who populate this new nation will emulate Abraham's journey of intellectual discovery, arriving at the ultimate truths in the universe
via rigorously methodical reason. Their "faith," therefore, is, as Abraham's
once was, the realization of efforts that are independent of parental rear-
ing, tradition, and parochial allegiances. The integrity of their new polity
will be guaranteed by their imitation of Abraham as teacher, fashioning
new constituents who will in turn be stimulated to their own independent pursuit of philosophical truth. However, their numbers, by virtue of
the Herculean prerequisites of their enterprise, will always be confined, as
Maimonides enumerates them in prophetic parlance, to *one of a city or two
of a family* (Jer 3:14) and *the remnant whom the Lord calls* (Joel 3:5). The larger
Jewish nation that lives on the periphery of reason will be nourished by
this national cadre of authentic Abrahamic disciples simply "through following traditional authority" and by being "correctly conducted toward
something by means of parables" (*GP* I:34, 75).

The Maimonidean midrashic rendering of this last phrase as *who preserve and perpetuate the rational faith of Abraham* precisely subverts its midrashic precursor. A classic talmudic reading of this phrase previously relates it to those who recite the liturgical *Amens:* "Resh Lakish said[,] 'He
who responds Amen with all his might has the gates of Paradise opened
for him[. A]s it is written[,] *Open ye the gates, that the righteous nation that
keepeth faithfulness (shomer emunim) may enter in*[. R]ead not *shomer emunim*[,]

but rather *she'omrim amen* [that say amen]."[93] The verse now resonates with both an appropriation and subversion of its original rabbinic refashioning.[94] On the one hand, it appropriates paradise as an allusion to the stakes involved in the *Guide's* teaching, which assures those who have mastered them of "rewards [that] are the greatest and most precious to which a human being can aspire."[95] On the other hand, however, it specifically rejects the "Amen" as a medium for obtaining such rewards for its readers who "master his doctrine and fully affirm it without reservation (i.e., answer amen to his teaching with all their power)."[96] One of the "amen's" most prominent normative roles within Jewish ritual is, by its formulaic response, as a vicarious means of discharging halakhic obligation. In other words, others perform, and the amen respondent endorses.[97] In this sense, the amen could never operate in the world of thought. To know is not to confirm vicariously but rather to achieve independently. The intellectual curriculum precludes surrogate means of advancement. Abraham's faith is perpetuated, not by "answering amen to his teaching," but by personal mimesis of the preliminaries leading up to that faith.

Once the *faithfulness* that is kept is taken as the *faith* of Abraham, the subversion deepens in an ironic inversion of its original rabbinic reference to the "amen." Its innovation as a means of vicarious participation addressed the phenomenon of widespread ignorance and illiteracy. Recitation of "amen" was a remedial measure intended to accommodate the uneducated and the ignorant and to facilitate their inclusion within the sphere of Jewish practice.[98] As Maimonides formulates it in his legal code:

> The congregational leader [*shaliah tsibbur*] fulfills the obligations of the congregation. How does this function? While he prays and they listen and respond "amen" to each and every blessing it is considered as if they themselves are praying. When does this apply? When they do not know how to pray, but one who knows fulfils his obligation only with his own prayer. [99]

"Amen," then, conjures up a model of limited learning and reliance on others who are self-sufficient to compensate for one's own deficiencies. Preserving Abraham's legacy of *emunah* inverts the rabbinic legacy of *amen*. The *righteous nation* Maimonides wished to forge with his *Guide* would carry the banner of Abraham's righteous faith, a faith so inspired by independent reason that its constituents would never have to resort to the "amen" of surrogate achievement.

In this study, the citation of a verse in the *Guide*, although significantly enhanced by its selection as a superscript, is emblematic of countless such verses strategically interspersed through it. As the reader advances through the text, each verse encountered previously becomes progressively textured and retextured by new text that recalls the earlier scriptural appearance. Revisiting, reformulating, and rereading those verses are triggered by associative strategies of terms, phrases, and text, which resonate with their initial articulation, resulting in a midrashic grid of text and Scripture. Any reader of Maimonides would be well advised to bear in mind Paul Ricoeur's view of a text as "more than a linear succession of sentences. It is a cumulative holistic process."[100]

Here Maimonides offered a tentative welcoming embrace by the promise of openings, unlocking gates and entries to a public presumed by the call to a "nation" whose admission is qualified by simple righteousness and faith. Once the reader arrives at the end of his journey through the text, drawn repeatedly to reexamine that welcome through the lens of a radically revamped "righteousness" and "faith," the opening becomes an aperture, and the nation is reduced to *one of a city or two of a family* (Jer 3:14). Only those who are both philosophically adroit and attuned to the midrashic hermeneutic can maneuver through the labyrinthine mesh of text and verse that weaves throughout the *Guide*. The entire *Guide* can be read in a sense as a midrashic proem that opens with *tsedeq* and concludes with a *tsedaqah* that has been refurbished by everything in between.

Rather than a philosophical treatise, the entire *Guide* is more appropriately read as a midrashic proem, with this opening verse to be analyzed playing the role of its *petihta*. Failure to follow this midrashic journey through the length of the *Guide* is not simply to miss a stylistic dimension of the *Guide* but to misread its substantive core. In subjecting this verse and others to such scrutiny, I abided by Marvin Fox's cautionary advice to all readers of the *Guide* never to ignore those verses that lead off the various sections of the *Guide*. He demands that they "should not be thought of as mere adornments with no substantive significance, but should be studied with care to see what message the author is conveying to his readers. One might say that this is the first test of the competence of the readers. Readers who ignore these verses or fail to investigate the implications fully have already shown insufficient sensitivity to the text."[101] Links with key terms or phrases that reappear at critical junctures in the text compel the reader to return to the earlier read verse, increasingly nuancing it with each new associative infusion of meaning. A midrashic interplay between verse and text is thus generated that is characteristic of many of the biblical and rabbinic citations interspersed through the body of the *Guide*. Verse and text form a dynamically integrated whole that in sum produces a Jewish book. Alongside its erudition, ingenuity, and the eminence of its author, it is this facet of the *Guide* more than any other that made it immeasurably more influential than other Jewish medieval texts whose mode of discourse was more faithful to the philosophical literary tradition.[102] As James Kugel has noted, "At bottom midrash is not a genre of interpretation but an interpretive stance, a way of reading the sacred texts,"[103] and in this sense Maimonides' project follows the contours of a longstanding Jewish tradition. Medieval Jewish philosophical texts must be added, or explicitly acknowledged, to the long list Kugel compiled of genres throughout Jewish history in which the midrashic "way of reading" has found expression.[104] Appreciating Maimonides' midrashic integration of verses in his work will assist in passing "the first test of competence" for all prospective readers of the *Guide*.[105]

NOTES

1. The literature is too vast to list here. The seminal work of Leo Strauss, "The Literary Character of *The Guide of the Perplexed*," in *Persecution and the Art of Writing* (Glencoe, Ill.: Free Press, 1952) sparked impassioned debate in the scholarly world that continues to flourish. For a sampling of the debate, see the discussion and sources cited by Yair Lorberbaum, "On Contradictions, Rationality, Dialectics and Esotericism in Maimonides' *Guide of the Perplexed*," *Review of Metaphysics* 55, no. 4 (2002): 711–50, nn. 23–25.

2. *Guide of the Perplexed*, translated by Shlomo Pines (Chicago: University of Chicago Press, 1963), intro., 15. Unless otherwise noted, all references to the *Guide* are to this edition, abbreviated as *GP*.

3. Daniel Boyarin, *Intertextuality and the Reading of Midrash* (Bloomington: Indiana University Press, 1994), 16.

4. Ibid., 23, where this tension is endemic to midrash.

5. Stefan Morawski, "The Basic Functions of Quotation," in *Sign, Language, Culture*, edited by Algirdas J. Greimas et al. (The Hague: Mouton, 1970), 690–705, at 692–93.

6. Ibid., 294.

7. Gerald Bruns, "Midrash and Allegory," in *The Literary Guide to the Bible*, edited by F. Kermode and R. Alter (Cambridge, Mass.: Belknap Press, 1987), 625–47, quote at 627.

8. See, for example, James A. Diamond, *Maimonides and the Hermeneutics of Concealment: Deciphering Scripture and Midrash in the* Guide of the Perplexed (Albany: SUNY Press, 2002).

9. See Alfred Ivry, "Strategies of Interpretation in Maimonides' *Guide of the Perplexed*," *Jewish History* 6, nos. 1–2 (1992): 113–30, who asserts, "In its stated purposes, then, the *Guide* is a work of biblical exegesis with a clearly stated hermeneutic" (118) as opposed to a philosophical composition in the traditional Western form. See also Shalom Rosenberg, "On Biblical Interpretation in the *Guide of the Perplexed*" (Heb.) *Mehqerei Yerushalayim BeMahshevet Yisrael* 1 (1981): 85–157.

10. Leo Strauss, "How to Begin to Study *The Guide of the Perplexed*," in *GP* xiv.

11. Not only does Maimonides share a form of midrashic discourse with the mystics, but according to Elliot Wolfson, his parabolic conception of prophetic truth provided them with an essential tool of their kabbalistic trade or a "rhetoric to frame an esoteric hermeneutic, which, in turn, facilitated the grounding of occult traditions in the corpus of classical rabbinic literature." See Elliot R. Wolfson, "Beneath the Wings of the Great Eagle: Maimonides and Thirteenth Century Kabbalah," in *Moses Maimoni-*

des (1138–1204): His Religious, Scientific, and Philosophical Wirkungsgeschichte in Different Cultural Contexts, edited by George Hasselhoff and Otfried Fraisse (Würzburg: Ergon Verlag, 2004), 209–37, at 221.

12. See Menachem Kellner's full-length study of this opposition in his *Maimonides' Confrontation with Mysticism* (Oxford: Littman Library, 2006).

13. For a concise summary of this debate, see Elliot R. Wolfson, "Jewish Mysticism: A Philosophical Overview," in *History of Jewish Philosophy,* edited by Daniel Frank and Oliver Leaman (New York: Routledge, 1977), 450–98, at 452–53. The very inclusion of this essay in a volume dedicated to a history of Jewish philosophy militates against the strict bifurcation of mysticism and philosophy.

14. Boyarin, *Intertextuality,* 22.

15. Wolfson, "Jewish Mysticism," 453.

16. Strauss, "How to Begin to Study," xiv.

17. See, for example, Eliezer Segal, "Midrash and Literature: Some Medieval Views," *Prooftexts* 11 (1991): 57–65, at 57–60; W. G. Braude, "Maimonides' Attitude to Midrash," *Studies in Jewish Biography, History and Literature in Honor of I. Edward Kiev,* edited by C. Berlin (New York: Ktav Publishing House, 1971), 75–82; Joshua Levinson, "Literary Approaches to Midrash," *Current Trends in the Study of Midrash,* edited by Carol Bakhos (Leiden: Brill, 2006), 189–226, at 196–99.

18. *GP* III: 43, 573

19. *GP* Intro., 19–20. I say "categorically" because Maimonides leaves the question open as to whether prophetic literature incorporates this seventh contradiction.

20. b*Hagigah* 3a–b. See David Stern's discussion of this passage in *Midrash and Theory: Ancient Jewish Exegesis and Contemporary Literary Studies* (Evanston, Ill.: Northwestern University Press, 1996), 18–22.

21. Ibid., 29.

22. This is strikingly consistent with the iconoclastic nature asserted by a prominent contemporary biblical scholar, of the "closed gate" here with that common motif in the ancient Near Eastern milieu. Walther Zimmerli in his *Ezekiel,* vol. 2, translated by J. D. Martin (Philadelphia: Fortress Press, 1983), 441, claims that, while others allowed periodic openings to accommodate sacred processions, "with complete uniqueness here the gate is to be closed 'once and for all' because Yahweh has 'once and for all' taken possession of his sanctuary, and no procession, however sacred, may repeat this event regularly after him." This is astonishingly consistent with Maimonides' view of the temple as a concession to the frailty of human psychology to which attendance must be kept at an absolute minimum.

23. Perhaps this is why Maimonides downplays the significance of prayer toward the temple in his Mishneh Torah (MT) where it is described simply as a longstanding custom but not as a halakhic requirement, the lack of which invalidates prayer. See MT *Prayer* 1:3. Gerald Blidstein attributes Maimonides' characterization of pre-rabbinic ritual conduct as custom rather than norm *as a consequence* of the rabbinic position on it as nonobligatory in his *Prayer in Maimonidean Halakha* (Hebrew) (Jerusalem: Mossad Bialik, 1994), 25.

24. Maimonides is here, as throughout the *Guide,* in stark opposition to the visionary nature of Jewish mystical experience, whose contours have been thoroughly and masterfully drawn by Elliot R. Wolfson in *Through a Speculum That Shines: Vision and Imagination in Jewish Mysticism* (Princeton, N.J.: Princeton University Press, 1994). Although Maimonides, under the influence of Western ocularcentrism, does adopt the visual as a principal metaphor for the cognitive, he does not allow for empirical divine ontic entities or hypostases that could be the object of visionary experience. This

starkly contrasts with what Wolfson has described of the ancient mystics, who are also paradigmatic of future Jewish mysticism, who paradoxically assume "the visibility of the essentially invisible God" (90).

25. For the distinction between necessary beliefs "for the sake of political welfare" and correct beliefs, see *GP* III:28, 512–14, and Hannah Kasher, "Mitos Ha'El *HaKo'es* BaMoreh Nevukhim," *Eshel Beer Sheva* 4 (1995): 95–111, which probes the precise meaning of God's anger as a necessary belief.

26. The term here is a subject of much discussion in the scholarly literature and has been rendered differently by virtually all of the classic translators of the *Guide*, both medieval and modern. See Schwartz's lengthy footnote in note 9 of II:22 in his Hebrew translation of the *Guide* (Tel Aviv: Tel Aviv University Press, 2002), 331, where he canvasses all the different possibilities, including inspiration, insight, and intuition. Whatever its precise meaning, it indicates some quicker thought process that reaches demonstrable truths without undergoing the lengthy and arduous path such conclusions normally demand.

27. For Maimonides, the ancient esoteric philosophical tradition originally in the possession of the Jews was lost but could be reconstructed by way of human reason (*GP* I:71). In contradistinction, for Nahmanides, whatever was lost of the mystical tradition remains irretrievable and cannot be independently reconstructed. See Moshe Idel, "We Have No Kabbalistic Tradition on This," in *Rabbi Moses Nahmanides: Explorations in His Religious and Literary Virtuosity,* edited by I. Twersky (Cambridge, Mass.: Harvard University Press, 1983), 51–73, at 62. However Idel's implications of this for reading Nahmanides have been persuasively challenged by Elliot Wolfson in his "By Way of Truth: Aspects of Nahmanides' Kabbalistic Hermeneutic," *AJS Review* 14:2 (1989): 103–78, at 111. For Idel, Nahmanides was an arch-conservative kabbalist from whose literary legacy we can glean very little of his mystical "secrets," whereas Wolfson has demonstrated that this is not entirely the case and that Nahmanides' writings are rife with kabbalistic allusions that beg his audience to speculate and decipher.

28. Josef Stern intriguingly suggests that Maimonides' admission of not having received his interpretation "from a teacher" reveals his consideration of his own interpretation as a *reading* of Scripture rather than the *meaning* of it. He draws an analogy between philosophical and legal interpretation, both of which can be the *meaning* only by way of received tradition that can trace itself back to Sinai. The lack thereof, though, does not detract from its correctness. Even accepting the cogency of Stern's argument, my point remains the same. Subjecting Scripture to philosophical hermeneutics is fraught with the anxiety of a rupture with Sinai while at the same time true. See Stern, "Philosophy or Exegesis: Some Critical Comments," in *Studies in Muslim Jewish Relations,* vol. 3, *Judaeo Arabic Studies,* edited by Norman Golb (Chur, Switzerland: Harwood Academic Publishers, 1997), 213–28, at 218–24.

29. *GP* II:36, 373. There is no essential link between the land of Israel and prophecy as there is in Judah Halevi. Prophecy ceases in exile due to natural causes because oppression and persecution are not conducive to the physical and psychological requirements that enable it. Political subordination to crude foreign powers causes sadness, which impedes the mental capacity for prophecy and is "the essential and proximate cause of the fact that prophecy was taken away during the time of *Exile*" (*GP* II:36, 373). This position is a consequence of his notion, on which there is a general scholarly consensus, that geographical holiness is historically contingent and not ontological. See Kellner, *Maimonides' Confrontation,* 107–15, and the studies he cites on 107 n. 68.

30. *GP* Intro., 5–6.

31. MT *Temple Vessels,* 7:3.

32. Ibid., 7:1

33. Ralph Lerner identifies this notion of simple justice with the all-consuming or passionate love (al-'ishq) described in III:51, which does not allow for any thought that is not God-directed. See his "Maimonides' Governance of the Solitary," in *Perspectives on Maimonides: Philosophical and Historical Studies*, edited by Joel Kraemer (Oxford: Oxford University Press for the Littman Library, 1991), 33–46, at 40. This state of unadulterated concentration corresponds to his halakhic formulation in MT *Repentance*, 10:3, where the analogy is drawn to an obsessive romance the likes of which is the subject of the *Song of Songs* and captured by the lover's declaration *For I am sick with love* (2:5).

34. Maimonides' view of the *tsaddiq* in this sense would be radically at odds with a "traditional" view such as that formulated by Gershom Scholem, where "The Zaddik, as the Talmud says, is not expected to be a man of words, he is to be a man of deeds . . . even though he may be devoid of intellectual attainments, if he were a simple and unsophisticated man, he still could be a Zaddik." See Scholem, "Three Types of Jewish Piety," in *Jewish and Gnostic Man* (Dallas, Tex.: Spring Publishers, 1987), 29–45, at 36–37. Maimonides' *tsaddiq* is in fact defined as such by virtue of his commitment to the pursuit of intellectual attainment.

35. *GP* II:36. See also MT *Foundations of the Torah* 7:4 and his Introduction to *Avot* (*Eight Chapters*) in I. Shilat's edition of *Rambam's Introductions to Mishnah* (Jerusalem: Maaleh Adumim, 1992), 247, based on b*Shabbat* 30b, b*Pesachim* 117a.

36. b*Avodat Zarah* 54b. *See* MT *Repentance* 9:2, *Kings and their Wars* 12:1; *GP* II:29, where even the phenomenon of miracles is covered by this rubric.

37. Lenn E. Goodman takes this Maimonidean passage regarding *tsedeq* as a catalyst for a full-length development of a theory of justice that is "ontological" by distinguishing "the moral virtue of justice (*tzedaqah*) from the mere doing of justice, the fulfilling of one's formal obligations." See his *On Justice: An Essay in Jewish Philosophy* (New Haven, Conn.: Yale University Press, 1991), 2.

38. See *GP* I:1, 22 and I:41, 91, which identifies the rational soul as the "form of man."

39. It is universally acknowledged that Maimonides derived his formulation from that of Aristotle in his *Nichomachean Ethics;* see, e.g., the English translation by Terrence Irwin (Indianapolis, Ind.: Hackett, 1985), 1106a28–b7. For another formulation of the doctrine of the mean by Maimonides, see his introduction to his commentary on *Avot*, known as "Eight Chapters" (English translation in R. Weiss, *Ethical Writings of Maimonides* [New York: Dover Press, 1975], 67–70). On the use of the term *de'ot* by Maimonides for ethical traits (rather than a more likely term such as *middot*), see R. Weiss, who attributes the choice to that which distinguishes man from brute—his intellectual form. Maimonides thereby "intellectualizes the character traits by calling them *de'ot*. He also stresses the effect of moral conduct upon the mind by treating character traits as *de'ot*" ("Language and Ethics: Reflections on Maimonides' Ethics," *Journal of the History of Philosophy* 9 [1917]: 430). Leo Strauss translates *de'ot* as "ethics" ("Notes on Maimonides' Book of Knowledge," in *Studies in Mysticism and Religion Presented to G. Scholem*, edited by E. E. Urbach, R. J. Zwi Werblowsky and Ch. Wirszubski [Jerusalem: Magnes Press, 1967], 269–83, at 270), while S. Schwarzschild prefers "morals" ("Moral Radicalism and Middlingness in the Ethics of Maimonides," in *The Pursuit of the Ideal*, edited by M. Kellner [Albany: SUNY Press, 1990], 37–160, at 143).

40. Herbert Davidson, "The Middle Way in Maimonides' Ethics," *PAAJR* 54 (1987): 31–72. For a ruler, who is also a prophet, the ideal form of political administration is a passionless one that assimilates divine attributes of action "so that these ac-

tions may proceed from him according to a determined measure and according to the deserts of the people who are affected by them and not merely because of his following a passion" (*GP* I:54, 126).

41. *bBava Metzia* 114b; MT *Lending and Borrowing* 3:5.

42. This might explain Maimonides' normative ranking of helping an unfortunate person to become self-supporting as the very acme of *tsedaqah* (charity) in MT *Gifts to the Poor* 10:7.

43. As Herbert Davidson has convincingly argued, the *Guide* offers a cogently developed ethical theory that "directs the perfect man to crown his knowledge of God with dispassionate behavior in areas affecting others" ("The Middle Way in Maimonides' Ethics," 71).

44. See, for example, Isaac Abravanel's conservative view of the verse. He takes the "gates" to refer to the chapters of the *Guide,* which only those who are "righteous" and who believe in the Torah may read, excluding heretics and those who subscribe to bad opinions. He then takes a swipe at Narboni, whom he considers a member of the latter in *Sefer Moreh Nevukhim im Arba'ah Perushim,* (Jerusalem, 1904, repr. 1960), 11. For an example of a contemporary scholar who understands *goy tsaddiq* as an ethical condition for entering through the gates, see Judah Even Shmuel's commentary on the *Guide,* Moreh Nevukhim (Heb.) (Jerusalem: Mossad HaRav Kook, 1960), 1:43. He considers the phrase to be the first prerequisite of ethics, while the second phrase, *shomer emunim,* stands for the second prerequisite of knowledge.

45. David Shatz, "Maimonides' Moral Theory," in *The Cambridge Companion to Maimonides,* edited by Kenneth Seeskin (New York: Cambridge University Press, 2005), 167–92. His argument is that the *Guide* reflects this kind of "consequent morality," while the MT largely develops a theory of "propadeutic morality," or one that is a prerequisite for the *vita contemplativa.*

45. See, for example, Morris Faierstein, "'God's Need for the Commandments' in Medieval Kabbalah," *Conservative Judaism* 36, no. 1 (1982): 45–59.

47. *mYomah* 8:9; *Sifra, Acharei Mot* 5; MT *Repentance* 2:5, 9; *Blessings* 11:2.

48. In *GP* III:35, Maimonides continues that these commandments are "called by them *between man and God* even though in reality it sometimes may affect relations *between man and his fellow man*" (*GP* 538). This is part of a systematic argument by Maimonides to collapse all these traditional distinctions between classes of commandments. Hannah Kasher notes an overtly distinctive perspective between this passage, which emphasizes the socio-political function of the commandments, and the very end of the *Guide,* which accentuates the intellectual as their final end. My reading here sees these two passages of the *Guide* as perfectly consistent. Even Kasher leaves open the possibility that III:35 covertly accords with the intellectualist stance of III:54 via the esoteric wink of "and understand this" with which Maimonides concludes his distinction between these categories of mitzvoth. See her "Commandments Between Man and God in the *Moreh Nevukhim*" (Heb.), *Daat* 12 (1984): 23–28, at 28.

49. See Moses Narboni, *Biur LeSefer Moreh Nevkhim* (Vienna: n.p., 1852) and Shem Tov's comment that they are considered "between man and God (*maqom*)" "because man conjoins with God in accord with his perfection and his knowledge and his level of ethical and intellectual achievement" at 48b–49a of part III. See also Hannah Kasher's citation of these commentators and her lucid discussion in "Commandments Between Man and God in the *Moreh Nevukhim*," 24.

50. Maimonides is here referring to the perfected soul, which is "the thing that remains of man after death" (*GP* I:40, 91). See also I:70, 173–174; MT *Foundations of the Torah,* 4:8–9; *Repentance* 8:1–2. For a concise overview of Maimonides' position on the

immortality of the soul, and in particular the thorny question whether there can be an individuated soul that survives the body, see Steven Nadler, *Spinoza's Heresy: Immortality and the Jewish Mind* (New York: Oxford University Press, 2001), 67–80.

51. On this I agree with Howard Kreisel's conclusion after canvassing the issue that "it is evident from Maimonides' approach that all of Israel does not have a portion in the World to Come, with the exception of a few individuals. The World to Come, he continuously hints, refers to the immortality of the perfected intellect." See Kreisel's chapter on "Intellectual Perfection, Knowledge of God," in *Maimonides' Political Thought: Studies in Ethics, Law and the Human Ideal* (Albany: SUNY Press, 1999), 208. Whether that perfected intellect can attain an individuated post-corporeal existence is another issue altogether that deserves its own treatment. On this, see *GP* I:74, 7th method, 221, where Maimonides explicitly endorses ibn Bajja's reasoning against individuated intellects, as well as II: Introd., prop. 16, 237, and Alexander Altmann's discussion in *Von der Mittelaterichen zur Modernen Aufklarung* (Tubingen: Mohr, Siebeck, 1987), 85–91. Maimonides' prevarication on this issue may follow the lead of Alfarabi, whose statements on individual immortality of intellects are "a stratagem designed to veil his precise views from conservative religious leaders." See Herbert Davidson's discussion in *Alfarabi, Avicenna and Averroes on Intellect* (Oxford: Oxford University Press, 1992), 53–57, quote at 57.

52. The stratification of the Maimonidean polity falls generally in line with his Islamic colleagues, yet perhaps with a slightly less cynical view of the masses. Though it is not within the power of the masses to understand philosophical truths about the world and God "as they truly are" (*GP* I:33, 71), they must be taught "on traditional authority" certain truths about the nature of God (I:35), which perforce would require cautioning them about the parabolic style of Torah. Avicenna and Averroes, on the other hand, advocate withholding from the masses even this. See Heidi Ravven's comments in "Some Thoughts on What Spinoza Learned from Maimonides about the Prophetic Imagination, Part 1. Maimonides on Prophecy and the Imagination," *Journal of the History of Philosophy* 39, no. 2 (2001): 193–214 n. 34, where she notes, "Maimonides wants to purify the masses of the worst imaginative excesses in their concept of God, whereas Averroes and Avicenna recommend the anthropomorphic conception of God as fitting for the masses."

53. Here I take issue with those such as Lawrence Berman, who argue that Maimonides adopts an Alfarabian position that views the philosopher as politician supreme, who "acquires knowledge of the world and God. He constructs an ideal state which resembles the world which proceeded from God." See Berman, "The Political Interpretation of the Maxim: The Purpose of Philosophy Is the Imitation of God," *Studia Islamica* 15 (1961): 53–61, quote at 58. The pivotal passage that fuels the debate on this issue and that Berman and others take as an explicit endorsement of his position is the very end of the *Guide*, which sets "loving kindness, righteousness, and judgment [*tsedaqah*]," as the ultimate goal of intellectual perfection. My reading here demonstrates how a key term, *tsedeq*, in the superscript is massaged and reshaped throughout the *Guide*, linking up finally with the end of *tsedaqah*, which transcends its regular social/ethical/political connotations.

54. Robert Cover, in his "Nomos and Narrative," *Narrative, Violence and the Law*, edited by M. Minnow et al. (Ann Arbor: University of Michigan Press, 1992), 95–172, elegantly argued for the mutual integration of law and narrative, using the biblical canon as his paradigm in which "every prescription is insistent in its demand to be located in discourse . . . and every narrative is insistent in its demand for its prescriptive

point, its moral" (96). Particularly suggestive for our purposes is his discussion of the dissonance between the biblical prescription regarding primogeniture and the narratives that overturn its rule of succession (113–20). In Maimonides' view of the Bible as well, there is a dynamic tension between such laws as belief in unity and prohibition against idolatry and the anthropomorphic narratives in which they are embedded. For Cover, "the biblical narratives always retained their subversive force" (119), whereas for Maimonides, an ideal understanding of biblical law is always subversive of its external narrative background.

55. See my discussion of the trivalent nature of prophetic parables in *Maimonides and the Hermeneutics of Concealment,* 15–18. See also Josef Stern, who suggests that circumcision is typical of "a mode of allegorical or parabolic interpretation that he employs not only for the narrative portions of Scripture but also of the commandments" ("Maimonides on the Covenant of Circumcision and the Unity of God," in *The Midrashic Imagination,* edited by Michael Fishbane [Albany: SUNY Press, 1993], 131–54, at 132, and esp. at 146–150.)

56. Kimhi a devotee of Maimonides, picks up on the Maimonidean slant to this verse by reading it as *"Enable me to understand* them [the decrees] *so that I may live* through them *for the world [forever]* to come." See *Mikraot Gedolot Haketer, Psalms II,* edited by Menachem Cohen (Ramat Gan: Bar Ilan University, 2003), 180. Kimhi understands this verse as declaring that it is the *understanding* of the mitzvoth, not the performance, by which man earns his share in the world to come or immortality.

57. For Maimonides, if the intellect is the only thing that survives the body, ipso facto any intellectual deficiency impedes such survival. This of course assumes that for Maimonides there is in fact some kind of individuated immortality. Howard Kreisel raises the intriguing possibility that Maimonides' failure to address anywhere how knowledge can lead to immortality of the intellect, coupled with his acknowledgment of the limitations of the human intellect, is evidence of an esoteric position that rejects immortality. Therefore, "even the notion that immortality is limited to the intellectually perfect would then be an 'exoteric' doctrine designed for some of his philosophically versed readers." See Kreisel, *Maimonides' Political Thought,* 141–42.

58. Avraham Nuriel, "The Concept of Belief in Maimonides" (Heb.), *Daat* 2–3 (1978–79): 43–47. This key distinction resolves the "contradiction" over which much ink has been spilled in the rabbinic academy between the first commandment listed in the *Sefer HaMitzvot* in the ibn Tibbon translation as "to believe" (*lehaamin*) in the existence of God, while the MT begins with the mitzvah "to know" (*leda*) that Being. What ibn Tibbon translated as "to believe" is *itiqad,* and therefore the MT is perfectly consistent with the Book of Commandments. See Nuriel's discussion on p. 43, and R. Haim Heller's first note to the first commandment of his edition of the *Sefer HaMitzvot* (Jerusalem: Mossad HaRav Kook, 1946), 35.

59. In his translation, Pines notes here that this means "the union of the Active Intellect with the intellect of the prophet" (403 n. 79). It is puzzling, then, how he can conclude in a later article that the dogma of the belief in prophecy as formulated by the sixth of his thirteen principles in the Mishnah Commentary is even more philosophical than that of the *Guide,* in that, "It is stated in this dogma but not in the *Guide that the intellects of the prophets were united with the Active Intellect."* See Pines, "The Philosophical Purport of Maimonides' Halachic Works and the Purport of *The Guide of the Perplexed,"* in *Maimonides and Philosophy, Papers Presented at the Sixth Jerusalem Philosophical Encounter,* edited by S. Pines and Y. Yovel (Dordrecht: M. Nijhoff, 1985), 1–14, quote at 3.

60. Both in *GP* II:41, 385, and II:45, 402.

61. Maimonides is obviously partial to this verse. See *GP* II:39, 379; III:24, 502; III:43, 572; III:51, 624; MT *Opinions* 1:7; *Gifts to the Poor*, 10:1.

62. The literature is vast on this topic. For a lengthy bibliography that covers 35 pages of publications only until 1995, see I. Dienstag, "Prophecy in the Thought of the Rambam: A Bibliography," *Daat* 37 (1996): 193–228.

63. Similarly, Lenn Goodman formulates Maimonides' virtue ethics as follows: "For moral development is a prerequisite of intellectual perfection, and the moral virtues are distinguished by a habitual, spontaneous, even pleasurable responsiveness to the counsels and judgments of reason" ("God and the Good Life: Maimonides' Virtue Ethics and the Idea of Perfection," in *The Tris of Maimonides: Jewish, Arabic, and Ancient Culture of Knowledge*, edited by Georges Tamer [Berlin: De Gruyter, 2005], 123–35, quote at 134).

64. In a highly illuminating discussion of the critical relationship between the imagination and the intellect for medieval philosophy, which is pertinent to Maimonides' conception of the prophet, Aaron W. Hughes accounts for the kind of "love/hate" attitude medieval philosophers had for the imagination. The imagination is the essential mechanism that draws the imageless goals of the intellect into the only language in which human consciousness converses: the image: "Images and the imagination, therefore, represent the prolegomena to noetic activity," and "[this] allows access to the incorporeal through an intricate process of symbolization." See Hughes, *The Texture of the Divine: Imagination in Medieval Jewish and Islamic Thought* (Bloomington: Indiana University Press, 2004), 85. For Maimonides, this activity would reach its zenith in the prophetic *vision* as opposed to *dreams* because of its content, which consists of the "cognition of scientific matters."

65. MT *Idolatry* 1:3 and its parallel in *GP* III:29, 516–17.

66. As Alexander Altmann states, prophecy is a natural process in which "the prophet's rational faculty operates in an optimal way and offers material to the imagination for mimetic activity" ("Maimonides on the Intellect and the Scope of Metaphysics," in *Von der Mittelalterlichen zur Modernen Aufklärung* [Tübingen: Mohr, Siebeck, 1987], 83). Here Abraham's imagination mimetically crafts parables out of the material provided to it by the intellect. For this reason it is partially misleading when drawing a Maimonidean portrait of Abraham, as Masha Turner does, to so neatly compartmentalize Abraham the philosopher and Abraham the prophet. See her "The Patriarch Abraham in Maimonidean Thought" (Heb.) in *The Faith of Abraham; In Light of Interpretation Throughout the Ages*, edited by M. Hallamish, H. Kasher, and Y. Silman (Ramat Gan: Bar Ilan University Press, 2002), 143–47.

67. It is worth noting that, contra Maimonides, who arguably blurs the distinction between philosophy and prophecy and does not seem to allow for any kind of supra-rational thought, the mystical tradition markedly distinguishes the two both in method and content. For but one prominent example, Abraham Abulafia, a kabbalistic expositor of Maimonidean thought, radically diverged from the philosophical approach. As Elliot Wolfson cogently argues, "It is not simply the case that prophecy is a more subtle form of comprehension than philosophy. What is revealed to the prophet through the technique of letter combination and permutation of the divine names does not only transcend but may ultimately contradict the dictates of philosophical reasoning." The second proposition of Abulafian prophecy would certainly have been anathema to Maimonides. See Wolfson, *Abraham Abulafia—Kabbalist and Prophet: Hermeneutics, Theosophy, and Theurgy* (Los Angeles: Cherub Press, 2000), 154.

68. Here also I concur with Altmann's assertion that the philosopher and the prophet share the identical scope of metaphysics as their cognitive goals, with the only distinction being that the prophet's intense imagination "is merely a tool for the translation of concepts into a language intelligible to the common man" ("Maimonides on the Intellect," 128–29). For imagination to be constructive, it must be somehow reined in by reason, whether entirely shut off from sensual perception or simply dominated by it. As Jose Faur captures it, imagination "constitutes a pathological retrogression from Adam's ability to reason" (*Homo Mysticus: A Guide to Maimonides' Guide for the Perplexed* [Syracuse, N.Y.: Syracuse University Press, 1999], 59).

69. *GP* II:48, 409–12.

70. Isaac Abravanel already noted this in his resolution of the problematic speech here, which should be precluded by a vision where speech means "parables or intellectual apprehensions." Alvin Reines's note clarifying this phrase underlies my analysis of the vision that follows: "Words, as units of thought occur in vision prophecy, 'heard' words perceived as sounds do not. Thus 'intellectual apprehensions,' words formed into conceptions that are divorced from corporeal association with sound, can appear in vision prophecy" (*Maimonides and Abrabanel on Prophecy* [Cincinnati, Ohio: Hebrew Union College Press, 1970], 227 n. 208).

71. Here also the literature is vast. For the earliest sustained account of Maimonides' theory of providence by Samuel ibn Tibbon, see Zvi Diesendruck, "Samuel and Moses ibn Tibbon on Maimonides' Theory of Providence," *Hebrew Union College Annual* 11 (1936): 341–56. For a more contemporary closely read and incisive treatment, see Charles Raffel, "Providence as Consequent upon the Intellect: Maimonides' Theory of Providence," *AJS Review* 12, no. 1 (1986): 25–71.

72. This is the very term used for each of his thirteen principles. It is also of note that throughout his discussion of providence, when he affirms his "belief" in the opinions he is endorsing in III:17, the term *itiqad* is used, which connotes philosophical demonstration rather than trust or faith in the matter. Kafih translates this as *daat,* and Schwartz as *emunah.*

73. MT *Foundations,* 2:2. Though Maimonides' position on this issue, as on others, does not remain static throughout his writings, which reveal ongoing revision and re-revision, my presentation here of love and of Abraham as "lover" follows his latest and most mature thinking on love as an expression of radical intellectualism. For a concise overview tracing the various stages in Maimonides' thought on this, see Kreisel, "The Love and Fear of God," in his *Maimonides' Political Thought,* 225–31.

74. Here I agree with Menachem Kellner's interpretation (also citing Lawrence Berman's "Ibn Bajah viHaRambam" [Ph.D. diss., Hebrew University, 1959], 37) that Maimonides' notion of human perfection entails two tiers of *imitatio dei,* one "before intellectual perfection and an imitation of God after such perfection. Put in other words, we obey God before intellectual perfection out of fear and after intellectual perfection out of love." See Kellner, *Maimonides on Human Perfection* (Atlanta, Ga.: Scholars Press, 1990), 39.

75. Without entering into the thorny issue of contradictions within Maimonides' moral theory as presented in *Deot* between the mandated "golden mean" and the equally mandated extreme in avoiding anger and haughtiness, perhaps this notion is the key to understanding the following exemplification of the extreme in *Deot* 2:3 by *tsaddiqim:* "The practice of the *righteous* is to suffer contumely and not inflict it, accept humiliation and not respond to it[,] *to be impelled in what they do by love . . .*" (emphasis mine). Extreme humility is a *consequence* of *love* which has been defined by Maimoni-

des as intellectually and not emotionally driven. Although there would of course be emotional manifestations of this love and fear, I would not emphasize that facet of it as much as Gilead Bar-Elli does in his "On the Concept of Awe (*Yira*) in Maimonides" (Heb.), *Iyun* 45 (1996): 381–88, esp. 385.

76. MT *Repentance*, 10:2.

77. Ibid., 10:6.

78. Ibid., 10:2. As Kreisel puts it, "Thus the worship of God in the context of Maimonides' thought should be viewed primarily as a means to the pursuit of the scientific knowledge by which the love of God is achieved. It is also the practical result of the attainment of the requisite knowledge and the love that necessarily follows" (*Maimonides' Political Thought*, 241).

79. The teacher/disciple relationship as father/son assumes halakhic significance where students are actually considered children. The obligation to "teach your children" extends to all people, for all students are children. See MT *Talmud Torah*, 1:2.

80. MT *Idolatry*, 11:4. One of the examples of prohibited "divination" (*naḥash*) is one who determines courses of action by signs "as Eliezer, Abraham's servant did." The reference is to Genesis 24:12–14, where Abraham's servant conditions his choice of a prospective bride for Isaac on "signs."

81. Although Maimonides himself subscribed to astrological theories, it was a scientific belief in the "physical stimulus of the stellar bodies," and not "that there exists a *spiritual* reciprocity between earth and heaven." See Y. Tzvi Langermann, "Acceptance and Devaluation: Nahmanides' Attitude Toward Science," *Journal of Jewish Thought and Philosophy* 1 (1992): 223–45, quote at 234. Problematic as is Maimonides' seeming endorsement of a theory of astral influence that sounds very much like astrology (*GP* II:10), it is strictly within the parameters of Aristotelian science and natural laws related to bodies affecting other bodies. See Y. Tzvi Langermann, "Maimonides' Repudiation of Astrology," *Maimonidean Studies* 2 (1991): 123–38, and esp. 140–43; and Gad Freudenthal, "Maimonides' Stance on Astrology in Context: Cosmology, Physics, Medicine and Providence," in *Moses Maimonides: Physician, Scientist, and Philosopher*, edited by F. Rosner and S. Kottek (Northvale, N.J.: Jason Aronson, 1993), 77–90, esp. at 80–84, where he places Maimonides' theories solidly within the Aristotelian cosmology, physics, climatology, and medicine of its time.

82. I have not subjected every word of this vision to the allegorical microscope, and in particular Eliezer's national origins *Damesek*. Here I follow Maimonides' admonishment to distinguish between hypersignificant parables, where "each word has meaning," and those where some words do not enhance meaning but rather serve to "render it more coherent or to conceal further the intended meaning" (*GP* Intro., 12). Though there are no strict guidelines for identifying the type we are dealing with, I follow his general cautionary advice that, once the "general proposition" of a parable has been singled out, not to investigate all the minutiae at the risk of "extravagant fantasies" (*GP* Intro., 14). Frank Talmage eloquently considered these words as a tribute to "a master, of one who knew how to practice restraint, of one who knew how not to outdo himself." See his "Apples of Gold: The Inner Meaning of Sacred Texts in Medieval Judaism," in *Jewish Spirituality: From the Bible to the Middle Ages*, edited by A. Green (New York: Crossroad, 1986), 313–55, quoted at 333.

83. b*Sabbath* 156a; b*Nedarim* 32a. According to other rabbinic lore, Abraham had established renown as an astrologer consulted by heads of state for his counsel in this area. See b*Baba Bathra* 16b, b*Yoma* 28b.

84. Maimonides mounted a strenuous assault on astrological *theology* in his *Letter on Astrology*, where he attributes the most disastrous catastrophe in Jewish history,

the destruction of the temple, to the Jewish preoccupation with a science of "nothingness and emptiness." More pertinent to our analysis here is that the obsession with astrology is credited to a naïve and uncritical acceptance of longstanding tradition. As Ralph Lerner has phrased it, "One might say that they are heirs to a tradition of credulity" (*Maimonides' Empire of Light: Popular Enlightenment in an Age of Belief* [Chicago: University of Chicago Press, 2000], 57–58).

85. My reading resolves Hannah Kasher's problem with the timing of the vision if the message is to extrapolate God's existence from the stars, which, she queries in her overview of the various Jewish responses to Gen. 15:5 from the middle ages to the modern period, would have certainly been accomplished before this vision. See her "'Look Toward Heaven'—on Jewish Thought in the Footsteps of the Midrashim" (Heb.), in *The Faith of Abraham; In Light of Interpretation Throughout the Ages*, 331–45, at 335–36.

86. *Bereshit Rabbah* 44:12.

87. The same term for "look" *(hibit)* appears also in Isaiah 51:1–2, *Look unto the rock whence you were hewn . . . Look unto Abraham your father*, which is interpreted by Maimonides to mean "Tread therefore in his footsteps, adhere to his religion, and acquire his character, inasmuch as the nature of a quarry ought to be present in what is hewn from it" (*GP* I:16, 42). The term *look* forms a literary link between Abraham and his disciples. To qualify, they must *look* at the way he *looked,* that is, philosophize the way he philosophized.

88. Indeed, according to Shlomo Pines, Maimonides holds out no possibility of metaphysical knowledge whatsoever. For Pines the ultimate goal of man is political in his "The Limitations of Human Knowledge According to Al Farabi, ibn Bajja and Maimonides," *Studies in Medieval Jewish History and Literature,* edited by I. Twersky (Cambridge, Mass.: Harvard University Press, 1979), 82–109. However, Herbert Davidson has vigorously and convincingly challenged that thesis in his "Maimonides on Metaphysical Knowledge," *Maimonidean Studies* 3 (1992–93): 49–103.

89. Many of the prominent medieval commentators such as Rashi, Radak, and Seforno take the subject of *vayaḥshevehu* as God, which is the case with Maimonides. Nahmanides, however, challenges this and considers Abraham the subject and God the object being qualified by *tsedaqah.*

90. Here I agree and disagree in part with Menachem Kellner's interpretation of this act of belief that he characterizes as "trust," thus allowing for noncognitive virtue in Maimonides' thought. Though I agree that Abraham here demonstrates "trust," it is virtuous only because it is cognitively based. While Kellner claims that Maimonides here welcomes simple, intellectually unsophisticated faith, I would argue that Abraham's faith is desirable precisely because it is a realization of "cognition of the intelligibilia" that Maimonides states explicitly is the subject matter of "visions." See Kellner, "The Virtue of Faith," in *Neoplatonism and Jewish Thought,* edited by Lenn Goodman (Albany: SUNY Press, 1992), 195–205.

91. Here I agree with those scholars who argue that Maimonides could not have viewed the entire *aqedah* episode as anything but a prophetic vision. See, for example, A. Nuriel's convincing arguments in "Maimonides on Parables not Explicitly Defined as Such" (Heb.), *Daat* 25 (1990): 88–91. Not the least of those arguments against the empirical historicity of the event is the impossibility of God's mandating the senseless and unjust death of any human being.

92. Supra, note 51. On this I prefer Altmann's naturalist stance as opposed to Abraham Joshua Heschel, who sees Maimonidean prophecy as a supra-rational attainment to which the philosopher of his own cognition has no access. See "Did Mai-

monides Believe He Attained Prophecy?" (Heb.), in *The Louis Ginzberg Jubilee Volume* (Philadelphia: Jewish Publication Society of America, 1946), 159–88, esp. 173.

93. b*Shabbat* 119b. See also b *Sanhedrin 110b,* which midrashically transforms the verse in the same way, proving that the recitation of Amen is what initiates a child into *the world to come.*

94. Maimonides' "reinvention" of an original midrashic restatement of a biblical verse is especially pertinent to the type dealt with here. He specifically characterizes "all the passages in the Midrashim enjoining *Do not read thus but thus*" (as in our case) as "witty poetical conceits" intended to "instill a noble moral quality" (*GP* III:43, 573) and therefore should not be taken literally. His own novel readings are legitimized since, as "poetic conceits," the original rabbinic readings were never meant to be taken literally, nor were they meant to be exhaustive interpretations of the verse in question.

95. Fox, *Interpreting Maimonides,* 155

96. Ibid.

97. As Ruth Langer states, "Communal prayer . . . serves the more mundane function of creating a mechanism by which those who cannot themselves recite the prayers, from lack of education or lack of ability, can meet their prayer obligations." See Langer, *To Worship God Properly: Tensions Between Liturgical Custom and Halakha in Judaism* (Cincinnati, Ohio: Hebrew Union College Press, 1998), 21.

98. See for example b*Rosh Hashanah* 34b.

99. MT *Prayer* 8:9. The destruction of the second temple left the illiterate and uninformed masses in a religious vacuum. The *shaliah tsibbur* emerged to fill that vacuum. He "functioned in the absence of the Temple and the sacrifices. He had become the means through which the masses complied with the Torah's warrants." See Hyman Sky, *Redevelopment of the Office of Hazzan Through the Talmudic Period* (San Francisco: Mellen Research University Press, 1992), 43.

100. Paul Ricoeur, "The Model of the Text: Meaningful Action Considered as a Text," *Social Research* 38, no. 3 (1971): 529–62, quote at 549.

101. Marvin Fox, *Interpreting Maimonides: Studies in Methodology, Metaphysics and Moral Philosophy* (Chicago: University of Chicago Press, 1990), 154. See also 260–64, where he subjects Genesis 21:33 to the same kind of analysis, turning a superscript into a critical clue in determining Maimonides' position on creation. I have dedicated many of my studies on Maimonides to demonstrating and deepening Fox's observations that Maimonides' choice of verses in the *Guide* are not "mere rhetorical flourish" or "arbitrary," but rather are deliberately selected "to communicate an important message to his readers and that, as is frequently the case, he was testing them in the process to see if they would discover the message on their own" (262).

102. When comparing Gersonides' legacy to Maimonides, Alfred Ivry astutely observes that "it is the *Guide,* not the *Wars,* which captured the imagination of most late medieval Jewish philosophers, and it is Maimonides' composition which influenced their own work. The exegetical mode of discourse remained attractive to Jewish philosophers, even if much of it was now turned to interpreting Maimonides' exegesis" ("Strategies of Interpretation," 126).

103. James Kugel, "Two Introductions to Midrash," in *Midrash and Literature,* edited by Geofferey Hartman and Sanford Budick (New Haven, Conn.: Yale University Press, 1986), 77–103, quoted at 91.

104. Ibid., 91–92. Kugel's list encompasses virtually every other genre of Jewish texts reflected in his summation that midrash is endemic "in short" to "almost all of what constitutes classical (and much of medieval) Jewish writing."

105. Maimonides, true to his rabbinic roots, possessed a midrashic mentality in the sense that when he reads Scripture, as Gerald Bruns has said of the midrashic oeuvre, he sees "not what lies behind the text in the form of an original meaning but what lies in front of it where the interpreter stands." See Bruns, "Midrash and Allegory," in *The Literary Guide to the Bible,* edited by Robert Alter and Frank Kermode (Cambridge, Mass.: Belknap Press, 1987), 625–46, at 627.

10

AESTHETICS AND THE INFINITE: MOSES MENDELSSOHN ON THE POETICS OF BIBLICAL PROPHECY

Michah Gottlieb

Recent discussions of Jewish aesthetics have challenged the once standard view that while Greek culture is essentially ocular, Hebraic culture is essentially aural.[1] On the standard view, the Jewish eschewal of the visual is rooted in the second of the Ten Commandments, which prohibits the fashioning of "a sculptured image or any likeness of what is in the heavens above or in the earth below or in the waters under the earth."[2]

In a novel approach to the problem of aesthetics in Jewish thought, Elliot R. Wolfson stresses the tension within Judaism between the sense that God can be perceived in physical form and the biblical prohibition against making visual representations of God.[3] One way that mystics and philosophers navigated this tension was by claiming that the mystic could visualize God through the imagination.[4] But recognizing the necessary limitation of any visualization of God,[5] mystics often interpreted these visions as hermeneutical operations of the imagination that clothed the perception of the divine in sensible forms. Given God's ineffability, these forms necessarily occluded God in the very process of revealing him.[6]

Like Wolfson, Kalman Bland criticizes the dichotomy between Greek ocular and Hebraic aural culture. But Bland's focus is different, for he is primarily interested in showing that this dichotomy reflects a distorted view of Judaism's attitude toward the visual arts. Following Moshe Barasch, Bland distinguishes between a "comprehensive" and a "restrictive" interpretation of the second commandment. The "comprehensive" interpretation "rejects every mimetic image" regardless of what the image depicts, while the restrictive interpretation only prohibits fashioning icons of the divinity.[7] Bland argues that the "restrictive" interpretation of the second commandment reflects a "pre-modern consensus," while the "comprehensive" interpretation is an invention of modern "Germanophone" Jewish thinkers. Writing in the wake of Kant and Hegel, these thinkers arbitrarily defined Judaism as "preeminently spiritual, coterminous with ethics, and quintessentially universal."⁸ Drawing on Romantic treatments of poetry, they reinforced this account by developing the myth of Jewish aurality and aniconism.⁹ In this way, Bland concludes that Judaism has not traditionally been averse to the visual arts.

Bland's work on German-Jewish aesthetics is pioneering and very suggestive. But by beginning with Jewish responses to Kant and Hegel, Bland omits the founder of German-Jewish philosophy, Moses Mendelssohn. In the introduction to his book, Bland writes that his task is "not to write the complete and final word . . . [but] to put things on the agenda . . . [with the] hope that our work is superceded." My intention is not to supercede Bland's work, but to build upon it.

Like later German-Jewish thinkers, Mendelssohn contrasts Hebraic and Hellenic art, but his contrast is different. For Mendelssohn, the dichotomy is not between Hebrew aurality and Greek visuality, but rather between alienating plastic/dead letter and correlating poetic/living script. While Hellenic poetry generally aims at inflaming the senses alone, Hebraic poetry aims at putting heart and mind in harmony by giving sensible expression to abstract metaphysical truths through vivid visual imagery.

Mendelssohn's biblical aesthetics are conditioned by the context in which he writes. While Bland identifies Kant and Hegel as the central polemic context for later German-Jewish aesthetics, I see Spinoza's treatment of prophecy as Mendelssohn's main concern. In Mendelssohn's view, the chief weakness of Spinoza's historical-critical approach is that it seeks the Bible's literal meaning at the expense of appreciating its literary features. The source of this is Spinoza's failure to understand aesthetics as a sphere with its own standards of validity. In consequence, Spinoza interprets prophetic visions literally as truth claims about God and nature, which unsurprisingly he finds philosophically wanting. Aesthetic considerations, however, show how these visions are better understood as religious poetry, whose purpose is to convey metaphysical truths in emotionally stirring ways.

It would be wrong, however, to reduce Mendelssohn's position to countering Spinoza. For Mendelssohn's biblical aesthetics emerge from a complex of factors, including his philosophical Wolffianism, theological optimism, commitment to religious pluralism, affirmation of biblical and rabbinic authority, opposition to Christology, and immersion in medieval Jewish philosophy. These factors, by no means exhaustive, are woven into a coherent whole through Mendelssohn's genius.

This chapter will have four parts. In the first part, I will discuss Spinoza's challenge to biblical authority and the dissemination of these views in Mendelssohn's time. In the second part, I will outline Mendelssohn's philosophical aesthetics and the connection between his aesthetics and philosophy of religion, which forms the background for his biblical aesthetics. In the third part, I will sketch Mendelssohn's claim that Hebrew aesthetics are superior to Greek aesthetics in facilitating the transmission of abstract metaphysical truths in moving ways without succumbing to idolatry, and I will connect this with his treatment of ritual law in *Jerusalem*. I will conclude with some methodological reflections.

SPINOZA'S CHALLENGE

Mendelssohn had a complex relationship with Spinoza. When Mendelssohn began his literary career, Spinoza was widely vilified as an atheist. In Mendelssohn's first published work, *The Philosophical Dialogues* (1755), he defended Spinoza by claiming that Spinoza made critical contributions to the development of the German-Enlightenment. But in his last works, *Morning Hours* and *To Lessing's Friends* (1785–1786), Mendelssohn was forced to fend off charges that his friend Lessing was a Spinozist, and he attacked Spinoza for his atheism.[10] But Spinoza's atheism was not all that Mendelssohn found problematic, for in his *Tractatus Theologico-Politicus* Spinoza had outlined an historical-critical approach to the Bible that threatened Mendelssohn's commitment to biblical and rabbinic authority.[11]

Mendelssohn considers Spinoza's approach to biblical prophecy especially troubling. Spinoza questions the validity of the biblical prophets' teachings about God and the universe. While Maimonides had claimed that the prophets had perfected intellects and that their visions should be understood as allegorical presentations of rational truths, Spinoza's historical method, which involves reading the Bible literally through a proper knowledge of Hebrew grammar and sensitivity to the context in which the Bible was originally written, leads him to conclude that the prophets are best understood as oriental soothsayers dominated by overactive imaginations.[12] So, for example, while Maimonides claims that Moses was a philosopher who affirmed the unity and incorporeality of God, Spinoza argues that careful study of the Bible shows that Moses was a primitive thinker who believed in the existence of multiple deities and who thought that YHWH was corporeal being dwelling in the heavens.[13] Spinoza concludes that since many of the prophets' metaphysical doctrines are irrational and contradictory, one need not accept the Bible's authority in the realm of speculation and that people should be free to think for themselves.[14]

The extent to which Mendelssohn had firsthand knowledge of Spinoza's biblical criticism is an open question.[15] But there is no doubt that Spinoza's approach to the Bible was well known to him through contemporary writers who adopted Spinoza's methodology and disseminated his views. Spinoza's view of biblical prophecy was made widespread through Lessing's sensational publication of Hermann Samuel Reimarus's *Fragments of the Unnamed Author,* to which Lessing appended "Counterpropositions," which affirmed that the Old Testament prophets taught metaphysical doctrines that contravened natural religion.[16] And in his *Education of the Human Race,* Lessing famously criticized the rabbis for trying to read rational doctrines back into the Bible through "petty, warped, hairsplitting" interpretations.[17]

In confronting the Spinozist challenge to prophetic authority, Mendelssohn is caught in a dilemma. On the one hand, his critical exegetical sense as well as his interest in opposing christological allegoresis lead him to accept Spinoza's emphasis on literal meaning (*peshat*), which demands knowledge of Hebrew grammar and sensitivity to historical context.[18] But as a Jew committed to biblical authority, Mendelssohn cannot accept Spinoza's conclusions regarding biblical prophecy.

The Archimedean point of Mendelssohn's reply to Spinoza is that Spinoza's exclusive emphasis on literal interpretation is far too limited. For Spinoza, literal interpretation involves translating prophetic pronouncements about God and nature into speculative, semantic truth claims that not surprisingly end up seeming primitive, unscientific, and confused. What Spinoza lacks is an appreciation that biblical prophecy should be understood using aesthetic criteria, which have their own standards of validity, rather than as primitive speculation. In a word, what leads Spinoza astray is his crude understanding of aesthetics.[19]

For Spinoza, human perfection involves the "knowledge of the union that the mind has with the whole of nature."[20] "Beauty," however, is a mode of imagining that is grounded, not in the nature of things, but rather in human enjoyment.[21] Spinoza adopts a relativistic, instrumentalist account of beauty, according to which people call those objects "beautiful" that they imagine exist for the purpose of being "conducive to their health [*valetudini conducat*]."[22] But since people have different bodies, it is no wonder that "so many controversies" have arisen about what constitutes beauty.[23] Furthermore, since the notion of beauty presupposes intentionality, it is based on the mistaken assumption that nature contains final causes.[24] In consequence, the person who understands reality through intellect alone observes no beauty.[25] And given that Spinoza identifies perfection with reality, beauty is not a perfection.[26]

In the *Tractatus Theologico-Politicus,* Spinoza opposes imagination and reason. He presents a negative view of the imagination, associating it with subjectivity and error while connecting reason with objectivity and truth.[27] Since the prophets were dominated by their imaginations, Spinoza thinks that they were not generally fit for philosophical contempla-

tion.[28] Given that Spinoza valorizes rational knowledge as true perfection
and does not consider beauty a perfection, it is not surprising that he severs
the aesthetic qualities of the Bible from objective, rational truth. For Spinoza, the imaginative fantasies of the prophets were means of promoting
moral and political obedience. These imaginative fantasies were only true
accidentally.[29]

In contrast to Spinoza's relatively scant treatment of aesthetics, for
Mendelssohn aesthetics was a major philosophical concern. Indeed, many
scholars have considered Mendelssohn's greatest philosophical contribution to be his work on aesthetics.[30] But what has been generally overlooked
is how Mendelssohn's aesthetics inform his approach to the Bible and constitute a crucial element in his response to Spinoza's biblical criticism.

Mendelssohn's aesthetics are grounded in his three-faculty doctrine of
the soul.[31] Although he presents this doctrine in various places in slightly
different forms, its basic outline is clear. The soul has three capacities: the
cognitive capacity (*Erkentnissvermögen*), the approval capacity (*Billigungs-
vermögen*), and the capacity for desire (*Begehrungsvermögen*).[32] Mendelssohn accepts Wolff's teleological psychology according to which human
beings' sole drive is to seek perfection, which Mendelssohn defines as "the
harmony of the manifold."[33] The term *Bildung* (education, formation) describes the process of perfecting one's faculties in general, but each faculty has its own distinctive perfection. Perfecting the cognitive capacity
involves knowing the true, and the process of achieving this is called "enlightenment" (*Aufklärung*).[34] Perfecting the capacity for approval involves
feeling the good and the beautiful, while perfecting the capacity for desire
involves seeking to actualize the good and creating beauty in the world.
The process of perfecting the capacities of approval and desire is called
"culture" (*Kultur*).[35] Mendelssohn summarizes his ideal of perfection in his
favorite motto: "Man's destiny: to seek truth, love beauty, will the good,
and do the best."[36]

In contrast to Spinoza, for Mendelssohn there is a deep connection between rational perfection and the appreciation of beauty. Mendelssohn defines beauty as a "sensuous knowledge of a perfection."[37] In doing so, he
follows Leibniz's understanding of sensation and Christian Wolff's definition of perfection: Leibniz defines "sensation" as confused knowledge, that
is, knowledge where one cannot clearly separate all the distinguishing features of a thing;[38] Wolff defines "perfection" as the harmony of a maxi-
mally diverse manifold.[39] For Mendelssohn, sensuous knowledge of perfection therefore involves "perceiving a large array of an object's features
all at once without being able to separate them clearly."[40] There are three
elements that make an object appear beautiful. First, the object has to be
perceived as a unity whose various parts serve the whole. Second, it has

to be perceived as complex, having many parts that can be taken in all at once. Third, these parts have to be sensed in such a way that one cannot distinguish these parts clearly. For example, a rose is beautiful insofar as we can sense it as a whole distinct from other things and take in its various parts—that is, its many petals, its stem, its leaves, and its thorns—all at once without clearly distinguishing the parts in the moment of perception. The sensation accompanying experiencing beauty is pleasure.

Consider an example of how the various faculties can be perfected, using the doctrine of divine providence. As regards the cognitive capacity, perfection involves clear knowledge of the unique law of divine providence according to which various individuals receive their just deserts.[41] When this law is not known clearly but is experienced sensibly, one feels beauty, which, for example, we appreciate in viewing artistic creations in which justice prevails.[42] The beauty that we appreciate in artistic works that depict the triumph of justice can in turn awaken our desire to promote justice in the world, which constitutes the perfection of our faculty of desire.[43]

In sum, both Spinoza and Mendelssohn agree that beauty presupposes final causality. But while Spinoza views final causality as an imaginative idea that is not a property of nature considered in itself, Mendelssohn thinks that final causality is demanded by the principle of sufficient reason and hence is an objective aspect of nature.[44] This then leads to their differing assessments of beauty. For Spinoza, beauty is an imaginative judgment inhering in the mind of the observer alone. Appreciation of beauty cannot then constitute a perfection, since perfection is equivalent with reality. For Mendelssohn, however, beauty constitutes the sensible correlate of contemplating perfection intellectually. While grasping perfection intellectually is the function of philosophy and leads to the perfection of the intellect, sensing this harmony yields aesthetic appreciation and leads to the perfection of the faculty of approval. This is a distinct perfection of equal value with intellectual perfection.[45]

MENDELSSOHN ON THE AESTHETIC EDUCATION OF MAN

For Mendelssohn, aesthetics serve a crucial pedagogic function. Although for Spinoza aesthetics are valuable as a means of encouraging political obedience among the masses regardless of whether the doctrines taught are true, for Mendelssohn aesthetics are a way of bringing the heart and the mind into harmony. Mendelssohn's account of the educational function of aesthetics grows out of a difficulty that he finds in Wolff's philosophical anthropology. While Mendelssohn accepts Wolff's claim that our sole drive is to achieve perfection, from early in his literary career he is bothered by the problem of how a person could willingly choose imperfection.[46] This is why Mendelssohn's first work on aesthetics, the *Letters on Sentiments,* concludes with an extended discussion of why a person would ever commit suicide.[47] In other aesthetic writings Mendelssohn addresses why we enjoy violent spectacles (e.g., cock fighting) or tragic theatre.[48] For our purposes, however, the most relevant problem that Mendelssohn confronts is how a person can will evil. In his earliest writings, Mendelssohn accepts Plato's solution to this problem: a person chooses evil because she mistakenly perceives it to be good.[49] But Mendelssohn soon realizes that this solution is incomplete, for there clearly are cases where people know the good intellectually, yet nevertheless choose evil. Mendelssohn first discusses this problem in his 1756 essay, "On Controlling Inclinations," but he addresses it most fully in his 1761 essay "Rhapsody."[50]

In "Rhapsody," Mendelssohn distinguishes between two ways in which we can know the good. There is insight that is purely theoretical but that has no effect on our actions, which he calls "speculative" (*speculative*) or "ineffective" (*unwirksame*) knowledge. But there is likewise insight that stirs us to action, which he calls "pragmatic" (*pragmatische*) or "effective" (*wirksame*) knowledge.[51] The "effectiveness" of knowledge is a function of three factors. First, there is the *degree* of the perfection represented. The greater the perfection represented and the more vivid our representation of it is, the stronger its effect on the will. Second, there is the degree of our *knowledge* of the perfection. The more clearly we know the perfection and with more cognitive certainty, the stronger the effect on our will. Finally, there is the *speed* with which we perceive the perfection. The faster that we perceive it, the more powerfully it will affect our will.[52]

On the basis of these distinctions, Mendelssohn notes that it is possible for a perfection known less clearly to have a greater power over our will than one known more clearly if we perceive the perfection more vividly and quickly. Perfections are perceived more vividly and quickly when they are taken in sensibly than when they are known intellectually.[53] Since art is a means of representing perfections sensibly, it can therefore be a far more powerful motivator than philosophy. Poetic images and similes are particularly effective ways of making ideas vivid.[54]

These distinctions help explain how we can know that something is evil in theory and nevertheless desire it. For while we may know intellectually that a particular action is vicious, if it is presented aesthetically in a way that stirs our senses to represent the action as leading to greater perfection in the short term, we can be seduced to choose the vicious course of action against our better judgment.[55] For example, we may know that regularly eating MacDonald's bacon double cheeseburgers will lead to the imperfection of our bodies, but if the bacon double cheeseburgers are presented in an appealing form, with smiling people looking satisfied after having eaten them, we can be led to act against our intellectual judgment. But while art can, in this way, be a force that divides our desires from our intellect, it can likewise be a way of putting our intellect and desires in harmony. By presenting true perfection in a sensibly pleasing light, art can spur us to virtuous action. Mendelssohn notes that history and fables can make abstract ethical principles concrete, and poetry, painting, sculpture, and rhetoric can "transform dry truths into ardent and sensuous intuitions . . . by transforming impulses into penetrating arrows and dipping them into enchanting nectar."[56] For Mendelssohn, metaphysics plays a crucial role in ethics because three metaphysical principles—God's existence, divine providence, and the immortality of the soul—are needed both to ground morality rationally and to motivate one to act ethically.[57] It is worth exploring these points.

In a number of places, most notably in his *Treatise on Evidence*, Mendelssohn makes clear that reason can demonstrate the highest principles of ethics without appealing to religion.[58] Ethical obligations are universal, rational laws, which follow from our nature as beings with intellect.[59] One of the ways in which we can know the fundamental law of ethics is by finding the common denominator of all of our natural drives. Given that Mendelssohn thinks that all of our actions aim at perfection, the fundamental law of ethics is "Make your intrinsic and extrinsic condition and that of your fellow human being in the proper proportion as perfect as possible."[60] Our extrinsic condition refers to our body, while our intrinsic condition refers to our soul. Our obligation to seek the perfection of others derives from our desire for our own perfection. Since our perfection is a function of our representations of perfection, we seek to create a world in which we represent others as attaining perfection as well.[61]

But while reason can uncover the universal law of morality, Mendelssohn argues in the *Phädon* that without belief in immortality of the soul, this law can become contradictory. He begins his argument by accepting Aristotle's definition of the human being as a *zoon politikon*, that is, a political animal. Mendelssohn interprets this to mean that without society a person can achieve neither safety nor perfection, for perfection includes both culture and enlightenment, which cannot be achieved in the state of nature.[62] But for a society to be able to protect itself, it must have a moral right to demand that its citizens sacrifice their lives for the state if the state requires this for its continued existence. According to Mendelssohn, without belief in the immortality of the soul, one's life on earth becomes the "highest good."[63] But if the highest law of morality is to seek perfection and this world is the only place in which perfection can be achieved, one has an "exactly opposite right" (*ein gerade entgegensetzte Rechte*) to preserve one's own life and so to refuse any request to lay down one's life for the state. Indeed, Mendelssohn goes so far as to claim that if one does not believe in immortality of the soul, then one is within one's right and perhaps even obligated "to cause the destruction of the entire world if this can help prolong one's life."[64] But if one recognizes in this extreme circumstance equally opposing moral rights, this creates intolerable confusion in the moral world.[65] For the idea of two contradictory rights is an absurdity, given that the moral law is a law of reason.[66] Hence, moral reason demands belief in the immortality of the soul.[67]

But it is not only moral reason that demands theological beliefs; these beliefs are likewise needed in order to be motivated to act ethically. In his defense of divine providence entitled *God's Cause,* Mendelssohn notes that while people generally recognize that morality is binding, they often notice the suffering of the righteous and the prospering of the wicked, which can cause them to despair of morality. It often seems that righteousness is an impediment to prosperity, because the wicked person who takes moral shortcuts is able to get ahead faster.[68] As such, benevolence can come to be seen as "a foppery into which we seek to lure one another so that the simpleton will toil while the clever man enjoys himself and has a good laugh at the other's expense."[69] While the wise man recognizes that benevolence is a crucial component of perfection and hence is its own reward, most people consider benevolence to be a sacrifice (*Verlust*) that demands compensation.[70] Since they do not see this compensation in this world, they require the belief that this injustice is rectified in the next world to be motivated to act ethically.[71]

But in order for the metaphysical truths of God's existence, providence, and the immortality of the soul to be effective motivators, they must not simply be uttered or defended through reason, they must be presented in sensibly stirring ways.[72] This helps explain Mendelssohn's concern with developing an attractive philosophical style for which he was famous in his day.[73] It is not only philosophy, however, that has an educational task. The purpose of religion is to educate people to convictions that will motivate them to fulfill their moral duties to one another. As such, religion will naturally be inclined to teach metaphysical truths aesthetically.[74] The problem is that aestheticizing religion runs the risk of idolatry.[75] One of the ways the Bible navigates this danger is by representing the divinity using oral, poetic imagery rather than visual images.[76]

MENDELSSOHN ON THE FUNCTION OF BIBLICAL AESTHETICS

While Mendelssohn's discussion of idolatry in *Jerusalem* has been treated frequently, it is worthwhile reviewing a few of its main elements. Mendelssohn's conception of idolatry is grounded in his assumption that idolatry grows from an original, proper conception of God.[77] Idolatry turns on the means used to represent God. Since the function of religion is to transmit metaphysical ideas in emotionally stirring ways, early religious teachers used hieroglyphs and other symbols to represent the deity. The use of these symbols, however, quickly descended into idolatry as people came to fetishize the symbols and superstitiously ascribed to them all sorts of magical, divine powers.[78]

For Mendelssohn, representing God using sensible images is not intrinsically problematic. Following Nachmanides, Mendelssohn adopts an extremely restrictive interpretation of the second commandment, according to which the commandment does not even prohibit the fashioning of idols, let alone visual art in general; it only prohibits the fashioning of idols with the intention of worshipping them.[79]

Mendelssohn interprets Jewish ritual law as a divine means to help Jews acquire living, effective knowledge of metaphysical truths, while avoiding idolatry. For the nature of actions is that they are transitory and as such cannot become objects of worship.[80] There are two ways that halakha transforms abstract metaphysical truths into effective knowledge. First, halakha directs the Jew to the contemplation of metaphysical truths, since ritual laws are correlated with metaphysical truths. Insofar as halakha governs a Jew's daily practice, theological truth is made part of daily living.[81] Second, halakha unites heart and mind through its essentially oral nature. The written law has never been sufficient for practice, but requires oral explanation and the living example of a teacher and a community. The living example helps truth penetrate the heart of the practitioner.[82]

While scholars have noted the educational function of the ritual law for Mendelssohn, they have tended to neglect the fact that biblical poetics serve a similar role for him.[83] Already in *Jerusalem*, Mendelssohn writes that the Bible is a work of "divine beauty" (*göttlichen Schönheit*) that contains an "inexhaustible treasure of rational truths and religious doctrines."[84] Mendelssohn develops his biblical aesthetics, however, only in his Hebrew writings. Central to Mendelssohn's account of biblical aesthetics is his understanding of the unique qualities of Hebrew.

While acknowledging that biblical Hebrew is not a philosophically precise language, Mendelssohn claims that what it lacks in philosophical precision it makes up for in imaginative richness.[85] Following Judah Halevi, Mendelssohn claims that biblical Hebrew is the oral language par excellence, which is able to preserve many of the features of oral communication in writing.[86] Oral communication is superior to written communication because it can convey meaning and arouse emotions through intonation, stresses, and gestures in a way that writing cannot. Biblical Hebrew is able to convey these emotions because Moses transmitted the Pentateuch with special accents (*te'amim*), which serve multiple functions.[87] On the one hand, they are like punctuation marks that indicate questions, emphases, endings, and so forth. But they are superior to conventional punctuation marks insofar as they also help the listener distinguish the different grammatical parts of the verse. For example, in Genesis 4:10 God confronts Cain after his having slain Abel:

Vayomer meh asita	*kol d'mai ahikha*
Then He said: "What	The blood of your brother
have you done?	
tzo'aqim elei	*min ha'adama*
cries out to me	from the ground!

Mendelssohn notes that there is a major pause indicated by the accent *etnahta* under "*asita*" ("have you done"). This indicates that the voice should be raised as a question. But there are likewise minor pauses indicated by the accent *zaqef qaton* under "*ahikha*" ("of your brother") and *tifha* under "*elei*" ("to me") before the verse closes with "*min ha'adama*" ("from the ground"). According to Mendelssohn, these minor pauses indicate different grammatical parts of the verse. "*Kol d'mai ahikha*" ("the blood of your brother") refers to the actor in the verse, "*tzo'aqim elei*" ("cries out to me") refers to the action, while "*min ha'adama*" ("from the ground") refers to the place where the action occurs. By distinguishing these different logical parts of the verse, the accents help "external speech [i.e., the verse] to be aligned to internal speech [i.e., thought] with great perfection."[88]

The accents also aid comprehension insofar as they also serve as musical tropes.[89] These tropes convey various emotions such as "love, hatred, anger, pleasure, warning, vengeance, joy and sadness."[90] While one may state a concept with great precision, if stated without voice modulation, it will remain "as a dish without salt that will not enter the heart of the listener."[91] Music, however, is able to "sweeten an idea like honey, such that its intentions enter the heart like stakes and pegs that are implanted in the hearts of the listeners."[92] By indicating how the verse is to be sung, the accents help the written word preserve the features of oral communication and penetrate the heart.

Mendelssohn's emphasis on the orality of Hebrew is especially evident in his approach to biblical poetry. Mendelssohn contrasts biblical poetry with Greek and Latin poetry. While Greek and Latin poetry are focused primarily on the enjoyment of sounds, the Bible's emphasis is on imprinting understanding on the heart. This explains the fact that while Greek and Latin poetry depend on metrical rules based on the number of long or short syllables or on rhyming, biblical poetry does not. For while meter and rhyming are pleasant to the ear, they are rigid structures that make conveying understanding more difficult. In addition, biblical poetry was designed to be set to music. However, it is very difficult to adapt metered and rhyming poetry to music without changing words around, which frequently distorts the poem's meaning.[93]

Biblical poetry also has a special structure that helps it connect the heart to the mind.[94] Following Azariah de Rossi and Robert Lowth, Mendelssohn claims that biblical poetry consists of short units of words (which modern scholars call "versets") that are parallel to one another. These parallels usually consist of versets that are of similar meaning but use different terms, or of versets that are opposed in meaning but use similar terms, though sometimes the parallel between the versets is only partial.[95] Employing short units is effective in transmitting concepts, for it allows frequent rest periods, giving the audience time to absorb the idea, reflect on its meaning, and remember it. Furthermore, by repeating concepts in different ways, the concept can penetrate the heart more easily, allowing one "to consider the matter on all sides until nothing is unclear or hidden."[96] Typically, versets have two to four components. At times versets with the same number of components follow one another, while at other times versets of differing length alternate with one another.

An example of parallelism adduced by Mendelssohn is Moses' poem in Deuteronomy 32. The parallelism of the first verse is as follows:

Ha'azinu	*Hashamayim*	*V'adabera*
V'tishma	*Ha'aretz*	*Imre-fi*
Listen	O Heavens	And I will speak
Hear	O Earth	The words of my mouth

While recent scholars have questioned the provenance of parallelism in Hebrew poetry and demonstrated the greater complexity in it than was recognized by Mendelssohn, parallelism remains a central concept in the modern study of biblical poetry. Thus James Kugel, one of the strongest recent critics of the emphasis on parallelism in the study of biblical poetry, nevertheless concludes that parallelism "is the most striking characteristic of this style."[97]

Aesthetic considerations also inform Mendelssohn's approach to biblical interpretation in his treatment of the "sublime" (*das Erhabene*), which he calls "the height of perfection in writings."[98] Mendelssohn's conception of the sublime is dependent on his account of beauty. As we have seen, there are three elements that make an object beautiful: (a) the object has to be perceived as a complete whole; (b) it has to be perceived as complex, having many parts that can be taken in all at once; (c) these parts have to be sensed in such a way that one can not distinguish these parts clearly.

Mendelssohn distinguishes between two types of beauty, which we may call "external" and "internal." External beauty refers to objects whose unity in multiplicity is revealed in their sensible form. But one can likewise perceive something as beautiful on account of its inner traits. For example, a person with a lovely face is beautiful in the external sense, while one who is able to unite the powers of her soul according to a unity of moral purpose, intelligence, or artistic vision, is beautiful in the internal sense.[99]

External and internal beauty can come together in the appreciation of a work of art. For example, not only do we take pleasure in appreciating an actual rose, but we likewise take pleasure in appreciating an artistic representation of a rose. Indeed, at times we enjoy the representation more than the object itself. For Mendelssohn this is because in appreciating artistic representations we enjoy a double pleasure. Not only do we enjoy the unity in multiplicity of the represented rose, we also take pleasure in the genius of the artist who is able to integrate the various powers of her soul to create a beautiful object according to a unified vision.[100]

Whereas one experiences beauty when sensing complexity in a unity that one perceives all at once, Mendelssohn notes that there are likewise objects that cannot be perceived as a unity because of their enormity. Such objects he calls "sublime." While the feeling that accompanies perceiving beauty is pleasure, the feeling that accompanies perceiving the sublime is "awe" (*Bewunderung*). Mendelssohn compares the experience of awe to a lightning bolt, which "stops us in our tracks, astounded."[101] Awe is a pleasant fear that we experience when we sense the immensity of the perfection of the object, which we realize is much greater than we can behold.[102]

As with beauty, we can distinguish external from internal sublimity. Externally sublime objects include those that are gigantic in size, such as "the unfathomable sea, a far reaching plain, or the innumerable legion of stars."[103] Internally sublime objects include those that exhibit vast "perfections of spirit," such as an "enormous intellect, enormous and uncommon sensibilities [*Gesinnungen*], a fortunate imagination joined with penetrating sagacity, and noble and passionate emotions that elevate themselves above the conceptions of commoner souls."[104] These two types of sublimity can be united in works of genius that represent sublime objects. In appreciating such works, we experience awe both at the objects represented and at the genius of the creative artist.[105]

There is an intimate relation between the sublime and the simple, or as Mendelssohn calls it, "the naïve."[106] Given the enormity of a sublime subject, if the representation of it is too complex, the observer will become dumbfounded, which will disrupt her feeling of awe. This occurs

with the use of too elaborate similes or excessive embellishment in painting. The most effective way of representing the sublime is through simple
representations in which the discrepancy between the simplicity of the
representation and the enormity of the object represented accent the object's perfection.[107] By not saying too much, the skilled artist is able to
awaken the observer to "think more than what is said to him."[108]

For example, one of the most effective tools for representing the internally sublime is to associate it with an image that is externally sublime,[109]
for "the impressions of the inner sense . . . [are] strengthened if the outer
senses are harmoniously attuned to it by a similar impression."[110] Hence,
the skilled artist can induce a heightened sense of awe by associating the
internally sublime object with a simple, externally sublime object.

Mendelssohn considers the Psalms a stunning example of the use of
sublime imagery.[111] In his 1771 essay "On the Sublime and Naïve in the
Fine Sciences," he discusses Psalms 36: 6–7:

> *YHWH b'hashamayim ḥasdekha, emunatekha ad sheḥaqim*
> *Tzidqatekha k'harerei el, mishpatekha tehom rabba*

> *Herr! Deine Gnade reicht über die Himmel, und deine Wahrheit über die Wolken.*
> *Deine Gerechtigkeit, wie die Berge Gottes, und dein Recht, eine unergründliche Tiefe!*

> Lord! Your grace extends above the heavens, and your truth above the clouds
> Your justice, as mountains of God and your law, an unfathomable depth.[112]

Associating divine justice with mountains conveys the unshakableness of
God's justice, while associating God's grace with the heavens, the abode
of the eternally happy angels, conveys the grandeur of divine love. But by
employing a naïve image obviously inadequate to the concept represented,
the psalmist is able to awaken in his audience a heightened feeling of awe
for God, who exceeds human comprehension.[113] Furthermore, the poetic
skill of the divinely inspired prophet inspires awe at the power of God to
move a person to produce such work of genius. Hence, the Psalms are a
remarkably effective means of instilling an emotionally moving sense of
God's power, wisdom, and goodness, which can in turn spur a person to
ethical action.

In sum, an important context for understanding Mendelssohn's biblical aesthetics is as a response to Spinoza's historical-critical approach to the
Bible. For Spinoza, beauty is a subjective judgment formed by the imagination. Lacking a theory of objective aesthetics, Spinoza interprets biblical
descriptions of God as primitive truth claims about God and nature. The
function of biblical aesthetics is to promote moral/political obedience—
they have no essential connection to truth.

Mendelssohn agrees with Spinoza that a function of biblical aesthetics
is to promote ethical action, but here the agreement ends. Unlike Spinoza,

Mendelssohn considers beauty a sensible representation of an objective perfection, which constitutes a perfection of the soul equal in value to rational perfection. Biblical aesthetics perfect feeling and desire by aligning heart and mind through the use of vivid imagery conveyed by means of the unique oral properties of Hebrew. For Mendelssohn, the metaphysical doctrines contained in the Bible are not just useful in promoting morality, they are true. Like later German-Jewish thinkers, Mendelssohn contrasts Hebraic and Hellenic aesthetics. For Mendelssohn, however, the contrast is not between Hellenic visuality and Hebraic aurality, but rather between alienating Hellenic plastic/dead letter and correlating Hebraic poetic/living script.

CONCLUSION

I have outlined Moses Mendelssohn's biblical aesthetics, indicating how they differ from the Germanophone conception of Jewish aesthetics described by Bland. Since this volume is dedicated to "new trends" in Jewish philosophy, I'd like to conclude with some methodological reflections, which I will set out by way of contrast with Bland.

First, Bland's treatment of Jewish aesthetics implies a normative conception of Judaism. Thus, he assumes a traditional Jewish approach to aesthetics (what he calls the "premodern consensus"), which German-Jewish philosophers distort by employing Romantic notions of poetry to invent the myth of Jewish aniconism. In this respect, Bland's methodological approach is reminiscent of Julius Guttmann's. For according to Guttmann, Judaism at its source is unphilosophical, and Jewish philosophy involves adapting originary Judaism to foreign ideas, which often resulted in the distorting of original Judaism.[114] I, however, do not see Judaism as a tradition with a clear and evident meaning that thinkers disfigure by importing foreign ideas. Rather, I see Judaism as a tradition whose boundaries are constantly being renegotiated. As such, while Mendelssohn's distinction between Hellenic and Hebraic art might have been an innovation alien to prior Jewish thinkers, I would not call this a distortion of some essential Jewish tradition. In this respect, I feel an affinity with Shlomo Pines, who eschewed the idea of normative Judaism or normative Jewish philosophy.[115]

Second, Bland makes clear that his research is guided by the assumption that "ideas and events are rooted in their historical contexts."[116] While I accept this assumption, central to Bland's thesis is his thematizing social and political circumstances, for example, assimilation and anti-Semitism as the catalyst for the development of German-Jewish aesthetics. Explaining the history of Jewish thought in light of social and political circumstances is very prevalent today.[117] While this approach can be illuminating, it can lead to analyzing a thinker primarily in terms of a set of "influences." I, however, strive to understand a thinker holistically. To this end, I seek to demonstrate how seemingly divergent statements reflect an integrated system of thought, and to draw inferences as to the author's views even when they are not explicitly stated. Here I feel an affinity with Harry Wolfson, who in studying a particular thinker set as his task "thinking out their philosophy in all its implications."[118]

Third, Bland claims that understanding the past on its own terms is impossible. As he puts it, postmodern thought has taught us that "the noble dream of neutral disinterested 'objectivity' in history writing has vanished."[119] While Bland does not expressly tackle the implications of this for the study of the past, some contemporary Jewish scholars have taken this recognition as a license to make past thinkers conform to contemporary points of view. Thus, Steven Kepnes has explicitly claimed that the aim of "postmodern Jewish philosophy" should be to adapt Jewish thought to the insights of Postmodernism.[120] I, however, tend to concur with Harry Wolfson's claim that "it is certainly no compliment to a philosopher of the past who is prominent enough for us to study him to say that only by being misunderstood does he become philosophically important."[121] I am, however, less sanguine than Harry Wolfson was about the possibility of understanding the past in a way that is not colored by my own subjectivity. But in my view, this recognition does not contradict the aim of understanding past thinkers on their own terms, but rather it is a means to this end.

In squaring this circle, I draw on methodological reflections that Elliot R. Wolfson has adumbrated in a fascinating recent article. In "Structure, Innovation, and Diremptive Temporality: The Use of Models to Study Continuity and Discontinuity in Kabbalistic Tradition," Wolfson engages the problem of whether kabbalistic thinkers should be studied as unique individuals or by using conceptual paradigms such as ecstatic vs. theosophical; mysticism vs. magic, and so on. While many see these two approaches as utterly opposed, Wolfson views them as complementary. Wolfson's argument is complex and subtle, but among his important insights is that understanding individuality requires imposing conceptual structure. As Wolfson puts it, "The variable [only] becomes apparent through the prism of the constant."[122] In other words, while any concepts used to understand the past will necessarily be imperfect, appreciation of the ways in which past individuals both conform and fail to conform to particular conceptual models is the best way to achieve understanding. The indispensability of using concepts to understand the past is clear from the fact that were we to take the claim that the task of the scholar is to understand the past independently of any conceptualization to its logical conclusion, we would ultimately find nothing to understand. For individuality is itself a concept without which one could never speak of particular thinkers, only of discrete thoughts. Furthermore, Wolfson notes the circularity of the claim that the past can never be understood through conceptual frameworks as this is itself a conceptual assumption applied to the understanding of the past.[123]

Employing Wolfson's insights, I conclude that the dichotomy between the positivist historian who aims at understanding the past "as it really transpired" and the subjectivist historian who claims that there is nothing "outside the text" is a false one. The fact that we approach the past through our subjectivity is not an impediment to understanding the past but rather the very condition for our understanding, for our present subjective concerns provide us with a frame through which to make sense of past thinkers. Assuming that a scholar has the requisite philological and philosophical training, her subjective concerns can then help bring to light new insights that may have eluded scholars who were animated by different concerns.[124]

The deepest insights into the past are achieved, in my view, not by seeing the ways in which the past *fits* our familiar conceptual frameworks, but rather by seeing how it diverges from these frameworks. The task of the historian of Jewish philosophy is neither to understand the past "objectively" (whatever this might mean), nor to restate what we already know in different terms. Rather, the aim is to use her subjectivity to illuminate aspects of the past not noticed by previous scholars with the hope of breaking open new horizons for understanding the past that offer new possibilities for understanding the present.

NOTES

1. See Elliot R. Wolfson, *Through a Speculum That Shines: Vision and Imagination in Medieval Jewish Mysticism* (Princeton, N.J.: Princeton University Press, 1994), 3–5, 13–16, 393–95; Kalman P. Bland, *The Artless Jew: Medieval and Modern Affirmations and Denials of the Visual* (Princeton, N.J.: Princeton University Press, 1999), 3–4, 13–15. For examples of authors who employ this typical contrast, see the sources quoted in Wolfson, *Through a Speculum*, 13, especially, Erich Auerbach, *Mimesis: The Representation of Reality in Western Literature* (Princeton, N.J.: Princeton University Press, 1953), 3–23; Walter Ong, *The Presence of the Word* (Minneapolis: Minnesota University Press, 1967), 3, 179–91; Martin Buber, *Darko shel Hamiqra* (Jerusalem: Mossad Bialik, 1978), 41–58.

2. See Exodus 20:3; Deuteronomy 5:8.

3. See E. R. Wolfson, *Through a Speculum*, 394.

4. Ibid., 7–8, 324

5. See Exodus 33:20; Deuteronomy 4:12, 15.

6. See E. R. Wolfson, *Through a Speculum,* 7–8, 181, 207. Aaron W. Hughes shows how a similar approach animates medieval Jewish Neoplatonists, who see terrestrial beauty as a means of attaining knowledge of the divine despite the inadequacy of these images. As beauty is perceived through the imagination, the imagination is "primarily hermeneutical . . . mak[ing] the incorporeal corporeal and . . . giv[ing] the formless form." See Hughes, *The Texture of the Divine: Imagination in Medieval Islamic and Jewish Thought* (Bloomington: Indiana University Press, 2004), 113, 147, 160.

7. See Moshe Barasch, *Icons: Studies in the History of an Idea* (New York: New York University Press, 1992), 13, 15–18 cited in Bland, *Artless Jew,* 59–60.

8. Ibid., 5, 14–16.

9. Ibid., 16, 20.

10. I explore these issues in my forthcoming book, *Faith and Freedom: Moses Mendelssohn's Theological-Political Thought* (New York: Oxford University Press, 2010).

11. Spinoza's approach to the Bible cannot be seen as an attack on biblical authority *in toto,* since he seeks to preserve biblical authority in the ethical sphere. See Michah Gottlieb, "Spinoza's Method(s) of Biblical Interpretation Reconsidered," *Jewish Studies Quarterly* 14 (2007): 286–317. Mendelssohn's difficulties with Spinoza's conclusions in the *Tractatus Theologico-Politicus* are multifaceted. Spinoza's rejection of Jewish chosenness and the authority of ritual law especially disturbed him. For the purposes of this paper, I focus on issues directly related to Spinoza's method of biblical interpretation. For detailed discussion of some of the other issues, see my forthcoming *Faith and Freedom,* chapter 2.

12. See Baruch Spinoza, *Tractatus Theologico-Politicus,* in *Spinoza Opera,* edited by Carl Gebhardt, vol. 3 (Heidelberg: Carl Winters, 1925), 15–44, 97–117 (henceforth: *TTP*); *Theological-Political Treatise,* edited and translated by Samuel Shirley (Indianapolis, Ind.: Hackett, 2001), 9–34, 86–104 (henceforth: *TPT*).

13. See Spinoza, *TTP,* 29–44, 70; *TPT,* 21–34, 60.

14. A second element of Spinoza's approach to the Bible that Mendelssohn found troubling was Spinoza's questioning the origin and integrity of the Masoretic Text and his mocking rabbinic interpretation. Edward Breuer has dealt with some of these issues in *The Limits of Enlightenment: Jews, Germans, and the Eighteenth Century Study of Scripture* (Cambridge, Mass.: Harvard University Press, 1996). I have some things to add to Breuer's excellent work on this subject, but I leave it to another occasion.

15. Most scholars assume that Mendelssohn read the *TTP* carefully. See Julius Guttmann, "Mendelssohn's *Jerusalem* and Spinoza's *Theological-Political Treatise,*" in *Studies in Jewish Thought,* edited by Alfred Jospe (Detroit, Mich.: Wayne State University Press, 1981), 361–86; Michael Morgan, "History and Modern Jewish Thought: Spinoza and Mendelssohn on the Ritual Law," *Judaism* 30, no. 4 (1981): 467–78; Ze'ev Levy, *Baruch Spinoza-Seine Aufnahme durch die jüdischen Denker in Deutschland* (Berlin: Verlag W. Kohlhammer, 2001), 31–58. Friedrich Niewöhner, however, challenges this prevailing assumption, claiming that Mendelssohn had no firsthand knowledge of the *TTP* ("'Es hat nicht jeder das Zeug zu einem Spinoza' Mendelssohn als Philosoph des Judentums," in *Moses Mendelssohn und die Kreise Seiner Wirksamkeit,* edited by M. Albrecht and E. Engel, N. Hinske [Tübingen: Max Niemeyer, 1994], 291–314). For our purposes, it is not important to decide this issue.

16. In the fourth fragment, published by Lessing in 1777, Reimarus argues that the Bible does not conform with reason as evidenced by its failure to teach rational doctrines such as the immortality of the soul, reward and punishment in a future life, and the union of pious souls with God. See *Gotthold Ephraism Lessing Werke,* ed-

ited by Wilfried Barner et al. (Frankfurt am Main: Deutscher Klassiker Verlag, 1989), 8:246–47 (henceforth: Lessing, *Werke*). Mendelssohn is clearly familiar with the Reimarus Fragments because Lessing showed him the entire manuscript in 1770, some seven years before he published them. See Alexander Altmann, *Moses Mendelssohn: A Biographical Study* (London: Littmann, 1998), 254–56. In Lessing's fourth "Counterpropositions" to the Reimarus Fragments, Lessing goes even further, noting that the Old Testament does not teach monotheism or the immortality of the soul. The Jews only developed these doctrines when they encountered philosophically informed nations while in Babylonian captivity (586–516 BCE). See Lessing, *Werke*, 8:328–30; Gotthold Ephraim Lessing, *Philosophical and Theological Writings*, translated and edited by H. Nisbet (Cambridge: Cambridge University Press, 2005), 75–77 (henceforth: *Philosophy and Theological Writings*). See also Lessing's *Education of the Human Race*, part of which he appended to the fourth "Counterproposition" and which he published in full in 1780, Lessing, *Werke*, 10:75–88; *Philosophical and Theological Writings*, 218–31. According to Julius Guttmann, Reimarus's critique of the biblical prophets is drawn indirectly from Spinoza by means of the English Deists William Warburton and Thomas Morgan. See Guttmann, *Religion and Knowledge* (Jerusalem: Magnes, 1979), 224 n. 3 (in Hebrew).

17. See Lessing, *Werke*, 10:88, #55; *Philosophical and Theological Writings*, 230, #51.

18. On the centrality of *peshat* for Mendelssohn, see Moses Mendelssohn, *Gesammelte Schriften Jubiläumsausgabe*, edited by Ismar Elbogen, Julius Guttmann, Eugen Mittwoch, and Alexander Altmann (Stuttgart-Band Cannstatt: F. Frommann, 1971), 14:244–45 (henceforth: Mendelssohn, *JubA*). On Mendelssohn's emphasis on the necessity of knowing Hebrew grammar for understanding *peshat*, see Mendelssohn, *JubA*, 14:249–67. On the importance of knowing historical context for understanding *peshat*, see Mendelssohn, *JubA*, 7:95, 304; 12.2, 22; 16:58–59; 18:133. See David Sorkin, *Moses Mendelssohn and the Religious Enlightenment* (Berkeley: University of California Press, 1996), 65–87.

19. James Morrison notes that Spinoza's writings "contain only a few brief and scattered remarks about art and beauty" and that Spinoza was "fundamentally alien, even hostile towards art and beauty" ("Why Spinoza Had No Aesthetics" *Journal of Aesthetics and Art Criticism* 47 [1989]: 359–65). The critique that Spinoza has an inadequate theory of aesthetics goes back to Leibniz. See Filippio Mignini, "Le problème de l'esthétique a la lumière de quelques interpretations de Leibniz à Hegel," in *Spinoza: Entre Lumière et Romantisme*, edited by J. Bonnamour (Fontenay: École Normale Supérieure, 1985), 123–42; Lee Rice, "Spinoza's Relativistic Aesthetics," *Tijdschrift voor Philosophie* 58, no. 3 (1996): 476–89. Rice presents a more positive reading of Spinoza's attitude toward aesthetics.

20. See Baruch Spinoza, *Tractatus de Intellectus Emendatione*, in *Spinoza Opera*, edited by C. Gebhardt, vol. 2 (Heidelberg: Carl Winters, 1925), 8 (henceforth: *TIE*); English translation: *Treatise on the Emendation of the Intellect* in *The Collected Works of Spinoza*, translated and edited by Edwin Curley (Princeton: Princeton University Press, 1985), 1:10 (henceforth: *TEI*); Spinoza, *TTP*, vol. 2, 59–60; *TPT*, 49–50.

21. See Spinoza, *Ethica*, in *Spinoza Opera*, Appendix to Part I, vol. 2, 81–82 (henceforth: Spinoza, *Ethica*. In referencing particular passages in the *Ethica*, I will use the following standard abbreviations: E= *Ethica*, followed by the part number; D=definition; A=axiom; P=proposition; C=corollary; S=scholium); English translation: *Ethics* in *The Collected Works of Spinoza*, 1:444 (henceforth: Spinoza, *Ethics*); Baruch Spinoza, *Complete Works*, translated by Samuel Shirley and edited by Michael Morgan (Indianapolis, Ind.: Hackett, 2002), letter 32, 848; letter 54, 899.

22. See Spinoza, *Ethica*, 82; *Ethics*, Appendix to Part I, 445; Spinoza, Letters in *Complete Works*, letter 54, 899 (henceforth: *Letters*). This is likewise evident in Spinoza's account of the medicinal value of art. See *Ethica*, EIVP45C2S, II:244–45; *Ethics*, 572. In the preface to Part IV of the *Ethics*, Spinoza gives the example of music, which he writes is good for one who is experiencing melancholy, and bad for one who is in mourning. See ibid, EIV, preface, II:208; *Ethics*, 545. Note that Shirley translates the term *valetudo*, not as "health" but as "well-being."

23. See Spinoza, *Ethica*, 81–83; *Ethics*, 444–45. It is important to consider how this fits with Spinoza's claim that one may use an "exemplar" of human nature as a model for human perfection. See Spinoza, *Ethica*, 208; *Ethics*, preface to Part IV, 545. If one can find certain things that promote health in people generally, it may be possible to form a notion of "objective" beauty in the sense of intersubjective agreement. Lee Rice tries to offer such a reconstruction of Spinoza's position in "Spinoza's Relativistic Aesthetics," *Tijdschrift voor Philosophie* 58, no. 3 (1996): 481–89.

24. Spinoza, *Ethica*, 2:77–83; *Ethics*, Appendix to Part I, 439–46. Given that human beings are part of nature, Spinoza would appear to level the difference between the natural and the artificial such that there can be neither natural nor artificial beauty. See Spinoza, *TTP*, 3:57–58; *TPT*, 48. However, there is an important scholarly debate over whether or not Spinoza allows final causality in respect to human beings. See Edwin Curley, "On Bennett's Spinoza: The Issue of Teleology," and Jonathan Bennett, "Spinoza and Teleology: A Reply to Curley," in *Spinoza Issues and Directions*, edited by Edwin Curley and Pierre François Moreau (Leiden: Brill, 1990), 39–53 and 53–57, respectively; For further discussion, see Michael Della Rocca, "Spinoza's Metaphysical Psychology," in *The Cambridge Companion to Spinoza*, edited by Don Garrett (Cambridge: Cambridge University Press, 1996), 252–57.

25. See Spinoza, *Letters*, letter 54, 899.

26. See Spinoza, *Ethica*, IID6, 2:85; *Ethics*, 447; Spinoza, *Descartes' Principles of Philosophy*, in *Collected Works of Spinoza*, Proposition 6, Lemma 1, Note 2, vol. 1, 251–52. But see Spinoza, *Ethica*, 2:208–209; *Ethics*, preface to Part IV, 545–46.

27. Shlomo Pines points out that in the *TTP* Spinoza's casts the imagination and intellect as opposed faculties. Unlike Maimonides, who thinks that the imagination can be brought under the dominion of the intellect, for Spinoza these faculties are so opposed that they exclude one another. So if the prophets possess lively imaginations, they cannot also have possessed perfected intellects. While overtly opposed to Maimonides, Pines points out that Spinoza could have drawn the conclusion that the prophets were not philosophers from an esoteric interpretation of Maimonides' *Guide of the Perplexed*, part II, chapter 29, and Pines notes how Spinoza was preceded in his view of the prophets by the 14th-century Spanish Jewish philosopher Isaac Pulgar in his dialogue *Ezer ha-Dat*. See Pines, "Spinoza's *Tractatus Theologico-Politicus* and the Jewish Philosophical Tradition," in *Studies in the History of Jewish Thought*, edited by W. Z. Harvey and M. Idel (Jerusalem: Magnes Press, 1997), 5:712–16. Aaron W. Hughes points out that in *Ezer ha-Dat*, Pulgar puts the view doubting the prophets' intellectual capacities in the mouth of a young man, and Hughes questions Pines's identification of the views of the young man with Pulgar's own. See Hughes, *The Art of Dialogue in Jewish Philosophy* (Bloomington: Indiana University Press, 2008), 92–98, 193 n. 86. For further discussion of the problem of prophetic error in medieval Jewish philosophy, see Charles Touati, "Le problème de l'inerrance prophétique dans la théologie juive du moyen âge," *Revue de l'Histoire des Religions* 174 (1968): 169–87. It is important to note that in the *Ethics* Spinoza does not cast the imagination and intellect as opposed to one another as he does in the *Tractatus*. See Gilles Deleuze, "Spinoza and the Three Ethics,"

in *The New Spinoza,* edited by Warren Montag and Ted Stolze (Minneapolis: University of Minnesota Press, 1997), 21–34; Edwin Curley, "Experience in Spinoza's Theory of Knowledge," in *Spinoza: A Collection of Critical Essays,* edited by Marjorie Grene (Garden City, N.Y.: Doubleday/Anchor Press, 1973), 35–59.

28. Spinoza does allow certain exceptions including Solomon, Paul, and Jesus. See Spinoza, *TTP,* 29, 41, 66–68; *TPT,* 27, 31, 56–57.

29. On role of Bible in promoting morality, see Gottlieb, "Spinoza's Method(s) of Biblical Interpretation Reconsidered," 307–16.

30. See Lewis White Beck, *Early German Philosophy* (Bristol: Thoemmes, 1996), 326; Ernst Cassirer, "Die Philosophie Moses Mendelssohn," in *Moses Mendelssohn zur 200 Jährigen Wiederkehr sense Geburtstages* (Berlin: Lambert Schneider, 1929), 55; Frederick Beiser, *Diotima's Children: German Aesthetic Rationalism from Leibniz to Lessing* (Oxford: Oxford University Press, 2010).

31. My understanding of Mendelssohn's aesthetics has been greatly advanced by Frederick Beiser's discussion in *Diotima's Children,* chap. 7.

32. See Mendelssohn, *JubA,* 3.2, 59–66, 69–71. Throughout his career, Mendelssohn speaks of three basic capacities, though his terminology changes. In a short piece from 1776, Mendelssohn divides the soul into the capacity for knowledge (*Erkentnisvermögen*), the capacity for feeling (*Empfindungsvermögen*), and the capacity for desire (*Begehrungsvermögen*). See Mendelssohn, *JubA,* 3.1, 276–77. In his 1763 *Treatise on Evidence,* he distinguishes between reason (*Vernunft*), sense and imagination (*Sinne und Einbildungskraft*), and inclination and desire (*Neigungen und Leidenschaften*). See Mendelssohn, *JubA,* 2:326. For a trenchant analysis of Mendelssohn's so-called "three-faculty theory" of the soul, see Beiser, *Diotima's Children,* chap. 7.

33. See Mendelssohn, *JubA,* 1:325–26; Mendelssohn, *Philosophical Writings,* edited by D. Dahlstrom (Cambridge: Cambridge University Press, 1997), 90–91 (henceforth: *Philosophical Writings*).

34. Mendelssohn, *JubA,* 6.1, 115; *Philosophical Writings,* 313–14.

35. Mendelssohn, *JubA,* 6.1, 115; *Philosophical Writings,* 313.

36. Mendelssohn, *JubA,* 3.2, 66; Alexander Altmann, "Mendelssohn on Education and the Image of Man," in *Studies in Jewish Thought,* edited by Alfred Jospe (Detroit, Mich.: Wayne State University Press, 1981), 399. See Mendelssohn, *JubA,* 15.2, 23–24.

37. Mendelssohn, *JubA,* 1:431; *Philosophical Writings,* 172.

38. See Bertrand Russell, *The Philosophy of Leibniz* (London: Routledge, 1997), 168.

39. See Mendelssohn, *JubA* 1:325–26; *Philosophical Writings,* 90–91.

40. Ibid.

41. Mendelssohn, *JubA,* 1:251–53: *Philosophical Writings,* 23–24.

42. See Mendelssohn, *JubA,* 15.2, 23–24.

43. See Mendelssohn, *JubA,* 3:1, 276–77; *Philosophical Writings,* 309–10. Mendelssohn's doctrine of human perfection forms an important contrast with that of his great medieval predecessor Maimonides and explains a difference in their respective approaches to beauty. Like Mendelssohn, Maimonides posits different faculties of the soul. But while Mendelssohn's conception of perfection is egalitarian, with each faculty having equal dignity and no perfection being subservient to another, for Maimonides these perfections are arranged hierarchically, with the *telos* of human existence being philosophical contemplation of God through the faculty of reason. In consequence, unlike Mendelssohn, for whom appreciation of beauty is an independent perfection on par with intellectual perfection, for Maimonides appreciation of beauty is of merely instrumental value, settling the individual's disposition to prepare

him for intellectual perfection. See Maimonides, "Eight Chapters," chapter 5 in Moses Maimonides, *Ethical Writings of Maimonides,* edited by Raymond Weiss and Charles Butterworth (New York: Dover, 1975), 75. In stressing its instrumental function, Maimonides' understanding of beauty resembles Spinoza's. The main difference between Spinoza and Maimonides is that for Maimonides imagination can be perfected and be brought under the dominion of the intellect and so transmit rational truths in sensible forms, which is what happens in prophecy. In contrast, at least in the *TTP,* Spinoza casts imagination as so opposed to intellect that it cannot be brought under its control and thus generally errs. See Spinoza, *TTP,* chaps. 1–2; Maimonides, *Guide,* II, 32. But see *Guide,* I, 73 where Maimonides describes imagination as the "contrary" of reason and see note 31 above. For further discussion of the role of imagination in prophecy for Maimonides and the contrast with Mendelssohn's account of prophecy, see note 78 below.

44. See note 29.

45. See *JubA,* 3.2, 68.

46. See Beiser, *Diotima's Children.*

47. See Mendelssohn, *JubA,* 1:271–75, 287–303; *Philosophical Writings,* 39–43, 55–70.

48. See Mendelssohn, *JubA* 1:268–69, 274–75, 290–91, 305–309, 383–97; *Philosophical Writings,* 36–37, 42–43, 58, 72–75, 131–44, 173–74.

49. See Plato, *Protagoras,* in *The Collected Dialogues of Plato,* edited by Edith Hamilton and Huntington Cairns (Princeton, N.J.: Princeton University Press, 1994, 344–48 (352a–357e of the standard pagination of Plato's works); Mendelssohn, *JubA,* 1:257, 260, 304–5, 412; *Philosophical Writings,* 28, 30, 71, 158.

50. See Altmann, "Mendelssohn on Education and the Image of Man," 394–401; Beiser, *Diotima's Children.*

51. Mendelssohn, *JubA,* 1:413; *Philosophical Writings,* 159; *JubA,* 2:326; *Philosophical Writings,* 304.

52. Mendelssohn, *JubA,* 1:414–15; *Philosophical Writings,* 160. Cf. *JubA* 2:327–28; *Philosophical Writings,* 305–6; Alexander Altmann, *Moses Mendelssohns Frühschriften Zur Metaphysik* (Tübingen: Mohr-Siebeck, 1969), 383–91; Mendelssohn, *JubA,* 8:112–13; *Jerusalem,* 42–43.

53. Mendelssohn, *JubA,* 1:416; *Philosophical Writings,* 161.

54. See Mendelssohn, *JubA,* 1:437; *Philosophical Writings,* 178.

55. This understanding of aesthetics is reflected in Mendelssohn's account of Adam's sin in the Garden of Eden. Like Maimonides, Mendelssohn takes prelapsarian Adam to reflect the ideal human state. But while Maimonides sees Adam's eating from the Tree of Knowledge of Good and Evil as his turning from his intellectual contemplation of the true and false to involvement with the imaginative fine and bad, Mendelssohn thinks that good and evil are intelligibles. Adam's ideal state was one of harmony between his powers of intellect (*koah ha-sekhel; Erkenntnissvermögen*), desire (*koah ha-teshuqah; Begehrungsvermögen*) and feeling (*koah ha-hush; Empfindungsvermögen*). He was perfect when he knew the good intellectually, felt it aesthetically as beautiful, and desired it. Adam's sin came about when the power of desire was severed from the true good by being overly strengthened and his thereby becoming drawn to apparent goods. See Mendelssohn, *JubA,* 15.2, 23–24. Zeev Harvey traces Mendelssohn's theory of the harmonious balance of faculties to Plato and Judah Halevi. See Harvey, "Mendelssohn and Maimon on the Tree of Knowledge," in *Sepharad in Ashkenaz,* edited by Irene Zwiep, Andrea Schatz, and Resianne Smidt van Gelder-Fontaine (Amsterdam: Edita, 2007), 185–89.

56. See Mendelssohn, *JubA*, 1:423; *Philosophical Writings*, 166–67. Compare *JubA*, 2:327–28; *Philosophical Writings*, 305–306; *JubA* 14, Commentary to *Ecclesiastes* 12:10, 206; *JubA* 14:76. Also compare Mendelssohn's essay, "What is Enlightenment?" where he writes that enlightenment is related to culture as theory to practice. See Mendelssohn, *JubA*, 6.1, 115; *Philosophical Writings*, 314. Also see *JubA*, 1:427–28; *Philosophical Writings*, 169–70. For discussion, see Beiser, *Diotima's Children*.

57. Mendelssohn, *JubA*, 8:131; *Jerusalem*, 63. In his "Counter-Reflexions," Mendelssohn enumerates three principles of Judaism: God's existence, divine Providence, and divine revelation of the Law. See Mendelssohn, *JubA*, 7:95.

58. See Mendelssohn, *JubA*, 2:315–30; *Philosophical Writings*, 295–310; *JubA*, 19:178–79; 15:2, Commentary to Genesis 2:9, 23–24.

59. Ibid.

60. Mendelssohn, *JubA*, 2:316; *Philosophical Writings*, 296.

61. Mendelssohn, *JubA*, 1:405–408; *Philosophical Writings*, 151–54; *JubA*, 2:316–17; *Philosophical Writings*, 296–97.

62. See Mendelssohn, *JubA*, 8:109, 116; *Jerusalem*, 40, 47; *JubA*, 15:2, Commentary to Genesis 2:18, "lo tov," 26.

63. Mendelssohn, *JubA*, 3.1, 116.

64. Mendelssohn, *JubA*, 3.1, 117; *JubA*, 1:295–96; *Philosophical Writings*, 61–63.

65. Mendelssohn, *JubA*, 3.1, 117.

66. See Mendelssohn, *JubA* 8:115; *Jerusalem*, 46.

67. In the introduction to the *Phädon*, Mendelssohn notes that this argument for the immortality of the soul is completely original. But while the argument can be elaborated by means of the strictest logic, Mendelssohn admits that in the *Phädon*, he presents it in a more popular, less rigorous way. In particular, Mendelssohn does not explain the philosophical basis of our moral obligations. He also does not philosophically deduce the state's right to demand that we sacrifice our lives in times of danger. A number of questions arise from Mendelssohn's presentation. Assuming that one does not believe in the immortality of the soul and that one's life in this world is the highest good, is there a moral obligation to enter society, given its right to demand that one sacrifice one's life? If there is no such obligation, is one created if one decides to enter society anyway?

68. See Mendelssohn, *JubA*, 14, Commentary to *Ecclesiastes* 9:10, 193.

69. Mendelssohn, *JubA*, 8:131; *Jerusalem*, 63; *JubA*, 14, Commentary to *Ecclesiastes* 9:10, 193.

70. See Mendelssohn, *JubA*, 3.2, 236–40. On the idea of benevolence as its own reward, see *JubA*, 8:111, 116; *Jerusalem*, 41, 47; *JubA* 6.1, 38, 47; *JubA*, 1:405–8; *Philosophical Writings*, 151–54.

71. See Mendelssohn, *JubA*, 3.2, 236–40.

72. At the end of the *Treatise on Evidence*, however, Mendelssohn does consider the possibility of a "fortunate genius" (*glückliche Genie*), who can be motivated by reason alone. See Mendelssohn, *JubA*, 2:329. For some reason, Dahlstrom does not translate this passage.

73. See Aaron W. Hughes's discussion of the literary style of Mendelssohn's *Phädon* in *The Art of Dialogue in Jewish Philosophy*, 138–66, esp. 153–55. Mendelssohn used the form of epistolary exchange in his 1755 *On Sentiments* (*Über die Empfindungen*). In addition to using the dialogue form in his 1767 *Phädon*, he used the dialogue form in his 1754 *Philosophical Dialogues* (*Philosophische Gespräche*) and in lectures 4, 14, and 15 of the 1785 *Morning Hours* (*Morgenstunden*).

74. Mendelssohn, *JubA*, 8:109–10; *Jerusalem*, 40–41. At first glance, Mendels-

sohn's account of the role of aesthetics in religion seems to have a deep affinity to Maimonides' account. Maimonides notes that the prophet must have a perfected imagination, through which he teaches metaphysical truths using parables and vivid imagery. So, like Mendelssohn, Maimonides holds that one function of prophecy is to present metaphysical truths aesthetically. But there are crucial differences between Maimonides and Mendelssohn on this score. For Maimonides, the aesthetic presentation of religious truth serves a cognitive as well as a moral/political function. On the cognitive level, the prophet uses imaginative imagery to transmit truths to the masses who would not attain this knowledge on their own. For example, Maimonides explains that the Bible describes God as having a body, because the masses imagine that only something physical can exist. However, once people are convinced that God exists, they are instructed that the terms indicating that God has a body have secondary meanings, which do not imply corporeality. So *ayin*, the term used for God's eye, can also mean "providence." See Maimonides, *Guide*, I:26, 44. On the moral/political level, the prophet uses imagery to transmit ideas about the divinity that foster obedience even though such ideas may be false. For example, the Bible often portrays God as getting violently angry with sinners, which Maimonides admits is philosophically untrue though politically useful. See *Guide*, III:28. So for Maimonides, religious aesthetics are needed to guide the masses, who are under the spell of the imagination; whereas for the philosopher, who is guided by intellect, they are unnecessary. In contrast, Mendelssohn thinks that the masses can attain true knowledge of God on their own through common sense and that this knowledge can motivate moral action. The function of aesthetic presentations of religious truth is to put the heart and mind in harmony. This, however, is something needed by all people, philosophers and common people alike. Hence, Mendelssohn's understanding of the role of aesthetics in religion is more egalitarian, blunting the elitist edge present in Maimonides' account.

75. See Mendelssohn, *JubA*, 8:173–91; *Jerusalem*, 107–25.

76. For a trenchant comparison between Maimonides and Mendelssohn's accounts of idolatry, see Lawrence Kaplan, "Maimonides and Mendelssohn on the Origins of Idolatry," in *Perspectives on Jewish Thought and Mysticism*, edited by A. Ivry, E. R. Wolfson, and A. Arkush (New York: Harwood, 1998), 423–56. For Mendelssohn's account of the role of common sense in religion, see Mendelssohn, *JubA*, 3.2, 33–34, 51–52, 80–83, 197–99; vol. 12.1, 148–51; vol. 12.2, 185–86.

77. Mendelssohn, *JubA*, 16:186; 8:179–82; *Jerusalem*, 113–16. See Lawrence Kaplan, "Maimonides and Mendelssohn on the Origins of Idolatry," 430–31; Michael Stanislawski, ""Towards an Analysis of the *Bi'ur* as Exegesis," in *Neti'ot Ledavid*, edited by Y. Elman, E. Halivni, and Z. Steinfeld (Jerusalem: Orhot, 2004), 144–52.

78. See Mendelssohn, *JubA*, 8:176–83; *Jerusalem*, 110–17; *JubA*, 16, Commentary on Exodus 32:4, 329.

79. See Mendelssohn, *JubA*, 6, Commentary on Exodus 20:4, 189. Compare Nachmanides on Exodus 20:3. While both Nachmanides and Mendelssohn do not see the second commandment as a general prohibition on fashioning idols, they do see such a general prohibition in Exodus 20:20, 34:17 and Leviticus 26:1. According to Mendelssohn, God only ordained the more general prohibition after the sin of the golden calf. See Mendelssohn, *JubA*, 16, Commentary on Exodus 34:17, 354.

80. Of course, rituals can become fetishized, a problem that Mendelssohn does not explicitly address in *Jerusalem*.

81. Mendelssohn, *JubA*, 8:84–185; *Jerusalem*, 118–19. For some recent interpretations of how halakha connects doctrine and life according to Mendelssohn, see Michael Morgan, "History and Modern Jewish Thought: Spinoza and Mendelssohn

on the Ritual Law," *Judaism* 30:4 (1981): 467–78; Arnold Eisen, "Divine Legislation as 'Ceremonial Script': Mendelssohn on the Commandments," *AJS Review* 15, no. 2 (1990): 239–68; Arkush, *Moses Mendelssohn and the Enlightenment,* 207–21.

82. Mendelssohn, *JubA,* 8:168–70; 184–85, 192–93; *Jerusalem,* 102–4, 118–19, 127–28.

83. I would suggest that part of the reason for this general neglect is the hackneyed slogan that Mendelssohn holds that laws can be revealed, but not doctrines. Recently, Allan Arkush has shown how problematic this view is. Arkush points out that in his "Counter-Reflexions" Mendelssohn writes that "the book of Job . . . the Psalms of David, all the prophets and all the Talmudic books" contain the doctrines of divine providence and immortality of the soul. And in *Jerusalem* itself, Mendelssohn makes clear that while pagans often cast God as malicious and angry, God revealed his merciful attributes to Moses. Arkush does, however, think that Mendelssohn at times claims that Judaism knows no revealed doctrines. In light of this contradiction, Arkush considers Mendelssohn's claim that Judaism knows no revealed doctrines to be a rhetorical slogan that derived from Mendelssohn's recognition that Judaism did not conform to natural religion. By using this slogan, Mendelssohn was able to sidestep contradictions between natural religion and Judaism. See Arkush, *Moses Mendelssohn and the Enlightenment,* 181–85.

Lawrence Kaplan does not see a contradiction in Mendelssohn. He notes that that in a key passage in *Jerusalem,* Mendelssohn writes that Judaism "knows of no *exclusive* (*ausschließenden*) revelation of eternal truths that are indispensable to salvation" (emphasis Mendelssohn's). According to Kaplan, Mendelssohn holds that while there are "no revealed Scriptural doctrines forced upon our belief, i.e., that we are commanded to believe, there certainly are revealed doctrines . . . presented to our understanding, i.e., that are commended to our knowledge." See Kaplan, "Maimonides and Mendelssohn on the Origins of Idolatry," 451 n. 31; see Mendelssohn, *JubA,* 8:164; *Jerusalem,* 97.

84. Mendelssohn, *JubA,* 8:166; *Jerusalem,* 99.

85. Nicolai, *Über meine gelehrte Bildung.* This text is quoted in full in Hermann Meyer, *Moses Mendelssohn Bibliographie* (Berlin: Walter de Gruyter, 1965), 113.

86. See Judah Halevi, *Kuzari,* translated by Hartwig Hirschfeld (New York: Schocken, 1964), 126–27 (part 2, par. 72). Indeed, it is significant that when discussing his method of biblical interpretation, Mendelssohn compares the style of the Bible to the way the "natural speaker" (*hamedaber hativ'i*) communicates. See Mendelssohn, *JubA,* 14:148–51.

87. On Mendelssohn's use of the accents in his biblical interpretation, see Edward Levenson, "Moses Mendelssohn's Understanding of Logico-Grammatical and Literary Construction in the Pentateuch" (Ph.D. diss., Brandeis University, 1972), 1–64. In his unfinished *Hebrew Grammar,* Spinoza says that he originally adhered to Halevi's view that the accents indicate emotions, which allow the written text to preserve the features of oral communication. But Spinoza tells us that on further reflection he decided that this was not true, since the accents frequently confuse the text. For example, the accents fail to indicate when a text is ironic or simple, and the same accent can be used to indicate "a period, a semicolon, and a colon." Spinoza thus concludes that the accents were actually a late invention of the Pharisees, who introduced them simply to prevent the Bible from being read too quickly in public. See Baruch Spinoza, *Compendium Grammatices Linguae Hebraeae,* in *Spinoza Opera,* edited by Carl Gebhardt (Heidelberg: Carl Winters, 1987), 5:8–10; *Hebrew Grammar,* in *Complete Works,* chap. 4, 594–95 (henceforth: *HG*). I have emended the English translation.

88. See Mendelssohn, *JubA*, 14:217. Compare Spinoza's discussion of this issue in Spinoza, *HG*, 595–99.

89. Mendelssohn, *JubA*, 14:217.

90. Ibid., 218.

91. Ibid., 217.

92. Ibid., 218.

93. See Mendelssohn, *JubA*, 16:125–28; 1:445–47; *Philosophical Writings*, 185–87. See Judah Halevi, *Kuzari*, 125–27 (part II, par. 70–74).

94. Mendelssohn, *JubA*, 16:126.

95. See *JubA*, 15.2, Commentary on Genesis 4:23, 46–49. This threefold classification of parallelism reflects Lowth's distinction between "synonymous," "antithetical," and "synthetic" parallelism. See Robert Lowth, *Lectures on the Sacred Poetry of the Hebrews*, translated by G. Gregory (London: J. Johnson, 1787), 2:24–59. Lowth's work was originally published in 1753 as *De Sacra Poesi Hebraeorum*, and Mendelssohn published a lengthy, glowing review of it in 1757. See Mendelssohn, *JubA*, 4:20–62. In a Hebrew letter from Mendelssohn to Lowth dated 26 April 1781 that Mendelssohn enclosed with a copy of his *Bi'ur* to Genesis and Exodus, Mendelssohn addresses Lowth as a "prince of Torah and wisdom (*sar hatorah v'hahokhma*)" and he thanks Lowth for his writings on biblical poetry, which were like "good wine to my palate." See Mendelssohn, *JubA*, 19:274. Recent scholars have challenged Lowth's classification. Thus, J. P. Fokkelman notes that "synthetic" parallelism is "a basket term that covers everything that cannot be called synonymous or contrasting" and as such is "a counsel of despair . . . which strikes at the root of the entire triadic structure." See Fokkelman, *Reading Biblical Poetry: An Introductory Guide*, translated by Ineke Smit (Louisville, Ky.: Westminster John Knox, 2001), 26.

96. Mendelssohn, *JubA*, 16:126. In his aesthetic writings, Mendelssohn notes that a similar effect can be achieved by using "unfinished sentences, interrupted references, or monosyllabic words." See Mendelssohn, *JubA*, 1:465–66; *Philosophical Writings*, 202–204.

97. See James Kugel, *The Idea of Biblical Poetry: Parallelism and Its History* (New Haven, Conn.: Yale University Press, 1981), 51. On parallelism, see Robert Alter, *The Art of Biblical Poetry* (New York: Basic Books, 1985) 3–27; J. P. Fokkelman, *Reading Biblical Poetry*, 15–36, 61–87.

98. Mendelssohn, *JubA*, 1:455; *Philosophical Writings*, 192.

99. Mendelssohn, *JubA*, 1, 433–34; *Philosophical Writings*, 174–74.

100. Ibid.

101. Mendelssohn, *JubA*, 1:461–62; *Philosophical Writings*, 198.

102. Mendelssohn, *JubA*, 1:458, 456, 398–399; *Philosophical Writings*, 195, 193, 144–45.

103. Mendelssohn, *JubA*, 1:456, 398; *Philosophical Writings*, 193, 144. I choose to call both the extensively enormous and intensively enormous "sublime," even though Mendelssohn seems to want to reserve the term "sublime" for those that are intensively large, while calling those that extensively large "gigantic" or "enormous." See Mendelssohn, *JubA*, 1:456, 459; *Philosophical Writings*, 193, 196. One reason for Mendelssohn's apparently wishing to use two different terms is that while the extensively large object arouses a pleasant shudder that ends in disgust, the intensively large object generates no feeling of disgust.

104. Mendelssohn, *JubA*, 1:461; *Philosophical Writings*, 198.

105. Mendelssohn, *JubA*, 1:459–60; *Philosophical Writings*, 196–97.

106. Mendelssohn, *JubA*, 1:462–63; *Philosophical Writings*, 199–200.

107. Mendelssohn, *JubA*, 1:488, 484–85; *Philosophical Writings*, 226, 222–23.

108. Mendelssohn, *JubA*, 1:463; *Philosophical Writings*, 200.

109. See Mendelssohn, *JubA*, 1:461; *Philosophical Writings*, 196.

110. Ibid.

111. Mendelssohn's translation of the Psalms appeared in 1783, but he cited many examples of sublime biblical poetry from the Psalms in the 1771 revised version of his essay "On the Sublime and Naïve in the Fine Sciences," which was originally published in 1761. See Mendelssohn, *JubA* 1:465; *Philosophical Writings*, 202; *JubA*, 16, Commentary on Exodus 33:23, 348.

112. Mendelssohn, *JubA*, 1:465; *Philosophical Writings*, 202. Robert Lowth likewise cites these verses as an example of the sublime. See Lowth, *Lectures on the Sacred Poetry of the Hebrews*, 1:353–54. Mendelssohn's translation basically follows Luther, with the exception of his translation of *ḥasdekha*, which Luther renders as "goodness" (*Güte*) and the fact that Mendelssohn somewhat oddly translates the first verse as God's grace and truth extending beyond the heavens, while Luther translates it more literally as saying that God's goodness and truth extend "to the heavens . . . and clouds" (*so weit der Himel . . . so weit die Wolcken gehen*). The rendering of "*ḥasdekha*" as "mercy" apparently follows Lowth, but I am unaware of a source for the translation "beyond the heavens." In his 1783 translation of the Psalms, Mendelssohn renders the verses more literally: "*Herr! Deine Güte reicht bis in die Himmel! Deine Treu, so hoch die Wolken gehn! Dein Recht, wie Gottes Gebirge! Dein Rathschluß-unabsehbare Tiefe!*" "Lord! Your goodness extends to the heavens! Your faithfulness as high as the clouds! Your justice, as mountains of God! Your will—a vast abyss!" See Mendelssohn, *JubA*, 10.1, 57. Here Mendelssohn also follows Luther in rendering *ḥasdekha* as "goodness" (*Güte*), but he now renders, *emunatekha, tzidqatekha*, and *mishpatekha* differently. In his long 1757 review of Lowth, Mendelssohn translates these verses according to Lowth's translation: "*Deine Gnade Jehova! reichet in die Himmel, Deine Wahrhaftigkeit in die Wolken. Deine Gerechtigkeit, wie die Berge Gottes, Deine Urtheile, eine unabsehliche Tiefe.*" "Your mercy, Jehovah extends to heaven. Your truthfulness to the clouds. Your justice as mountains of God, your judgment, a vast abyss." See Mendelssohn, *JubA*, 4:39–40.

113. Ibid.

114. See Julius Guttmann, *Philosophies of Judaism: A History of Jewish Philosophy from Biblical Times to Franz Rosenzweig*, translated by David W. Silverman (New York: Schocken, 1964). Bland approvingly quotes Guttmann's claim that philosophy is alien to essential Judaism. See Bland, *Artless Jew*, 5.

115. See Ze'ev Harvey, "On Professor Shlomo Pines and His Approach to Jewish Thought," in *Jubilee Volume for Professor Pines*, vol. 1, edited by Moshe Idel, Zeev Harvey, and Eliezer Schweid (=*Jerusalem Studies in Jewish Thought*, 7 [1986]: 4–11).

116. Bland, *Artless Jew*, 10.

117. For recent examples of this approach, see the excellent work of Eugene Sheppard, *Leo Strauss and the Politics of Exile* (Waltham, Mass.: Brandeis University Press, 2007); Samuel Moyn, *Origins of the Other* (Ithaca, N.Y.: Cornell University Press, 2005); David N. Myers, *Resisting History: Historicism and Its Discontents in German-Jewish Thought* (Princeton, N.J.: Princeton University Press, 2003).

118. See Wolfson, *Crescas' Critique of Aristotle* (Cambridge, Mass.: Harvard University Press, 1929), 27. The subtitle of Wolfson's book *The Philosophy of Spinoza* is "unfolding the latent processes of his reasoning." In the Spinoza book, Wolfson makes a distinction between what he calls the "explicit author" and the "implicit author." Identifying the implicit author requires understanding the inner thought processes of a particular thinker, while identifying the explicit author involves understanding the

author's use of literary sources and terminology to express his thought processes. See Harry Wolfson, *The Philosophy of Spinoza* (Cambridge, Mass.: Harvard University Press, 1934), vii. While I regard Wolfson's assumption of an implicit author as very fruitful, I think that he went too far in assuming that the explicit author always used preexisting philosophical sources to express his ideas.

119. Bland, *Artless Jew*, 10.

120. See *Interpreting Judaism in a Postmodern Age*, edited by Steven Kepnes (New York: New York University Press, 1996), 1–5; *Reasoning after Revelation*, edited by Steven Kepnes, Peter Ochs and Robert Gibbs (Boulder, Colo.: Westview, 1998), 13. Also see my review of two recent works on Spinoza, Michah Gottlieb, "Defending Spinoza?" *AJS Review* 30, no. 2 (2006): 427–33.

121. See Harry Wolfson, *Philosophy of Spinoza*, vi.

122. Elliot R. Wolfson, "Structure, Innovation, and Diremptive Temporality: The Use of Models to Study Continuity and Discontinuity in Kabbalistic Tradition," *Journal for the Study of Religions and Ideologies* 6:18 (2007): 150–51.

123. Ibid., 154.

124. See Emanuel Levinas, "Revelation in the Jewish Tradition," in *The Levinas Reader*, edited by Seán Hand (Oxford: Blackwell, 2000), 191–96. Franz Rosenzweig declares passions and subjectivity the conditions of knowing truth. See Rosenzweig, *Understanding the Sick and the Healthy*, translated by Nahum Glatzer (Cambridge, Mass.: Harvard University Press, 1999), 35–53. Also see E. R. Wolfson's discussion of Rosenzweig's approach to systematicity in "Structure, Innovation, and Diremptive Temporality," 156–58.

CONTRIBUTORS

Kalman P. Bland is Professor of Religion and Jewish Studies at Duke University. A medievalist specializing in Jewish intellectual history, his publications include a critical edition of *Moses Narboni's Commentary to Ibn Rushd's Epistle on the Possibility of Conjunction with the Active Intellect* and a monograph, *The Artless Jew: Medieval and Modern Affirmations and Denials of the Visual*. He is currently investigating medieval Jewish and Islamic philosophic conceptions of the human-animal boundary.

Almut Sh. Bruckstein is a philosopher, curator, and director of *ha'atelier—platform for philosophy and art*. In addition to numerous essays in medieval and modern Jewish philosophy and aesthetics, she is author of *Vom Aufstand der Bilder: Materialen zu Rembrandt und Midrasch; Die Maske des Moses: Studien zur jüdischen Hermeneutik;* and *Hermann Cohen's Ethics of Maimonides.*

James A. Diamond is Joseph and Wolf Lebovic Chair of Jewish Studies at University of Waterloo, Ontario. He has published widely on medieval Jewish thought, and his most recent book is *Converts, Heretics and Lepers: Maimonides and the Outsider.*

Sergey Dolgopolski is Assistant Professor of Religious Studies and Jewish Studies at the University of Kansas. His publications include *Of the Talmud's Rhetoric: A Poststructuralist Analysis (Affect and Figure)* (in Russian) and *What Is Talmud? The Art of Disagreement.*

Michah Gottlieb is Assistant Professor of Jewish Thought and Philosophy in the Skirball Department of Hebrew and Judaic Studies at New York University. He is the author of several articles on medieval and modern Jewish thought, including "Moses Mendelssohn's Metaphysical Defense of Religious Pluralism." He is the editor of a new collection of Mendelssohn's writings entitled *Selected Works of Moses Mendelssohn: Writings on Judaism, Christianity, and the Bible,* forthcoming. His book *Faith and Freedom: Moses Mendelssohn's Theological-Political Thought* is also forthcoming.

Dana Hollander is Associate Professor in the Department of Religious Studies at McMaster University, where she is also an Associate Member of the Department of Philosophy and a Member of the MA Program in Cultural Studies and Critical Theory. Her primary research and teaching areas are twentieth-century French and German philosophy, modern Jewish thought, and German-Jewish studies. Her most recent publication is *Exemplarity and Chosenness: Rosenzweig and Derrida on the Nation of Philosophy.*

Aaron W. Hughes is Associate Professor of History and the Gordon and Gretchen Gross Professor in the Institute of Jewish Thought and Heritage at the University at Buffalo, SUNY. In addition to numerous articles and book chapters, he is author of *The Texture of the Divine: Imagination in Medieval Islamic and Jewish Thought* (Indiana University Press, 2004), *Jewish Philosophy A–Z,* and *The Art of Dialogue in Jewish Philosophy* (Indiana University Press, 2008).

Martin Kavka is Associate Professor in the Department of Religion at Florida State University. He is author of *Jewish Messianism and the History of Philosophy* as well as multiple articles and essays in the fields of philosophy of religion and modern Jewish philosophy.

Steven M. Wasserstrom is The Moe and Izetta Tonkon Professor of Judaic Studies and the Humanities at Reed College in Portland, Oregon. His publications include *Between Muslim and Jew: The Problem of Symbiosis under Early Islam; Religion after Religion: Gershom Scholem, Mircea Eliade, and Henry Corbin at Eranos;* and *The Fullness of Time: Poems by Gershom Scholem,* selected, edited, and introduced by Steven M. Wasserstrom.

Elliot R. Wolfson is Abraham Lieberman Professor of Hebrew and Judaic Studies at New York University. He is author of *Through a Speculum That Shines: Vision and Imagination in Medieval Jewish Mysticism; Language, Eros, Being: Kabbalistic Hermeneutics and Poetic Imagination; Venturing Beyond: Law and Morality in Kabbalistic Mysticism; Alef, Mem, Tau: Kabbalistic Musings on Time, Truth, and Death;* and *Open Secret: Postmessianic Messianism and the Mystical Revision of Menaḥem Mendel Schneerson.*

INDEX

visual culture, 4, 151
Volk, 58

Walker, D. P., 209
Wissenschaft des Judentums, 1, 13,
    55, 70
witness, 28–29, 35

Wolff, Christian, 327, 330–331, 331–332
Wolfson, Elliot R., 34, 53, 149, 153,
    187–188, 214, 258, 288, 326, 341–
    342
Wolfson, Harry A., 25, 176, 178, 341

Zimmer, Heinrich, 178–179